National Portrait Gallery

DAVID GARRICK

by Thomas Gainsborough

A
BIOGRAPHICAL
DICTIONARY

OF

ACTORS, ACTRESSES, MUSICIANS, DANCERS,

MANAGERS & OTHER STAGE PERSONNEL

IN LONDON, 1660–1800

Volume 6: Garrick *to* Gyngell

by

PHILIP H. HIGHFILL, JR., KALMAN A. BURNIM

and

EDWARD A. LANGHANS

SOUTHERN ILLINOIS UNIVERSITY PRESS

CARBONDALE AND EDWARDSVILLE

Extracts from the letters of David Garrick are reprinted by permission of the publishers from *The Letters of David Garrick,* David M. Little, George M. Kahrl, and Phoebe de K. Wilson, editors. Cambridge, Mass.: The Belknap Press of Harvard University Press. Copyright © 1963 by the President and Fellows of Harvard College.

Publication of this work was made possible in part through a grant from the National Endowment for the Humanities.

Library of Congress Cataloging in Publication Data (Revised)

Highfill, Philip H., Jr
  A biographical dictionary of actors, actresses, musicians, dancers, managers & other stage personnel in London, 1660–1800.

  Includes bibliographical references.
  CONTENTS: v. 1. Abaco to Belfille.—v. 2. Belfort to Byzand.—v. 3. Cabanel to Cory.–v. 4. Corye to Dynion.–v. 5. Eagan to Garrett.–v. 6. Garrick to Gyngell.
  1. Performing arts—London—Biography. I. Burnim, Kalman A., joint author. II. Langhans, Edward A., joint author. III. Title.
PN2597.H5   790.2'092'2   [B]   71–157068
ISBN 0–8093–0833–9 (v. 6)

List of Illustrations

PLAYBILLS, TICKETS, ACCOUNTS, AND CASTS

Volume 6

Garrick *to* Gyngell

Garrick, David *1717–1779, actor, manager, patentee, playwright, poet.*

David Garrick's grandfather, David de la Garrique, was a Huguenot of good family who fled France in 1685 after the revocation of the Edict of Nantes. His eldest son Peter was brought to England in 1687 at the age of eighteen months. The family established itself in the little colony of French exiles in London. When Peter was 21, an ensign's commission was purchased for him in Tyrrel's regiment of dragoons, which was stationed at Lichfield. There he met and married Arabella Clough, who was the daughter of a vicar-choral of Lichfield Cathedral, Anthony Clough, and his wife Elizabeth, née Bailye, who was of Irish descent.

David, the second son and third child of Peter and Arabella Garrick, was born on 19 February 1717 at the Angel Inn at Hereford and was baptized on 28 February at All Saints Church in that city, where Peter, by then a lieutenant, was on recruiting duty.

The Garricks returned to Lichfield soon after David's birth and, except for one rather exotic interruption, there David remained through his twentieth year. He was put to study at the Lichfield Grammar School under the same ferocious Rev John Hunter who had whipped Samuel Johnson so brutally as to gain his lasting detestation and who would often palliate his cruelty to a boy being flogged by remarking "this I do to save you from the gallows." Garrick learned very little under that taskmaster. Neither did he seem to profit from the tutelage in trade of his uncle David, a wine dealer in Portugal, who brought his namesake to Lisbon about 1728 but did not keep him long. David seems to have made a social success clowning and reciting for the English merchants of Lisbon, but he showed no aptitude for the counting house.

Like all Lichfield youngsters of promise, Garrick enjoyed the patronage and advice of the learned and kindly Gilbert Walmes-ley, Registrar of the Ecclesiastical Court, who resided in the Palace of the absentee Bishop of Lichfield. The stories which are usually told concerning the precocity of notable actors are told of Garrick too, and doubtless some are true. He was said to have assembled a troupe of youngsters to perform *The Recruiting Officer* at the Palace, when he played Sergeant Kite to the applause of Walmesley and others. He is supposed to have asked the young Samuel Johnson, with whom he was already well acquainted, to write a prologue for him and to have been refused.

David's childhood in Lichfield seems to have been happy, though straitened by poverty. His family was large, close-knit, and affectionate. He had an elder brother, Peter, and an elder sister, Magdalen, and four younger siblings—Jane, William, George, and Merrial; and there were three others who died in infancy. Peter was sent early into the navy, and so it was the 16-

Harvard Theatre Collection

DAVID GARRICK

engraving by Cooper, after Pine

year-old David who acted as surrogate father when Captain Garrick went out to Gibraltar in 1731, leaving behind his debt-burdened and lonely wife and family. The letters from David to Captain Garrick, dating from the first surviving one, on 21 January 1733, to one of May 1736, reveal much of the character of the adolescent boy and, by reflection, of his indulgent and understanding father. One of the earliest letters, written when David was 16, shows a rather overanxious desire on his part to convince his father of his filial duty:

I cant but tell my Dear Pappa that one part of his Letter put a damp upon my pleasure, in which you thought I was neglectfull of Writing. It would be the worst of ingratitude, and I ought to be esteem'd ye worst of Wretches, did I neglect, what I thought would give ye least pleasure and Satisfaction to one of the best of Fathers. If those Persons who have not in any measure receiv'd what tenderness & Affection, I have, from their Parents, are accounted Reprobates, if they omitt to pay all ye Regard and obedience to them they possible can, what on ye contrary can be said for him who in every instance of Life, has had ye greatest indulgences from a most kind father, whose study has always been to promote the welfare of his Children, such a one I think that does not return Paternal love with filial affection is ye most odious Monster, and rather fit for ye Society of Brutes than that of Men.

Few of David's missives to his father are so priggish, but the propitiatory tone, which was in later years to recur in letters to others, died out only gradually. Most letters reported the news of the rather claustrophobic, petty-genteel inbred society of Lichfield, where the Garricks, despite their poverty, were well connected and popular. The Captain was anxious both about his family's health and their financial well-being, and it was young David's diplomatic duty to convey necessary truths about their indebtedness and his mother's frequent illnesses without unduly alarming or depressing his father. He accomplished the delicate feat for a while by the expedient of mixing sad news and urgent requests for money with diverting small talk of all sorts:

My Mamma was got very well and stir'd abroad, but on the 9th of this Month she had a very severe Relapse which continu'd for a Week, but she is at present much better but very weak, attended with a Lowness of Spirits, which compells her to drink Wine which gives a great deal of uneasiness upon two accounts, as it goes against her inclination, and Pockett. We are making all possible interest we can for y^r Leave to come over, we have not as yet had ye good News but Live in Daily expectation of it: Mr Walmisley is going to London very soon and he does not doubt but put the finishing stroke to it. We have a great many Officers here a Recruiting from Ireland, I was in great hopes I should have Recruited my Self this Spring, For Mr Hervey who is a Cornett in my Lord Car's Reg^{nt} had given me & Mr Walmisley a promise for his Commission, If his Brother in Law Sr Thos Aston had died who at ye Time was struck with a dead Palsie, Mr Hervey being Heir to it through his Wife Sr Thos Aston's Sister, or rather she was the Heiress; but Sr Thomas is now perfectly recover'd. My Sister Lenney & Sister Jenny send their Duty to you and being in great Want for some Lace for Heads, and my Mamma being but very Low in ye Purse by reason of her Illness could not afford y^m so much Money, They with ye greatest Duty & Obedience request a small Matter to purchase their Head ornaments. . . .

In May 1736 David's father returned to his thankful family. But he died less than a year later. He was buried in the Lichfield Cathedral ground on 11 March 1737, but David was absent from the funeral, having departed for London nine days before. In 1736 Samuel Johnson, under the patronage of Gilbert Walmesley, had opened the rather pathetic little school at Edial, near Lichfield. Johnson had attracted few students, among them David Garrick and his younger brother George (the accounts crediting him with enrolling only the Garrick brothers are certainly wrong). Tom Davies thought that Johnson "was not better disposed to teach the precepts of learning with that exactness which is necessary to form the classical scholar, than young Garrick was willing to learn them." Perhaps Garrick did not learn much under either Hunter or Johnson. Johnson himself was to remark of him later: "He finds out the Latin by the meaning rather than the meaning by the Latin." But Walmesley wrote to Colson that he was "a good scholar."

The school at Edial soon languished for lack of pupils, and Garrick and his instructor, only nine years his elder, set out for London on 2 March 1737 to try their fortunes. Johnson had nearly nothing, and Garrick, though his uncle David had left him £1,000, had no money he could yet draw upon. (The death of Garrick's father at nearly the same time he and Johnson went to London left David no better off than before. Captain Garrick had failed in an attempt to sell his commission for £1,000 just before his death and had left David out of his will, almost certainly because of the previous bequest of David's uncle.) The pair arrived in London almost destitute but managed, miraculously, to borrow £5 of a bookseller named Wilcox.

Garrick was then 20 and had not yet shown any real interest in any of the occupations suggested to him. Walmesley, with his usual courtesy, had arranged for him to continue to study with the Rev Mr John Colson at Rochester, with a view to preparing for a career at the bar. But after a few months Colson was called to a chair at Cambridge, and Garrick's formal education ended. Garrick did, indeed, rather prematurely enter himself at Lincoln's Inn, paying down his £3 3s. 4d. for that privilege on 9 March 1737. But when in 1738 he came of age he quickly forgot the law as a course of life. He threw his inheritance of £1000 from his Uncle David into a new

wholesale wine business, Garrick Brothers, in Durham Yard, in which his elder brother Peter invested the £1000 left him by Captain Garrick. David's activity as salesman for the firm took him to the coffee houses and taverns of the theatrical district. One of his first acquaintances there was Charles Macklin, already an established actor. It was not long before David knew a good many actors, and not very much longer before his youthful love of plays and acting began to push the vintner's trade to the back of his mind.

In the spring of 1740 Garrick took two of Fielding's most popular characters and some of the liveliest comic clichés and tinkered together the first version of *Lethe: or Æsop in the Shades*, which in one or another conformation was to be revived until the nineteenth century. Garrick's first dramatic production, it played for the first time on Henry Giffard's special benefit night at Drury Lane on 15 April 1740. This time Johnson acceded to Garrick's request to write a prologue, penning one twitting his student's rashness in commencing author:

Oft has our Bard in this disastrous Year,
Beheld the Tragic Heroes taught to fear.
Oft has he seen the Poignant Orange fly,
And heard th' ill Omen'd Catcall's direful Cry.
Yet dares to venture on the dangerous Stage,
And weakly hopes to 'scape the Critick's Rage.

The prologue ends with a hope, characteristic of Johnson's staunch didactic method, that the farce would tend to the reformation of stage manners.

By 5 July 1740 David was writing from London to brother Peter in Lichfield reminding him of a promise to join a campaign to influence the Duke of Grafton, then Lord Chamberlain, in behalf of Giffard's desire to reopen his playhouse in

Goodman's Fields, which had been closed by the Licensing Act of 1737.

Samuel Johnson had found employment with the publisher Edward Cave on the *Gentleman's Magazine*, quartered in rooms above St John's Gate. There Garrick, at Cave's urging, gave a performance in the title role of Fielding's *The Mock Doctor*, with the printers as supporting players, reading their parts. For the production Garrick wrote a special prologue, which Cave printed, signed only "G.," in his September 1740 issue. Garrick later acted at St John's Gate in a burlesque of *Julius Caesar* and began, with Cave's connivance, his long-time practice of publishing anonymous verses and criticisms in the periodicals.

It has been repeatedly suggested that the death of Garrick's mother in September 1740 removed the most formidable inhibition to his life as a professional performer. But Peter, elder brother and partner, still remained to be convinced. David's approach to that difficulty was characteristically circuitous. For some time he had been, as an intimate acquaintance of Henry Giffard, an attentive student of the backstage procedures of the little theatre in Goodman's Fields where Giffard was evading the Licensing Act of 1737 with the transparent device of charging for admission to the music and offering plays "gratis." In the winter season of 1740–41, a sudden illness seized Richard Yates at the theatre while Garrick was behind the scenes, and Yates "was not able to begin ye Entertainment so I put on ye Dress [of Harlequin] & did 2 or three Scenes for him" in the pantomime *Harlequin Student*. Garrick wrote a little later, "but Nobody knew it but him and Giffard."

In June 1741 Giffard took a small company—Yates, Vaughan, Harry ("Dagger") Marr, Miss Hippisley, Mr and Mrs Dunstall, and Paget—adventuring to Ipswich, a market town some 60 miles northeast of London. The newspaper notices show that among the rest at the little theatre in Tankard Street was a "Mr Lyddall." Garrick's choice of that nom de guerre to conceal from Peter and other censorious relatives his growing apostasy from commerce is probably explained by the fact that Lyddal was the maiden name of Mrs Giffard. It has been often stated, on the authority of Thomas Davies, in his *Memoirs of the Life of David Garrick, Esq* (1780), that Garrick's first regular appearance was at the Ipswich theatre as Aboan in Southerne's old tragedy *Oroonoko* (which would have given him a second layer of protective disguise, inasmuch as the role required blackface). But though Garrick evidently played the part at Ipswich, it may not have been his first one there. Others he is known to have essayed that summer included some which remained in his repertoire for many years: Lord Foppington in *The Careless Husband*, Orestes in *Iphigenia*, Sir Harry Wildair in *The Constant Couple*, Dr Caius in *The Merry Wives of Windsor*, and Chamont in *The Orphan*. On 21 July, for the benefit of Marr and Miss Hippisley, Garrick played Captain Duretête in *The Inconstant*, the mainpiece, and had the satisfaction of appearing in the afterpiece, his own *Lethe*, as Ventre-Bleu.

There was no word of his Ipswich outing in his letters to Peter, who was at Lichfield in the summer of 1741, and, strangely, there is no evidence that rumor had yet connected Garrick with the stage. But he may have been flying a signal to Peter to prepare him for the inevitable discovery when he spoke, in a letter on 11 July, of being "at present very busy with Jack Arthur," the Covent Garden clown and machinist, "upon Our Catapult-project. We have laid out above Six pounds already in Timber and ye Carpenter has almost finish'd y^e Catapulta. . . ."

At Goodman's Fields, between the two parts of "A Concert of Vocal and Instrumental Music," on 19 October 1741 Colley Cibber's version of *Richard III* was presented before a thin house with "The Part

THEATRE IN TANKARD STREET IPSWICH WHERE GARRICK MADE HIS FIRST PUBLIC APPEARANCE, 21ST JULY 1741.
IT WAS STANDING TILL ABOUT 1800 WHEN THE PRESENT THEATRE WAS BUILT UPON THE SAME SITE.

From the collection of Edward A. Langhans

Theatre in Tankard Street, Ipswich

engraving by Dale

of King Richard by a GENTLEMAN (*who never appear'd on any Stage*)." A critic in the London *Daily Post and General Advertiser* the following day said flatly that the anonymous gentleman's "Reception was the most extraordinary and great that was ever known upon such an Occasion." The statement was not the usual puff devised by management to boost a young performer over his first hurdle. In the light of what followed, it looks ineloquent and understated. Garrick sensed at once the stunning effect his interpretation of Richard had on his first London audience, and he sat down next morning in his lodgings in Mansfield Street to confront Peter with the irreversible facts:

Dear Peter

I rec'd My Shirt safe & am now to tell You what I suppose You may have heard of before this, but before I let you into ye Affair tis proper to premise Some things that I may appear less culpable in y^r Opinion than I might Otherwise do. I have made an Exact Estimate of my Stock of wine & What Money I have out at Interest & find that Since I have been a Wine Merchant I have run out near four hundred pounds & trade not encreasing I was very Sensible some way must be thought of to redeem it. My Mind (as You must know) has been always inclin'd to y^e Stage, nay so strongly so that all my Illness & lowness of Spirits was owing to my want of resolution to tell You my thoughts when here, finding at last both my Inclination & Interest

Walker Art Gallery, Liverpool

DAVID GARRICK, as Richard III

by Hogarth

requir'd some New way of Life I have chose y^e most agreeable to my Self & tho I know You will bee much displeas'd at Me yet I hope when You shall find that I may have ye genius of an Actor without ye Vices, You will think Less Severe of Me & not be asham'd to own me for a Brother— I am willing to agree to any thing You shall propose about ye Wine, I will take a thorough Survey of ye Vaults & making what You have at Lich^d part of ye Stock will either Send You Y^r Share or any other way You shall propose— Last Night I play'd Richard ye Third to ye Surprize of Every Body & as I shall make very near £300 p Annum by It & as it is really what I doat upon I am resolv'd to pursue it—I belive I shall have Bowers Money wch when I have, it shall go towards my part of ye Wine

You have at Lichf^d pray writ[e] me an Answer immediately. I am D^r bro[ther]

Y^rs Sincerely

D Garrick

I have a farce (Y^e Lying Valet) coming out at Drury Lane.

While at his escritoire that morning Garrick made the same explanation and plea for understanding to at least one other disapproving relative, his first cousin, the attorney Peter Fermignac, adding

As My Brother will Settle at Lichfield I design to throw up ye Wine Business as soon as I can conveniently & I desire You'll let my Uncle know— if You should want to Speak with Me yᵉ Stage Door will be always Open to You or any other part of yᵉ house, for I am Manager with Mʳ Giffard & You may always command

> Yʳ most humˡᵉ Servant
> D: Garrick

David had hoped thus to enlist the persuasive powers of his cousin on his side. Just the opposite occurred, for Fermignac immediately spread the news, and his own disapproval, among members of his branch of the family.

On seven of the next eight nights of performance at Goodman's Fields the steadily less-anonymous "gentleman" played Richard to ever-swelling crowds of the fashionable from the West End who had got wind of the prodigy. Thomas Davies reconstructed his reception:

Mr. Garrick's easy and familiar, yet forcible style . . . at first threw the critics into some hesitation concerning the novelty as well as propriety of his manner. They had long been accustomed to an elevation of the voice, with a sudden mechanical depression of its tones, calculated to excite admiration and entrap applause. To the just modulation of the words, and concurring expression of the features from the genuine workings of nature, they had been strangers for some time. But after he had gone through a variety of scenes, in which he gave evident proofs of consummate art, and perfect knowledge of character, their doubts were turned into surprize and astonishment, from which they relieved themselves by loud reiterated applause.

To Garrick this was the very breath of a splendid new-found life. To his brother Peter it was degrading notoriety, the more notorious the more degrading. David was hurt but stubborn, replying

The Uneasiness I have receiv'd wᵗʰ Yʳ Letter is inexpressible; however 'twas a Shock I expected & had guarded Myself as well as I could against it . . . I am not so much to blame as You Seem to think I am. . . . &

indeed the Trade we have if You will reflect very seriously can never be Sufficient to Maintain Me & a Servant hansomely— As for yᵉ Stage, I know in yᵉ General it deserves Yʳ Censure, but if You will consider how hansomely & how reputably Some have liv'd . . . & as My Genius that Way (by yᵉ best Judges) is thought Wonderfull how can You be so averse to My proceedings . . . As to Company yᵉ Best in Town are desirous of Mine.

Peter still refused to accept David's decision, and David grew more insistent:

I am very Sorry You still Seem so utterly Averse to What I am so greatly Inclin'd & to What yᵉ best Judges think I have yᵉ Greatest Genius for— . . . Mʳ Pit, who is reckon'd yᵉ Greatest Orator in the house of Commons, said I was yᵉ best Actor yᵉ English Stage had produc'd . . . the Prince has heard so great a Character of Me that we are in daily Expectations of his coming to See Me— I have been told that You are Affraid Giffard has had my Money, Upon my honour he does not owe Me a farthing . . . You can't imagine what regard I meet with, yᵉ Pit & Boxes are to be put togeather & I shall have all my friends (who still continue so to Me tho You cannot be brought over) if You come to town yʳ Lodgings will cost you Nothing I having a Bed at Arthur's for You.

The fiction of anonymity was continued in the Goodman's Fields bill of 28 October, when Clodio in *Love Makes a Man* was played "By the Gentleman who perform'd King Richard," that designation being certain now to draw more theatregoers than any actor's name whatever. The Gentleman was also in the bills for Chamont in *The Orphan* on 6 November and for Jack Smatter, Garrick's first original role, in the stage adaptation of Richardson's *Pamela*, which received 14 performances during the season. The device of anonymity was of no further use by 28 November. Garrick played Chamont, seeing that night for the first time anywhere his real name in a playbill. On 30 November he played Sharp, the lead in his own new farce *The Lying Valet*, and also acted Chamont, the first of many occasions during the season on which he played in both mainpiece and afterpiece. For the still dubious Peter he laid it on with a trowel: "the Valet takes prodigiously, & is approv'd of by Men of genius & thought yᵉ Most diverting Farce that ever was perform'd; I believe You'll find it read pretty well, & in performance tis a general Roar from beginning to End."

Garrick kept himself frantically busy, winning success after success: he acted Lothario in *The Fair Penitent* on 2 December, the Ghost in *Hamlet* on 9 December, Fondlewife in *The Old Bachelor* on 5 January 1742, Costar Pearmain in *The Recruiting Officer* on 14 January, Aboan in *Oroonoko* on 23 January, and Witwoud in *The Way of the World* on 27 January.

After seven consecutive highly acclaimed performances of Bayes in *The Rehearsal*, the pace and excitement overwhelmed Garrick. Never really robust, he had played right through a bad cold in December and January, and in February he fell ill of a fever, causing a deferral, on the eighteenth, of *The Rehearsal*. It was resumed on the twentieth. Now for the first time Garrick encountered the envy which accompanies all adulation. The gossips whispered that he was malingering, neglecting the stage but disporting himself at the ridottos. Instead of ignoring gossip, the thin-skinned young man defended himself, as he was to do, unwisely, so often in his career. He published an indignant denial in the London *Daily Post and General Advertiser*:

Whereas it has been industriously reported to my prejudice, that I was at the Masquerade in the Habit of a Madman; this is to assure the Gentlemen or Ladies, who are offended at me, without Cause, I was not at either of the Masquerades this Season, as can be testify'd by several Gentlemen in whose Company I was. If any Person has a Mind to be further satisfy'd, I will fully convince them of the Truth of this Advertisement. David Garrick.

On 22 February he played Master Johnny in the farce *The Schoolboy*.

The True and Ancient History of King Lear and His Three Daughters, Nahum Tate's sadly inferior version of the tragedy which is often considered the sublimest production of Shakespeare's art, is the version which, by and large, held the stage from the late seventeenth century until the early nineteenth century. The blinding of Gloucester occurs offstage; the Fool is omitted entirely; Goneril and Reagan poison each other; Cordelia and Edgar are united in love; Lear, Kent, and Gloucester are all spared and go off to philosophical retirement. Yet the part of Lear himself is left relatively intact, though all too many of his lines are mangled. This version was Garrick's vehicle when he essayed Lear for the first time on 11 March 1742, and even this abomination he made so movingly effective (though not at first and not without the critical coaching of Charles Macklin) that some performances were said to have been interrupted by the weeping of the audience.

On 15 March 1742 Garrick introduced his great Lord Foppington in *The Careless Husband* to Goodman's Fields. His benefit bill on 18 March (when he chose *Lear*) advised those seeking tickets to apply at his lodgings in Mansfield Street, Goodman's Fields. On 22 March he was Duretête. On 1 April he played Pierre in *Venice Preserv'd* and on 6 April Brazen in *The Recruiting Officer*, both for the first time. As the season drew to a close, several of Garrick's roles—Lear, Richard III, Sharp—were repeatedly advertised as being played "positively for the last time this season." But always, "At the Desire of several Persons of Quality," he played them again. As the West End emptied night after night and there were unbroken lines of carriages from Temple Bar to Goodman's Fields, the managers of the patent theatres exerted more and more pressure for a closure of Giffard's illegal operation. On 24 May they succeeded, and the bills acknowledged "the last Time of the Company's performing there." Two nights later, 26 May, having signed articles for the following season at Drury Lane Theatre, Garrick opened his long association with Drury Lane, playing Bayes in *The Rehearsal*. He had confided to Peter on 30 January 1742: "My Lord Essex has sent word Just now he would be glad to See me for Rich [the Covent Garden manager] but I have fixt my Mind upon Drury Lane, tho 'tis quite a secret." He played his Lear on 27 May and closed his personal season on 31 May triumphantly, as he had begun it, playing Richard III, this time "By Command of their Royal Highnesses the Duke, and the Princesses Amelia, Caroline, and Louisa."

Perhaps the greatest wonder of that wonderful season was that the young provincial should have kept his balance. On 19 April he wrote his already-relenting brother:

[the] favour I meet with from yᵉ Greatest Men has made me far from Repenting of my Choice. I Am very intimate with Mʳ Glover, who will bring out a Trajedy next winter upon My Accᵗ. I have sup'd Twice Wᵗʰ yᵉ Great Mʳ Murray Councellʳ & Shall with Mʳ Pope by his Introduction [Alexander Pope, after seeing Garrick for the first time, is reported by Davies to have said "he was afraid the young man would be spoiled, for he would have no competitor"] – I sup'd wᵗʰ yᵉ Mʳ Littleton yᵉ Prince's Favourite last Thursday night & Met with yᵉ highest Civility & complaisance, He told me he never knew wᵗ Acting was till I appear'd & Said I was only born to act wᵗ Shakespear writ, these Things daily occurring give me great Pleasure I din'd with Lᵈ Hallifax & Lᵈ Sandwich Two very ingenious Noblemen Yesterday & am to dine at Lᵈ Hallifax's next Sunday with Lᵈ Chesterfield, I have yᵉ Pleasure of being very intimate too with Mʳ Hawkins Brown of Burton, in short I believe nobody (as an Actor) was

ever more carress'd & My Character as a private Man makes [them] more desirous of my Company – (all this Entre nous as one Brothʳ to Another) I am not fix'd for next Year, but shall certainly be at yᵉ Other End of yᵉ Town – I am offer'd £500 guinea & a Clear Benefit or Part of yᵉ Management; . . .

The former Lichfieldian, later Bishop of Bristol, the Reverend Thomas Newton wrote that the famous old actress

Mrs. [Mary] Porter is no less in raptures than the rest; she returned to town on purpose to see you, and declares she would not but have come for the world. You are born an actor, she says, and do more at your first appearing, than ever any body did with twenty years' practice; and, Good God, says she, what will he be in time! And when somebody in company mentioned your not doing Lord Foppington so well, she made answer, that she was sure it was impossible for you to do any thing ill; you might perhaps excel less in that, but you must excel in every thing.

Garrick had, however, some psychological ballast to keep him on the ground as the frenzy over his acting increased. Advice was free and plentiful, from friends and strangers. Rev Thomas Newton kindly wrote to correct minutely his action of Richard III. When Richard compares the young Princes to spiders and says to Buckingham "I would have some friend to tread upon them," Garrick's "action is only with your hand, but surely it should rather have been with a little stamp of your foot *to tread upon them*." Newton not only wrote but called upon Garrick, who accepted his tutelage affably. The advice moved on from art to life. "You know," remarked Newton, "Roscius was familiar with Cicero, and the greatest men of his time; and Betterton used frequently to visit Bishop Sprat and Atterbury, and other divines, as well as the best of the nobility and gentry, not as a mimic and buffoon, to make diversion for the company, but as an agreeable friend and companion." And so Garrick was increasingly to do.

Garrick should now have been physically and emotionally exhausted. For seven months, studying at least 18 leading roles for 136 performances (in 20 of which he played in both mainpiece and afterpiece), he also spoke many epilogues, some of them of his own writing. His exertions had earned him what Davies called "a full moiety of the profits" before Goodman's Fields Theatre was closed down, plus the £300 which had first been stipulated as his salary, with the proceeds also of a crowded benefit night when the stage was "turn'd into an Amphitheatre." The variegated year which had catapulted him to fame and brought the heady praise of paragraphers and the flattering attentions of the learned and the great had also awarded him the fickle favors of the charming Irish actress Margaret Woffington.

In early June 1742, accompanied by Peg Woffington and the dancer Barbarina Campanini (both of Covent Garden), Garrick set out from London for Dublin. The trip, including a rough voyage, consumed two weeks. In mid-June Garrick joined the summer company at Smock Alley. Garrick reported enthusiastically:

Dublin
My Dear Peter   June 23^d [1742]
I am got safe to Ireland & have had Success Equal to that in England. My Lord Orrery who is a Demi-God has wrote Such affectionate Letters to all ye Noblemen & Gentlemen of his Acquaintance that I am more caress'd here than I was at London— Delane has play'd against Me, but wanting allies has quitted ye field— I will certainly call upon You at my Return— I am quite well & ye Change of Air has agreed vastly with Me— when I am more Settled. I will write more in ye Mean Time, believe Me (with Love and Services to B^{rs} and S^{rs}

    Y^r most affect^e Friend and Broth^r
    D Garrick
direct for Me at My Lodgings in Aungier's Street, Dublin.

He had opened on 18 June 1742 as Richard III. He played only one new part but was accepted enthusiastically in Bayes (especially), Lear, Pierre, Sharp, Fondlewife, Foppington, Master Johnny, and Clodio. His one new part, Hamlet, was destined to be one of his most memorable. He had been studying it for months (part of the time from the vantage point of the Ghost). He knew it was a role of vast importance for his London future, and on the night of his second benefit, 12 August, with Peg Woffington his Ophelia, he tried it out on the Dubliners.

Eager throngs of curious playgoers pushed into Smock Alley to view the prodigy in each of his roles. An epidemic of some hot-weather malady then sweeping Dublin was called "Garrick fever." He ended his season playing Captain Plume on 19 August to Mrs Woffington's Sylvia in *The Recruiting Officer*. Garrick wrote to Peter on 22 August "My Affairs are quite finish'd here & with great Success, applause & w^t Not, I shall call upon You in 15 or 16 Days Time, I have an Invitation from Ld Tyrawley to come with him & I believe shall Stay for ye Hon^r of his Lordship's Company—"

The Anglo-Irish society had lionized the young visitor, and the biographers of the author, actor, and manager Thomas Sheridan credit Garrick's social and stage successes with precipitating Sheridan's decision to risk his own respectability by embarking on a stage career. Garrick-adulation from strangers continued in newspaper eulogy and private letters. So did instruction. A lengthy letter of 14 August 1742 from some anonymous Dublinite acknowledged the deservedness of the applause Garrick had received in Hamlet but pointed out some errors ("which I insist upon that you reform"), including "false pronunciation of several words," for example: "*Matron, Israel, villain, appal, Horatio, wind;* which you pronounced, *metron, Iserel, villin, appeal, Horetio.* . . ."

On 23 August 1742 Garrick sailed back for England, his companions on the voyage being Delane and two people with whom he was to have long and emotional relationships—one of the greatest of eighteenth-century England's native musicians and its most prolific composer of first-rate theatrical music, T. A. Arne, and his sister, the actress Susanna Maria, the second Mrs Theophilus Cibber. They had been employed at Dublin's Aungier Street Theatre for the summer.

Peg Woffington followed Garrick back to London, and there, immediately or later, they evidently set up housekeeping on an expenses-shared basis. (At Garrick's first benefit that season, 13 January 1743, his patrons were sent for tickets to his "lodgings in the Great Piazza, Covent Garden," at his second, 3 March, to "Garrick's, Bow Street, Covent Garden.") We know virtually nothing about the relationship, though it is certain that the pair continued lovers. Though Charles Macklin visited them and perhaps even lived in the same house awhile, it seems equally certain that stories which circulated later that he made a third in a *menage à trois* were false. William Cooke, in his *Memoirs of Charles Macklin* (1806), gathered some fugitive anecdotes of the Garrick-Woffington relationship, most of them contributed (and perhaps invented) by Macklin after he fell out with Garrick in 1743. One of them gives Garrick the character of skinflint, which not all his many well-documented benefactions in later years could completely erase: he was said to have refused to relinquish a costly pair of diamond shoe buckles when he and Peg returned each other's gifts at parting. More credible, perhaps, is Samuel Johnson's memory of Garrick's reproof of Peg for wastefully making their visitor's tea too strong: "Why this tea is as red as blood!" The association finally became uncomfortable, one gathers, both for the rather meticulous Garrick and for the careless Woffington. At one time Garrick supposed he

might marry her, and Murphy says he even bought the wedding ring, but her notorious inconstancy and Garrick's developing conservatism worked to blunt that intention. (He found it necessary to write Peter denying the rumor that he was on the verge of marriage to her.) They resolved to part but remained friends. After his marriage to Eva Maria Veigel Garrick avoided speaking of the association.

Garrick opened his first season at Drury Lane under the management of the charming and irresponsible Charles Fleetwood on 5 October 1742 playing Chamont in *The Orphan*. He was the least experienced of the principals in the excellent company of 58 actors and actresses, among them: John Beard, Delane, Mr and Mrs Mills, Havard, Yates, Macklin, Mrs Clive, Mrs and Miss Macklin, Mrs Pritchard, Miss Young, and, of course and especially, Peg Woffington. But they already appeared to some extent as his inferiors. Some of them openly resented his sudden rise, but before the season was over they looked to him as a leader.

Garrick astonished the town with his Lear, dazzled it with his Archer, but disappointed it as Millamour in Henry Fielding's wretched *Wedding Day*. On 16 November 1742 Garrick played Hamlet "By Command of Their Royal Highnesses the Duke, and Princesses Amelia, Carolina and Louise," causing a critical and popular sensation. He was, also for the first time in London, Hastings in *Jane Shore*—a solid success—and Sir Harry Wildair in *The Constant Couple*—which puzzled some of his audience and annoyed others because they had naturally expected Peg Woffington, showing her figure in that, her most famous part. The sensitive Garrick felt the audience's mere tolerance and before long he dropped the part from his repertoire. On 23 March 1743, for Macklin's benefit, he introduced his Abel Drugger in *The Alchemist*, which was to be perhaps the comic character most appreciated by his audiences. Garrick played 14 roles during a winter

Harvard Theatre Collection

DAVID GARRICK, as Abel Drugger

engraving by Dixon, after Zoffany

counts just who fomented the insurrection. Garrick had absented himself from the theatre for three weeks in May, the first act of defiance against Fleetwood, but Arthur Murphy, relying on the testimony of Isaac Reed, said it was Macklin who "invited them to enter into a general confederacy." But Garrick certainly emerged as the spokesman for the group. Neither is it clear whether all of the actors were resolute "to set up a new company, if possible," as Murphy said Garrick and Macklin were, or simply wished to draw their pay and improve their conditions at Drury Lane.

"An Embodied phalanx was . . . drawn up against the manager, who had notice early in September, that none of the junto would act under him, if he did not accede to their terms. Fleetwood stood at bay," concluded Murphy. A petition was presented to the Crown for a license to operate a third winter theatre at the Haymarket summer house.

The Duke of Grafton, who was then Chamberlain, received the petition of the players with coldness: instead of examining into the merit of their complaints, he desired to know the amount of their annual stipends. He was much surprised to be informed, that a man could gain, merely by playing, the yearly salary of 500 *l.* His Grace observed, that a near relation of his, who was then an inferior officer in the navy, exposed his life in behalf of his King and country for less than half that sum. All attempts to convince the Duke that justice and right were on the side of the petitioners, were to no purpose.

through which Drury Lane, despite good houses, was drawn deeper and deeper into debt by the dissolute Fleetwood. Before the end of the season bailiffs were attaching the costumes and properties, and salaries were so far in arrears that finally a rebellion was concerted among the leading performers. Garrick, Charles Macklin, William Havard, Edward Berry, Charles Blakes, Hannah Pritchard, Kitty Clive, Mr and Mrs William Mills, and others signed a "formal agreement," says Davies, "by which they obliged themselves not to accede to any terms which might be proposed to them by the patentee without the consent of all the subscribers." It is not clear from early ac-

At the moment of Grafton's refusal, the psychology of the strike had turned suddenly into that of lockout by management. Fleetwood had combed the countryside for provincial performers and with them and a few of those principals (like Yates, Henry Giffard, and Peg Woffington) who had not signed the agreement, he prepared to open his 1743–44 season. The dissident actors had nowhere to go in London and many had no prospects anywhere else. Fleetwood would reinstate them but certainly not without Garrick. Garrick could not now avoid the humiliating capitulation urged upon him by his companions. Yet such a course was made ethically nearly impossible for Garrick by Fleetwood's adamant refusal to rehire Macklin. Fleetwood had befriended Macklin through some hard times (including his trial for killing his fellow-actor Hallam) and he now saw him as a monster of ingratitude.

Garrick tried to appease Macklin by offering to pay him a weekly sum out of his own pocket and by obtaining a promise from Rich to engage Mrs Macklin at Covent Garden for £3 a week. Macklin would have none of it. Garrick announced that he would return to Drury Lane. On the morning of 6 December 1743 a pamphlet, *The Case of Charles Macklin, Comedian*, appeared (inspired by Macklin, but probably written by Corbyn Morris), bitterly denouncing Garrick as a dishonorable breaker of solemn compacts. A band of Macklin's adherents, recruited at the Horn Tavern by Dr Barrowby, stationed themselves in the pit at Drury Lane. When Garrick attempted to perform Bayes

he was not suffered to speak. Off! off! resounded from all parts of the house. The play went on in dumb shew, scene by scene, from the beginning to the end; Garrick, during the whole, standing aloof, at the upper part of the stage, to avoid the rotten eggs and apples, which showered down in great plenty.

Garrick caused an answering "case" to be published on 7 December, which on 12 December drew a *Reply*. Meanwhile, before the performance of 8 December, Fleetwood stationed in the theatre 30 pugilists, armed with bludgeons and under the direction of a friend of Garrick's, Mr Wyndham of Norfolk. When the disturbance resumed, "they fell upon Macklin's party, and drove them out of the pit."

The rioting at the theatre was soon forgotten, and by November 1744 Macklin was again at Drury Lane, but the breach between him and Garrick was never quite repaired. Garrick had been introduced to two of the uncomfortable lessons of leadership: how easy it is to be trapped between two courses of action equally difficult and how it feels to be booed and hissed.

During the 1743–44 season Garrick had added to his repertoire Townly in *The Provok'd Husband*, Biron in *The Fatal Marriage*, and the title character in William Havard's new tragedy *Regulus*. But the high point of his season had been the addition of *Macbeth* on 7 January 1744. Some motive of self-doubt made Garrick prepare for the event by writing and publishing an anonymous pamphlet entitled *An Essay on Acting, in which will be consider'd the Mimical Behaviour of a certain fashionable faulty actor. . . . to which will be added a short criticism on his acting Macbeth*, in which he derided, among other things, the notion of a man of his low stature playing a martial hero. Perhaps it was to forestall criticism. He was to write similar pamphlets afterwards, never to any discernable effect. Rejecting the Davenant alteration of *Macbeth*, which was current, and basing his text on that of Theobald, Garrick also consulted both Johnson and Warburton. He thus thoughtfully prepared an acting text which, despite some crucial cuts—like the banishment of the porter at the gate—was much closer to Shakespeare's original than anything which had been seen since before 1660. Garrick in the title part, supported by the magnificent Lady Macbeth of Hannah Pritchard, earned enormous praise, and Macbeth remained one of his most affecting characters until Mrs Pritchard's death in 1768, after which he relinquished it to others.

In 1744–45 Drury Lane Theatre continued downhill under the mismanagement of Fleetwood, who sought to recoup by raising prices. The result was a riot, a paper war, and, finally, in December, Fleetwood's sale of his playhouse and patent to Norton Amber, Richard Green, and James Lacy. Garrick now lodged in James Street, Covent Garden, where he would reside until April 1747. He added in the 1744–45 season several of his more important roles: Zaphna in *Mahomet the Imposter*, Tancred in *Tancred and Sigismunda*, Scrub in *The Stratagem*, and Sir John Brute in *The Provok'd Wife*. ("He may possibly act Master Jacky Brute, but he cannot possibly be Sir John Brute," contemptuously remarked Quin, who owned the role at Covent Garden. But Quin was wrong.) On 20 February 1745 Garrick played the title role in *King John*, from a text to which, once again, he restored a good many lines previously cut. He was reported to be impressive in some of John's scenes, but his size militated against him both as the King and as the Bastard Faulconbridge, which he played first in Dublin the following season. He quickly eliminated both from his repertoire. Also, on 7 March 1745, Garrick played Othello for the first time. Criticism was polite about Garrick's presentation, but his diminutive stature made him uncomfortable in the role. He repeated it a few times and then relinquished it. It was indeed a fortunate abnegation, for the stalwart Spranger Barry, perhaps the century's finest Othello, would be coming from Ireland to Drury Lane in the fall of 1746.

Garrick sustained an injury playing Richard III on 12 February 1745 which caused *The Rehearsal*, planned for 15 February, to be postponed. He was very ill in April, but he wrote the Rev John Hoadley on 22 May from Teddington, "I am now (thank God) recovering Daily, & my Physicians tell me I shall be a much better Man (bodily I mean) than I was before; if so I'll crack ye Drum of y^r Ear Next winter." But he was again out of action for a week in early October 1745. Garrick referred the cause of these frequent illnesses to his having overworked himself in "principal

characters . . . King John, Tancred &c &c" in a letter to Francis Hayman, the Drury Lane scene painter.

But, except for uncertain health, Garrick's phenomenal luck was running even stronger than usual in 1745–46. The Pretender, Prince Charles Edward, began his military campaign in July 1745, and throughout the following year the alarums and excursions of the Jacobite rebellion depressed theatre attendance in London. But apparently there was no such effect in Dublin. Garrick's long and irritated association with Lacy had already begun. When Lacy had taken over the patent from Fleetwood, Garrick had assumed that Lacy would abide by the terms of his articles. They explicitly stated that a debt of some £250 owed by the theatre to Garrick would be paid by 20 June 1745 and that if it were then Garrick would either sign with Drury Lane Theatre or not act at all or act in some other kingdom. Lacy (as Garrick contended) had not only refused to honor those provisions, cheating Garrick of his arrears in salary, but had also insisted that he play as often as Lacy thought proper, and even suggested a reduction in salary. Garrick was further incensed by Lacy's false charge that the actor had in the previous season played infrequently and had added too few new parts. Angry and unpleasant correspondence ensued.

But the altercation at least gave Garrick a chance to escape London for a while. After a ritual gesture toward volunteer service against the rebels and a feint toward the eager manager John Rich at Covent Garden, Garrick responded affirmatively to a cold but sincere invitation from Thomas Sheridan to come to Ireland to act and to co-manage Dublin's United company at both Smock Alley and Aungier Street.

Garrick and some friends had established a social club at the Queen's Arms Tavern, St Paul's Churchyard. He wrote to "his Brethren" from the Bedford Coffee House on the eve of his departure for Dublin, apologizing for not joining them. He was, he said, "with Mr Rich drawing up a Memorandum" establishing his salary of 600 guineas for the Covent Garden season of 1746–47. Pinning down the job and salary at Covent Garden a year ahead of time was a typical example of Garrick's prudential forehandedness. (Garrick's letter is dated 23 November 1745 by Kahrl and Little, following their source, the *London Morning Post* of 30 September 1786; but either that date or Fitzgerald's for Garrick's arrival in Dublin – 24 November – is obviously incorrect.)

When Garrick arrived in Dublin he stepped at once into a controversy over whether he was to be paid, as Sheridan had suggested, on equal shares with Sheridan, or, as Garrick preferred, in a (large) set sum. According to Davies, Sheridan settled the dispute "by taking out his watch and insisting on an answer in a few minutes," and Garrick "submitted."

The season was a brilliant one, with George Anne Bellamy and young Spranger Barry vying for attention and Garrick and Sheridan often acting together or exchanging each other's favorite roles. Garrick reeled off before the Dublin audiences at least 20 parts: Hamlet, Richard III, Archer, Bayes, Lothario, Macbeth, Chamont, Lear, Captain Plume, Sir John Brute, Master Johnny, Tancred, Othello, Sir Harry Wildair, Hastings, Sharp, King John, Iago, Orestes, and the Bastard (in *King John*).

George Anne Bellamy, not always the most honest of testators, claimed in her *Apology* that she caused Garrick to play King John to empty boxes when he and Sheridan denied her the part of Constance and cast her as Arthur. She was the illegitimate but acknowledged daughter of the Irish Lord Tyrawley, and (she says) her word was so influential in Dublin society that she easily invoked her theatrical boycott on Garrick. Garrick received one more snub that winter, of a kind that he relished

even less than playing to diminished houses. When Lord Chesterfield, then Lord Lieutenant of Ireland, was lighted ceremoniously into his box by the two managers on a command night, he treated Sheridan with affability but completely ignored Garrick. (The politically astute Chesterfield was probably only being diplomatic, deliberately deferring to the Irishman Sheridan for the effect it would have on the Dublin audience. For the very next year Garrick's friend Walmsley reported from Bath that Chesterfield had said that "you are not only the best tragedian in the world, but the best, he believes, that ever was in the world.")

Garrick set out for London with his Dublin season's earnings of £600 on 3 May 1746 and arrived a week later. He found affairs at Drury Lane in almost as bad a condition as under Fleetwood's management. The combined woes of bad houses and the failure of Green and Amber's banking concern had defeated Lacy's efforts to reorganize the enterprise. Garrick was beginning to see an opportunity in all that. But he bided his time. Though he had written from Dublin to Somerset Draper on 1 December 1745 that "I have no inclination to Covent-garden; I am afraid of the house, and other things," in mid-May 1746 he signed formal articles for the winter season of 1746–47. But even before the 1746–47 season opened, under a special profit-sharing agreement he earned over £300 during 15 days in mid-June 1746 with his first appearances on the Covent Garden stage, playing Lear, Hamlet, Richard III, Othello, Archer, and Macbeth. Three of those performances were by command of the Prince of Wales.

The Covent Garden company which Garrick joined for the 1746–47 campaign was already in most respects stronger than the one at Drury Lane. Although it had no Woffington and no Clive, the presence of Quin, the tragedy queens Mrs Cibber and Mrs Pritchard, and the fine comedian

Woodward more than compensated. The coming of Garrick practically insured the best season Rich had ever enjoyed. Contrary to some expectations, the rough and skeptical veteran Quin received Garrick with kindness and cooperation. Both the devices which Garrick and Sheridan had found useful in Dublin were tried: Quin and Garrick in succession in the same character, Richard III, and in tandem in the same play, and Quin as his famous Falstaff in *1 Henry IV* and, on 6 December 1746, Garrick as Hotspur, though that part was so unsatisfactory that Garrick never acted it again.

The contrast between Quin's stately, formal, traditional style of acting and Garrick's fresh interpretations was nowhere more obvious than when they assumed the principal male roles in *The Fair Penitent*.

By gracious permission of Her Majesty Queen Elizabeth II

GARRICK's proportions compared to QUIN'S

by Hogarth

Richard Cumberland left us his vivid memories of one of those performances.

For the first time in my life I was treated with the sight of Garrick in the character of Lothario; Quin played Horatio . . . I enjoyed a good view of the stage from the front row of the gallery, and my attention was rivetted to the scene. I have the spectacle even now as it were before my eyes. Quin presented himself upon the rising of the curtain in a green velvet coat embroidered down the seams, an enormous full bottomed periwig, rolled stockings and high-heeled square-toed shoes: with very little variation of cadence, and in a deep full tone, accompanied by a sawing kind of action, which had more of the senate than of the stage in it, he rolled out his heroics with an air of dignified indifference, that seemed to disdain plaudits, that were bestowed upon him. . . . [W]hen after long and eager expectation I first beheld little Garrick, then young and light and alive in every muscle and in every feature, come bounding on the stage, and pointing at the wittol Altamont [Lacy Ryan] and heavy-paced Horatio—heavens, what a transition!—it seemed as if a whole century had been stept over in the transition of a single scene; old things were done away, and a new order at once brought forward, bright and luminous, and clearly destined to dispel the barbarisms and bigotry of a tasteless age. . . .

Garrick was compensated for the comparative failure of his Hotspur by the unqualified success of his own new farce, *Miss in Her Teens*, in which he played the fop Fribble, on 17 January 1747. Garrick presented a variety of his best characters, stimulated to a widening and varying of his portrayals by the interpretations of supporting actors who were new to him. His great comic triumph of the season was the amiable rake Ranger in *The Suspicious Husband*, the new comedy written especially for Garrick's talents by his friends Benjamin and John Hoadly, for which Garrick himself had written prologue and epilogue. But despite the multiplying artistic successes and satisfactory income at

Covent Garden, there were forces pushing Garrick irresistibly back toward Drury Lane.

For many months Lacy had sought to retrieve Garrick, and Rich was strangely passive about retaining him, as usual unwilling to give any straight dramatic actor credit for Covent Garden's success. When Lacy repeated his offer to sell a half interest in Drury Lane, Garrick agreed. On 9 April 1747 Garrick and Lacy signed an agreement of partnership in the patent and the house. For his £8000 Garrick purchased the responsibility for "setting or altering the business of the Stage" while Lacy was to supervise "the economy of the household." Lacy's business sense quickly taught him that the arrangement was sensible, and he interfered with the artistic management on only one or two occasions. By the end of their third season together, each partner had regained his investment. Garrick never really liked Lacy, and it is doubtful that Lacy cared much for Garrick, but the partnership held profitably together for 27 years, until Lacy's death.

Garrick's energies in the summer of 1747 had been partially donated to pumping new vitality into the Drury Lane company. He had no trouble wrenching Susanna Maria Cibber and Hannah Pritchard away from Covent Garden, though he had immediately to mollify William Pritchard, his new treasurer, who wrote from Bristol, suspicious that Mrs Cibber was to take precedence over his wife. He also brought John Arthur, William and Elizabeth Havard, and Henry Vaughan from Covent Garden and others from various places. The newcomers joined the first-line players Spranger Barry, the Yateses, Kitty Clive, and the Macklins and a number of fine secondary actors, singers, and dancers.

Once again Garrick applied to his old teacher Samuel Johnson for a rousing prologue. He received the famous poem whose last two stanzas deftly state the dilemma of the performers in the patent theatres and appeal to the audience to elevate the standards of the stage:

> Hard is his lot, that here by fortune
>   plac'd,
> Must watch the wild vicissitudes of taste;
> With ev'ry meteor of caprice must play,
> And chase the new-blown bubbles of the
>   day.
> Ah! let not censure term our fate our
>   choice,
> The stage but echoes back the publick
>   voice.
> The drama's laws the dramas patrons
>   give,
> For we that live to please, must please
>   to live.
>
> Then prompt no more the follies you de-
>   cry,
> As tyrants doom their tools of guilt to
>   die;
> 'Tis yours this night to bid the reign
>   commence
> Of rescu'd Nature, and reviving Sense;
> To chase the charms of Sound, the pomp
>   of show,
> For useful mirth, and salutary woe;
> Bid scenic virtue form the rising age,
> And Truth diffuse her radiance from the
>   stage.

Garrick, for reasons both diplomatic and theatrical, chose to open the first season of his direction of stage affairs with *The Merchant of Venice*, on 15 September 1747, with his old friend and hardly reconciled enemy Charles Macklin playing Shylock. The bills of that night noted "As the Admittance of Persons behind the Scenes has occasioned a general Complaint on Account of the frequent Interruptions in the Performance, 'tis hop'd Gentlemen won't be offended, that no Money will be taken there for the Future." (Many gentlemen *were* offended at that most necessary reformation, and a brief and puny rebellion, led by Lord Hubbard, occurred on 22 February 1748. But it resulted only in scattered catcalling and a hurled apple, and, except for benefit nights, the beaus were banished

from Drury Lane's stage forever. Beginning with the 1762–63 season they were not even to be seen on benefit nights.)

Just before opening night Garrick fell ill and the value of the theatre's plethora of talent began to count, as Barry's Hamlet, Lowe's Macheath, and Macklin's Iago appeased an audience eager to see the new manager on the stage again. On 15 October, still pale and queasy, Garrick played Archer in *The Stratagem* with Macklin, excellent as always, as Scrub and Peg Woffington, provocative as always, as Mrs Sullen. During the season Garrick ran through most of his established repertoire and, despite the unaccustomed duties as manager and his precarious health, added three new roles: Prologue-Chorus to *Henry V*, Young Belmont in Edward Moore's new comedy *The Foundling*, and Jaffeir in *Venice Preserv'd*. About *The Foundling* the prompter Cross observed in his diary: "This C. was written by Moore—it is a good play—it was acted 11 times successively—Garrick's peculiar qualifications and happy use of them, added amazing spirit to the piece, and gave more consequence to Young Belmont than can well be imagined—."

There were major changes in the Drury Lane company before the beginning of the 1748–49 season. Peg Woffington was lured away by Rich, and so were Dennis Delane, Luke Sparks, Mrs Ridout (who rejoined her husband), and Lowe the singer. But Garrick added to his roster John Beard, young Tom King, and Henry Woodward. Garrick himself, immersed in the problems of his new company, held off acting until the eighth night, 27 October 1748, when he was Ranger. On 14 November he introduced a carefully rehearsed Benedick in *Much Ado About Nothing*, acting from a severely cut text of his own devising. His interpretation of the character was greatly successful and remained one of his two or three best comedy roles for the rest of his career.

During the season Garrick had the difficult duty of staging Samuel Johnson's stately but frigid tragedy *Irene*, which went off well enough the first night until the heroine was to have been strangled with a bowstring. Cries of "Murder! Murder!" went up from the wits in the galleries, and Mrs Pritchard had to retreat to the wings alive. Garrick loyally kept the piece on the boards through the traditional (third, sixth, and ninth) author's nights. A more successful feature of the season was the revival of *Romeo and Juliet*, with Barry and Mrs Cibber. The tragedy, which had not been seen in London for 80 years, was altered by Garrick to provide for an awakening by Juliet to witness the death throes of Romeo. On 9 March 1749 Garrick played Iago for the first time in London, for Barry's benefit. (He essayed the part again in 1753 and then abandoned it.) On 15 April he played Eumenes in the new classical tragedy *Merope*, by his friend Aaron Hill. It was, said Cross, "Receiv'd with great applause." At some time in 1747 Garrick had met the talented Viennese dancer Eva Maria Veigel, who performed under the stage name "Violette." Apparently David and Eva Maria fell immediately in love, but their union was at first thwarted by the Countess of Burlington, under whose patronage and protection Violette lived and who had high matrimonial ambitions for her protegée. Among the romantic stories which surround Violette are several which detail the efforts of the young lovers to communicate with each other (Garrick was said, for example, to have resorted to female disguise in order to pass notes to her). Finally the Countess relented, and on 22 June 1749 David Garrick and Eva Maria were married twice, since the bride was Roman Catholic, first by Garrick's old friend the Rev Thomas Francklin at his

National Portrait Gallery
DAVID GARRICK
by G. Dance

National Portrait Gallery
EVA MARIA GARRICK
by G. Dance

chapel in Russell Street, Bloomsbury, "at eight o'clock in the morning," Mrs Garrick recalled over 60 years later, "and immediately afterwards in the chapel of the Portuguese ambassador, in South Audley Street."

Among Garrick's papers, after his death, were found:

VERSES SENT TO ME ON MY MARRIAGE
What! has that heart, so wild, so roving,
So prone to changing, sighing, loving,
Whom widows, maids, attacked in vain,
At last submitted to the chain?
Who is the paragon, the marvellous she,
Has fix'd a weathercock like thee?

Garrick's reply, attached, was:

'Tis not, my friend, her speaking face,
Her shape, her youth, her winning grace,
Have reach'd my heart;—the fair one's mind,
Quick as her eyes, yet soft and kind,
A gaiety with innocence,
A soft address, with manly sense,
Ravishing manners, void of art,
A cheerful, firm, yet feeling heart,
Beauty, that charms all public gaze,
And humble, amid pomp and praise
. . . .
These are the charms my heart have bound,
Charms often sought, so rarely found!
Nor think the lover's partial voice
In flattr'ing colours paints his choice.
When you MARIA hear and see
You will not wonder such a she
Has fix'd a weathercock like me.

Garrick settled on his bride £4000 (and £70 per annum of the obligatory "pin-money") and Lady Burlington donated the interest income of £5000 derived from her estates in Lincolnshire. The pair honeymooned first at Chiswick, the miniature Italian palazzo of Lord Burlington on the Thames near London, and then in a cottage near Merton, Surrey. On 14 October 1749 the Garricks moved into the capacious house at No 27, Southampton Street, which

was their town house for the next 23 years. It was only a short distance from Drury Lane Theatre. Garrick had bought the lease in July, paying 500 guineas for it, "*Dirt* and all," wrote Mrs Garrick to Lady Burlington, " 'tis reckon'd a very good Bargain." After his alliance with Eva Maria, Garrick courted the Burlingtons assiduously, and gradually a real intimacy developed with the Earl and Countess, and especially with their only daughter Charlotte, her husband the Marquis of Hartington (later fourth Duke of Devonshire), and their children.

Garrick during the season 1749–50 extensively employed John Oram the scene painter and laid out much money for new costumes. He expanded the corps of dancers to 30. The acting company remained fairly stable; it picked up only minor figures. Garrick, appearing on 28 October for the first time after his marriage, impudently chose Benedick as his character. The "Jests in Benedick were receiv'd with uncommon applause," noted Cross. William Shirley's historical pageant-play *Edward the Black Prince, or the Battle of Poictiers* was brought out with great fanfare on 6 January 1750, with Garrick as Edward. Cross testified that "it was receiv'd with great Applause—only a little groaning at some of the Love Scenes." On 15 February the afterpiece *Don Saverio* "A new musical entertainment compos'd & wrote by Mr Arne . . . was much hiss'd but suffer'd to be given out again." Garrick revived Dr John Dalton's 1738 alteration of Milton's masque *Comus*, for which Arne had set the music, and gave one of the several performances for the benefit of Milton's only surviving grandchild, Mrs Forster. He made William Whitehead's inferior tragedy *The Roman Father* palatable with his portrayal of Horatius and helped Mrs Clive launch her *The Rehearsal; or, Bayes in Petticoats*: "A new farce partly singing part speak^g. Went off well," said Cross. There was an outbreak of ugliness from Samuel Foote who (having himself cruelly mimicked half the town) wrote Garrick a nasty letter threatening "a short farce that will be wormwood to some, entertaining to many" if the revived *Friendship in Fashion* at Drury Lane should contain a rumoured caricature of him by Woodward.

The latent suspicions between the Drury Lane managers burst forth, as Lacy questioned the boundaries of their respective governance. Yet, writing later, Davies thought that "Mr. Garrick and Mr. Lacy divided the business of the theatre in such a manner as not to encroach upon each other's province. Mr Lacy took upon himself the care of the wardrobe, the scenes, and economy of the household; while Mr Garrick regulated the more important business of treating with authors, hiring actors, distributing parts in plays, superintending rehearsals, &c." And so it must have seemed to the observer. Garrick had also been sorely vexed during the year by the arrogance of Barry who, notwithstanding the fact that he had been handed Othello, Hamlet, Macbeth and others of Garrick's parts, still sulked and professed himself unappreciated.

The Garricks' social life most often centered on the Burlingtons, in town and country. Garrick visited Lord Burlington at his new house on the estate of Londesburgh Park in Yorkshire, riding, shooting, and binding himself closer to Lady Burlington. Those expeditions were not without incident. To the Marquis of Hartington—now become a close confidant who depended upon Garrick for news of his mother-in-law's disposition—Garrick wrote from Londesburgh on 8 June 1750:

. . . We got to this place on Wednesday Night, being detain'd at Lord Rockingham's a Day & a half—tho, we are all Well & Merry, I can't say we arriv'd here absolutely without Accidents; for Lady Burlington & her Grace of Garrick, were fairly turn'd heels upward in the once horse chair; & tho there was no

broken Arms & Legs, We have a swell'd Face & a black Eye or two. . . .

and, ruefully, on 13 July 1750,

. . . I murder a Rabbit now & then, & have been fatal to ye woodpeckers, but from a five Years cessation of Arms, I really cannot distinguish between tame & Wild Pigeons; for unluckily I fir'd among a flock of 'Em Yesterday upon ye Wolds, & incurr'd a penalty of twenty pounds by act of Parliam^t—I shall look before I shoot, ye next time, for such Mistakes have no Joke in 'Em—half a Dozen Partridges were brought in to Day kill'd by long Ralpho; I think they are rather too Small, but as they are not ye Produce of My Lord's Manor, they will be relish'd better with bread Sauce & a little Shalot—.

The Drury Lane season of 1750–51 opened without Barry, who had defected to Covent Garden. A loss more grievous was Mrs Cibber, whose health had not permitted her to act at all in the 1749–50 season and who now also left for Covent Garden. King went to Ireland. But a prize acquisition was the beautiful, dissolute, and difficult George Anne Bellamy.

The two patent houses opened the 1750–51 season with prologues of matching truculence. As a calculated act of defiance toward Charles Macklin, who had signed on with Covent Garden after two years in Ireland instead of returning to Drury Lane, Garrick had opened his season on 8 September by offering *The Merchant of Venice* with Yates as Shylock.

It had long been known that Rich was preparing the irresistibly sentimental team of Spranger Barry and Susanna Maria Cibber to sweep the town with *Romeo and Juliet* for Barry's debut at Covent Garden. Garrick had never played Romeo but he had been rehearsing the part strenuously with Miss Bellamy as his Juliet. The tragedy was announced by both houses for 28 September, and for twelve successive nights the London public could see nothing else.

Many did not care to see anything else. But I. H———tt, writing in the *Daily Advertiser*, summed the matter up for many others:

> *"On the Run of* Romeo and Juliet*"*
> *Well—what tonight, says angry Ned,*
> *As up from bed he rouses,*
> *Romeo again! and shakes his head,*
> *Ah! Pox on both your houses!*

Barry's handsome physique and mellow voice extended Garrick's genius to the full and Mrs Cibber's seasoned excellence made her advancing years (she was 36) seem unimportant, though George Anne Bellamy's fresh favour (at 19) attracted charmed attention from the town's beaus. Francis Gentleman remembered in 1770 that Garrick had earned the most applause but Barry the most tears. A judicious lady is said to have remarked, when asked to make a judgment as to the Romeos: "Had I been Juliet to Garrick's Romeo,—so ardent and impassioned was he, I should have expected he would have *come up* to me in the balcony; but had I been Juliet to Barry's Romeo,—so tender, so eloquent, and so seductive was he, I should certainly have *gone down* to him!" Mrs Garrick had an opinion, too: ". . . Mr Barry is too jung (in his ha'd) for Romeo, & Mrs Cibber is too old for a girl of 18. . . . I wish thie woold finish both, for it is too much for My Little Dear Spouse to Play Every Day." Yet her spouse and George Anne Bellamy won the contest by outlasting their exhausted competitors. But Garrick was not a gallant winner. He crowed loudly to Lady Burlington:

I can give Y^r Lad^p the Satisfaction, & I flatter Myself that it will be so to You, of assuring You that ye Battle is at last Ended, & in our favour—our Antagonists yielded last thursday Night & we play'd ye Same Play (Romeo & Juliet) on ye Fryday to a very full house to very great applause; Mr Barry and Mrs Cibber came incog to see Us, & I am very well-assur'd

they receiv'd no little Mortification—Miss Bellamy has surpriz'd Every body, & I hope before Y^r Lad^p returns, that she will almost be a Match [for] Madam Cibber, who I believe now begins to repent of leaving Drury Lane— I have written an Epilogue for Clive, which is an Answer to Barry's almost universally Exploded prologue— We have got ye Laugh on our Side, & by turning the whole to Joke, We are at present in ye highest Spirits— I have receiv'd great favour indeed from ye Town in ye Character of Romeo; & I am so extreamly well, that no fatigue hurts Me, & I have not once lost my Voice or Powers for thirteen Nights togeather, which is amazing.

Garrick then referred the whole triumph back to what seems to have been his nagging need to prove to the Countess the success of his marriage: "I need not tell Y^r Lad^p that this is all owing to my happiness at Home—."

On 3 December Garrick essayed Osmyn in Congreve's *The Mourning Bride* with good success, and he added it to his permanent repertoire. Garrick's third new attempt that season was in the title role of Edward Moore's comedy *Gil Blas*, on 2 February 1751. Cross recorded that "the first 3 Acts went off without much hissing, but the two last were but indifferently treated; a great party for & against it, but it was given out again—great crowding to get in & ye Pit took possession of many of the Boxes, wch confus'd ye accounts," and on 4 February, the next night of playing, there was "Great applause." "I believe," wrote Cross, "the author had many friends." But by the seventh performance there was "a great deal of Hissing," an apple was thrown at Mrs Pritchard, and Garrick was forced to come forward and plead for indulgence to complete a run of nine nights for the sake of the author.

Garrick acted in one more innovation that season, Malet and Thomson's *Alfred, a Masque*, on 23 February. On 26 December the first of half a dozen pantomimes devised by Henry Woodward for Drury

Lane opened a decade of competition between Garrick and Rich for preeminence in dance, music, and spectacle.

On 19 March, just as the annual benefits were beginning, the Prince of Wales died, and the theatres were closed for a period of national mourning. They reopened on 8 April. During the interval David and Eva Maria went off for a week to drink the waters of "the Bath." Garrick came back to work on 8 April and plunged into the midst of the jealous strife and bustle of the benefits.

It had been an arduous season, beginning with the exhausting *Romeo and Juliet.*

Garrick had performed major roles 97 times, acted in three afterpieces, spoken 15 prologues, brought out several new works, and coached his 82 performers through 186 nights of performance. He had quelled the usual disturbances, fended off the usual proposals of amateur thespians and aspiring authors, and suffered the expected irritations from Lacy, his brother manager. He had found time to lobby for the election of his friend Sir Thomas Harrison as Chamberlain of London. In addition, he had, during the spring of 1751, tutored his brother George in the negotiations which gained him the hand in marriage of Cath-

The Museum of London

DAVID GARRICK as Ranger and HANNAH PRITCHARD as Clarinda

by Hayman

erine Carrington, even going so far as to write model letters of supplication.

On Sunday, 19 May 1751, the Garricks left London for a long excursion to Paris, traveling with their friend Charles Denis. Garrick wrote Somerset Draper on 21 May from Boulogne. They had arrived the night before after a swift, rough passage of three hours from Dover which left Mrs Garrick "a little sick" but David "as hearty as the most stinking tar-barrel of them all." Garrick began at once to keep a diary, setting down, as he later wrote to Peter Garrick, "the particulars of my liking and dislike" of that "best place in the world to make a visit to," France. But Garrick's introduction to his ancestral country was unpropitious. ". . . I never saw so much Dirt, Beggary, imposition & Impertinance as I did at Boul^e, The Custom house Officers . . . were very uncivil & strict . . . & shewed not ye least politeness to . . . us."

Once in Paris the Garricks plunged into a round of sightseeing and theatre-going, visiting 15 palaces and 17 churches and attending the theatre or opera 13 times. Their professional eyes were in general displeased by the performances. Dancing which was "much approv'd of" at the Comédie Italienne "would have been hiss'd off ye English Stage—." At the Opéra in the Palais Royal "ye scenes were well conducted & had a good Effect ye habits seemingly rich, the singers & dancers very numerous; but ye singing abominable to *me* & ye dancing very indifferent." He thought the actor Lekain had "feeling & spirit" but "Duminil [Dumesnil] ye celebrated actress has not *yet* touch'd me." "*Grandval* play'd this Night [10 June], but he did not touch me, he has a manner, & some affectation—*ill-dress'd*." "*Carlin* ye Arlequin is undoubtedly a Genius in his way" and "*Gautier* [was] not a bad Actress." Only Mlle Clairon, not yet come to her full powers, and "*Chassee*, ye bass singer" (Claude Louis-Dominique de Chassé de Chinais) pleased Garrick very much. Garrick cast a critical eye at the house appointments and production arrangements of the Comédie Française:

NB the Appearance of ye house was not so bad as I expected from ye report of others, ye glass branches give it a rich look, but ye candles instead of lamps at ye front of ye stage are very mean & ye building on ye stage wholly destroys all *vraysemblance* (as ye french call it) & with all their perfection, occasions ten thousand absurdities—they have but one piece of musick before ye play & they have only 8 or at most 10 hands in their Orchestra.

Yet "I am not certain there is not an advantage to ye actors & audience from ye shape of their theatre—." He was most "magnificently" entertained at supper by an actor of the Comédie Française, Jean Sauvé, "a very sensible man, but not in ye first rank of his profession," who told Garrick "several things of their disagreeable Dependence on ye L^{ds} of ye B^d Chamb^r," and of being imprisoned for displeasing them.

Actors were as yet mere lackeys in France, of course, not even entitled to the sacrament or Christian burial, and Garrick's English celebrity had not spread very far on the Continent. He was not, therefore, welcomed into the circles of the nobility in the manner to which he had already become accustomed in his own country, although there was one exception; when they "Went to see y^e *Hotel de Taillard* & indeed worth seeing, ye Count himself tho lame had ye Civility to come in his chair upon Castors & attend us through ye Rooms. . . ." He contented himself with waiting upon the ancient Lady Sandwich, widow of the third Earl and a daughter of the Restoration poet, the second Earl of Rochester, and making courtesy visits to members of the little colony of genteel British expatriates: "Mr *York*, (whom I sat wth an hour) Lord Huntington, Mr Stanhope, Lord Stormont. . . ." He "had an invitation to drive with Ld Albemarle [the English Ambassador], but could not, on account of going to Versailles." With

Versailles Garrick was not much impressed, deprecating the grandeur of its fountains when compared with those of Chatsworth, seat of his friend the Duke of Devonshire. But he admired the wood carving and Coustos's Pieta in Notre Dame, "the most splendid Church I ever saw." His brisk curiosity and interest in humanity took him to the great orphan asylum, the Enfants Trouvés or Hôspice de L'Allaitement, where he found "yᵉ Children much handsomer than one would imagine as yᵉ People of all kinds we meet in yᵉ Street, Gardens & other publick places are by much yᵉ ugliest I ever saw—."

An eager tourist, Garrick investigated the Sorbonne, the Paris cloister of the Carthusians, the Carmelites, and the English Benedictines, the pensioners at the Hôtel des Invalides, the Collège de Mazarin, the great library at the "Golden Basilica" of St. Germain des Prés, the church of St. Sulpice, the old Luxembourg palace built for Marie de Medici (to see "Rubens's Gallery"), the tapestries at the house of the Gobelins, the garden of the Palais Royal. Mrs Garrick stayed behind and Denis accompanied David when his morbid curiosity or sociological diligence took him among the stinks and horrors of the Hôtel-Dieu, the Place de Grève, the General Hospital, the Bastille, and the open charnel house of the Churchyard of the Innocents.

By late July 1751 Garrick wrote Hoadly he had "return'd with my better half, safe & sound from Paris & as true an Englishman as Ever. . . . I am much, very much pleas'd with my Jaunt, & am ready & willing to take yᵉ Same & for a Month longer, whenever Business will permit. . . ." He seemed almost triumphant. To Peter he wrote: "The great fault of our Countrymen is, yᵗ when they go to Paris, they keep too much among themselves; but if they would Mix wᵗʰ yᵉ French as I did, it is a most agreeable jaunt." Yet there seems also an air of relief at a return to British society, where theatrical performers—especially the

Garricks—were more than tolerated. (There was even a rumor that the Garricks had quitted France hastily to avoid arrest. There are extant official documents which indicate that Garrick was suspected of trying to lure French dancers to London, which was against the law.) Later, in July, the Garricks were at Chiswick House, being cosseted and flattered by the possessive Burlingtons, and in August they went off for more of the same at Londesborough.

Garrick had returned to London refreshed in spirit, with a widened appreciation of the possibilities of the multifaceted art of the theatre, and enormously increased in confidence. His opinion of his partner Lacy ("Timbertop") had changed only for the worse, however. From Londesborough he wrote Draper that George had told him that "the Great Lacy" had in his absence signed the ropedancer Anthony Maddox for a series of engagements. "I cannot possibly agree to such a prostitution on any account; and nothing but downright starving would induce me to bring such defilement and abomination into the house of William Shakespeare. What a mean, mistaken creature is this Par[tn]er of mine!" Yet it was one of the few times that Lacy had openly interfered with the performance side, and Garrick had sense enough to appreciate the positive contributions of the man with whom he was contractually yoked. "Oh, I am sick, sick, sick of him!" Garrick could exclaim to an intimate like Draper and, the aggression worked off, follow the explosion with "I am working and studying here like a horse," with a list of his intended parts.

Garrick had already gone about the annual business of bringing fresh talent into the company, acquiring from Dublin three excellent actors—the heavy tragedian Henry Mossop, the strong performer of rakes and young lords David Ross, and young John Dexter, a virtual amateur, but of great potential. Garrick himself, in the season 1751–52, acted 93 times and spoke three prologues. His new parts were Kitely in *Every Man in His Humour*, which he rewrote, and, on 17 February 1752, the original Mercour in the Rev. Philip Francis's tragedy *Eugenia*, which not all Garrick's talents could keep afloat for more than six nights. Garrick's magnificent Lear was again widely commended.

In 1752–53 the Drury Lane company swelled to 88 exclusive of the band. The theatre had lost some minor people but had gained the obstreperous but valuable Theophilus Cibber and Thomas Davies and his beautiful wife, who had come from Ireland, and a dozen promising secondary players. In 185 nights of playing the theatre added four new works. Garrick took the leading part of Beverly in Edward Moore's moral tragedy *The Gamester*, attacking gambling, which was presented on 7 February to plaudits from audience and critics. The poet Edward Young's equally moral classical tragedy *The Brothers*, produced on 3 March, was less successful, though the critics acclaimed Garrick as Demetrius.

In 1753–54 Garrick presided over his largest company to that point, 92 performers, a dozen more than Covent Garden mustered. Drury Lane also distanced its competition in number of nights played by 192 to 183. Though he had lost Mrs Bellamy, Theophilus Cibber, and Ned Shuter to Rich, and the successful but diffident Dexter had returned to Ireland, Garrick's company was decidedly the better one. In fact, for the first time during his management Drury Lane was comfortably ahead of the rival house in almost every department.

Garrick played the Bastard in *King John* for the first time at Drury Lane on 23 January 1754, but "being hoarse went not so well as expected," noted Cross. In March for Mossop's benefit Garrick revived *Zara* after 17 years and played Lusignan. On 18 March, for Mrs Pritchard's benefit, he extracted his three-act farce *Catherine and Petruchio*, from *The Taming of the Shrew*.

It held the stage for 90 years. During the year Garrick injudiciously played Dumnorex in William Glover's frigid failure *Boadicea* and Virginius in Henry Crisp's twice-refused tragedy *Virginia*, in which, however, there were at least a few incidents of interest. The tyro Miss Graham redeemed the pale part of Marcia with her excellent acting. Garrick caused "a thunder of applause such as had never been equalled in the theatre" with his dreadful gaze bent on the tyrant Claudius and the two words "Thou Traitor!" which "He uttered in a low tone of voice that spoke the fullness of a broken heart." No more successful was William Whitehead's turgid *Creusa, Queen of Athens*, which died almost immediately despite the efforts of the whole panoply of tragedy power, headed by Garrick as Aletes. He began to discern the decline of the power of ponderous pseudo-classical tragedy to fill theatres.

Garrick's letters in 1752 and 1753 had revealed his ambition to acquire a country seat, quite natural in a gentleman of refined tastes and expanding income and social horizons. Peter Garrick was excitedly asked to investigate what David had been told was "one of the prettiest freehold Estates in yᵉ County of Derby." But Derby was too far from London and though, as David said, "I own I love a good Situation prodigiously, & I think the four great Requisites to make one are, Wood, Water, Extent, & inequality of Ground," neither his income nor his social station could ever let him aspire to a Chatsworth or a Blenheim. Though he "must have a River," something smaller than a palace and nearer Westminster had to be found. So in January 1754 Garrick rented Lacey Primatt's largish yellow-brick house on several acres of ground at Hampton, 13 miles from his theatre. Satisfied with its situation near the river, he bought the property in August and began making the improvements which eventually included a new white Palladian front by Robert Adam, tasteful gardens in the new style by "Capability" Brown, and a classical riverside temple to Shakespeare.

Garrick had obliged "the gentlemen of Calcutta by sending them some plays, scenes, etc." and in return they sent Indian chintzes for bed and curtains. Some were detained in the customs and had to be wheedled out by Garrick. Chinese wall-paper, Chippendale chairs, blue-and-gold bookcases, and the exacting process of hiring suitable country serving-people for the dwelling began to seize more and more of Garrick's time. It was to be his country retreat for the next 25 years and to provoke Samuel Johnson to sigh when he saw it: "Ah, David! It is the leaving of such a place that makes a death-bed terrible." Letitia Hawkins recalled that "at Hampton, and in its neighbourhood, Mr. and Mrs. Garrick took the rank of the *noblesse*; — his highly-finished manners, and his lady's elegance of taste, making their house and themselves very attractive" to the incessant stream of visitors. "I see him now," she wrote in 1824, "in a dark blue coat, the button-holes bound with gold, a small cocked-hat laced with gold, his waistcoat very open, and his countenance never at rest, and, indeed, seldom his person; for in the relaxation of the country, he gave way to all his natural volatility. . . ."

Garrick again devoted his time to management until the 1754–55 season was well under way, turning over several of his roles to Mossop, Ross, and Woodward. He appeared first on 3 October, as Archer, next on 11 October as Romeo, and on 16 October as Hamlet, thereafter performing his standard parts at intervals of several nights: Chamont, Richard, Macbeth, Jaffeir, Lothario, and, in March, his superb Lear, for his benefit, to a capacity house of £220. He flogged John Brown's dull *Barbarossa*, in which he played Achmet, to 11 nights from its opening on 17 December. Garrick had learned that Covent Garden was preparing to revive something like the Shakespearean text of *Coriolanus*. Working

quickly, from Sir Thomas Hanmer's scholarly edition, Garrick made the excisions he deemed necessary for the stage presentation. Those were extensive, but no additions were made. Presumably Garrick had planned to assume the role, but press of business made him give it to Henry Mossop. It appeared on 11 November 1754 and for eight other performances that season, but to thin houses.

Garrick also produced (and probably wrote) the opera *The Fairies*, altered from the first four acts of *A Midsummer Night's Dream*, with music by J. C. Smith, on 3 February. He wrote prologues and epilogues in aid of several of the masques, operas and pantomimes which were becoming such an important part of the bill. It was a season of revivals. Garrick produced *The Mistake* ("Not acted these 30 Years"), in which he played Don Carlos, and *Measure for Measure*, missing from the repertory for five years. He also revived Buckingham's old comedy *The Chances*, on 7 November, and was roundly chided by "A Gentleman of Oxford" in *The Devil Upon Crutches in England* for "the most barefaced bawdry Farce . . . that ever disgraced the stage, in which the Manager, who has caus'd it to be reviv'd, is to perform the principal part [Don John]." Garrick in February disappointed and alienated John Home by refusing to stage his tragedy *Douglas*.

There were vexations more serious that season than captious critics and sore authors, including continuing difficulties with temperamental performers and dangerously turbulent audiences:

Whereas several complaints, by letter and otherwise, have been lately made to the Managers of Drury Lane Theatre, of the ill Behavior of some persons in the Upper Gallery, who throw down Apples, Potatoes, and other things into the Pit.: This is therefore to assure the Ladies and Gentlemen that the Managers will take all imaginable care to discover and prosecute any person or persons, who shall, disturb, or insult them for the future. If any person will discover who it was that flung a hard piece of cheese, of near half a Pound Weight, from one of the Galleries last Thursday Night [11 Feb.] and greatly hurt a young Lady in the Pit, shall receive Ten Guineas from Mr Pritchard, the Treasurer of the Theatre.

By 1754 the Garricks' position in the innermost circles of London fashion was secure, due greatly to their circumspect and genteel behavior and to his accomplishments, but also to the patronage of the Burlingtons. With that family they were on such close terms that they occasioned some jealousy on the part of its various members vying for their favors. Garrick was consulted and even appealed to in settling their intimate differences. Several letters to and from him in 1754 reveal him as a peacemaker between Lady Burlington and her son-in-law the Marquis of Hartington, Lord Lieutenant of Ireland, soon to become the fourth Duke of Devonshire. It was apparent that Garrick enjoyed the confidence and the consequence.

After prolonged and complicated negotiations, beginning in the summer of 1754, Garrick, on 31 January 1755, had signed a contract with the Swiss ballet master and choreographer Jean-Georges Noverre to bring his greatly successful *Les Fêtes Chinoises* from Paris to Drury Lane. But England was on the brink of war with France, and the passions of the London audiences were rising. When on 6 November "Mr Garrick ended the 3ᵈ Act [of *Jane Shore*] with 'Die wᵗʰ pleasure for my Country's good'—a person in the Gall: cry'd no french Dancers then," wrote Cross the prompter. Completely futile were Garrick's quick newspaper assurances that Noverre was Swiss, of a "Protestant family in the Canton of Berne, his wife and sisters Germans," and that of the more than 60 performers only nine were French, fewer than he generally employed. When the entertainment was staged on 12 November 1755 before a large audience which included the King,

the dancers were hissed. Some officers interpreted the hissing as disrespectful to the King and drove several persons out of the pit and galleries. The disorder was confined to noise on 13 and 14 November, but on the next night, wrote Cross,

When Garrick appear'd one from the Slips cry'd out Monsieur, & great Numbers Hiss'd —the play went on—wᶜʰ done, the Mutiny began, amazing noise—no palting, except one Apple; yᵉ pit to yᵉ Boxes cry'd—now draw yʳ Swords, wᶜʰ makes us think, the Riot was occasion'd by the Box people being so busy & turning some out of the pit & Gall: before. Some benches were pull'd up, & Mr Lacy gave up the Dance to appease 'em—being Sat: our friends were at yᵉ Opera, & the common people had leisure to do Mischief.

Lynham, in *The Chevalier Noverre*, quotes the *Journal Étranger* of 25 November 1755:

The blackguards . . . tore up the benches and threw them into the Pit on the opposing party; they broke all the mirrors, the Chandeliers, &c., and tried to climb onto the stage to massacre everybody; but, as there is a magnificent organization in this theatre, in three minutes all the decor had been removed, all the traps were ready to come into play to swallow up those who might venture up, all the wings were filled with men armed with sticks, swords, halberds, &c., and behind the scenes the great reservoir was ready to be opened to drown those who might fall on the stage itself.

The disturbance subsided on 17 November when it seemed that an agreement had been reached which would allow the Festival, "hotly call'd for by the boxes," to be played three times a week, with the pit to decide the entertainments on the alternate three nights. But on 18 November the riot broke out afresh, "& broken heads were plenty on both Sides." Justice Fielding came "with Constables & a Guard," and "numbers went & broke Garrick's Windows in Southampton Street . . . Garrick was oblig'd to give up the Dancers—."

Garrick and Lacy were not only out of pocket some £4000 for the expensive scenery and costumes of *The Chinese Festival*, the salaries of the swollen dance company, and the damage done to the theatre but Garrick had counted very heavily on large receipts during a long run. Lacy had looked with disfavor on the affair from the beginning and had counselled its abandonment after the first disorder. Here was another bone of contention between them. On 21 November Garrick returned to the boards for the first time since the fracas had begun, playing Archer in *The Stratagem*:

Soon as Mr Garrick appear'd, a great Clap, with some hissing upon wch he said—Gentlemen it is impossible to go on with these hisses, I don't know what offence I am guilty of—they clap'd greatly—& he proceeded—Let one Gentleman speak for the rest & I'll give an Answer—there was a moments pause, & then a general cry of—Go on with the Play, &c., all ceased—& all continu'd quiet.

All continued quiet for the rest of the season. On 27 February Dr John Brown's tragedy *Athelstan* took the stage to "Great Applause," with Garrick in the title part, but it was 18 March before it saw its ninth and last night. Several new farces and afterpieces were staged, and Garrick revived *The Fair Quaker of Deal* after 30 years, *Rule a Wife and Have a Wife* after 15 (he playing Leon for the first time), *The Orphan* after 12, and *All's Well that Ends Well* after 18 (but it "went off Dull," wrote Cross). On 21 January 1756 Garrick played Leontes in his new alteration of *The Winter's Tale*, whose title he presently changed to *Florizel and Perdita*. He furnished a prologue in which he avowed " 'Tis my chief wish, my joy, my only plan / To lose no drop of that immortal man," for which remark he has been derided, with a good deal of justification, by generations of critics. His version, however,

By gracious permission of Her Majesty Queen Elizabeth II

DAVID GARRICK, as Kitely

by Reynolds

seems to have been prepared, as were others of his alterations, with the limitations of his audiences in mind. It was brutally attacked by Theophilus Cibber in his *Two Dissertations on the Theatres*, but better critics of Garrick's time, including Thomas Davies, defended it persuasively. Garrick took the pastoral half of Shakespeare's romance, fitted it up with music and dancing, and made a resounding stage success of it. It was usually played in a double bill, the other part of which was his *Catherine and Petruchio*.

The success of *Florizel and Perdita* induced Garrick, on 11 February 1756, less than a month later, to work a similar drastic change on *The Tempest*. He employed J. C. Smith to furnish music, as he had done with *The Fairies*, and either he (though he denied it) or someone under his direction pruned Shakespeare and spliced in lines from the Dryden-Davenant version and fitted in Smith's 32 songs. The opera was, after a tolerable first night, a failure, and even Garrick's friends among the critics parted company with him on this attempt. Murphy remarked that Garrick had " 'wished to lose no drop of that immortal man,' and here he lost a *tun* of him." Tate Wilkinson thought the piece "dreadfully heavy." Garrick also provided a new scene for his popular *Lethe* and a new character for himself to play, Lord Chalkstone. The long season of 187 performances, begun so badly, ended with modest profit to the house and to Garrick.

The season following, 1756–57, saw an increase in gross income at Drury Lane. Frances Barton, who would make a great name as Fanny Abington and who would give Garrick more woe than any others of the many difficult actresses who tried his temper over the years, joined the company. On 28 October 1756 Garrick was seen as King Lear in a text which offered some modest "Restorations from Shakespeare," as the prompter Cross noted, restorations which would grow in number, as Garrick made this one of his finest roles, though he never completely eradicated Tate's depredations.

The most resounding success of the season resulted from Garrick's employment of children to act his farce *Lilliput*, which ran for 17 performances in December, notwithstanding the opposition of the *Theatrical Examiner's* critic who flayed it as "a most petit, trifling, indecent, immoral, stupid parcel of rubbish," calculated to "debauch the minds of infants." Garrick wrote and staged an afterpiece, *The Male Coquette* (billed at first as *The Modern Fine Gentleman*). The Marine Society benefited by £280 to clothe young volunteers for the sea service on 11 May, when Garrick spoke the prologue and epilogue "in the character of a sailor." Garrick on 20 April 1757 had purchased through, and in the name of, James Clutterbuck the manor of

Hendon in Essex for £13,038. (On 10 July 1767, most of the property was conveyed to Garrick.)

In 1757–58 the Drury Lane company of 81 put on 181 performances, despite closing for ten days during mourning for Princess Caroline. The company remained relatively stable. Again Garrick and Lacy refurbished the interior of the theatre before the start of the season. There were pamphlet attacks, general and personal, levelled both on the theatres and the managers by James Ralph in *Case of the Authors . . . Stated with Regard to Booksellers, the Stage, and the Public*, by William Shirley in *Brief Remarks on the Present State of the Drama*, and by the anonymous author of *The Theatrical Examiner*.

Garrick also had to endure a long diatribe from Marguerite Louise Noverre, who attacked him and Lacy for having reduced Jean Georges Noverre's salary in the 1756–57 season when he showed up three months late. Garrick was thrust into an angry correspondence quarrel when he refused the irascible poet and bookseller Robert Dodsley's tragedy *Cleone*. A ten-year friendship with the playwright James Ralph ended when Garrick refused one of Ralph's pieces. Three people were crushed to death in a crowded passageway of Drury Lane Theatre on Boxing Day. Garrick sustained John Home's bombastic new tragedy *Agia* through ten performances by his acting of Lysander, thus finally cementing a friendship greatly strained both by Garrick's refusal of *Douglas* and by its subsequent success at Edinburgh and Covent Garden. (In May Home led an hilarious party of intellectual Scots—the architect brothers Robert and James Adam, the lawyer Alexander Wedderburn and his army officer brother David, the Rev John Black, the historian Dr William Robertson, and the Rev Alexander Carlyle—to Hampton to teach Garrick to play golf.)

On 20 October 1757 Garrick offered

(perhaps in contrition for his impiety in the matter of the opera of the previous season) a *Tempest* billed "As written by Shakespeare" and in which, indeed, only some 432 lines had been cut and 14 added. Garrick played Henry IV in *2 Henry IV* for the first time ever, on the occasion of Woodward's benefit on 13 March 1758. Again, his text shows his concern to restore, rather than prune, Shakespeare's words. On 30 March, having turned the role of Hamlet over to Mossop at his benefit Garrick announced he would play his old part of the Ghost, but, noted James Winston, "he afterwards declined it having a new part in the farce." That part was Pamphlet in *The Upholsterer*, by which Garrick sought to favor the author, his quarrelsome friend Arthur Murphy. But it "Went off Indiff," said Cross. The gross receipts for 1757–58 climbed well over the £30,000 mark by season's end.

In the quiet season of 1758–59 Drury Lane escaped riots but lost nine days in January because of the death of the Princess Royal. Garrick's company of 80 actors put on 185 nights of performance, nevertheless. Garrick acquired, almost by accident, during the season one of his finest and most constant players, John Moody.

A Mr Apreece, objecting to being caricatured in a farce of Foote's, caught Garrick in the controversy before the matter was settled by the intervention of the Lord Chamberlain. Dr John Hill, enraged by the failure of his farce *The Rout* (on 20 December 1758), talked and wrote bitterly against Garrick. Illness plagued the company toward the end of the season, and Garrick was forced to borrow players from Rich. The manager himself was taken ill while acting Lear on 25 October and was not very well through the rest of the year. He gave several compassionate benefits, notably, on 3 February, for "Mr Crisʳ Smart, an Ingenious young man in poetry, but now confin'd in a Mad house." For that night Garrick wrote and produced his own two-act comedy *The Guardian* and played the hero, Heartly.

The persistant Arthur Murphy's *Orphan of China* lasted through nine performances, thanks to Garrick's acting the principal part of Zamti and to a command performance by the Prince of Wales. During the regular season he sponsored, as usual, a number of revivals of old pieces, including David Mallet's *Eurydice*, in which he for the first time played Periander.

But the most important venture of the 1758–59 season was the staging of *Antony and Cleopatra* on 3 January, in a version altered by Garrick and the scholar Edward Capell, in which Garrick played Antony. There is no record of the play's having been performed after Shakespeare's time before that occasion. Garrick had prepared elaborate scenery and colorful new costumes, but Cross thought on the first night that it "did not seem to give yᵉ Audience any great plasure, or draw any Applause. . . ." Perhaps it puzzled the audience, being very different from anything they had seen. Yet for the six times it played it drew good houses. Garrick thought later that it might have been continued, for "it gain'd ground Every time it was play'd, but I grew Tir'd, & gave it up,—the part was laborious. . . ."

In July the Garricks ran down to Wickham, Hampshire, on a long-promised visit to the Rev Dr Thomas Garnier, a fellow Huguenot, afterwards Dean of Winchester. On the way, at Winchester, they stayed with Dr Joseph Warton. While at Wickham they dropped down to Kennedy's theatre at Portsmouth and saw young Tate Wilkinson act Hamlet. Wilkinson was invited to the Garniers', and Garrick walked him around Portsmouth and bought his boat cloak from him. Wilkinson never forgot the flattery.

The company of 1759–60 was neither as strong nor as weak as it had sometimes been, but Garrick (despite pamphleteers' plaints that he did not act often enough) continued to be the chief attraction and greatest revenue-producer as well as the mainspring of planning and production. He directed his 84 actors, dancers, and singers to 186 varied performances, producing two new mainpieces and six new afterpieces. A brace of these—*The Desert Island*, a dramatic poem in three acts, and the comedy *The Way to Keep Him*, both by Murphy—had set off another round of recriminations between that cantankerous spirit and Garrick. Garrick had said that he could not perform parts in both, and Murphy had twice taken back his manuscripts in dudgeon. Finally Garrick wrote and spoke a prologue for *The Desert Island* "In the character of a Drunken Poet" and played Lovemore in *The Way to Keep Him*, bringing forth the works on the same night—a procedure which again displeased Murphy. But the playwright was pacified when the twin bill achieved 11 performances.

John Home brought Garrick his third massive tragedy, *The Siege of Aquileia*, and, superstitiously (for Garrick still had his unfortunate refusal of the successful *Douglas* in mind), the manager accepted it. Garrick worked it up, learned the principal role, Aemilius, and, with the assistance of two commands from the obliging Prince of Wales, laboriously pushed it to the ninth night, for Home's third benefit. Among the afterpieces produced were Garrick's own Christmas pantomime, *Harlequin's Invasion*, on 31 December (historic because it was the first pantomime with a speaking Harlequin) and James Townley's *High Life Below Stairs*, which provoked a near riot in the footmen's gallery and Goldsmith's censure in *The Bee*. It emerged anonymously and was generally fathered on Garrick, despite his denials.

On 17 March 1760, for Mrs Cibber's benefit, Garrick essayed Pierre in *Venice Preserv'd* for the first time in 15 years. On 24 April, for O'Brien's benefit, he allowed Steele's *Tender Husband* to be revived and indulgently accepted—for that night only

—the role of Sir Harry Gubbin. On 14 April for Mrs Yates's night, he acted Chamont for the first time in four years, and on short notice.

The year had been peaceful, except for the turbulence of the footmen at *High Life Below Stairs*. Otherwise Cross recorded scarcely a catcall. But Garrick's professional and social successes had excited Edward Purdon to attack him, in his 33-page *Letter to Garrick on Opening the Theatre*, for deficiencies, as Purdon thought, in casting and scene display; but Garrick was defended immediately, and the rate of encomiastic comment on his acting continued to swell, led by the laudatory pamphlet *Obvious Reasons Why David Garrick Should Not Appear on the Stage* (he so far overtops his fellows that he gives them no chance for distinction).

Garrick completely changed the look of his company by wholesale refusal to renew articles and by energetic searches for new talents before the season of 1760–61. The prize and surprise of the season was Tom Sheridan, who had been in England working on plans for lectures and not acting at all for some two years after quitting his Dublin managership. Through the good offices of Benjamin Victor, Sheridan had agreed with Garrick "to be together on shares on those nights he performs," an arrangement to that time unique at Drury Lane. On some nights, Sheridan took principal roles ordinarily taken by Garrick. On others, they shared attention—as Horatio and Lothario in *The Fair Penitent*, for instance. Davies reminds us that "a coldness had subsisted between them for some time," yet the relationship held together despite Garrick's jealousy, aroused by the preference of the newly crowned George III for Sheridan's King over Garrick's Bastard in *King John*. Though, said Davies, their admiration was mutual and they were both gentlemen, "one could not bear an equal, nor the other a superior." Sheridan's contract was not renewed.

Garrick's company of 87 performed only

179 nights in 1760–61. The loss of 19 playing days for both theatres (25 October through 17 November 1760) because of mourning for George II was somewhat compensated for by the determined efforts of George III, the young "Patriot King," to build upon the cordiality his subjects showed him as the first of his house born in England by coming frequently to the theatre. Of course full houses were realized on nights of command performances.

Garrick deferred his first appearance until 30 September, the fifth night of the 1760–61 season, when he appeared as Benedick. He added only three new roles: Lovemore in the revision of Murphy's *The Way to Keep Him*, Oakly, the lead, in his friend George Colman's successful comedy *The Jealous Wife* (which the prompter Hopkins noted "met with greater applause than anything since the *Suspicious Husband*,") and Mercutio, for Holland's benefit night, which was deferred, said Hopkins "that Mr Garrick may have time to be prepared in the Character. . . ." He was, indeed, most accommodating to his actors during the benefit season, stepping into farce for Foote's benefit, playing the title part in *The Guardian*. He acted the low comedy Scrub character in *The Stratagem* for O'Brien and re-studied Duretête in *The Inconstant* for the first time in eight years. He graciously (and wisely) turned over King John, Othello, Macbeth, Lord Townly, Cato, and other prime parts to Sheridan, Romeo to Holland, Orlando to Palmer.

Garrick played Hastings in *Jane Shore* and Lothario in *The Fair Penitent*, Lysander in *Agis*, and Lear (the latter because the King required it), but for the most part he stayed in his well-worn roles in comedy: Bayes, Abel Drugger, Kitely, and Don Carlos. He wrote and staged another of his musical interludes, *The Enchanter; or, Love and Magic*. He was as usual principally engaged with the small routines and large excitements of his unique position—helping Havard prepare his *New Coronation Ode*, coaching the younger players, penning pro-

logues, comforting Miss Piercy, who "in running off the stage, which was greatly crowded, fell down and broke her arm," and trying to deserve the commands of a newly-crowned George III, who in the space of one week bespoke three performances at Drury Lane. He was also worried over rumors that the monarch was listening with favor to proposals for a third winter patent theatre. His social life continued vigorous. He had struck up a friendship with Edmund Burke about 1757, and he introduced Burke to Samuel Johnson at a dinner at his house on Christmas Day, 1760, bringing together two of his warmest friends.

In the summer of 1761 Garrick had to spend less time than usual culling his company, which was now in admirable balance. The death on 2 November 1761 of Garrick's old acquaintance and managerial rival the eccentric John Rich at Covent Garden caused ambivalent feelings at Drury Lane. Rich had won the last round in the seesaw battle of spectacle. The coronation of George III and Queen Charlotte had brought on the obligatory stage "coronations" at both patent houses. Davies left the following account of Drury Lane's disgrace on this occasion:

This had been an usual practice, on such occasions, from the days of James the First to the present time. This spectacle had been remarkably magnificent, and attended with great profit to the managers of Drury Lane in 1727, who exhibited themselves, and their best actors. Booth, Wilks, Cibber, Mills, and Mrs. Porter, acted the principal characters in Shakespeare's Henry the Eighth.

Mr. Garrick knew very well that Rich would spare no expense in the presentation of his show; he knew too that he had a taste in the ordering, dressing, and setting out these pompous processions, superior to his own; he therefore was contented with reviving the Coronation with the old dresses which had been often occasionally used from 1727 to 1761. This show he repeated for near forty nights successively, sometimes at the end of a play, and at other times after a farce. The exhibition was the meanest, and the most unworthy of a theatre, I ever saw. The stage indeed was opened into Drury Lane; and a new and unexpected sight surprised the audience, of a real bonfire, and the populace huzzaing, and drinking porter to the health of Queen Anne Bullen. The stage in the mean time, amidst the parading of dukes, dutchesses, archbishops, peeresses, heralds, &c. was covered with a thick fog from the smoke of the fire, which served to hide the tawdry dresses of the processionalists. During this idle piece of mockery, the actors, being exposed to the suffocations of smoke, and the raw air from the open street, were seized with colds, rheumatisms, and swelled faces. At length the indignation of the audience delivered the comedians from this wretched badge of nightly slavery, which gained nothing to the managers but disgrace and empty benches. Tired with the repeated insult of a show which had nothing to support it but gilt copper and old rags, they fairly drove the exhibitors of it from the stage by hooting and hissing, to the great joy of the whole theatre. It is difficult to guess the reason which induced a man of Mr. Garrick's understanding to pursue a losing game so long. Though he knew that nothing could withstand the grand sight which Rich was preparing, I suppose he thought that the people by seeing one Coronation often, would not have a very keen stomach for another.

In 1761–62 Garrick acted a little less often than he had earlier in his career. Although he appeared as Lear twice and Macbeth several times and played Tancred in *Tancred and Sigismunda* for Mrs Cibber's benefit, he generally avoided tragedy, again preferring Fribble, Heartly, Drugger, Sir John Brute, Benedick, and Don Felix. He was the original Sir John Doriland in *The School for Lovers*. He indulgently witnessed Holland in Hamlet, Richard III, and Orlando, Havard in Prospero, O'Brien in Archer. His high point of exertion in 1761–62 was the preparation and staging of his alteration of *Cymbeline*, in which he played Posthumus. His version, a drastic simplification, showed his agreement with his friend Johnson's famous dictum that the

original constituted an "unresisting imbecility" full of "faults too evident for detection, and too gross for aggravation," and upon which criticism was wasted. Garrick's audiences approved the result of his alteration, which was to see some 100 performances before he retired. The character of Posthumus gave him one of his most cherished acting opportunities. Francis Gentleman in *The Dramatic Censor* (1770) exclaimed:

his revival of this play, were there no other motives but fresh opportunity of displaying his unparalleled powers, merits a large portion of public praise; for we are bold to affirm, that considering an actor must make the part, not the part an actor, his astonishing talents were never more happily exerted . . . the falling off from him to any other person who has since done it, is greater than in any other character; the tenderness of his love, the pathos of his grief, the fire of his rage, and the distraction of his jealousy, have never been surpassed, and possibly, in Posthumus, will never be equalled.

In 1762–63 Garrick produced two new mainpieces and five afterpieces and encouraged Benjamin Victor in his alteration of *Two Gentlemen of Verona* on 22 December 1762 in which the text of Shakespeare reappears in some scenes but is damaged in others. It was, however, the first appearance of the play in the eighteenth century. The long peace the theatres had enjoyed was shattered by Thaddeus Fitzpatrick and his adherents when, on 25 January 1763, they rioted and broke the chandeliers to demonstrate their disapproval of Garrick's attempt to abolish the absurd practice of admitting spectators for half price at the end of the third act. Garrick's capitulation emboldened Fitzpatrick and his gang to make the same demands upon Beard at Covent Garden. When he refused, they demolished the interior of his theatre, on 24 February. Beard, too, gave in.

Garrick was becoming not only very tired

but also disgusted with audiences, authors, society, and (especially) actors. In a letter of 6 November 1762 to his brother Peter he burst out:

I am very glad that You are all so merry at Lichfield with Your balls, Players &c for my part I detest Balls, & the name of Players makes me Sick— I have a goodly parcel of 'Em Myself, & a pretty choice set of Devils they are; however they are less damnable with Me, than Any body Else; but Woe to ye Manager who is not the first Actor in his Company.

And though he added that "our Theatre is most amazingly improv'd & I really think it the first Playhouse in Europe," as the season wore on it became apparent that he was more than ready to rest from the perpetual labor of keeping it so. A peace had been signed between Britain and France. Garrick longed to travel again abroad.

On 15 September 1763, accompanied by Eva Maria and a King Charles spaniel named Biddy, Garrick departed for Paris. He had left the theatre in the charge of Lacy and George Colman and had provided for his absence as an actor by coaching the bright and handsome young William Powell in a number of his leading roles. Garrick resolved to keep another journal. It sputtered out after a few entries, but his copious and vivacious correspondence supplies a virtually complete record of the journey. Garrick was returning to the Continent at 46 in the full flower of a fame which made him, even to foreigners, a personage and a curiosity. At Paris, sponsored by Richard Aldworth Neville, the British Minister Plenipotentiary, he met the popular writer Marmontel, the sages Diderot and D'Alembert, and the critic Grimm, and was respectfully deferred to by the leading actors Mlle Clairon, Mlle Dumesnil, and Préville. The *Gazetteer and London Advertiser* heard "that on Mr Garrick's arrival at . . . [Paris], the company of Comedians waited on him with the freedom of their houses in a gold snuff box." Garrick's tension was gone. He wrote to Colman euphorically and pridefully:

You can't imagine, my dear Colman, what honours I have receiv'd from all kinds of People here— the Nobles & the Litterati have made so much of Me that I am quite asham'd of opening my heart Ev'n to You. Marmontel has wrote me ye most flattering Letter upon our supping togeather, I was in Spirits & so was the *Clairon*, who sup'd with us at Mr Neville's— She got up to set me a going & spoke something in Racine's Athalie most charmingly— upon which I gave them the Dagger Scene in Macbeth, ye Curse in Lear, & the falling asleep in Sr John Brute, the consequence of which is, that I am now star'd at ye Playhouse, & talk'd of by Gentle & Simple as ye most wonderfull Wonder of Wonders— the first Person I find going to England shall bring you Marmontel's Letter—D'Alembert was one of ye Company & Sings my praises to all ye Authors of the *Encyclopedie*. I am glad to hear of ye Prologue, if they love to hear me abus'd, they will have great Pleasure this winter, for I am told they have begun already, but I am happy & in Spirits, & shall not read any Newspapers on this Side the Alps—.

To George Garrick he wrote happily from Montmélian, "a small Village in Savoy," with poetic descriptions of the countryside, a request for Churchill's *Ghost*, instructions to take care "of Hogarth's Pictures, if ye Sun comes upon them they will be spoilt," and the news that "I have had a most warm invitation from *Voltaire*, whom I shall take in my return; tho I am rather angry with him for saying in his last thing, that tho Shakespeare is surprising, there is more *Barbarism* than *Genius* in his Words—O the damn'd fellow!"

Onward the Garricks progressed, over the terrible pass at Mount Cenis, where their coach was broken, into Italy, appalled by "the Nastiness in ye Inns," disgusted by the "miserable Bouffi Opera" at Turin, with "ye worst dancing I ever saw. . . ." To the Duke of Devonshire, Garrick wrote from Florence at the end of November 1763 of his reception in Milan by the Austrian Minister, Count Karl Joseph von Firmian, the sail in a felucca from Genoa to Leghorn, and their "magnificent" apartment "upon the banks of ye Arno" where the English of Firenze meet "almost Every Night," one of whom "is beat constantly by Mrs Garrick at chess." The Garricks bore introductory letters to the poet and art historian Count Francesco Algarotti, who, in turn, gave them letters to the Marquis Monvi, the Marquise Scappi, and the Cardinal Legate at Bologna for their return journey.

Rome was next on the itinerary. The *London Chronicle* of 26/28 January 1764 quoted a letter from Garrick "to a person of distinction" at London: "I scarce, my Lord, know what sensation to call it, but I felt a strange unusual something at entering the very city where the great Roscius exerted those talents that rendered him the wonder of his own age; and of which, I fear, the living actors convey but a faint idea to ours." Garrick spent nearly all of the two weeks of his initial visit to Rome in astonished admiration of the antiquities. He reported his sensations from Naples to Colman on Christmas Eve 1763:

I cannot quit you, till I say something about Rome: I hardly slept the night before I arriv'd there with ye thoughts of seeing it— my heart beat high, my imagination expanded itself, & my Eyes flash'd again, as I drew near the *Porta del Popolo*; but the moment I enter'd it, I fell at once from my Airy Vision & Utopian Ideas into a very dirty ill looking *place*, (as they call it) with three crooked streets in front, terminated indeed at this End with two tolerable Churches— w^t a disappointment! my Spirits sunk & it was wth reluctance that I was drag'd in the afternoon to see the Pantheon— but my God, w^t was my Pleasure & Surprize! — I never felt so much in my life as when I Entered that glorious Structure: I gap'd, but could not speak for 5 Minutes— It is so very noble, that it has not

been in ye Power of Modern Frippery, or Popery (for it is a Church you know) to extinguish Its grandeur & Elegance—Here I began to think myself in *Old* Rome & when I saw the ruins of the famous amphitheatre— Omnis Caesareo cedat labor Amphitheatro— I then felt my own littleness— & was convinc'd that the Romans were as much superiour to the Moderns in Every thing, as Vespasian's Amphitheatre was to Broughton's— it is impossible, my dear Colman, to have any Idea of these things from any Prints that have been made of 'Em,— all modern performances look better upon paper, but these Ruins are not to be conceiv'd, but by *ye sensible & true Avouch of your own Eyes*. Tho I am pleas'd, much pleas'd with Naples, I have such a thirst to return to Rome, as cannot possibly be slak'd till I have drank up half ye Tiber, which, in it's present state, is but a scurvy draught neither.

By 17 December 1763 the Garricks had arrived at Naples "after a most disagreeable Journey" (he later described its difficulties to the Duke of Devonshire—how their chaise had "broke down in ye Middle of ye Post, in ye Severest Storm of thunder Lightning, & rain that I ever saw," in which Mrs Garrick had caught cold which settled as "a Rheumatism in one of her hips"), but, he told Colman, "at present the weather is inconceivably fine, & we are basking ourselves in a warm sun with the Mediterranean at our feet, and Mount Vesuvius in our view—tho it is Xmas, we have green Peas Every day, & dine with our Windows open—."

To brother George, from Naples on 2 January 1764, he spoke of having been greatly obliged by "the two Dances," George and Nathaniel, architect and painter, brothers of his Drury Lane colleague James Dance, who acted under the name Love. He promised to write to the historian of music Charles Burney to "let him know the present State of Musick in Italy" and boasted of his social successes in Naples: "We Dine & sup with Lord Spencer, Lord Exeter, the Minister, Consul, &c &c &c almost Every day & Night, we have balls more than twice a Week & parties innumerable—." On 31 January David declared to his brother his intention of staying at Naples until "about the 23d of next month; then We shall return to *Rome* for a Month or more, then we shall set out for *Bologna* in our way to *Venice*, & from thence through Germany in our way to England—this is our intended Route, which I will dispatch wth all convenient speed, but am affraid that I shall not see Your fat face, or kiss ye brawn of it, till ye middle of June—."

But the itinerary went sadly awry, as the same letter to George presaged, for "our Mirth has been lately damp'd by my poor Wife's keeping her bed & room for many Days, with a most obstinate Rheumatism in her hip—she had been blister'd &c &c &c tho she is better, yet [she] still continues lame & Weak. however she hopes to be at A Carnaval Masquerade . . . in ye Dress of a lame Old Woman; I have scolded and phys'd about it, but if she can wag, she goes—." Her painful and exhausting disability grew worse. Though Eva Maria strove gallantly to keep up, she did not, with David, "attend Lord & Lady Spencer . . . to Herculaneum" or "Mount to see ye top of Vesuvius" or accompany David on the day he was "wet to ye Skin in ye Elysian fields at Baiae." Garrick inspected the offerings of the San Carlo Opera and reported to Burney after listening to "the famous Gabrielli, who had indeed astonishing powers, great compass of voice and great flexibility, but she is always ye same. . . ." He thought that, all in all, the music of the Neapolitan house, "vocal and instrumental, has lost its nature, and it is all dancing on ye slack rope, and tumbling through ye hoop. . . ." More pleasing to him was a ceremony he attended

of the making of a nun, she was the daughter of a duke, and the whole was conducted with great splendor and magnificences. The church was richly ornamented, and there were two

National Portrait Gallery

DAVID GARRICK

studio of Zoffany

large bands of Music. . . . and to crown the whole the principal part was sung by the famous *Caffarelli*, who, though old, has pleased me more than all the singers I have heard. He *touched* me; and it was the first time I have been touched since I came to Italy.

But Garrick was also touched, and horrified as well, by the sights of woe he was forced to witness in the great famine which began early in 1764 and which was to leave over half a million Neapolitans dead of starvation. It was one of the reasons his stay in Naples was terminated. By mid-March the Garricks had returned to Rome, "which of all Places in the World is the most worth coming to & writing about," he told Colman, adding "I am antiquity-hunting from Morning to Night & my poor wife drags her lame leg after me." At Rome he saw the eccentric English artist Joseph Nollekens, invited him to breakfast, and sat for a bust, the first Nollekens had ever modelled and for which Garrick gave him

12 golden guineas. Eva Maria was for a while improved, but in April David began feeling peckish, with "disagreeable nervous flutterings. . . ."

Nevertheless in May they pressed on to Parma, where they met the Duke of York, then touring the Italian states, dined with him, and were presented by him to the Duke of Parma. Garrick acted the dagger scene from *Macbeth* with terrific effect, and the appreciative Duke of Parma sent him a gold snuffbox. The Garricks went on to Venice, whence the Duke of York was also bound. From there, on 6 June, David wrote George Garrick anxiously about Eva Maria's crippled condition. But even in weariness and anxiety Venice worked upon Garrick's imagination:

[T]his Venice is ye most particular Place in ye whole world— it glares upon you at first, & inchants You, but living a Month here (like ye honey moon) brings you to a temperate consideration of things, and you long for y^r terra firma liberty again. I am tir'd to death; tho I have seen here such sights I had no conception of but in Fairy land & have seen the visions of the Arabian Night realiz'd by the Venetian *Regate*; This show was given ye 4th of this Month in honour of our King & to Entertain the [visiting] Duke [of York]. I shall be a Week in telling you all I saw & felt that Day Such Elegant luxury! which plainly shew'd, that the Contrivers were as little formidable in war & Politicks, as they were superiour to all ye World as Managers of a Puppet-Shew— I have taken my Evening walks of Meditation on the Rialto, & have fancy'd myself waiting for my friend Pierre, but the whole Idea has vanish'd at the Sight of a Venetian Noble, who can give you no Idea in look & in dress but that of an Apparitor to a Spiritual Court in the Country— but then their Courts of Justice! & their Lawyers! If there is any thing more particularly ridiculous than another, it is one of their Pleadings— It was some Minutes before I recover'd my Senses, & when I found I was really awake & in a Court of Justice, I was ready to burst wth laughter— it is inconceivably strange, & more whimsical & outrée than

the Italian theatre— & yet all sober People agree that their decrees are generally just & impartial.

From Venice also Garrick wrote, restively, to George for news of domestic doings and bade him watch for "Florence wine ship'd from Leghorn in the Raven Captn Alex^r Scott, and some essences for Mrs Garrick," which shipment the British Consul at Leghorn, Sir John Dick, had overseen. "I fret to be at home, I dread the Italian suns, & I am affraid that my presence is necessary to make a Plan for ye next Winter." He wanted to return "a Month before ye opening of ye house."

But Eva Maria's lameness had to be cured first. They were to leave Venice immediately, on 13 June, and backtrack to Padua "to be near the famous Mud of Abano, which the physicians here tell us, will certainly restore" her. A fortnight of treatment at Abano restored her sufficiently to enable them to turn northward. On 10 and 14 July Garrick received letters, warm and respectful, from Joseph Baretti at Venice, relaying from Countess Bujovich a "marvelous remedy against the sciatica," a "plaister" of "Venetian soap and the yolk of an egg," and a commentary on a commission given him by Garrick to buy 30 sequins' worth of Italian books. Letters from a Mr J. Minifie, an Englishman at Milan, Count Marsili at Padua, and Richard Brompton at Rome spoke of the effort to acquire old books and paintings and modern books and prints both for Garrick and for his friend Count Firmian.

Garrick had written to Edmund Burke on 21 June 1764 from Padua, still confident of being in London about the second week in August 1764, though he would not touch English soil until April 1765. The rest of the Garricks' tour was chequered— the triumph of their social successes dimmed by Mrs Garrick's pain, the interest in seeing strange places flawed by homesickness and repeatedly chilled by bereavement. Garrick received news of the death of "Lenny," his sister, and learned in succession of the passing of five old friends: an unidentified Mr Hubert, the writer Robert Lloyd, William Hogarth the painter, Charles Churchill the satirist, and—more affecting than all the rest—the Duke of Devonshire. For a time, the Duke's death was kept from David "by the management of the best of women and wives," for he himself fell deathly ill at Munich in August after a hard journey from Padua through the Brenner pass and Innsbruck. Eva Maria diagnosed the malady as "a Violent Billious fiver" in a letter of 22 August 1764 addressed to George Garrick. It may have been typhoid fever. Whatever it was, as Garrick wrote the Rev William Arden from Munich on 15 September 1764, it left him

but the Shadow of myself, that Self which at Naples, & at Venice, made no contemptible figure ev'n at Your Side, & which was always ready & willing to Second You in Every Article of the fat & fine! but alass, my good Friend, all the Combustibles I had been long storing up there & Elsewhere took fire at this place, & I have been confin'd more than a Month to my bed, by the most dangerous bilious Fever, that Ever poor Sinner Suffer'd for the small fault of a little innocent Society — . . . As You have been troubled with part of my Misfortunes, You must have the Sequel; when I had got quit of my Fever, & was so well to ride out twice a day, I was seiz'd with a fit of the Gravel & Stone collected, by my lying in bed so long, which threw me back another week, so that tho I cannot creep thro an Alderman's thumb ring, yet I can thread the Smallest tumbler's hoop, & I think at my return to England of enter^g myself at Saddler's Wells as much fitter for that place, than for the Sock or Buskin at Drury Lane . . . I am most truly ye Knight of ye Woefull Countenance & have lost legs arms belly cheeks &c & have scarce any thing left but bones & a pair of dark lack-lustre Eyes that are retir'd an inch or two more in their Sockets & wonderfully set off ye yellow Parchment that covers ye cheek bones—thus I really am, but out of

all danger, for I recover daily, have no Cough, & am in tolerable Spirits—.

He also agreed with his wife's diagnosis in a letter written at Nancy to Voltaire, probably in November 1764, refusing an invitation and suavely reproving the sage of Ferney for his harsh estimate of Shakespeare:

I think myself greatly honour'd by a paragraph in a letter which You were pleas'd some time ago to write to Mr Camp at Lyons, and had it been in my power to have follow'd my inclinations, I should have paid my respects at Ferney long before this time. . . . You were pleas'd to tell a Gentleman that You had a theatre ready to receive me; I should with great pleasure have exerted what little talents I have, & could I have been the means of bringing our Shakespeare into some favour with Mr Voltaire I should have been happy indeed!
No enthusiastick Missionary who had converted the Emperor of China to his religion would have been prouder than I, could I have reconcil'd the first Genius of Europe to our Dramatic faith.

By 10 November 1764 the Garricks were in spacious apartments of the Hôtel de Malthe in the Rue St Niçoise, Paris, conveniently close to the Opéra, and with a garden gate opening directly onto the Tuileries. Despite attacks of the stone (the first of a long series which would terminate in his death) and of gout and several threatening resurgences of fever, Garrick gradually slipped back into the social round, as his letters show. He wrote Colman of the prescription—"l'Exercise du Cheval, et beaucoup de dissipation"—that

all the french Doctors have prescrib'd, & I have had three of 'Em———wch with three German ones, & two of my own Country, make the Number Eight—Eight Physicians, my good friends, & still alive! . . . I am a little ye worse for wear, & was so alter'd a fortnight ago, that I was not known, till I spoke; but now, my Cheeks are swelling, my belly rounding, & I can pass for a tolerable looking French Man; but my nerves, S^r: my Nerves—They are agitated at times; & the Duke of Devonshire's death had very near crackt them—.

On 19 November 1764, "after dining with the Controller of the Finances," Clément Charles-François de L'Averdy, a favorite of Madame Pompadour, Garrick was "taken with a Shiv'ring fit, at the french playhouse, & went home much indispos'd—." He "then grew Sick, but after puking a little, was better." But the pressures of fame and flattery kept him ambulatory and interested:

I am so plagu'd here for my Prints or rather Prints of me—that I must desire You to send me by ye first opportunity *six* prints from my Reynolds's picture . . . You must likewise send me a *King Lear* by *Wilson, Hamlet* d^o *Jaffier* & Belv by *Zoffani*, speak to him for two or 3, & what Else he may have done of Me—There is likewise a print of Me, as I am, from Liotard's picture Scrap'd by Mac-Ardel. . . .

As both David and Eva Maria improved in health, they revolved in wider and wider circles of French society. They were entertained at the château of the Duc d'Orléans at Le Raincy, where Garrick was sketched by de Carmontelle. Garrick renewed an acquaintanceship with the actor Préville. A body of legend exists concerning their "contests" in acting, in which they confounded folk in the streets by pretending drunkenness and madness and which Garrick finally "won" by falling off his horse and feigning death so well that he alarmed even Préville. At the salons of Mons and Mme Helvetius and the celebrated hostess Mme Geoffrin he was respectfully received by both ephemeral fashionables and important intellectuals who were contributing to the ferment of Parisian society in that pre-revolutionary time: the poet Saint-Lambert, the abbé Morellet, the historian Duclos, the journalist Suard, the abbé Bonnet, the mathematician Clairaut, the playwright and translator de la Place, the wit Mlle Lespinasse, and, most importantly for lasting friendship and correspondence, the novelist and ex-actress Mme Riccoboni, for whom Garrick conceived a platonic passion which was fully reciprocated. Acquaintance was also renewed with Mlle Clairon, with Lekain, with Grimm, D'Halbach and others. For many of those, and on several evenings, Garrick graciously essayed his greatest parts, usually in mime. For some six months artists and philosophers united to praise the talent and charm of the Garricks. A single exception was the songwriter and dramatist Charles Collé. Collé left a bitter lament in his secret journal that he had lavished a good dinner on "those two donkeys," had sung them his songs and paid "two visits for one with which that histrion had deigned to honour me," had made him presents of printed plays—but had utterly failed to induce Garrick to perform for his supper.

(It has been conjectured by Frank Hedgecock that Garrick's success with the French was a result of his frequent illustration of the practices of the natural actor in "that *drame bourgeois* which Diderot and Grimm had long been preaching amid the decadence of classic tragedy and under the influence of the English theatre and novel" but that he was also in Paris at just the time to be the beneficiary of the interest in Shakespeare generated by Voltaire's inflammatory opinions.)

Garrick had kept in fairly close touch with Drury Lane affairs through his brother George and George Colman during the many months and vicissitudes of his absence but had relinquished any real control, realizing that Lacy had the advantage of the ground. Besides, he had craved relaxation of tension and escape from importunate playwrights and job-seekers. So in the early months of his grand tour he had been detachedly humourous about such foibles of actors and playwrights as came to his attention and unwontedly complacent about reports of the phenomenal success of young William Powell at Drury Lane. His continental reception as an important personage had kept his ego sufficiently massaged without the praise and deference which acting and managing had brought. At some points in the journey the world of Drury Lane had seemed remote. He had written George Colman from Venice on 12 June 1764: "I have no Joy now in thinking on ye Stage, & shall return (if I must) like a Bear to the Stake—and this baiting, my good friend, is no joke after forty—."

But as the time for his departure from France drew nigh, Garrick's letters to his two surrogate Georges at Drury Lane contained less and less about David's Parisian social triumphs. They began to enquire anxiously and then to pronounce authoritatively about theatre personnel and operations. Young William Powell, who had assumed many of Garrick's parts and was winning critical success, had written in March 1764 with a dutiful expression of gratitude for Garrick's tutelage, and on 12 December 1764 Garrick replied with an avuncular letter, almost a courtesy-book model of advice, professional and personal, to the young actor. A letter of 27 January 1765, to the Drury Lane actor James (Dance) Love, shows Garrick already quietly clearing the way for his re-assumption of power:

You will greatly oblige me, when any new thing is brought upon ye Stage, to let me know it's success—and pray tell me truly, if there is no hopefull Young Man springing up that I could make Use of in Obrien's room— . . . Give me an Acc^t I beseech You (an impartial one) of any Youngsters of Either Sex, who promise something— I have my reasons for this desire, so pray be particular and distinguish their Merits, if you can percieve any— I have many Schemes, & a hint from You will be of Service— Say nothing of this letter to any one Person, but answer me fully. You see that I confide in you.

By 3 March 1765, Love (now too near the throne?) needed snaffling a little:

I am very sorry that You was not fix'd upon for ye Character of Sr John Brute— it is a favourite one of Yours, & very deservedly so, & I allotted it to you, because I thought You the most fit person to supply my place— but, my good friend, my Judgment at that time was not to overrule Mr Lacy's, who certainly had a right to give the part where he thought it would be best for the Theatre— He & I think differently in that particular, & that is ye only comfort I can give you for your disappointment: You have good Sense & Experience & therefore should see these things in their true light— Mr Lacy is left sole Manager & has a right to think & Act by himself till my return— . . . but there is no wrong to you, as you did not play ye Part before, & if you had, I cannot but think that a Manager has an undoubted right to change the Characters from one to another to ye best of his Judgment.

Garrick had also lost some of his complacency at the threat to his ascendancy with the London audience represented by young Powell's success: "If you really differ with *him* [Lacy] in Opinion, that *Powell* is a better Actor than *David Garrick*, can you desire better consolation than that the afores^d D. Garrick thinks you a better Sr John Brute than Mr Thomas King— I may be partial, & so may you, & so may he—."

Garrick's re-orientation, however, was not to be easy. To Colman he wrote in March:

I can very readily believe what You tell me of my Brother Consul [Lacy]— He will never forgive my being the means of his making a figure in the world— . . . pray does Powell continue to visit you, & get a little Sense from you, or is he topsy turvey like ye rest & thinks like Ric^d ye 3^d that *he is himself alone?* . . . I must intreat you to be very sincere with me— do the Town in general really wish to see me on ye Stage? or are they (which I rather think ye truth) as cool about it as their humble Servant? — I have no maw for it at all, & yet something must be done to restore our credit: that I may be able to play, & as well as Ever, I will not deny, but that I am able to do as I have done, wear & tear, I neither must or can, or will—.

The final months in Paris were a welter of shipping and packing, farewells and correspondence. Garrick had an unhappy inspiration: why not prepare his re-entry onto the stage with some clever, indirect reminder to the London public of his talent? He broached the subject in a letter to Colman of 8 March 1765:

I shall send you next Monday a little parcel— a great secret— tis a Fable I have written, yᵉ *Sick Monkey*, to be publish'd at my return— Severe upon myself— I have likewise got a print engrav'd by Gravelot, I shall send you the plate— I would have Becket be in yᵉ Secret & print it but not publish it under his name for it may be suspected— I shall cut it, & you may cut more, or return what I have *quered*— You'll find your Self there as a *Galloway*— I have given some of my friends, whom I love, a little fillip— for Heaven's sake take care to be Secret—.

Garrick pursued the matter in another letter to Colman of 7 April 1765:

I have sent you yᵉ nonsense that I threatened you with in my last— I am rather pleas'd with the Notion, & shall continue so, till you undeceive me. I have copy'd it hastily, but you can make it out— if you approve yᵉ Scheme pray let it be printed ready for my Arrival— I shall either send or bring a little Copper plate by Gravelot, representing yᵉ Fable with great taste & spirit— I would have it printed in Quarto, & well— if you will correct the Sheets for me, I shall be happy— 'tis written in too great hurry to be correct, but you will lick yᵉ Cub, or knock it on yᵉ head, if it is Shapeless.

Garrick's crafty secrecy and his apprehension proved ludicrously useless. The silly little beast-fable caused no furor at all. In Colman's words, *The Sick Monkey* "fell *still-born* from the Press."

The Garricks left Paris on 24 April 1765 and arrived in London three days later. Their little dog Phill, left with the Burney children, had been so cosseted and pampered that he refused to accept his master again. He was returned to the Burneys and replaced by Dragon, an English mastiff. James Love was ready to open his new theatre at Richmond, and Garrick set about making a brisk prologue. He began assessing his position in the theatre, *vis à vis* his partner, and the position of Drury Lane in the whole London theatrical scheme. George Colman and George Garrick had got on well in his absence, and both friend and brother had been faithful to Garrick's trust. Both were distrustful of and distrusted by Lacy. But the house had prospered, partly through the astonishing success of Powell, but also because of the assiduity of Colman. Garrick returned to a company which was as strong as the one he had left.

On 25 July Garrick wrote to his friend Lekain in Paris that, despite the fact that he had been received again by "mes compatriotes d'un maniere le plus honorable pour moi," he had almost decided to abandon acting and confine himself to direction. His hesitation dissolved, however, in the face of a royal command, and on 14 November he returned, as Benedick, to the applause of his countrymen.

Garrick acted only four roles during the season. But at every appearance he demonstrated his old hold over the audience. On 23 January 1766, at another command performance, he played both Lusignan in *Zara*, the mainpiece, and Lord Chalkstone in his own *Lethe*, the afterpiece. The prompter Hopkins wrote: "It is almost impossible to express how finely he played both characters. The *Prologue* was called for. Mr Garrick went on directly to speak it— as soon as he appeared a general clap and a loud huzza,—and there was such a noise from the House being so crowded, few heard anything of the prologue." That night Jean Jacques Rousseau was a guest in Garrick's box.

Powell and Holland were allowed to retain most of the leading roles they had assumed in Garrick's absence. Garrick was to add no new parts until 20 January 1776, in his last season. He was resolved, he told his brother, gradually "to draw my neck as well as I can, out of the collar, and sit quietly with my wife and books by my fireside." But that notion was altogether romantic. A decade of furious activity was ahead. The 1765–66 season was a mélange of satisfactions and vexations. Covent Garden had a Theatrical Fund, so Drury Lane must have one; Garrick established it, decreed an end-of-season benefit, and contributed largely himself. He installed the new-fangled wing lights he had brought back from France. He continued to work with Colman on their comedy *The Clandestine Marriage*. Garrick demurred at playing the comic character Lord Ogleby, but Colman thought he must. A quarrel sprang up when Colman, at Bath, heard gossip that Garrick was claiming credit for the conception of the character. Intemperate correspondence flew between them. The play opened on 20 February 1766 with Tom King (much against his will) playing Ogleby and Kitty Clive as the eccentric Mrs Heidelberg. It was enormously successful with the public and was acclaimed by critics the best comedy of the decade. Tempers cooled all around. The piece played 19 times during the season until, on 17 May, King broke his thigh in a fall from his horse.

Garrick's active re-entry into the affairs of Drury Lane had again excited the jealous opposition of James Lacy. John Paterson, who had witnessed the contractual agreement between the managers, was applied to by Garrick for a recollection of the terms of a subsequent verbal agreement. In letters of January and March Paterson sustained Garrick's understanding that Lacy was to keep out of stage management entirely. But he also reported Lacy's refusal to sign a memorandum ratifying any such understanding.

From the first week of March until the end of April 1766 the Garricks were at Bath, he treating "a very serious fit of gout" by drinking the mineral waters and riding early in the morning. (But he "ventured to ride out too Soon, & had a sad bout of it— I shook it into my Stomach & head—.") He busied himself writing epilogues and sending letters of managerial admonition to George Garrick and corresponding socially with Colman, Lekain, and others. On 10 April he visited the newly erected Bristol Theatre and was reported to be well pleased with it. He wrote both prologue and epilogue for its opening night, 30 May. During the summer George Colman and his common-law wife went to Paris, leaving the young George, then only three years old, behind in the care of servants. Garrick, who was extremely fond of children, visited "ye sweet Boy" often and assumed a general guardianship until his family's return.

Garrick rushed energetically into the new season 1766–67. Over the course of 191 nights, Garrick brought forward four of his own new productions—an alteration of Wycherley's *The Country Wife*, which Garrick called *The Country Girl*, on 25 October 1766, his farce *Neck or Nothing* on 18 November, his original dramatic romance *Cymon*, with music by Michael Arne, on 2 January 1767, and his very well-received *Linco's Travels* on 6 April, "a New Humourous Little Piece." The unfortunate manager was also hounded by Richard Glover into allowing his *Medea* to be prepared for Mrs Yates's benefit; and after eight years of harassment by Joseph Reed, Garrick finally produced his tragedy *Dido*, for Holland's benefit. Another brief period of strained relations between Garrick and Colman ensued when Colman negotiated to buy the patent of Covent Garden from John Beard and delayed telling

Garrick of the matter until it was accidentally discovered.

Garrick added a few players of note in the 1767–68 season. From Dublin he engaged the brilliant tragedian Spranger Barry and the excellent actress and singer Anne Street Dancer, soon to become Barry's wife, for £1500, Barry making his first appearance at Drury Lane for a decade on 21 October 1767, playing Othello. The Barrys were to be featured performers at Drury Lane for the following seven years, but frequently in disagreement with their manager. Drury Lane prospered through 189 nights while its rival, Covent Garden, nearly sank under the quarrels of its new managers Colman, Harris, and Rutherford. Among six new pieces and numerous revivals Garrick contributed his own burlesque, *A Peep Behind the Curtain*. A new note began to appear habitually on Drury Lane's playbills: "No money returned after Curtain is drawn up."

The season ended on 31 May, with Garrick playing Hamlet for the benefit of the theatrical fund. But he gathered several players at loose ends in London in August—George Anne Bellamy, Henry Woodward from Covent Garden, Charles Dibdin, Mrs Scott, Mrs Stephens—and, with some of his regular company, reopened Drury Lane on 18 August and 8 September at the request of the visiting 19-year-old King Christian VII of Denmark. Garrick himself played Ranger in *The Suspicious Husband* and Sir John Brute in *The Provok'd Wife*. The *London Post* reported his reward for this courtesy on 14 October: "Mr Garrick had the honour of being with the King of Denmark Tuesday morning last, and conversed with him for near half an hour on the state of the Stage in England and France." The King gave him a gold snuffbox studded with diamonds as "a small mark of the great regard he had for his extraordinary talents."

Garrick's relations with his partner Lacy were freshly exacerbated in the summer of 1768 by "some disagreeable circumstances," as he wrote John Paterson in August, and he was newly "resolv'd to close our theatrical Connection as soon as possible." The fact was that "Mr Lacy, who seems to be alone insensible of my Merit & Services . . . thinks and speaks very injuriously and unjustly of my Brother, has very ill requited my Services and has lately done some things which I think shews a Spirit contrary to that of our Articles." A portion of the letter (prudently deleted before posting) revealed also Garrick's suspicion that Lacy wanted now "to Superintend I suppose the Rehearsals & casting of ye Parts" even "while I was rummaging my brains to fill up the many vacancies We have at present in our Comp^y."

Garrick's personal acting talents were employed above 20 times in the 190 nights of the 1768–69 season, particularly toward the beginning. On the third night of the season he played *Macbeth*, again commanded by the King of Denmark. The infatuated young King also procured performances of Garrick as Richard III (the first time Garrick had acted the part in six years), Ranger in *The Suspicious Husband*, and Lusignan in *Zara*. Before the end of October the manager had also acted Archer in *The Stratagem*, Don Felix in *The Wonder* (twice), and, for his own sovereign, Benedick in *Much Ado about Nothing*. Once again he brought his season to a close, on 23 May, with a benefit for the theatre's retirement fund, playing Archer and speaking an occasional epilogue of his own devising.

Kitty Clive, perhaps the foremost comedienne of the entire century, withdrew from the stage after 41 years, on her benefit night, 24 April 1769. Garrick complimented her by playing Don Felix to her Flora in *The Wonder*. During the long period in which she had been in Garrick's company, an initial mutual distrust had gradually tempered to a grudging respect and finally to a frank affection, punctuated

From the Collection at Parham Park, Sussex

DAVID GARRICK as Steward of the Shakespeare Jubilee

by van der Gucht

by explosive incidents. They were to remain fast friends during the remaining decade of Garrick's life.

Garrick's health was uneven throughout the season. On 3 January he wrote Helfrich Peter Sturz at the Danish court "I can scarcely hold my pen in my hand, and [am] just risen from a sick-bed," and on 9 March he wrote James Clutterbuck that he had "had a very sad bout indeed with Stone, Gout, fever & Jaundice. . . ." Worse, it seemed to David, Mrs Garrick had been very ill for a week. But plans were maturing for an event which would take Garrick's attention away from inconveniences like illness, fractious actresses, riotous audiences, demanding relatives, and his irritating fellow patentee.

The Stratford Shakespeare Jubilee of 1769 was almost wholly the invention of David Garrick. It sprang out of his social and emotional needs, and it reflected many of the features of his character: his vanity and susceptibility to flattery, his reverence for Shakespeare, his delight in managing complicated enterprises, and his love of ceremony. James Boswell, Charles Dibdin,

DAVID GARRICK, as Steward of the Shakespeare Jubilee. Plaster medallion by Tassie, after van der Gucht

and Benjamin Victor left contemporary descriptions, and three modern book-length accounts, those of Christian Deelman, Martha England, and J. M. Stockholm, have told the story in great detail. The Little-Kahrl edition of the *Letters* furnishes many other details. The essential elements are few. Garrick had long been excited with the notion of a festival which would do honor to Shakespeare. He had been on the Continent in 1764, the obvious year for such an event. In 1767, when Stratford began to erect a new town hall, the burgesses, at the suggestion of the Steward of the Court of Records, Francis Wheler, had requested Garrick to send "some statue, bust or picture" of Shakespeare, along with a portrait of himself to be placed in the town hall "that the memory of both may be perpetually together."

In 1768, Garrick began making definite plans for a Jubilee. His epilogue capping the Drury Lane season, which he spoke on 18 May 1769, sprang the surprise on the audience. He bade them farewell until September:

> My eyes till then no sight like this will
> see,
> Unless we meet at Shakespeare's jubilee
> On Avon's banks, where flowers eternal
> blow;
> Like its full stream our gratitude shall
> flow.
> There let us revel, show our fond regard;
> On that loved spot first breathed our
> matchless bard.
> To him all honour, gratitude is due.
> To him we owe our all—to him and you.

Garrick at once ran into the predictable satire of his friend and enemy Samuel Foote, who ridiculed the idea in performances of his *The Devil upon Two Sticks* at the summer theatre in the Haymarket. Foote heard that Garrick was planning an elaborate ode to Shakespeare, so he immediately published his plan to write his own ode "Set to very whimsical music" and recite it at Stratford. Neither that recitation nor his projected production of something in embryo, which he called *Drugger's Jubilee*, ever became actual, but Foote's constant devilish threats wore on Garrick's nerves. Predictably, also, Lacy grumbled and opposed the whole project.

The newspapers of the summer and fall of 1769 were awash with squibs and satires and serious letters supporting and attacking the proposition of the Jubilee, with the *Public Advertiser* the principal organ of the ridiculers. The *St. James's Chronicle* invariably defended the conception. Other publications were more even-handed, publishing both abuse and encomium. Garrick shook off the illness of the spring with the good weather of June and took Mrs Garrick and George to Stratford to direct the final preparations. Latimore and Boar, architects, supervised the cutting of trees on a wooded spot called Bomstead Mead, on the banks of the Avon above Clopton Bridge. There they erected the Rotunda, a building nearly as large as the Rotunda at Ranelagh. The painter Benjamin Wilson, artistic director, equipped it with crimson velvet draperies and chandeliers with 800 candles. John French, Drury Lane's resident lighting expert, supervised the installation of the lighting. Gainsborough painted the famous portrait of Garrick with his arm around a pedestal on which stands the bust of Shakespeare.

Meanwhile Garrick was terrifically busy at the multiple tasks of writing his *Ode upon Dedicating a Building and Erecting a Statue to Shakespeare* for Thomas Augustine Arne to set to music, writing dozens of "ballads" for Charles Dibdin and others to set for group singing, designing an official medal for the observance, and overseeing organization of the myriad features of the Jubilee itself—the ball, the horse races, and the procurement of a 327-pound turtle to be cooked in the town hall. More than 150 actors, musicians, composers, and technicians preceded the thousands of nobles and

gentry, tradesmen and apprentices who flocked from London to Stratford on 5 September 1769 to do honor to Shakespeare. Among them were James Boswell, rhapsodizing, and Samuel Foote, sneering. Samuel Johnson was absent.

The festivities opened well despite painful crowding and the overcharging of visitors by the townspeople. On 6 September Stratford awoke at dawn to cannon and bells. Mummers serenaded Garrick, who was, later in the day, given his insignia of office as Steward of the Jubilee—a wand and medallion carved from the mulberry tree purportedly planted by Shakespeare at New Place and cut down by the Rev Mr Francis Gastrell in 1756. Garlands were placed on Shakespeare's statue in the church, and Dr Thomas Augustine Arne conducted his oratorio, *Judith*. The day climaxed with a banquet and ball in the Rotunda and elaborate fireworks by the eminent pyrotechnists Domenico and Henry Angelo and Benjamin Clitherow.

On the next day, 7 September, torrential rains caused the Avon to overflow, the fireworks to fizzle, and enthusiasms to dampen. A grand procession of Shakespeare's characters was rained out. But Garrick's recital of his *Ode*, accompanied by Arne's musicians, thrilled the auditors. The Jubilee dragged doggedly on through 8 September with a horserace for the Jubilee Cup on Shotley Meadows—the horses knee-deep in water—and another ball. In the entire course of the celebration no play or poem by Shakespeare was performed or recited.

The Jubilee ended with a deficit of £2000, which was assumed by Garrick. Though he respectfully declined an invitation to involve himself in a Stratford Jubilee the following year, he moved the aborted procession of Shakespeare's characters onto the Drury Lane stage in the 1769–70 season. Its presentation was delayed by the illness of the Barrys until 14 September but afterwards played 90 times, as an adjunct to a concoction by Garrick called *The Jubilee*, made up largely of the songs composed for the Stratford affair. That enterprise was supposed to have allowed Garrick to recoup his Stratford losses. George Colman at Covent Garden paid Garrick the compliment of a rival exploitation of the Stratford celebration by producing a quickly written comedy *Man and Wife; or, The Shakespeare Jubilee*.

But Garrick's most lasting pride seems to have been in his *Ode*, which he declaimed several nights at Drury Lane while waiting for his stage *Jubilee* to jell. The admiring Hopkins noted: "Mr G speaking in this performance is equal to anything he ever did and met with as much applause as his heart could desire." Garrick sent "this trifle" to Joseph and Thomas Warton, both of whom returned flattering praise, and to Jean Baptiste Antoine Suard: "I have sent you my last Child, begot and brought forth in the heighth of Zeal, (I wish I could say poetic rapture) for ye God of my Idolatry–." He even sent it to Voltaire, saying, with perhaps calculated ambiguity, "I have

taken the liberty of offering my small poetical tribute to the first Genius in the World–." He sent it also to Charles Macklin, who returned an unfavorable criticism, to Garrick's evident chagrin. In a long letter Garrick answered some 15 points of Macklin's disagreement. Thomas Sheridan was also, perhaps, an unappreciative recipient. He may have written a squib against it. In an aside to the Rev Evan Lloyd, Garrick exclaimed "Sheridan is ye Blockhead has abus'd me & my ode. . . ."

That 1769–70 Drury Lane season was otherwise prosperously uneventful. A large company of some 95 performers gave 196 performances. Garrick was chided in pamphlets and newspapers for not being more enterprising in his offerings. He himself acted late in the season and rather seldom thereafter. The *Freeholder's Magazine* believed that the company had "now no capital performer, besides himself," and suggested remedies. Garrick wrote to Elizabeth Griffith in February refusing to help her translate a comedy by Marivaux, saying that he had matters of much "Consequence

Harvard Theatre Collection

DAVID GARRICK, delivering his Jubilee Ode on the stage of Drury Lane Theatre

engraving by Lodge

upon my hands, & for which I have given up the pleasures of yᵉ Dauphin's Marriage [to Marie Antoinette in Vienna on 15 February 1770] which Mʳˢ Garrick & I had resolv'd to partake of." The consequential matters included the merger, in January preceding, of the *London Packet* with the already-combined *Saint James's Chronicle* and *Public Advertiser*. Garrick had a share in that enterprise, along with George Colman, Thomas Davies, and others.

Garrick had many managerial difficulties that season and some personal ones as well. The Barrys were sometimes ill and oftener feigned illness. The excellent tragedian and Garrick's close personal friend, Charles Holland, died on 7 December 1769. Garrick wrote Lloyd "I am too bad to attend the doleful Ceremony" at the graveside in Chiswick churchyard; but he furnished an epitaph for Holland's monument there. The manager was vexed and embarrassed when his brother George fought a bloodless duel with the actor Robert Baddeley over shabby treatment George thought Baddeley had given Sophia Baddeley, his wife. George was roundly ridiculed in the public prints. David Garrick's desire to retire to country ease revived. To Jean Baptiste Antoine Suard he wrote in August 1770 that he had "a sort of flying gout, which I must keep under by the Bath waters. I will tell you a secret which is known only by my wife and a few select friends; at the end of the next theatrical campaign, I shall write up over my door *caestus artemque repono*."

The manager's restless activity outside the theatre was constantly increasing along with his property and his celebrity. At Hampton he was already one of the squirearchy. The Gazetteer of 7 September 1770 noted that "Mr. Garrick has given two Silver Cups, to be played for at Cricket, between Chertsey and Hampton—on Moulsey Hurst." In January 1771 he purchased from Col Thomas Clarke the manor of Copford, five miles from Colchester. In May he wrote the Rev Dr John Douglas

accepting "the office of one of yᵉ Stewards for yᵉ Sons of yᵉ Clergy," a "Corporation for the Relief of the Poor Widows, and children of Clergymen," chartered in 1678. Hosts and hostesses vied for the joy of receiving the charming Garricks. In 1771 they were entertained by General Henry Seymour Conway and Lady Hilesbury, widow of the fourth Duke of Argyll, at Park Place, near Henley-on-Thames, by the second Baron Edgecumbe, later first Earl of Mount-Edgcumbe, at his seat, Mount-Edgcumbe in Devonshire, by Lord Pembroke at Wilton, and by their old friend Lord Lyttelton at Hagley. (To the Lyttelton family Mrs Garrick was always "Pid-Pad"—"all parties of pleasure without Garrick and Pid-pad appear dull and insipid," wrote Lyttelton.)

Garrick dined at Bishop William Warburton's with Dr Richard Hurd and they discussed literature. He took Eva Maria to the masked ball of the Tuesday Nights Club, at Almack's, an occasion when Miss Monckton wore £30,000 in jewelry. Suppliants for sinecures sought his intercession with the great. (A long, witty letter of 26 July from Richard Burke, Edmund's brother, thanked Garrick warmly for obtaining from the Commissioner of the Customs permission for Burke to take a year's leave from his post of Customs officer in Grenada, West Indies.) Untalented playwrights continued to press in on Garrick from every direction: the testy Rev Charles Jenner at Cambridge, Col William Elsden, Quartermaster General in the service of the Portuguese at Lisbon, the bluestocking Mrs Elizabeth Montagu, Rev William Hawkins, Prebendary of Wells Cathedral. Bodily ills had increased as demands on Garrick's time had multiplied. In February 1771 he had been "attack'd in both legs & one knee without rest in yᵉ Night, or Spirits in yᵉ Day—." In a letter of 3 May 1771 to his good friend Edmund Burke he remarked that "dining Yesterday wᵗʰ an Archbishop I have got yᵉ Gout in My Knee."

Garrick began the theatrical season of 1771–72, as he wrote Rev William Hawkins, "very ill, & in the greatest theatrical bustle I have ever known." He had begun it, he confided to the Rev Evan Lloyd later in the season, "with great Uneasiness, several fits of ye Stone, & much business in hand," which "almost overset" him. But "by advice, & much Philosophy," he had regained "health, voice, Spirits & Strength, & lost my belly— in short I have play'd with some credit, & the people are really mad after Me as if I was a new face—I tell not this in vanity, but in ye spirit of truth—."

His theatric kingdom grew with nearly every season. In fending off Bennet Langton's proposal that he audition a Mrs Vernsberg, Garrick wrote on 14 March 1772 that "indeed our Theatre at present is so cramm'd with unemploy'd Actors, that we shall be oblig'd at ye End of this Season to discharge Some, who are a mere Weight upon the property— others, whom we keep because they have been some time wth Us, have very little to do. . . ." The theatre was open 186 nights and Garrick and Lacy cleared £6000 after expenses.

Garrick himself played fewer than 20 times in 1771–72, principally in comedy: Benedick, Drugger, Kitely, Leon, Lusignan, Ranger, Archer, Fribble, Bayes (for the first time in four years), then twice, at season's end, Richard III. (Hopkins's comments after the first night of *Richard III* were "Mr G very fine—Voice clear to the last great applause," and, for the second performance, for the benefit of the retirement fund: "Mr G better than before if possible.") Garrick wrote and produced a masque, with Charles Dibdin's music, called *The Institution of the Garter; or, Arthur's Round Table Restored*, in which Tom King revelled as Sir Dingle, the Court Fool. Hopkins noted this "Entertainment is got up at vast Expense both in Scenery & Dresses," and it earned "very great applause."

But the principal success of the season was in heavy tragedy. Garrick's exasperating friend Arthur Murphy was finally disarmed of all complaint by the assiduity with which Garrick and the actors went about preparing his *Grecian Daughter* for its premiere. Even before its fifth act was finished, in January 1772, Garrick wrote Murphy from Hampton: "I brought The Grecian Daughter with me here, have examined her well, and wonderfully pleased with the Lady. Mrs. Garrick was more affected than ever I knew her to be with any play. . . . The part of the Daughter is one of the finest for an actress in all the dramatic circle." When the play was produced on 26 February, Hopkins judged that it had "great Merit, it is very carefully got up and well perform'd, & receiv'd uncommon Applause Mrs Barry Display great Tragick Powers & receiv'd the vast Applause she merited— She will gain great Reputation in the part."

The season had not been without disagreeable incident. Garrick endured a serious attack of gout in November which kept him from the theatre for a week. His pain had hardly subsided when he was alarmed on 8 November by a threatening letter from the powerful and anonymous political satirist "Junius." Garrick had incurred Junius's displeasure innocently by passing along to Nicholas Ramus, Senior Page of the Back Stairs to George III, the casual remark of Henry Sampson Woodfall, Junius's publisher, that the satirist would write no more. Ramus had of course apprised the Royal household of the joyful news. Junius wrote Garrick:

I am very exactly informed of your impertinent inquiries, and of the information you so busily *sent* to Richmond, and with what triumph and exultation it was received. I knew every particular of it the *next day*. Now mark me, vagabond. Keep to your pantomimes, or be assured you shall hear of it. Meddle no more, thou busy informer!— It is in *my* power to make you curse the hour in which you dared to interfere with JUNIUS.

Garrick's reply, relayed necessarily through Woodfall, wavered between manly defiance, hurt feelings over "vagabond," and circumstantial apology. Junius never retorted.

The eccentric actor-critic-playwright Francis Gentleman, under the *nom-de-plume* Sir Nicholas Nipclose, also launched a satirical attack on Garrick in *The Theatres: A Poetical Dissection*—an attack which surprised Garrick, inasmuch as he had loaned Gentleman money and Gentleman had in 1770 dedicated his major work, *The Dramatic Censor*, to him. Garrick called him a "dirty, dedicating knave" and thought that Mrs Abington (with whom the manager feuded furiously during the season) was responsible.

The largest enterprise, aside from theatrical affairs, to engross Garrick's time and that of Eva Maria during the season of 1771–72 was the move from No 27, Southampton Street, to their grand new house in the Adam brothers' Adelphi Terrace. The Terrace was still incomplete when the Garricks began their complicated move on 28 February 1772. Their house was large, in the classical style, and furnished consonantly, with Adam-designed furniture. The green and yellow drawing room had an elaborate plaster ceiling with nine medallion paintings encircling the central circular panel by Antonio Zucchi, R.A., second husband of Garrick's friend the painter Angelica Kauffmann. Visitors noticed both that the drawing-room was magnificent and that most of the rest was gloomy and ill lit. The Garricks were "fix'd" in the new abode by mid-March, but Mrs Garrick was "almost kill'd wth ye fatigue of removing," David wrote Bennet Langton.

The theatrical year had been difficult indeed, and the summer brought no remission. In July the Garricks went to the Duke of Richmond at Goodwood and to Knighton on the Isle of Wight, along with John Wilkes, to visit the Hon. Thomas Fitzmaurice, younger brother of the Earl of Shelburne. But the peace Garrick sought

Folger Shakespeare Library

GARRICK's House in the Adelphi

engraving by Storer

was denied him. His friend, the respected writer of farces and musicals Isaac Bickerstaff, had in May fled to the Continent, accused of the capital crime of homosexuality. Garrick wrote to Robert Johnson in May "shock'd . . . beyond imagination" at the affair. On 24 June Bickerstaff wrote Garrick from St Malo a despairful letter expressing respect and thankfulness for past favors. Garrick endorsed it "from that poor wretch Bickerstaff— I could not answer it."

William Kenrick was a querulous, publicity-seeking, lying, drunken, mischief-making playwright and pamphleteer who had attacked nearly every successful writer in London—including Johnson, Fielding, Smart, and Goldsmith. He had turned his malevolent attention to Garrick in 1766 after the failure of Kenrick's *Falstaff's Wedding* at Drury Lane and again in the winter of 1767–68, when he charged unequal division of the profits of his comedy *The Widow'd Wife* and challenged Garrick to a duel. He had then declined to fight. In the spring of 1772 he had angrily demanded a speedy and favorable answer to the submission of his play *The Duellist* to Drury Lane, then had published insinuations that Garrick and two friends had planned to waylay and assault him.

In July 1772 Kenrick published a poetic lampoon titled *Love in the Suds Being the Lamentation of Roscius for the Loss of His Nyky*, a scurrilous attempt to involve Garrick in the Bickerstaff tragedy. Prefixed was an insolent letter to Garrick signed W. K. The silly libel ran through five editions, despite Garrick's attempts to suppress it. Garrick instituted suit in the Court of the King's Bench. Public sentiment was virtually all on his side, and he received much published support, including, oddly enough, that of his old enemy Joseph Reed. With typical inconsistency and cowardice, Kenrick inserted an abject apology in the newspapers of 26 November 1772. Advised by his solicitor, Peter Fountain, and other friends, Garrick dropped the prosecution. "Kenrick," wrote Garrick with relief to George Faulkner, "has made a publick recantation which has blacken'd him more— He had done what we wanted, & I am content. . . ."

Garrick was, in the fall of 1772, subjected to an anonymous attack in the *Public Ledger* by its publisher Francis Newberry. It was the introduction to another year of troubles. An unbalanced Presbyterian parson, the Rev David Williams, wrote Garrick curious, threatening letters, also anonymous. Garrick sued Newberry too and received an apology. About Williams he did nothing. There were other sorrows and disappointments. Garrick's old friend and first manager, Henry Giffard, died on 20 October. In November there was a tedious wrangle with Tom King, who was aggrieved that he did not make as much money as Harry Woodward did at Covent Garden—£500. Fanny Abington contributed her mite to Garrick's vexatious autumn and to the prostrating headaches which had begun with the Kenrick matter. The comedienne complained that a part in a new comedy which she imagined the author, Murphy, had promised her had been assigned to Mrs Barry. In his reply Garrick could not refrain from remarking "I never yet Saw Mrs *Abington* theatrically happy for a week together." The near-paranoid Murphy became convinced that he was the object of a plot, Barry attempted on Garrick's behalf to placate him, and a tediously verbose correspondence flowed. It was staunched only when Garrick wrote Murphy tersely:

Sir
I am too much indispos'd to write long Letters, & too old, & too happy to love Altercation— . . . I really have no more to say upon the Occasion, & am sorry that You have renew'd your old Way of making War, when I thought We had concluded a lasting Peace.

There was also a brief falling out, soon made up, with Dr John Hawkesworth, who did not accept Garrick's recommendation of Thomas Becket as publisher for Hawksworth's three-volume account of South Sea voyages. In March 1773 Garrick wrote Henry Sampson Woodfall in dudgeon over some slighting remarks the publisher had made about Garrick's contribution to the affairs of the *Public Advertiser*. Garrick declared his intention to dispose of his share in the enterprise. Garrick's ailments were episodic but frequent. He often closed letters by speaking of the gout in his writing hand. Several times he described to friends the pain of kidney stones. (To the brothers Adam: "I was attack'd terribly with a fit of ye Stone, & had it all yesterday Morning till I was deliver'd of twins—to ye great Joy of my Wife & family—I was 4 hours upon ye rack & now as free from pain as Ever I was, I am weak wth my delivery. . . .")

Meanwhile the 1772–73 season forged ahead, a season in which Garrick's company of well over 100 performed 188 nights. The theatre made money. Profits were nearly £5000. But there was much grumbling in the newspapers about the entertainments and a restlessness in a company which had lost some at least of its meridian power. Garrick, as he had done for some seasons, stuck to his resolve to learn no more new characters, and the public now saw him relinquishing more of his old ones. It had to get used to seeing Aickin as Pierre and Barry as Lear and even, sometimes, Cautherley as Don Felix. Garrick played about 20 times, including twice in Lear in February, when, Hopkins said, he was "never better. monstrous Applause." Garrick wrote and produced his farce *The Irish Widow*, which remained fairly popular for some years.

Garrick also worked especially diligently to stage Messink and Dibdin's pantomime *The Pigmy Revels*. That production, which opened as the annual Christmas pantomime but played 36 times during the season, perhaps owed its unusual popularity to its scenery, which may have been the first work Londoners saw by the Alsatian genius Philippe Jacques De Loutherbourg (1740–1812). De Loutherbourg had first been introduced to Garrick's attention by a letter from Jean Monnet, director of the Opéra-Comique, who called him "un de nos plus grand peintres, et garçon fort aimable." He had come to London in search of painting commissions in 1771, at first residing with Garrick's friend the fencing- and riding-master Domenico Angelo. Garrick asked him for ideas about some new production and received a comprehensive proposal for the alteration of the entire lighting and mechanical systems of Drury Lane. De Loutherbourg proposed integration and the closest cooperation between the scenic functions and those of the costumier, ballet master, and composer. He virtually offered himself as the coordinator of these func-

tions, and Garrick engaged him. The account books show payments to De Loutherbourg of £300 between 20 March and 18 June 1773, but the productions in which he assisted that season are not certainly known. He remained with Drury Lane, introducing fresh marvels each year, until 1781.

On 17 December 1772 Garrick politely evaded Lord North's desire to see him as Macbeth, giving illness as the reason— "'tis the most violent part I have. . . ." He added that he was deliberating a *Macbeth* "in yᵉ old dresses—." The next evening, 18 December, Garrick acted Hamlet in his own alteration, about which the critic of *Town and Country Magazine* used the word "mutilated" and about which Garrick himself came at last to feel doubtful. There are changes throughout, but the most striking ("impudent," Garrick later admitted) are in Act V, which banished the gravediggers, the word play between Hamlet and Osric, and the fencing. In the concluding scene of the tragedy—33 lines, nearly all by Garrick—Hamlet kills the King, the Queen runs away, Hamlet "runs on Laertes's sword and falls." The "Good-night, sweet prince" speech is retained. In a letter to Pierre-Antoine de Laplace Garrick boasted: "just before Christmas I appear'd in the Character of the *Young* Hamlet, and receiv'd more applause than when I acted it at five and twenty—."

It was true, so far as anyone at Drury Lane could see. Hopkins's *Diary* attested "Mr Garrick played divinely & Merited the great Applause he receivd It is alterd much for the better in regard to the part of Hamlet & I think the alterations very fine and proper." It was, of course, a professional theatrical judgment. The scholars would be heard from later. Garrick was very conscious of his audacity and especially pleased to be boasting of it to the French. In a letter to the Abbé André Morellet on the day following the one to Laplace, he remarked "this is a great revolution in our theatrical history, for wch 20 years ago instead of Shouts of approbation, I should have had ye benches thrown at my head—." The letter to Laplace had the pleasant—and perhaps sought-for—effect of further spreading Garrick's continental fame. Laplace wrote on 24 January that he had placed a detailed account of the alteration in *L'Observateur françois à Londres*.

In April 1773 Garrick played a favorite part, Don John in *The Chances*, in a command performance. Hopkins noted: "this Comedy is reviv'd with great Alterations by Mr G. Play'd with great Spirit & much Applauded the Alterations are vastly lik'd it will now be a living play."

The Garricks fled to their social enjoyments in June 1773 with more than usual relief. They visited, among others, Richard Rigby at Mistley, the Earl of Shelburne at Bowood House, Wiltshire, Lord Camden at Camden Place near Chislehurst, and, near summer's end, the Spencers at Althorp, Northamptonshire; and they entertained frequently at Hampton. But it was not a summer full of fun or free of care. The leading hero of Covent Garden Theatre, William "Gentleman" Smith, had fallen out with his manager Colman and, in endeavoring to secure a place at Drury Lane, had been haughty with George Garrick over a matter of salary. The ensuing correspondence (in which, by way of discipline, Garrick systematically reduced Smith to abjectness) stretched over three months. There were also that summer anonymous nuisance letters, rumors of revived schemes for a third theatre, and pestiferous authors. Garrick complained to Richard Berenger in July about life's unfairness:

I am here [at Hampton] with my family spending my time as innocently and thoughtlessly as the Theatre & my slanderers will permit me— I look upon myself as lawfull Game in the winter, when I am justly hunted & shot at from all quarters; but surely a manager ought to have the same priveledges with hares

& Partridges, & not be disturb'd till such a Day, as should be settled by Parliament.

One consolation for Garrick's troubles during 1773 was his election to the society which had been founded in 1764 by Reynolds, Johnson, Burke, Goldsmith, Beauclerk, Langton, and Chamier. He had already been seconded to the fashionable Almack's Club by Topham Beauclerk. But Garrick was intelligent enough to appreciate that election to *The* Club was an honor of far greater magnitude. It was one which he had long yearned for. The honor perhaps would have come much sooner had Garrick not been injudiciously confident of election. Hawkins wrote that Johnson had objected "He will disturb us by his buffoonery" and had actively worked to exclude him. Boswell's refutation was emphatic:

The truth is, that not very long after the institution of our Club, Sir Joshua Reynolds was speaking of it to Garrick. "I like it much, (said he,) I think I shall be of you." When Sir Joshua mentioned this to Dr. Johnson, he was much displeased with the actor's conceit. *"He'll be of us,* (said Johnson) how does he know we will *permit* him? The first Duke in England had no right to hold such language." However, when Garrick was regularly proposed some time afterwards, Johnson, though he had taken a momentary offence at his arrogance, warmly and kindly supported him, and he was accordingly elected, was a most agreeable member, and continued to attend our meetings to the time of his death.

Mrs Piozzi also exaggerated the difficulty. She quoted Johnson as asserting "If Garrick *does* apply, I'll black-ball him." Boswell was at pains to refute that story too. Boswell's editor, Powell, points out that Garrick was only the sixth new member admitted after The Club's foundation in 1764 and that he was admitted a year before either Fox or Gibbon. (Hannah More in her *Memoirs* said that "upon Garrick's death, when numberless applications were made to succeed him, Johnson was deaf to them all; he said, 'No, there never could be found any successor worthy of such a man'; and he insisted upon it there should be a year's widowhood in the club, before they thought of a new election.")

Again, during the 190-night season of 1773–74, Garrick acted sparingly and avoided the energy-sapping parts of heavy tragedy, concentrating on production and direction of three new mainpieces and three farces during the season. But his most spectacular production in the 1773–74 season was one he wrote himself and for a special purpose. It was the seasonal extravaganza, *A Christmas Tale*. Though Hopkins thought Dibdin's music for it "the worst he ever composed," the piece was repeated successfully through January. Hopkins said that it had been written "in a hurry & on purpose to Shew Some fine Scenes which were design'd by Mon^s De Loutherberg particularly a Burning Palace &c. which was extremely fine & Novel."

The *Morning Post* of 22 January 1774 reported:

Last night at Drury-lane Theatre, the comedy of the Wonder concluded with a new country dance, in which Mr. Garrick surprised the audience. His activity was beyond description, and was accompanied with huzzas and bravos from all parts of the house. The dance was encored: However, when the curtain drew up for the dance to be repeated, some gentlemen had feeling enough to cry out "it was too much;" but Mr. Garrick, with a significant look, informed them he was equal to the task, and the dance was performed again.

Garrick's long-time co-manager James Lacy died at Isleworth that same night. Their long-standing mutual animosity had not broken the surface of their profitable relationship for years. Garrick had spent those years teaching Lacy that his business was in the front of the house, not backstage. He must therefore have read with a sinking heart and a sense of *déjà vu* the curt letter of 25 February from 25-year-old Wil-loughby Lacy, heir to his father's share of the patent, informing Garrick that the young man had consulted a lawyer "who, on reading the articles, was clearly of the opinion that I have an equal right with you in the management of every branch of the business relative to the theatre. This being the case, I am sure you would not wish to deprive me of any right I am entitled to, as, from my conduct, I hope you have no reason to think I shall make an improper use of it."

Willoughby Lacy knew much less about the theatre than his father James had known when he had begun the partnership with Garrick. Furthermore, he had an ambition to act and in fact had already performed enough in country companies to demonstrate his lack of talent to everyone but himself. Nevertheless, Garrick set himself to the tasks of being agreeable and helping Lacy learn to act and manage.

The winter of 1773–74 was an exceptionally hard one for David Garrick. In January he was housebound for a fortnight by severe cold and hoarseness. Having to exchange wrong-headed but experienced James Lacy for his weak and insolent son thrust heavy new front-office burdens onto Garrick's shoulders. In the late winter and spring George Garrick was desperately ill, and the petty details which he normally took care of accumulated. In a letter to the *St James's Chronicle* Tom Davies attacked his former manager, under the disguise (which Garrick penetrated) of "Anti-Mendax," for allowing the prompter William Hopkins "to deliver the Plays of Shakespeare in a State of Mutilation, as acted at his Theatre, to Mr. [John] Bell" for the edition edited by Francis Gentleman. Francis Gentleman again attacked him, in March 1774, thinly veiled as "Censor Dramaticus." Nor was Garrick's physical condition comfortable. He wrote Mrs Elizabeth Montague, in mid-May, that his "foot was flanell'd up wth y^e Gout . . . y^e foul Fiend—."

Harvard Theatre Collection

GARRICK's Estate at Hampton

engraving by Stadler, after Farington

In the summer of 1774 Garrick, pleased with the work on the Adelphi, gave Robert Adam orders for a classical façade to his villa at Hampton. He busied himself in fending off volunteered plays from amateur playwrights and scrawling letters with his gouty fingers to a variety of other correspondents, including his nieces Arabella and Catherine Garrick, George's daughters, at school in Paris. He bargained with Mary Ann Yates and won her back from Covent Garden for the ensuing season. Elizabeth Younge gave him anxiety about her salary, too. The vixen Abington was at him about roles, "Except for the very charming part which you Made for me in the Chances, I have not been permitted to speak one comic line in any new Piece these six years past— and Indeed Miss Pope is in possession of all the comic characters in Every class without Exception, while my Rolle has been confined to Melancholy walking gentlewomen only." It was, of course, an exaggeration. Garrick replied wearily:

What still complaining, my dear Mad^m, of my Injustice? Still seeking redress by producing a Catalogue of Grievances? for heaven's sake let ye poor Manager have some respite from his many labours, & enjoy a few unmurmuring Weeks in the Summer; the Month of September will be soon here, & then it will be as Natural for you to find fault with him, as for him to find fault with you.

Dodd, who had run away to Dublin with Mrs Bulkley, was "money bound in Dublin" and had to be bailed out.

On 20 August the Garricks paid off accumulated social obligations (and belatedly celebrated their twenty-fifth wedding anniversary, which had occurred on 22 June) with what the *London Chronicle* called "a splendid entertainment or Fête Champêtre, at [their] gardens at Hampton." The eminent French pyrotechnist at Ranelagh, Morel Torré, "conducted a most brilliant fire-work." Garrick had been responsible, on Monnet's recommendation, for Torré's immigration and prosperity and now was repaid. After "an elegant concert of music," the "Temple of Shakespeare, and gardens, were illuminated with 6000 lamps, and the forge of Vulcan made a splendid appearance." Present were "a great number of Nobility and Gentry," who "expressed the utmost satisfaction on the occasion." But Kitty Clive had refused to come, and Garrick wrote his "dear Pivy" that

in short your Misconception about that fatal Champetre (the Devil take the Word) has made me so cross about every thing that belongs to it, that I curse all Squibs, Crackers, Rockets, Air-Balloons, Mines, serpents & Catherine Wheels, & can think of nothing & Wish for nothing, but laugh, Jig, humour, fun, pun, conundrum carriwitchet & Catherine Clive! —

In mid-summer Lord Camden had written "I do very much, dear Garrick, wish for a quiet day with you, when you are not interrupted every minute with authors and actors." But an attack of jaundice had laid Camden low, and he wrote on 20 August that he had not been "fit for convivial riot" and renewed his invitation: "will you and your wife come and see us out of charity, and sacrifice wit for a few days to friendship?" The Garricks went down to Camden Place at once. When they came back David had a badly sprained leg, "among other misfortunes," he wrote Richard Cumberland, and was "afraid of a long confinement." The disability may have been exaggerated by Garrick, who was trying to avoid involvement in some private theatricals being sponsored by Cumberland and William Hanbury at Kelmarsh, Northamptonshire, in September. And Garrick could not afford just then to offend Cumberland, who was at work on his comedy *The Choleric Man*. Garrick was counting on it heavily in the season which loomed just ahead.

Petty ills dogged him into the beginning of the season. When he wrote the Earl of Upper Ossory on 3 September to thank him for the gift of "as fine a haunch of Venison as Ever Quin roll'd an Amorous Eye at," he addressed the letter "Mr Garrick from his bed," where he was confined by gout and a broken blood vessel.

For Willoughby Lacy's Drury Lane debut on 8 October 1774, when he was billed as "A Young Gentleman," Garrick wrote a "New Occasional Prologue." It was a futile bow to the venerable custom of concealing the names of debutants, for every editor in town knew his identity. The *Westminster Magazine* was disappointed in this "friend and pupil of our English Roscius. . . . His figure is . . . lank, awkward, and unengaging; his voice distinctly powerful, but inharmonious; his action *outré*, vulgar and forced: his attitudes unnatural affected and disgustful; and his delivery a continued rant. . . ." Lacy's hauteur quickly diminished.

Garrick never drove harder to prepare a season's bill of fare than in the waning weeks of summer and in the fall of 1774, though often racked by gout and plagued by Mrs Abington. In the 188 nights before the end of the 1774–75 season, he pushed into production a total of 11 new pieces, two of them of his own authorship. Garrick's contributions were *The Meeting of the Company; or, Bayes's Art of Acting*, a prelude on 17 September (which the loyal Hopkins noted was "full of fine Satyr and an Excellent Lesson to all performers," adding "it was receiv'd with great Applause"), and *Bon Ton; or, High Life Above Stairs*, produced for King's benefit on 18 March. Hopkins said that farce had been "Written 15 or 16 years ago" and that "Mr G. out of Friendship for Mr King gave it him to get up for his Benefit—It was very well perform'd & receiv'd with the highest Applause."

The summer of 1775 passed quickly for the Garricks and was broken by visits in August both from and to the Duke of Newcastle and his family and in September to

Lord and Lady Camden at Camden Place, for the hop-gathering festivities. Garrick posted his usual enquiries to trustworthy friends about young performers who were making a stir on provincial circuits. On 31 July 1775 he wrote Henry Bate: "If you pass by Cheltenham on Your Way to Worcester, I wish you would see an Actress there, a *Mrs Siddons*, She has a desire I hear to try her Fortune with Us; if she seems in Your Eyes worthy of being transplanted, pray desire to know upon what conditions She would make ye Tryal, & I will write to her the post after I receive Your Letter—." According to Mrs Siddons, Tom King, at Garrick's request, had already witnessed her performance in June.

Garrick brought to a close his 34 years of connection with the London theatres and his 29 years of management in a season which in several respects surpassed all his previous ones. In 1775–76 his Drury Lane company of well over 100 persons produced 67 plays and 32 afterpieces in 189 performances. The house gleaned the greatest income (£37,917) and laid out the most money for salaries, sets, maintenance, and costumes (£33,453), although profits to Lacy and Garrick were only a modest £4,463.

Jane Pope was feuding with Garrick over salary. She had written him demanding a raise, "determin'd at length to shake all affection off, & like the Swiss to perform only with those that pay the best." Garrick had suspended his favor, and she had taken herself off to Dublin to repent of her impertinence. Kitty Clive talked her back into Garrick's graces before the end of the year. But the most important addition to the roster was, of course, Sarah Siddons. She made her Drury Lane debut under the usual denomination "A Young Lady," playing Portia in *The Merchant of Venice*, on 29 December 1775. Hopkins was restrained in his judgment: ". . . a good figure rather handsome—wants Spirit and ease her Voice a little course very well receiv'd." The

Middlesex Journal was also censorious of her vocal abilities. She was monotonous and there was "also vulgarity in her tones." Garrick and his judicious friends King and Bate saw a little deeper. Garrick protected her from the spite of Mrs Yates and Miss Younge, seated her by him at rehearsal, and sought to smooth the rough edges of her provincial habits through half a dozen comedy parts. He also allowed her to be Lady Anne to his own Richard III.

Only one new mainpiece was introduced during the season, the comedy *The Runaway*, the first of 14 dramatic productions by Hannah Cowley, a "Lady-Author . . . very clever & very modest," whose manuscript Garrick had been inspecting—and probably correcting—for a year and a half. He furnished an epilogue, she a prologue. The whole, wrote Hopkins the prompter, "was receiv'd with very great Applause" on 15 February 1776 and entered the regular repertory. The season brought forth also the exiled Isaac Bickerstaff's musical farce *The Sultan; or, a Peep into the Seraglio*, George Colman's farce *The Spleen; or, Islington Spa*, Henry Bate's comic opera *The Blackamoor Wash'd White*, William Heard's farce *Valentine's Day*, Garrick's own prelude *The Theatrical Candidates* and his *May Day; or, the Little Gipsy*. The latter, as Hopkins noted, was a "Musical Farce of one act [which] was wrote by Mr G on purpose to introduce Miss [Harriet] Abrams. . . ," a fifteen-year-old Jewish girl, a sister of John Braham, who was to have a long and celebrated career as a singer. (Garrick was enchanted with her: "She is very young and small, has a very sweet Voice and a fine Shake, but not Power enough yet." He had told Colman, "she is surprizing! — I want to introduce her as the little Gipsy with 3 or 4 exquisite Songs—.")

All those pieces met with some degree of success, except Heard's, which, being "badly perform'd" at Reddish's benefit, was "much hiss'd," and Henry Bate's *Blacka-*

moor Wash'd White, which occasioned the last in-house disturbance (a near riot) in which Garrick was personally concerned. Bate, afterwards Sir Henry Bate Dudley, was a clergyman and editor of the *Morning Post*. He had married a sister of the actress Mrs Hartley and was called "a very warm friend" by Garrick, who had procured him a curacy in 1774. He was an eager controversialist and his aptness to fisticuffs and duelling had earned him the sobriquet "the Fighting Parson." Bate had correctly surmised that his enemies would oppose the play and had stationed hired bruisers in the pit. But that had only increased the uproar, which Garrick finally came onstage to quiet. Hopkins wrote in his prompter's diary that "Mr G. told them that his Theatrical Life would be very Short and he should be glad to end it in peace—A man in the Pit said if you have a mind to die in Peace don't let this Farce be play'd again. . . ." It was withdrawn by Bate.

On 29 December 1775 Garrick had written to George Colman offering, as he had promised, first refusal of his rights in Drury Lane Theatre:

I must now seriously acquaint You that I shall most certainly part with it— I Saw a Gentleman Yesterday of great property, & who has no objection to the price Viz: 35000 pounds for my Part— I must desire you to speak out . . . for I must See the Party again on Saturday Evening. . . . My disorder increases & distresses me much; my Friend [the physician] Pott is to search for yᵉ cause next Week— I beg that Your letter may be determinate—.

Colman had replied that he had no interest in sharing a theatre with anyone. It was the answer Garrick had expected. The "Party" Garrick had referred to was Richard Brinsley Sheridan. On 18 January 1776 a sale contract was signed which would, by July, give control of Drury Lane into the hands of Willoughby Lacy (who had refused to sell his share), Sheridan, Sheridan's

father-in-law (the musician Thomas Linley), and the wealthy obstetrician James Ford (physician-extraordinary to Queen Charlotte). The actual management would quickly devolve on Sheridan.

Garrick's break with the theatre was not a clean break, for he still held a large mortgage on Lacy's share (secured by the whole property). But for the immediate present, Garrick was jubilant as he contemplated the release from various cares which quitting the management would bring. On 3 January 1776 he wrote the Rev Dr John Hoadly

I shall take my leave of the Stage, & bid Farewell to the plumed troops & the big Wars, & welcome content & the tranquil Mind— in Short— I will not stay to be Sixty with my Cap & bells— Active as I am, & full of Spirit, with the drawback of a *gravel-complaint*:

Mʳˢ Garrick & I are happy wᵗʰ the thoughts of my *Strutting & fretting no more upon yᵉ Stage*, & leaving to Younger Spirits the present race of Theatrical Heroines with all their Airs, indispositions, tricks & importances which have reduc'd the Stage to be a dependant upon the Wills of our insolent, vain, & let me add insignificant female trumpery— there must be a revolution, or my Successors will Suffer much, I had a resource in my own Acting, that counter-acted all the Evil designs of these Gentry—Linley will be of great Service— Sing Song is much the Fashion, & his knowledge of Musick & preparing fit Subjects for the Stage, will be a Strength, that the Proprietors may depend upon, when the Heroines are prankish—.

And on 23 January 1776 his beloved old ally and adversary, the crusty Kitty Clive, wrote to him:

Is it really true, that you have put an end to the glory of Drury-lane theatre? *if it is so*, let me congratulate my dear Mr. and Mrs. Garrick on their approaching happiness; *I know* what it will be; you cannot yet have an idea of it; *but* if you should still be so wicked not to be satisfied with that *unbounded*, uncommon degree of fame you have received as an actor, and which no other actor ever did receive— nor no other actor ever *can* receive;— I say, if you should still long to be dipping your fingers in their theatrical pudding (now without plums), you will be no Garrick for the Pivy.

In the height of the public admiration for you, when you were never mentioned with any other appellation but the Garrick, the charming man, the fine fellow, the delightful creature, both by men and ladies; when they were admiring every thing you did, and every thing you scribbled,—at this very time, *I, the Pivy*, was a living witness that they did not know, nor could they be sensible, of half your perfections. I have seen you, with your magical hammer in your hand, *endeavouring* to beat your ideas into the heads of creatures who had none of their own—I have seen you, with lamb-like patience, endeavouring to make them comprehend you; and I have seen you, when that could not be done—I have seen your lamb turned into a lion: by this your great labour and pains the public was entertained; *they* thought they all acted very fine,—they did not see you pull the wires.

There are people *now* on the stage to whom you gave their consequence; they think themselves very great; now let them go on in their new parts without your leading-strings, and they will soon convince the world what their genius is; I have always said this to every body, even when your horses and mine were in their highest prancing. While I was under your control, I did not say half the fine things I thought of you, because it looked like flattery; and you know your Pivy was always proud: besides, I thought you did not like me then, but *now* I am sure you do, which makes me send you this letter.

What a strange jumble of people they have put in the papers as the purchasers of the patent! I thought I should have died with laughing when I saw a man-mid-wife amongst them: I suppose they have taken him in to prevent *miscarriages!*

The spring of 1776 made the most strenuous demands upon Garrick's physique and psyche, and also on his diplomacy. As soon as word leaked to Fanny Abington

that Garrick was finally decided upon retirement, she decided to divert part of the attention to herself by announcing her own withdrawal from the stage and to seclusion in Wales for the rest of her life. She informed her manager of this "fixed determination" on 4 March. Further, that "worst of bad women" wished Garrick to play for her retirement benefit. He did so, matching his Archer to her Mrs Sullen in *The Beaux' Stratagem* on 7 May. But she returned to Drury Lane 1776–77 and did not finally retire from the stage until 1799. There were the usual nerve-jangling encounters with Lacy and upsetting stage accidents. Hurst narrowly escaped losing an eye in a mock-duel with Palmer on 18 April, and on 9 May, just after Garrick finished performing Benedick for the last time, "the whole set of Clouds fell down upon the Stage but did no Damage."

Even aside from the theatre, social, family, and business pressures were incessant during his last season. Garrick often relaxed in the bonhomie of The Club with Johnson and his circle. But his innocent gregariousness also drew him into less desirable company, despite a vigilant regard to propriety which bordered on prudery. He had boasted to his brother Peter on 21 March 1776 of his reception to the Savoir Vivre Club:

I receive Every honour that a Man can do from all Sorts of people, & I was yesterday enroll'd a member among the first & greatest people in this Kingdom— We have a New house built in the best Taste in ye middle of St James's Street, & it is furnish'd like a palace— Each Member pays 12 Guineas at Entrance— It is ye first Society for titles & property in the known world—

Garrick speaks of "14 Dukes at the head of us," and although he was then careful to deprecate the effect of all this on him, he was obviously impressed. Alas, the Savoir Vivre Club, which had been founded by General Joseph Smith in pique because he had been excluded from Almack's, turned out to be merely a gaming place and was closed by May 1776, when Smith went to jail for bribery.

All Britain seemed determined to attend Garrick's final performances. Notables, both friends and strangers, importuned him eagerly and sometimes rudely for seats in the sold-out houses. Parties of worshippers from Edinburgh and Dublin coached into London. Mme Suzanne Necker (the mother of Mme de Staël) arrived from Paris with her husband, the finance minister of Louis XVI. Many of those visitors expected to be entertained at the Adelphi or at Hampton. The More sisters came and Hannah stayed, settling into the Garrick household to witness many of the farewell performances in April and May. She went back to Bristol before the climax, but Garrick kept her faithfully informed by letter.

The emotional hubbub increased as the season drew to a close. On 20 January 1776 Garrick had played his first new part in a decade, Sir Anthony Branville, in a revival of Frances Sheridan's comedy *The Discovery*. On 1 March he had advertised his last performance of Lusignan in *Zara*. He spent the next month gathering his strength. Then, between 11 April and 10 June, he gave Abel Drugger, Benedick (twice), Kitely, Hamlet (twice; on the second, and last, time the proceeds were for the theatrical fund), Sir John Brute, Leon, Lear (three times), Don Felix (twice), Archer, and Ranger (for the first time in two years, twice).

In his *Memoirs* Joseph Cradock reported that Garrick had said to him: "I can play Richard; but I dread the fight and the fall. I am afterwards in agonies." (An anonymous memorialist in the *Monthly Mirror*, recalling some performance of 1768 or earlier, wrote: "I saw him once, after having played the part of Richard, stretched, like the expiring Germanicus in Poussin's picture, on a sofa, panting, pale, speechless, covered with perspiration, and unable to raise his arm.") The town had not seen him

in the part in five years. Yet, *Richard III* had been the vehicle which had carried Garrick to greatness, and his audience begged for it, so he manfully struggled through Richard three times in the final two months. On 3 June, when he played the part, the crush was so great that standees made it impossible for those seated to see the stage, and the start was delayed for two hours, but Garrick wrote Hannah More next day that he had "play'd it last Night better than Ever−," but "What a Trial of breast, lungs, ribs & What not−." He had been at Court in observance of the King's birthday "& Such work they made with Me, from ye Archbishop of Canterbury to the Page of ye Back Stairs, that I have been suffocated wth Comp^{ts}−." His Majesty had demanded Richard for the following night.

But for his very last appearance on the boards of Drury Lane, on Monday, 10 June 1776, Garrick eschewed tragedy. For an occasion on which he, his actors, and the audience would all be overwrought, he thought comedy would be better. He chose to play the suave Don Felix in *The Wonder*. The profits of that night were again for the theatre's retirement fund. Several comments on the historic last evening are extant, including those of Hopkins and of Garrick himself. Hopkins wrote in his diary: ". . . he spoke the Usual prologue & after the play he went forward & address'd the Audience in so pathetic a Manner as [to] draw Tears from the Audience & himself & took his leave of them forever."

Arthur Murphy in his *Life of Garrick* furnished the text of the simple farewell speech, which was, as he said, "on the next day published in the newspapers, and from them reprinted in the magazines":

Ladies and Gentlemen,
It has been customary with persons under my circumstances to address you in a farewell epilogue. I had the same intention, and turned my thoughts that way; but I found myself

Harvard Theatre Collection

DAVID GARRICK, as Don Felix

engraving by Collyer, after Dodd

then as incapable of writing such an epilogue, as I should be now of speaking it.

The jingle of rhyme and the language of fiction would but ill suit my present feelings.

This is to me a very awful moment: it is no less than parting for ever with those, from whom I have received the greatest kindness, and upon the spot, where that kindness and your favours were enjoyed.

(Here his voice failed him; he paused, till a gush of tears relieved him.)

Whatever may be the changes of my future life, the deepest impression of your kindness will always remain here—here, in my heart, fixed, and unalterable.

I will very readily agree to my successors having more skill and ability for their station than I have had; but I defy them all to take more uninterrupted pains for your favour, or to be more truely sensible of it, than is your grateful humble servant.

Murphy declares that "Having uttered these sentiments, he bowed respectfully, to all parts of the house, and in a slow pace, and much hesitation, withdrew for ever from their presence. . . . Every face in the theatre was clouded with grief. . . ." Garrick wrote Madame Necker that: "After I had left the stage . . . they would not suffer the *petite piece* to go on; nor would the actors perform, they were so affected."

Two days later Garrick's mood was mixed. He wrote Hannah More:

I never pass'd two days with more real pleasure than I did Yesterday & today at Hampton, reliev'd from the Slavery of Government: such a Night as Monday last was never Seen! —Such clapping, Sighing, crying, roaring, &c &c &c—it is not to be describ'd! —in short— it was as we could Wish, et finis coronat Opus —ye Bell rings—exit Nonsense—.

Garrick sent Tom King a relic and a note on 25 June: "Accept a Small token of our long & constant attachment to Each other— I flatter Myself that this Sword, as it is a theatrical one, will not cut Love between us, and that it will not be less valuable to You for having dangled by my side some part of the last Winter." Mrs Garrick wrote Hannah More that she had saved for her the buckles Garrick had worn on the last night of his career, and Anna Laetitia Barbauld wrote a distich of which Garrick was inordinately fond: "Thy Buckles, O Garrick, thy Friends may now Use. / But no Mortals hereafter shall stand in thy Shoes."

A Committee of the Theatrical Fund, 13 prominent Drury Lane actors, headed by Tom King, presented Garrick with a medal designed by Reynolds. "The device— Garrick, habited as a Roman Actor, undrawing a curtain, and discovering Nature, embracing her favourite child Shakespeare. Mr. Cipriani . . . made a drawing in colours . . . and it was executed in enamel by Mr. Howes, of Fleet-street," recalled John Williams in 1797.

The popular Garricks continued to receive more invitations than they could accept—from Sir James Caldwell in Ireland, from Lord Chief Justice and Lady Mansfield, from the Burneys. At Lord Halifax's house Garrick shared with Lord Sandwich and party a huge green turtle brought back from the Indies by Admiral Sir Edward Hughes. He and Eva Maria visited the Henry Bunburys at Barton. They went again to Richard Rigby at Mistley. In July 1776 the Garricks' old and intimate friends Lord and Lady Spencer and some of their kin visited Hampton, and in October the Garricks visited the Spencer estate, Althorp ("Felicity Castle"), returning by way of Ampthill, where they stayed with the Earl and Countess of Upper Ossery.

Garrick witnessed a fox hunt at Althorp, but he was not mounted. The surviving "Chace Books" noted that "Lady Spencer and Mr Garrick were out in the cabriolet and viewed the fox several times over Holdenby Grounds." Often now, Garrick could not sit a horse with comfort. Both the gout and the stone had grown steadily worse, though he bore the torture with the wry gallantry expressed in a letter of 12 December 1776 to Lady Spencer: "I am writing this with one knee as big as my head, & two large cloth shoes, to give the Gout room to divert itself. I write with great pain, or I would send some nonsense which would, by way of variety, relieve the surfeit of Charrades."

His gout was not helped by his convivial habits and love of the table. He had written Henry Hoare the younger on 27 July 1776: "two Glasses of Champaign wch I drank Yesterday with Earl Spencer at Wimbledon, are now tickling the ball of my great toe—."

Garrick's illnesses were a matter of news and of public as well as private concern. On 17 January 1777 General John Burgoyne wrote an affectionate note: "The day before I left town I heard you had a slight touch of the gout; at Bath, Beauclerk told

me it was a serious fit; and at my return yesterday, which is repeated in the papers to-day, I find the report that the attack had amounted to confinement, fever, acute pain, and all the attendant inconveniences and trials of that earthly plague." But by 18 January that attack had abated.

Garrick resisted all suggestions that he perform, but he carefully prepared a reading from his own works before the Royal Family at Windsor in February 1777. He thought his reception cool, and he was hurt. Johnson, when told this, thought that "he should not, in a Royal apartment, expect the hallooing and clamour of the One Shilling Gallery." Even the publication, that year, of Hannah More's *Ode to Dragon, Mr. Garrick's House-dog at Hampton* was insufficient balm.

He was still ready to help young theatrical aspirants like Mary Robinson (afterwards "Perdita") polish their talents. John Bannister has in his memoirs an amusing story of how he called upon Garrick and recited Hamlet's speeches while the great actor shaved. Garrick attended Bannister's rehearsals of *Zaphira* at Drury Lane in the following year until he was given to understand that his presence was interpreted as interference by old Tom Sheridan. Garrick's relationship with the new management had already begun to erode, for he had begun to have trouble collecting interest owed him by Lacy.

Rumors that Garrick was due for a knighthood had spread as far as France by the end of May 1777, when he received a letter from the bluestocking Joel Henrietta Pye, the wife of an army officer then resident in Paris: "I know not how to congratulate you," she wrote, "because I know of no title that can add lustre to the name of Garrick."

In October 1777 the Garricks went into North Wales to spend a couple of days with Sir Watkin Williams Wynn at Wynnstay. The passion of Sir Watkin was for amateur acting—carefully bolstered with visiting professionals. But Garrick did not act, agreeing only to "superintend" the gentle Thespians who were getting up Henry Carey's famous farce *Chrononhoton-thologos*. In December he wrote Luke Gardiner (later Baron and Viscount Mountjoy) in Ireland, responding to a plea for advice about that gentleman's amateur productions by sending costume sketches by the scene painter James Messink. And Garrick continued to write prologues and epilogues for friends on request.

In the spring of 1778 there was an occurrence which Garrick may well have considered his finest triumph and most valuable compliment. He was in the strangers' gallery of the House of Commons one day when, the debate growing heated, the Speaker ordered a closed session. Thomas Davies reported the scene and action:

Mr. Burke rose, and appealed to the honourable Assembly, whether it could possibly be consistent with the rules of decency and liberality, to exclude from the hearing of their debates, a man to whom they all were obliged; one who was the great master of eloquence; in whose school they had all imbibed the art of speaking, and been taught the elements of rhetoric. For his part, he owned that he had been greatly indebted to his instruction. Much more he said in commendation of Mr. Garrick, and was warmly seconded by Mr. Fox and Mr. T. Townshend, who very copiously displayed the great merit of their old preceptor, as they termed him. . . .

The House almost unanimously concurred in exempting Mr. Garrick from the general order of quitting the gallery.

"Almost unanimously"—all except a Mr Baldwin, a Member from Shropshire, who, wrote Garrick to Hannah More, "complain'd that a celebrated Gentleman was admitted into the house when Everybody Else was Excluded, & *that I gloried* in my situation. . . ." This, wrote Garrick, had provoked his "Muse" and he has proudly read the verses *contra* Baldwin "to Lord North, Lord Gower, Lord Weymouth Mr Rigby &c &c [and] they were all pleas'd. . . ."

In July 1778 Garrick had a sharp attack of the stone which, as late as mid-September, he wrote Cradock, "almost renders me incapable of reading, writing or judging— I am, like a State Prisoner, debarr'd the Use of Pen, Ink & paper— I am going into Hampshire for Change of Air, & thence, if I recover but slowly, to Bath— so that my Stay there or Absence from Town will prevent for Some time my Even Seeing a Theatre— indeed, Sir, I am grown unfit for any thing, but sitting in a great chair, or walking, or rather at present, creeping about my Garden—."

The journey into Hampshire was imprudent. It soon involved a stay with Lord Palmerston at Broadlands, a stop with Joseph Warton at Winchester, where the King was reviewing militia (and where he also viewed Garrick and made amends for the failure of the Windsor reading with a well-turned compliment), and visits to some country acquaintances. The journey was punctuated by various pains. As Garrick wrote Richard Cox later, "I had no sooner got rid of the Stone, but I was attack'd with the Bile, & underwent the torment of Martyrs." Though he chafed under the necessity, Garrick obeyed Dr Cadogan's advice "to be at rest at Hampton" eating "Nothing but plain boil'd & roast; & bread & cheese" and resisting all invitations like Cox's. But the resolution wavered by September, and he began planning epilogues for Sheridan and even going to plays on occasion.

His appearance was no longer youthful, but that was due to pain and not to the reason Dr Johnson gave in his quip to Mrs Thrale in 1778: " 'David, madam,' said Johnson, 'looks much older than he is; for his face has had double the business of any other man's; it is never at rest; when he speaks one minute, he has quite a different countenance to what he assumes the next; I don't believe he ever kept the same look for half an hour together, in the whole course of his life; and such an eternal, restless, fatiguing play of the muscles, must certainly wear out a man's face before its real time.' "

Despite the run-in with old Tom Sheridan and the coolness of young Lacy, Garrick was friendly with Richard Brinsley Sheridan and often lent him assistance with theatrical problems. Early in September 1778, he stayed late at Drury Lane Theatre after a performance to give advice about some new scenery. He caught a cold in the chilly house. In November, though he had been "ill with a Cold & Cough wch tear my head & breast to pieces," he took much trouble detailing corrections in Hannah More's manuscript play *Fatal Falsehood*. He even roused himself to attend meetings of The Club.

Garrick felt well enough to undertake a visit to his old friends the Spencers at Althorp for New Year's. He and Mrs Garrick arrived in the middle of the night and encountered bad weather. Garrick fell ill again. A local doctor, William Kerr of Northampton, diagnosed shingles. On 13 January the Garricks set out for home, arriving at the Adelphi on the afternoon of the fifteenth. David felt somewhat better the next day, but it was a temporary respite. He gradually sank, despite all the efforts of the best physicians. Mrs Garrick's entry in her journal for 20 January 1779 was brief: "At a quarter before eight, my Husband sighed, and Died without one uneasy moment, the Lord be Praised."

Garrick was buried in Westminster Abbey, near the monument to Shakespeare, on 1 February. His funeral was splendid. His pallbearers, all old friends, were the Duke of Devonshire, the Earl of Ossery, Earl Spencer, Viscount Palmerston, Lord Camden, Sir Watkin Williams Wynn, the Right Honorable Richard Rigby, the Honorable Hans Stanley, John Paterson, Esq, and Albany Wallis, Esq. Richard Brinsley Sheridan was chief mourner. A dozen actors from each of the winter patent houses attended, along with the members of The Club, hundreds of close friends, and innumerable admirers. The procession stretched from the Strand to the Abbey. R. B. Sheridan's *Ode on the Death of David Garrick* was only the most celebrated of the versified expressions of grief which inundated the press. Johnson was to write in his *Life of Edmund Smith* the famous declaration: "I am disappointed by that stroke of death which has eclipsed the gaiety of nations, and impoverished the public stock of harmless pleasure." Mrs Garrick later had the words incised on her husband's monument at Lichfield.

By the terms of the second of Garrick's two wills, dated 24 September 1778 and proved on 5 February 1779, the fledgling British Museum was to receive the bulk of his large library. Mrs Garrick was to receive the houses at Hampton and the Adelphi, with their contents. She also was to have £1,000 to be paid her immediately after his death "out of the first Money that shall be received by my Executors," and the lump sum of £5,000 paid one year after his death, plus an annuity of £1,500, which was to be at her sole disposal, free of any future husband's "Debts Controul or intermeddling." But Garrick had sometimes been troubled by the attraction exerted on Eva Maria by her Viennese connections, and he added a proviso that "if she shall leave England and reside beyond Sea or in Scotland or Ireland . . . which I hope will not happen," then she should be reduced to an annuity of £1,000 and should lose the real property.

Garrick's brother George was devised £10,000, his sister Merriel Docksey and his brother Peter £3,000 apiece, his nephew Carrington Garrick £6,000, his nephew David Garrick £5,000, ("besides what I agreed to give him on his Marriage"), his niece Arabella Schaw £6,000, his niece

By permission of the Trustees of the British Museum

"Immortality of Garrick"

engraving by Caldwell and Smith, after Carter

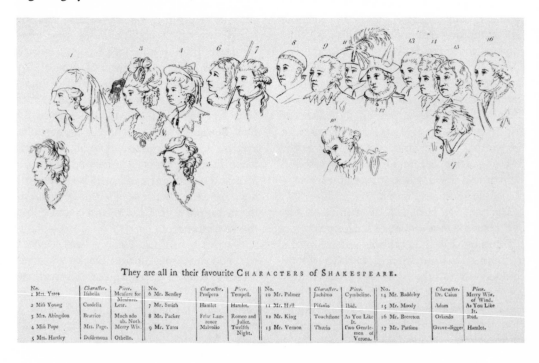

They are all in their favourite CHARACTERS of SHAKESPEARE.

No.	Character.	Piece.	No.	Character.	Piece.	No.	Character.	Piece.	No.	Character.	Piece.
1 Mrs. Yates	Isabella	Measure for Measure.	6 Mr. Bensley	Prospero	Tempest.	10 Mr. Palmer	Jachimo	Cymbeline.	14 Mr. Baddeley	Dr. Caius	Merry Wiv. of Wind.
2 Miss Young	Cordelia	Lear.	7 Mr. Smith	Hamlet	Hamlet.	11 Mr. Hull	Pisanio	Ibid.	15 Mr. Moody	Adam	As You Like It.
3 Mrs. Abingdon	Beatrice	Much ado ab. Noth.	8 Mr. Packer	Friar Laurence	Romeo and Juliet.	12 Mr. King	Touchstone	As You Like It.	16 Mr. Brereton	Orlando	Ibid.
4 Miss Pope	Mrs. Page	Merry Wiv.	9 Mr. Yates	Malvolio	Twelfth Night.	13 Mr. Vernon	Thurio	Two Gentlemen of Verona.	17 Mr. Parsons	Grave-digger	Hamlet.
5 Mrs. Hartley	Desdemona	Othello.									

Catherine Garrick £6,000, and his "Wife's Niece [Mrs Fürst] who is now with us at Hampton" £1,000. Any surplus after the discharge of debts and payment of specific bequests was to be divided among Garrick's relatives.

But, although Garrick seems not to have overvalued his net worth, as it was once thought he did, it is still not clear how much the several legatees received, or how soon. Ireland, the undertaker who managed Garrick's funeral, went bankrupt while awaiting payment of his bill of £1,500. Popular opinion was expressed by the *Gentleman's Magazine:* he was "immensely rich." That opinion was the twin of the notion, also widespread, that he was parsimonious. The truth was that he was acquisitive, careful with his money, delighted to see it grow, happy to be able to live high in the world, but at the same time was warmly, impulsively generous. Johnson once declared: "I know that Garrick has given away more money than any man in England that I am acquainted with, and that not from ostentatious views. Garrick was very poor when he began life; so when he came to have money, he probably was very unskilful in giving away. . . . But Garrick began to be liberal as soon as he could. . . ."

The evidence extant makes Johnson's opinion (which he repeated in several companies) seem hardly an exaggeration. The known list of Garrick's benefactions, both of money and time, is too long to complete. A selection will nail down the point. He not only gave young Joseph Simpson £100 to arrange his release from debtors' prison but also wrote repeatedly to the young man's estranged father, effecting a reconciliation. He sent Andrew Newton ten guineas to buy tea and snuff for a poor old woman with whom he was barely acquainted. He loaned large sums to his friend Thomas Racket and seems never to have been repaid. In addition to working actively badgering his friends in behalf of the The-

atrical Fund and playing repeatedly and gratis for its benefit, he also contributed from his own pocket. Samuel Sharp recalled to Garrick a scene at the house of Voltaire, who addressed Garrick saying "that when Madem. Clairon was sent to prison, you made her an offer of five hundred louis; and I was not a little flattered to see him turn round to the company and ask if there was a Duke or Mareschal in France, generous and honourable enough to do such an action."

During Samuel Foote's frightful ordeal following amputation of his leg in February 1766, both Garricks were unwearyingly assiduous in attention. Garrick wrote him "should you be prevented from persuing any plan for y^r Theatre [in the Haymarket], I am Wholly at y^r Service, & will labour in y^r vineyard for you, in any Capacity, till you are able to do it, so much better, for yourself." (But Foote seems seldom to have reciprocated such generous feelings. When Foote died at Calais on 21 October 1777, Garrick wrote to Lady Spencer: "He had much wit, no feeling, sacrific'd friends & foes to a joke, & so has dy'd very little regretted even by his nearest acquaintance.")

Robert Jephson, Master of the Horse to two successive Lords Lieutenant of Ireland, was the recipient of large loans from Garrick, never repaid. Benjamin Victor, deep in debt, wrote to thank Garrick for subscribing to his works. Garrick endorsed the letter: "I gave him up his note of 70 *l.* which with interest come to above 100 *l.*" When Mrs Pye's husband was snatched from her to the American war, Garrick relieved her financial distresses. His repeated favors to his nephews moved Kitty Clive to write "all the world is repeating your praises . . . *I wish that Heaven had made me such an uncle.*" Few of his beneficiaries were long grateful. The eccentric Francis Gentleman applied successfully for loans again and again, both before and after libelling Garrick. Mossop the actor waited until he was on his deathbed to repent of the poor return he had made for Garrick's many kindnesses.

Except for prominent politicians, Garrick was probably the target of more personal attacks than any other public figure of his time, just as he was the recipient of more adulation. The constant praise was eagerly received but it made the frequent barbs sting more by contrast. Most of the adverse criticism came from jealousy of Garrick's professional fame. Some proceeded from a general dislike of seeing an actor enjoy acceptance into the highest circles of society. Samuel Johnson was not wholly exempt from that feeling, for he had had to watch his old pupil become the darling of the metropolis while he toiled obscurely in Grub Street. Johnson, with his constitutional gloom, appreciated the quality which made Garrick the "cheerfullest man of his age" and he was not insensible to Garrick's critical ability. He would allow Garrick to have an opinion on Elphinston's translation of Martial. But he would sometimes disparage him as artist and man, either out of a philosopher's contempt for the whole tribe of actors or because he desired to argue against Boswell or another who was at the moment championing Garrick: "Garrick's great distinction is his universality. He can represent all modes of life, but that of any easy fine-bred gentleman."

Boswell was troubled, or affected to be, that Johnson

had not mentioned Garrick in his Preface to Shakespeare; and asked him if he did not admire him. JOHNSON. "Yes, as 'a poor player, who frets and struts his hours upon the stage;' as a shadow." BOSWELL. "But has he not brought Shakespeare into notice?" JOHNSON. "Sir, to allow that, would be to lampoon the age. Many of Shakespeare's plays are the worse for being acted . . ." BOSWELL. . . . "Indeed, I do wish that you had mentioned Garrick." JOHNSON. "My dear Sir, had I mentioned him, I must have mentioned many more: Mrs Pritchard, Mrs Cibber—nay, and Mr Cibber too; he too altered Shakespeare."

That ostensible attempt to bring Garrick level in ability with other notables of his profession, and to indicate that for Johnson the profession itself merited no respect, was compounded of sincerity and affectation. The wind could veer, even in one exchange, from: "Garrick's gaiety of conversation has delicacy and elegance" to: "What, Sir, a fellow who claps a hump on his back and a lump on his leg, and cries 'I am Richard the Third?' Nay, Sir, a ballad-singer is a higher man. . . ."

But when Johnson talked for effect or to discipline Davy, he was not being true either to his judgment or his affections. He is reported to have remarked to William Jones on the way to Garrick's funeral: "His profession made him rich, and he made his profession respectable." Johnson's distrust of the craft of acting and his love of his old pupil could give rise to comic paradox. Goldsmith once attacked Garrick's compliment to the Queen in the revision of *The Chances* as "mean and gross flattery." Irked, Johnson launched into a defense of Garrick which involved a disquisition about the "formular" nature of flattery given to royalty. But then (said Boswell) his anger at Goldsmith suddenly spilled over onto actors and thence onto Garrick: " 'And as to meanness,' (rising into warmth,) 'how is it mean in a player,—a showman,—a fellow who exhibits himself for a shilling, to flatter his Queen?' " But the exchange well illustrates an ambivalence which Johnson often admitted: "Sir Joshua Reynolds observed, with great truth," says Boswell, "that Johnson considered Garrick to be as it were his *property*. He would allow no man either to blame or praise Garrick in his presence, without contradicting him."

Cumberland's *Memoirs* described Johnson's behavior at Garrick's funeral: "I saw old Samuel Johnson standing beside his grave, at the foot of Shakespeare's monument, and bathed in tears." Johnson was "very willing to pay that last tribute to the memory of a man I loved" by writing a Life of Garrick and even, Murphy wrote, "if Mrs Garrick would desire it of him, to be the editor of his works. . . ." But Mrs Garrick never asked.

Social and literary activity were to Garrick secondary delights. The center of his life was Drury Lane Theatre. He carried his widening experience and understanding of men and language to the playhouse, where he fused the arts of acting, managing, and directing in the fire of his genius. R. B. Sheridan, in his *Verses to the Memory of Garrick*, penned a plaint which was already a cliché:

> The Actor only, shrinks from Time's
>   Award;
> Feeble Tradition is His Memory's Guard
> . . . .
> Ev'n matchless Garrick's Art to Heav'n
>   resign'd,
> No fix'd Effect, no Model leaves behind!

Yet, contemporaneous description of Garrick's speech and action at least establishes that in the estimation of virtually everyone who ever saw him perform he was not only the finest actor of his age but far outdistanced his nearest competitors in all but a few parts. Most of those he abandoned early.

Garrick's peculiar responsiveness to the nuances of Shakespeare was the result of hard, respectful study working on a highly developed emotional sensivity. Early in his career he established his preeminence in the interpretation of nearly the entire list of those of Shakespeare's capital characters which reached the stage in the eighteenth century. Long before the Jubilee of 1769 Shakespeare and Garrick were inseparably associated in the minds of theatregoers.

It would be impossible at this distance to decide which, among the giant inhabitants of the tragedies, were most impressive when Garrick assumed their personalities. Othello and Hotspur were received mildly and were felt by Garrick himself to be inappropriate to his physique or style and were early discarded. Others, like Richard III, were immediate sensations but were nevertheless developed and polished over the length of Garrick's service. Perhaps the most convenient example of this development is his Lear, which he first played on 11 March 1742 at Goodman's Fields, when he was only 24 years old. Though audiences seemed satisfied, Charles Macklin was severe on Garrick's failure to convey fully the decrepitude of age. Macklin also found him wanting in dignity in the prison scene and carped at the management of his vocal tones, specifically in the curse which Lear levels on Goneril in the first act. Garrick had invited criticism from the old professional and he received it humbly and constructively. He set about in his rehearsals to remedy matters, and within six weeks his portrayal amazed his mentor: "the curse had such an effect that it seemed to electrify the audience with horror. The words 'Kill-kill-kill' echoed all the revenge of a frantic king, whilst he exhibited such a scene of the pathetic discovery of his daughter Cordelia, as drew tears of commiseration from the whole house." The aged Macklin remembered, long after Garrick's death, that "the little dog made it a *chef d'oeuvre*, and a *chef d'oeuvre* it continued to the end of his life."

Garrick's consummate greatness in the part shines through the testimony of all who wrote of it. John Hill in *The Actor* described the "little, old, white-haired man . . . with spindle-shanks, a tottering gait, and great shoes upon his little feet," who appalled audiences with his violence and wounded pride. Foote addressed Garrick in *An Examen of the New Comedy, Call'd the Suspicious Husband* in 1747, still early in Garrick's career, calling up a picture of his action in cursing Goneril: "You fall precipitately upon your Knees, extend your arms—clench your Hand—set your Teeth—and with a savage Distraction in your Look —trembling in your Limbs—and your Eyes pointed to Heaven . . . begin . . . with a *broken, inward, eager* Utterance; from thence rising every Line in Loudness and Rapidity of Voice."

Harvard Theatre Collection

DAVID GARRICK, as Hamlet

by B. Wilson

Though Garrick never called back the Fool, whom Tate had banished from the text, or did away with the "happy" ending —among other restorations urged on him by Foote and others—from 1756 onward he spoke many more of Shakespeare's lines than the earlier century had been permitted to hear. Many theatregoers felt that in speaking them he reached the height of his art.

But Garrick's most popular Shakespearean part was Hamlet, whether he used the truncated text he inherited from Robert Wilks or the "impudent" version he himself tinkered up in 1772–73. The careful reportage of the German visitor Georg Christoph Lichtenberg (translated by Mare and Quarrell) brings the action back before our mind's eye.

Hamlet appears in a black dress, the only one in [the battlement scene]. . . . Horatio and Marcellus, in uniform, are with him and they are awaiting the ghost; Hamlet has folded his arms under his cloak and pulled his hat down over his eyes; it is a cold night and just twelve o'clock; the theatre is darkened, and the whole audience of some thousands are as quiet, and their faces as motionless, as though they were painted on the walls of the theatre; even from the farthest end of the playhouse one could hear a pin drop. Suddenly, as Hamlet moves toward the back of the stage slightly to the left and turns his back on the audience, Horatio starts, and saying, "Look my lord, it comes" points to the right, where the ghost has already appeared and stands motionless, before anyone is aware of him; [Garrick's] hat falls to the ground and both his arms, especially the left, are stretched out nearly to their full length, with the hands as high as his head, the right arm more bent and the hand lower, and the fingers apart; his mouth is open: thus he stands rooted to the spot, with legs apart, but no loss of dignity, supported by his friends, who are better acquainted with the apparition and fear lest he should collapse. His whole demeanor is so expressive of terror that it made my flesh creep even before he began to speak. The almost terror-struck silence of the audience, which preceded this appearance and filled one with a sense of insecurity, probably did much to enhance this effect. At last he speaks, not at the beginning, but at the end of a breath, with a trembling voice: "Angels and ministers of grace defend us!" words which supply anything this scene may lack and make it one of the greatest and most terrible which will ever be played on any stage. The ghost beckons to him; I wish you could see him, with eyes fixed on the ghost, though he is speaking to his companions, freeing himself from their restraining hands, as they warn him not to follow and hold him back. But at length, when they had tried his patience too far, he turns his face towards them, tears himself with great violence from their grasps, and draws his sword on them with a swiftness that makes one shudder, saying: "By Heaven! I'll make a ghost of him that lets me." That is enough for them. Then he stands with his sword upon guard against the spectre, saying: "Go on, I'll follow thee," and the ghost goes off the stage. Hamlet still remains motionless, his sword held out so as to make him keep his distance, and at length, when the spectator can no longer see the ghost, he begins slowly to follow him, now standing still and then going on, with sword still upon guard, eyes fixed on the ghost, hair disordered, and out of breath, until he too is lost to sight. You can well imagine what loud applause accompanies this exit. It begins as soon as the ghost goes off the stage and lasts until Hamlet also disappears. What an amazing triumph it is.

Lichtenberg describes Garrick when he comes on to speak the soliloquy "To be, or not to be": "with his thick hair dishevelled and a lock hanging over one shoulder; one of his black stockings has slipped down so as to show his white socks, and a loop of his red garter is hanging down below the middle of his calf." He begins the speech "sunk in contemplation, his chin resting on his right hand, and his right elbow on his left, and gazes solemnly downwards." The words were spoken softly, but because of the "absolute silence" they were "audible everywhere."

Lichtenberg, like everybody else, found Garrick quite as admirable in comedy. In the part of Sir John Brute in *The Provok'd Wife*, according to Lichtenberg's description, Garrick even used features of Hamlet's disordered costume for comic effect:

Mr. Garrick plays the drunken Sir John in such a way that I should certainly have known him to be a most remarkable man, even if I had never heard anything of him and had seen him in one scene only in this play. At the beginning his wig is quite straight, so that his face is full and round. Then he comes home excessively drunk, and looks like the moon a few days before its last quarter, almost half his face being covered by his wig; the part that is still visible is, indeed, somewhat bloody and shining with perspiration, but has so extremely amiable an air to compensate for the loss of the other part. His waistcoat is open from top to bottom, his stockings full of wrinkles, with the garters hanging down, and, moreover—which is

vastly strange—two kinds of garters; one would hardly be surprised, indeed, if he had picked up odd shoes. In this lamentable condition he enters the room where his wife is, and in answer to her anxious inquiries as to what is the matter with him . . . breaks into coarse talk, and suddenly becomes so wise and merry in his cups that the whole audience bursts into a tumult of applause. I was filled with amazement at the scene where he falls asleep. The way in which, with shut eyes, swimming head, and pallid cheeks, he quarrels with his wife, and, uttering a sound where "r" and "l" are blended, now appears to abuse her, and then to enunciate in thick tones moral precepts, to which he himself forms the most horrible contradiction; his manner, also, of moving his lips, so that one cannot tell whether he is chewing, tasting, or speaking: all this, in truth, as far exceeded my expectations as anything I have seen of this man. If

Harvard Theatre Collection

DAVID GARRICK, as Sir John Brute

by unknown engraver, after J. Roberts

you could but hear him articulate the word "prerogative"; he never reaches the third syllable without two or three attempts.

Garrick was, indeed, as Johnson proclaimed him, "the only actor I ever saw, whom I could call a master both in tragedy and comedy." Though we should not perhaps today call him a "natural" actor, in the context of his century he was so. Johnson thought that "A true conception of character and natural expression of it were his distinguished excellences." And Garrick himself remarked that he would never engage a performer "who should be marked with that blackest of all Sins of Nature— Affectation." Not that he himself eschewed startling effects and odd contrivances. But, as William Shirley wrote, though "he falls from fury into tears with a breath" he was "pure and entire in both sensations." *The Rational Rosciad* derided him for

> *His frequent turning round about,*
> *His handkerchief forever in and out,*
> *His hat still moulded to a thousand*
> *   forms,*
> *His pocket clapping when his passion*
> *   storms*

He was not above employing a device to make his hair stand on end when he confronted the Ghost in Hamlet, or of having the carpenter saw short the hind legs of his chair that he might the more easily tip it over at the second confrontation with that same Ghost. He was a showman. But his grace and certainty in action and his sure control of voice made the formal, regular declamation and gestures of Quin and others of the generation which preceded Garrick seem antique. As Lichtenberg remarked "With him there is no rampaging, gliding, or slouching, and where other players in the movements of their arms and legs allow themselves six inches or more in scope in every direction farther than the canons of beauty would permit, he hits the mark with admirable certainty and firmness."

The notable French actress, Garrick's friend Madame Suzanne Necker, came to London to witness the close of his career in June 1776. After she returned to France she wrote him: "I will travel no more. I have, in Mr Garrick's acting, studied the manners of all men, and I have made more discoveries about the human heart than if I had gone over the whole of Europe."

Garrick spent long hours in the green room and on the stage at rehearsals, trying to instill his view of proper action and speech in successive generations of younger actors. He was always ready with precept and example, yet he was determined not to encourage beginners simply to imitate him. And to Garrick a sustainedly successful career of performance was the product of more than technical proficiency. It proceeded from a resolutely disciplined course of conduct. He had, during the summer of 1763, given fatherly encouragement and much instruction to the talented young actor William Powell. During Garrick's absence on the Continent, Powell had won sudden and great acclaim at Drury Lane and in March 1764 had written Garrick to thank him for having "laid the foundation of all, by your kind care of me." Busy with his travels and bedevilled by his wife's illness, Garrick had neglected to reply until December, but then he responded graciously and carefully to Powell, outlining his prescription for a solid professional prosperity:

The News of Your great Success, gave me a most Sensible Pleasure, the continuance of that Success will be in Your own power; and if you will give an Older Soldier leave to hint a little advice to You; I will answer for its being sincere at least, which from a Brother Actor is no Small Merit. . . . You have Acted a greater variety of Characters than I could expect in the first Winter, and I have some fears that Your Good nature to Your Brother Actors (which is commendable when it is not injurious) drove You into parts too precipitately—however, you Succeeded, & it is happy, that you had yᵉ Whole Summer to correct the Errors of hast[e], which the publick will ever excuse in a Young performer . . . but now is the time to make sure of your Ground in every Step you take— You must therefore give to Study, and an Accurate consideration of Your Characters, those Hours which Young Men generally give to their Friends & fflatterers. The common excuse is, that they frequent Clubs for the Sake of their Benefit; but nothing can be more absurd or contemptible.— Your Benefits will only encrease with your fame, & Should that Ever Sink by your Idleness, those friends who have made you idle, will be the first to forsake You— When the publick has mark'd you for a favourite (& their favor must be purchas'd wᵗʰ Sweat & labour) You may chuse what Company you please, and none but the best can be of service to you. The famous *Baron* of France us'd to say that an Actor should be nurs'd in the lap of Queen's, by which he meant that the best Accomplishments were necessary to form a great Actor.— Study hard, my friend, for Seven Years, & you may play the rest of your life,— I would advise You to read at Your leisure other books besides the plays in which you are concern'd . . . . But above all, never let your *Shakespear* be out of your hands, or your Pocket— Keep him about you, as a Charm— . . . one thing more, And then I will finish my preaching; Guard against *the Splitting the Ears of the Groundlings who are capable of Nothing but dumb Shew*, & noise,— don't sacrifice your taste and ffeelings to the Applause of Multitude; a true Genius will convert an Audience to His Manner . . . *be not too tame neither. . . .*

The advice was well considered. A year later Garrick was writing to Powell for a copy of the letter because, he said, "I was collecting my thought, from scatter'd papers, upon our profession," preparatory to writing a book upon acting and other theatrical problems. In the absence of such a treatise, we judge his potency in instruction, direction, and management principally by the magnificent success of Drury Lane Theatre during his tenure. As his best comedienne Kitty Clive observed to him, he had

"been for these thirty years contradicting an old established proverb—you cannot make bricks without straw; but you have done what is infinitely more difficult, for you have made actors and actresses without genius; that is, you have made them pass for such, which has answered your end, though it has given you infinite trouble."

Garrick's scholarly qualifications, though of the amateur variety, certainly allowed him to compete in the conversational jousting at The Club and in other intellectual circles. He had had the early friendship of Walmesley, the classical floggings of Dr Hunter, and the ministrations of the Rev Mr Colson, as well as the improving association with Johnson at Edial and afterward. His daily business and correspondence over thirty years and in both English and French was with authors and scholars, as well as not a few actors and musicians of knowledge and taste. Hambly Cope sent to Garrick from Leghorn a copy of Garrick's *Miss in Her Teens*, which he had translated into Italian "as I know you are a perfect Master of the Italian language." (There seems to be no other evidence.) His large library contained many rare volumes, including early quartos and folios of Shakespeare's works, which he generously loaned to advance the editorial labors not only of Samuel Johnson but of George Steevens, Thomas Percy, and other savants. Steevens told him: "Your collection of old plays is far from complete, though much the greatest that I know of. . . ."

In 1765 Steevens thanked Garrick for the loan of several scarce quartos to be used in a reprint of 20 of Shakespeare's plays in quarto before 1623. Steevens acknowledged that he "could never have carried [the work] into execution but for the assistance you lent me" and added:

I am contented with the spirit of the author you first taught me to admire, and when I found you could do so much for him, I was naturally curious to know the value of the materials he supplied you with; and often when I have taken my pen in hand to try to illustrate a passage, I have thrown it down again with discontent when I remembered how able you were to clear that difficulty with a single look, or particular modulation of voice, which a long and laboured paraphrase was insufficient to explain half so well.

In 1772, when Steevens was on the point of issuing his revision of Johnson's edition, he wrote a long letter to Garrick which stands in striking contrast to Johnson's evident attempt to keep Garrick as far away from the scholarly text as possible:

The legitimacy of an edition of Shakespeare can no more be ascertained to satisfaction, without the testimony of the Poet's High Priest, than that of a Prince can be lawfully proved, unless the archbishop attends in person. I am therefore desirous that you should glance your eyes over the enclosed papers, which are to announce the birth, or (not to speak profanely) the regeneration of Dr. Johnson's Edition to the world.

In March 1775 Steevens asked Garrick for ten old plays and remarked: "I heartily wish I was possessed of anything which you could stand in need of half so often, that I might find some way of returning those favours which I have so frequently solicited and constantly received."

Garrick, in turn, was a frequent borrower and user of books belonging to Wilkes, Colman, and Horace Walpole. Warburton corresponded with Garrick as with an intellectual equal, and though the drama was the most frequent subject of their discourse, it was by no means the only one.

Garrick's unsurpassed critical sense of what a play needed in order to be both actable and acceptable to the appetites of his audience was, of course, more necessary to him in the theatre than were his classical and other literary attainments. His instincts were not infallible; he refused both Home's *Douglas* and Goldsmith's *Good Natured Man*, and he accepted many dramatic works damned by audiences and critics. But the acceptance of dubious dramas can often be attributed to the pressures he was constantly under, not only from aspiring playwrights, good and bad, but from their patrons and advocates. Some of the latter were powerful or highly placed, some had persuasive literary or academic credentials, and some were personal friends whom Garrick was concerned to please if he could. His good friend Sir Joshua Reynolds pressed him hard to produce a drama, *Zaphira*, by a nephew, Joseph Palmer. Garrick had the greatest difficulty making Reynolds understand that he had then a two-year supply of plays readying for production. He wrote Colman concerning that affair "I hate this traffick wth friends." Yet much of the unavoidable search for new plays and afterpieces was traffick with friends or with those who would pretend friendship in order to put forward their productions. Reynolds was reasonable, finally. Many others were not.

Typical of the troublemakers was "that strange heap of insincerity and contradiction" the Rev Dr Thomas Francklin, who wrote "in violent wrath," said Garrick, when his *Siege of Aleppo* was refused, and who badgered Garrick about his tragedy *Matilda* for two years, from 1773 until its production in 1775. Garrick wrote Thomas Evans in October 1774 complaining about some "falsehood" Francklin had told Woodfall the printer: "I have a play of his to Act, I reliev'd his Want within this Fortnight wth a good round Sum, & procur'd him the reversion of a very good living. . . . I avoid him as a Friend, but I do him justice as a Manager." Garrick's vexed correspondence with Francklin yields one especially significant sentence, wrung from Garrick by illness and exhaustion: "Whenever you put a play into my hands You desire my remarks, seem to express an Eagerness for them, but I always found that my Criticism was a very ill office." Indeed it was true; except for the collaboration with Colman (which had also generated a quarrel), Garrick avoided open literary partnership, but his mark is on most of the new and revised plays which he accepted, notwithstanding that assisting authors toward production was a thankless business. He was even obliged to hide the authorship of some of his own farces, as he wrote Lord Bute as early as 1759, because "I have so many Enemies among the Writers on Account of my refusing so many of their Performances Every Year, that I am oblig'd to conceal Myself in order to avoid the Torrent of abuse that their Malice would pour upon me—."

He infuriated the Rev William Hawkins, who had been Professor of Poetry at Oxford, by rejecting five of his plays over the years, and Hawkins threatened an appeal to the public. Garrick tried reasonable remonstrance: "[H]ave I refus'd, to see [your play]? I know my Duty too well— I am oblig'd by my Situation to read all You are pleas'd to Send me, but I have ye same right to reject a Play, which I think a bad one, as You have to compose it." But, as Steevens quipped in 1774, after another incensed bard had gone to the newspapers with his plaint: "Pray who is this offended author who appeals from Your judgment to the public? Your enemies always take care to justify your conduct by exposing their own productions."

So Garrick read and re-read, revised, and offered suggestions to and suffered the indignation of a succession of petulant aspirants: Benjamin Wilson, John Cleland, Robert Dodsley, John Shebbeare, William Julius Mickle, James Ralph, Joseph Reed, and dozens of others. Plays were "rained" on him, as he said, not only from his encouraged suppliers and repetitive tormentors but from total strangers: The Rev Charles Jenner at Cambridge, Col William Elsden, in the service of the Portuguese at Lisbon, the Rev Sanford Hardcastle,

Rector of Adel, Yorkshire. Even his physician, Dr Ralph Schomberg, contracted the itch and submitted an alteration of *Richard III*, and Garrick, "to cure him of Scribbling," wrote him a hard critical letter, "a rough purge to be cleans'd of his playwriting. . . ."

The entire difficulty may be summed up in the irony reflected in a letter from Garrick to Colman on 28 December 1774, the day after the death of the Irish actor Henry Mossop: "a most disagreeable affair has happen'd—Mossop on his death-bed sends me his play, begging that I would Ease his Mind in his last moments, by taking his play & doing all in my power with it for ye service of his Creditors." Garrick was Mossop's largest creditor—in the amount of £200. The play was not good enough either to produce or to print.

Garrick's own original productions for the theatre—some 20 comedies, farces, masques, "preludes," interludes, comic operas, and satires, plus dozens of songs and occasional prologues and epilogues, and the *Ode* in celebration of Shakespeare—were principally *jeux d'esprit* written swiftly, under the spur of immediate theatrical necessity, and filled with topicality and perishable persiflage. Nearly all well served their immediate purposes, and a few, like *Bon Ton; or, High Life above Stairs, Lethe; or, Aesop in the Shades*, and *A Peep Behind the Curtain* were durable. Scholarly opinion has oscillated between extreme denigration and qualified approval of the various alterations of Shakespeare but has seemed recently to accept, with some modifications, George Winchester Stone's estimate that, on balance, Garrick was a major influence in the restoration and clarification of the text in the theatre: "He both committed and permitted certain tamperings with the texts, yet his audiences witnessed more authentic Shakespeare than they or their ancestors had seen since before 1700."

In addition to the works penned for production Garrick left a large body of gracefully-turned light verse, published and unpublished. He was called upon to write numbers of epitaphs. He was, as he boasted to Samuel Johnson, "a little of an epigrammatist myself," and his journals and letters often demonstrate a keen and figurative wit. Together, in fact, the 1362 items in the superbly edited, definitive three-volume *Letters of David Garrick* (1963, David M. Little and George M. Kahrl, editors; associate editor Phoebe De K. Wilson) constitute a collection of considerable literary charm as well as an indispensable source of biographical facts. They were often written hastily in the midst of business ("my Brother George backed by the Crowing of the Prompter summons me away—." "I am writing now in ye greatest haste . . ."; "I hope You'll excuse My hurry, I am this Moment dressing for ye laborious part of King Lear"), but at their best they rise to the level of literature.

A complex personality is refracted through Garrick's letters to his wide variety of correspondents and is often reflected from their letters to him, preserved in *The Private Correspondence of David Garrick* (1831–32, James Boaden, editor), in *Letters of David Garrick and Georgiana Countess Spencer 1759–1779* (1960, edited by Earl Spencer and Christopher Dobson), and in manuscript in the Forster Collection in the Victoria and Albert Museum, in the Folger Shakespeare Library, and elsewhere. Garrick is shown to be a man of optimistic outlook—Johnson's remark "Cheerfullest man of his age" seems just for one whose natural ebullience and energies could not be long repressed by pain, responsibility, or a killing workload. The letters also show Johnson's offhand remark, that Garrick had friends but no friend, to be unfair. Johnson himself, Lady Spencer, Hannah More, Edmund Burke, Tom King, Lord Camden, Colman, the Duke of Devonshire, John Hoadly—all those, surely, were close

Harvard Theatre Collection

GARRICK Between Tragedy and Comedy

engraving by C. Corbutt, after Reynolds

friends. And yet, there was something to Johnson's remark. Garrick was for over three decades one of the most sought-after men in England and he had one of the widest ranges of acquaintance. The response of his gregarious nature to the overtures of flattery often left little time for that privacy which the cultivation of intimate friendship demands.

The oft-reiterated charge that Garrick, like Cibber, "loved a lord" is undoubtedly justified, but it needs to be qualified. The effusive formal compliment and sycophantic tone of some of his earlier London letters, for instance those to the formidably learned Countess of Burlington, were subdued and warmed to unselfconscious badinage after Garrick discovered his social value to people of title and wealth. Justice also compels the observations that it was usually the aristocracy who sought out his company and correspondence and that he was on the whole more attracted to intellect than to power. Garrick was aware of the charge of snobbery, as he was of the charge of stinginess, and was nettled by it. To John Cleland's complaint that he was "so infested with Lords, Counts, Marquises, Dukes, &c." that it was difficult to do business with him, Garrick replied "if You suspect me of being fond of worthless Titles, you wrong me— I wou'd no more avoid the Company of a Man because he was a Marquis, than I wou'd keep him Company if he was a fool or a Scoundrel. . . ."

Boswell once "slily introduced Mr. Garrick's fame, and his assuming the airs of a great man," and the following *defensio* was excited:

JOHNSON. "Sir, it is wonderful how *little* Garrick assumes . . . Consider, Sir: celebrated men, such as you have mentioned, have had their applause at a distance, but Garrick had it dashed in his face, sounded in his ears, and went home every night with the plaudits of a thousand in his *cranium*. Then, Sir, Garrick did not *find*, but *made* his way to the tables, the levees, and almost the bed-chambers of the great. Then, Sir, Garrick had under him a numerous body of people; who, from fear of his power, and hopes of his favour, and admiration of his talents, were constantly submissive to him. And here is a man who has advanced the dignity of his profession. Garrick has made a player a higher character." SCOTT. "And he is a very sprightly writer too." JOHNSON. "Yes, Sir and all this supported by great wealth of his own acquisition. If all this had happened to me, I should have had a couple of fellows with long poles walking before me, to knock down every body that stood in my way. Consider, if all this had happened to Cibber or Quin, they'd have jumped over the moon.—Yet Garrick speaks to *us*." (Smiling.)

That Garrick loved to shine in company —any company—was generally agreed. And in most companies he did shine because he was expected to. Only in The Club, and then only occasionally, did his "significant smart manner" seem to justify many of the jibes Goldsmith put into his mock-epitaph in *Retaliation* (which had been written, according to Garrick's account, in retaliation for Garrick's extempore mock-epitaph on Goldsmith: "here lies NOLLY Goldsmith, for shortness call'd Noll, / Who wrote like an angel, but talk'd like poor Poll"):

> Here lies David Garrick, describe me
>   who can,
> An abridgment of all that was pleasant
>   in man;
> As an actor, confest without rival to
>   shine,
> As a wit, if not first, in the very first line,
> Yet with talents like these, and an excel-
>   lent heart,
> The man had his failings, a dupe to his
>   art;
> Like an ill judging beauty, his colours he
>   spread,
> And beplaister'd, with rouge, his own
>   natural red.
> On the stage he was natural, simple, af-
>   fecting,

*'Twas only that, when he was off, he was
    acting:*
*With no reason on earth to go out of his
    way,*
*He turn'd and he varied full ten times
    a day;*
*Tho' secure of our hearts, yet confound-
    edly sick,*
*If they were not his own by finessing and
    trick,*
*He cast off his friends, as a huntsman his
    pack;*
*For he knew when he pleased he could
    whistle them back.*
*Of praise, a mere glutton, he swallowed
    what came,*
*And the puff of a dunce, he mistook it
    for fame;*
*'Till his relish grown callous, almost to
    disease,*
*Who pepper'd the highest, was surest to
    please.*
*But let us be candid, and speak out our
    mind,*
*If dunces applauded, he paid them in
    kind.*
. . . .

But peace to his spirit, wherever it flies,
*To act as an angel, and mix with the
    skies:*
*Those poets, who owe their best fame to
    his skill,*
*Shall still be his flatterers, go where he
    will.*
*Old Shakespeare, receive him, with
    praise and with love,*
*And Beaumonts and Bens be his Kellys
    above.*

But Goldsmith, said Garrick, "never would allow a superior in any art, from writing poetry down to dancing a hornpipe," and certainly there was some jealousy as well as much truth in the characterization.

Garrick in his middle fifties was still an arresting figure; "though low in stature," he was "regularly made, and well propor-tioned," according to William Hawkins's description in 1775: "[H]is face is strongly and finely featured, but on the whole not handsome . . . his eyes . . . big, the pu-pil large, strong, lively, active, and variable; their colour dark, surrounded and set off with a due proportion of white, that gives to their every motion, a brilliancy . . . His complexion is dark; and lastly his voice . . . from its harmony, sweetness, and moreover it's pliancy . . . has ever been admired."

Except when he received the insult direct or when his authority as manager was under insistent attack, he was of a peace-able, relenting nature. He rejoiced that during their tranquil and affectionate mar-riage of nearly 30 years he and Eva Maria, a woman of exceptional beauty and amia-bility, had never spent a night apart. Dur-ing the 43 years that she survived him Mrs Garrick never wavered in her retro-spective devotion to her Davy, though she received several advantageous proposals, including one in 1782 from the great Scot-tish lawyer and judge, James Burnett, Lord Monboddo.

Evidently Garrick kept his marriage vows despite the temptations thrust toward him by the most attractive women of his day. His early liaison with Peg Woffington is well documented. Other such pre-marital connections were hinted by the gossip pub-lications. David and Eva Maria had no children, but talk went around that David had fathered at least one child before his marriage. *Theatrical Biography* (1772) spoke of the "almost *paternal* influence of Mr. Garrick" over the actor Samuel Cautherley, and *The Thespian Dictionary* in successive editions through 1805 said flatly that Cautherley "was a supposed natural son of Mr. Garrick." Certainly Cautherley's career was assiduously pro-moted by Garrick, who educated and coached him and who seems to have as-sumed a guardian's role. In a letter to Mrs Garrick in 1800 Cautherley acknowledged "the many kindnesses confer'd on me, while under your Hospitable Roof (for almost Twenty years). . . ." (Garrick left noth-ing to Cautherley in his will, but on 3 July

1771, the day before Cautherley's marriage to Susanna Blanchard, valuable securities were settled on the bride through George Garrick, and Mrs Garrick left £100 to Cautherley's daughter and £50 to his son in 1822.) But Cautherley was only a third-rate performer despite Garrick's teaching; he was also ungrateful and difficult as an employee; and he and Garrick quarrelled and parted finally in 1775. The 1775 edition of *Theatrical Biography*, in Jane Hippisley Green's biographical sketch, implicated that actress and David Garrick in a liaison: "a chopping boy bore witness to their loves whose death is since to be lamented . . . as it was the only child our English Roscius ever had. . . ." It is impossible to say whether or not the remark was in some way related to the allegation that Garrick fathered Cautherley. In 1805 James Winston, in his *Theatric Tourist*, circulated an unsubstantiated rumor that the

actor Edward Cape Everard was the illegitimate son of Garrick.

David's fame and financial success had quickly dissipated the doubts felt by his siblings and cousins over the propriety of his becoming an actor. By 1750 he had become cynosure and virtual chief of the clan. By 1750 also his younger brother George had joined him at the theatre. George remained throughout the years of Garrick's career, taking care of the petty details of managing a large patent theatre which would otherwise have devolved upon David. George was loyal, but improvident, and David frequently supplemented the salary given him as factotum at the playhouse and (after 1752) as stable-keeper in the Royal Household. David subsidized George's sons Carrington and David through expensive educations and tried to assist them in starting careers. He saw that George's daughters, Arabella and Catherine,

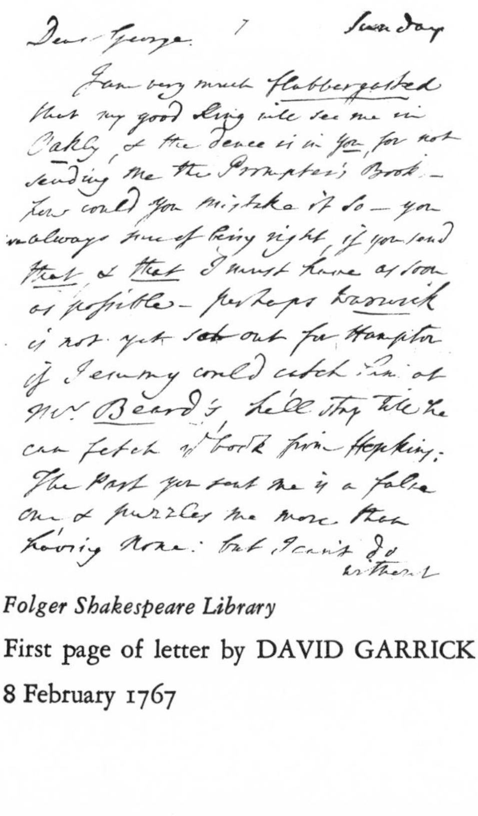

Folger Shakespeare Library

First page of letter by DAVID GARRICK to GEORGE GARRICK

8 February 1767

were provided with a Parisian convent school, proper dowries, and fatherly advice. Garrick's relationship to his older brother Peter, who had made a success of the wine business, was warm. David and Eva Maria visited Peter in his large Lichfield house as often as they could. Less close or cordial were David's feelings for his surviving sister Merrial, though he often helped her and her husband Thomas Docksey with loans. Garrick's sister Jane died unmarried in 1745, as did Magdalen in 1764. His brother William disappeared from his correspondence early.

Besides the editions of letters mentioned there have been a number of biographies and specialized studies of David Garrick and of his associations and accomplishments. Thomas Davies's *Memoirs of the Life of David Garrick* (1780) and Arthur Murphy's *The Life of David Garrick* (1801) are by contemporaries who knew him well. Percy Fitzgerald's *The Life of David Garrick* (1899) is still useful. Carola Oman's *David Garrick* (1958) is the best recent biography. Mrs Clement Parsons, in *Garrick and His Circle* (1906), and Frank A. Hedgecock, in *A Cosmopolitan Actor David Garrick and His French Friends* (1913), examine some social connections. Ryllis Clair Alexander edited the *Diary of David Garrick Being a record of his memorable trip to Paris in 1751* (1928), and George Winchester Stone edited *The Journal of David Garrick, 1763 Describing his visit to France and Italy in 1763* (1939). Elizabeth P. Stein, in *David Garrick, Dramatist* (1938), stresses the value of his theatrical writings. Kalman A. Burnim in *David Garrick Director* (1961) gives a balanced estimate of Garrick's techniques and abilities as producer and director. A new biography by George M. Kahrl and George Winchester Stone and an edition of Garrick's theatrical works by Frederick L. Bergmann and Harry W.

Pedicord are in preparation. James Boswell's *The Life of Samuel Johnson, LLD* (1791), *The Diary and Letters of Madame D'Arblay* (ed. Charlotte Barrett and Austin Dobson, 1904–5), *The Early Diary of Frances Burney, 1768–1778* (ed. Annie Raine Ellis, 1889), *Elizabeth Montague, Queen of the Bluestockings . . . Letters from 1720 to 1761* (ed. Emily J. Climenson, 1906), *Mrs. Montagu . . . Her Letters from 1762 to 1800* (ed. R. Blunt, n.d.), and Letitia-Matilda Hawkins's *Anecdotes, Biographical Sketches and Memoirs* (1822) contain much information on Garrick. G. W. Stone's 1938 Harvard dissertation, "Garrick's Handling of Shakespeare's Plays and His Influence upon the Changed Attitude of Shakespearian Criticism During the Eighteenth Century," is a detailed examination of the Shakespeare alterations, restorations and productions, as well as Garrick's acting in Shakespearean roles. A series of articles by Stone continued the examination. Frederick L. Bergmann's 1953 George Washington University dissertation performs a similar service for Garrick's non-Shakespearian alterations. The largest manuscript collection of Garrickiana—correspondence, part-books, prologues, epilogues, promptbooks, songs, epitaphs—is in the Folger Shakespeare Library.

No other actor in the history of the English theatre prior to the development of the camera was the subject of as many portraits, original or engraved, in private or stage character, as was David Garrick. It is likely, indeed, that Garrick was the subject of more original paintings than any figure in English history. His listing in the *British Museum Catalogue of Engraved British Portraits*, moreover, is exceeded only by that for Queen Victoria. The *Catalogue of Engraved Dramatic Portraits in the Harvard Theatre Collection* lists more than twice as many portraits for Garrick as for any other performer.

The following list includes and supplements the engravings noted in the British

Museum and Harvard catalogues. Additionally, it includes numerous original paintings, drawings, and portraits in other media to be found in various galleries, libraries, and museums, and in the hands of private collectors in the United Kingdom, the United States, and Europe. No claim is made for completeness. We believe, however, that this is the most extensive iconography on Garrick ever published. Most of the paintings and drawings have been seen by us either in the original or in photographs. We have looked at many of the engravings, but not all. We have attempted to sort out the various known versions of the paintings and engravings, but since we have not seen all it is probable that some portraits are listed more than once.

The portraits are not described in detail. More information about the details and provenance of a picture may often be found in the catalogue of the gallery owning it or in studies of the artist. Sales and exhibition catalogues have been especially helpful. *The Artist and the Theatre* by Raymond Mander and Joe Mitchenson, and *The Georgian Playhouse*, the catalogue of the exhibition devised by Iain Mackintosh, assisted by Geoffrey Ashton, at the Hayward Gallery, London, in 1975 have been indispensable. Additional information provided to us by Messrs Ashton and Macintosh is gratefully acknowledged.

The iconography is organized as follows:

I. Original paintings and drawings of Garrick in private character, including those of him in nonstage groups, known now to exist or to have existed, listed alphabetically by *artist*. Engraved versions are sublisted alphabetically by engraver.

II. Engraved portraits in private character for which no original paintings or drawings are known or identified although an artist may have provided a design, listed alphabetically by *engraver*.

III. Engraved representations, depictions, or views (not in stage characters) for which no original paintings or drawings are known, listed alphabetically by *engraver*.

IV. Original and engraved portraits in stage roles listed alphabetically by name of the *character* portrayed. Within the character listing, the items are given alphabetically by artist or engraver. Engraved versions of original portraits are sub-listed.

V. Portraits (including Garrick in stage characters) in other media: sculptures, medallions, wood carvings, wall coverings, porcelain, tiles, etc. Other Garrick artifacts.

For more convenient reference, we have placed in parentheses the numbers of the descriptions, when applicable, of engravings listed in the *Catalogue of Engraved Dramatic Portraits in the Harvard Theatre Collection.*

I. ORIGINAL PAINTINGS AND DRAWINGS IN PRIVATE CHARACTER, INCLUDING NON-STAGE GROUPS.

1. By Pompeo Batoni. Painted in Rome, 1764. Holding the Vatican edition of Terence. Once in the possession of the Rev Sir Richard Kaye. Now in the Ashmolean Museum, Oxford. Reproduced in the illustrated catalogue of a *Portrait Exhibition at Oxford*, 1906, and in the catalogue of *The Georgian Playhouse* exhibition at the Hayward Gallery in 1975. A copy by an unknown artist, after Batoni, and inscribed by a later hand, "David Garrick Esq, Rome 1764," was presented to the Garrick Club in 1926 by an anonymous donor in memory of Rowland Berkeley.

2. By George Carter, about 1782. A large canvas, sometimes called "The Apotheosis of Garrick," or "The Immortality of Garrick." With many of his contemporary actors in various attitudes and characters. Exhibited at the Royal Academy in 1784. In the Art Gallery of the Royal Shakespeare Theatre, Stratford-upon-Avon.

    a. An engraving by J. Caldwell and S. Smith was published, with a key plate to the figures, by G. Carter, 1783.

3. By Penelope Coates. Watercolor on

ivory. In the Art Gallery of the Royal Shakespeare Theatre, Stratford-upon-Avon.

4. By Charles Nicholas Cochin (*fils*), at Paris, 1764.

a. Engraving by C. N. Cochin & Dupuis. (1)

b. Copy by unknown engraver. Published by J. Hinton as a plate to *Universal Magazine*, and also by E. Evans. (2)

5. Attributed to George Dance. Pencil drawing. In the National Portrait Gallery.

6. By Nathaniel Dance. Painting, Garrick holding a copy of *Macbeth* in his hand. In the Folger Shakespeare Library. Bought from Gabriel Wells, December 1923. Perhaps this is the portrait, completed by Dance in October 1773, which Garrick presented to Andrew Newton at Lichfield. (See David Little and George Kahrl, *Letters of David Garrick*, No 805.) On 23 March 1776, Boswell mentioned in his "Journal" seeing this "fine portrait" in Newton's house.

7. By Nathaniel Dance. Painting owned by Lord Mansfield in 1773. Present location unknown.

a. Engraving by T. Cook, published by J. Bell, 1779. (6)

b. Engraving by T. Cook, published by J. Bell, 1786. (6)

c. Engraving by J. Hall, from Lord Mansfield's picture, published by J. Bell, 1773. (3)

d. Reverse engraving of c., published by J. Bell, 1773. (4)

e. Engraving by J. Hall, published by J. Barker, 1793. (5)

8. By Nathaniel Dance. A portrait of Garrick which had hung in Evans's Supper Rooms, Covent Garden, was sold at Christie's on 22 July 1871. It was exhibited at the New Gallery in 1914. A photograph is in the Witt Library.

9. By Nathaniel Dance. Two pencil drawings, the same. Seated, arms folded and resting on table. In the Beard Collection, Victoria and Albert Museum. In the

Folger Shakespeare Library is a pencil drawing of the same, with notation: "David Garrick, from a Sketch in Pencil made by the late George [*recte* Nathaniel?] Dance, Esq.ʳ——by Mrs Samˡ. Lolly Daughter of the Revᵈ Thomas Rackett." Two single portraits of Mr and Mrs Garrick "at the Breakfast Table" were drawn by Dance on 16 March 1771. W. E. Image, who married Kitty Garrick's goddaughter, claimed, "Mr Garrick always considered it the best likeness ever made of him."

10. By William Dance. In the Harvard Theatre Collection.

a. By unknown engraver. Published by R. Stewart, 1779. (130)

b. By unknown engraver. Published by E. Hedges, 1781. (131)

c. By unknown engraver. Published at Shrewsbury by C. Hulburt. (132)

11. By Dance (George, Nathaniel, or William?). A portrait of Garrick by "Dance" was purchased at Christie's on 18 June 1954 by the London dealer M. Bernard. Present location unknown.

12. By De Carmontelle, at Paris, 1764. Sketch of Garrick in tragic and comic parts. In the Musée Condé. According to David Little and George Kahrl, *The Letters of David Garrick* (II, 454 n), the duc d'Orleans "commissioned the artist Carmontelle to paint Garrick's portrait for his collection of notabilities."

13. By P. J. De Loutherbourg. Pen and ink sketch made shortly before Garrick's death. Present location unknown.

a. A facsimile engraving by R. Sawyer, after De Loutherbourg, was published by Colnaghi & Co, 1825.

14. By Edward Edwards. Pencil drawing. In the Victoria and Albert Museum.

15. By Thomas Gainsborough. Garrick with the Bust of Shakespeare. In 1768 Gainsborough was commissioned by the Stratford Corporation to paint a portrait of Garrick for the Shakespeare Jubilee of 1769. The artist reworked a picture which he had exhibited at the Royal Academy in

1766. The painting, for which Gainsborough was paid £63 by the Corporation and which Mrs Garrick thought was the best likeness of her husband, hung in the Stratford Town Hall until it was destroyed in the fire of 5 December 1946.

a. Engraving by H. Adlard. (11)

b. Engraving by W. Devrient. Published by Schumann. (13)

c. Engraving by V. Green. Published by J. Boydell, 1769. (9)

d. Engraving by J. Scott. Published by H. Graves & Co. 1872. (10)

e. Engraving by W. Sharp. Published by W. Walker, as a plate to *Effigies Poetica,* 1823. (12)

16. By Thomas Gainsborough. Painted for Garrick and exhibited at the Royal Academy in 1770. Then owned by Albany Wallis, Garrick's executor. Eventually it was bought by Lord Asham, through Agnew, in 1900, and thence came into the possession of Lady Swinton, at Swinton Park. It was acquired by the National Portrait Gallery in 1975. An autographed copy was painted for James Clutterbuck, and passed to his third daughter and heiress, Mrs John Buxton, and in 1958 was at Tockenham Manor in the possession of Major G. J. Buxton. A second autographed copy was painted for Dr Ralph Schomberg; eventually it was bought by a Mr Martin at Christie's on 7 May 1804, and passed to F. Fleischman, then to Mrs Oscar Ashcroft. It is now in the Mellon Collection. Another copy was offered in the Mahon sale at Christie's on 16 May 1928; a photograph is in the Witt Library.

a. Engravings by T. Collyer were published by J. Kearsley, 1776 (14) and as a plate to *Westminster Magazine,* 1779. (15)

b. Engraving by J. Newton. Published by J. Wallis, 1783. (18)

c. Engraving by unknown engraver. (16)

d. Engraving by unknown engraver. (17)

17. By Thomas Gainsborough. Seated, looking to right, paper in right hand. When engraved by W. Boucher as a plate to Knight's *Life of Garrick* in 1894, the picture belonged to a Mrs Kay. Version and present location unknown to us. (19)

18. By Thomas Gainsborough. A sketch, offered in the Burdett Coutts sale at Sotheby's, 16–17 May 1922.

19. By Francis Hayman. Garrick with William Wyndham. Formerly in the Lowther Collection, it was sold at Sotheby's on 17 March 1971.

20. By William Hogarth. Pencil sketch, comparing the physical proportions of Garrick and James Quin. Once owned by J. P. Kemble; now in the possession of Her Majesty Queen Elizabeth II, at Windsor Castle.

a. Engraving by T. Cook. Published by Longman, Hurst, Rees & Orme, 1 November 1808, and as a plate to J. Nichols and G. Steevens, *The Genuine Works of William Hogarth,* 1810. (25)

b. By an unknown engraver. Published by Laurie & Whittle, 1797. (24)

21. By William Hogarth. Garrick seated at a table, with his wife standing behind and leaning across to pluck his pen from his hand. Painted in 1757 for Garrick, who evidently never paid for it. The painting remained in Hogarth's studio until after Garrick's death, when it was given by Hogarth's widow to Mrs Garrick. It was bought at Mrs Garrick's sale at Christie's on 23 July 1823 for £75 11s. by E. H. Locker of Greenwich Hospital, who sold it to George IV about 1826. Now in the possession of Her Majesty Queen Elizabeth II, at Windsor Castle.

a. Engravings by H. Bourne were published by P. D. Colnaghi & Co (20) and in the *Art Journal,* 1855. (21)

b. Engraving by J. Sartain. Published in *Eclectic Magazine.* (22)

c. By unknown engraver, of Garrick alone, with facsimile autograph. (23)

22. By William Hogarith (?), after the

portrait done by Reynolds in 1776 (No 42, below). Bought in the Danton sale at Baltimore on 18 February 1930 by S. Kutch, of that city.

23. By N. Hone. Sold in the Carlberg sale at the National Arts Galleries, New York, on 27 May 1931, and sold again in the Dunham sale at Parke-Bernet, New York, 9–10 May 1947. A photograph is in the Witt Library.

    a. By unknown engraver. Copy in the British Museum.

24. By John Hoppner. A copy of Gainsborough's portrait for the Stratford Town Hall (above, No 15). In the Folger Shakespeare Library.

25. By or after Thomas Hudson. Seated at table, book in right hand. Sold in the Garnier sale at Christie's (lot 143) on 27 July 1928.

    a. Engraving by J. Dixon. Published by R. Wilkinson, 1779. (27)

    b. Engraving by C. Spooner. Published by R. Sayer. (28)

    c. Engraving by J. Watson. Printed for John Bowles at the Black Horse, Cornhill. (29)

    d. By unknown engraver. Printed for John Bowles & Son at the Black Horse, Cornhill. (30)

    e. By unknown engraver. Printed for John Bowles, at No 13, Cornhill. (31)

    f. By unknown engraver. Printed for Carington Bowles, at No 69, St Paul's Church Yard. (32)

    g. By unknown engraver. No painter, engraver, or publisher named. (33)

    h. By unknown engraver. Published by J. Cundee as a plate to the *Thespian Dictionary*, 1805. (34)

26. By Angelica Kaufmann. At the Burghley Estate, Stamford, Lincolnshire.

27. By Louisa Lane. Miniature painted on horn. The portrait passed to the artist's brother, the Rev Theophilus Lane, Rector of St Michael's, Crooked Lane; then it was in the possession of the Rev Trevor Garrick (a descendant of George Garrick) un-

til his death during World War II. See Mander and Mitchenson, *The Artist and the Theater*, p. 68.

    a. Engraving by James Heath. Published by W. J. White, 1819. (35, 36)

28. By Jean Liotard. Pastel done in France, 1751. Once at Chiswick House, this drawing is now in the collection of the Duke of Devonshire at Chatsworth.

    a. Engraving by C. Barth. (39)

    b. Engraving by J. McArdell. Published by the engraver and by Robert Sayer. (37, 38)

29. By Jean Liotard. Painting, at one time reported to be at the Burghley Estate, Stamford, Lincolnshire, but not now there. A copy, after Liotard, is in Drury Lane Theatre.

30. By Alessandro Longhi. Presumed to be a painting of Garrick in conversation with a group in a salon at Venice, with Mrs Garrick seated at left of group. In the Lady Lever Art Gallery, Port Sunlight. This painting has been incorrectly titled "Garrick in the Green Room," and attributed to Hogarth. The painting's present curator questions the identification of the main subject as Garrick.

    a. Engraving by W. J. Ward, titled "Garrick in the Green Room," with a key plate by G. Daniels which erroneously identifies the English actors presumed to be present. Published in 1829 by J. W. Southgate, who owned the original at that time.

31. By Philip Mercier. A painting of Margaret Woffington, seated, holding a miniature portrait of Garrick in her left hand. In the Garrick Club. In *British Galleries of Art* (1825), the painting is said to have been commissioned by Garrick.

32. By J. Northcote. A copy of the portrait by Reynolds (below, No 42). Owned by the Duke of Bedford, it was sold at Christie's on 18 December 1925 to Hope Johnstone for 15 guineas; it is now in the collection of Lord Olivier.

33. By Thomas Patch. Garrick in Flor-

ence in 1763. With a group including Sir Horace Mann. In the Royal Albert Memorial Museum, Exeter.

34. By Robert Edge Pine. In the National Portrait Gallery.

a. Engraving by Annan & Swan. Published as a plate to Doran's *Annals of the English Stage*. (45)

b. Engraving by R. Cooper. Published by E. Baldwyn and R. Cooper, 1815, reissued 1817 (41), and by E. Evans 1840. (42)

c. Engraving by W. Dickinson. Published by Pine and Dickinson, 1778. In the Harvard Theatre Collection is a proof made before a pillar in background was deleted; dated 1 December 1776. (43)

d. Engraving by W. Holl. Published in *Biographical Magazine*, 1819. (49)

e. Engravings by unknown engravers: published by Johnson, Wilson & Co, 1860 (44); published as a plate to *Illustrated Shakespeare* (48); and two others (46) (47).

35. By Robert Edge Pine. In the Folger Shakespeare Library. Bought at the American Art Association, 19 February 1925.

36. By Robert Edge Pine. In the Garrick Club. Presented by Lockett Agnew in 1918. Garrick Club *Catalogue* No 186.

37. By Robert Edge Pine. Miniature. In 1865 it was listed as in the collection of the late George Daniels. Present location unknown.

38. By Robert Edge Pine. Seated at table, pen in hand. In the Art Gallery of the Royal Shakespeare Theatre, Stratford-upon-Avon.

39. By Robert Edge Pine. Seated, left elbow resting on a table, book in hand. Right hand resting on knee. In 1818 the original picture was in the possession of the widow of the late George Wilson. Present location unknown.

a. Engraving by F. W. Pailthorpe. published by Frank T. Sabin. (53)

b. Engraving by J. Rogers. Published

as a plate to Oxberry's *Dramatic Biography*, 1827. (51)

c. Engraving by W. Skelton. Published by Colnaghi & Co, 1818. (50)

d. Engraving by C. Warren. Published 1822. (52)

40. By Arthur Pond. Present location unknown.

a. Engraving by J. McArdell. (59)

b. Engraving by N. Parr. Published as a plate to Thomas Whincop's *Scanderbeg*, 1747. (62)

c. Engraving by J. Wood. Published by the engraver, 1745; evidently the earliest engraved portrait. (61)

d. By unknown engraver. With title, "David Garrick (Gentleman) One of their Majesty's Servants as he appeared (aged 25) in London." (60)

41. By R. Pyle. Painting of William Powell, seated at a table. On the wall behind are a portrait of Garrick and a bust of Shakespeare. In the Garrick Club.

a. Engraving by S. Okey, Jr.

42. By Joshua Reynolds, 1776. Seated at table, hands clasped, resting on a paper inscribed "Prologue," on a table before him. There are, it seems, three versions of this portrait by Reynolds himself, and at least six copies after Reynolds. The original was painted for Mrs Thrale and was shown at the Royal Academy in 1776; it was purchased at the Piozzi sale by Dr Burney for 175 guineas. In 1865 it was in the possession of the widow of Archdeacon Burney. An exact duplicate is at Knole. Another, purchased at Christie's on 7 March 1930 through Gabriel Wells, is at the Folger Shakespeare Library. Copies, after Reynolds, are in the National Portrait Gallery, the Garrick Club, the Hereford City Museum, and at the Folger Library. Perhaps one of these, or another copy, was the one exhibited at the British Institution in 1823 and owned by the Earl of Amherst in 1857. A version of the Reynolds, attributed to Hogarth, was offered in the Danton sale at Baltimore on 18 February 1930, when

it was bought by S. Kutch, of that city. A copy by J. Northcote, belonging to the Duke of Bedford at Woburn Abbey, was sold at Christie's on 18 December 1925 to Hope Johnstone for 15 guineas; it is now in the collection of Lord Olivier. Numerous engravings, in various states and alterations, were done.

a. Engraving by W. Bromley. Published as a plate to *Biographical Magazine* by Harrison & Co, 1794. (74) Another version also appeared, undated. (75)

b. Engravings by A. G. Downing. (79, 80)

c. Engraving by W. Evans. Published as frontispiece to Davies's *Life of David Garrick*, 1806. (73)

d. Engraving by J. Geremia. (64)

e. Engraving by R. Laurie. Published by J. Stevens, 1779. (63)

f. Engraving by S. W. Reynolds. Published by the engraver. (65) Also published by Hodgson, Boys & Graves, as "Printed for the Thrale Collection," 1834. (66)

g. Engraving by W. Ridley. Published as a plate to Parsons's *Minor Theatre*, 1793. (76)

h. Engraving by M. Saugrain. In the British Museum.

i. Engraving by Schiavonetti. Published as a plate to Murphy's *Life of Garrick*, 1801, and as a plate to *European Magazine*, 1809. (67)

j. Engraving by Thoenert. (77)

k. Engravings by P. Thomas. Published by T. Kelly, 1829, 1830, and undated. (68, 69, 70)

l. Engraving by P. Viel. With inscription "Avec Privilège du Roi." (78)

m. Engraving by T. Watson. Published by Watson and Dickinson, 1779. (71)

n. Engraving by W. H. Worthington. Published as frontispiece to Boaden's *The Private Correspondence of David Garrick*, 1831. (72)

o. Engravings, two, by unknown engravers. (81, 82)

43. By Joshua Reynolds. With Mrs Garrick, seated on a garden seat, Garrick reading to her. Painted for the Hon T. Fitzmaurice and exhibited at the Royal Academy in 1773. Now in the possession of Major General E. H. Goulburn, D.S.O.

44. By Joshua Reynolds. "Garrick Between Tragedy and Comedy." Exhibited at the Society of Artists in 1762, it was bought by the second Earl of Halifax. In 1857 it was in the possession of John Julius Angerstein. Although Angerstein's collection became the foundation of the National Gallery, this painting remained in the family until 1882, when it was sold to Agnew's and then sold to Lord Rothschild, in whose family collection it remains. Mander and Mitchenson in *The Artist and the Theatre* note "a number of copies in existence," some possibly from Reynolds' studio. A small copy, after Reynolds by an unknown artist (sometimes said, without authority, to have been Benjamin West), was sold by W. F. Shaw at Christie's on 1 April 1890. It was owned subsequently by Sir Henry Irving, and eventually came into the hands of Somerset Maugham who left it to the National Theatre. Another small copy, by an unknown artist, is in the Garrick Club. Another version was bought for £231 by A. Morton from the collection of Lord Rivers at Christie's on 3 May 1926. Another, "after Reynolds," was up for sale at Christie's on 10 April 1953. Numerous engravings of the original, the first by E. Fisher in 1762, were done in various versions and titles:

a. Engraving by A. Cardon. Published as a plate to Britton's *Fine Arts of the English School*, 1811 (87) and by E. Evans. (88)

b. Engraving by H. Dawe. (90)

c. Engraving by E. Fisher. Published by E. Fisher, J. Boydell, E. Bakewell, and H. Parker, 1762. (83)

d. Engraving by J. E. Haid, with title "L'Homme entre le Vice et la Vertu." Published by J. J. Haid, at Augsburg. (84)

e. Engraving by Norman *fils*. (92)

f. Engraving by C. Corbutt. Published by R. Sayer and C. Bowles. (85)

g. Engraving by S. W. Reynolds. Published by Hodgson, Boys & Graves, 1834. (89)

h. By unknown engraver. Printed for Carington Bowles. (86)

i. By unknown engraver. Published by Gebbie & Husson Co. (93)

j. By unknown engraver. Undated, without text; presumably the smallest portrait of Garrick ever engraved (1⅜″ × 1¾″). (91)

45. By Joshua Reynolds. Standing, leaning on shoulder of Mrs Garrick, "who holds their sleeping daughter on her lap." Present location unknown. At one time in the possession of Mr T. Grissell. Photographs are in the Enthoven Collection and the British Museum. Identification of subjects questionable. The Garricks had no children.

46. By Joshua Reynolds. Details and provenance unknown to us. In the collection of Lord Olivier.

47. By Joshua Reynolds. Sketch of bust, left profile. In the Harvard Theatre Collection.

a. Engraving by J. C. Bromley. Published by Longman & Co, 1815. (94)

48. After Joshua Reynolds. In the Folger Shakespeare Library. This is the painting listed in the Daly Sale (No 42) at the Anderson Galleries on 27 November 1912. A copy of the above, bought from Robson and Co through Gabriel Wells in October 1924, is also in the Folger. The identifications of sitter and artist are questioned.

49. By George Romney. A portrait described as of David Garrick by George Romney was sold at Christie's on 18 June 1859.

50. By James Scouler. Called Garrick and his wife. At the Victoria and Albert

Museum. Reproduced in *Country Life*, 15 October 1964. Exhibited at the Royal Academy Bicentenary, 1968–69. The sitters do not look like the Garricks.

51. By John Keyse Sherwin. Pencil drawing. In the National Portrait Gallery.

52. By John Keyse Sherwin. With five curls on side of wig, robe with ermine trimming. Present location unknown.

a. Engravings by the artist in two states; one without title (115), the other with title "Engraved from an Original Painting." (116)

b. Engraving by unknown engraver, after Sherwin. (117)

53. By A. Soldi. A painting depicting Roubiliac finishing his bust of Garrick. In the Garrick Club. The bust, as painted by Soldi, is an excellent likeness to the finished sculpture. See below, No 256.

53a. By James Stewart (a pupil of Reynolds), c. 1770. Portrait in oils, 30″ × 25″. In the collection of Lord Olivier.

54. By Benjamin Van der Gucht. At the Althorp Estate, Northampton. Probably the portrait exhibited by the artist at the Royal Academy in 1779, "a head of the late Mr. Garrick, being the last picture he sat for." Said to have been painted for Hannah More. A copy, perhaps by Van der Gucht, was presented to the Garrick Club in 1900 by Sir Squire Bancroft.

55. By Benjamin Van der Gucht. "Garrick as Steward of the Jubilee." In the Collection at Parham Park. A copy by or after the artist is in the Garrick Club.

a. Engraving by J. Saunders. Published by the engraver, 1773. (97)

56. By Jean-Baptiste Van Loo? Owned by the Messrs Tooth in 1947, then by Somerset Maugham, who left it to the National Theatre. (The similarity of this portrait to the engravings by McArdell and J. Wood, both after Pond, is noticed by Mander and Mitchenson in *The Artist and the Theatre*.) The frame is inscribed by an unknown hand, "J. B. Van Loo c.1742," but the picture is thought to have been painted

in 1740 or 1741, the first portrait of Garrick. Recent expert opinion in London rejects the subject as Garrick and doubts the attribution to Van Loo.

57. By Victor Vispré. Pastel on paper. In the Garrick Club. Presented in 1924 by Major R. Woodhouse.

58. By Benjamin Wilson. In the Collection of Lord Kenyon. Exhibited at the Tate Gallery in 1925 as by Richard Wilson, but at the National Museum of Wales, Cardiff, in 1951 as by Benjamin Wilson. In his *Richard Wilson* (1953), W. G. Constable writes, "In the Kenyon family since *c.* 1830. The present owner has always heard it ascribed to Benjamin Wilson, with whose work it agrees in style completely." A photograph is in the Witt Library.

59. By Thomas Worlidge. Pencil drawing. In Art Gallery of the Royal Shakespeare Theatre, Stratford-upon-Avon.

60. By Thomas Worlidge. Pencil drawing. In the Victoria and Albert Museum.

61. In the manner of Joseph Wright of Derby. Called a portrait of Garrick. In the London Museum.

62. By Johann Zoffany, c. 1762. With Mrs Garrick, on the steps of the Shakespeare Temple at Hampton. With two dogs, a boy, a servant coming on with tea, and a view of the reach of the river. This painting was bought after Mrs Garrick's death by Lambton at Christie's for £28 7s. in 1823 and has descended by inheritance through the Earls of Durham to the present owner, the Viscount Lambton. Another version, owned by the Dowager Lady Mickelham of Strawberry Hill, was sold at Scott and Fowler's, New York, on 28 May 1923 (lot 557).

63. By Johann Zoffany? Mr and Mrs Garrick playing picquet? When published in an engraving by an unknown engraver as a plate to Doran's *Annals of the English Stage*, the picture was the property of Henry Graves. It is now in the Art Gallery of the Royal Shakespeare Theatre, Stratford-upon-Avon; the catalogue of that collection finds doubtful the attribution to Zoffany and the identification of the Garricks as sitters.

64. By Johann Zoffany, c. 1765. Mr and Mrs Garrick taking tea upon their lawn at Hampton. The clergyman is identified as Mr Bodens and the angler as George Garrick. This painting was bought after Mrs Garrick's death by Lambton at Christie's for £49 7s. in 1823 and has descended by inheritance through the Earls of Durham to the present owner, Viscount Lambton.

64a. By Johann Zoffany, 1762. Garrick is seated on his lawn, writing; there is a view of Hampton House. In the collection of Lord Egremont.

65. By Johann Zoffany. Painting of Garrick, bald-headed. Evidently the "original" done by Zoffany for the elder George Colman, and then owned by Thomas Harris, the manager of Covent Garden; presumably the portrait in the possession of George McKenny in 1824. Now in the possession of Mrs J. C. Conway of Turville Court, Buckinghamshire.

Another version, now attributed tentatively to Zoffany, but perhaps by a copyist, is in the National Portrait Gallery. It was at one time thought to have been painted by Luke Sullivan. This version was left by Mrs Garrick in 1822 to her husband's nephew Nathan Egerton Garrick; she had bought it from a Mrs Bradshaw, "to whom it had been given as a present." It came to the National Gallery from the grandson of Nathan Egerton Garrick in 1885, and was transferred to the National Portrait Gallery in 1898.

Another, a "Free Version by an Unknown Artist, founded on a Portrait by John Zoffany," was given by Somerset Maugham to the National Theatre. In this painting hair has been added to Garrick's head.

For a discussion of the several versions and the various engravings, with and without hair, made from the painting in the National Portrait Gallery, see Mander and

Mitchenson, *The Artist and the Theatre*, pp. 65–72, and p. 189.

   a. Engraving by Johann Sebastian Müller. On same plate with a portrait of Shakespeare. Published as a plate to the *London Magazine*, 1769.

   b. Both the British Museum *Catalogue of Engraved British Portraits* (No 64) and the *Catalogue of Engraved Dramatic Portraits in the Harvard Theatre Collection* (No 105) list an engraving by Müller as a plate to Smollett's *History of England*, 1757, but such an engraving, as pointed out by Mander and Mitchenson, does not exist for that date, and the print referred to "is in reality a cut-down version" of the 1769 engraving and "must perforce be of a subsequent date." In the Harvard catalogue are listed six engravings by Müller, in different states, all undated, and two engravings, after Müller and Zoffany, by unknown engravers. (105–112)

66. By Johann Zoffany. Oil sketch, unfinished. In the Garrick Club. In his *History of the Garrick Club*, Percy Fitzgerald stated that the portrait once belonged to Robert Baddeley. Probably this is the "Garrick's head" which, in Baddeley's will, proved on 18 December 1794, was left to Mrs Catherine Strickland to use for her life; it was then intended to be housed with his other theatrical pictures and effects in "Baddeley's Asylum" for indigent actors, which was never opened. The portrait came to Billy Dunn, who transferred it to one Stephenson, a banker, who passed it to Charles Mathews, from whom it went to the Garrick Club.

67. By Johann Zoffany. In the National Gallery of Ireland. The painting was acquired from William Permain, of London, in 1903. Said to be a portrait of Garrick, but the sitter does not look like him.

68. By Johann Zoffany. In the Folger Shakespeare Library. Bought from Gabriel Wells, 6 December 1923. The identification of Garrick as sitter is questioned.

69. By Johann Zoffany. Small oval. Details and provenance unknown to us. In the collection of Lord Olivier.

70. Attributed to Johann Zoffany. In the Players, New York. Bought by unknown person at the sale of the effects of the London Dramatic College, April 1861.

71. By unknown artist. Holding a copy of *Hamlet*. Painting in the Garrick Club. Presented by the Duke of Fife in 1888. Previously at Duff House. "It was stated to be by Reynolds and to have been acquired by James, Earl of Fife, a friend of Reynolds," according to the Garrick Club *Catalogue*.

72. By unknown artist. Watercolor. In the Art Gallery of the Royal Shakespeare Theatre, Stratford-upon-Avon.

73. By unknown artist. Pen and wash drawing. In the British Museum.

74. By unknown artist. Pencil and red crayon drawing. In the British Museum.

75. By unknown artist. In Roman costume. Pencil and colored wash drawing. In the British Museum.

76. By unknown artists. Two drawings. Reported in 1968 to be at Old House, High Tower, Hereford, but not there now.

77. By unknown artist. According to a notation in the art file at the Huntington Library and Art Gallery, a three-quarter-length portrait said to be of Garrick by an artist of the eighteenth-century English school is at the "Theatre Birmingham." We have been unable to locate this portrait, but a photograph of it in the Witt Library indicates that the sitter probably was not Garrick.

78. By unknown artist. Portrait in oils, 22″ × 26″. In the collection of Lord Olivier.

79. By unknown artist, British school. In the W. L. Peacock Collection. A photograph is in the Witt Library.

80. By unknown artist. Watercolor of Garrick and Mrs Siddons. Formerly in the possession of the American Shakespeare Theatre, it was sold (as part of lot 55) at

Sotheby Parke Bernet, New York, on 15 January 1976.

II. ENGRAVED PORTRAITS IN PRIVATE CHARACTER FOR WHICH NO ORIGINAL PAINTINGS OR DRAWINGS ARE KNOWN OR IDENTIFIABLE.

80a. Engraving by L. Dickinson, 1824. "From a portrait in the possession of the engraver." (101)

81. Engraving by Edwin. Plate to the *Mirror of Taste*, Philadelphia, 1811. (102)

82. Engraving by S. Freeman, after Reynolds. Plate to the *Monthly Mirror*. 1807. (95)

83. Engraving by "T. M. G." (103)

84. Garrick in Bristol, with inscription in German. Engraving by A. Geiger, after Schoeller. (150)

85. Engraving by Hall, after Zoffany. (99)

86. Engraving by F. Hillemacher, 1862. (104)

87. Engraving by S. Ireland, after Hogarth. Garrick standing with Hogarth, silhouette profile. Published as plate to Ireland's *Graphic Illustrations of Hogarth*, 1799. (26)

88. Engraving by R. Laurie, after R. Dighton. Published by W. Richardson, 1779. (7) As Memorial to David Garrick. Similar to Sherwin's pencil drawing in the National Portrait Gallery (see No 51).

89. Engraving by J. Lodge, after T. Worlidge. Published by "M. A." (98)

90. Engraving by W. Read. Plate to *Dramatic Table Talk,* 1825. (113)

91. Engraving by B. Reading. Published by W. Richardson, 1785. (114)

92. Engraving by J. Romney, after Dodd (and Brighty). Published by C. Dyer. (8)

93. With William Hogarth; sitting for his picture. Engraving by R. Evans Sly. A puzzle containing 30 different likenesses of Garrick and sketches from Hogarth's best pictures. Published by T. Houston & R. Evans Sly, 1845. (151)

94. Engraving by I. Taylor, after T. Pingo. Oval medallion within a wreath, from the seal executed for the Theatrical Fund. Published as frontispiece to Davies's *Life of David Garrick*, 1780. (57) A reverse engraving by W. Esdall was published at Dublin. (58)

95. By unknown engraver, after Pond. With a companion portrait of Mlle Violetti (Mrs Garrick). Published as a plate to *London Magazine*, 1749. (125)

96. With George Colman, titled "The Rival Managers." By unknown engraver. Plate to *Lady's Magazine*. (123) A similar plate by an unknown engraver was published in *Hibernian Magazine*. (124)

97. Copy of Dublin farthing. By unknown engraver. Issued by Murphy, Dublin, 1792. (133)

98. With Shakespeare. By unknown engraver. Published by C. & G. Kearsley on the title page of the fifth edition of *The Beauties of Shakespeare*. (138)

99. Medallion portrait with another of Garrick as Scrub. By unknown engraver. Published on title page to *Darley's Comic Prints of Characters, Caricatures, Macaronies*, 1776. (139)

100. Death Mask, the eyes inserted. By unknown engraver, after R. E. Pine. Publshed by Pine, 1779. (54)

101. In addition, in the Harvard Theatre Collection are 11 engravings, in various states, without description or date, by unknown artists: *Catalogue of Engraved Dramatic Portraits*, Nos 118–22, 126–29, 134, 149.

III. ENGRAVED REPRESENTATIONS, DEPICTIONS, OR VIEWS (NOT IN STAGE CHARACTERS) FOR WHICH NO ORIGINAL PAINTINGS OR DRAWINGS ARE KNOWN.

102. Satirical print: Garrick between Comedy and Tragedy and two theatre artisans. In his right hand he holds a paper inscribed "Arthur's Round Table." Engraving by M. D[arly]. Published by John Bell as title page to Nicholas Nipclose [Francis Gentleman], *The Theatres*, 1772. (313)

103. Medallion bust held by Cupid standing on a monument, Tragedy and Comedy at base. Engraving by T. Letton, after De Loutherbourg. (141) "To the Lovers of the Drama." As a Memorial to David Garrick. The face of Garrick is taken from Reynolds portrait done for Mrs Thrale. See above, No 42. The monument was probably inspired by a sketch—pen, pencil, watercolor—by C. F. Burney, now in the British Museum, of a "Garrick Memorial Concert." Orchestra and choir, with monument centered.

104. Delivering his Ode to Shakespeare on the stage of Drury Lane Theatre. Engraving by John Lodge. (314)

105. Nature and Genius introducing Garrick to the Temple of Shakespeare. Engraving by John Hamilton Mortimer. Published 1779.

106. Satirical print: "The Theatrical Steel-Yards of 1750." At one end of the steelyard is Garrick waving his helmet in triumph and weighing down the united performers of Covent Garden Theatre. Engraving by Patrick O'Brien. Published 27 April 1751.

107. Standing in a room, Comedy and Tragedy on pedestals, small medallion portrait of Shakespeare at top. Engraving by Peltro, after T. Thwaites. (140) Mistakenly identified in the Harvard catalogue as Garrick, this print is of James Cawdell on the Sunderland stage; it was published as frontispiece to *The Miscellaneous Poems of James Cawdell, Comedian*, 1785.

108. Standing beside bust of Shakespeare, with group of Shakespearean characters. Title: "O'erstep not the modesty of nature." Engraving by I. Taylor. (96)

109. In character, reclining on couch, with allegorical figure floating into room. Pegasus and group of figures facing Comedy and Tragedy in background. Engraving by W. Walker. (309)

110. Delivering the Ode to Shakespeare, surrounded by Shakespearean characters. Engraving by C. Watson, after R. E. Pine.

Published by J. Boydell, 1784. (55) A copy by an unknown engraver was done without the surrounding figures. (56)

111. Delivering his Ode to Shakespeare, in the Rotunda at the Stratford Jubilee, surrounded by musical performers. By unknown engraver. Plate to *Town and Country Magazine*, May 1769. (315)

112. Seated on the shoulders of Tragedy and Comedy. Shylock (Macklin) prostrate at their feet being urged into the fires of purgatory by the demons of Satan. Title: "Roscius in Triumph, or the downfall of Shylock, alias Mackbeth." By unknown engraver. (312)

113. With a Ranter (an amateur auditioner), Garrick seated, the Ranter reciting a soliloquy of Hamlet. By unknown engraver. Published by Colnaghi, Sala & Co, and F. Jukes, 1798. (152)

114. A bust of Garrick, with Mrs Yates as the Tragic Muse reciting the monody to his memory. By unknown engraver. Published by Harrison & Co, 1783. (135)

115. Comedy standing before a monument of Shakespeare, holding a portrait of Garrick, Tragedy on her right. By unknown engraver. Plate to Dibdin's *Overtures, Songs, Airs and Choruses in the Jubilee, or Shakespeare's Garland*. (136)

116. Medallion bust, supported by Fame, Tragic and Comic Muses. By unknown engraver. Plate to *Town and Country Magazine*, February 1779. (137)

117. Satirical print: "The Theatrical Contest 1743." The actor-figure marked "H" is Garrick. He is supported by "S," who is Mrs Woffington. By unknown engraver. Published by G. Foster, 24 October 1743. Details and background of this print are given in the British Museum *Catalogue of Political and Personal Satires*, No 2599.

118. Satirical print: "The Soho Masquerade Conference, between the Premier and his Journeyman." Garrick in riding habit points crop at Lord North in Harlequin trousers. By unknown engraver. In the Huntington Library.

119. Satirical print: "Britannia Disturb'd or an Invasion by French Strolers." Garrick is pictured as Fribble, with Rich as Lun, in the lap of Britannia, who says, "Lunn and Frible are my only Theatrical Children I will Cherish no Foreign Vagrants." By unknown engraver. Published about 1749? Example in the Folger Shakespeare Library.

120. Frontispiece to *The Sick Monkey, a Fable* [1765], depicts Garrick as a monkey reclining on cushions. The text congratulates Garrick upon his return to England from his grand tour. By unknown engraver.

IV. ORIGINAL AND ENGRAVED PORTRAITS IN STAGE CHARACTERS.

121. As Abel Drugger in *The Alchemist*. Engraving by W. Darling. (156)

122. As Abel Drugger. Engraving by Mary Darly, after "F. K." (155)

123. As Abel Drugger. Ink and watercolor by Jean-Louis De Faesch, after Zoffany. In the Folger Library. See also No 129.

124. As Abel Drugger. Gouache on vellum by Jean-Louis De Faesch, after Zoffany. In the Harvard Theatre Collection.
 a. By unknown engraver. Published by R. Sayer and J. Smith, 1770. (166)

125. As Abel Drugger. Engraving by J. Nixon. Published 1784. (168)

126. As Abel Drugger. Line and watercolor by J. Roberts. In the British Museum.
 a. Engraving by Thornthwaite. Plate to *Bell's British Theatre*, 1777. (158)

127. As Abel Drugger, with Edmund Burton as Subtle and John Palmer as Face. By Johann Zoffany. The painting was exhibited at the Royal Academy in 1770; it was purchased by Sir Joshua Reynolds for £100 and then sold by him to the Earl of Carlisle for £150. Now in the possession of the Hon George Howard at Castle Howard.
 a. Engraving by J. Dixon, published by the engraver, 1771. This engraving is reproduced in this dictionary, Vol. II, 436; in the caption we have erroneously identified Face, the center figure, as William Parsons; it is John Palmer, as correctly stated in our text on p. 437.

128. As Abel Drugger. Two oil sketches on canvas by or after Johann Zoffany. In the Ashmolean Museum, Oxford. Thought to be studies for the larger picture at Castle Howard.

129. As Abel Drugger. By Johann Zoffany. The single figure of Garrick from the larger scene with Burton and Palmer. In the Garrick Club. Another version is reported to be in the Players, New York, the gift of Joseph Jefferson.
 a. Engraving by Alford. (164)
 b. Engraving by J. Dixon. Published by R. Sayer, 1791. (159)
 c. Engraving by S. W. Reynolds. Published by Colnaghi & Co, 1825. (160)
 d. Engraving by A. Ribault. (163)
 e. Engraving by T. Wright. Plate to Oxberry's *New English Drama*, 1821. (161)
 f. By unknown engraver. (162)
 g. By unknown engraver. (165)

130. As Abel Drugger. By unknown engraver. (157)

131. As Abel Drugger. By unknown engraver. Plate to the Universal Museum. (167)

132. As Archer, in *The Beaux' Stratagem*. By Jean-Louis De Faesch, who visited England in 1767. See David Little and George Kahrl, *Letters of David Garrick*, No 442.
 a. By unknown engraver. Published by Jefferys & Faden, 1773. (170)

133. As Archer, with Thomas Weston as Scrub. Ink and watercolor by Jean-Louis De Faesch. In the Folger Shakespeare Library. See also No 132.

134. As Archer, with Thomas Weston as Scrub. Drawing on vellum by unknown artist (De Faesch?). In the Harvard Theatre Collection.
 a. An engraving by an unknown engraver was published by J. Smith and R. Sayer, 1771. (169)

135. As the Auctioneer in *Taste*. Engraving by J. McArdell. Published by R. Sayer, 1769. (171)

136. As Bayes in *The Rehearsal*. Watercolor by J. Roberts. In the British Museum.

    a. Engraving by R. Pollard. Plate to *Bell's British Theatre*, 1777. (172)

137. As Bayes. Pen, ink, and wash drawing by unknown artist. In the British Museum.

    a. By unknown engraver. Published by Wenman, 1777. (13)

138. As Benedict in *Much Ado About Nothing*. By unknown engraver. Published by Wenman, 1778. (174)

139. In the character of a Countryman, speaking the prologue to *Barbarossa*. Engraving by Cook, after Dodd. Published 29 October 1779.

140. As Demetrius in *The Brothers*. Engraving by J. Collyer, after Dodd. Published as a plate to *New English Theatre*. 1777, by Lowndes & Partners. (176) A reverse copy was engraved by L. Darcis. (177)

141. As Demetrius, with George Anne Bellamy as Erixene. Watercolor by J. Roberts. In the British Museum.

    a. Engraving by Thornthwaite. Plate to *Bell's British Theatre*, 1777. (178)

142. As Demetrius. By unknown engraver, as a plate to an edition of the play. Published by Wenman, 1778. (179)

143. As Don Felix in *The Wonder*. Engraving by J. Collyer, after D. Dodd. Published as a plate to *New English Theatre* by T. Lowndes & Partners, 1777. (180)

144. As Don Felix, with Mrs Barry as Violante. Gouache on vellum by Jean-Louis De Faesch. In the Harvard Theatre Collection.

    a. By unknown engraver. Published by J. Smith and R. Sayer.

145. As Don Felix, farewell performance. Painting by Robert Edge Pine. In the Garrick Club.

146. As Don Felix. Painting by Robert Edge Pine. In the Garrick Club (No 478).

Another version by Pine was sold by the New York Public Library through the Coleman Galleries in 1943. Present location unknown.

147. As Don Felix. By unknown engraver. Plate to *Royal Female Magazine*.

148. As Don Juan in *The Chances*. Painting by De Loutherbourg. In the Victoria and Albert Museum. Probably exhibited at the Royal Academy in 1774. A smaller version of the painting, perhaps by a copyist, is in the Garrick Club.

    a. Engraving by J. Hall, after E. Edwards's version of the De Loutherbourg. Published as a plate to *New English Theatre* by T. Lowndes & Partners, 1777. (184)

    b. Engraving by C. Phillips, after De Loutherbourg. Published 1776.

    c. Engraving by C. Phillips, modified version, showing Garrick in a ruined building. Published 1775.

149. As Don Juan. Watercolor sketch thought to be by De Loutherbourg, 1774, but perhaps by a copyist. In the Victoria and Albert Museum.

150. As Don Juan. Pencil sketch, after De Loutherbourg. In the British Museum. Perhaps a tracing of the engraving by Phillips, No 148 b, above.

151. In the character of a Drunken Sailor, speaking the prologue to *Britannia*. Pen and wash drawing by Isaac Taylor. In the British Museum.

    a. Engraving by the artist. Published as a plate to *Theatrical Bouquet* by Lowndes, 1778. (185)

    b. Engraving by the artist. With name of engraver and publisher removed, undated. (186)

152. In the character of a Drunken Sailor, speaking the prologue to Britannia. By unknown engraver. Published as a plate to the *Spouter's Companion,* by J. Cooke (187); a copy was published by Sabin in 1880 (188); another copy, reduced, engraved by "AB," was published in America, 1850. (189)

153. As Edward in *Edward the Black Prince*. Engraving by Terry. Published by J. Harrison & Co, 1779. (190)

154. As the Farmer in *The Farmer's Return*, with Mary Bradshaw as the Farmer's Wife, Edward Cape Everard (when Master Cape) and Ann Heath as the Children. Drawing by William Hogarth. In a private collection. A photograph is in the Witt Library.

  a. Engraving by J. Basire. Published as frontispiece to the edition of Garrick's interlude, 1762. (191)

  b. Engraving by T. Cook. Published as a plate to Nichols's *Genuine Works of Hogarth*, 1807. (193)

  c. Engraving by Hogarth. Published by E. T. Brain & Co. (194)

  d. Engraving by unknown engraver. Published by Laurie & Whittle, 1804. (192)

  e. Engravings (three) by unknown engravers. (195–197)

155. As the Farmer. Study for the single figure. Engraving by S. Ireland, after Hogarth. Plate to Ireland's *Graphic Illustrations of Hogarth*, 1794. (198) Copies by Ireland also appeared, undated. (199, 200)

156. As the Farmer, with Mary Bradshaw as the Farmer's Wife, Edward Cape Everard (Master Cape) and Ann Heath as the Children. Painting by Johann Zoffany. Exhibited at the Society of Arts in 1762, then owned by Garrick. It was bought at Mrs Garrick's sale in 1823 by a Mr Sequier for £33 12s. for the collection of the Earl of Durham. Now owned by Viscount Lambton.

A replica version by Zoffany once belonging to the Earl of Yarborough was sold at Christie's on 12 July 1929; it was owned by Mrs Maud Russell until 1963, when it came into the Mellon Collection. A third version is in the collection of Lord Leigh.

  a. An engraving by J. G. Haid was published by J. Boydell, 1766.

157. As Fribble in *Miss in Her Teens*, with Miss Hippisley as Biddy Bellair, Mrs

Pritchard as Tag, and Woodward as Captain Flash. Engraving by C. Mosley, 1747. Three versions, all published on 17 January 1747, are described in the British Museum *Catalogue of Political and Personal Satires* (No 2855).

158. As Hamlet, with Mrs Hopkins as Gertrude. Ink and watercolor by Jean-Louis De Faesch. In the Folger Shakespeare Library.

159. As Hamlet. Engraving by Ducarme, after "R. T." Plate to *Galerie Universelle*. (210)

160. As Hamlet. Engraving by Fonrouge, after "R. T." (211)

161. As Hamlet. Engraving by Formentin. Published by Decrouan, Paris. (207)

162. As Hamlet. Engraving by Gjöthström & Magnusson, after "F. M." (209)

163. As Hamlet, with Gertrude and the Ghost. Engraving by C. Grignion, after Francis Hayman. Published as a plate to Jennens's edition of *Shakespeare*, 1771–1774. (205) Mander and Mitchenson point out that this print is a variation of Hayman's painting of Spranger Barry and Mrs Elmy in *Hamlet,* in the Garrick Club.

164. As Hamlet. Painting by Benjamin Wilson. Location unknown.

  a. Engraving by J. McArdell. Published by B. Wilson, 1754, and by R. M. Laurie. (202)

  b. Engraving by Liebe. (204)

  c. Engraving by unknown engraver. Published by R. Sayer & J. Smith, 1769. (203)

  d. Engraving by B. Wilson. Head, probably of Garrick as Hamlet; without inscription (*Catalogue of Engraved British Portraits in the British Museum*, No 136).

165. As Hamlet, with the Ghost. Painting by Johann Zoffany. In the Folger Shakespeare Library. Listed as No 103 in the Irving sale at Christie's, 16 December 1905.

166. As Hamlet. Painting by unknown artist, of the English school. In the Museo

Teatrale alla Scala, Milan. Identification, as Garrick, is doubtful.

167. As Hamlet, in the "play scene," with others. By unknown engraver. Plate to *Universal Museum*, March 1769. (206)

168. As Isaac Mendoza in *The Duenna*. Sketch by Johann Zoffany. In the Folger Shakespeare Library. Though the subject has been identified in some sources as Garrick, he is probably Quick, who first represented Mendoza. Garrick never played the role.

169. As Jaffeir, with Mrs Cibber as Belvidera, in *Venice Preserv'd*. Painting by Johann Zoffany, exhibited at the Society of Artists in 1763. There are at least four versions of this painting.

The original version belonged to Garrick. At the sale of Mrs Garrick's pictures in 1823 it was bought for 25 guineas for the Earl of Durham. It was offered for sale at Christie's on 18 April 1932, but withdrawn. It is now in the collection of the Viscount Lambton.

A second version, probably that from which the engravings were done, was once owned by Sir Henry Irving. It was bought by Mr Parsons at the Irving sale at Christie's on 16 December 1905. The widow of a later owner, C. Newton Robinson, sold it at Christie's on 3 April 1914, to Messrs Knoedler for Somerset Maugham, who gave it to the National Theatre, its present owner.

The third version is in the Garrick Club and was part of the Charles Mathews Collection. Perhaps this was the painting owned by George Steevens, the editor of Shakespeare, who in his will of 1800 left his "picture of Mr. Garrick and Mrs. Cibber, in the characters of Jaffeir and Belvedera, painted by Zoffanij," to George Keate, Esquire, of Charlotte Street, Bloomsbury.

A fourth version is in the Budapest Museum of Fine Arts.

a. Engraving by J. McArdell. Published by the engraver, 1764. (212)

b. Engraving by Stayner. Published by C. Sheppard. (213)

c. Engraving by [Benjamin?] Wilson. Published by R. Sayer.

For a discussion of the several paintings, see Mander and Mitchenson, *The Artist and the Theatre*, pp. 5–11.

170. As King Lear. Gouache on vellum by Jean-Louis De Faesch. In the Harvard Theatre Collection. Single figure similar to that in Wilson's painting.

a. By unknown engraver. Printed for R. Sayer and J. Smith, 1769. (218)

171. As King Lear. Painting by G. Francis, at Hartford, Connecticut, dated 1810. Purchased from Walter Schatzki by the Folger Shakespeare Library in January 1945; sold in 1962 to the American Shakespeare Festival Theatre, Stratford, Connecticut; sold to Mrs Jan Henry James for $250 at Sotheby Parke Bernet in New York on 15 January 1976. This painting is a copy of the scene by Benjamin Wilson.

172. As King Lear, seated on ground, with Kent, Edgar, another man. Engraving by Ravenet, after Francis Hayman. Published as a plate to Jennens's edition of *Shakespeare*, 1771–1774. (221)

173. As King Lear, in the storm, with Bransby as Kent and Havard as Edgar (Havard incorrectly cited as the Fool in some sources). By Benjamin Wilson, c. 1760. Lost.

a. Engraving by Liebe. (219)

b. Engraving by J. McArdell. Published 1761. (214)

c. Engraving by C. Spooner. Published by Robert Sayer, 1761. (215)

d. By unknown engraver, after Richard Houston ("R^d Houston delin^r ab Originali"). Published by John Ryal, 1761. (216)

e. By unknown engraver. Plate to *Court Magazine*, 1761. (217)

174. As King Lear, figure similar to portrait by Wilson. Engraving by Terry. Published as a plate to an edition of the play, by Harrison & Co, 1779. (220)

175. As Kitely in *Every Man in His Humour*. Painting by Joshua Reynolds, 1768.

Probably given by the artist to Edmund Burke. At the Burke sale at Christie's on 5 June 1812 it was sold to the Prince Regent. Exhibited at the British Institution in 1827. By 1857 it was in the possession of Queen Victoria. Now in the Collection of Her Majesty, Queen Elizabeth II, at Windsor Castle. Shown in *The Georgian Playhouse* exhibition at the Hayward Gallery, 1975. A copy, after Reynolds, is in the National Portrait Gallery.

    a. Engraving by J. Finlayson. Published by Parker & Finlayson, 1769. (222)

    b. Engraving by J. Scott. Published by H. Graves & Co, 1864. (224)

176. As Kitely, with two other figures. By Johann Zoffany. From the collection of Sir William Knighton, it was sold at Christie's on 31 July 1925.

177. As Leon in *Rule a Wife and Have a Wife*. Engraving by Pollard & Jukes, after R. Rushbrooke. Published by J. Cary, 1786. (225)

178. As Leon. Engraving by Pollard & Jukes, after R. Rushbrooke. Published by J. Cary, 1786. (226)

179. As Leon. By unknown engraver. Published by Laurie & Whittle, 1802. (227)

180. As Lord Chalkstone in *Lethe*. Engraving by Goodnight. (229)

181. As Lord Chalkstone, eyeglass in right hand, with three other figures. Engraving by G. Smith. Published by M. Dickenson and also by C. Sheppard. (228)

182. As Lord Chalkstone, with Ellis Ackman as Bowman and Astley Bransby as Aesop. Painting by Johann Zoffany. Exhibited at the British Institution in 1814 by the owner, Sir George Beaumont. Subsequently it was lent to the National Portraits Exhibition, South Kensington, in 1868; to the Grosvenor Gallery in 1888; to the Leicester City Art Gallery in 1939. This painting, and a companion canvas by Zoffany of Bransby as Aesop, Parsons as the Old Man, and Watkins as John, remained with the

Beaumont Trustees at Coleorton Hall, Leicester, until their sale at Sotheby's on 30 June 1948 to A. Tooth & Sons, from whom in that year they were acquired by their present owner, the Birmingham City Art Gallery for £1850 (with the aid of a grant of £950 from the National Art Collections Fund). This painting is reproduced in this dictionary, Vol. 1, 28.

    An inferior version of this same scene, perhaps by a copyist, was given by Somerset Maugham to the National Theatre. For a discussion see Mander and Mitchenson, *The Artist and the Theatre*, pp. 13–23.

183. As Lord Chalkstone, single figure. By Johann Zoffany. There are two versions of this painting. One, probably that which was exhibited at the Society of Artists in 1766, was sold at the Garrick sale in 1823 to a Mr Wansey, in whose family it remained until it was sold at Christie's on 13 July 1951 to Messrs Mallet, agents for William Randolph Hearst. It had been exhibited at the British Institution in 1865 and at the Royal Academy in 1888. The second version is in the Garrick Club. Acquired with the Charles Mathews Collection in 1835. Probably the picture which was sold at Christie's on 8 July 1814; it was sold again on 10 March 1815, to a Mr Davis. The picture was exhibited at the Tate Gallery in 1951.

    a. Engraving by John Smith. Published by R. Sayer & J. Smith, 1770. (230)

184. As Lusignan, with Miss Younge as Zara, in *Zara*. Engraving by J. Collyer, after E. Edwards. Plate to *New English Theatre*, 1777. (232)

185. As Lusignan. Ink and watercolor by Jean-Louis De Faesch. In the Folger Library.

186. As Lusignan. Gouache on vellum by Jean-Louis De Faesch. In the Harvard Theatre Collection.

    a. By unknown engraver. Published by J. Smith and R. Sayer, 1770. (231)

187. As Lusignan, with Mrs Yates as

Zara. Engraving by W. Walker, after J. Roberts. Plate to *Bell's British Theatre*, 1776. (233)

188. As Macbeth, in the Witches' cave. Engraving by Bannerman, after P. Dawe. Published by Sayer & Bennett, 1777, and by R. Sayer & Co, 1789. (234)

189. As Macbeth. Three gouaches on vellum, in different postures, by Jean-Louis De Faesch. In the Harvard Theatre Collection.

    a. One of the above gouaches, showing Garrick holding a dagger in each hand, belonged to the Duchess of Northumberland in 1769, when an engraving of it by an unknown engraver was published by R. Sayer & J. Smith. (240)

    b. An engraving by Liebe, a copy of engraving (a), was also published.

190. As Macbeth, with Mrs Pritchard as Lady Macbeth. Watercolor by Henry Fuseli. In the Kunsthaus, Zurich.

    a. Engraving by J. Heath, 1804.

191. As Macbeth, with Mrs Pritchard as Lady Macbeth? Painting by Henry Fuseli. In the Tate Gallery. Said to be Fuseli's development of his drawing, above, but probably not actually of Garrick and Mrs Pritchard. For a list of exhibitions and provenance, see *Henry Fuseli*, edited by Gert Schiff, the catalogue of the Fuseli exhibition at the Tate Gallery in 1975.

192. As Macbeth. Watercolor by W. Loftis. In the Folger Shakespeare Library. "The Likeness of Dress taken from a Print done in the year 1768." This is the only portrait in the Loftis series at the Folger which the artist did not claim to have done "from life."

193. As Macbeth, the dagger scene. Engraving by I. Taylor, after D. Dodd. Published as a plate to an edition of the play, by Harrison & Co, 1780. (243)

194. As Macbeth. Engraving by C. White, after T. Parkinson. Plate to Bell's *Shakespeare*, 1775. (235)

195. As Macbeth, with Mrs Pritchard as Lady Macbeth. By Johann Zoffany. In the

Garrick Club, acquired with the Charles Mathews Collection in 1835. A different version by Zoffany, perhaps the original, was in the hands of George Keate when an engraving of it was done by V. Green and published by J. Boydell in 1776 (236); it is now in the Baroda Museum.

196. As Macbeth. By unknown engraver. Published by T. Bowen, 1769. (242)

197. As Macbeth. By unknown engraver. Plate to Bell's *Shakespeare*, 1776, and in other impressions. (237–39)

198. As Osmyn in *The Mourning Bride*. India ink drawing by Isaac Taylor, the elder. In the British Museum.

    a. Engraving by W. Walker. Plate to *New English Theatre*, 1776.

199. As Periander in *Eurydice*. Watercolor on vellum by J. Roberts. In the British Museum.

    a. Engraving by Wilson. Plate to *Bell's British Theatre*, 1795. (245)

200. As Periander. Drawing in India ink by Thomas Stothard. In the Victoria and Albert Museum.

    a. Probably the engraving by an unknown engraver, published by Harrison & Co, 1781, is after the Stothard drawing. (246)

201. As Ranger in *The Suspicious Husband*. Gouache on vellum by Jean-Louis De Faesch. In the Harvard Theatre Collection.

202. As Ranger, with Mrs Pritchard as Clarinda. By Francis Hayman, 1747. There are two versions of this painting. The original is at the London Museum, and was shown in *The Georgian Playhouse* Exhibition at the Hayward Gallery in 1975. The other was in the possession of the Garrick Club until 1970, when it was sold to Paul Mellon; it is now in the Yale Center for British Arts. The latter was painted for Benjamin Hoadly, the play's author; it was sold at the Harris sale in 1819 and at the sale of the Rowland Stephenson collection in 1829, when it presumably came to

Charles Mathews, from whom it was acquired by the Garrick Club in 1835.

203. As Ranger, with Mrs Abington as Clarinda. Engraving by Thornthwaite. Plate to *Bell's British Theatre*, 1776. (27)

204. As Ranger. Pen, ink, and wash drawing by unknown artist. In the British Museum.

    a. By unknown engraver. Published as a plate to an edition of the play, by Wenman, 1776. (248)

    b. By unknown engraver. Smaller version of (a). Published by Harrison & Co, 1779. (249)

205. As Richard III. By Thomas Bardwell, 1742. In the Russell-Cotes Art Gallery, Bournemouth.

    a. An engraving by G. Quinton, after Bardwell, was done for the *European Magazine*, but was never published. A rare copy of the engraving is in the Harvard Theatre Collection. (270)

206. As Richard III. By Nathaniel Dance, c. 1769. Exhibited at the Royal Academy in 1771. Now in the Town Hall, Stratford-upon-Avon. Although the picture was originally intended for Garrick, the artist sold it to Sir Watkin Williams-Wynn, who offered a more substantial price of £150. For many years it hung at the Williams-Wynn family residence, No 20, St James's Square, in a frame made especially by the brothers Adam, the architects of the house. It was sold at Sotheby's on 5 February 1947 to the Stratford Corporation for the nominal sum of £55, to replace the Gainsborough of Garrick lost in the fire of December 1946.

The painting is 7' 9" × 4' 11". Three smaller versions, or copies, are known. In the Folger Shakespeare Library is a version (48" × 31½") presumably by Dance, which was bought from Curtis Walters in March 1925. In the Garrick Club is a small copy (34¼" × 23") by Henry Morland, after Dance, which was acquired with the Charles Mathews Collection in 1835. In the National Theatre is a late copy by an inferior artist (25¼" × 16½") which was acquired in the Somerset Maugham bequest. See Mander and Mitchenson, *The Artist and the Theatre*, pp. 181–85, for a discussion of all the versions except the Folger portrait.

There were six engravings of the original:

    a. Engraving by H. Dawe. The artist is incorrectly said to be Zoffany. (251)

    b. Engraving by John Dixon. The first engraving, exhibited by the engraver at the Society of Artists in 1772. Published by J. Boydell, 1772. (250)

    c. Engraving by Landon, bust only. (252)

    d. Engraving by R. Sands, with ornamental frame. (253)

    e. Engraving by R. Sands without frame. Published by Vernor, Hood & Sharpe, 1811. (254)

    f. Engraving by S. W. Reynolds. Published by Colnaghi & Co, 1825.

207. As Richard III. Pastel by B. Dandridge (24" × 18"). In the Johnson Birthplace Museum, Lichfield, Staffordshire.

208. As Richard III. Ink and watercolor by Jean-Louis De Faesch. In the Folger Shakespeare Library.

209. As Richard III. By P. J. De Loutherbourg. Exhibited at the Royal Academy in 1774 (No 166). Now lost.

210. As Richard III. Pen and wash drawing by Henry Fuseli. In the Kunsthaus, Zurich. For photograph and details see *Henry Fuseli*, edited by Gert Schiff, the catalogue of the Fuseli exhibition at the Tate Gallery, 1975.

211. As Richard III. By Francis Hayman, 1760. In the National Theatre, from the Somerset Maugham bequest. Exhibited at the Society of Artists in 1760. Later in the collection of Lord Howe. Sold with the family treasures by Messrs Trollope at Gopsal on 21 October 1918. When owned by Somerset Maugham it was shown at the "History of Shakespearean Production" Exhibition at Leighton House, Kensington,

June–July 1953, and in the "Garrick, Johnson and Lichfield Circle" Exhibition at Lichfield, September–October 1953. It was recently shown in the "Garrick to Kean" Exhibition at Orleans House, Twickenham, from 18 May through 8 September 1974, and at "The Georgian Playhouse" Exhibition at the Hayward Gallery from 21 August through 12 October 1975.

a. Engraving by William Bromley. Published by J. Boultree at Chester, 1811. (278)

212. As Richard III. Engraving by "R. J. G." 1775. (277)

213. As Richard III. By William Hogarth, 1745. Richard in his tent, the night before the battle of Bosworth Field, starting up from the dream. In the Walker Art Gallery, Liverpool. The painting was commissioned by Lord Duncombe of Duncombe Park, Yorkshire, for £200 and was inherited by the Earls of Feversham. It was acquired by the Walker Art Gallery from Agnew's in 1956. Shown at the "Shakespeare and the Theatre" Exhibition at the Guildhall Library, 27 May–27 June 1964.

There are at least 14 engravings of this most famous of Garrick paintings.

a. Engraving by C. Grignion and Hogarth. Published 1746. (255) Another copy in eighteenth century. (256)

b. Engraving by T. Clerk. Published by R. Scholey. (259)

c. Engraving by G. Cook. Published by Vernor, Hood & Sharpe, 1807. (258)

d. Engraving by T. Cook & Son. Plate to Nichols's *Genuine Works of Hogarth*, 1808. (257)

e. Engraving by Dent. (266)

f. Engraving by Dent. (267)

g. Engraving by E. I. Portbury. Plate to Tallis's *Drawing Room Table Book* and Trusler's *Works of William Hogarth*. (260)

h. Engraving by E. I. Portbury. Published by E. T. Brain & Co. (261)

i. Engraving by E. L. Riepenhausen. German print. (262)

j. Engraving by A. Romanet. Title in French. (268)

k. By unknown engraver. As a plate to an edition of the play, published by B. Edmont, 1756. (263)

l. By unknown engraver. (264)

m. By unknown engraver. (265)

214. As Richard III. By Henry Morland, after Dance. In the Garrick Club. See also No 206.

215. As Richard III. Engraving by J. Ogborne, after S. Harding. Plate to *Biographical Mirror*, 1810. (269)

216. As Richard III. Engraving by J. K. Sherwin. Printed by J. Bell & C. Etherington, published by Hull. (271)

217. As Richard III. Pen and wash drawing by unknown artist. In the British Museum. Perhaps the design for the plate by an unknown engraver for an edition of the play published by Wenman, 1777. (272)

218. As Richard III. Drawing by unknown artist. In the Harvard Theatre Collection.

a. By unknown engraver. Published by R. Sayer & J. Smith, 1771. (276)

219. As Richard III. Watercolor on vellum by unknown artist. In the Harvard Theatre Collection.

a. By unknown engraver. (275)

220. As Richard III. By unknown engraver. (274)

221. As Richard III. By unknown engraver. Plate to *Galerie Dramatique*. (273)

222. As Richard III. By unknown engraver. (279)

223. As Richard III. By unknown engraver. (280)

224. As Richard III, with Norfolk, in battle scene. Sometimes attributed to Zoffany, sometimes to William Beechey. This painting, now in the National Theatre, does *not* picture Garrick, but is evidently of John Bannister and John Pindar, and by an unknown artist. See Mander and Mitchenson, *The Artist and the Theatre*, pp. 224–27.

225. As Romeo, with Mrs Bellamy as Juliet, in the tomb. Painting by Benjamin

Wilson, 1753. Recently owned by the American Shakespeare Festival Theatre at Stratford, Connecticut, the painting is now owned by Yale University.

    a. Engraving by R. Laurie. Published by R. Sayer. (281)

    b. Engraving by Ravenet. Published by J. Boydell, 1765. (282)

    c. Engraving by Stayner. Published by C. Sheppard. (283)

226. As Romeo. Head and shoulders, similar to the head and shoulders in the engravings of the larger picture after Wilson. A copy after Benjamin Wilson. In the Garrick Club. In earlier catalogues given as by De Wilde.

    a. Engravings, by Wilson(?), in Harvard Theatre Collection, without inscription and date. (284, 285)

    b. By unknown engraver. Copy of (a), printed for T. Purland, 1851. Only 20 copies issued and the plate destroyed. (286)

    c. By unknown engraver. Engraved for the collector Billie Wright; only two copies were printed. One was inserted into his extra-illustrated *Life of Garrick*, and the Harvard copy is the other. The plate was destroyed. (287)

227. As Scrub in *The Beaux' Stratagem*. Engraving by T. Holloway. (291)

228. As Scrub. By unknown engraver, after Holloway. (292)

229. As Scrub, medallion portrait, with another of Garrick in private character. By unknown engraver. Published on title page of *Darley's Comic Prints of Characters, Caricatures, Macaronies*, 1776. (139)

230. As Sir John Brute in *The Provok'd Wife*. Pen and watercolor drawing on vellum by J. Roberts. In the British Museum.

    a. By unknown engraver. Plate to *Bell's British Theatre*, 1776. (289)

    b. Engraving by Thornthwaite, after De Wilde's copy of Roberts. Plate to *Bell's British Theatre*, 1794. (288)

    c. By unknown engraver. Reversed, with German title. (290)

231. As Sir John Brute. Engraving by I. Taylor. Plate to *New English Theatre*, 1776. (293)

232. As Sir John Brute, with Vaughan, Hull, Clough, Watkins, and Phillips as Watchmen. By Johann Zoffany. There are two versions of this painting. One, probably the version exhibited at the Society of Artists in 1765 as "Mr. Garrick's Drunken Scene in *The Provok'd Wife*," was bought by Garrick himself. He left it to his brother George. It remained in the family for many years until sold as the property of the late Henry E. Trevor, a descendant, on 15 May 1929 at Sotheby's, to a Mr Henson. Presently it is owned by the Wolverhampton Art Gallery and was exhibited in *The Georgian Playhouse* exhibition at the Hayward Gallery in 1975. The second version was bought by the Earl of Mulgrave at the sale of Zoffany's effects in 1811. After 1834 it came into the hands of the Marquis of Normanby. Although sold at Christie's in 1897 it was repurchased by the family and is in the present Marquis of Normanby's collection.

    a. Engraving by J. Finlayson. Published by Zoffany, Finlayson & Parker, 1768. The engraver exhibited his work at the Society of Artists in 1769.

233. As Sir John Brute. Single figure from larger group. By Johann Zoffany. In the National Theatre. Originally this picture was owned by Garrick and was bought at the Garrick sale in 1823 by Lord Essex for 12 guineas. It was sold by the Earl of Essex in 1922 to Spiller, who sold it to Somerset Maugham, from whom it was acquired by the National Theatre. It was lately seen at an exhibition, "Garrick to Kean," at Orleans House, Twickenham, from 18 May through 8 September 1974, and in "The Georgian Playhouse" exhibition at the Hayward Gallery in 1975. For a discussion of this and the larger versions, see Mander and Mitchenson, *The Artist and the Theatre*, pp. 47–53.

    a. Engraving by John Smith. Published by R. Sayer, 1769. "From an original picture of the same size in the possession of Her Grace the Duchess of Northumberland" (Perhaps a sketch by Zoffany?). (294)

234. As Sir John Brute. Drawing by unknown artist. In the Folger Shakespeare Library, with notation by George Daniel, "Garrick in the character of Sir John Brute, original drawing."

235. As Sir John Brute. Watercolor drawing on vellum by unknown artist (De Faesch?) after Zoffany. In the Harvard Theatre Collection.

    a. By unknown engraver. Published by R. Sayer and J. Smith, 1772. (296)

236. As Sir John Brute, seated in a chair. By unknown engraver. Printed for J. Smith, 1769, and reissued as published by J. Smith & R. Sayer. (297)

237. As Sir John Brute. Line and watercolor by unknown artist. In the British Museum.

238. As Sir John Brute. By unknown engraver. (295)

239. As Tancred, with three other figures, in *Tancred and Sigismunda*. Engraving by J. Neagle, after T. Stothard. Published by T. Cadell, 1788. (300)

240. As Tancred, with Sigismunda in background. Drawing in India ink by Isaac Taylor, the elder. In the British Museum.

    a. Engraving by Collyer. Plate to *New English Theatre*, 1776. (301)

241. As Tancred. Engraving by Thornthwaite, after J. Roberts. Plate to *Bell's British Theatre*, 1778. (298)

242. As Tancred, with Miss Younge as Sigismunda. Engraving by Thornthwaite, after J. Roberts. Plate to *Bell's British Theatre*, 1776. (299)

243. As Tancred. By Thomas Worlidge, 1752. In the Garrick Club. Presented by F. J. Nettlefold in 1940; in 1920 in the collection of Wynne Morgan.

    a. Engraving by Worlidge. Printed for E. Jackson, 1752. (302)

244. As Tancred. By Thomas Worlidge.

In the Victoria and Albert Museum. This half-length portrait is similar to the full-length painting in the Garrick Club.

    a. Engraving by Worlidge. Sold by him. (303) Three other engraved states by Worlidge, one published by J. Bowles, are in the Harvard Theatre Collection. (304–306)

245. As Tancred. By unknown engraver. Published by Wenman, 1777. (307)

246. In four of his principal tragic characters: Lear, Macbeth, Richard III, and Hamlet. On one plate. By unknown engraver. (311)

247. In character. Engraving by A. Biasoli, after S. Marceau. Published by Batelli & Fanfani at Milan, 1818. (308)

248. In character. Ink and watercolor by Jean-Louis De Faesch. In the Folger Library.

249. In character, standing, pegleg. Engraving by R. Sawyer, after Hogarth. (310)

250. In the possession of the National Theatre, from the Somerset Maugham bequest, is a painting which at one time was believed to be by Zoffany and of Garrick in an unknown play. The picture, however, is now attributed to De Wilde and the subject is identified as Charles Mathews. See Mander and Mitchenson, *The Artist and the Theatre*, pp. 128–33.

V. SCULPTURES, WOOD-CARVINGS, MEDALLIONS, WALL-COVERINGS, PORCELAIN, TILE, ETC (INCLUDING GARRICK IN STAGE CHARACTERS). OTHER GARRICK ARTIFACTS.

251. Bust, head. By Lucius Gahagan. For the exterior of the Garrick Head Hotel, 1831.

252. Contemporary wax portrait. By Gardener. In the possession of Her Majesty, Queen Elizabeth II.

253. Contemporary wax portrait. By Isaac Gosset.

254. Marble bust. By Joseph Nollekens, c. 1764. Garrick paid 12 guineas in gold for

it and gave it to the Rev William Arden, whose widow later presented it to Lord Spencer. At the Althorp Estate, Northampton.

255. Bust. By Phillipson. In the sale of the artist's stock-in-trade held by Christie, 1785.

256. Bust in plaster (25″ high). By Louis François Roubiliac, 1758. In the National Portrait Gallery. Probably the plaster model for a marble bust of Garrick by Roubiliac which was sold at Mrs Garrick's sale in 1823. Garrick also posed for the figure of Roubiliac's famous statue of Shakespeare (1758) which stood in the Shakespeare Temple at Hampton and was bequeathed by Garrick to the British Museum. A reduced marble version of the Shakespeare statue is in the Royal Shakespeare Theatre Gallery and Museum. A terracotta model (which probably preceded the plaster model) is in the Folger Shakespeare Library (22″ high). It was sold at the Hudson sale in 1758 and at the Hudson sale in 1907. Then it was owned by Mrs Ludwig Nord and later by Sir Israel Gollancz, from whom it was purchased by A. S. W. Rosenbach for the Folger. Another terracotta is at the Victoria and Albert Museum.

257. By John Van Nost, the younger. Terracotta statuette (14⅞″ high) of Garrick as Roscius. In the Brighton Museum and Art Gallery. Photograph in *Country Life*, 7 February 1974. In February 1778 "a cast figure of Mr Garrick in the character of Roscius" was bought by Sir Watkin Williams Wynn from Van Nost for two guineas. When John Thomas Smith and his wife visited the Garrick villa at Hampton in 1829 they "were shewn a small statue of Garrick in the role of Roscius but by whom it was sculpted they were unable to learn." Perhaps the casts for these statuettes were made from the Brighton terracotta.

258. Bust, black basalt (3¾″ high). Wedgwood. In the Folger Shakespeare Library.

259. Plaster cast of Garrick's head, mounted on black slate (15″ × 12″). By unknown sculptor. In the Folger Shakespeare Library.

260. Bust. Supplied to Wedgwood by Hoskins and Grant, 1779.

261. Terracotta bust. By unknown sculptor. At one time reported to be at the Burghley Estate, Stamford, Lincolnshire, but not there now.

262. Bust, wax portrait. By unknown sculptor. In the Garrick Club, on the Grand Staircase. Presented to the Club by the late Edward Percy Smith, M.P., the dramatist.

263. By William Hackwood. Portrait on a blue jasper dipped dark blue, modelled from the cast of a medal by Thomas Pingo. On a Wedgwood and Bentley piece. In the Wedgwood Museum.

264. By Anne Louisa Lane. A miniature of David Garrick, purportedly made of his hair. In the Garrick Club.

265. By James Tassie. Portrait on a plaster medallion, as the Jubilee Steward, after Van der Gucht. In the National Portrait Gallery of Scotland.

266. On a refreshment token, designed by C. James and struck by Sims, for use at the Harp Tavern in Russell Court, London, after Garrick's death.

267. As Abel Drugger. On a delftware tile in the City of Manchester Art Gallery. The picture is that engraved by Thornthwaite, after J. Roberts, 1777. (See No 126.)

268. As King Lear in the storm, with Bransby as Kent and Havard as Edgar. Carving on a mulberry wood casket by Thomas Davies, after the painting by Wilson. The casket was made to contain the freedom of Stratford-upon-Avon granted to Garrick on 11 October 1768. The casket, the freedom, and the letter from the town clerk are in the British Museum.

269. Wall hanging with scenes from *Lethe*, the figure of Lord Chalkstone after

Zoffany's portrait. In the Victoria and Albert Museum.

270. As Sir John Brute. On a delftware tile in the City of Manchester Art Gallery. The picture is that engraved by Thornthwaite, after De Wilde and Roberts, 1794. (See No. 230.)

271. As Richard III. Intent, starting up from sleep. Two Staffordshire figurines; one 9½″ high, the other 6¾″ high. Examples in the Folger Shakespeare Library. A number of statuettes of Garrick as Richard III, of Bow, Derby, and Staffordshire porcelain are to be found in various museums and in the hands of private collectors. For information see George Savage, *Eighteenth-Century English Porcelain* (1952), P. D. Gordon Pugh, *Staffordshire Porcelain Figures* (1971), and articles in *Theatre Notebook*, XI, 53–55, 108, 128–30; XIII, 159; and XXIX, 17–18. Among the leading authorities on theatrical porcelains are Messrs Mander and Mitchenson, who have catalogued several hundred pieces, about 150 in their own collection.

272. As Tancred. Two Bow porcelain figurines; one 9″ high, the other 7¾″ high. Examples in the Folger Shakespeare Library.

273. As Tancred. On the Knave of Hearts with a pack of cards, engraved and colored by hand by Thomas Foubert. In the collection of the Worshipful Company of Makers of Playing Cards.

274. On his monument in Westminster Abbey, unveiled in 1797. By H. Webber. Engravings of the monument were done: by J. Barlow, published by W. Bent, 1797; by Audinet, after Stothard, published by G. Cawthorn, 1797; by H. S. Storer, published in Cole's *Residences of Actors*; and by several other unknown engravers.

275. "Project for a Memorial to Garrick." Drawings submitted for the design of the monument in Westminster Abbey include those by John Bacon, now in the Harvard Theatre Collection, by Agostino

Carlini and Giovanni Battista Cipriani in the Witt Collection, Courtauld Institute of Art, and possibly by Joseph Nollekens in the Heim Gallery. The commission was awarded to John Hickey, who died before he could begin, and then was passed to Henry Webber, whose monument was unveiled in May 1797.

276. "A View of the Seat of the late David Garrick Esquire at Hampton with the prospect of the Temple of Shakespeare in the Garden." By Isaac Taylor. The painting, owned by Garrick, was sold in the 1823 Garrick sale to the Earl of Durham.

277. Garrick's medal as Steward of the Jubilee, carved in mulberry wood by Thomas Davies, is in the Shakespeare Birthplace Trust, Stratford-upon-Avon.

278. The "gloves of Shakespeare" given to Garrick by the Mayor of Stratford-upon-Avon, 1769, are in the Royal Shakespeare Theatre, Stratford-upon-Avon.

279. A stage wig reported to be Garrick's is in the collection of Lord Olivier.

280. The silver tea set owned by Garrick, made in 1774 by James Young and Orlando Jackson, was sold for $7500 in a Parke-Bernet auction at New York in March 1970.

281. A medal commemorating the two-hundredth anniversary of the Garrick Jubilee was struck in 35mm and 58mm, in various metallic combinations, at Stratford-upon-Avon in 1969. The obverse of the medal has a representation of Shakespeare based on the Soest portrait. In the upper center of the reverse, framed by a stage curtain, is a representation of Garrick, carrying his wand of office, and admiring his mulberry-wood medallion. Words from the Jubilee Ode appear in the legend under his figure.

282. Furniture, artifacts, and other memorabilia owned by David Garrick are in the Garrick Club, the Folger Shakespeare Library, and the Victoria and Albert Museum, as well as in various other museums and in the possession of private collectors.

Garrick, Mrs David, Eva Maria, née Veigel, called "Violette" *1724–1822, dancer.*

Eva Maria Veigel was born in Vienna on 29 February 1724 in the house called "Zum weissen Hasen," No 323, at the corner of the Tiefer Graben and Heidenschuss, according to George Kahrl in *The Letters of David Garrick*, the daughter of Johann Veigel (or Faigel) and his wife, Eva Maria Rosina. The story that she was the illegitimate daughter of the Earl of Burlington, given wide currency by Charles Lee Lewes in his *Memoirs*, seems to be without foundation.

Eva Maria was placed early as a pupil to the accomplished ballet dancer and choreographer Franz Anton Hilverding and was by age ten dancing with the Imperial Ballet Company at the Kärtnertortheater in Vienna. She was taken up by the Court,

Harvard Theatre Collection

EVA MARIA GARRICK

engraving by Sherlock, after Read

patronized by the Countess Rabutin, and invited to dance at the private parties of Prince Eugene of Savoy. An obituary notice written for the *Gentleman's Magazine* in 1822 by one of her executors, George Frederick Beltz, declared that it was "at the express command of her Sovereign," the Empress Maria Theresa, that she adopted the professional name "Violette"—a translation into French of her surname. The author of the obituary had heard from another of her executors, the Rev Thomas Rackett, that "The Empress Queen, perceiving that her husband, the Emperor Frederick I, regarded Mademoiselle Violette with marked attention, to prevent any unpleasant circumstances proposed [a] journey to England, and forwarded powerful recommendations in her favour."

Violette signed a contract with the Italian company at the King's Theatre when she was 22. She embarked from Helvoetsluys to England in February 1746, chaperoned, according to Beltz, by three members of a British family named Rossiter who were returning from transacting business in Austria. For reasons not now clear, she traveled dressed as a boy (at least, so recalled the Rev Dr Alexander Carlyle many years later, in his memoirs). The young student Carlyle and two companions had met Violette and her escorts during a stormy sixteen-hour Channel crossing which left them all prostrate. At an inn at Colchester, the young men had protected the girl from insult by servants who had discovered her sex and objected to her disguise.

A bill of the King's Theatre for 11 March 1746 advertising the opera *Artamene* carried the comment: "Madem. VIOLETTE, a New Dancer from Vienna, will perform this day for the first time." William Wentworth, Lord Strafford, in a letter dated 27 March 1746, described her rather memorable London debut: "She surprised the audience at her first appearance . . . for at her beginning to caper she shewed a neat pair of black velvet breeches, with roll'd stockings; but finding they were unusual in England, she changed them the next time for a pair of white drawers." She must have danced during most of the some dozen and a half performances of the opera before 6 June, when Horace Walpole wrote: "The fame of the Violetta increases daily."

But Eva Maria had attracted the interested attention of another prince, this one the Prince of Wales, who asked her to come privately to Carlton House to receive the instruction of the dancing master Denoyer. She saw this as not only professionally demeaning but, given the Prince's reputation, hazardous, and so she refused. Walpole suggested a chain reaction in which the Prince's friend Lord Middlesex, master of the opera house (who was already upset that Violette was eclipsing his mistress Mlle Nardi) dismissed the musical director for taking Violette's part, caused the principal male dancer to be arrested for debt, and withheld salary from Violette, whom Walpole described as "the finest and most admired dancer in the world." Whether she was dismissed or left of her own accord, she appeared no more at the King's Theatre. (In *The London Stage* the notation "Mrs Garrick," opposite the Second Witch in the pantomime *The Imprisonment of Harlequin* at Warner's Booth at Southwark Fair on 8 September 1746, is perhaps an editorial anticipation. Violette probably was in the part, but she was certainly not yet carrying Garrick's name.)

On 3 December 1746 Eva Maria danced for the first time at Drury Lane, along with Giuseppe Salomon (the first time also of his "appearing on that stage"), his son, Muilment, the Mechels, and others. On the following night she appeared with the same people in two dances, *The German Camp* and *The Vintage*, "with new habits, scenes, Machines, and other Decorations for the Dances," and those were repeated on 17 December. On 29 December the corps performed Salomon's "New Grand Dance call'd *The Turkish Pirate; or a descent on the Grecian Coast*," featuring Violette and Salomon again. When Violette did not appear in all of the dances she was scheduled for on 14 January, a night patronized by their Royal Highnesses the Prince and Princess of Wales, the audience was vociferous in protest. Eva Maria inserted an apologetic notice in the *General Advertiser* of 16 January: she had not known the dances were scheduled until it was too late to prepare herself properly, but she was grateful for the "indulgence" accorded her.

By the time of that perturbation in the theatre, Eva Maria had been taken under the affectionate protection of the Earl and Countess of Burlington and was living with them at Burlington House. According to some reports the solicitous Countess used to accompany her to the theatre and stand in the wings, ready to throw her pelisse over the girl's shoulders when she had finished dancing. Walpole professed to see political influence at work in protecting her from a renewal of the audience's turbulent displeasure:

One night that she had advertised three dances and danced but two, Lord Bury and some other young men of fashion began a riot, and would have had her sent for from Burlington House. It being feared that she would be hissed on her next appearance, and Lord Hartington, the cherished of Mr Pelham being son-in-law of Lady Burlington, the ministry were in great agitation to secure a good reception for the Violette from the audience, and the Duke [of Devonshire] was even desired to order Lord Bury (one of his lords) not to hiss!

Violette appeared again on 21 January 1747, and on 22 January a writer in the *General Advertiser* complimented her and her partners for the delight and innocency of the "kind of Serious Pastoral Ballet" which they practised, so inoffensive to "the Modesty of the Ladies": "To say they are excellent in their way is barely doing 'em justice; but in these Dances they may be said to have excell'd themselves." Violette showed "an Elegance peculiar to herself that shone thro' her whole performance." In fact, "never did three dancers in a Pas Trois altogether equal the execution of Sg Salomon, Madem. Violette, and Mr Cook."

On 11 February Mlle Violette achieved the distinction, rather unusual for any performer, and particularly so for a dancer, of a benefit night "By his Majesty's Command," when "eight rows of the pit were rail'd into the Boxes." Her benefit tickets for the occasion were designed by William Kent and engraved by George Vertue. So far as the playbills show, she danced only four more times that season, finishing on 20 February, when were advertised "The Two last new Entertainments by Salomon, Mlle Violette, and Cook." She was probably referred to in the bills of 23 April when one "Violetty" was named as dancing, and also on 16 May, when "Violetta" appeared in a *Wooden Shoe Dance* with Leviez. The name both times was without the addition "Mlle."

Various stories are told of the vigilance exercised by the eccentric Lady Burlington over the conduct and company of her young ward. The Countess is said to have discouraged the advances of one predatory nobleman at a ball by removing her glove and significantly moving her own wedding ring up and down on her finger. She was neither vigilant enough nor adamant enough, however, to fend off the ardent attentions of David Garrick or to withstand Eva Maria's pleas that she be allowed to marry the rising young actor. Several highly colored and unauthenticated stories were told about the courtship: that Garrick disguised himself as a woman in order to pass letters to Eva Maria, that the Countess softened her resolve to find a more suitable match only after Eva Maria had pined and declined into a dangerous state of health, and so on.

Garrick was acting at Covent Garden in 1746–47, when Eva Maria danced at Drury Lane, but he had seen her perform and had met her on several social occasions during her first year in London, and his ardour was irrepressible. He pursued her all during his first two seasons as manager at Drury Lane, and in the spring of 1749 he pressed matters to a conclusion with the Burlingtons. On 22 June David and Eva Maria were married, first at eight o'clock in the morning in a Church of England ceremony by Garrick's (then) friend Rev Thomas Francklin "at his Chapel near Russell Street, Bloomsbury," reported the *General Advertiser* of 23 June. They were "afterwards on the same day" married, "according to the rites of the Roman Catholic Church, by the Rev. Mr. Blyth, at the Chapel of the Portuguese Embassy in South Audley Street."

After her marriage, Mrs Garrick left her career as a dancer behind. Her intimacy with the Burlingtons gave the young couple easy entree into the most fashionable circles, and their grace and amiability were eagerly sought by hostesses. Mrs Garrick was evidently much beloved by all kinds and degrees of people and her quiet, sweet, but firm personality was the perfect complement to that of her restless, vivacious husband. Mrs Mary Greville Delany thought that "the more one sees her the better one must like her; she seems never to depart from a perfect propriety of behaviour, accompanied with good sense and gentleness of manners. . . ." Sterne wrote: "I love Garrick on the stage better than anything in the world, except Mrs. Garrick off it."

Sir John Wilmot, Garrick's schoolfellow and Chief Justice of Common Pleas, commenting on a suit with which Garrick was wrongfully threatened, remarked "I think I had rather you should go to gaol, and then Mrs. Garrick (to whom I beg my love) may come and live with me. . . ." Lord Lyttelton and his family were en-

By gracious permission of Her Majesty, Queen Elizabeth II

DAVID and EVA MARIA GARRICK

by Hogarth

chanted with her and invented a loving nickname, "Pid-Pad." After a visit to the Isle of Wight their host Thomas Fitzmaurice wrote the Garricks, pleasantly addressing Eva Maria as "Your Majesty": *"Our Queen's Health* was our first, and a bumper toast, every day after dinner, during the solitary remainder of last week; nor has better health to your Majesty ever been forgot." Giuseppe Baretti wrote from Venice in 1764 that he still remembered the dish of tea Eva Maria had poured for him the first time he came to London: "She did it in so graceful a manner, I could still paint her in that pretty attitude." Mrs Thrale judged in her diary:

That Woman has lived a *very wise Life*; regular and steady in her Conduct, attentive to every Word she speaks, & every step she treads—decorous in her Manners, & graceful in her Person. My fancy forms the Queen just like Mrs Garrick[;] they are *Countrywomen*, & have, as the Phrase is, had a hard Card to Play; yet never lurched by Tricksters, nor subdued by superior Powers, they will rise from the Table unhurt either [by] others or by themselves—having play'd a *saving Game*.

At David Garrick's death some papers were found containing, as he had noted, "VERSES SENT TO ME ON MY MARRIAGE," chiding Garrick as a Benedick and asking "Who is the paragon, the marvellous she, / Has fix'd a weathercock like thee?" Garrick's reply was also found:

'Tis not, my friend, her speaking face,
Her shape, her youth, her winning grace,
Have reach'd my heart;—the fair one's
     mind,
Quick as her eyes, yet soft and kind,
A gaiety with innocence,
A soft address, with manly sense,
Ravishing manners, void of art,
A cheerful, firm, yet feeling heart,
Beauty, that charms all public gaze,
And humble, amid pomp and praise
. . . .

These are the charms my heart have
     bound,
Charms often sought, so rarely found!
Nor think the lover's partial voice
In flatt'ring colours paints his choice.
When you MARIA hear and see
You will not wonder such a she
Has fix'd a weathercock like me.

After 30 years of marriage, during which, he said, they never spent a night apart, David still held that same opinion of his wife. Their domestic life was tranquil and affectionate. Her relatives' financial requirements sometimes taxed his patience, but David would not quarrel with her over that. He teased her about her Teutonic accent and syntax (she was never entirely comfortable with the English language): "She is *crown fadder* than a *Big*," he wrote Lady Spencer, with his wife at his elbow, and (for he wrote many of her letters for her) "Mrs Garrick bresentz her pest respects to her tearest Laty Sbencer. . . ." She chided him for his gout-inducing attachment to the pleasures of the table. But they never had a falling-out, and when in 1768 some malicious person circulated a rumor that they were on the verge of parting, it apparently gave both David and Eva Maria much concern.

There were no children of the marriage, a fact regretted by both. Evidently their parental instincts were fulfilled in part by their solicitude for David's nieces and nephews, especially George's children. There was also the mysterious matter of Samuel Cautherley, the protégé whom Garrick educated and trained for the stage, but who finally disappointed his master. Several early sources stated, others hinted, that Samuel was Garrick's natural son, the product of a pre-marital liaison. If that was so, Mrs Garrick showed a long and remarkable tolerance. In 1800 Cautherley wrote her acknowledging "the many kindnesses confer'd on me, while under your Hospitable Roof (for almost Twenty years). . . ." In her will she left a "Miss

Cautherly" £100 and "Mr Cautherly of Ludgate Street Chemist" £50.

David Garrick left his wife comfortably provided for (see his entry for details of his will). But neither he nor she could have foreseen that she would outlive him by 43 years and die at age 98. Except for a painful and dangerous attack of sciatica suffered during the Garrick's second continental tour in 1764, she enjoyed generally good health throughout her long life. As her years advanced she began to worry about money, and before the end of her life she began to hear the same unjust charges of parsimony which had troubled her husband. As late as 1807 David's executors still had in hand some £50,000, after paying all specific bequests. Garrick had provided that any such surplus should be divided amongst the next of kin. Mrs Garrick claimed to fall under that designation and sued for an equal portion, but the court ruled against her. She had need to be prudent, and more and more as years went on and the cost of maintaining the house in the Adelphi and the estate at Hampton rose. But she was far from stingy. She gave away some thousands of pounds to her own relatives and made many small philanthropies.

William Oxberry, writing his *Dramatic Biography and Histrionic Anecdotes* around 1824, had

heard, that in the character of the late Mrs Garrick, there was a singular mixture of parsimony and liberality. She has been known to give fifty pounds at one time to the poor at Hampton, and on the instant deny herself the common comforts of life. Her wine-cellar she has not opened for years together, and a dish of tea was the usual extent of her hospitality. She always stated herself to be poor, as an apology for the ruinous condition in which the house and offices at Hampton now are. To save fuel, and secure herself from damp, a room in the attick served her "for parlour, for kitchen, and hall." She kept one female servant at Hampton, who resided with her many

years; and to compensate the poor woman and a numerous family (for her wages were small indeed), the house and grounds were shewn to visitors, unknown to the old lady. . . . Mrs Garrick's greatest pride was (when health would permit) in promenading her picturesque grounds, and explaining, with enthusiastic delight, the age and date of each tall tree, planted by herself and Mr. Garrick. . . . During the summer months, she would indulge in an occasional walk on the lawn and terrace on the bank of the Thames, at the end of which Garrick built the mausoleum for the statue of Shakespeare, and the celebrated chair: here Mrs. Garrick would sip her tea, and, in the society of one female or so, recount the pleasures she enjoyed in the same place, in the society and conversation of her husband, and their noble and learned guests.

Oxberry added that until the end of her life she was "a rigid Catholic; and, when at Hampton, if health and weather permitted, used to attend the Chapel at Isleworth on a Sunday."

Oxberry's report seems collected and not first-hand observation and acquaintance. Yet, the touches in his sketch are confirmed by other sources. After David's death in 1779, Eva Maria drifted a little toward eccentricity, but no more so than most aging people of independent personality are likely to do. Even before his death she had shown herself interested in mesmerism, mysticism, and alchemy, corresponding on arcane subjects with Drury Lane's great scene designer Philippe Jacques de Loutherbourg, though apparently she did not follow him in his near-disastrous venture into faith-healing.

The oddly brilliant Scottish judge, metaphysician, and experimental scientist James Burnett, Lord Monboddo twice proposed to Mrs Garrick in 1782, but she refused him. She settled into her quiet, semi-secluded life at Hampton, surrounded by mementoes of her life with David, seeing a few friends, and going sometimes to the theatre. A manuscript inventory of Drury Lane Theatre, dated 27 August 1819, now in the

Folger Library, details the sumptuous appointments of "Mrs Garrick's Anti Room" (*sic*) and "Mrs Garrick's Box." Another inventory taken four years after her death specified that those were called "Mrs Garrick's" still.

She kept up a brisk correspondence with her Austrian relatives, David's kin, the Countess Spencer, and other old friends, and especially with Hannah More, who flew to her side at Garrick's death and for some time was a frequent or even constant houseguest (upon Mrs Garrick's death she spoke of having spent "twenty winters" in her house). Eva's letters, many of which survive at the Folger, show a sturdy common sense, and a buoyant enjoyment of life. They give a good indication of her interests, many of which were philan-

Harvard Theatre Collection

EVA MARIA GARRICK, at age 97

by Cruikshank

thropic. An answer to one of her inquiries, from Hugh Bailye, Chancellor of Lichfield, assured her he had not been able to procure her any anecdotes respecting the earlier part of Mr Garrick's life because most contemporaries had died. Perhaps she had contemplated a Life, or perhaps she was simply showing that singleminded devotion to her "Davy" which never faded. Dean Stanley remembered her in his *Memorials of Westminster Abbey* (1868) near the very end of her life as "a little bowed-down old woman, who went about leaning on a gold-headed cane, dressed in deep widow's mourning, and always talking of her dear Davy."

Mrs Garrick died in the Adelphi Terrace house on 16 October 1822. Beltz's obituary in the *Gentleman's Magazine* declared that "She expired in her chair, without any apparent suffering, and so unexpectedly, that she had, on the preceding day, signified her intention of witnessing, in her private box, the re-opening of Drury Lane Theatre, in its improved state." She was buried by David Garrick's side in the Poet's Corner of Westminster Abbey, on 25 October 1822. Her will, signed on 28 January 1819, with codicils of 28 November 1821 and 15 August 1822, left a large number of bequests to the administration of her executors, the Rev Thomas Rackett, Rector of Spettisburg, Dorsetshire, and George Frederick Beltz, Esq., Lancaster Herald. David Garrick's niece Catherine Payne was left £1000; his nephew Nathan Egerton Garrick, "the portrait painted by Zoffany of my said husband in which he is represented without a wig," £300, and "the Gold Enamelled Snuff Box given to my late Husband by the Duke of Parma"; her own "God daughter Eva Maria de Saar daughter of my late Nephew Louis de Saar of Oldenburgh in Hungary the Sum of One thousand pounds in addition to whatever share she may eventually [be] entitled to of the residue of my Estate."

David's nephew Christopher Garrick and

his wife were to receive sentimental gifts of "the silver plate which was bought when I was married on the twenty second day of June 1749 that is to say Tea Kettle and Lamp Coffee Pot two Ladles for Cream a Complete Tea Chest three pair of Candlesticks," and a considerable inventory of other items, including the "table service of pewter which my dear husband made use of when a Bachelor and which it is my wish should always remain with the head of the ffamily bearing the name of Garrick." Christopher also was to have the "picture of my said husband in the character of Richard the Third which belongs to me having been purchased after his decease." Each of his four children was to have £100.

Of interest, among the multiplicity of bequests to her old servants and friends, were the following: "My Gold Rope which I usually wear" to Evans Prothero of Pembrokeshire; to "the Dowager Lady Amherst my Ring set with Diamonds bearing King Charles's Oak in it and my small Gold Box used for . . . sticking plaister"; "to Lady Anson, wife of Lieutenant General Sir William Anson . . . my Dejeuner Set of Dresden porcelain." "I give to Mrs Siddons a pair of Gloves which were Shakespeares and were presented by one of his ffamily to my late dear husband during the Jubilee at Stratford upon Avon." Her charities were considerable: she gave to the Rev Mr Arthur of Warwick Street Chapel £100 for himself and another £100 "for the relief of the Charity Children of the said Chapel." She gave £100 each to Saint George's Hospital, Middlesex Hospital; the "indigent Blind Charity"; the Refuge for the Destitute; the London Orphan Asylum. She also left £300 to be invested, the interest of which was to go to buy coals for the poor of the parish of Hampton.

Portraits of Mrs Garrick include:

1. Attributed to George Dance, but probably by Nathaniel Dance. Pencil drawing, 1771. In the National Portrait Gallery.

See David Garrick's list of portraits, No 9.

2. By Thomas Gainsborough. Probably owned by Frances Rigby, Lady Rivers (d. 1860), then by Dr Hodges. Sold anonymously in 1911, and in the Thomas Glen Coats sale in 1920, when it was bought by Hotham. Sold anonymously on 29 July 1948, bought by Bier. Present location unknown to us. According to E. K. Waterhouse: "Too damaged for certain judgement, but probably once a genuine picture of the end of the 1770s: in riding habit, turned half to left."

3. By Thomas Gainsborough. Sold at Christie's in 1900. Present location unknown to us. A photograph is in the Harvard Theatre Collection.

4. By William Hogarth. Standing behind her husband, who is seated at a table. See David Garrick's list of portraits, No. 21.

5. By Nathaniel Hone. Present location unknown. The portrait file at the Huntington Library suggests that the identity of the sitter is uncertain.

6. By G. Knapton. In her youth. Present location unknown. Noted in the portrait file at the Huntington Library. See also No 20.

7. By Jean Liotard. In the collection of the Duke of Devonshire at Chatsworth.

8. By Alessandro Longhi. With her husband and others in a salon at Venice. See David Garrick's list of portraits, No 30.

9. Attributed to the Rev M. W. Peters. Subject called Mrs Garrick. In the Garrick Club. Presented by William Commerwell about 1854.

10. By Catherine Read. The original painting was in the possession of S. Edwards when an engraving of it by W. P. Sherlock was published by Anthony Molteno in 1802. A miniature copy, after Read, is in the Garrick Club; it was listed erroneously in the Mathews Collection catalogue (No 312) as by Cipriani.

11. By Joshua Reynolds. Holding sleeping child on her lap, her husband standing at her side. Identification of sitters ques-

tionable. See David Garrick's list of portraits, No 45.

12. By Joshua Reynolds. With her husband, on a garden seat. See David Garrick's list of portraits, No 43.

13. By Johann Zoffany. When a young woman. Present location unknown. A photograph is in the Fogg Museum of Art, Harvard University; reproduced in *The Letters of David Garrick*, edited by David M. Little and George M. Kahrl (I, 117).

14. By Johann Zoffany. Taking tea with her husband upon their lawn at Hampton. See David Garrick's list of portraits, No 64.

15. By Johann Zoffany. With her husband on the steps of the Shakespeare Temple at Hampton. See David Garrick's list of portraits, No 62.

16. Attributed to Johann Zoffany. Elderly features. In the Garrick Club. Bequeathed in 1936 by Harry Graham. Formerly in Sir Henry Irving's Collection, sold at Christie's, 16 December 1905.

17. By Johann Zoffany? With her husband playing picquet. See David Garrick's list of portraits, No 63.

18. Portrait engraving by J. Bretherton, after T. Orde.

19. Portrait engraving by R. Cruikshank. At age 97. Published by Colnaghi & Co, 1822, and as a plate to *Dramatic Magazine*, 1 February 1830.

20. By unknown engraver. Full front, when young, shawl around shoulders. Not listed in the Hall catalogue, but in the Harvard Theatre Collection. No text or inscription except, in pencil, "Mrs Garrick." Perhaps this is an engraving of the portrait by Knapton.

21. By unknown engraver. With a companion engraving of her husband. Published as a plate to *London Magazine*, 1749.

Garrick, George *1723–1779, house servant.*

George Garrick was born in Lichfield on 22 August 1723, the sixth child and third

son of Captain Peter Garrick and his wife Arabella. One of George's brothers was the distinguished actor and manager David Garrick, in whose employ he was for many years. Of George's life in Lichfield little is known. Along with David, he was evidently one of the few pupils of Samuel Johnson in his ill-starred school at Edial. But nothing is known of his education after that enterprise failed in 1737. The following decade of his life is virtually a blank.

On 24 May 1746 David wrote their elder brother Peter that he had procured George a place with David's "very good Friend Mr Paterson the City Sollicitor," who was "ye most Amiable, sensible sweet fellow, that ever the Law produc'd. . . ." It was a fine opportunity. David thought that a stiff admonition should be administered by Peter, who had been head of the family since the death of Captain Garrick in 1737: "He can't be there till Midsummer, so let him prepare his affairs . . . in ye mean Time let him not be idle. I have given George a Character which I think he deserves & wch will infallibly (if he does not deceive me) make him a happy & an Eminent Man." The question of George's happiness is moot. He was never to be eminent. We do not even know whether or not he secured the position with Paterson who, David wrote on 9 August, "has lessen'd his Office of One Clark to make room for George."

By 1747 George had crept under David's wing at Drury Lane Theatre, where he remained, semi-dependent, for the rest of his life, despite several attempts by David to find other patronage for him: in 1758 to the Duke of Newcastle for a position in the Customs; in 1765 or 1766 to Lord John Cavendish and others for a post in the Treasury; in 1768 to Lord Mansfield for the office of Marshal of the King's Bench Prison; and in 1776, just before David sold his Drury Lane patent, to Richard Rigby, Paymaster of the Forces, for any sort of job at all. There were doubtless other attempts on David's part to lighten the financial load, which increased gradually as George's family grew.

About 1752, in the Savoy Chapel, George married Catherine, the daughter of Nathan Carrington, a King's Messenger. His father-in-law procured for him the minor sinecure of stable-keeper in the Royal Household and George and his wife moved into Somerset House. Sustained by the small salary of his office, a larger one from Drury Lane Theatre, and an allowance (and "loans" which he seldom if ever repaid) from David, plus some aid from his father-in-law Nathan Carrington, George sired five children: Carrington, who was sent to Eton and Cambridge, was ordained in the Church of England and became Vicar of Hendon, a parish in the gift of his Uncle David; David, who studied at the Academy of Geneva (tuition paid by his Uncle David), became briefly a cornet of dragoons and then gratefully accepted an estate in Norfolk from Uncle David when he married Emma Hart in 1778; Nathan, also educated at Eton, in part by Uncle David and partly by Nathan his grandfather; and Arabella and Catherine, whom a fond Uncle David had educated in Paris and to whom he left £6,000 apiece.

A letter of George to David, dated 5 July 1767, requested a loan of £200 and reminded David that his salary at the theatre at that time was £200, out of which he had to pay "for stamps, engrossments, &c. upwards of 50*l.* So that there remains clear 150*l.* which your kind allowance makes 250*l.*" His boys' schooling cost him £120 and their clothes £40. Apparently the plea was heeded, as were most such, though David endorsed the letter "Ill Management." Nevertheless, in his first will, made that year, David left his brother residuary legatee, after Eva Maria Garrick, of his estates at Hampton and Hendon.

In 1771, his first wife Catherine having died, George Garrick married the actress Elizabeth Tetley. (They had one son,

George, who took up acting as his career, and apparently a second one, also, of whom nothing is known.) On 18 May 1774 he was elected, with his brother David, Willoughby Lacy, and Thomas King, a Trustee of the Drury Lane Fund.

That George was useful to David there is no doubt. As the brother of Drury Lane's manager he carried sufficient weight of authority to transmit the routine orders necessary for the management of the house. As time went on he took more and more responsibility, though he did not act and had nothing to do with the stage business. (So far as is known, he was on the stage only once during a performance. That was on the occasion, 9 November 1768, when "at the end of the Pantomime [was given] a Grand Masquerade in imitation of that given the King of Denmark at the Opera House, and lighted up after the same manner—." The prompter Hopkins's diary said that "Every performer belonging to the House was on, even Mr Garrick and his brother.")

George's duties were various, though he apparently never held an official titled position in the theatre or settled any important matter without consultation with David. He protected David, and for that matter Lacy, from many minor irritants in the ceaseless negotiations with actors, authors, tradesmen, and house servants. He soothed refractory personnel, sent accurate reports of theatrical operations to Garrick when he was traveling, ran errands, made appointments, placed squibs in the papers, and rebuffed undesirables. He seems sometimes to have been responsible for sending parts and even the prompter's book to Hampton when David was to act a new role. He was especially useful during the preparations for the Stratford Shakespeare Jubilee in 1769 and in representing (along with George Colman) David's interests when Eva Maria and David took their extended continental trip from 1763 to 1765. He received his brother's confidences regarding

By permission of the Board of the British Library

GEORGE GARRICK's duel with ROBERT BADDELEY

artist unknown

the most delicate and secret matters and was often asked to provide David with some tactical advantage in the continuing contest for mastery between David and Lacy: "Just give me a clue to walk into the labyrinth of Lacy's brain, that I may be upon my guard," wrote David on one occasion.

As David's deputy, George was often the recipient of anger and abuse, and sometimes of ridicule. On 17 March 1770 he fought a duel in Hyde Park with the Drury Lane comedian Robert Baddeley. It was a ludicrous affair, as most such rencounters were. George had objected to Baddeley's receiving the salary of his wife, the notorious Sophia Baddeley; one angry word had led to another and finally to a challenge. Baddeley's second was a Mr Mendez, one of his wife's cast lovers. Sophia is said to have burst upon the scene in a hackney coach, just after her husband had fired and missed. She threw herself on her knees and implored Garrick to spare Baddeley's life. George fired into the air, the combatants shook hands, and the *Westminster Magazine* immediately lampooned the partici-

pants in "A Short History of DUELLING, illustrated by a wooden picturesque Representation of a late Theatrical Engagement." The woodcut, full-page, featured Mrs Baddeley in a prayerful attitude and the duelists, both presenting pistols with their left hands. The caption is "The SINISTER (or Left-Handed) THEATRICAL DUEL."

George could, nevertheless, show calm self-possession in real emergencies. On a night in November 1772 when the King and Queen were in attendance, according to the *Memoirs* of the Duchess of Northumberland, a false alarm of fire was given and a panic ensued, in which "In trying to get into the Orchestra, one Gentleman ran the Spikes through his Thigh, & many lacerated their hands & were otherwise much hurt." The Queen's Gentlemen moved to rescue her. But "Mr. George Garrick & Mr. Johnson appear'd on the Stage assuring them that there was not the least Circumstance of Truth in the Report. There was happily no mischief done, & the Confusion was soon over."

Though David and George seemed to feel deep affection for each other, George's

Shakespeare Jubilee Ticket signed by GEORGE GARRICK

improvident habits and perhaps also his feelings of inferiority and beholdenness to his brother put a strain on the relationship. There was almost a breach when, in January 1771, David discovered that George had "been possess'd sometime of a Country-house of horses, Chariot &c without so much as in yᵉ least hinting it to Me. . . ." David thought that "had you been possess'd of yᵉ fortune of Lord Clive such a Brother (as . . . I think I have been to You) should have been in common civility at least acquainted with it—I have never heard of it but from yʳ Neighbors, to whom I have always express'd my ignorance—an old Clergyman attack'd me at Court on yᵉ Birthday as Your Neighbor in yᵉ Country —What is this Mistery?" David was always reluctant to quarrel, but, his anger now raised, he opened his thoughts on a number of other injuries—"Neglect, unkindness, & I will not add injustice to Me," and, finally, George's mismanagement (if not worse) of accounts he was charged with collecting,

and in particular the management of money matters connected with an estate left by their cousin Peter Fermignac, who had died in 1770.

In the spring of 1774 George Garrick fell ill, and in a series of letters to various people from April to July, David spoke of the "doubling" of his managerial tasks at the theatre because of his brother's absence. David, writing to George's young daughters in Paris on 3 July, told them that their father would be going to Bath for his health. Much of George's time for the following three years was spent at the spa. The nature of his illness is not known. In a fretful and self-pitying letter of 27 December 1776, which protests that David had "affected me much with your great kindness, and I could now dash out my brains that I should either have neglected or offended you," George vacillated from such expressions of gratitude to the charge that David's "withdrawing your love and affection . . . at times," had "been the cause of my many and very long as well as very expensive illnesses." David replied with indignation.

But those recriminations, developing late in their relationship and perhaps inevitable given the personalities of the two men, were neither frequent nor serious enough to separate them. George remained at the theatre, so far as is known in his old capacity, after David sold his share of the patent and retired in 1776, for on 15 December 1777 David wrote to him at the "Stage Door of Drury Lane Theatre." But George's health continued poor.

David Garrick died on 20 January 1779, having in a revised will left George £10,000. At four o'clock in the morning of 3 February 1779, just two days after David was buried with pomp in Westminster Abbey, George died at his house in Russell Street, Covent Garden. His own funeral was somewhat less elaborate. A clipping in the Burney Collection at the British Museum notes that "Twelve horsemen preceded the hearse, and six mourning coaches, in which were relations and friends, attended it; the procession closing with the empty coach of the deceased." He was buried at Hendon, Middlesex.

In his will, dictated to an executor William Ward of Hatton Street from his death bed on 29 January 1779, George Garrick left £4,000 to his children, and to his wife £6,000 — and household effects. No mention was made of landed estates.

George Garrick's invariable question on returning to the theatre after any absence, no matter how brief, had been: "Has David wanted me?" When wonder was expressed at how closely his death followed on his brother's, Richard Cumberland pronounced what seemed to many the epitaph: "David wanted him."

George Garrick is pictured on the bank of the Thames, fishing, in a scene of the Garricks taking tea upon their lawn at Hampton, painted by Johann Zoffany. See the list of portraits of David Garrick, No

64. George Garrick is also pictured in a crude engraving purporting to depict his "duel" with Robert Baddeley, published in *Town and Country Magazine*, March 1770. He was said to be shown in a painting (previously believed to be by Hogarth) of "Garrick in the Green Room," but he is not, for that picture is actually by Alessandro Longhi and may show David Garrick in a salon at Venice. Jubilee tickets signed by George Garrick are at the Folger Shakespeare Library and the Shakespeare Birthday Trust, Stratford-upon-Avon.

Garrick, Mrs George. *See* TETLEY, ELIZABETH.

Garrick, Mrs Nathan Egerton. *See* GRAY, SARAH JANE.

Garrow, Mrs Joseph. *See* ABRAMS, THEODOSIA.

Garse. *See* GARCIA.

Garton, Jonathan [*fl. 1767–1784*], *treasurer.*

Jonathan Garton served as the treasurer of Covent Garden Theatre from 1767–68 through 1782–83. His salary for the former season was 8s. 10d. daily; in 1780–81 he received £230 for the season, and in 1782–83 he was paid £238. At his benefit on 9 May 1768 he was deficient by £9 11s. 6d., but he received £118 11s. on 1 May 1769 and £152 3s. on 7 May 1770, both times, presumably, before house charges were subtracted. At the beginning of his tenure as treasurer on 5 September 1767 Garton's surety bond for £5000 was posted by George Durant, Esq.

In his testimony given in connection with a law suit against the manager George Colman in 1769, Garton described his duties:

to receive the monies taken at said Theatre from the receivers at the different doors there & keep an account thereof & thereout to pay the salaries of the officers performers & servants & the Renters & Tradesmen their several demands thereon & other outgoings thereof — at the close of each season to balance the general account & pay into each of the Propr what appears to be their respectiv shares or proportions of the net profits.

On 27 September 1784 Jonathan Garton and the dancer John Slingsby were granted administration of the estate of Joseph Younger, the late Covent Garden prompter, having been named as executors in his will dated 31 August 1784. During that year, after which nothing more is known of Garton, he was living in Charlotte Street, Bloomsbury.

Gartreight. *See* **CARTWRIGHT.**

Garvey, Miss, later Mrs S. Raworth [*fl.* 1764–1779], *singer, actress.*
Faulkner's Dublin Journal reported on 17 November 1764 that a young gentlewoman would make her first appearance at the Smock Alley Theatre as Madge in *Love in a Village* on 19 November. She played Madge again on 26 November and 5 December, and on the latter date her name was given as Miss Garvey. In August 1765 she sang at Finch's Grotto Gardens in London, after which she went to York in 1768.
Tate Wilkinson in *The Wandering Patentee* said that Miss Garvey joined his troupe at York to supply the loss of Mrs Mahon. There about 1769 Miss Garvey married the young singer S. Raworth and acted as Mrs Raworth in 1771, 1772, and 1773. In the latter year she and her husband were in the cast of *The Macaroni.* They left York after 1773. Wilkinson told the story of Mrs Raworth's departure:

[She] came to take her leave, and begged permission to assure me — that she neither liked me as a manager or a man; for she knew that being a manager I must be a rascal: However she parted from me, she averred, without enmity; but there was one thing which she could

never forgive. I asked her what dreadful offence I had been guilty of, and whether I could not make her some atonement? She tartly replied — "Atonement, Sir! never — for when I asked to play Miss Fanny Sterling, you handed me to the glass, bid me look at myself, forget I was a lady, and declared I was ugly; which no woman can ever forgive!"

Wilkinson said that Raworth went to Chester, where he died. Mrs Raworth is known to have performed in 1779 at Leeds, Norwich, and York.

Garvey, Edmund *c. 1738–1813, scene painter.*
Edmund Garvey was born about 1738. He is said to have been of Irish parentage, and his earliest exhibits were at the Dublin Exhibitions. He worked in Dublin and Bath, painting landscapes in oil and watercolor. In 1767, when he exhibited with the Free Society of Artists, he is said to have been living at Mr Hargreave's, near Slaughter's Coffee House, St Martin's Lane. The following year he was living again in Bath, where he remained until about 1777. In London he regularly exhibited at the Royal Academy, having been elected an associate in 1770 (he became a full member in 1783). Many of his landscapes were continental views, and it is likely that he spent some time abroad in the early 1760s.
Garvey was employed as a scene painter at Covent Garden from 5 June 1777 to 26 May 1778, during which period he was paid £170. He helped paint the scenery for *The Norwood Gypsies*, which opened on 25 November 1777. He stayed on at Covent Garden for at least another season, his name being listed among the painters who prepared the scenery for *The Touchstone*, which opened on 4 January 1779.
Edmund Garvey died in 1813 and was buried at St Paul, Covent Garden, on 3 June of that year at the age of 75. His address was given in the registers as Chandos Street, as it was in his will, dated 7 February 1808. In his will he left all his estate

to his sister, Barbara Garvey of Shilbourny, Ireland, except for bequests as follows: £100 each to the children of James Fitzpatrick and his late wife Jane, of Shilbourny; £10 to Mrs Ann Carver; £10 to Garvey's former servant Mary Harford; £100 to Maria Van der Gucht, widow of Benjamin Van der Gucht (no doubt the portrait painter who died in 1794); £100 to Edward Dowland of Whitechurch, Dorset; £100 each to friends and executors Martin Arthur Shore, R.A., of Cavendish Square, and Patrick Davis of the Inner Temple; and a choice of pictures to friends Thomas Edwards Forman and John Curtis. A codicil, undated, added mourning rings for Mr and Mrs Dowland, the two Misses Wolfrey of Whitechurch, Mr and Mrs Clinton, and Mr and Mrs Lary. The will was proved on 10 August 1813.

Gash. *See* GACHES.

Gaskin, Mr (*fl.* 1783–1785), *dresser.*
Mr Gaskin served as a dresser at the King's Theatre in the Haymarket from 1783 to 1785.

Gasparini, Signor, stage name of Gasparo Visconti (*fl.* 1702–1706), *violinist.*
Born in Cremona, Gasparo Visconti, called Gasparini, came to England in the fall of 1702. On 3 December at York Buildings was presented "An Italian Consort, with Additions of New Songs by the Gentlewoman, and Symphonies by Signor Gasparine." On 22 December at Drury Lane he was advertised as recently arrived from Rome; that night he played "several Entertainments of Musick by himself, and in Consort with others"—the implication being not that he performed his own compositions but rather that he played both solo and ensemble works. He seems not to have been a composer, though Grove suggests that he was, and he should not be confused with the prolific composer Fran-

cesco Gasparini, as Grove points out. He was a member of the Drury Lane company in 1702–3, as was Signora Gasparini.

Through the 1704–5 season Gasparini was a regular attraction at Drury Lane, usually playing Italian sonatas, some of them by Corelli. Often he offered solos, but on occasion he performed with other musical artists, among them Dieupart and Paisible. The dancer Du Ruel sometimes joined Gasparini in "an Eccho." Gasparini also appeared at York Buildings, Hickford's Dancing School, and at private concerts. According to a letter of 6 May 1706 he was scheduled to play at Vice Chamberlain Coke's house. By 1703 Gasparini was performing with his own students, and in 1705 and 1706, when Gasparini's public appearances ceased, his scholars were often cited in the Drury Lane bills. On 6 May 1706 Nicolino Haym wrote to Vice Chamberlain Coke concerning an *Ode to Discord* which he had just composed; the violin parts were very difficult, he said, and he recommended Gasparini to play first violin. But by that time Gasparini seems to have given up his performing career.

Gasparini, Signora, stage name of Signora Gasparo Visconti (*fl.* 1702–1703), *actress.*
Percy Fitzgerald in his *New History* printed a roster of the Drury Lane troupe in 1702–3; included among the actresses was Signora Gasparini and, among the instrumentalists, her husband. No roles are known for her, and *The London Stage* does not list her.

Gasson, Margery *b. c. 1783, oddity.*
Margery Gasson, advertised as being six and a half years old and pregnant, was exhibited at Mr Beckett's, No 31, Haymarket in 1789.

Gataker, Mr (*fl.* 1747), *actor.*
Mr Gataker played Moneses in *Tamer-*

lane at a playhouse in Red Lion Street at the Cole Hole on 27 January 1747.

Gately, Roger [*fl.* 1702], mountebank.

The *Post Man* on 8 September 1702 reported that Roger Gately and other strolling players were required to pay 2*s.* daily to town constables. All the cited strollers were called mountebanks, and since the notice appeared in a London paper, they were probably active there.

Gates, Mr [*fl.* 1672], musician.

Mr Gates and four others were ordered apprehended on 15 July 1672 for practicing music without a license.

Gates, Mr [*fl.* 1790], actor.

A Mr Gates played Baptista in *The Spaniard Well Drub'd* at the old Yates and Shuter booth at Bartholomew Fair in 1790.

Gates, Bernard 1685–1773, singer, composer.

Bernard Gates was born in London in 1685, the second son of Bernard and Maria Gates of the parish of St Margaret, Westminster. As indicated in his father's will of 1702 (proved by Maria Gates in 1718), young Bernard had brothers named Gabriel and Abell and a sister Eleanor. Chamberlaine's *Angliae Notitia* (1702) listed Bernard as one of the Children of the Chapel Royal, and on 27 March 1705, long after the young man's voice had changed, he was granted £9 worth of clothing as a former Chapel boy. On 4 February 1708 he sang bass at a concert at York Buildings, and on the following 15 July he was sworn a Gentleman of the Chapel Royal, replacing John Howell.

About 1710 Gates and other London musicians formed the Academy of Ancient Music at the Crown and Anchor Tavern in the Strand. The Academy was under the direction of Pepusch, who was assisted by

Courtesy of the Faculty of Music, Oxford

BERNARD GATES

artist unknown

Gates, Johann Ernst Galliard, Maurice Greene, and the men and boys of the Chapel Royal and St Paul's Cathedral choirs. According to Dean's *Handel's Dramatic Oratorios and Masques*, Gates sang in all of the London performances of Handel's church music from 1713 to 1743, his first such appearance, perhaps, being on 6 February 1713, when he sang at court in the "Ode for the Birthday of Queen Anne." On the following 7 July at St Paul's, Gates sang in Handel's *Utrecht Te Deum and Jubilate*. It was apparently for his services in the Chapel Royal that Gates was paid the £40 annually mentioned in the *Calendar of Treasury Books* in 1715–16. He sang at a concert at Stationers' Hall on 27 March 1717.

On 15 August 1722 Gates sang at the Duke of Marlborough's funeral at Wesminster Abbey; on 11 January 1723 he participated in a concert at Buckingham

House; and on 5 January 1725 he sang in a *Te Deum* (probably Handel's *Utrecht Te Deum* again) at the Royal Chapel in St James's Palace. Perhaps by that time Gates had been appointed to some of the important positions we know he ultimately held: Master of the Children of the Chapel Royal and of Westminster Abbey, a member of the Westminster Abbey choir, and the sinecure office of Tuner of the Regals (small organs) in the King's household.

At the Inner Temple on 2 February 1726 Gates sang at a concert; on 14 January 1731 as Master of the Children of the Chapel Royal he directed a concert at the Academy of Vocal Music which he had helped found on 7 January 1726 at the Crown Tavern in the Strand. On 23 February 1732 at the Crown and Anchor in the Strand (not, as is reported in some sources, at Gates's own house in James Street, Westminster), Gates and his Chapel boys performed Handel's *Esther*. Singing in the choir on that occasion were John Randall and John Beard. The performance marked a turning point in Handel's career and encouraged him to compose more oratorios.

In 1734 Gates withdrew his boys from the Academy of Ancient Music, creating for the group a temporary difficulty, for they had trouble carrying on without treble voices. On 17 December 1737 Gates was one of the basses who sang Handel's funeral anthem on the death of Queen Caroline. He was one of the original subscribers to the Royal Society of Musicians when it was founded on 28 August 1739. On 27 December 1743 at the banqueting house Gates sang in Handel's *Dettingen Te Deum*.

On 9 June 1744 Handel wrote to Jennens to say that he had taken the King's Theatre and engaged a number of singers, including Gates and his Chapel boys, but the 1744–45 season there was not a success. Gates is said by Dean to have participated with his boys in performances at the Foundling Hospital from 1749 to 1751. On

13 June 1749 the minutes of the meeting of the General Committee of the Hospital show that Gates had been paid seven guineas for singing—with the boys—on 1 and 15 May, but Gates had returned £5 19s., saying that he wished to be reimbursed for only the coach fare to get the boys to and from the performances. He responded similarly in 1751. His boys sang at the Hospital again in 1754, but the accounts do not show whether or not Gates himself was involved. In 1757 Nares succeeded Gates as Master of the Children, and Gates retired the following year to North Aston, Oxford. He died on 15 November 1773 at the age of 88 and was buried in the north cloister of Westminster Abbey on 23 November.

Gates had written his will at North Aston on 5 October 1772. To his sister Eleanor Downes (widowed and then living in London) he left an annuity of £50, and to her son Bernard he left all of his estates, farms, and tenements in North Aston. The bequest to young Downes was to descend to Downes's offspring; if Downes should have no children, the property was to go to the musician Thomas Dupuis of King's Row, Upper Grosvenor Street, London, with a further remainder to Dr Samuel Arnold. Gates left £150 to his niece Elizabeth Musgrave, widow of Charles Musgrave, and he left generous bequests to his various servants. Gates directed that his chaise horse be kept on his North Aston estate, without being worked, and that the animal should be allowed to die naturally and be buried without mutilation.

Gates requested that upon his death his body should be carried to the Swan and Two Necks in Tothill Street and then to Westminster Abbey for burial near his wife and daughter. He asked that a marble slab be placed over his tomb in the Abbey cloisters, inscribed with the list of musical posts he had held. By a codicil dated 20 March 1773 Gates left additional gifts to his servants. His executors, John Griffin and Samuel Churchill, proved the will on 28 November 1773.

Bernard Gates's mother had died in 1725. In her will, dated 22 June 1724, she had appointed Bernard her executor, and he proved the will on 1 June 1725. The will directed that Bernard should receive two landscapes and a chimney piece. Bequests were also made to several relatives and friends of Mrs Gates, and her four children were named residuary legatees, sharing equally. Bernard's sister Eleanor was, by 1725, married to John Downes, a painter of Whitechurch, Shropshire. Mrs Gates left her best feather bed to her granddaughter Atkinson Gates, Bernard's daughter. Bernard's wife Elizabeth (1689–1737) was brought up by a Mrs Elizabeth Atkinson; on 18 March 1726 Elizabeth Atkinson's will was proved by Mrs Bernard Gates, who inherited the bulk of the estate.

Bernard Gates's wife Elizabeth had died on 10 March 1737 at the age of 48 and had been buried in the Abbey cloisters on 15 March. The Abbey registers tell us something further about Gates's children: Atkinson was his first child, born on 14 April 1717, christened on 23 April at St Margaret, Westminster, and buried in the Abbey cloisters the following 6 June. A son Bernard was born on 18 June 1719, christened at St Margaret's on 30 June, and buried at the Abbey on 11 July. The only child to live past infancy, so far as the registers show, was a second daughter Atkinson: she was born on 23 June 1718, christened at St Margaret's on 1 June, died on 24 November 1736, and was buried in the Abbey cloisters on 28 November.

A portrait of Bernard Gates, perhaps by John Russell, is at the Faculty of Music, Oxford. A poor and anonymously engraved print of that portrait was published by T. Williams in 1784 as a frontispiece to *Selection of Biography.* The engraving is captioned "From an Orig.[1] Painting in the Possession of M[r] Dupuis" (Thomas Saunders Dupuis, Gates's student and heir, who gave the painting to Oxford sometime between 1784 and 1795).

Gattolini, Signor [*fl. 1787*], *singer.*
At the King's Theatre Signor Gattolini sang Don Orlando in *Giannina e Bernardone* on 9 January 1787, Berto in *Il tutore burlato* on 17 February, and Curio in *Giulio Cesare in Egitto* on 1 March.

Gatward, Mrs [*fl. c. 1673–1675*], *actress?*
The Lord Chamberlain's accounts cited Mrs Gatward as a member of the King's Company—an actress perhaps—about 1673–1675.

Gaudenzi, Teresa [*fl. 1783*], *singer.*
Signora Teresa Gaudenzi sang Marinetta in *L'albergatrice vivace* at the King's Theatre on 16 December 1783. She was then advertised as making her first appearance —and that was the last time she was mentioned in the bills.

Gaudry. *See also* **GAWDRY.**

Gaudry, Master [*fl. 1789*], *actor, dancer?*
A Master Gaudry played an unspecified part in *The Battle of Hexham* at the Haymarket Theatre on 12 September 1789.

Gaudry, Miss [*fl. 1757–1769*], *singer.*
A Miss Gaudry was a concert and chorus singer who lent her talents intermittently to special benefits and other one-night stands and to brief engagements between 1757 and 1760. Her name first appeared on 17 August 1757, when she sang an "English song" as part of *A Medley Concert and Auction* put on by a band of irregulars at the Haymarket. She repeated that offering on seven successive performance nights and then, on 31 August, varied to "When all the Attic Fire was fled," from *Eliza,* which she sang at two performances, and then, on 8 September, to "Kitty or the

Female Phaeton," which she sang for several additional nights. On 12 September, on the occasion of a "Benefit for Miss Gaudry, the Marine Cook, the Lilliputian Clown, and Lilliputian Harlequin," there was also a "Dialogue by Mr and Miss Gaudry." Her interlocutor was probably Joseph Gaudry. The fact that she shared her benefit with juveniles suggests that she herself was very young.

Such performances by "Mistress Midnight"—either Christopher Smart or Theophilus Cibber—and the company were offered fairly frequently through November 1757. They were resumed on 26 December, now definitely under Cibber's management, according to his announcement of 24 December, and continued until 6 January 1758, after which Cibber began to offer more conventional bills of mainpieces and afterpieces intermittently for the rest of the season. Neither of the Gaudrys seems to have been concerned in the plays.

Miss Gaudry returned to what was now called *Mrs Midnight's Concert and Oratory* on 14 February 1760, to figure in the foolishness presented at the Haymarket by Signor Twangdillo, Mynheer Broomsticado, and Signora Tambourina. It was the last such "concert" until 8 September following, when Mrs Midnight, Signora Mimicotti, Broomsticado, and the rest rallied to Mr Gaudry's benefit. Miss Gaudry was not specified in the bill, unless she was the "Young Gentlewoman" who sang. Miss Gaudry had, however, been named as taking a "Vocal Part" in a concert for the benefit of Phillips and Tariot on 2 June 1760. Perhaps she spent the intervening time at Marylebone Gardens singing in burlettas, for that is where Joseph Gaudry was, we know from his benefit plea. No casts were listed in the bills of the Gardens that season.

Gaudry, Anne, later the second Mrs **John Fawcett the younger** *c. 1780–1849, actress, singer, dancer, pianist, wardrobe mistress.*

From the Collection at Parham Park, Sussex

ANNE GAUDRY

by Harlow

The 1804 and 1806 editions of Oulton's *Authentic Memoirs of the Green Room* relate a few particulars of the daughter of "the musical Mr. Joseph Gaudry, who belonged for some years to the theatre royal, Drury Lane, and who died [in 1782] when his daughter was only two years of age." *The London Stage* furnishes her performance record through 1800. The Drury Lane bill of 10 December 1787 listed "Duke of York by Miss Gawdry" in *Richard III*. She repeated that part several times. On 31 January 1788 she was the Child in the first performance of Hannah Cowley's turgid tragedy *The Fate of Sparta*, which was abandoned after nine nights. She did not appear in the bills again until 14 October 1788 when she turned up once more as the Duke of York. But though *Richard III* was announced "With new Scenes, Dresses and Decorations," it was offered only three more times that season.

Little Miss Gaudry came first to the Hay-market as the Prince of Wales in the first presentation of George Colman's popular melodrama *The Battle of Hexham*, on 11 August 1789, and the company reeled off 17 performances of the piece during the rest of the summer.

Oulton's account reported that

After having been two or three years on the stage, her mother fearing a theatrical situation was too precarious for a young woman, gave her a very fine musical education, and with the assistance of a kind friend, procured her the tuition of Mr. Clementi.

However, she continued on Drury Lane stage till the age of fourteen, when her size rendered her unfit for any business, being too tall for children's characters, and too short for young women. . . .

Her mother, says Oulton, withdrew her then from the stage and put her to piano practice again.

The record of the bills shows Anne Gaudry's theatrical apprenticeship to have been slow and uncertain, with few performances and with minor parts, in the Drury Lane company from 1790 through the spring of 1795: the Duke of York, Blunt's Boy in *Many Masks*, Black Boy in *The Way to Keep Him*, one of the Spirits in *Cymon*. Sometimes she rose, but no higher than Marietta in *The Pirates* or Ann in *Dido, Queen of Carthage*, then was submerged again in the chorus of Goatherds and Villagers in *The Mountaineers* or the choruses of *The Cherokee* or *Jack of Newbury*.

Just before her mother whisked her away from the stage, in the summer of 1795, Anne joined Colman's Haymarket troupe. And it was Colman at the Haymarket to whom she returned when, "her wishes still being bent upon a theatrical life," in Oulton's words, she was seen again in the bills in 1800. At the Haymarket she sang and acted Sam's Wife and Quashi's Wife in *Obi*, Caroline in *The Irishman in London*,

Miss Godfrey in *The Liar*, Pink in *The Young Quaker*, Narcissa in *Inkle and Yarico*, Miss Godfrey in *The Liar*, and Rachel in *The Prisoner at Large*. For those exertions she earned 15s. per week in 1789–90 and £1 from 1790–91 to 1793–94. There are in the Drury Lane account books for 1791–92 and 1792–93 many partial and occasional payments to her for dancing, e.g., 10 March 1792 "Miss Gaudry 3 nights dancing 1.7.6." Doane's *Musical Directory* in 1794 listed "Miss Gawdry," a singer, as resident in Craven Buildings, Drury Lane, and as participant in the spring oratorios at Drury Lane Theatre.

Perhaps her pianistic talent was exercised more than once in concert, but only one such venture is now known. For Bannister's benefit at the Haymarket on 3 August 1797 there was heard, among other attractions, "A concerto by Dussek played on the Grand Piano Forte, by Miss Gaudry." It was said to be her first appearance "in public," the claim referring only, no doubt, to her piano playing. The *Monthly Mirror* for June 1800 praised her singing and gave us our only glimpse of her person and personality: a "pleasing countenance, a light and elegant figure, and a voice of much tenderness and delicacy."

Miss Gaudry was signed on by Harris at Covent Garden early in the nineteenth century, and there her employments were much the same as they had been at the Haymarket. About 1806 she married the younger John Fawcett, whose first wife had died in 1796. Anne and John Fawcett had at least three children—two sons, one of whom became a clergyman, and a daughter. Shortly after her marriage Anne Gaudry Fawcett succeeded Mrs Kemble in the management of the Covent Garden wardrobe at £3 weekly. The Covent Garden account books show her to have been still so employed in 1821–22, and James Winston recorded for her a salary of "5 or 6£" for some function at the Haymarket in the summer of 1817.

Fawcett died in 1837, leaving Anne most of his property, including "the Garrick Medal presented to me by the Covent Garden Theatrical fund," which he had chaired so long. Anne's letter of 10 December 1837 to the Fund, now in the Garrick Club, concerning her own application for a dividend, added "I acknowledge most gratefully being in possession of perfect health."

Anne Gaudry Fawcett died on 13 October 1849. Her husband's will had mentioned "the portrait of myself and Wife painted by Harlowe." That portrait, by G. H. Harlow, shows Anne as Mrs Fawcett and is at Parham Park, along with another painting by Harlow of her three sons, the Masters Fawcett.

Gaudry, Joseph I. *d. 1782, singer, actor, dancer, music copyist.*

Joseph Gaudry was probably that Gaudry who sang "The Lark Concerto" in a *Medley Concert* given by Theophilus Cibber's band of buffoons at the Haymarket on 12 September 1757 for the "Benefit of Miss Gaudry, the Marine Cook, the Lilliputian Clown, and Lilliputian Harlequin." Joseph Gaudry and a Miss Gaudry (who was not Anne) also spoke "a Dialogue." Though that occasion was the first in which Gaudry appeared in the bills, similar entertainments, in many of which Miss Gaudry had figured, had been given throughout that summer and the previous one. Their "Dialogue" was repeated at *An Impromptu Faragolio* on 26 September.

Joseph Gaudry was very likely also that Gaudry who sang in a series of burlettas in the Great Room at Marylebone Gardens in the summers of 1759 and 1760. On 16 April 1759 the Pergolesi *La serva padrona* was performed "By Particular Desire," and played over 30 times during the summer season. From 10 May it alternated with the equally popular *La cicisbea alla moda* ("vocal parts by Signora Seratina, Miss Glanville, Reinhold, Gaudry"). Gaudry had also

secured the part of Pandolfo in the burletta *The Tutor* at Drury Lane, but it failed after its first offering, on 14 December 1759.

La serva padrona performances resumed at the opening of Marylebone Gardens on 3 June 1760, and there were more than two dozen repetitions. *La stratagemma* ("By Sga Saratina, Reinhold, Gaudry, &c.") was given some 18 times, from 18 June, and was followed by a dozen presentations, from 10 July, of *La cicisbeo alla moda.*

No casts were cited for *La serva padrona* in either season, but Gaudry shared his benefit with Miss Glanville when the opera was performed on 16 August 1759, and it is reasonable to assume that he sang in all three productions that summer. He may have thought that he had participated enough to earn a benefit in the summer of 1760. When he did not get one (Miss Glanville and Signora Seratina did) he induced friends to organize one for him at the Haymarket Theatre: "Benefit for Gaudry and Mrs Midnight [Christopher Smart]," read the bill of 8 September; "Mr Gaudry hopes to have the favour of the company of Ladies and Gentlemen, as he has been deprived of the Benefit at Marybone Gardens." He sang "The Echo of Anacreon" and offered "a Rhapsody on the Death of General Wolfe." Also, he was named, along with Reinhold and Signora Seratina, when *La serva padrona* was transferred to the Haymarket on 14 July 1761 to play some two dozen times through 25 August. Moreover, Gaudry had been one of the principals, with Reinhold and Mrs Vernon, at the Haymarket opening on 23 June 1761 in what was now billed as *The Stratagem*; and he sang in that burletta a dozen times that season. From 28 July through 7 August he, Reinhold, and Sga Seratina were the principal singers in *The Ridiculous Guardian*, "A new English Comic Burletta from the Italian," music by Hasse; and on 13, 14, and 15 August the same principals figured in *The Co-*

quette, another translation, with Galuppi's music. On 22 August Gaudry not only sang, in a concert with Reinhold, Signora Seratina, and Mrs Smith, but concluded the program by dancing a minuet with Miss Twist.

After the Haymarket's summer season of 1761 the Gaudry name did not appear in a London theatrical notice for a decade. There were, however, two male Gaudrys, J. and R., in Roger Kemble's company playing at Coventry, Worcester, Droitwych, Bromgrove, and Bath between August 1766 and June 1768. At least one was singing at Salisbury in 1768, and the poetic critical dialogue *Candour*, published there that year, came down on one of the Gaudrys rather roughly

> GAUDRY *no Marks of real Merit brings*
> *The Creature cannot speak—he sweetly sings—*
> *Strong Affectation, superficial Art,*
> *Mark ev'ry Line, and mangle ev'ry Part:*
> *Yet, in an Age like this, he still must please,*
> *He sings with Taste, with Judgement, and Ease.*

Some Gaudry sang at Bristol in 1769.

The Gaudry who next appeared in London was presumably Joseph, judging from a number of circumstances. The Covent Garden bill for 6 June 1771 carried a program of "Catches and Glees. Under the direction of Dr Arne," who had assembled "a considerable number of the best 'catch' singers and instrumental performers." Gaudry shared billing with Mrs Scott, Mrs Woodman, Phillips, and Mrs Barthélemon.

Joseph Gaudry did not appear in any published London record for another five years. It was he who appeared from time to time each season in Drury Lane's musical productions from December 1776 through 29 May 1781. But he was also playing engagements out of London. There is a notation dated "3 Jany 1781" in the Committee

Books of the Norwich Theatre: "Ordd that the Treasurer pays a Bill of one pound six shills & three pence to Mr J. I. Gawdry unless the same had been before allowed to Mr Griffith."

Gaudry's first exertion for Drury Lane —one voice among many which intoned the dirge for the elaborate funeral procession of Juliet—was typical of his services. He earned £2 10*s*. weekly in 1776–77 as the Falstaff of *Harlequin's Invasion* and as one of a chorus of Spirits in *The Tempest*. He was also, however, assigned the inconsiderable role of Sir Harry (later called Sir Toby) Bumper in the first production, on 8 May 1777, of Sheridan's *School for Scandal*.

Gaudry was chorus-bound for most of his Drury Lane tenure, rising only occasionally to parts like Mat o' th' Mint in *The Beggar's Opera*, Steady in *The Quaker*, Merlin or the Daemon of Revenge in *Cymon*, Scander in *Selima and Azor*, Serjeant Drill in *The Camp*, Trusty in *The Election*, Don Diego in *The Padlock*, the second Sailor in *Fortunatus*, and the title role in the afterpiece *Belphagor*. He was employed occasionally in warbling entr'acte songs— "Poor Thomas Day" or "How Merrily we Live" or *"Beviamo tutti tre"*—and he regularly earned small sums for copying music at the theatre from 1778 through 1780. Which Gaudry—Joseph or Richard—was singing in concert at the Edinburgh Musical Society on 8 March 1782? Both were in town.

Joseph Gaudry died at Edinburgh on 2 April 1782, according to the Fawcett notebook in the Folger Library. Ralph Wewitzer in his *A Brief Chronology of Actors* (1817) also assigned April as the month. The usually authoritative record of the Drury Lane theatrical fund, copied by James Winston, also in the Folger Library, said 2 October but gave no first name. The *Authentic Memoirs of the Green Room* (1804, 1806) called Joseph Gaudry the father of the talented actress, dancer, and musician Anne Gaudry, later the second wife of the younger John Fawcett.

Gaudry, Richard   *d. 1803?, singer, actor, composer.*

According to *Grove's Dictionary*, which invokes lines in the poem *Candour*, Richard Gaudry and his wife were playing and singing with strollers at Salisbury in 1768. But it is by no means clear that that pair were not Joseph Gaudry and his wife. We know from the manuscript ledger record of Roger Kemble's company, now at Harvard, that both "J. and R." Gaudry were at Coventry, Worcester, Droitwych, Bromgrove, and Bath between 18 August 1766 and early April 1768. J. was there until 31 May, but "Gaudry left the company clandestinely Apr 4, 1768." Grove believes that Richard and his spouse were again at Salisbury in 1776, citing the credit on the libretto of *The Perplexed Lovers, or The Double Marriage* (though Nicoll's "Hand-list" says "Music selected by *G.* Gaudry"). However, Clark, in *The Irish Stage in the County Towns*, located Richard Gaudry at the Capel Street Theatre in Dublin in 1773 and at a theatre in Kilkenny on 22 July and 14 August 1776. There is a probability of confusion with Joseph Gaudry at one or several of those times and places. *The Sprightly Horn*, as sung by a Mr Gaudry, was published in Dublin about 1775, according to the *Catalogue of Printed Music in the British Museum*. W. J. Lawrence, in a note to his article "Eighteenth-Century Magazine Music" in the October 1911 issue of *The Musical Antiquary*, cited the publication of *Corydon. A song* "by R. Gaudry" in Dublin in April 1776 and added that "Gaudry was then singing and acting at Crow Street" Theatre, Dublin. Lawrence's transcriptions in the University of Cincinnati library place Richard at the Fishamble Street Music Hall, Dublin, in 1777. Richard Gaudry was very likely in London in 1780, for on 19 June at Sadler's Wells was performed his *Riddle-me-re, or,*

The Serjeant Taylor. But Dibdin remembered Richard Gaudry's singing at Edinburgh in the 1781–82 season. Mrs Norma Armstrong finds Richard Gaudry on the bill of Edinburgh's Theatre Royal, Shakespeare Square, for 15 December 1781, as Hecate in *Macbeth* and on that for 13 March 1782 as Thomas in *Thomas and Sally*. In between those dates he played a variety of roles, including Amiens in *As You Like It*, Aubrey in *The Fashionable Lover*, Blandford in *Oroonoko*, Macheath in *The Beggar's Opera*, Careless in *The School for Scandal*, Don Antonio in *The Duenna*, Don Diego in *The Padlock*, Hawthorn in *Love in a Village*, Henry in *The Deserter*, the title role in *Robinson Crusoe*, Sealand in *The Conscious Lovers*, Sileno in *Midas*, and Tom Tug in *The Waterman*.

From Edinburgh he apparently went on to Dublin, for a "Mr Guadrey," certainly Richard, was advertised at the Haymarket Theatre in London as being from the Irish capital when he sang Sir Felix Friendly in *The Agreeable Surprise* on 31 May 1783. He was the original Twig in John O'Keeffe's *The Young Quaker* on 26 July. He sang, with Wood and Brett, when a musical oleo called *A Fête* was given on 1 August, and on 13 August he was both the original Clump in John Dent's afterpiece *The Receipt Tax* and King of the Fiddlers in *Chrononhotonthologos*. He finished his first full summer season of London appearances on 28 August, again in a new piece, Stuart and O'Keeffe's *Gretna Green*, but in a part unspecified.

Gaudry must have returned to the provinces in the winter season of 1783–84, for he was named on no London playbills again until 22 March 1784, at that time playing La France in *The English Merchant* at the Haymarket in a special benefit for Mrs Cuyler. He resumed his summer Haymarket appearances on 14 June 1784 and sang and acted there also in the summers of 1785 and 1786. In the winter season of 1784–85 he achieved his first few performances at a

London patent house, appearing at Covent Garden Theatre for the first time on 28 September 1784 as Pedro in *Catherine and Petruchio* in a special "Benefit for the Widow and Children of the unfortunate Mr Linton," a Covent Garden band member who had been murdered by robbers. For 1785–86 only one performance by Gaudry at Covent Garden was recorded, on 18 January 1786, and he was on only ten times in 1786–87. But surviving accounts show that he was paid £1 5s. weekly, so doubtless he was sharing in the chorus singing to earn his pay. At his only known benefit he was, on 2 June 1787, given tickets to sell, along with 11 other singers and dancers.

Richard Gaudry joined the ill-starred adventure of Palmer at the Royalty Theatre in 1787, and surviving bills of that house show a Gaudry to have been a principal singer in the musical pastoral *The Birthday* on 3 July and 31 October 1787, Thespis in *Hobson's Choice* on 3 July, Macaroni in *Harlequin Mungo* sometime in November, and Jupiter in *Apollo Turn'd Stroller*, a musical pasticcio, on 3 December 1787. He played Macaroni again on 1 January 1788 and danced *The Milk Maid* with Miss Burnett on 9 September. Following that date the performance record is blank until 30 September, when Gaudry played Sir Peter Pride in the afterpiece *Barnaby Brittle* in a special performance at the Haymarket. So far as the bills show, he performed nowhere else in London that season, nor was he ever again cited in a London part. The Gaudry who shared tickets and was paid small sums for dancing at Drury Lane from 1792 onward was surely not Richard, but Stephen.

Perhaps Richard Gaudry had returned to Ireland. The date of his first payment of 13s. to the Irish Musical Fund was 4 April 1793 and the date of his last one was 10 March 1795, according to the Fund's subscription ledger. On 13 May 1798 the ledger mentioned the discontinuance of some assistance the Fund had given him, his health having improved by that date. On 1 June 1801 he was granted half a guinea per week "until further notice," but on 6 July that allowance was discontinued. He was recorded as present at a meeting of the Fund's governors on 4 January 1802.

Gaudry was a journeyman chorus-singer and actor of small parts in farces and melodic comedies. There were only a few momentous incidents in his professional life in London. He had sung the "American Ballad" (that is, "Yankee Doodle") as the Ballad Singer in the first performances, on 26 December 1786 and after, of Miles Peter Andrews's *The Enchanted Castle*. He was the original French Innkeeper in O'Keeffe's *Fontainbleau*. His other identifiable assignments were seldom very important: the Counsellor in *The Lawyer's Panic*, an Irishman in *The Apprentice*, Don Quixote in *Barataria*, Damaetas in *Midas*, Mercury in *Poor Vulcan*, the Cook in *The Devil to Pay*, Count Pierpoint in *He Wou'd Be a Soldier*, De Jarsey in *The Maid of Bath*, an unspecified part in the first performance of Leonard Macnally's *Richard Coeur de Lion*, a member of the numerous chorus singing the "Solemn Dirge" in Juliet's funeral procession or in *Macbeth*.

The *Catalogue of Printed Music in the British Museum* lists the following of Richard Gaudry's works: *And are all thy vows come to this?* "Set by Mr Gaudry, the Words by Miss E. C. Keene" (1780?); *Hope. A favorite Sonnett* (1795?); *June. A favourite Song* "sung by Mr Burket at Ranelagh" (1785?); and *Ye Shepherds ye Nymphs and ye Swains* "the Words by Miss E. C. Keene" (1780?). In 1795 a *Collection of Masonic Songs* was published by "Brother Richard Gaudry."

Richard Gaudry's first wife, identified by the *General Magazine* as the wife of the performer at the Royalty, died at their house in Mansel Street, London, on 15 March 1788. The 1794 report of Dublin's Deputy Keeper of Public Records cited the marriage, at some time in 1790, of Richard Gaudry to Louisa Verschoyle. Account books of Covent Garden Theatre show a Mrs "Gawdry" earning £2 weekly in 1803–4, £2 10s. in 1804–5, and £3 in 1805–6.

But the Minute Books of the Governors of the Irish Musical Fund show that on 27 July 1803 a Mrs Gaudry was granted one guinea until the Society should settle her weekly allowance, and perhaps she was Louisa Vershoyle Gaudry. The allowance was fixed on 1 August 1803 at half a guinea per week. She was a claimant on 5 January 1807 for 11s. 4d. per week. On 6 July 1807 she was granted two guineas; on 3 July 1808 she obtained two guineas for one of her children who was seriously ill. The fragmentary list shows her receiving £29 1s. 6d. per annum from 1809 through 1815. In 1816 the failure of the Grand Canal, in which the Fund securities were invested, caused the suspension of her pension. In 1817 payments of 12 guineas per annum were resumed. There is another cumulative record in 1822 showing payments of £13 13s. to 23 July, when they break off abruptly.

The Richard Gaudry who was proposed as a professional subscriber to the Irish Musical Fund on 21 June 1822 was no doubt Richard Otto Gaudry, the organist of St Ann's, Dublin, and, according to W. J. Lawrence, the son of the Richard of this entry.

Gaudry, Mrs Richard the first *d. 1788, singer, actress.*

The first Mrs Richard Gaudry, according to the brief notice of her husband (erroneously called "Joseph Gawdry") in *The Thespian Dictionary* (1805) "Assisted in choruses, &c." and died on 15 March 1788. The death date is confirmed by a notice in the *Morning Chronicle* of 18 March and by the *General Magazine* of March, which called her the wife of Richard Gaudry "of the Royalty." The chorus singing was at Drury Lane from April 1778 to December

1780, during which time she joined her husband and others in the choruses to *The Tempest* and in several pantomimes.

Mrs Gaudry also sang and acted at Edinburgh in 1781–82, where she was allowed several named parts: Altea in *Rule a Wife and Have a Wife*, Inis in *The Wonder*, Jenny Diver in *The Beggar's Opera*, a Lady in *The Belle's Stratagem*, Lady Freelove in *The Jealous Wife*, Mademoiselle Florivel in *The Deuce is in Him*, Miss Bridgemore in *The Fashionable Lover*, Mrs Fulmer in *The West Indian*, and a Shepherdess in *Robinson Crusoe*.

Gaudry, Stephen [*fl.* 1792–1800], *dancer.*

On 21 January 1792 the Drury Lane account book, now in the Folger Library, carried the entry "Gaudry 5 nights for dancing 1. 12. 6." "Gawdry" appeared with 15 house functionaries and minor musicians on a list of those delivering tickets, on 29 May 1792. There are entries for 3 and 24 March 1792 and 12 January 1793, for 10s., 7s., 7s. 6d., and £1 10s., respectively. On 9 February 1793 the entry was "Gaudry & Edwin 8 nights each 2/0/0."

A Gaudry, specialty unspecified but possibly the same, was put on the pay list for £1 per week on 25 April 1795. He was still on the list for 3s. 4d. per day, which was confirmed (£1 per week) on 3 December. He was again on the company list—but with no salary and no specialty given—in 1797, and again in July, 1800. "Gawdry" was with 19 others on a ticket list on 3 July 1799.

Gaudry had died sometime before December 1802 when the actress and singer Ann Gaudry was identified as the "relict of the late Mr. Gaudry of Drury Lane Theatre." He was called Stephen Gaudry by *The Gentleman's Magazine* in January 1803.

Gaudry, Mrs Stephen, Ann *d. 1802, actress, singer.*

The Mrs Gaudry who died in October

1802 was described by the *Monthly Mirror* of December 1802 as the "relict of the late Mr Gaudry of Drury Lane Theatre." The *Gentleman's Magazine* of January 1803 furnished his first name, Stephen. The only male Gaudry at Drury Lane at the end of the eighteenth century was the dancer who is recorded sporadically in the theatre's account books from January 1792 through July 1800. Mrs Stephen Gaudry was sometimes paid in 1789–90 as "Mrs A. Gawdry," otherwise simply as "Mrs Gaudry" (or "Gawdry").

Mrs Gaudry's first opportunity in London was at the Haymarket in the summer of 1787, so far as the bills show. She assumed the part of Margaret in *Much Ado About Nothing* on 25 May. Unhappily, an announcement in the following day's *Public Advertiser* acquainted the public with the decision to shut down the theatre until the end of the season at the winter houses (15 June). There were not enough actors to staff the Haymarket until that time. Very likely Mrs Gaudry was given walk-ons or chorus bits before she was next named in the bills. On 14 August, at the treasurer William Jewell's benefit performance, Meadows, Chapman, Matthews, Mrs Forster, Mrs Edwards—and Mrs Gaudry—sang a "Musical Epilogue."

Mrs Gaudry was idle until the following summer when she again sought work with the Haymarket company and was allowed to be a Coach Passenger in the first five successful performances of George Colman's new *Ways and Means* on 10 July and afterward. She was the Cobbler's Wife in Wewitzer and Invill's new pantomime *The Gnome* on 5 August 1788, a Country Lass in *Love and War* on 13 August, and the original Margaretta in O'Keeffe's farce *A Key to the Lock*, which was "attempted to be represented, [but] . . . not heard out," according to the *Public Advertiser*.

In the next season Mrs Gaudry's only recorded theatrical effort was as one of the many chorus singers in the some 20 performances of Colman's *The Battle of Hex-*

ham after it came out on 11 August. But Mrs Gaudry, like many of the singers and dancers who made the musical drama of the late century possible, served many more times than the prompter gave her credit for when he prepared printer's text for the playbills. That is graphically shown by a paylist in the account books of Drury Lane Theatre, where she sang in the winter season of 1789–90. From 4 November 1789 through 11 June 1790 there were entered 16 payments to Mrs Gaudry at the rate of five shillings per night, involving 101 nights, in a season totalling 197 nights. She was paid at the same rate in 1790–91 and through 1799–1800.

Mrs Gaudry was absent from the Haymarket in 1790 but returned in 1791, was there again in 1792, and returned each year through 1801. She was also briskly employed during the winter of 1793–94 when Colman took advantage of the disbanding of the Drury Lane company during the rebuilding of that house and kept the Haymarket open all year.

Though principally a chorus singer, Mrs Gaudry was, as has been noted, occasionally given an identifiable part. Some of them were a Priestess in *The Cave of Trophonius*, Madelon in *The Surrender of Calais*, a Bacchant in *Comus*, a Bridesmaid in *Royal Clemency*, and Anna in *Dido, Queen of Carthage*.

Gaun. *See* CAUN.

Gaurie, Miss [fl. 1728], *actress*.

Miss Gaurie played Gypsy in *The Rivals*, an entertainment produced by Mrs Violante on 21 February 1728 at the Haymarket Theatre.

Gauron, Mr [fl. 1789–1803], *dancer, actor*.

Mr Gauron (or Gourion, Gorion, Jouron) was first noticed in London bills when, on 12 May 1789 at the Royal Circus, he played Monsieur Scaroon in *I Don't Know What!* On 9 April 1792 he was at

Sadler's Wells in the cast of *Meadea's Kettle,* and during the summer of that year he played a Valet and a Peasant in *La Forêt Noire* at the same house. Gauron continued at the Wells during the summers through 1797, appearing as a Commissioner in *Sans Culottes,* Cochon in *The Honours of War,* a Mariner in *William Tell,* and Hubba in *Alfred the Great.*

He had joined the Covent Garden company in 1792–93, appearing as a Cook in *Harlequin's Museum* on 26 December 1792 and a Creolian Insurgent in *The Governor* on 11 March 1793. At the same theatre in 1797–98 he danced one of the Domestics in *Oscar and Malvina.*

Gauron moved to Drury Lane in 1798–99 and was noticed in the bills somewhat more frequently, though he still played only minor roles. Through June 1803 at Drury Lane he was assigned such parts as a Slave in *Blue-Beard,* a Villager in a dance called *The Scotch Ghost,* a Vassal in *Feudal Times,* and a Slave in *The Egyptian Festival.* His salary at Drury Lane was £1 weekly. During the summers of 1800 and 1801 Gauron is known to have performed at the Haymarket Theatre.

Gautherot, Louisa, née Deschamps
d. 1808, violinist.

On 27 February 1789 Madame Louisa Gautherot played a concerto on the violin at Covent Garden Theatre, the event being advertised as her second appearance in England since her arrival from Paris. The date of her first appearance has not been discovered. After her performance on 27 February Mme Gautherot appeared fairly regularly as a violin soloist at the oratorios at Covent Garden, usually playing a "concerto." On 13 May 1790 she and Mountain offered a violin and tenor duet between the acts at a regular play performance, and at Cecilia Hall in Edinburgh in July 1792 she performed with the clarinetist Mahon. Doane's *Musical Directory* of 1794 gave no street address in London for Mme

LOUISA GAUTHEROT

engraving by F. Bartolozzi, after Violet

Gautherot, but Doane mentioned her participation in the oratorios at Covent Garden. Louisa Gautherot died in 1808, remembered as among the most celebrated violinists of the 1790s. Her portrait, engraved by Bartolozzi, after P. Violet, was published in 1791. According to the *Catalogue of Engraved British Portraits in the British Museum,* Mme Gautherot's maiden name was Deschamps. A Miss Gautherot, possibly Louisa's daughter, was a music teacher living in Bedford Square in 1823.

Gautier, Mons [*fl.* 1718], *singer.*

Monsieur Gautier made his first appearance on the English stage on 3 January 1718 at the Lincoln's Inn Fields Theatre when he sang the Professor in *The Professor of Folly,* "A New Dramatick Entertainment of Vocal and Instrumental Musick after the Italian Manner, in Grotesque Characters." He was doubtless related to the dancer

Mlle Gautier who was in London at that time.

Gautier, Mlle ɪ*fl. 1717–1719*ɪ, *dancer.*

Mademoiselle Gautier, from the Opéra in Paris, made her first appearance on an English stage dancing with Dupré at Lincoln's Inn Fields on 25 October 1717. During the 1717–18 season she danced a chaconne and a *Harlequin* with Dupré from time to time, appeared in *The Prophetess*, was a Grace in *Mars and Venus*, and danced Oriana in *Amadis*. At her solo benefit on 19 February 1718 her gross receipts came to £49 6s. She remained at Lincoln's Inn Fields until the end of the 1718–19 season, repeating her role in *Amadis*.

Gawdry. *See also* **GAUDRY.**

Gawdry ɪ*fl. 1794–1795*ɪ, *doorkeeper.*
During the 1794–95 season Covent Garden Theatre paid a doorkeeper named Gawdry 15s. per week.

Gawdy. *See* **SHADWELL, MRS THOMAS.**

Gay, Mr ɪ*fl. 1794–1802*ɪ, *tailor.*
Mr Gay was one of the tailors at Drury Lane Theatre from as early as 14 April 1794 to as late as 16 September 1802, according to the theatre accounts. His salary during the entire period remained at £1 16s. weekly. The playbills noted his contribution to the preparation of the "dresses" for a number of spectacle productions during the late 1790s, including *The Iron Chest* on 12 March 1796, *Vortigern* on 2 April, *Mahmoud* on 30 April, *Robinson Crusoe* on 26 December, *Blue-Beard* on 16 January 1798, *Feudal Times* on 19 January 1799, *Pizzaro* on 24 May, *The Egyptian Festival* on 11 March 1800, *De Montfort* on 29 April, and, at the Haymarket Theatre, *Obi* on 2 July 1800 and *The Corsair* on 29 July 1801.

Possibly Gay was related to the John Gay who was the proprietor of the Norwich theatre from 1769 to 1786, to the actor Gay who played at York from 1770 to 1774, or to the actor Gay who performed in Philadelphia in 1789 and 1790.

Gayet, Mr ɪ*fl. 1778*ɪ, *pyrotechnist.*
The *Bristol Journal* of 7 November 1778 carried an advertisement concerning Gayet's "Grand Collection of Fireworks." The display had been postponed from 5 November to the tenth and the fireworks were to be let off on College Green. The notice indicated that Gayet had worked in London:

From the great Satisfaction Mr. GAYET'S Performances have given at Ranelagh, Vauxhall, and Marylebone, he flatters himself the Ladies and Gentlemen of this place will readily oblige him with their Company and Encouragement on the above Evening. – Tho' his Apparatus is prepared at a great expence, the Price is left to the Generosity of every Spectator.

Gayet gave his address in Bristol as at the Ship and Castle in Marsh Street and indicated that he could arrange for private displays.

Gaylard, Charles James ɪ*fl. 1749*ɪ, *actor?*
On 3 July 1749 a benefit performance of *The Fair Penitent* "By young gentlemen" was given for Charles James Gaylard at the James Street Theatre. Gaylard was possibly one of the players or the organizer of the event.

Gaynes, Mr ɪ*fl. 1770s*ɪ, *puppeteer.*
The puppeteer Mr Gaynes exhibited at the Cassino Rooms in the 1770s. He sometimes worked with the puppeteer Sharpe.

Gayward, Mr ɪ*fl. 1752*ɪ, *actor.*
Mr Gayward played Harlequin in *Harle-*

quin Triumphant at Bence's booth at South-wark Fair on 22 September 1752.

"Gazette, Sir Gregory." *See* SHUTER, EDWARD.

"Gazette, Tim." *See* COSTOLLO, PATRICK.

Gearing, Mr [*fl.* 1789–1797], *house servant?*

The Drury Lane accounts list a Mr Gearing as a staff member on 19 September 1789 at a salary of 9*s.* weekly. His function was not noted, but he was probably a house servant. His name was mentioned again in the accounts in 1797.

Geery, Mary. *See* KNIGHT, MARY.

Gehot, Joseph *b. c.* 1755, *violist, composer.*

Joseph Gehot was born in Liège, Belgium, about 1755 (Grove suggests about 1750 and other sources say about 1756, but Gehot was 25 in July 1780.) He traveled in France and Germany before coming to England. Since two of Gehot's songs were introduced by Shield in *The Cobler of Castlebury* at Covent Garden Theatre on 27 April 1779, perhaps Gehot was by that time in London. He was certainly in the city on 2 July 1780, when he was recommended for membership in the Royal Society of Musicians. His record showed that he had studied and practised music for a livelihood for over seven years, that he was married but had no children, that he was 25 years old, and that he played the tenor (viola) at Ranelagh Gardens, the Ladies' Concerts, the Pantheon, and Bach's concerts. Gehot's date of admission into the Society is not known.

By 1783 Gehot was playing in the band at the King's Theatre; in May and June 1784 he participated in the Handel Memorial Concerts at Westminster Abbey and the Pantheon; his burletta *The Maid's Last*

Shift was presented at the Royal Circus in 1787; and in the summer of 1789 at Astley's Amphitheatre Gehot's music for *The Marriage by Stratagem* and *The Royal Naval Review at Plymouth* was heard. He also wrote music for *Royal Grove, She Would be a Soldier*, and *The Enraged Musician*, all of which were performed at the Royal Circus or Astley's before 1790. He was doubtless the "Gepot" who played in the St Paul's concert in May 1790. During the 1790–91 season Gehot played at the Pantheon and at the King's Theatre.

He left for America in 1792, performing first in New York and then settling in Philadelphia by 1794 and serving as a theatrical musician. Grove says that Gehot died in obscurity; his death date is not known. Though some sources call him Jean or John Gehot, he signed himself Joseph in 1780. Gehot published a number of duets, trios, quartets, and military pieces, and he wrote two treatises, one on theory in 1784 and the other, *The Complete Instructor for every Instrument*, in 1790.

Gell, Master [*fl.* 1795–1801], *actor.*

Master Gell, the son of William Gell perhaps, played the Page to Regan in *King Lear* at Drury Lane Theatre on 20 November 1795. He was still acting that role in 1800, and he appeared at the Haymarket Theatre in the summer of 1801.

Gell, William [*fl.* 1793–1800], *dresser, watchman, actor.*

The William Gell who was paid £1 11*s.* 6*d.* on 4 July 1793 for "Dressing Soldiers at Mr. Colemans"—that is, at the Haymarket Theatre—was probably the same Gell who was cited in the Haymarket accounts several times in 1794 and 1795 as a watchman. His salary as watchman was 12*s.*, and he continued in that capacity to at least 17 October 1795. On 2 July 1800 at the Haymarket Gell swelled the cast of *The Jew and the Doctor* by playing one of the Planter's Servants. William was probably the father of Master Gell, who acted from 1795 to 1801.

Gèllier, Master [*fl. 1743*], *dancer.*

According to Egerton MS 2320 at the British Museum, one of the dancers at Drury Lane in 1743 was Master "Gèllier."

Gelmeena, Signor [*fl. 1777*], *puppeteer, musician.*

With the conjuror Breslaw, Signor Gelmeena and other members of an Italian troupe performed in Cockspur Street in late March 1777. The program included a droll piece called *Musica Arabatia*, in which Gelmeena appeared with Armalena and Nicola (a whistler). From 19 June to 15 July Breslaw and the Italians played in the Great Room in Panton Street; Chinese shadow puppets were presented by Gelmeena, Brunn, and Ambrose.

Gemea, Mrs Tobias. *See* CHETWOOD, RICHABELLA.

Geminiani, Francesco   *1687–1762, violinist, composer.*

Grove states that Francesco Geminiani was baptized in Lucca on 5 December 1687 (earlier sources had suggested the musician was born about 1666). Geminiani studied under Carlo Ambrogio Lonati, called "Il Gobbo," in Milan and under Alessandro Scarlatti and Corelli in Rome. He then went to Naples and was made leader of the band there, but, according to Barbella's account as retold by Dr Burney, Geminiani "was soon discovered to be so wild and unsteady a timist, that instead of regulating and conducting the band, he threw it into confusion; as none of the performers were able to follow him in his *tempo rubato*, and other unexpected accelerations and relaxations of measure." In his native Lucca from 1707 to 1710 Geminiani played violin in the band of the Signoria.

He came to London in 1714 and was quickly accepted as a teacher, composer, and

Harvard Theatre Collection

FRANCESCO GEMINIANI

engraving by McArdell, after Jenkins

virtuoso performer (though he did not play frequently either in public or private). His Opus 1, consisting of 12 violin sonatas, was published in London in 1716. Matthew Dubourg was one of Geminiani's earliest pupils, and over the years the Italian master taught, among others, Joseph Kelway, Cecilia Young, Michael Christian Festing, Charles Avison, and William Savage. He also became interested in art and set himself up as a dealer in paintings, but Dr Burney said Geminiani had insufficient knowledge or taste in art, and at one point his underhanded practice of passing off copies for originals and assigning false names to pictures landed him in prison, from which he was extricated by one of his pupils, Lord Essex.

The *Session of Musicians* (May 1724), which imagines Apollo judging the virtues of London composers, speaks only of Geminiani as a performer:

Next him Ge[mi]n[ia]ni *did appear,*
With Bow in Hand and much a sob'rer
        air;
He simper'd at the God, as who would
        say,
You can't deny me, if you hear me
        play.
Quickly his meaning Phoebus *under-*
        stood,
Allowing what he did was very good;
And since his Fame all Fiddlers else
        surpasses,
He set him down first Treble at Parnas-
        sus.

In fact, Geminiani had not composed much since his arrival in London; his Opus 1, of 1716, was not followed by Opus 2, six concertos, until 1732.

The violinist performed on occasion for the Academy of Ancient Music and provided them with music of his to perform, and during the life of the Philo Musicae Society from 1724 to 1727 he was the musical director at their concerts held at the Queen's Head Tavern near Temple Bar. Despite his infrequent public appearances, Geminiani was acknowledged London's greatest violin virtuoso during the 1720s. In 1728 Lord Essex obtained for the violinist the post of Master and Composer of the State Music of Ireland, but Geminiani did not take the position. He either handed it over or saw it handed over to his student Dubourg.

In 1731 Geminiani conducted a weekly concert at Hickford's Room, playing first violin. The following year Arrigoni and San Martini conducted the performances, though they were still called "Geminiani's Concert." When the violinist went to Dublin in December 1733 he set up a Great Room in Dame Street where Italian concerts were offered through 1740. In Dublin Geminiani also accepted students and spent some time composing and writing *Rules for Playing in True Taste*, published in 1739, and *Guida armonica*, published in 1742.

He returned to London in 1740 and held benefit concerts at the Haymarket Theatre in 1741 and on 19 March 1742. Latreille reported that Geminiani was living in Dufour's Court, Broad Street, Soho, in the spring of 1745. It was rumored in March of that year that he would perform at the Haymarket; an epigram appeared on 2 March in the *General Advertiser*:

When Orpheus, dying, sought his native
        skies
Snatching his bow, he thus in transport
        cries:
'This bow, long lost, extinct its power of
        sound
'Shall, by an artist be in Albion Found
'Touch'd by his hand, new joys it shall
        inspire,
'And wond'ring Britons think they hear
        my lyre.'

His playing was much praised, but his conducting at concerts still left much to be desired. He conducted a *Concert Spirituale* at Drury Lane during Lent, 1749, which was much applauded, Burney said, but the violinist's unsteady manner and the under-rehearsed quality of the performing distressed judicious auditors.

At Drury Lane on 11 April 1750 Geminiani again conducted a concert. A puff for it had appeared in the *General Advertiser* on 16 March:

When Mr Geminiani came first over here, the great excellence of the Violin was unknown in this kingdom, and the great improvement our countrymen have made on that instrument is entirely owing to him. The valuable works he has produc'd in the instrumental way, are greater indications of his merit, as an author, than any I can offer in his behalf; this is the only Benefit he ever made [sic], therefore I persuade myself that the Public (who are justly famous for their Generosity on such laudable occasions) will give him the encouragement his Merit deserves.

At the benefit Geminiani performed a concerto and a solo of his own composition and conducted the orchestra.

Courtesy of the Royal Society of Musicians

FRANCESCO GEMINIANI

attributed to Hudson

He then went to Paris for five years, where he continued composing, one of his pieces being *La Forêt enchantée*, based on Tasso and published in 1756. The work, which was partly a scenic spectacle not unlike those produced by the designer Servandoni, was presented at the theatre in the Tuileries on 31 March 1754. Geminiani returned to London the following year and then went to Ireland in 1759 to serve as violin master at Cootehill. In 1760 he visited Dubourg in Dublin and there lost, through a robbery at his house in College Green, the manuscript treatise on music on which he had been working. However, he had published, in 1748, a useful work on *The Art of Playing the Violin*, which set down the principles established by Corelli; the treatise was the first thing of its kind. On 3 March 1760 in Dublin Geminiani held a benefit concert at which he played several solos, but he was getting on in years

and appeared less frequently than he had before. On 17 September 1762 Francesco Geminiani died in Dublin. He was buried at St Andrew's on 19 September. The report that he was aged 96 years when he died seems to have been a gross exaggeration. His music continued popular after his death, and "Geminiani's Great Room in Spring Gardens, Dame Street," in Dublin, was still in operation as late as 1782, when Chinese shadow puppets were exhibited there. The *Catalogue of Printed Music in the British Museum* contains an extensive list of the violinist's compositions which, according to Burney, are full of tricks but lacking in cohesion.

Portraits of Geminiani include:

1. By William Hoare, c. 1735. Present location unknown.

2. By Howard. Present location unknown.

3. By Thomas Hudson (?). At the Royal Society of Musicians.

4. By T. Jenkins. In the collection of the Earl of Wemyss. Engraving by T. McArdell. An engraving by C. Grignion, after McArdell, was published in Hawkins's *General History*, 1776.

5. By Latham, 1737. Present location unknown.

6. By an unknown artist. At the Royal College of Music.

7. Engraving by Bettelini, c. 1805, after Luigi Scotti's painting of a group of composers.

8. Engraving by P. Aveline, after E. Bouchardon. A medallion supported by the Genius of Music and the three Graces, with Apollo above.

Gendon, Mlle ₁fl. 1742₁, *dancer.*

On 21 September 1742 and subsequent dates through 8 October Mademoiselle Gendon participated in a *Tyrolean* Dance at Drury Lane.

"General Jackoo." *See* **"Jackoo, General."**

Genovini, Carlo [*fl.* *1761–1762*], *pyrotechnist, machinist.*

The Italian pyrotechnist Carlo Genovini (sometimes Genuini or Genorinij), identified as an "artificer from Rome," exhibited a mechanical contrivance at the Haymarket Theatre on 29 April 1761 which consisted of a globe that separated into four parts to reveal the inventor in the middle. Prices were advanced for that night only to a half-guinea in the boxes, 5*s.* in the pit, and 3*s.* in the gallery, and Genovini advertised his hopes for a good house, for he had "performed in most of the principal courts of Europe." Several months later at Ranelagh Gardens on 12 June 1761, at the conclusion of Dr Arne's masque *The Judgment of Paris*, Genovini displayed a fireworks entertainment called the *Chinese Festival*, for which he had promised to

avoid common effects such as rockets and to "confine himself to works of real ingenuity."

A light ediface will be fixed near the Chinese Temple, and a boat will sail at the end of the canal, containing several persons performing on musical instruments, the boat moving to the Temple, and giving fire to the ediface, it will display ingenious conceits; particularly the operations of the fireworks will change to ten different colours.

In the summer of 1762, at the Star and Garter Tavern, situated in what is now Eaton Square, Belgravia, Genovini gave regular exhibitions of fireworks, as well as a special display on 1 September in honor of the birth of the Royal Prince and on 17 July "by Desire of the Cherokee King and his Chiefs." The ingenious pyrotechnics

Public Record Office

License for GIULIO GENTILESCHI, 1660

showed stars, moving suns, "a guilloche of a varied coloured rose," cascades, and a machine, 32 feet long and 40 feet high, "painted in a theatrical manner," with Britannia triumphant on top, called "the Temple of Liberty." At that time Genovini lived at No 6, Castle Lane, Westminster. Presumably he returned to Italy soon after.

Perhaps he was related to Giuseppe Genovini, a dancer, who performed with a company of Italian burletta players in Dublin from January to July 1761 and also at Smock Alley Theatre in that city in 1761–62.

Gentileschi, Giulio [fl. 1660], impresario.

On 22 October 1660 Charles II granted Giulio Gentileschi, the son of the painter Orazio Gentileschi who had served Charles I as a picture buyer, a license to build a theatre, import a company of singers, and offer "opere musicale, con machine mutationi di scene et altre apparenze." The project apparently never materialized.

Gentili, Filippo Giacomo [fl. 1793–1797], dancer, choreographer.

The full name of the dancer Filippo Giacomo Gentili is on the libretto of La secchia rapita, which was published in 1793 at Milan, where he was a member of the opera company. Announced as from that city, Gentili made his first appearance in London at the King's Theatre on 5 February 1793 in a dance called Les Epoux du tempe, a piece in which he continued to perform throughout the season. On 26 February he danced Mercury in a heroic pantomime ballet, Venus and Adonis. That ballet was repeated on 9 April 1793, when he also appeared in La Faune infidèle. On 23 April Gentili danced the role of Lesbian in Ifigenia in Aulide. With Mlle Millard, the Gardels, and others, he offered a new dance divertisement on 8 June.

Gentili remained at the King's Theatre for four more seasons of similar work. In 1793–94 he appeared in two of Noverre's ballets, Adélaide; ou, La Bergère des Alpes and L'Union des bergères, and also in D'Egville's Le Bon Prince. At Drury Lane Theatre on 2 July 1794, at a special benefit for the relief of the families of the men who had fallen in the recent military actions under Lord Howe, Gentili performed with other dancers from the opera in a ballet by D'Egville composed for Sheridan's afterpiece The Glorious First of June. On 21 July 1794 Gentili was paid £66 13s. 4d. by the Drury Lane treasurer.

In 1795–96 Gentili received a salary of £500 from the King's Theatre. He also danced at Drury Lane in Little Peggy's Love, a new ballet "in the Scots' Stile," for the benefit of Stephen Storace's widow.

In his final season in London, 1796–97, Gentili was busy at both the King's and Drury Lane. He began the season by composing The Triumph of Love to introduce Mlle Parisot to the stage of Drury Lane. That ballet was originally intended for its first performance on 20 September 1796, but was delayed until 1 October. The press reported that the piece was "speedily produced" and promised to be very magnificent, as "no expense has been spared." On 5 October 1796 the theatre paid Gentili £10 10s. for his choreography and for dancing the role of Olimpio. His ballet The Scotch Ghost, in which he danced the role of Jamie, was first presented at Drury Lane on 29 October and was repeated throughout the season. For his composition of that piece he was paid £10 on 4 February 1797.

At Drury Lane he also danced in a revival of the spectacular afterpiece, Robinson Crusoe, which was presented 19 times between 26 December and 31 January, and danced Joseph in The Labyrinth; or, The Country Madcap, which he also devised, at its first performance on 6 March 1797; he played Scaramouch (for the first time) in a performance of Don Juan on 19 May 1797. At the King's Theatre that season

Gentili appeared in *Little Peggy's Love*, *L'Amour et Psiché*, *Apollon Berger*, *Pizarre; ou, La Coquette du Perou*, *L'Heureux Retour*, *Sapho et Phaon*, *Le Trompeur trompé*, *Le Triomphe de Cupidon*, and finally in *Acis et Galatie* on 17 June 1797. At the end of that season, evidently, Gentili returned to the Continent.

"Gentle." *See* CAUTHERLEY, SAMUEL.

"Gentleman." *See* LEWIS, WILLIAM THOMAS, and SMITH, WILLIAM 1730?–1819.

Gentleman, Francis 1728–1784, *actor, elocutionist, playwright, critic.*

Francis Gentleman was born in York Street, Dublin, on 23 October 1728. His father was an officer in the British army who had evidently been recruited as a ranker but who had after "forty years service . . . during which time he had seen many coxcombs of fortune, title, or interest, put over his head . . . obtained a Captain's commission." He was "blessed with a wife" and Francis "with a mother who by invariable conduct proved herself a worthy pattern of both characters." The words are from the preface to Gentleman's comedy *The Modish Wife*, 1775, a rambling narrative which is the chief source of information about his early activities. Its puzzling chronology is broken by critical excursions and laced with prudential morality, trite maxims, and self-serving protestation. But its main outlines, which can sometimes be proved against and often supplemented by other sources, seem firm.

Though Gentleman traces his lineage no further back than his parents, it is probable that the family was Anglo-Irish. They may have been originally from London, for the author of the anonymous *History of the Robinhood Society* (1764), whom we believe to have been Gentleman, claims that the Society's predecessor club, a "Societie for Free and Candyd Enquirie," was founded jointly by Sir Hugh Myddleton and the author's "grandfather"—who is identified only as "G.——." The claim is probably moonshine (Myddleton died in 1631), but there were many of the name of Gentleman in the parish registers of London and vicinity in the seventeenth and eighteenth centuries, including one Franciscus Gentleman, buried at St Martin-in-the-Fields on 19 September 1665.

Francis Gentleman was a sickly infant but was devotedly nursed to health and at the age of ten "or a little after" placed at school under the Rev Mr Butler in Digges Street, Dublin, where he formed an acquaintance with fellow students John Dexter and Henry Mossop, whose later careers as actors crisscrossed his own. Mossop, especially, was his close friend: "During the space of five years we were inseparable. . . ." But schooling ended early for Gentleman. "At fifteen I had the misfortune to obtain a commission in the same regiment with my father. . . ."

In the Jacobite rebellion of 1745–46 Gentleman continued on active duty but saw no battle action. Some of the time was spent in "a camp of 5000 men" at Bennet's Bridge, near Kilkenny, "which tho' a pleasing show, was certainly an idle affair, discipline being in a most relaxed state." The regiment returned to Dublin, where by then Mossop and Dexter were resident members of Trinity College. "The former complaining grievously of the narrowness of his allowance," young Francis, "in a romantic fit of friendship . . . gave him my commission, purposing to accomplish myself for the church." The arrangement was not "ratified by government." Francis remained in an army he by now detested and was ordered to take a company to Cashell, "neither the Captain nor Lieutenant attending." The youthful ensign's men plundered hen roosts all along the line of march. At Cashell the lad was befriended by Dr Price, the Archbishop of the See, who took him riding every morning to keep him from the company of his dissolute, fox-hunting brother officers.

Gentleman came next under the friendly command of Captain Henry Boyle Walsingham, son of the speaker of the House of Commons, a great rake but liberal of his wealth to poorer officers. While stationed at Kinsale, Walsingham and Gentleman decided to escape the boredom of inaction by joining a regiment being raised "for the Dutch service." The pair exchanged to a newly formed company intended for field service in 1745. The British Army was reduced to its former dimensions after the peace of Aix-la-Chapelle in 1748. Gentleman's father, who had risen to the rank of colonel, had died in 1745, and Francis, because of his transfer no longer a regular, was forced out of the service. He had "been foolish enough to give a hundred guineas for advance of rank" in the temporary regiment, and now, like so many officers all over Britain, he found himself relegated to half-pay status.

At twenty, without much formal education, but with much useless experience, he looked about for a means of existence. His father had left him only the "right to some freehold property," which he could not dispose of, being under age. He turned to Thomas Sheridan, manager at Smock Alley Theatre, who gave him "a most gentleman-like reception," casting him first as Aboan in *Oroonoko* on 16 February 1749 and then in a succession of small parts. Gentleman succeeded "beyond my most sanguine expectations" he said, "notwithstanding a most inconsequential figure and uncommon timidity. . . ." He remained with Sheridan "a season and a half." Extant Dublin records show him in the Smock Alley company in 1749–50.

About that time Gentleman received news of a legacy of £800 from an uncle, "till then totally unknown to me even by name," who had died in the East Indies. Gentleman's "little freehold," when sold, would produce £700 additional. He at once

threw over acting and set out for London. His departure was accelerated by a coolness which had developed between him and Mossop, who had also gone on the stage and had become both successful and haughty.

There had been more displays of high temperament than Mossop's at Smock Alley in 1748–49. Sheridan had been carrying on a feud with his most illustrious actor, Charles Macklin, and in March 1749 had fired the whole Macklin family—Mr, Mrs, and Miss. Macklin, characteristically, sued and after settling for £300 dawdled on back toward London. The London winter season being almost over, the Macklins remained at Chester, where they collected a summer company made up of London cronies like Sparks and Palmer. Gentleman found them there when he crossed St George's Channel on his way to London and "protracted my journey three months," he says. Whether or not he acted there is unclear.

At Chester he met Samuel Derrick, a linendraper who did not care for "the vocation he was placed to." Derrick followed Gentleman to London. They then moved out to lodgings at Richmond "for sake of better air." (In Derrick's *A Collection of Original Poems*, 1755, are stanzas titled "A Voyage from Dublin to Chester. In an Epistle to Lieutenant Francis Gentleman, Anno 1746," in which "Frank" is hailed as the author's best friend. Some poems contributed to the volume by "G.——" are almost certainly by Gentleman.) At Richmond Gentleman waited a year for a settlement of his inheritance, living extravagantly in expectation, "but how was I surprised to find, that three *honest* lawyers . . . had, upon perusing my uncle's will, explained away 600 *l.* out of the 800 *l.*"

While at Richmond Gentleman committed the first of several assaults on Ben Jonson's texts by altering *Sejanus*, dedicating it to John Boyle, Earl of Orrery and Cork. For his dedication he received a commendation and 20 guineas, which he declared to be the only profit he ever received from such encomia—a pitiable statement if true, for he was an insistent and abject dedicator for the rest of his life. *Sejanus* was published in December 1751 with a preface "Wherein the [Drury Lane] manager's reasons for refusing it [on 26 November 1751] are set forth." (Isaac Reed had "heard," however, that "it was acted at Bath with some degree of applause.")

Gentleman made several other literary attempts during the year at Richmond. Very little is known about his play *Osman* beyond the fact that it was a tragedy. Stephen Jones, in the 1812 edition of *Biographica Dramatica*, said that it had "never yet appeared in print, although about the year 1751 proposals were published both for the printing and acting it by subscription," at the Haymarket. The plan failed, but the play was acted at Bath on 11 November 1754. Gentleman began in 1751 his campaign of flattering Garrick when Manby and Cox published the anonymous 24-page Hudibrastic satire *Fortune, a Rhapsody*, inscribed to the manager. *The Monthly Review* stigmatized it as a "vague declamation against Fortune, for bestowing her favours only on the undeserving." The idea was filched from Rousseau.

The "disagreeable stroke" of Fortune administered by the peculating lawyers, said Gentleman, "precipitated me into fresh dissipation, which shortly narrowed my circumstances much, and occasioned me to accept an engagement for Mr. *Simpson's* theatre at Bath." Gentleman first, however, strolled for awhile "under the gothic management of one Mr. *Phillip's* [*sic*], an old theatrical coxcomb, vain of playing, and covetous of money." At Bath Gentleman shone among the "very imperfect jumbled crew" and wrote and saw acted a five-act tragedy, *The Sultan, or Love and Fame*, which he dedicated to the Countess Cowper. He remained at Bath eight months, studying "a multiplicity of parts." James Quin, then at the height of his success, took notice of him, giving him two guineas on his benefit night.

Evidently Gentleman left Bath during the summer after his first successful season, but he spent two more winter seasons there, 1752–53 and 1753–54. The chronology of his narrative is much confused. He remembered that "During summer, between the second and third seasons at Bath, I came to London and found Mr. *Derrick* studying law and practical philosophy in that agreeable academy the Fleet. . . ." Gentleman joined Sir Francis Delaval, Foote, and Dr Thompson in relieving Derrick's exigency. Yet a project in which he and Derrick were jointly concerned, called, like Gentleman's project and better-known work, *The Dramatic Censor*, was deliberated, conceived and aborted in 1752. The first, and probably only, number of that shilling pamphlet, subtitled "remarks upon the conduct, characters, and catastrophe of our most celebrated plays," consisted only of "Remarks upon the Tragedy of Venice Preserved; with some observations on the performers. By Mr. Derrick." A second number was projected. It would contain "critical remarks on *Richard III*. By Mr. Gentleman," but it is doubtful that the second number ever appeared. Gentleman and Derrick both reached metropolitan notoriety in 1752, being stigmatized by Madam Roxana Termagant (Bonnell Thornton) in *Have at You All: or, the Drury-Lane Journal*, No XIII, as puffers of their own works. They attained the dubious distinction, in 1753, of being mentioned by William Kenrick in *The Pasquinade*.

Gilliland affirmed that "previous to 1756 Mr. Gentleman and Copper Captain [Henry] Brown successively presided at the helm of theatrical affairs" at Bath. That can hardly have been so, inasmuch as Brown was manager in 1751, when Gentleman arrived. Very likely Gilliland got the order of service reversed. Gentleman was busily writing plays: "The second season I produced *Zaphira*, a tragedy, on the same story as Dr John *Brown's Barbarossa*, but performed [on 18 January 1755] before that gentleman's piece came out at *Drury-*

lane. . . ." The *Critical Review* declared (January 1770) that *Zaphira* "contains many lines and sentiments that would not disgrace the best of our modern tragedies" but that it was more suitable for the French stage, "for which it is entirely calculated." It had respectable runs at York and Scarborough later on and in 1769 was revived in London at the Haymarket but was never printed. The same season Gentleman "fitted up an alteration of *Shakespeare's Richard the Second* . . . which was very well received," on 17 March 1755. About his third Bath season (1753–54) he was silent, except to say that it was under the "mild and gentleman-like management" of Thomas King.

Gentleman's vague narrative swallows the next four or five years at a gulp: "Departing from Bath, I shall omit several excursions made to places of less note, and only observe that during a year's vacation from dramatic connections, I had an opportunity to see the *London* stages in their meridian glory. . . ." During 1754 Gentleman turned out two works which were in their vastly different ways typical of strains which appeared in his later productions. First was a lecture on toleration entitled *Religious and Political Liberty: an Oration,* published by Bouquet. It was the text of a speech he had given at a club which the *Monthly Review* identified as "a society of disputants well known in the city of London . . . *The Friday Night's Club,* at the *Queen's-arms,* a beer-house, in *Newgate-street.*" The second was a poem, *Narcissa and Eliza,* styled a "dramatic Tale" by its author. Its sensationalism, "sensibility," and didactic morality were qualities to which Gentleman, as critic, would later award his highest praise. *Narcissa and Eliza* is a long and solemn story in heroic couplets, concerning the daughters of one Anselmo, who inherit £20,000 apiece. Narcissa immediately goes to London, gambles her portion away, runs into debt, fishes for a title, but is finally brought to shame by a nobleman ("being overreached by his subtlety and assiduity"—to adopt the formulation of the *Gentleman's Magazine*). She is finally forced to prostitution and is found in a dying condition by her sister, who had remained at home, married humbly, and prospered.

Tate Wilkinson's *Memoirs* placed Gentleman in the Portsmouth theatre in the summer of 1758, but those recollections cannot be quite accurate on some points. Wilkinson said that

in consequence of some pique which had happened on my playing all the principal parts the year before, several had taken it so much in dudgeon that a great desertion [of Portsmouth] ensued. The hero, Mr. Cook (alias Gentleman) who, though very lame and in years, had been the stock Romeo, Mr. Gates, Mrs. Price . . . Mrs Mozeen, Mr. and Mrs. Fitzmaurice, all had invited themselves on a jolly party for Scotland, where they had removed the winter before, and were fixed for some time in the Edinburgh company of comedians, and were there when Mr Foote paid his first visit. . . .

Now, Gentleman says nothing about being lame, and he was certainly not "in years" at age 30. Perhaps Wilkinson meant old for the role of Romeo. James Dibdin, in *The Annals of the Edinburgh Stage,* picked up the suggestion and imaginatively expanded it in a note:

The following paragraph from the *Edinburgh Chronicle,* published the next year (December 3rd, 1759), evidently refers to this gentleman: "I once imagined our ladies had more humanity, the gentlemen a better taste, than to sit tame spectators, as they last winter did, while good old Lear was barbarously murdered on the stage, not by his daughters, but by a limping fiend of an actor. How ridiculous was it to see Lord Townley, with one leg short and the other long, like a hen on a hot girdle [*sic*], hirpling through the stage."

Gentleman's own account of how he got to Scotland and what he did there is very different:

Having received an invitation from *Edinburgh*, I went thither, and met there, on my arrival, an extreme disagreeable disappointment; Mr Digges and Mrs Ward, two very popular favorites, instead of joining the company . . . decamped to *Dublin* . . . and reduced me to the same disadvantageous state I was first in at *Bath*, obliging me to take a porter's load on a school-boy's back. Judge of my regret when I was *obliged* to march on, with a very insignificant figure [the "lameness"?], the first night in *Othello* [14 November 1758] and the second in *Hotspur*, parts I would ever have wished to decline; after all I met indulgence, and the season for six weeks, during which time I had the misfortune to be *acting* manager—a most disagreeable station —went smoothly on; at length, considering some friends I had brought to the company . . . ill used, I resigned, with secret joy.

Neither had Gentleman been at Edinburgh in the winter of 1757. A cordial letter from Garrick to the Scottish playwright the Rev John Home, dated 19 October (1758) seems to establish that:

The Bearer of this is one *M*r *Gentleman*, born & Educated a Gentleman; He has gone through great variety of distress, still preserving his probity & honour—

He is now going to try his fortune upon the Edinburgh Stage; What his theatrical talents are I cannot say—His Knowledge & Understanding are much Superior to those of our common Stage-Adventurers—Should he have a Benefit, or any Scheme to Support himself, I would desire Your Assistance with convenience to Yourself—I am sure My Account of his Probity and Distress are sufficient to Make You his Friend without any other Consideration.

It is not recorded whether or not Gentleman came under obligation to Home for any favor. He evidently was already in Garrick's debt for several. In a letter from Gentleman to Garrick, dated from Edinburgh on 11 September 1759, Gentleman regretted that he had been unable to return the sum loaned by Garrick. Gentleman had

been victimized by the perfidy of the theatre's management, had resorted to reading public lectures, and since the next season at Edinburgh would be worse than the one just past he wished to get a place in the Drury Lane company. In a postscript, Gentleman adds: "Not having heard from Mr. Derrick since I wrote to him to put the manuscript of *Osman* into your hands, at which time I enclosed an address to you, I know not what to think, but have been very uneasy."

Gentleman, without prospects, wandered on to Glasgow where he was invited to "assist some persons of respectable families in the proper pronunciation of English." It was also intimated to him "that a professorship of English oratory might be obtained" for him. (Glasgow had no theatre.) Very probably, as suggested by Frederick A. Pottle in *James Boswell, the Earlier Years*, Gentleman's journey to Glasgow had something to do with the fact that his acquaintance, the young Boswell, had been obliged by his father in 1759 to transfer his studies from the College of Edinburgh to that of Glasgow. The possibility remains, indeed, that Gentleman, as Pottle had suggested in *The Literary Career of James Boswell, Esq.*, may have assisted Boswell in writing the 50-page pamphlet *A View of the Edinburgh Theatre During the Summer Season, 1759*, which was published in London in 1760.

Also in 1760 the excellent press of Robert and Andrew Foulis at Glasgow published Gentleman's alteration of Southerne's *Oroonoko* with a verse-dedication to Boswell. Much more important, Boswell recalled in *The Life of Samuel Johnson* that Gentleman had first whetted his interest in the Great Cham:

Mr. Gentleman . . . had given me a representation of the figure and manner of DICTIONARY JOHNSON! as he was generally called; and during my first visit to London . . . Mr. Derrick the poet, who was Gentleman's friend and countryman, flattered me with hopes that he would introduce me to Johnson. . . .

And of course Derrick later introduced Boswell to the actor-bookseller Thomas Davies, who performed the historic introduction to Johnson. When and how Gentleman became acquainted with Johnson—if he did—is not known. (It is curious indeed that, although Boswell in 1791 boasted of Gentleman's dedicatory epistle, Gentleman, despite his propensity to name-dropping, did not mention either Boswell or Johnson in his preface to *The Modish Wife*.)

Gentleman's wretched but somehow theatrically successful farce *The Tobacconist*, which he had ripped from Jonson's *The Alchemist*, was his second Edinburgh publication in 1760. It may have been played at Edinburgh; it was certainly seen in London.

Though the gentry of Glasgow urged him to abide, "a sudden wandering seized [his] brain" and he pushed on to Carlisle, where he paused to await "a remittance from *Ireland*, thro' London." After a fortnight he learned that his "draft had been evaded" and "highly chagrined at this . . . in the heat of vexation, joined a company of *Thespians*, then exhibiting there." With those strollers he encountered "the only scene of real theatrical wretchedness, both as to performances and finances," that he ever saw. But "some remains of cash, and a tolerable benefit, brought me through bearably," he says. "At the end of five weeks," Gentleman "received an invitation from Mr. *Whitley* . . . a reputable, bustling, and judicious manager," and took the road to Scarborough to join his company. On the way he fell to drinking with strangers in an inn at Kirkleatham, was mistaken for a French spy, was arrested by an officious innkeeper-constable, and was very nearly summarily hanged before he was taken to a magistrate and his identity established.

Whitley's company stayed at Scarborough a week after Gentleman's arrival and then went on to Manchester, a place whose "affable and social" townspeople pleased Gentleman mightily and where he produced his dramatic satire *The Mentalist; or Passion Doctor*, which "rendered" him "pecuniary advantage." (It had at least one other performance, at York, 26 May 1767, as an afterpiece, at the benefit of Flour, the prompter.) It may also have been at that period that he wrote the "interlude," *The Scarborough Lass*, which the 1812 *Biographia Dramatica* credited him with. It was never published. A quarrel arose between Gentleman and Whitley at season's end, and Gentleman headed once more for London. But he was once more deflected, joining "a company, as it was called, of kidnapped comedians, picked up from *London, Dublin* &c. led by one *Bardin*, a noted adventurer, who, without any consent . . . from the magistrates, most ignorantly and impudently intruded himself and unhappy Co. upon the town of *Liverpool*; where the *wise Mayor* had, at that time, conceived a *wise* prejudice against theatrical performances. . . ."

Gentleman suggested the well-worn device of masking the performance with an enterprise more acceptable to the Mayor:

my scheme was to stile, and to occupy the *theatre* as a school of *Oratory*, for the explanation of moral and practical philosophy, both according to the ancients and moderns; to render this plausible, and indeed incontrovertible . . . I gave before each of the pieces a short introductory lecture upon the general subject and tendency of the play; a point not amiss to be practical [in London], instead of farcical unmeaning prologues.

The ruse sufficed for a week, and then the magistrates pounced. One of the company, a "miserable illiterate wretch," when asked on examination how he lived, answered "by the stage," and the jig was up for everybody. Bardin, "our valorous manager, ever renowned for being the first in, and the first out of a scrape, secreted himself, as I was credibly informed, in a coalhouse. . . ." The group of actors dissolved and "several who came down in the coach were glad to return in the basket; others swam upon credit to Dublin," while Gentleman and Hurst of Drury Lane remained and turned again to the expedient of actual public lecturing.

Gentleman went next to Chester, where he met Whitley again but did not play in his company. He did, however, induce Whitley to perform for four nights his new tragedy *The Modish Wife*. He also "pieced together a little interlude, calculated for an admirable set of children," called *The Fairy Court*, which ran for 15 nights.

Gentleman next joined a traveling company managed by one Bates and (though the language of the preface becomes here especially opaque) left the company after further misfortunes at Scarborough, went to Malton near York, and met and married "a most deserving female." He remained there—in what employment he does not say—for four years and wrote his two-volume *A Trip to the Moon, A Set of Fables* and a poem called *The General*, all printed at York.

The *Fables* (1764) were dedicated "by *permission*" to the Prince of Wales but though they were presented and "graciously received," and though Gentleman had "a very polite letter from a Lady of Quality, eminent in her station at court," he received no further emolument. The *Trip* (1764, 1765) was signed by "Sir Humphrey Lunatick, Bart." It is heavily in the tradition of Lucian, Swift, and Cyrano de Bergerac, and though whimsical, it is also didactic, as the *Monthly Review* observed in reviewing the second volume: "there is something of a Shandyan levity gathered here and there through his pages, which suits not with the moral spirit and serious tendency of the whole. . . ."

The General (1764), "By the Author of A Trip to the Moon," was dedicated to the Marquis of Granby, John Manners, a brilliant and generous soldier. In his preface to *The Modish Wife* Gentleman said that

A gentleman, who knew my father's and my former situation, recommended me to his Lordship, shewing him, at the same time, some of my productions; the consequence was, that he would provide *comfortably* for me, a promise I had afterwards from the Marquis's own mouth. Near Twelve months I waited in pleasing expectation, then came to town, and had not been above a quarter of a year, when death, my frequent friend in such cases, before and since, robbed me of my foremost hope, and a favourite son in the same day.

(Granby died on 18 October 1770, £37,000 in debt.)

The General was, however, more than a blandishment for Granby. Aside from a long and bitter attack on Charles Churchill (whose *Rosciad* it most resembles in style and form) *The General* is successively adulatory of the Duke of Devonshire, Earl Temple, the Marquis of Rockingham, Archbishop Drummond, Sir George Saville, and William Pitt, a list which indicates Gentleman's Whiggish political persuasion. The performance was obviously designed to cast a wider net for patrons.

Another production of 1764, *The History of the Robinhood Society*, was almost certainly Gentleman's. The society, which met at a Butcher's Row tavern every Monday night for some years, was seriously reprobated by sober folk, despite the prominence of many of its quondam members—Derrick, Goldsmith, Foote, Macklin. Some people were convinced that it was an infective locus of treason. On 14 November 1768, Sylas Neville wrote in his diary that he

went to the Robin Hood Disputing Society or Spouting Club, where all sorts of people may harangue on moral & political subjects which few of them understand. In such clubs young men whose passions are strong & their reason weak are furnished with arguments against the sacred obligations of virtue. . . .

Ralph Allen in his *Clubs of Augustan London* says that the Robin Hood Society "developed a reputation for licentiousness, blasphemy, deism, atheism, and disloyalty to the crown that was bound to make it grist for the mills of Grub Street." It was attacked by Fielding in the *Covent Garden Journal,* by Arthur Murphy in the *Gray's Inn Journal,* by Hawkesworth in his *Adventurer,* and by others.

The *History of the Robinhood Society* contains vignettes of some members. One of them is of a

Mr. G*NT**M*N

A very ingenious Gentleman, the Son of a Colonel of the *Irish* Establishment, Author of SEJANUS, a Tragedy, and many other wellwrote Pieces. He is now a Lieutenant on Halfpay, and lives at *Worcester.* As an Orator he was excellent; having an Energy of Expression, a Facility of Utterance, and a Reach of Thought few can equal. Fortune, who, in the Distribution of her Favours, proves herself a blind and ignorant Judge of Merit, has been peculiarly severe to this Gentleman. He was promised, by a late deceased worthy Lord [Granby], to be provided for; but nothing has been done for him, and he now lives upon a scanty Pittance; a deplorable Instance that men of the greatest Merit, Learing [*sic*] and Genius, may sit sighing in Rags and Poverty, while pliant Knaves, Fools, and Coxcombs, bask in the Sunshine of a Court, and almost bend beneath the Load of Fortune's Favours. He has not infrequently wrote in Conjunction with Mr. D*RR**K.

An arresting feature of *The History,* considering its probable authorship, is the eloquent and bitter philippic against critics, especially critics of elocution, as venal, cruel, and pedantic. That could well have

been disastrous for his own critical career, had not most of Gentleman's later criticism been, like the *History,* pseudonymous. It provoked a spleenful reply from the *Critical Review* which also, a little later, reviewed a shilling pamphlet, *A Defense of the Robinhood Society* (1764), which was "Filled with the same stupid illiberal stuff that runs through the history which we have already reviewed; and, if we are not greatly mistaken, both of them are the productions of the same pen."

How Gentleman made shift to survive from about 1761 to 1770 is a mystery. He performed only once, so far as is known. His longer publications cannot have sold well. Doubtless he scribbled anonymous paragraphs for the papers, and he may have been flung an occasional guinea or two by one of his dedicatees. In dedicating *Characters: An Epistle* (1766) to the Earl of Carlisle he abandoned subtlety, signing his name. His poetry had much improved since *The General,* but as the edition of the *Critical Review* (which printed 42 of Gentleman's best lines) remarked: "All his characters are applicable not only to one person but to ten thousand. The rake, the benevolent man, the miser, the epicure, the enthusiast, the pedigogue, &c." Evidently the Earl of Carlisle, like the rest of the noble sponsors Gentleman courted, looked the other way. Gentleman thenceforth usually directed his muse to the stage and his dedications to theatrical people.

In the fall of 1769 Garrick put together his curious and colorful commemoration of the Shakespeare Jubilee. In order to recoup his sizeable losses at Stratford he brought a "procession of Shakespeare's Characters," a feature of the festival, the same season to Drury Lane where, expanded by the addition of a slight fable, it ran for over 90 nights. The spectacle was called *The Jubilee* and has several times been confused bibliographically with a two-act comedy which Francis Gentleman wrote to exploit the farcical goings-on in Warwickshire, *The*

Stratford Jubilee. A New Comedy of Two Acts as it has been lately exhibited at Stratford npon [sic] *Avon, with Great Applause. To Which is prefixed Scrub's trip to the Jubilee* (1769). Gentleman declared in the preface that he had written the play (and presumably *Scrub's Trip*) in eight days. The comedy was published almost as soon as written (16 September 1769) but has never been acted, despite the claim on the title page. It was dedicated to Foote, with whom Garrick was currently at odds. Stephen Jones remarked in the *Biographia Dramatica* that Gentleman had "attempted to asperse Mr. Garrick, though under very recent pecuniary obligations to him; but the offensive passages were erased by a bookseller." The "aspersion," added to the dedication to Foote, was probably already sufficient to provoke Garrick's later characterization of Gentleman—"dirty, dedicating knave"—but *The Stratford Jubilee* was published anonymously, and Garrick had not yet found out its authorship. Very shortly he did.

Gentleman had appeared as actor on one London playbill, that of Covent Garden for 12 May 1768, on the occasion of Charles Dibdin's benefit. But his bad luck had held, for the death of the King's sister, Princess Louisa Anne, had occurred that morning, and all performances had been cancelled. His alteration of Southerne's *Oroonoko*, called *The Royal Slave*, had been produced on Barry's benefit night on 11 March 1769 but had foundered after that one performance.

When Gentleman did, finally, reach the London boards it was due to the ill luck of someone else. His old acquaintance Tom Weston had deferred his benefit for many nights of the Haymarket's 1769 summer season because of a protracted illness. On the season's last night, 19 September, Weston shared the receipts with Miss Ogilvie but did not appear in the role of Richard III, as he had planned to do. The playbill carried this explanation:

Mr Weston's late precarious State of Health making it extremely doubtful whether he could go through so long and laborious [a] part as Richard, he humbly recommends to the Public Mr Gentleman's friendly intention of undertaking the Character for that Night, and will for the Capital Entertainment of his Friends, speak a new *Occasional Prologue*. . . .

The "Occasional Prologue" was Gentleman's brand new *Scrub's Trip to the Jubilee*. On 27 September the Lord Chamberlain permitted some of the Haymarket company, with some provincials, to give Mrs Gardner and Tom Death a special benefit at which Gentleman played Sullen in *The Beaux' Stratagem*. But the summer season was at an end, Garrick was freshly offended, and Covent Garden did not seem interested in acquiring Gentleman's talents. There remained only Samuel Foote and the Haymarket. Gentleman decided it was time to cash in his recent dedication to Foote.

In 1768 he had persuaded Sir Francis Delaval to urge his comedy *The Modish Wife* on Foote, who had kept the play for two years. But in the spring of 1770 Foote told Gentleman he could not, after all, bring it out, "pleading the insufficiency of his company to do a five-act piece." Foote devised, however, a peculiar compensation for Gentleman's long anxiety, according to the *Modish Wife* preface:

In lieu of rejecting [sic] my piece Mr. *Foote* very kindly, and then conveniently for me, offered a summer engagement, which I gratefully accepted, played, and was, without any agreement, gratified by Mr. *Foote's* generosity. . . . With this gentleman I passed three agreeable and advantageous summers, an expedition to *Edinburgh*, one of the intervening winters was, though pleasant, rather a ballance against me, as I took no benefit. . . .

The year 1770 was perhaps the most eventful year in the errant and painful life of Francis Gentleman. It was the year of the death of his favorite son and also of his pitiful hopes of patronage from the Marquis of Granby. But it was also the year he first planted his feet solidly on a London stage and the year of the inauguration of one of the two most important publications of his career, *The Dramatic Censor*. His *The Sultan: or, Love and Fame* was published by a combination headed by Bell and Etherington in January 1770. The advertisement in its endpapers read: "The Subscribers to an Octavo Volume of Poems by the Author of this Tragedy; are respectfully requested to take Notice, that the Said Volume will certainly be delivered on or before the 1st of next June." (There is, however, no record of the publication of the poems.) He also revised his alteration of *Sejanus*, sharpening it to a pointed and personal attack on the Earl of Bute. It was published by Bell and Etherington at London and York and a second edition, also in 1770, was scathingly dedicated to Bute. Finally, by the terms of an agreement Gentleman signed on 12 January 1770, along with representatives of a group composed of George Colman, David Garrick, Thomas Davies, and some others, he was "desired to accept the superintendence" of a newspaper publishing venture in which the *Saint James's Chronicle* and the *Public Advertiser*, already merged, were to be combined with the *London Packet*.

The details of Gentleman's journalistic episode are not known. He was evidently editor of the combined enterprise for a few months only. (*The Cambridge Bibliography* lists Alexander Chalmers as co-editor.) But his other publication of 1770 is an important title in any history of criticism in the eighteenth century.

Monthly numbers of the anonymous *The Dramatic Censor* were announced by the printer-publisher John Bell in January 1770 to sell for a shilling a copy. John Wheble was announced as a publishing partner in the fourth advertisement, and from the sixth number through the twelfth the publishers were Bell of London and

The DRAMATIC CENSOR. 111

Macbeth.
while judgment was obliged to slumber, or seek safety in silence, from popular prejudice.

Among many theatrical circumstances much to be lamented, is that terrible necessity which forces Mr. SMITH into an undertaking so opposite to every one of his requisites, except figure; we are confident his good sense agrees with us, that saddling him with the part is an imposition upon that good nature and integrity which stimulate him to work through thick and thin, for the support of Covent-Garden house.

Macduff is a part of no great action, except on discovery of the King's murder, and the fourth act scene; Messrs. RYAN and HAVARD both did him great justice, yet we must be of opinion that Mr. REDDISH depicts him with superior strength and beauty: his feelings are manly, yet tender; spirited without excess; and to us convey whatever an author intended, or an audience can wish.

Banquo's chief merit is as a ghost; here Mr. Ross made the most striking, picturesque appearance we have ever seen, and with peculiar grace even beautified horror: All the rest of the men in this play are unworthy notice.

Lady Macbeth, as to the detestable composition of her character, has been sufficiently animadverted on, therefore little more is necessary than to observe, that though there does not appear much call for capital merit, yet several first-rate actresses have made but a languid figure in representing her.

Notwithstanding Mrs. WOFFINGTON was extremely well received, and really did the part as
                                                              well

Harvard Theatre Collection

Dramatic Censor, by FRANCIS GENTLE-MAN

Etherington of York. Early in 1771 the numbers were collected in two volumes, the first of which was dedicated, with fulsome adulation, to Garrick, and the second to Foote. Gentleman's criticism is often pretentious, everywhere unlearned (though affecting learning), and suspiciously insistent on the "impartiality" of the Censor. His "leading principle," which was "to develope vice from [its] poetical masquerade; to strip off the serpent's shining coat, and to show the poison which lurks within," and the parallel insistence on "delicacy," and positive didacticism are formidable deterrents to the modern reader.

But the criticisms of some 50 plays and of the acting of 45 performers, plus "A summary of the Most Known Dramatic Writers," furnish an invaluable testimony to critical fashions in mid-to-late eighteenth-century London. Gentleman's tests for "blasphemy" and "immorality" were ludicrously strict and probably affected, but beneath the conventional concern for piety and "beauties," beneath the incrustation of tedious digression, Gentleman's criticism is always that of an actor who has swayed audiences in his time and of an elocution teacher who has coached pupils in the values of words well spoken. Its flaws aside, *The Dramatic Censor* is unique for its time. It stands with Cibber's *Apology* and Chetwood's *History*—each a different sort of work—as one of the three most considerable and extended critical commentaries on both plays and performers written by an actor until the nineteenth century.

When Foote opened the Haymarket for the summer season of 1770 on 17 May with an excellent company, Frank Gentleman was present in an unspecified part in *The Devil Upon Two Sticks*. He was often employed that summer in his old roles of Governor Cape in *The Author* and Sullen in *The Beaux' Stratagem*, and as Renault in *Venice Preserv'd*, Gloucester in *King Lear*, Sir Thomas Testy in *Hob in the Well*, and Hubert in *King John*. On 22 June, also, the bill advertised "a *Prologue* written and spoken by Mr Gentleman." On Weston's benefit night (15 October) Gentleman was advertised as speaking "an Occasional Prologue" and the entr'acte entertainment was said to be *Scrub's Trip to the Jubilee*. A final night of acting ("By Authority") at the Haymarket on 29 October, when Gentleman played Renault again, saw him in a pick-up company of people usually strangers to London.

In the winter of 1770–71 Foote took his company, including Gentleman, to Edinburgh as an experiment. From 10 December through 23 March he played Cacafogo in *Rule a Wife and Have a Wife*, Bluff in *The Old Bachelor*, Fairfield in *The Maid of the Mill*, Cape in *The Author*, Lord Brumpton in *The Funeral*, Adam in *As You Like It*, Old Mirabel in *The Inconstant*, and Subtle in *The Tobacconist*. Gentleman returned with the rest to the Haymarket in the summer of 1771 and played his former collection of parts, adding Quidnunc in *The Upholsterer*, Subtle in *The Englishman in Paris*, Alderman Pentweazle in *Taste*, Goodwin in *The Brothers*, Fulmer in *The West Indian*, Antonio in *The Merchant of Venice*, and Sir William Meadows in *Love in a Village*.

On 15 July 1771 and on several other dates that season, Gentleman's *The Tobacconist* was given, he playing the role of Sir Epicure. The two-act farce taken from *The Alchemist* had caused little stir when acted in Edinburgh ten years before. Now, after some rewriting, it became a favorite vehicle for Tom Weston, playing Drugger, both at the Haymarket and at Drury Lane. Bell published the shilling edition in 1771. The *Critical Review*, the *London Chronicle*, and the *Monthly Review* approved the farce. The *Town and Country Magazine* reprinted a scene. "Ben Johnson's Ghost" signed an "Epigram on Mr Francis Gentleman's late alteration of some . . . Plays" in the *Scots Magazine*:

> *Mark the commandments, Frank,*
>   *Go no further—*
> *Is it not written,*
>   *Thou shalt do no murther?*

On 16 September he spoke a prologue and took an unspecified part in his own farce, abstracted from Jonson's *Epicoene* and called *The Coxcombs*. The *Whitehall Evening Post* reported that it was hissed. The prologue and one scene were then reprinted by *The Oxford Magazine*. (But the farce was repeated at the Haymarket, and Weston took it for his benefit at Drury Lane on 21 April 1772.) While at Edinburgh Gentleman published privately *The Orator. An Essay on Reading and Declamation.*

Gentleman also busied himself in 1771 writing an 80-page satirical survey of the acting styles of some 70 performers called *The Theatres: a Poetical Dissection*, published, probably, in the fall of 1771, under the pseudonym Sir Nicholas Nipclose. An only sporadically effective imitation of Churchill's *Rosciad*, it was dedicated to Garrick's enemy Frances Abington, and it praised Foote. Its preface furiously excoriated Garrick for venality, artistic insensitivity, jealousy, snobbery, and failing powers. A satirical-allegorical engraving pictured Roscius, with fruitlessly beseeching Thalia and Melpomene at his side, treading gleefully on manuscripts marked "B. John—," "S——pear," Rowe, and so on, and holding a paper marked "Arthur's Round Table" and a parchment entitled "Processions Forever." The motto was: "Behold the Muses Roscius sue in Vain / Taylors & Carpenters usurp their Reign."

The reason for this ungrateful and (one would have thought) professionally suicidal attack on Garrick was probably Garrick's indignant response of 9 October 1771 to a letter (dated only 1771, from Downing Street, Westminster) in which Gentleman had charged Garrick with stealing the idea of the masque *The Institution of the Garter* (which was then preparing at Drury Lane) from a plan which Gentleman had submitted "ten years ago." Gentleman had charged also that Garrick's alteration from Southerne, *Isabella or The Fatal Marriage*, had been brought out at Drury Lane after Gentleman "had laid before you a plan of alteration" and "the *Oronoko* also came forth at the same theatre after a like suggestion, and when I actually printed one at Edinburgh." Garrick's reply, beginning

"Since I have been a manager, I never receivd a Letter that surpris'd me so much as yours," rejected the charges totally and with asperity.

Certainly that passage-at-arms plus *The Theatres*, led eventually to the scrap of verse found among Garrick's papers:

> *Tell me, Dame Abington, how much you gave*
> *To that same dirty, dedicating knave?*
> *Alas! that you should think to gather fame,*
> *From one that's only Gentleman by name!*

Was the quatrain penned soon after the publication of *The Theatres*? The amateur ropemaker-playwright Joseph Reed, in an attack on Foote (manuscript in the Harvard Theatre Collection), testified:

While I was in the managers [Garrick's] seeming good graces a quarrel happend between him and Mr Foote One of the mimics [Foote's] dram drinking performers# had publish'd a scurrilous poem called (as I remember) *the Theatres dissected* in which he had made very free with the Character of the celebrated Roscius and had even graciously condescended to take satirical notice of *me*. Mr Garrick suppos'd (as he justly might) that Mr Foote had put the Author on writing the piece, a violent quarrel ensued and continued for above a twelvemonth unhappily for me a reconciliation was effected which put an end to my rising Expectations. . . .
 # Francis Gentleman (if that were his real name)

Yet for a considerable time after the publication of *The Theatres* Garrick *seems* to have been bent on conciliation with all parties. He assured Foote, in a letter of 31 December 1771, that he had not taken offense at some anonymous (and as yet unidentified) attack on him apparently implicating Foote, and then proceeded:

—by my word, I have as much forgotten the poem of ye Theatres, as if it had never existed & upon my honor I never heard of a Word You had said in ye Boxes ye other Night, but what express'd your great partiality & regard to me—As to y^r being angry with one of y^r Company, who has been suppoz'd ye Author of ye Poem, You ought not in justice discharge him; the Author is as yet unknown, and You had much better exert y^r humanity towards a hundred undeserving people, than injure one innocent Man.

Whether Garrick's closing piety was sincere or proceeded from his well known aversion to a brawl in print, Gentleman seems to have been not only mistaken but censurable. For if *The Theatres* had not been published by the date of Gentleman's upbraiding letter to Garrick (early October), it certainly had been prepared for publication long before, and it is hard to believe that any mollifying reply by Garrick to Gentleman's charges would have deterred its publication.

What impelled Gentleman to throw in with Frances Abington in her never-ending warfare with her manager cannot even be conjectured now. Certainly his careful buttering-up of Foote and especially his calculation that the Garrick-Foote enmity would last were bad tactical mistakes. The ironical proof lies in the last sentence of Garrick's letter to Foote. Very likely Gentleman never guessed that his "victim" Garrick had saved him from being discharged by his "patron" Foote.

Gentleman's self-destructive tendencies which he remarked in the preface to *The Modish Wife* ("being ever more prone to revenge injuries on myself than other people") impelled him in *The Theatres* also to insult Colman, "tiny George," manager of Covent Garden and his only other possible chance for permanent theatrical employment in London, and, for good measure (besides many fellow-actors), Hugh Kelly, Richard Cumberland, William Whitehead, John Hoole, Isaac Bickerstaff, Joseph

Reed, Dr. Thomas Francklin, Oliver Goldsmith, Samuel Johnson, and George III. His red herring "attack" on "FRANKY GENTLEMAN, from Liffey's side," is comically transparent. As we see from Garrick's letter to Foote, before the end of the year the gossip in the profession was that Gentleman was Nipclose.

In the summer of 1772, Gentleman was again fully employed at the Haymarket, but he added nothing to his repertoire. However, his farce *The Anatomist* was revived to play three times, and his "new dramatic pastoral farce" *Cupid's Revenge* was introduced on 27 July and repeated a dozen times. Theodore Hook wrote the music for the libretto by Gentleman; some of its songs are charming. It was published in the summer of 1772, dedicated to "Hon. Arthur Duff, Esq. of Rothmay, North Britain."

Gentleman's fortunes now again took a downward turn. Mossop came briefly back into his ken early in 1773 with a grandiose scheme for making Gentleman manager at Dublin, which Gentleman heartily distrusted even before the bailiffs came to conduct Mossop to the Fleet, ending negotiations. In March 1773 Gentleman's wife died, "a companion equal to every idea of matrimonial happiness," and "health, recollection, and every mental exertion were for some months thrown into absolute confusion." And finally

About a fortnight before Mr Foote's theatre began, I was struck with an information that he had no more occasion for my assistance; this, at a time of peculiar embarrassment, . . . known to the manager, was that I could not at that time account for, nor have I to the present moment [1774] a single idea of explanation.

Nevertheless, he continued, he wrote for Weston "in four days" the critically successful satire on high life called *The Panthe-*

onites. It was praised by the *Critical* and *Monthly* reviews, but it played only once at the Haymarket after its opening on 3 September 1773. (Weston, who evidently liked his new part of Daniel Drugger, "great grandson to Abel Drugger," less well than that of old Abel, played it at Drury Lane on 26 April and 5 May 1774, and then it expired.)

On 18 September 1773 Gentleman's comedy *The Modish Wife* achieved its only metropolitan performance as the mainpiece in a specially licensed benefit performance for Mrs Williams at the Haymarket. (The play, with its valuable preface, was published by Bell and Evans on 9 February 1775, dedicated to the Countess of Mexborough.)

In 1772 Gentleman had been commissioned by his friend and publisher John Bell to take from the playhouse promptbooks of Hopkins of Drury Lane and Younger of Covent Garden the texts of those Shakespearean plays then in the repertoire and prepare explanatory footnotes and introductory material. Gentleman's name did not appear, and in the advertisements the edition was said to be by "the authors of The Dramatic Censor." Consequently, the edition came to be known as the "Bell edition." It was published both in convenient playhouse separates for each play and in an attractive bound edition, the first five volumes of which were announced in the *Daily Advertiser* of 30 December 1773. The edition eventually extended to nine volumes, including the plays then not current in the repertoire, the poems, and a *Life* written by Gentleman. In footnotes Gentleman also contributed critical comments on acting as well as his familiar suggestions for improving the morality of the texts. Thirty-six sumptuous copperplate engravings by prominent artists rounded out this unique edition which was reprinted again and again by John Bell and, after his bankruptcy, by John Barker.

An unidentified newspaper clipping in the Enthoven collection, dated 11 January 1774, announced that

Sir Nicholas Nipclose, after three years dormancy since the appearance of his poetical dissection The Theatres, has devoted all his leisure and genius to a most satisfactory, elaborate, elucidated edition of all Mr. Garrick's Prologues and Epilogues, with adequate notes: As also Mr. Whitehead's Birthday Odes, since his Lauretship, similarly set forth; supposed to be the best poetical collection and critical remarks, that have appeared in any language.

The notice added that publication had been postponed in order to include Garrick's prologue to *The Christmas Tale*. A sarcastic epistle dated from Drury Lane 10 March 1774 and signed Censor Dramaticus —surely Francis Gentleman—was published in a newspaper (not named by James Boaden, who reprinted it in his *Private Correspondence of David Garrick*). The letter cited a correspondent who had expressed a wish that "the Roscius of Drury-lane would oblige the public with a . . . collection of all the prologues and epilogues he has . . . composed" and who had also desired "to know the reason why he withholds that treasure from the public. . . ." Censor Dramaticus thought the reason obvious. It was simply that the "little great man" had a "warehouse of old and obsolete wit and humour," from which he produced popular "*petits-pièces*" full of "inoriginality, as well as insignificancy," but which like that "incoherent rhapsody" the *Jubilee Ode*, succeeded because of the "graces" of Garrick's declamation.

It was Gentleman's last outbreak of spleen and jealousy against Garrick, who within a year disarmed him of his poor weapon of satire. Garrick finally got the better of it by an almost incredible demonstration of returning good for evil. On 9 February 1775 *The Modish Wife* was published with a preface in which Garrick's management and acting were gently praised and no word set down of past disagreements. By 8 March Garrick had sent Gentleman a commendation and a sum of money. On 14 March, in a letter dated from Castle Yard, Holborn, Gentleman was fawning and cringing as abjectly as if he had never abused Garrick:

Your very condescending favour, though dated the 8th, did not reach my hands till last night; as to its SOLID contents, being more than I found any idea of, they forcibly call on gratitude, and shall by no means fail of that feeling, which a heart capable of proper sensibility, can entertain. . . . Let me assure you, that my *promulged* theatrical sentiments have been *adopted* ones, received from persons I thought much better judges than myself, and on whose integrity I judged it safe to rely.

There was more of the same, in which he spoke of his "confirmed veneration for Mr Garrick's eminent abilities" and rejoiced that "*any* part of my little biographical sketch gave amusement. . . ."

Gentleman importuned Garrick for five guineas' "temporary assistance" in a letter of August 1775. "Some amendment of health has enabled" him to execute a long meditated scheme. He has been "invited" to "Eaton and Oxford" to give "dramatic lectures, of a nature different from any yet attempted; liberal . . . and useful. . . ." He added somewhat pitifully, "but my externals have so unfavourable an appearance, that I cannot produce myself with any comfort or hope of success." Garrick sent the money, and was effusively thanked on 29 August 1775, in a letter enclosing a note-of-hand and a manly resolve to pay up—some day. Gentleman was, as he had said in concluding his eccentric preface in January 1775, "still scrambling on the surface of existence. . . ."

How long Gentleman remained in London after 1775 is not known. Evidently he had little means of subsistence. His faithful friend Weston had brought his farce *The Pantheonites* to Drury Lane as an afterpiece for three performances—long enough

to earn his author's fee—in the spring of 1774. One wonders if the "Gentlewoman" for whose benefit his *Modish Wife* was played at a special performance at the Haymarket on 3 January 1780 was really Gentleman. ("End of mainpiece a Variety of *Rhetorical Imitations* by a Gentleman.") And there are suspicious touches to the bill of a specially-licensed performance at the Haymarket on 21 April 1782: the afterpiece was *The Tobacconist*, Drugger by "A Gentleman"; the mainpiece, *Love at a Venture*, a new comedy, author unknown, the actors all strangers to London. No avowed work of Gentleman's played in London for the rest of the eighteenth century except an alteration of his alteration, *The Tobacconist*, and an alteration of Gluck's *Orpheus and Eurydice* (at Covent Garden for three performances in February and March 1792), which he had produced at Smock Alley Theatre, Dublin, in 1783. By 1783 he was working at Smock Alley, probably as prompter.

Francis Gentleman died, in his accustomed poverty, in George Lane, Dublin, on 21 December 1784, aged 56. The number of Gentleman's children is unknown. Besides the "favourite son" who died on 18 October 1770, there were at least two other children, mentioned in a letter to Garrick dated only 1775. One may have been the only one of the children whose baptismal date is known, "Patty Daug̃:ʳ of Francis Gentleman by Ruth his Wife," christened at St Paul, Covent Garden, on 26 September 1769.

In his autobiographical preface Gentleman had remarked: "I heartily wish I had been fated to use an awl and end sooner than the pen, for nothing but a pensioned defender of government, a sycophant to managers, or a slave to booksellers can do anything more than crawl." The falseness of that bitter declaration was illustrated in the careers of many of Gentleman's friends and enemies, and his own fecklessness and improvidence, as well as his treachery, can be blamed for much of his woe. Yet the man had considerable talent and he does seem to have been greatly unfortunate.

No portrait of Gentleman survives, but George Parker met him at a gathering in a house in Russell Street, Covent Garden, in 1781 and left a description which is picturesque. Gentleman was "of an extraordinary appearance, talking to a large congregation of ALL SORTS on the *equity, justice,* and policy of the American war." His "garb . . . was his *whim,*" Gentleman declared to Parker, and his "circumstances were by no means so narrow" as his dress indicated.

He wore a very ragged surtout coat, without a waistcoat: his hat, wig &c. were all of a piece. In his left hand he held a pot of porter, and with his right enforced by his action the weight of his argument. He was a perfect master of his subject, and of the language. He exemplified his knowledge of the English Constitution, by running thro' the annals of Great Britain, from its earliest period to the year 1777, with the greatest accuracy and precision, never hesitating one moment. His principles were perfectly *Whig,* and he adduced numerous cases . . . to prove the Crown of England was in the gift of the people. . . . [He] astonished all . . . by the greatness of his capacity, and the force of his abilities. . . .
On my talking to him indifferently about the weather &c. he turned his back, and pulling out a bologna sausage and a crust of bread, eat his dinner, without noticing any one, observing the remainder of the afternoon with the most rigid rules of taciturnity, though he had his full-pot five times replenished with porter.

An obituary in the *Dublin Morning Herald* for 29 December 1784 stated that he had been "afflicted with a severe rheumatic disorder" and that "for the last seven years of his life" he had "struggled under sickness and want to a degree of uncommon misery." The obituary concluded:

The many years this unfortunate gentleman lived upon the precarious bounty of some worthy individuals of the stage in this kingdom, only served to linger out a deplorable existence; though the qualities of his head and heart were worthy of a better fate. For some time past, he principally owed his support to the humanity and attention of Mr. Younge, who yesterday saw him decently interred, on the subscription raised by the performers of Smock-alley for that purpose; his blameless, though unfortunate, life having secured him the esteem of all who knew him.

Genuini. *See* GENOVINI.

George. *See also* GIORGI *and* GOUGE.

George, Mr ₍fl. 1745–1749₎, *actor.*
An actor named George played the Miller in *The King and the Miller of Mansfield* for his own benefit at Shepherd's Market, May Fair, on 28 February 1745. On 24 August 1748 he played Sir John Lovewell in *The Unnatural Parents,* a droll performed at Lee and Yeates's booth at Bartholomew Fair. At Yeates's Great Tiled Booth on the Bowling Green, Southwark, he acted Mat in *The Beggar's Opera* on 2 January 1749 and Kite in *The Recruiting Officer* on 9 January 1749. In those plays the characters of Mrs Slammekin and Lucy, respectively, were acted by Mrs George (fl. 1743–1749), probably his wife. Perhaps he was related to John George, who was a billsticker at Drury Lane Theatre between 1741 and 1746.

George, Mr ₍fl. 1788–1820₎, *box-keeper.*
A Mr George was a boxkeeper at Drury Lane Theatre for at least 32 years between 1788–89 and 1819–20, during which time he shared regular annual benefits with numerous other house servants. His salary in 1789–90 was 15s. per week, a figure still in effect in 1800–1801; by 1803–4 it had been reduced to 12s. per week, by 1812–13 it was raised to 18s., but in 1815–16 it was again reduced to 12s., at which level it remained through 1819–20.

George, Mr ₍*fl. 1793*₎. *See* **WATHEN, GEORGE.**

George, Mr ₍*fl. 1794*₎, *violinist, pianist.*

A Mr George of No 42, Wigmore Street, Cavendish Square, was listed in Doane's *Musical Directory* (1794) as a violinist and pianist and as a member of the Academy of Ancient Music.

George, Mrs ₍*fl. 1743–1749*₎, *actress.*

Mrs George made her first appearance on any stage at Drury Lane Theatre on 14 November 1743 as Miss Prue in *Love for Love,* a role she repeated on 21 December. She next acted Lucy in *The London Merchant* on 16 May 1744, when she shared a benefit with Ray, Barclay, and Green. In the fall of 1744 she joined Theophilus Cibber's company at the Haymarket Theatre for several months, playing Lady Graveairs in *The Careless Husband* on 25 September and then Lucy in *The Recruiting Officer,* Lady Capulet in *Romeo and Juliet,* and Isabella in *The Prodigal.* At the James Street Theatre on 8 March 1745 Mrs George acted Calisto in *The Fair Penitent* and Melissa in *The Lying Valet.* At Yeates's Great Tiled Booth on the Bowling Green, Southwark, she played Mrs Slammekin in *The Beggar's Opera* on 2 January 1749 and Lucy in *The Recruiting Officer* on 9 January 1749, performances in which Mr George (fl. 1745–1749), probably her husband, also appeared.

George, Georgina, later Mrs John Oldmixon *d. 1835, singer, actress.*

According to contemporary biographical notices Georgina George's real surname was Sidus, and she was reported to have been the daughter of a clergyman at Oxford. But a manuscript in the Bodleian Library which contains a copy of a sworn statement by her father, dated 27 November 1780, reveals his name as Tobias George. It was as Miss

George that Georgina began singing in concerts around Oxford by 1780. When she disappointed G. Monro by not appearing for his annual concert at the Oxford Music Room on 16 November 1780, he began a public quarrel with Dr Philip Hayes, her teacher, whom Monro accused of preventing her performing. It was then that Tobias George, her father, offered the letter referred to, in which he shouldered the blame for refusing permission for his daughter, evidently still a minor, to sing for Monro. She did, however, sing on many other occasions and on 10 April 1783 had a benefit at the Oxford Music Room.

In the summer of 1783 Miss George joined Colman's company at the Haymarket Theatre, where she made her first appearance as an actress, as Rosetta in *Love in a Village,* on 2 June. After seven more performances as Rosetta, in which she became a favorite of the town, she played Euphrosyne and the First Bacchant in *Comus* on 27 June 1783. On the morning after her debut the *Morning Post* lavished high praise upon her and predicted she would become one of the finest singers on the stage. The *Morning Herald* judged her a singer without "an equal on the English stage," who had the advantages of "a fine voice . . . great execution, a correct ear, and a very finished shake," although she was undisciplined and inexperienced in acting, "having scarce seen half a dozen plays in her life." Her figure was reported to be "genteel, and appeared to the greatest advantage, from her being dressed with neatness and taste." Seilhamer says that when she acted Euphrosyne for the second time (1 July) a man dressed like a clergyman sitting in the boxes so disturbed her by hissing and shouting that Miss George fainted. Seilhamer's suggestion that the disturber was her father seems unlikely, and perhaps the whole story was fabricated. She performed Mandane in *Artaxerxes* on 16 July, Florina in *The Birth Day* on 12 August, Nysa in *Midas* on 26 August, and

Harvard Theatre Collection

GEORGINA GEORGE

engraving by Orme, after Howell

one of the Italian girls in *The Critic* on 29 August. In a hodgepodge musical piece called *A Fete* on 1 August she sang Boyce's song "With Horns and with Hounds," and at the end of Act I of *The Green Room* on 27 August she delivered "a favourite *song*."

Although without experience, Miss George possessed a good natural voice which caught the public's ear. She was a petite, vivacious person, with large features and expressive eyes. Her voice was melodious and sweet and had a wide range.

Intent on building up her reputation as a distinguished performer when she later appeared on the American stage, Seilhamer seems to have exaggerated the effect she had on early Haymarket audiences by hailing her as the English Allegranti. Recognized as a promising singing actress, Miss George was engaged at Drury Lane for the winter season (hardly, we assume, at the

high salary of £10 per week stated by Seilhamer) and made her first appearance there on 25 September 1783 as Rosetta. Her next appearance was on 7 October as principal Bacchant in *Comus*, a part she played with spirit and sang with some excellence. But the *Theatrical Review* of that date was disappointed with her girlish manner, finding her deficient in the song "Would you taste the noon-tide air" in comparison to Anne Catley: "CATLEY was luxurious in countenance, deportment, and singing. Miss GEORGE was cold, tedious, and uninteresting."

On 30 October she made her first attempt as Diana in *A School for Fathers,* on 4 November as Sally in *Thomas and Sally*, and on 18 November as Annette in *The Lord of the Manor.* Her other roles in her first season at Drury Lane included Charlotte in *The Metamorphosis* on 5 December 1783 and Huncamunca in *Tom Thumb* on 28 April 1784. On 20 May she sang a duet with Williames in *A Musical Oglio*. For her benefit on 14 April she had offered Sylvia in *Cymon* and sang "Queen Mary's Lamentations" and "The Soldier tir'd of War's Alarms" as entr'acte pieces. Tickets could be had of Miss George at No 23, King Street, where she was still living in 1787. According to figures cited in *The London Stage* for her benefit performance in 1784, Miss George made a profit of £24 6*d.*, but a notation in a Drury Lane account book (now in the Folger Shakespeare Library) indicates she suffered a deficit of £34 11*s.* 6*d.*, which she paid to the theatre on 17 April 1784.

Miss George's career at Drury Lane never really blossomed into one of distinction, although she served ably for several more seasons in the roles of pretty young ladies. In 1784–85 she played Venus in *Arthur and Emmeline*, Urganda in *Cymon*, Aurelia in *Liberty Hall*, Phoebe in *Rosina*, and Corinna in *The Confederacy*, as well as her familiar Rosetta, Diana, and principal Bacchant. She also appeared regularly as one of the singing witches in *Macbeth*; on 24 February 1785 the *Public Advertiser* took her and Mrs Wrighten to task for a "monstrous marring" of this play by laughing and talking all the time on stage. For her benefit on 6 April 1785, as Corinna in *The Confederacy*, she suffered another deficit, of £15 according to the account books (but according to *The London Stage* she realized a profit of some £91 4s.).

In 1785–86 a long illness limited Miss George's activities at Drury Lane. She made only occasional appearances in the chorus of *Macbeth*, played in several performances of *Arthur and Emmeline*, *The Lord of the Manor*, *Comus*, and *Cymon*, and was a featured singer in the spring oratorios. Her benefit on 25 April 1786, however, brought her a good sum of £175 0s. 6d. At the end of the season she was discharged from her regular engagement and thereafter made only a few appearances there in the oratorios of 1787 and 1788. She seems never to have performed at Covent Garden Theatre.

During that period she had kept up regular summer engagements at the Haymarket, playing such roles in her line as: in 1784, Tippet in *Two to One*, Adela in *The Roman Peasant*, Susan in *The What D'ye Call It?*, Jenny in *The Deserter*; in 1785, Diana in *Love in a Village*, Fib in *A Turk and No Turk*, Araminta in *The Fair Quaker*, Miss Plumb in *Gretna Green*, Phoebe in *Rosina*; in 1786, Priscilla Tomboy in *The Romp*, Miss Jenny in *The Provok'd Husband*, Lucy in *The Beggar's Opera*, Teresa in *The Siege of Curzola*, Rhodope in *A Peep Behind the Curtain*; and in 1787, Juno in *The Golden Pippin*, Wowski in *Lionel and Clarissa*, and Fanny in *The Test of Love*. At the Haymarket, Miss George enjoyed greater success. Dunlap, the American manager, reported seeing her in the "Noble Peasant" in 1785 (but he must have meant *The Roman Peasant* in 1784) and was very much impressed. When she played Priscilla Tomboy in *The Romp* for the first time at the Haymarket for her benefit on 3 August

1786, she was favorably compared to Mrs Jordan in the role by the *Gazetteer*: ". . . we must bear testimony to the spirit, the volatility, the gamesomeness of Miss George. She sang the songs with such taste and excellence as to excite a tumult of applause and, in all but one or two, a general encore. She has reason to be fully satisfied with her benefit, both from the accession of fame and of cash, for the house overflowed in every part." But when she played Miss Jenny in *The Provok'd Husband* on 19 July 1786, the *Morning Chronicle* (24 July) complained of her constant spinning around like a top and running to the back of the stage: "She too is very apt to *stay* at the back of the stage. She knows when it is her turn to speak, joins the party, speaks, spins, and away again! Pray, Miss George, sometimes do your friends the favour to stay amongst them, and attend to what is going forward." The same year, John Williams wrote equivocally of her in *The Children of Thespis*:

> See George *in the sweet paths of melody
>   tread,*
> By dull frigid Insensibility led:
> Tho' careless to please, her meek essays
>   delight. . . .

In the summer of 1786 Miss George also sang at Ranelagh. About that time it was mistakenly given out in the press that she was to marry a Mr Martyr—the laboriously waggish paragrapher calling her "St. George, the Martyr." In the autumn, no longer engaged at Drury Lane, she was with Joseph Fox's company at Brighton, and in November, December, and February she made occasional appearances singing arias at readings given by Lacy at Free-Masons' Hall. She was back at the Haymarket and at Ranelagh for the summer of 1787.

In the autumn of 1787 Miss George joined John Palmer's venture at the Royalty Theatre in Wellclose Square. She made her first appearance there on 27 September as

Susan in *Thomas and Susan*, prompting the *Gazetteer* to commend Palmer for "engaging this little syren" about whom there was no doubt but that she would "be as great a favorite in the East as she was in the West." On 31 October she sang with Master John Braham in *A Scotch Pastoral Entertainment*. On 3 December 1787 she performed the roles of Pallas and Nysa in the premiere of *Apollo turn'd Stroller; or, Thereby hangs a Tale*, a musical pasticcio by Sir John Oldmixon, whom she was to marry in the early spring of 1788.

Little of certainty is known about Sir John Oldmixon. Possibly he was the grandson of John Oldmixon (1673–1742), the historian and pamphleteer who was mentioned in Pope's *Dunciad*. The elder Oldmixon's daughter Eleanor, who sang at Hickford's Room in 1746, married the musician Giovanni Battista Marella; their son, according to Seilhamer, changed his name to Oldmixon and later was knighted by the viceroy for his services under the Duke of Portland in Ireland. Oldmixon dropped his title when he went to America. John Bernard, who knew him at Bath in 1784 and reported him as a noted beau of the time, professed to have used Oldmixon as a model for his playing of Lord Sparkle in Mrs Cowley's *Which is the Man?*: "Bernard, I saw your *Sparkle* last night," Sir John was supposed to have said to the actor on one occasion, "they say you imitate me, but your dress was incorrect; you wear only twelve curls to a side—I never wear under sixteen."

Although presumably she had become "Lady" Oldmixon, Georgina George continued to perform under her maiden name, playing an engagement in Edinburgh, where she appeared on 10 March 1788 in the title role of *Rosina*. She also played Rosetta in *Love in a Village*, Clorinda in *Robin Hood*, Diana in *Lionel and Clarissa*, and Nysa in *Midas*. On her return journey to London she was taken by a fever which threatened her life and made her engage-

ment at the Haymarket for the summer impossible. Having recovered by the autumn, she performed for several weeks at the Crow Street Theatre, Dublin, in November and December 1788 and then was in Edinburgh again from January to May 1789 to appear in *Robin Hood* and the several roles she had played there the previous year.

Miss George returned to the Haymarket for the summer of 1789 to play her familiar roles of Miss Plumb, Rosetta, Wowski, Trippet, and Araminta. She also performed the Milk Girl in the premiere of Colman's *Ut Pictura Poesis; or, The Enraged Musician* on 18 May 1789, Isabella in *The Portrait* on 31 July, and Maud in *Peeping Tom* on 12 September. When she had her benefit as Wowski in *Inkle and Yarico* on 12 August, her address was No 8, Panton Street. Her last performance at the Haymarket, and in London, was as Cowslip in *The Agreeable Surprise* on 15 September 1789. On 15 October 1789 the *Oracle* announced that she was one of the performers who had been dismissed from the Haymarket company when the younger Colman assumed the management.

She was performing at Crow Street in 1790 and 1791, at Limerick in 1790, and at Cork in the summer of 1791. At Cork she was placed in competition with the more famous vocalist Mrs Billington, who had a reputation for ill temperament and loose morals. When they appeared together on the stage one of the other actors compared them to "St George and the Dragon." Also during the early 1790s, Miss George acted at Edinburgh.

On 22 May 1793 the *Gazetteer* announced that Miss George, along with Mrs Chalmers, Miss Broadhurst, Mrs Melmoth, and Mr Fennell, had been engaged by Thomas Wignell for his new theatre in Philadelphia. Georgina made her debut at the Chestnut Street Theatre on 14 May 1794 (not 1793, as is often given) as Clorinda in *Robin Hood*. Now she was called Mrs Oldmixon in the bills. A notation on a manuscript now in the Folger Library says that she had only just recently married Oldmixon and was pregnant: *"Miss George* was oblig'd to assume . . . [the] Name of *Oldmixon* here because she was in the way that Women wish to be who Love their Lords & because the Trans-Atlantics have more regard to Appear-[ance]s than People on this side of the Water."

After Clorinda, Mrs Oldmixon's other roles in Philadelphia included Fanny in *The Maid of the Mill* on 16 May, Roxalana in *The Sultan* on 19 May 1794, Caroline in *The Prize* on 26 May, Miss Tittup in *Bon Ton* on 28 May, Diana in *Lionel and Clarissa* on 2 June, Margaretta in *No Song No Supper* on 6 June, Euphrosyne in *Comus* on 25 June, and Rosina in *The Spanish Barber* on 7 July. She acted at Philadelphia regularly between 1795 and 1798 and also at Baltimore, where her name was on bills as Sally in *The Purse* on 29 July 1795, Roxalana on 2 September 1795 (when she sang "Loose were her tresses seen" with "divine melody, grace, and elegance"), and Diana on 7 September 1795, as well as Mrs Malaprop in *The Rivals* on 28 September 1796. In 1798, at a salary of $37 per week, she became associated with Dunlap's company at the newly built Park Theatre. She acted again in Philadelphia in 1799 and 1800.

After some six years of retirement, during which she presumably gave birth to some of the seven children she was reported to have borne, she returned to the Park Theatre in 1806 as the Nurse in *Romeo and Juliet* and played other older roles, although her singing voice was reported still good. By 1813 she retired again from the stage but gave occasional concerts, residing principally at Philadelphia and Germantown, where at one time she conducted a seminary for young ladies.

In November 1818 the *Gentleman's Magazine* announced that Sir John Oldmixon, who had once been known in fash-

ionable life but who had left England "from pecuniary embarrassments," had lately died obscure and neglected in America, where he had turned to farming. At some point he and Georgina had been divorced. His children, it was reported, "are singularly, and indeed unhappily situated— one half being born in, are citizens of the United States; while the other half (Englishmen) are actually lieutenants in the British navy."

"Lady Oldmixon," as the *Gentleman's Magazine* of June 1835 called her in an obituary notice, died in Philadelphia on 3 February 1835. William Wood's statement that she had died at the age of 62 is manifestly wrong, for that would place her birth in 1773, only ten years before she made her debut at the Haymarket.

A Miss George who acted in musical roles at Philadelphia in 1828 does not seem to have been related.

According to William Dunlap, the historian of the early American stage, a portrait by Russell of Miss George with John Palmer was at one time exhibited at Somerset House. A portrait engraving of Miss George by Orme, after Miss Howell, was published at London by Billington & Freeman, 1787. In the Harvard Theatre Collection is a process print, a slight variation of the Orme engraving, which bears the legend "From an original miniature of 1786 in the possession of Dr. C. C. Lamdin, Philadelphia."

George, James [*fl. 1775*], *musician.*

A James George, "musician," lived in 1775 with his wife Mary in Rose Lane, Spitalfields, according to the registers of Christ Church, Spitalfields.

George, [James?] [*fl. 1785–1789*], *actor.*

A Mr George acted Lazarillo in a single performance of *'Tis Well It's No Worse* at the Haymarket Theatre on 25 April 1785. He or another actor of the same name played the King of the Fiddlers in *Chrononhotonthologos* at the White Horse Inn, Parson's Green, Fulham, on 9 November 1789. *The London Stage* identifies the latter actor as the James George who, with other performers from the Smock Alley Theatre in Dublin, signed a letter published in the *Hibernian Journal* on 30 January 1786. But we believe that signator to have been the James George who died in 1798; he had been a member of the Irish Musical Fund in 1798–99 and was probably in the band at Smock Alley. We have not been able to find a clear connection between the Dublin James George and the London actor, though there may have been one.

George, John   ₁*fl. 1741–1746*₁, billsticker.

John George, who is identified by a manuscript in the British Museum as a billsticker, shared benefits with many other minor personnel at Drury Lane Theatre on 23 May 1741, 24 May 1743, 8 May 1745, and 16 May 1746. Perhaps he was related to the Georges who acted occasionally in London during that decade.

Georgi, James. *See* GEORGE, JAMES.

Georgi-Banti, Brigitta. *See* BANTI, SIGNORA ZACCARIA.

Geortini. *See* GIARDINI.

Gepot. *See* GEHOT.

Gerard, Mons   ₁*fl. 1753–1754*₁, dancer.

Monsieur Gerard came from Paris and made his first English stage appearance at Drury Lane on 26 March 1753 in a solo *Masquerade Dance.* On 31 March he danced the Peasant in *La Chacone des caractères.* During the 1753–54 season at the same theatre he performed a *Rural Dance* with Mlle Lussant, danced with Mme Lussant (the same person?) in *The Old Bachelor,*

was in a piece called *Gipsey Tambourine,* appeared in a *Masquerade Dance* in *The Man of Mode,* was a Peasant in the pantomime dance *The Savoyard,* and danced a minuet with Miss Batchelor. He was scheduled to share a benefit on 15 May 1754, but, as the prompter Cross noted in his diary: "he run away."

Gerard, William   ₁*fl. 1759–1768*₁, scenekeeper.

In 1768 William Gerard testified in favor of Colman in the lengthy litigation concerning Covent Garden; Gerard claimed knowledge of the theatre's affairs because he had "been scene keeper in sd Theatre 9 years."

Geree. *See* GAREE.

Gerey. *See* GERY.

Gerhardi. *See* GHERARDI.

German. *See also* GARMAN and JERMAN.

"German Giant, The." *See* MILLER, MAXIMILIAN JOHN CHRISTOPHER.

"German Man, The"   ₁*fl. 1698–1699*₁, contortionist.

The *Flying Post* of 10–13 December 1698 contained the following advertisement:

There is arrived from *Germany,* a Man born without Arms; He Fences with his Foot, Flings a Dart or Sword through a Board; lays one Foot behind his Neck and Hops on the other; stands on a Stool and reaches a Glass from under it with his Mouth, holds a Cane so fast with his Foot, that the strongest Man cannot pull it from him; writes with his Feet and Mouth Five several Languages, cuts the Pen himself; lays one Foot on his Neck and with his other brings a Glass into that Foot, &c. He is to be seen at Mr. *Strutts* at the *Civet Cat* over against *Exeter Change* in the

Strand. Was never in *England* before and will stay but a short time.

The puff was repeated in the paper through 3 January 1699.

"German Man, The Little." *See* **"LITTLE GERMAN MAN, THE."**

Germiniani. *See* **GEMINIANI.**

Gerrard, Mrs ₍*fl.* 1736₎. *See* **GERARD, MISS.**

Gerrard, Miss ₍*fl.* 1733–1740₎, *dancer, actress, singer.*

Miss Gerrard was first noticed in playbills on 23 October 1733 when she played the title role in *Flora* at the Goodman's Fields Theatre. On 26 October she appeared as Flora in *The Lovers' Opera*; on 26 December she was Jenny in *The Beggar's Opera*; on 2 January 1734 she sang "The Milk Pail Song" between the acts; on 8 January she augmented that with a dance; on 26 April she acted Phebe in *The Distrest Mother*; and on 1 May she offered *The Milk Pail Dance* as part of a dialogue with Jenkins called "The May Morning's Adventure." At Bartholomew Fair on 24 August Miss Gerrard concluded her first year's work playing Betty in *The Imposter*.

Miss Gerrard stayed at Goodman's Fields through the 1735–36 season, but she appeared at the Haymarket on 26 June 1736 as Polly in *The Beggar's Opera* and Dorcas in *The Mock Doctor*, and she was probably the "Mrs Gerrard who acted Engine in *The Innocent Wife* at Southwark Fair the following 7 September. She moved with the Goodman's Fields troupe to the Lincoln's Inn Fields playhouse for the 1736–37 season. During the winters with that group she acted such new roles as the Yeoman's Wife in both *Britannia* and *Harlequin in the City*, a Haymaker and a Scaramouch Woman in *The Necromancer*, Iris in *Jupiter and Io*, Phoebe in *The Beg-*

gar's Wedding, Penelope in *Tunbridge Walks*, Arbella in *The Honest Yorkshireman*, Jenny in *Patie and Peggy*, the Widow in *Sauny the Scot*, Emmeline in *King Arthur*, Harriot in *The Lover His Own Rival*, Wheedle in *The Miser*, and Mrs Lovepuppy in *The Worm Doctor*.

After 1736–37 Miss Gerrard acted less regularly. She was not performing in London in 1737–38 but she appeared as a Sea Nymph in *The Sailor's Wedding* on 23 August 1739 at Bartholomew Fair. She did not act in London again until the fall of 1740, when at Goodman's Fields she played four roles: Myrtilla in *The Provok'd Husband*, Betty in *A Bold Stroke for a Wife*, Honoria in *Love Makes a Man*, and Lamorce in *The Inconstant* (on 19 November). After that she seems to have left the London stage for good.

Gerrard Alexander ₍*fl.* 1694–1697₎, *singer.*

Alexander Gerrard was one of the Children of the Chapel Royal, but by 12 December 1694 his voice had broken. John Gerrard, probably the lad's father, was paid £20 on that date for one year's maintenance for Alexander. Clothing was granted Alexander on 10 January 1695; mourning linen was awarded him some time later that year; and on 31 March 1697 clothing materials were again granted.

Gerum, Mr ₍*fl.* 1735₎, *actor.*

On 22 August 1735 at Lincoln's Inn Fields a Mr Gerum played Antonius in *Caius Marius*.

Gervasia, Signor ₍*fl.* 1768₎, *mandolin player.*

On 3 March 1768 at the Haymarket Theatre Signor Gervasia played a mandolin concerto.

Gery, Mons ₍*fl.* 1734–1735₎, *scene man.*

Monsieur Gery was one of the scene men

in the troupe of players brought to England by Francisque Moylin in the fall of 1734. They performed at the Haymarket Theatre from 26 October 1734 through 2 June 1735 and also played at Goodman's Fields for two performances in May and June.

Gethin, John ₁*fl. 1716–1724*₁, *singer.*
On 9 November 1716 John Gethin was sworn a Gentleman of the Chapel Royal in ordinary. He was perhaps the father of Thomas Gethin, who at that time was receiving payments as a former boy singer in the Chapel and of Roger Gethin, who was cited as a former Chapel boy in 1721. A "Gething Jr" sang at Drury Lane Theatre in October 1724, and the designation would suggest that the elder Gethin, John (if we have sorted out the Gethins correctly), was then still active. We take the Drury Lane singer to have been Thomas, since records of him continue to 1725, whereas Roger was mentioned in contemporary accounts only in 1721. The Gethin who sang at Drury Lane in 1725 was, again, probably Thomas, and since he was not then called "Jr," his father John was doubtless no longer active in London music circles.

Gethin, Roger ₁*fl. 1721*₁, *singer.*
A Lord Chamberlain's warrant of 8 July 1721 awarded clothing and an allowance to Roger "Gethins," a former Chapel boy whose voice had changed. We would guess that his correct name was Gethin and that he was, perhaps, a son of John Gethin and brother of Thomas Gethin. We have found no other references to Roger, so after he left the Chapel Royal he probably gave up a musical career.

Gethin, Thomas ₁*fl. 1715–1725*₁, *singer.*
The *Calendar of Treasury Books* contains an entry covering the period from December 1715 to December 1716 awarding £40 to Thomas "Gethyn" and John Duncombe,

two Children of the Chapel Royal whose voices had changed. Thomas continued his singing career, performing as a countertenor at the Cannons Concerts about 1717 to 1720 for £10 per quarter, and he was, as of 23 April 1720, a Gentleman of the Chapel Royal. We take the Mr "Gething Jr" who sang in Italian and English at Drury Lane Theatre on 14 October 1724 to have been our subject; he was advertised as making his first appearance on any stage. The designation "Jr" suggests that an elder Gethin was performing or was well known in London at the time, and the likeliest candidate would be John Gethin, who was sworn into the Chapel Royal about 1716 and about whom we know no more.

On 22 April 1725 "Gething"—Thomas Gethin, most likely—sang again at Drury Lane for his benefit, and on 30 April he and Mrs Hill sang at her benefit concert at Stationers' Hall. The 1725 notices did not refer to Gethin as Junior, which suggests that the elder Gethin was no longer active.

The Westminster Abbey registers show that Thomas Gethin's daughter Elizabeth died at the age of five and was buried in the south cloister of the Abbey on 15 June 1721. Gethin's wife Elizabeth died on 10 October 1725 at the age of 35 and was buried in the Abbey cloisters on 13 October. The registers indicate that Thomas was still alive at that time.

Gevan. *See* JEVON.

Ghendi. *See* GHERARDI.

Ghentbrugh. *See* VANBRUGHE.

Gherardi, Master ₁*fl. 1764*₁, *dancer.*
Announced as making his first appearance on the English stage, Master Gherardi danced with Miss Street in a dance called *The Carpenters and the Fruit Dealers* at Drury Lane Theatre on 23 May 1764. He was the son of the director of the dances at that theatre, and his dancing partner was

his father's pupil. The dance was repeated only one more time, on 24 May, before the season ended. Young Master Gherardi was next at the Haymarket Theatre during the summer season of 1764, where with Miss Street and Master Clinton (another of the elder Gherardi's students) he appeared in the same dance on 26 and 28 June and in *The Dutchman and the Provincials* on 10 July. Both dances were repeated throughout the summer season, which ended on 14 September 1764.

Gherardi, [Jean-Baptiste?] [*fl. 1740?–1768*], *dancer, ballet master.*

On 25 August 1760, Signora Mattei, new director of the opera at the King's Theatre in London, announced that a Mr Gherardi, who was famed both for serious and comic dancing and for choreography, was engaged as the first male dancer and ballet master for the next season. Possibly Gherardi was the Jean-Baptiste Gherardi who performed as a harlequin and dancer at the Académie Royale de Musique in Paris from 1740 to 1746 and at various theatrical centers in Europe until 1758. If so, then he was the son of Jean-Baptiste Gherardi (b. 1696), also a dancer, and was the fourth generation, at least, of an Italian family that had been performing from as early as the middle of the seventeenth century. The elder Jean-Baptiste Gherardi was the son of Evariste Gherardi (1663–1700), a famous harlequin, and his wife Elizabeth Daneret (called Babet-la-Chanteuse), also a performer at the Comédie-Italienne in Paris. Evariste, in turn, was the son of another well-known player, Giovanni Gherardi. The family is noticed in the *Enciclopedia dello spettacolo*.

In any event, Mr Gherardi made his debut at the King's Theatre on 22 November 1760, when he danced with Mlle Asselin, Polly Capitani, and Tairot. He continued to dance in specialty numbers throughout the season, and on 28 April 1761 he danced in the first performance in England of

Bertoni's comic opera *La pescatrice*. After the opera season, several new dances composed by Gherardi were introduced at the Haymarket Theatre on 23 June 1761. They included *Les Chasseurs et les Bergères*, *The German Coopers*, and *The Gardeners* and were executed by his students Miss Buckinger, Miss Street, Miss Tetley, and Miss Twist. The dances were repeated throughout the summer season under Foote's management. On 6 August Gherardi received a benefit which had been deferred from 30 July by bad weather.

Gherardi was not re-engaged for 1761–62 at the King's Theatre. Presumably he remained in London, for in August of 1763 his students again danced at the Haymarket, and he, no doubt, was employed there. Again, in 1763–64, Gherardi seems to have enjoyed no regular theatrical appointment, but his students continued to appear at Drury Lane and the Haymarket. They now included Master Clinton, Miss Ford, and his own son, Master Gherardi (sometimes Gherardy), who made his debut in a dance called *The Carpenters and Fruit Dealers* at Drury Lane on 23 May 1764.

In 1764–65 Gherardi was again at the King's Theatre as ballet master; his creations there included *The Chinese Wedding* on 24 November 1764, but the bills for that season do not reveal much of his activity. Thereafter he seems to have given up his theatrical connections in London, although perhaps he remained in the city for several more years. On 30 May 1768, Duquesney and Miss Street were described as scholars of Gherardi when they danced at the Haymarket.

Gherardi, Pietro [*fl. 1777–1790*], *singer.*

The singer Pietro Gherardi, whose full name is on a libretto of *Avaro* printed in Florence in 1777, made his first appearance on the London operatic stage at the King's Theatre on 28 March 1780 in the role of Don Anselmo in *L'amore soldato*. In his other appearances at the King's that spring he sang principal roles in *La schiava* and *La buona figliuola* and Mons L'Allumette in *Il duca d'Atene*. Gherardi was reengaged for the following season, 1780–81, in which he performed Dottore Matteo in *L'arcifanfano*, Barone in *Il barone di Torreforte*, Sandro in *Zemira e Azor*, Don Fabrizio in *La Frascatana*, and a principal role in *L'omaggio*. He gave his final performance in London as Don Fabrizio on 19 June 1781. Gherardi's full name appeared on a libretto of *Andromaca* which was published at Venice in 1790. The young Signora Gherardi who sang at the King's Theatre in 1782–83 may have been his daughter or wife.

Gherardi, Teresa *b. c. 1765, singer.*

At the age of 17, Signora Teresa Gherardi, who perhaps was related to the singer Pietro Gherardi (fl. 1777–1790), made her first appearance in England at the King's Theatre on 2 November 1782 in the role of Giacomina in *Il convito*. She sang Zelinda in *Medonte* on 14 November, Giacomina in *Il trionfo della costanza* on 19 December, Elvira in *Cimene* on 16 January 1783, a principal role in *Ifigenia in Aulide* on 18 February, Fatima in *Zemira and Azor* on 27 February, Droghetta in *I vecchi burlati* on 27 March, Laodamia in *Creusa in Delfo* on 29 April, Argène in *L'Olimpiade* on 1 May, a principal character in *La buona figliuola* on 3 June, and Rosalinda in *Avaro* on 14 June.

Gheri, Signor [fl. 1799–1800], *dancer.*

Signor Gheri made his first appearance dancing Jamie in *The Scotch Ghost* after the mainpiece at Drury Lane on 2 December 1799. The dance was repeated many times during the season, and on 2 June 1800 Gheri also appeared in an untitled new ballet and in a dance called *The Lucky Escape*.

Ghirardo. *See* GIRALDO.

Ghiringhelli. *See* CHIRINGHELLI.

Ghizziello. *See* "GIZZIELLO."

Giacomazzi, Margarita [fl. 1749–1750], *singer, instrumentalist.*

On 6 March 1749 Signora Margarita Giacomazzi, who had recently arrived in London from Italy, appeared at Covent Garden as a singer after the mainpiece was performed. Latreille reported that she held a benefit at the Haymarket Theatre on 17 April, a performance which is not listed in *The London Stage*. On 16 September 1749 at the Assembly Room, St Augustine's Back, Bristol, a vocal and instrumental concert was presented by her for her benefit. She was in Croza's opera company at the Haymarket in London in November and December 1749, but no notice was taken of her in the bills. That troupe moved to the King's Theatre in January 1750. On 31 March Signora Giacomazzi sang Turno in *Il trionfo di Camilla*, and on 10 April she sang at the benefit concert for indigent musicians and their families. Croza's season ended on 28 April, and the impresario left with many of his debts unpaid. Margarita Giacomazzi seems also to have departed London.

Giacomo, Giorgio, stage name of Giorgio Giacomo Berwillibald [fl. 1716], *singer.*

Giorgio Giacomo Berwillibald sang Amiceto in *Lucio Vero* on 1 February 1716 and Aurillo in *Cleartes* on 18 April at the King's Theatre. At Hickford's Music Room on 9 June he gave a benefit concert at which he was identified as "Servant to his Serene Highness the Margrave of Brandenburgh Anspach, Brother to Her Royal Highness the Princess of Wales."

"Gianetta." *See* BACCELLI, GIOVANNA.

Giani, Signor [fl. 1791–1796], dancer.

On 5 November 1791 Signor Giani danced in *Don Juan* with the Drury Lane company at the King's Theatre. The following 31 December he was a Knight in *Cymon,* but the account books indicate that on 7 January 1792 Giani was discharged. He was back with the troupe in October 1794, though the playbills for the 1794–95 season make no mention of him. On 7 July 1796 he participated in a dance titled *L'Heureux Naufrage* at the King's Theatre, but on the twelfth of the month he was omitted from it.

Giani, Signora [fl. 1789], singer.

Signora Giani sang a minor character in *Il barbiere di Siviglia* at the King's Theatre in the Haymarket on 11 June 1789.

"Giantess, The Saxon Lady." *See* "SAXON LADY GIANTESS, THE."

"Giant Hatter, The." *See* BAMFIELD, EDWARD.

Giardini, Felice de' 1716–1796, violinist, composer, conductor, teacher.

Felice de' Giardini was born in Turin on 12 April 1716. He was sent to Milan to study the harpsichord, composition, and singing under Paladini and was choirboy in Milan Cathedral. But he had already expressed a partiality for the violin and his father recalled him to Turin to study under Lorenzo Somis.

In 1728 when he was 12, he went to Rome and a little later joined the orchestra of the Teatro San Carlo at Naples. His technique was exceptionally brilliant and he was fond of displaying it even when doing so was inappropriate. Burney said that he was fond of recalling how he was cured of this conceitedness:

I had acquired great reputation among the ignorant for my impertinence; yet one night,

By permission of the Trustees of the British Museum

FELICE GIARDINI

engraving by Tomkins, after Gainsborough

during the opera, Jomelli, who had composed it, came into the orchestra, and seating himself close by me, I determined to give the Maestro di Capella a touch of my taste and execution; and in the symphony of the next song, which was in the pathetic style, I gave loose to my fingers and fancy; for which I was rewarded by the composer with a violent slap in the face; which . . . was the best lesson I ever received from a great master in my life.

But Jomelli afterwards showed great kindness to the young musician.

In 1748 Giardini left Naples for a tour which took him through Germany, on to Paris in 1750, and then to London. He played for the first time in England at Hickford's Room in Brewer Street, on 18 May 1750, at a benefit for Signora Cuzzoni. Burney remembered that Cuzzoni "was grown old, poor, and almost deprived of voice, by age and infirmities," and that "there was but little company; yet, when

Giardini played a solo of Martini of Milan's composition, the applause was so long and loud, that I never remember to have heard such hearty and unequivocal marks of approbation at any other musical performance." He favored Signora Cuzzoni by performing again at her benefit, along with the singers Guadagni and Signora Frasi, on 27 April 1751.

Giardini had no doubt established himself in the intervening year as a concert player, though no bills are known and few are available for several years thereafter. On 23 August 1751 Garrick wrote to the Marchioness of Hartington and mentioned that "Geortini" had given a concert at York that day. On 24 March 1752 Giardini furnished a "New Overture" and played a concerto on the violin, when he joined Beard, Galli, Wass, Vincent, and Signora Frasi in a concert at the King's Theatre, "Benefit for the Increase of a Fund for the support of Decayed Musicians or their Families."

In December 1751 Giardini established, with the second Thomas Vincent, oboist, subscription concerts at the Great Room, No 21, Dean Street, Soho, which, with some remissions, ran for over 30 years. (By 1762 his establishment seems to have been conducted on the order of a supper theatre. The Duchess of Northumberland entered in her diary on 9 December 1762: "In the Evening went to Giardini's. Only 30 people stay'd to Supper. . . . They began after supper to sing Catches. . . ." She mentioned "Giardini's" again in 1773 as one in a list of some 80 "public amusements this Year.")

After the death of Michael Christian Festing, in 1752, Giardini took over as leader of the band at the Italian opera at the King's Theatre. The connection lasted, with some long interruptions, for 40 years. Burney testified that in the band Giardini "introduced new discipline, and a new style of playing, much superior in itself, and more congenial with the poetry and

Music of Italy, than the languid manner of his predecessor Festing."

In 1756, after Vaneschi's bankruptcy, Giardini and the singer Regina Mingotti assumed "for awhile the sovereignty of the opera kingdom, by which gratification of ambition they were soon brought to the brink of ruin. . . ." In 1757 they resigned the management, but evidently Giardini continued to lead the band. At the close of the season, 11 June 1763, when Signora Colomba Mattei left the opera management and England, Giardini and Signora Mingotti took over once again, but after "an inauspicious season" in 1763–64 their reign finally ended. Extant bills show that Giardini was leader of the opera band in 1772–73, 1776–77, and 1782–83.

Giardini had been listed as first violin when Handel's *Acis and Galatea* had been given at the Haymarket for the benefit of Signora Frasi on 2 April 1753, and at Arne's benefit at Drury Lane on 27 March 1754 "De Giardino" directed a performance of *Alfred* "Done in the Manner of an Oratorio." He was much in demand as an attraction to benefit nights, and scattered notices of that sort appeared until 1790, placing him at all the major theatres and at many of the theatrical and musical taverns. At various times he was leader of the bands at the Pantheon, and Ranelagh, Vauxhall, and Marylebone Gardens.

Wilkinson mentioned Giardini as leader of the band at the Assembly Rooms in York in 1765. For a number of years in the later sixties and in the seventies he organized, played, and led the band in benefit performances for the Lock Hospital, in its Chapel. At the Pantheon on 4 April 1774 he played a violin solo after the second part of the oratorio *The Resurrection*, but he was then called "Giordini." On 4 June 1774 he appeared at the head of a band when the King's birthday was celebrated at a banquet at Somerset House. In a letter to Sainsbury, now in the Glasgow University Library, the oboist John Parke said he had "attended [at the residence of the Prince of Wales], with Giardini, Schroeter, and Crosdill, who were his royal Highness's Chamber Band." He presided musically over many public ceremonies, as at the opening of the building of the Incorporated Society of Artists on 11 May 1782.

During all his varied activities his house swarmed with pupils. Burney said that his

great hand, taste, and style of playing, were so universally admired, that he had soon not only a great number of scholars on the violin, but taught many ladies of the first rank to sing; and after he had been here a few years, he formed a morning *academia*, or concert, at his house, composed chiefly of his scholars, vocal and instrumental, who bore a part in the performance. . . .

Among his pupils were the violinists Charles Ashley and William Dance. He was also "employed . . . to teach several of our playhouse singers. . . ."

Burney's opinion was that Giardini could have been a fine harpsichord player, "but he told me himself that he was perfectly cured of that vanity, at Paris, by the performance of Madame de S. Maur, a scholar of Rameau, who played in such a manner, as not only to make him ashamed of his own performance, but determined him never to touch the instrument again in serious practice." Perhaps Giardini kept his hand in, however, for *Mortimer's London Directory* listed him in 1763: "Composer, teaches singing, and the Harpsichord."

In 1784 Giardini left England and returned to Italy, determined on retirement; but he soon reconsidered, and by 1789 he was once again in England. On 7 January 1790 he began a final season of opera at the Little Theatre in the Haymarket. During the time he was out of the country his old and friendly rival Wilhelm Cramer had gained the advantage as the premier violinist, and Johann Peter Salomon had become his principal challenger. Loewenberg

FELICE GIARDINI

engraving by S. W. Reynolds, after J. Reynolds

has stated in *Grove's Dictionary* that "soon after" 1790 Giardini left London and that he arrived in St Petersburg "about 1793." Van der Straeten has him arriving "with a theatrical company" in Moscow in 1791. But Haydn noted on 21 May 1792 that he had heard Giardini at Ranelagh: "He played like a pig." Doane's *Musical Directory* (1794) listed "Giardini,–/Violin. Opera. No 7 Shepherd St Mayfair." Giardini died at Moscow, in poverty, on 8 June 1796.

According to Alexis Chitty in *Grove's Dictionary* Giardini in December 1752 had married at London the excellent young singer and dancer of the Concerts Spirituel in Paris, Maria Caterina Violante (d. 23 April 1791). She was of the numerous and illustrious family of singers, actors, and dancers, several of whom were at later times in London. (Details of their careers may be found in Grove.) She herself did not perform in London. Her appearances in the Concert Spirituel up to 1757 were under the name of Vestris-Giardini.

Evidently Giardini remarried, for on 3 April 1814 a Mrs Giardini asked for financial assistance from the Royal Society of Musicians. Relief was refused, and she was asked to "report to the annual general meeting."

Sainsbury's *Dictionary of Musicians* (1824) makes Giardini out to have been a splenetic, difficult man, "Careless of his own interest, and inattentive to all those means which have promoted his success in the world."

Giardini collaborated with Charles Avison on an English oratorio, *Ruth* (1765), and wrote the music for William Mason's lyrical drama *Sappho* (1778) and choruses for Mason's *Elfrida* (1779). His operas were *Rosmira* (1757), *Siroe* (1763), *Enea e Lavinia* (1764), and *Il re pastore* (1765). He also wrote much instrumental music (see Grove). Twelve numbers of his *Miscellaneous Works*, published in London about 1790, are itemized in the *Catalogue of Printed Music in the British Museum*, along with many catches, glees, songs, and instrumental pieces.

Portraits of Giardini include:

1. By Thomas Gainsborough, painting. At Knole. Perhaps this is the portrait which was engraved by C. Tomkins and published by H. Graves.

2. By Gainsborough, painting. At Old Warden.

3. Engraved portrait by F. Bartolozzi, after G. B. Cipriani. Published as a plate to his *Sonatas*, 1765.

4. Engraved portrait by Lambert, Jr., after G. B. Cipriani. At the Hoftheater, Vienna.

5. Engraved portrait by S. W. Reynolds, from a sketch by Sir Joshua Reynolds.

6. Giardini was pictured in a large group of musicians engraved by Bettelini, after Luigi Scotti, about 1805.

7. Possibly Giardini was one of the musicians pictured in a red chalk drawing by Gainsborough of a musical party. If that drawing, which is in the British Library, is of a party at Bath, as has been suggested, the other musicians pictured may be Mrs Linley, Elizabeth Linley, and the elder Thomas Linley.

Giay, Mons [*fl.* 1733–1734?], *horn player.*

On 6 October 1733 at the Haymarket Theatre Messrs Giay and Charle (Charles), advertised as lately arrived from Paris, played a concerto for French horns. They repeated it at subsequent performances and on 20 October offered an untitled duo. The playbill for 4 February 1734 advertised music for French horns but failed to cite the players; perhaps Giay and Charles were the performers.

Gibbetti. *See* GIBETTI.

Gibbon, Mr [*fl.* 1713–1726], *manager, performer?*

Mr Gibbon managed a troupe of ropedancers who performed at the tennis court in James Street on 26 November 1713 and apparently continued offering their "agilities" through the Christmas season. On 7 September 1726 at Southwark Fair Gibbon ran "Mr Gibbin's and Mrs Violante's Great Booth." Gibbon may also have been a performer, though the bills did not say so.

Gibbon, Mr [*fl.* 1797–1805?], *actor.*

A Mr Gibbon—not James Deverell Gibbon, though possibly related to him—acted at Drury Lane Theatre in 1797–98. He played Lenox in *Macbeth* on 7 November 1797, a Messenger in *Othello* on 23 November, Gadshill in *1 Henry IV* on 25 November, a Knight in *The Countess of Salisbury* on 8 December, Antonio in *The*

Tempest on 9 December, Harold in *The Castle Spectre* on 14 December (though he was dropped from the cast four days later), Valentine in *Twelfth Night* on 13 February 1798, the First Gentleman in *Measure for Measure* on 3 March, Conrade in *Much Ado About Nothing* on 24 May, a Gentleman in *Don Juan* on 13 June, Trueman in *The Clandestine Marriage* on 15 June, and the Second Brother in *Comus* on 18 June. His benefit tickets were admitted on 13 June.

He was probably the subject of the following report in the *Monthly Mirror* in October 1801:

A Mr. Gibbon, who played, last season, Obadiah, in Honest Thieves, for Mrs. Glover, at Covent Garden, and Don Manuel, in She would and She would not, for Mr. Trueman, at Drury-Lane, came forward [on 16 October 1801] under a regular engagement, in the part of Verdun. He possesses a tolerable portion of vis comica, and upon the whole, was pretty successful; but to follow Munden in such a character was a hazardous experiment, and we think Mr. Gibbon felt the difficulty of the task he had undertaken.

The Drury Lane accounts cited a Mr Gibbon from 1801–2 on, confirming the report, but by 1805 the references were not to our subject, we believe, but rather to the singer James Gibbon, who seems to have joined the troupe about 1803–4.

It is likely that Gibbon the actor had performed outside of London between 1798 and 1800, and he may have been the Gibbon who, with his wife, the former Mrs Belfille, acted at Wolverhampton in January 1802—though our subject was supposed to have been at Drury Lane that season. It is very likely that he was the Gibbon who played Touchstone in *As You Like It* at Gloucester on 24 July 1805.

Gibbon, James Deverell *1779–1852, singer, actor.*

According to the *Theatrical Inquisitor*

in August 1814, James Deverell Gibbon (identified only as Mr Gibbon) was born in Derby on 17 December 1779. He and his parents moved to Ashby-de-la-Zouch, Leicestershire, and there he studied under the Rev John Prior. Young Gibbon was bound apprentice to a cabinet maker and, while serving, turned to music. He became a favorite of Dr Kirkland, a promoter of oratorios and musical meetings in Ashby-de-la-Zouch, and sang treble parts in some of Handel's choruses. After he completed his apprenticeship Gibbon came to London—we may guess that he was then about 21 and the year about 1800. Indeed, a Mr Gibbon sang at Vauxhall Gardens about 1800, and the Drury Lane accounts cited a

Harvard Theatre Collection

JAMES D. GIBBON, as Vincent

engraving by Carver, after De Wilde

Gibbon from 1801 on (but he may have been the actor Gibbon and not our subject).

But the *Theatrical Inquisitor* stated that upon arrival in London James looked up a relative, Mr Hodson of the Piazza Coffee House, Covent Garden, applied to Cross of the Royal Circus, played a small part there in *Cora,* toured with the company to Liverpool and Edinburgh, returned to London to finish out the season at Astley's Amphitheatre, and *then* applied to Kemble at Drury Lane, where he was given a five-year contract beginning, apparently, in 1803–4. We take it that the Gibbon cited in the Drury Lane accounts from about 1803 on was James and that the actor Gibbon had by then left the troupe.

The accounts named Gibbon regularly through 1808–9, once calling him James. He was a member of the singing chorus at a weekly salary of £3 in 1805, £4 in 1806, and £5 in 1807. During his tenure at Drury Lane Gibbon also appeared at Vauxhall Gardens in June 1802 and, perhaps, other times. He may have been the Mr Gibbon who, with his wife, the former Mrs Belfille, acted at Wolverhampton in January 1802, though that seems unlikely, since our subject was clearly at Drury Lane during the 1801–2 season. However, he may well have been the Gibbon who played Touchstone in *As You Like It* at Gloucester on 24 July 1805.

The *Theatrical Inquisitor* account of James Gibbon stated that after the Drury Lane Theatre burned in 1809 Gibbon was dropped from the troupe and had to seek employment elsewhere. Wewitzer's *Pocketbook* placed Gibbon at the Lyceum in 1809, and the *Monthly Mirror* said that Gibbon sang in Dublin under the management of Henry Johnson. The Minute Books of the Irish Musical Fund show that on 11 March 1810 a Mr "Gibbons" was appointed to assist at the annual Handel commemoration concert; he was, we would guess, our subject.

Gibbon returned to London and was engaged by Elliston at the Surrey Theatre. The Royal Circus accounts show a J. Gibbon there on 13 July 1812 playing Apollo in the pantomime *Seven Wonders of the World.* A Mr G. Gibbon (an error for J., or a second person?) performed at the Circus in 1811, 1812, and 1813; he arranged a burletta called *Animal Magnetism* on 6 November 1811, played Plainway in *Raising the Wind* on 3 November 1812, and had a leading role in the musical *Siberian Exile* on 28 June 1813. James Gibbon was certainly working at the Royal Circus on 19 February 1816, for the playbill gave his full name and announced that he would sing "The Lass that Loves a Sailor."

The *Theatrical Inquisitor* stated that on 16 July 1814 Gibbon had played Ferdinand in *The Duenna* at the Lyceum Theatre. There the paper ended its account, with an admonition to Gibbon to live a more adventurous life in order to give the paper better copy. A picture of Gibbon accompanied the brief biography. It was an engraving by J. Carver after S. De Wilde of Gibbon as Vincent in *The Jovial Crew.*

The *Memoirs* of the younger Charles Dibdin cited a singer J. Gibbon at Sadler's Wells in 1818, and James Winston on 9 June 1824 noted in his diary that a Mr Gibbon, a vocalist, supped with his daughter at the Craven's Head. Both references are probably to James Gibbon.

On 21 August 1852, according to the *Gentleman's Magazine* of October 1852 (which supplied his full name), James Deverell Gibbon was killed in an accident in Lambeth workhouse:

The unfortunate gentleman was very feeble, and had for some time been an inmate of the workhouse. On Sunday he had permission to go out, and on his return, was descending . . . stone steps into the yard [when] his hand gave way as he was leaning on the railing, and he fell over into the area below, a height of about sixteen feet. His head pitched first on the stones, and Mr. Brooks, the task-master, described the concussion as like 'some one breaking a cocoa nut with a hammer.'

Gibbon's profile portrait appears in a group of English singers which was printed as frontispiece to Hodgson's *New Skylark*, 1823, reprinted 1840.

Gibbons, Mr *d. c. 1673, actor.*

The Duke's Company prompter, John Downes, stated in his *Roscius Anglicanus* that a member of the troupe named Gibbons died about 1673. No roles are known for Gibbons, and *The London Stage* lists him only for the 1673–74 season, which he presumably did not complete.

Gibbons, Mr [*fl. 1784*], *violinist.*

Mr Gibbons played tenor (viola) in the Handel Memorial Concerts at Westminster Abbey and the Pantheon in May and June 1784.

Gibbons, Mr [*fl. 1786*], *actor.*

A "Young Gentleman" making his first appearance on any stage spoke a monologue called "Parents and Children" at Hammersmith on 28 June 1786. In later bills his name was revealed as Mr Gibbons. He acted Jaffeir in *Venice Preserv'd* on 5 July, Lord Gayville in *The Heiress* on 10 July, Don Carlos in *A Bold Stroke for a Wife* on 19 July, Lord Townly in *The Provok'd Husband* on 24 July, and Sir George Touchwood in *The Belle's Stratagem* on 26 July.

Gibbons, Mrs [*fl. 1754–1757*], *dancer.*

Mrs Gibbons danced at Drury Lane in the 1750s, the first mention of her name being on 2 May 1754 when her benefit tickets were accepted. On 3 May 1755 she shared a benefit with two others; on 7 May 1756 she shared one with three others, as she did on 18 May 1757, the last time she was mentioned. Though her benefits would

suggest that she held a position of some responsibility in the theatre, the playbills for those years cited her only twice: she danced in *The Chinese Festival* on 8 November 1755, and at her shared benefit on 18 May 1757 she performed a louvre with Shawford.

A Catherine Gibbons, possibly a daughter of Mrs Gibbons the dancer, was left a small bequest in the will of Josceline Shawford on 7 February 1760 (probate 2 January 1764). Catherine was described in 1760 as a minor and the sister of John Morris—which does not quite make sense, unless "sister" should be taken to mean stepsister.

Gibbons, Mrs [*fl. 1767*], *singer.*

Mrs Gibbons sang at Marylebone Gardens under Thomas Lowe in August and September 1767. On the last night of the season, 18 September, she was one of the singers in a performance of *Solomon*.

Gibbons, Christopher *1615–1676* *organist, virginal player, composer.*

Christopher Gibbons, the second son of the famous musician Orlando Gibbons and his wife Elizabeth, was christened at St Margaret, Westminster, on 22 August 1615. He may have received some early musical training from his father at the Chapel Royal, but Orlando died when Christopher was ten, and the lad is said to have been adopted by his uncle Edward Gibbons, the organist of Exeter Cathedral. In 1638 Christopher was appointed organist of Winchester Cathedral, and when the civil war brought an end to the Cathedral music, he fled with the dean and prebends in 1644 and served in one of the garrisons.

Gibbons supported himself during the Commonwealth by teaching organ and virginal. On 12 July 1654 John Evelyn heard him at Oxford: "Next we walked to Magdalen College, where we saw the library and chapel, which was likewise in pontifi-

Courtesy of the Faculty of Music, Oxford

CHRISTOPHER GIBBONS

artist unknown

cal order, the altar only I think turned ta-blewise, and there was still the double organ, which abominations (as now es-teemed) were almost universally demol-ished; Mr. Gibbon, that famous musician, giving us a taste of his skill and talents on that instrument."

When Sir William Davenant produced *The Siege of Rhodes* at Rutland House about September 1656, Christopher Gib-bons was one of the small band of musi-cians who accompanied the performers. On 17 November 1660 Gibbons replaced Thomas Warwick as virginal player in the King's Musick at a salary of £86 annually. He also became organist of the Chapel Royal and Westminster Abbey and private organist to Charles II. The Lord Chamber-lain's accounts cited Gibbons frequently during the 1660s, though the citations rarely stated more than that he continued at his posts. Samuel Pepys, too, mentioned Gibbons several times during that decade: for Lord Sandwich on 19 May 1661 Gib-

bons and other musicians played some songs and symphonies; on 13 June 1662 Pepys dined with Gibbons and others; on 23 De-cember 1666 Gibbons promised Pepys he would set a bass to a piece of music for him; on 24 February 1668 Gibbons helped Pepys search for an organ for his house; and on 3 July 1668 Pepys and Gibbons were at the Sun Tavern in King Street, and Gibbons promised to get Pepys some music for his flageolets.

On 2 July 1663 Charles II wrote "To our trusty and welbeloved the Vice-Chancellor, Doctors, Proctors and Masters of the Uni-versity of Oxford" as follows:

Whereas the bearer, Christopher Gibbons, one of the organists of our Chapell Royall, hath from his youth served our Royall father and our selfe, And hath soe well improved him-selfe in musique as well in our owne Judge-ment as the judgement of all men well skilled in that science as that he may worthily receave your honer and degree of Doctor therin, wee in consideracon of his merritt and fittness thereunto, have thought fitt by these our Let-ters to recommend him unto you. And to sig-nify our gracious pleasure to be, that he be forthwith admitted and created by you, Doc-tor in Musique. He performing his exercises and paying all his due fees, any statute or cus-tome whatsoever be contrary notwithstanding.

Gibbons was granted the degree on 7 July 1664.

On 7 January 1668 Christopher Preston was assigned to replace Dr Gibbons in the King's Musick when Gibbons should die. That often meant a musician was very old or not in good health, and, significantly, after 1669 the accounts made no mention of Gibbons until his death in 1676, and he may well have been ailing. Anthony à Wood called Gibbons a "grand debauchee" who "would often sleep at Morning Prayer when he was to play the organ." Certainly Christopher was far from the talented mu-sician his father Orlando had been. He composed a number of fantasies and anthems, and with Matthew Locke he wrote music for Shirley's *Masque of Cupid and Death*, performed on 26 March 1653, but his music was not distinguished and most of it languishes today in manuscript.

On 23 September 1646 at St Bartholomew the Less in London, according to Joseph Chester's notes in the Westminster Abbey registers, Gibbons had married Mary Kercher, the daughter of Dr Robert Kercher, who was then canon of Winchester and later became a canon of St Paul's in London. Mary Kercher Gibbons died in 1662 and was buried in the North Cloister of Westminster Abbey on 15 April of that year. Christopher married a second time, to Elizabeth Ball (or Bull), who outlived him and was buried in the cloisters of the Abbey on 27 December 1682. Gibbons and his second wife had three daughters.

Christopher Gibbons died on 20 October 1676; he was buried in the cloisters of the Abbey on 24 October, and the following day Christopher Preston, after a considerable wait, was given Gibbons's post as virginal player in the King's Musick. Gibbons's nuncupative will described him as from the parish of St Margaret, Westminster. The memorandum stated that on or about 17 October 1676 Christopher declared his will, leaving everything to his wife Elizabeth. That was done in the hearing of Elizabeth Rabliss and Ann Ball; Ann, Elizabeth Gibbons's sister, signed with her mark. Elizabeth proved the will on 6 November 1676. Her own will, written on 19 March 1678, was proved on 22 January 1683, less than a month after "Elizabeth Bull" was buried at Westminster Abbey on 27 December 1682.

There is no explanation of why Mrs Gibbons was recorded in the burial register under her maiden name, especially since she was buried, as she requested, near her late husband, whom she clearly identified as the musician Christopher Gibbons. Mrs Gibbons left her copyhold estates in "Freesolke," Southamptonshire, to her daughter Elizabeth. To her cousin Henry Sherborne of "Bedfont" Mrs Gibbons left £279 10*s*. "or thereabouts" in money due her late husband from the King. Mrs Gibbons mentioned a daughter Anne and a daughter Mary who was not in England in 1678. Also cited were Mrs Gibbons's sister Ann Ball, a brother Leonard Ball, and a nephew (her late husband's godson) Orlando Ball.

Curiously, there was another Elizabeth Ball or Bull in the vicinity of Westminster Abbey. The registers for St Margaret, Westminster, cited an Elizabeth Ball, née Burnley, whose husband was named William; they were married in 1666. One wonders if the burial notice in December 1782 of Elizabeth Bull referred to Christopher Gibbons's widow or another woman. Just as curious is the fact that there was another Christopher Gibbons (with a wife named Elizabeth and a son named Orlando) in London—a cousin of our subject, perhaps. On 8, 15, and 22 April 1655 at St Clement Danes banns were published for the marriage of Christopher Gibbons of St Giles, Cripplegate, gentleman, and Elizabeth Filbridge of St Clement Danes, widow. On 20 February 1656 their son Orlando was born; he was baptized six days later. Orlando died in infancy and was buried on 11 December 1657. Mary Gibbons, their next child, was born on 13 September 1658 and christened on 29 September. Their daughter Ann was baptized on 7 June 1660. Three different women named Elizabeth Gibbons were buried in our period at St Clement Danes: one on 3 September 1665, a second on 8 December 1667, and a third on 17 February 1670.

A portrait of Christopher Gibbons, "A. V. Dyck fecit," is at the Faculty of Music, Oxford. The portrait was engraved by J. Caldwall and published by Hawkins in his *General History*.

Gibbons, John *\[fl. 1784–1794\]*, *singer.*

The Reverend John Gibbons sang bass

in the Handel Memorial Concerts at Westminster Abbey and the Pantheon in May and June 1784. Doane's *Musical Directory* in 1794 listed him as a minor canon at St Paul's Cathedral living at No 3, St Paul's College. He sang in the choirs at Windsor and Westminster Abbey.

Gibbs, Mr [*fl. 1719–1720*], *treasurer.*

Mr Gibbs, the treasurer of the Lincoln's Inn Fields Theatre, received benefits on 5 May 1719 and 5 May 1720. He may well have served at the theatre more years than those citations indicate, and it seems probable that he was related to Edward Gibbs of the Restoration period and Gibbs the pitkeeper of the 1730s.

Gibbs, Mr [*fl. 1732*], *house servant.*

On 12 May 1732 at Lincoln's Inn Fields Mr Gibbs and three other house servants shared a benefit. It is possible that Gibbs was the man of that name who served the theatre as treasurer in 1719 and 1720, but if so, his position in the company had certainly dropped in importance.

Gibbs, Mr [*fl. 1732–1736*], *pitkeeper.*

Mr Gibbs, the pitkeeper at the Goodman's Fields Theatre, shared a benefit with Temple on 19 May 1732, had solo benefits on 21 May 1733 and 20 May 1734, and had his benefit tickets accepted on 3 May 1736. He was probably related to other house servants named Gibbs who were active in the late seventeenth and early eighteenth centuries.

Gibbs, Mr [*fl. 1759–1760*], *actor, singer?*

Mr Gibbs's name was first seen in a London theatrical bill when he played Ben in *The Beggar's Opera* at Covent Garden Theatre on 20 March 1759. He took the part of Lysimachus in *The Humourous Lieutenant* on 7 April following. In the season of 1759–60 he was a Butcher during the long run enjoyed by the pantomime *The Fair* and played Dervise in *Tamerlane*, Scentwell in *The Jovial Crew*, Steer in *The Spirit of Contradiction*, Pounce in *The Tender Husband* and Clump in *The Funeral*. At the beginning of the season of 1760–61 Gibbs was carried in the paylist of performers at the rate of 3s. 4d. per day, but he is not recorded as having performed again there or anywhere else in London.

Gibbs, Mr [*fl. 1782*], *actor.*

A Mr Gibbs, who had evidently performed at Sadler's Wells, spoke an epilogue as part of an entertainment given at Coopers' Hall in King Street, Bristol, on 2 March 1782. The troupe was headed by Mr Andrews and claimed that it would perform a "great Variety of new and pleasing EXHIBITIONS of SADLERS' WELLS" during the fair. We have found no record of Gibbs's activity in London.

Gibbs, Mrs [*fl. 1676–1678*], *actress.*

Mrs Gibbs was possibly a younger sister of the actress Anne Gibbs Shadwell. Mrs Gibbs acted minor and secondary parts for the Duke's Company at the Dorset Garden Theatre, her first recorded role being Henrietta in *Don Carlos* on 8 June 1676. Thereafter she played Beatrice in *The Wrangling Lovers* on 25 July, Mrs Essence and the epilogue to *Tom Essence* in late August, Arbella in *Madam Fickle* on 4 November, Clara in *The Cheats of Scapin* in November or December, Iras in *Antony and Cleopatra* on 12 February 1677 and probably earlier, Clarina in *The Counterfeit Bridegroom* in September, Chloe in *Timon of Athens* in January 1678, Maundy in *Sir Patient Fancy* on 17 January, Victoria in *Friendship in Fashion* on 5 April, and Flora in *The Counterfeits* on 28 May.

Gibbs, Anne. *See* SHADWELL, MRS THOMAS.

Gibbs, Edward *[fl. 1665]*, *house-keeper*.

A warrant in the Lord Chamberlain's accounts dated 29 June 1665 listed Edward Gibbs as the housekeeper at the King's Company playhouse in Bridges Street.

Gibbs, Edward *[fl. 1749–1763]*, *instrumentalist*.

Documents among the Lord Chamberlain's papers in the Public Record Office show Edward Gibbs to have been a musician in the King's Band under the successive Masters Maurice Greene and William Boyce from 1749 through 1759, with a stipend of £40 plus livery each year. A lengthy document, dated only 1763, empowered one Abraham Lara, merchant, of London to collect annually £20 of the salary of Edward Gibbs of Lympsfield, Surrey, musician in ordinary to the King, in consideration of an indebtedness to Lara of £250.

Harvard Theatre Collection

MARIA GIBBS, as Cowslip

engraving by Ridley, after Clarke

Gibbs, Maria née Logan, later the second Mrs George Colman the younger *b. 1770, actress, singer*.

Maria Logan was said by William Oxberry in his *Dramatic Biography* (1826) to have been born in 1770, one of three daughters of an Irish theatrical couple. They were probably the performers of that name whom Clark in *The Irish Stage in the County Towns* located at Kilkenny in 1767, 1768, and 1770, Belfast in 1770, Smock Alley, Dublin, in 1772, 1774, and 1775–76, Crow Street, Dublin, in 1776–77, 1778–79, and 1781–82, and Cork in 1773. (Mrs Logan, without her husband, acted at Cork also in 1776, 1779, and 1780.)

Maria appeared for the first time "on any stage" billed only as "a Very Young Lady," at the Haymarket Theatre on 18 June 1783 in the part of Sally in *Man and Wife*. She played the part only four times and nothing else that summer. But she must have left an impression, for she was invited by

Harris to perform Sally at Covent Garden on 7 May 1784 and on that occasion was called "A Very Young Lady, the same that performed it at the Haymarket." On 28 June following she returned to the Haymarket, seemingly in minor triumph, to play the title part in the "dramatic novel," *Polly Honeycombe*. She was then identified as Miss Logan "Who, last Year, perform'd the part of Sally in MAN AND WIFE." But strangely, she was seen no more at the Haymarket that season, or anywhere, for several years.

When next Maria did appear it was in the company at John Palmer's ill-fated Royalty Theatre in the summer of 1787. Palmer was reported by Oxberry to have been her godfather. An earlier (and less trustworthy) source, the *Authentic Memoirs of the Green Room* (1799), put forward another story—that she "was supposed to be a natural daughter of the late Mr. Palmer's, but it was an artful report, propagated by Joseph Surface [Palmer] himself . . . to be her only admirer, and check the ardour of rivals, by seemingly parental affection." Neither assertion is provable.

Maria had changed her name to Mrs Gibbs by the spring of 1787. She played Miss Biddy in *Miss in Her Teens* under that designation when the Royalty opened its doors on 20 June 1787, according to a cast for that night printed in the *Thespian Dictionary* in 1805. But the powerful interests of the patent theatres prevented the Royalty from performing plays thereafter. The house reopened on 2 July with a program of burlettas and then Palmer staged only musical pieces. Oxberry said that "Mrs G., by the secession of the more initiated troops of Thalia, got into possession of a very considerable line of business. In a piece called *Thomas and Susan,* (taken from *The Poor Soldier*), she played Kathleen, and most of the principal characters in the serious pantomimes that were performed there. . . ." She also became Palmer's prologue spokeswoman, "the instrument by which satirical allusions, or pointed invectives [against the patent-house managers], were conveyed to the town . . . [and] was marked for exclusion from the boards of the Haymarket" by the elder Colman.

Maria Gibbs played Louisa in *The Deserter of Naples* for her patron Palmer at Drury Lane Theatre on 2 June 1788. Her activities for the five years following that date are unknown. She seems to have been blacklisted by management. But by the early 1790s the elder Colman's grip on the Haymarket management had been loosened by physical and mental illness and his son had assumed direction of the theatre's affairs. The Palmers—John, John the younger, and Robert—were playing regularly at the Haymarket after 1789, and through their influence Maria was introduced to the company, coming out on

15 June 1793 as Bridget in *The Chapter of Accidents.* Thus began an unbroken series of successes which made her second only to Dora Jordan in their frank and merry line of comedy. She succeeded Becky Wells in her famous Cowslip in *The Agreeable Surprise*, and the younger Colman created for her Mary in *John Bull*, Cicely in *The Heir at Law*, Annette in *Blue Devils*, and Grace Gaylove in *The Review.*

Mrs Gibbs began her first full winter season at Drury Lane on 27 September 1794. She played there in the winter seasons of 1795–96 and 1796–97 (at £6 per week) and transferred to Covent Garden in 1797–98 (still at £6), where she remained for several seasons more. She played at one winter patent house or another off and on far into the nineteenth century, but her true theatrical home was always the little Haymarket house, for which her voice was said to have been more suited than for Drury Lane and Covent Garden.

Before the end of the eighteenth century she played Kitty Pry in *The Lying Valet*, Letty in *Tit for Tat*, Kitty Barleycorn in *The London Hermit*, Kitty Sprightly in *All the World's a Stage*, Patty in *Inkle and Yarico*, Patch in *The Busy Body*, Kitty in *Ways and Means*, Louisa in *Royal Clemency,* Kate Hardcastle in *She Stoops to Conquer*, Corinna in *The Confederacy*, Flora in *The Wonder*, Anne Lovely in *A Bold Stroke for a Wife*, Rose in *The Recruiting Officer*, Dorinda in *The Tempest*, Maria in *Heigho for a Husband!*, Lady Jane Danvers in *The Box-Lobby Challenge*, Bloom in *I'll Tell You What*, Mary in *Summer Amusement*, Julia in *How to be Happy*, Viletta in *She Wou'd and She Wou'd Not*, Biddy in *Miss in Her Teens*, Miss Jenny in *The Provok'd Husband*, Miss Plumb in *Gretna Green*, Maria in *The Citizen*, Mary in *The Prisoner at Large*, Araminta in *The Young Quaker*, Emily in *Three and the Deuce*, Lady Jane in *Know Your Own Mind*, Annabel in *The Man of Ten Thousand*, Blanch in *The Iron Chest*, Catherine in *Catherine and Petruchio*, Mrs Cadwallader in *The Author*, Susan in *The Follies of a Day*, Belinda in *The Provok'd Wife*, Miss Fuz in *A Peep Behind the Curtain*, Ruth in *The Honest Thieves*, Cicely Homespun in *The Heir at Law*, Nancy in *The Beggar on Horseback*, Lucy in *The Guardian*, Jessy Oatland in *A Cure for the Heartache*, Foible in *The Way of the World*, Amelia in *Retaliation*, Rose in *Botheration*, Lucy in *He's Much to Blame*, Fanny in *A Mogul Tale*, Hannah in *Throw Physick to the Dogs*, Lady Griffith's Shade in *Cambro-Britons*, Betty Blackberry in *The Farmer*, Sophia in *The Road to Ruin*, Lydia Languish in *The Rivals*, Dorothy in *Love When You Can*, Eliza in *The Jew*, Maud in *Peeping Tom*, Dolly in *Fortune's Frolick*, and Molly Beezom in *New Hay at the Old Market*. In her later years she played elderly eccentrics like Mrs Sterling in *The Clandestine Marriage*. Every season at Covent Garden from 1804–5 through 1814–15 she drew £10 per week.

Every early critic spoke of her beauty and her ability to inspire, in the words of the author of *Authentic Memoirs of the Green Room*, belief in "rustic innocence, simplicity, and artless truth." That writer, in fact, seems to have been swept away by his emotions:

Her fine blue eyes, bright as the "fish-pools of Heshbon," to adopt an Oriental figure—boast a facinating power, and melt the heart to love! Whilst the luxurious swell of her bosom lights up the torch of desire—and thrills the aching nerve with pleasure almost too fierce for sufferance. There builds Ida's dove his nest!—there reclines Cytherea's truant son! and seeks his couch of down! Her disposition perfectly accords with the expression of benignity, which irradiates her countenance—mild, affable, and gracious. . . .

Oxberry, who by 1826 had known her throughout most of her long career, was more restrained but no less flattering:

Harvard Theatre Collection

MARIA GIBBS, as Grace Gaylove

by unknown engraver, after Buck

Mrs Gibbs had genius, talent, and industry . . . . Next to Mrs Jordan, [she] was decidedly the best actress in her line. Her Curiosa, in *The Cabinet*, is one of the richest specimens of comic acting extant. In such parts as Nell (*Devil to Pay,*) she is capable of rivalling Mrs. Davison, or Fanny Kelly. . . . Her figure and face, too, contain more vivacity, and her voice has more of the fullness and jollity of humour in humble life, than either of the other ladies. Mrs. GIBBS is one of the best laughers upon the stage; a qualification of the utmost importance to a comic actress . . . . A good and judicious laugher may lead auditors where she pleases.

She drew Thomas Bellamy's attention (in his poem "The Theatres," in *Miscellanies*, 1795): "But who is this, with lively glance and free;/ Whose countenance beams mind, and soul, and fire,/ Whose flexile form and easy frolic air/ Speak her alliance to the comic muse?/ 'Tis GIBBS! the pretty! Gibbs, by all admir'd." And even dyspeptic John Williams found it difficult to put forth his wonted correction when he came to her name in *A Pin Basket to the Children of Thespis* in 1797:

> *When in acting, she seems not fulfilling*
> *   her duty,*
> *But solacing men with the blaze of her*
> *   beauty*
> . . . .
> *She's so fidgetty, sideling, and full of*
> *   stage sleight,*
> *One imagines she wishes to be out of*
> *   sight*
> . . . .
> *But some charm highly potent is carried*
> *   about her,*
> *That suspends the whirled lash, and we*
> *   would but can't flout her.*

William Robson in *The Old Playgoer* in 1846 remembered her especially as Mary Thornberry in Colman's most famous success, *John Bull*:

She was one of the most interesting and beautiful women on the stage, where many were eminently beautiful, and the naive simplicity, pathos, and tenderness with which she filled the character, were fully in keeping with the great talent that surrounded her. Mrs. Gibbs was, from first to last, a loveable woman; you could not help liking her.

The personal life of Maria Logan Gibbs is largely mysterious. As stated above, she seems to have had theatrical parentage, and she had two sisters, both actresses, Mrs Cary and a Miss Logan. The date of Maria Logan's marriage to Gibbs (if there was such a marriage) is not known; nor is her husband known. There was a Gibbs on stage in the eighteenth century at Covent Garden in the seasons of 1758–59 and 1759–60, playing a handful of very minor

characters. He seems far too early to have been Maria's husband.

Maria caught the eye of young George Colman probably before she went to the Haymarket. He did not get along with his wife, Catherine Morris Colman, and by about 1795 or earlier he had made Maria Gibbs his mistress. Their affair initially attracted some satire, like that of "Peter Pindar" in *The Cap* (1795), and some moralistic abuse, such as this from the *Monthly Mirror* of August 1796, aimed at Maria and purporting to be theatrical criticism:

Mrs. Gibbs, a poor *water-gruel* actress! thinks she can play like Miss Farren, and therefore we have been sickened with her Maria, Catherine, Belinda, Susan &c. We really cannot see what it is that entitles this insipid thing to the first benefit in the season, unless she takes precedence as the mistress of the manager, by way of encouragement to others of the Cyprian corps, *who glory in their shame.*

The pair were devoted and lived together until the end of George Colman's life. If there was a marriage ceremony, its exact place and date has eluded search. But Maria was received everywhere as George Colman's wife, and she brought him at least one child, his second son, Edmund Craven Colman, born (probably in June) 1802. She was at George Colman's side when he died in 1836, and the attending physician, Dr H. S. Chinnock, left a testimonial to her worth:

The perfect domestic happiness [Colman] enjoyed, the constant, invariable attention of Mrs. Colman, the affectionate character of her disposition, her anxious solicitude, combined with the most perfect judgment, has not only been observed by me, but also, as constantly mentioned by him as one main, even the principal source of his comfort. Never could he bear her from his sight.

After Colman's death in 1836 she lived in retirement at Brighton. The date of her death is unknown, but she was apparently still alive in 1844.

Portraits of Maria Gibbs include:

1. Engraved portrait by T. Cheesman, after S. De Wilde. Published by C. Chapple, 1807.

2. Engraved portrait by R. Cooper, after De Wilde. Published as a plate to *La Belle Assemblée* by J. Bell, 1812.

3. As Blanch in *The Iron Chest*. Painting by De Wilde. In the Garrick Club.

4. As Blanch. Watercolor by De Wilde. In the Garrick Club.

5. As Cicely Homespun in *The Heir at Law*. Engraving by J. Thomson, after De Wilde. Published as a plate to *The Theatrical Inquisitor*.

6. As Cowslip in *The Agreeable Surprise*. Drawn and engraved by G. Cruikshank. Published as a plate to *The British Stage*, October 1818.

7. As Cowslip. Engraving by W. Ridley, after Clarke. Published by Vernor and Hood, 1800, as a plate to *The Monthly Mirror*.

8. As Grace Gaylove in *The Review*. Aquatint by A. Buck. In the Harvard Theatre Collection. Published in 1816.

9. As Lady Elizabeth Freelove. Engraving by J. Rogers, after De Wilde. Published by G. Virtue, 1826, as a plate to Oxberry's *Dramatic Biography*.

10. As Miss Hoyden in *The Relapse*. Engraving by Wilson, after De Wilde. Published by G. Cawthorn, 1795, as a plate to *Bell's British Theatre*.

11. As Rosa in *Obi*. Engraving by Alais, after C. Linsell. Published by J. Roach, 1801, as a plate to *Memoirs of the Green Room*.

12. As Selina in *The Tale of Mystery*. Painting by De Wilde. In the Garrick Club.

Gibetti, Signora [*fl.* 1766–1767], singer.

On 6 August 1766 a notice in the *Public Advertiser* informed Londoners that Signora Gibetti (or Gibelli, in the *Gazet-* *teer*) would sing the third woman parts at the King's Theatre during the 1766–67 opera season. She took the role of Paoluccia in *La buona figliuola* beginning on 25 November and had a part in *La buona figliuola maritata* beginning on 31 January 1767. The season ended on 20 June.

Gibons. *See* GIBBONS.

Gibraltar [*fl.* 1765?–1807?], performing horse.

The equestrian Philip Astley's two favorite and most celebrated mounts have been confused with each other since the earliest accounts. One was the "white charger" called Gibraltar or "The Spanish Horse." The other was Billy, or "the Little Learned Horse," or "the Little Learned Military Horse." Apparently both were trained to perform astonishing tricks. There is a possibility that the attributes of other animals have in the course of time been conflated with those of Billy and Gibraltar to produce the misunderstandings to be found in modern works on circus and hippodrama.

In a minutely circumstantial account of Philip Astley in "The Manager's Notebook" in *The New Monthly Magazine* the writer (probably James Winston) says that "After eight years of honourable service, [Astley] obtained his discharge, and the General [Elliott] gave him, as a mark of his esteem, a charger, which charger lived to the age of 42." The account continues to a description of the earliest of Astley's methods of advertising: "On the nights he performed, he placed himself, on his white charger, in his regimentals, at the end of Pedlar's Acre . . . [where] he gave out his bills. . . ." Plainly, in the context, Winston is asserting that Elliott's gift was presented immediately upon Astley's discharge in 1768 and that the donated horse was a "white charger." Winston then quotes an early Astley advertisement in which there is a short poem describing the actions of a horse which plays dead at the word of command, and whose name is Bill ("Rise young Bill . . ."). All of those events are given as of 1768.

A newsclipping in the Huntington Library dated 27 April 1769 states: "Yesterday his Majesty reviewed Elliott's and Burgoyn's [*sic*] regiment of light horse on Wimbledon Common. . . . During the review, his Majesty seemed very much pleased with Mr. Astley's learned horse, which he made kneel down, lie down, and sit up like a dog, at the word of command." Nothing in that report gives us a certain clue as to the identity of the horse, inasmuch as "learned" only later became associated with "little" in the advertisements. Perhaps the charger was accomplished too.

In 1773, the "Manager's Notebook" account states, Astley announced that he would no longer parade his company through the streets: "In the parading he mentions," explains Winston, "he commenced the procession, mounted on his white charger, dressed *à la militaire*, in a light blue coat, followed by trumpets; two of the riders, in their costume, with his little learned pony looking out of a hackney-coach window, distributing bills for his British Riding School."

James Decastro, who knew Astley well, quotes in his *Memoirs* a bill of 27 November 1780 which speaks of "The Little Conjuring Horse," presumably our "Bill" who was "the little learned pony." An extant program of 1786 describing an Astley evening salutes Philip Astley "who will be mounted on the Gibraltar Charger which was lately presented to him by Lord Heathfield (late General Elliott). The Charger will be surrounded by a chain of fire, and Mr. Astley will salute the audience with an Olive branch in Fire-works."

At least two horses are obviously discriminated in these several accounts: a large, white charger called Gilbraltar (who was either presented by General Elliott in 1768 and was consequently already well advanced in years in 1786 or—as the bill

seems to claim—had only "lately" been presented, in which case he was perhaps younger) and a small, clever pony named Bill (who was also elderly if he was the one who beguiled the King in 1769).

James Decastro, who served the Astley enterprises for 35 years after being hired by Philip Astley in 1785, gives in his *Memoirs* a short resumé of Astley's career. In a footnote he says the following:

This charger was called the "Spanish Horse," and lived to the age of 42 in his service. Mr. W. Davis, the present proprietor and manager of the Royal Amphitheatre, was so fond of this same horse from its wonderful tractability and extreme docility, that when, from his loss of teeth by age, he was unable to eat his corn; and from a lively remembrance of his former services, he very humanely . . . allowed the decrepit, aged, and nearly worn-out animal, out of his own private purse two quartern loaves per day.

N.B.—This beast was accustomed, at a public performance, to ungirt his own saddle, wash his feet in a pail of water, fetch and carry a complete tea equipage, with many other strange things. He would take a kettle of boiling water off a flaming fire, and acted in fact after the manner of a waiter at a tavern or tea gardens.

At last, nature being exhausted, he died in the common course of it, and Mr. Davis, with an idea to perpetuate the animal's memory, caused the hide to be tanned and made into a thunder-drum, which now stands on the prompt side of the theatre, and when its rumbling sounds die on the ear of those who know the circumstance, it serves to their recollection as his "parting knell."

Decastro's chronology is vague, but William Davis was performing feats of equitation at Astley's Amphitheatre as early as 1789, perhaps earlier. He and his partners of the Royal Circus took over a half interest in Astley's business in 1804, Philip Astley died in 1814, and Davis became joint proprietor with John Astley in 1817. Assuming that both horses were three-year-olds when acquired and that both were acquired in 1768, they would have been about 39 years old when Davis assumed some share in the management in 1804. But the claim of extraordinary longevity is made for only one horse, that "charger" which Decastro also calls "The Spanish Horse"—presumably the one called Gibraltar in the bills.

Though we never find in Amphitheatre bills (they are rare) that Gibraltar ever did anything more talented than stand still while his master handled pyrotechnics, it is impossible not to give credence to Decastro's specific recollection that the horse was highly trained. Considering Astley's wizardry with animals, there is nothing inherently improbable in that. And we have sufficient evidence of the education of Bill (sometimes "Billy"), the Little Learned Horse (Little Military Horse, Little Learned Military Horse, or Little Conjuring Horse). It remains only to observe that the universal tendency of show people to stretch the unusual into the prodigious may have urged Decastro to add a few years to Gibraltar's age. Decastro was followed exactly by Edward W. Brayley in *Historical and Descriptive Accounts of the Theatres of London* (1826) and Brayley was followed by Erroll Sherson in *London's Lost Theatres of the Nineteenth Century* (1925).

Gibson. *See also* GILSON.

Gibson, Mr [*fl. 1762–1763*], *actor.*
On 25 October 1762 a Mr Gibson acted the roles of the Counsellor and Donald MacGregor in *The Orators* at the Haymarket Theatre. The bill announced that "At the Request of several Scotch Nobility" the performance was for the benefit of Gibson, who had "perform'd Donald MacGregor in *The Orators* 38 Days." The 1762 edition of that entertainment, styled as "Oratorical Lectures," did not include Gibson's name as one of the participants, but the piece, by Foote, had opened at the Hay-

market on 1 May 1762, and was repeated, indeed, some 38 times over the summer. The following summer of 1763 at the Haymarket, Mr Gibson played Sir Charles M'Ruthen in *The Englishman Return'd From Paris* on 5 August and Crab in the same work on 22 August. He appeared again in *The Orators* some five times, with his last performance occurring on 3 September 1763.

Gibson, Mr [*fl. 1780*], *actor.*
A Mr Gibson acted the role of Dash in *The Humours of Oxford* at the Haymarket Theatre on 28 March 1780.

Gibson, Mr [*fl. 1794–1805*], *violinist.*
A Mr Gibson, of Little Abbingdon Street, Westminster, was listed in Doane's *Musical Directory* in 1794 as a violinist, a member of the New Musical Fund, a player in the Handelian commemorative performances in Westminster Abbey, and a performer at Drury Lane Theatre. He was an honorary subscriber to the New Musical Fund in 1805.

Gibson [Richard?] *d. 1799, boxkeeper.*
A Mr Gibson was a boxkeeper with a constant salary of 12s. per week at Drury Lane Theatre from as early as 1776–77 through 1797–98, sharing annual benefits regularly with other house servants. According to notes by Wewitzer and Burney on manuscripts in the British Museum, Gibson died in 1799. Possibly he was the Richard Gibson, late "of Grafton Street in the parish of St Anne Soho, Westminster," who in his will drawn on 12 March 1798 left all his possessions to his wife Eleanor, who proved the will on 18 May 1799.

Gibson, Stephen [*fl. 1667*], *drummer.*
Stephen Gibson was appointed a drummer extraordinary (that is, without fee

until a position became vacant) in the King's Musick on 22 October 1667.

Gibson, William *1713–1771, actor, manager.*

William Gibson, who was born in 1713, spent 32 years as an actor at Covent Garden Theatre, yet, as with so many of his contemporaries who toiled nightly in the London theatres during the eighteenth century, little is known of the details of his life. He was said to have been the son of one William Gibson, who was an eminent Quaker preacher, and as a young man in London he possessed "the peculiarities of the speech and garb" of the Quakers, from which he gradually weaned himself.

He became acquainted with Bridgwater and Hippisley, both actors in London, who took a liking to him. The latter, it is said, invited Gibson to his summer company in Bristol for "instruction and protection" and then gave him a letter of recommendation to Dennis Herbert, a provincial manager, with whom he remained engaged, according to Broadbent's *Annals of the Liverpool Stage,* "a considerable time." He gained some reputation in Herbert's company as a soft-sighing lover. Lewes, who referred to him as a "new-made Christian," stated that Gibson had not been baptized until he entered the Church of England at about the age of 30.

When Gibson made his debut at Covent Garden as Bellmour in *The Old Bachelor* on 17 September 1739, the bills stated it to be "the first time of his performance on a public theatre," a claim manifestly wrong.

The fact that in his first season at Covent Garden Gibson acted some 24 different roles credits him with considerable previous experience in the provinces. After Bellmour he played Philip in *The Rival Queens* on 1 October 1739, Hotman in *Oroonoko* on 4 October, Cabinet in *The Funeral* on 6 November, Snap in *The Royal Merchant* on 20 November, and Pymero in *The Island Princess* on 10 De-

cember. During the remainder of the season he acted Alcandar in *Oedipus,* Moreton in *2 Henry IV,* Gray in *Henry V,* Fetch in *The Stage Coach,* Rake in *The Provok'd Wife,* Seyward in *Macbeth,* Hellebore in *The Mock Doctor,* a Beggar in *The Beggar's Opera,* Noodle in *The Tragedy of Tragedies,* Charles in *The Busy Body,* the Poet in *The Twin Rivals,* Friendly in *The School Boy,* Cunningham in *The Irish Widow,* the Merchant in *The Royal Merchant,* Young Fashion in *The Relapse* (on 13 May 1740 for his benefit shared with Bencraft and the French Boy and Girl), the Governor in *Love Makes a Man,* Blunt in *The London Merchant,* and an unspecified role in *The Rehearsal.* Those parts, none in a capital line, were of the sort he was to fill, with a few exceptions, throughout his long career in London.

In his second season, 1740–41, at Covent Garden, during which he was paid 5s. per night, he added to his repertoire Donalbain in *Macbeth,* Rosencrantz in *Hamlet,* Perdiccas in *The Rival Queens,* Humphrey in *The What D'ye Call It,* Modely in *The Country Lasses,* Marcus in *Cato,* Bellamour in *Wit Without Money,* Pedro in *The Spanish Fryar,* Easy in *The Fair Quaker of Deal,* Albany in *King Lear,* Fabian in *The Fatal Marriage,* Vainlove in *The Old Bachelor,* Selim in *The Mourning Bride,* Worthy in *Greenwich Park,* Lovewell in *The Gamester,* Catesby in *Jane Shore,* Cuproli in *Abra Mule,* the King in *The King and the Miller of Mansfield,* and Alonzo in *Rule a Wife and Have a Wife.*

In 1741–42, Gibson assumed about two dozen more roles, including some in Shakespeare's plays: Fenton in *The Merry Wives of Windsor,* Catesby and Tressel in *Richard III,* Le Beau in *As You Like It,* Time in *The Winter's Tale,* Lodovico in *Othello.* A complete list of Gibson's parts would number in the many dozens and would consist of a veritable census of minor roles in the eighteenth-century English theatre.

Although almost his entire career was

passed under Rich's management at Covent Garden, on several occasions he acted elsewhere. While the oratorios were on at Covent Garden in February 1743, Gibson played Valentine in *Love for Love* on the eighteenth and Airy in *The Busy Body* on the twenty-fifth in a theatrical booth on the Bowling Green in Southwark. At the beginning of the season 1747–48 he was absent from Covent Garden in September and October because he was a member of a summer company at Richmond, Surrey, where the season extended into the autumn. He had similar engagements at Richmond in 1748 and 1749, and in the latter summer he also acted at Twickenham.

After the end of the 1751–52 season Gibson interrupted his engagement at Covent Garden, presumably to devote the following season to travel. The decision almost cost him his life, for Richard Cross, the Drury Lane prompter, entered in his diary on 27 December 1752: "We have advice that the *John* (Capt Smith) from Leith, which was supposed to be lost, got into Gottenburgh on the first of this month. The vessel had several passengers on board, among others Mr Gibson belonging to Covent Garden Theatre."

After a year away, Gibson returned to his old stand at Covent Garden Theatre on 26 September 1753 as Brumpton in *The Funeral* and settled into his familiar line, the only difference being that now more and more roles of older characters began to enter his repertoire, since he was now into his middle age. In 1753–54, for instance, he played such roles as Escalus in *Romeo and Juliet*, Duke Frederick and Adam in *As You Like It*, Omar in *Tamerlane*, Bedamar and Priuli in *Venice Preserv'd*, Solanio in *The Merchant of Venice*, and Sir John in *The Conscious Lovers*. Over his remaining 17 years on the stage he added such characters as Tiresias in *Oedipus*, Brabantio in *Othello*, Sir W. Meadows in *Love in a Village*, the King in *Macbeth*, Sir Peter Pride in *The Amorous*

Widow, Capulet in *Romeo and Juliet*, King Henry in *Richard III*, Gloucester in *King Lear*, Cymbeline, Old Knowel in *Every Man in his Humour*, Thorowgood in *George Barnwell*, and Claudius in *Hamlet*.

In 1746–47 Gibson's salary was £1 per week; by 1749–50 it had risen to £3 per week. In 1761–62 he was earning about £70 per season. According to a list provided by Arthur Murphy, Gibson's salary in 1767–68 was then up to £1 per day or £6 per week, a relatively respectable figure. In his last years, for which figures are available, he received £68 3s. 6d. for his benefit on 24 April 1767, £45 8s. 6d. on 15 April 1768, £95 1s. on 11 April 1769, and £60 8s. 6d. on 23 April 1770.

Sometime in 1767 Gibson seems to have had a disagreement with David Garrick, manager of Drury Lane, perhaps over negotiations about employment at that theatre, but more likely over Mrs Bennet, whom Gibson lived with for many years. She left Drury Lane employment after 1766, probably dismissed by the management. On 24 July 1761 Tom King, a leading actor at Drury Lane, wrote to Garrick from Liverpool: "I have seen Mr. Gibson since I had the pleasure of receiving your last letter, the necessary parts of which I communicated to him. His answer was, that he was much obliged to you for the civility used on the occasion, but could not give up his opinion as to your intentions, or his resolution in regard to Mrs Bennet."

During the latter part of his career, Gibson was also the manager of a small theatre in Drury Lane, Liverpool, where he acted in the summers. With Isaac Ridout (d. 1761), another London actor, he became associated in the management of the Liverpool house (which had a modest capacity of some £70) in the middle of the 1750s. Ridout died in 1761, leaving his half-moiety to his sister Elizabeth, but the principal responsibilities for management continued with Gibson.

In 1768 Gibson began his campaign to

erect a larger theatre in Liverpool and to obtain letters patent from Parliament for a Theatre Royal. He petitioned the Corporation of Liverpool to support his application. After several delays, finally on 9 November 1769 his petition to Parliament was stamped by the Common Seal of the Corporation:

It is ordered that the petition of the Mayor and Council of this Borough and Corporation now read to this Council to the Honourable the Commons of Great Britain in Parliament assembled, for obtaining an Act to enable his Majesty to Grant his Letters Patent to Mr. William Gibson, his executors, and administrators for the term of 21 years, to build a new Theatre in Liverpoole, and to perform plays, etc., therein during the Term, be passed under the Common seal by Mr. Mayor and Bailiffs, and be presented to Parliament at the now ensuing sessions, according to the Terms and conditions in a late order of Council made for such purpose.

On 10 January 1770 the petition was favored by the Commons but was rejected by the Lords. The Corporation backed Gibson for another try with three petitions which finally passed both houses in January 1771.

Capitalized at an estimated cost of £6000, raised in five-percent-interest shares of £200 which were fully subscribed within an hour after the sale opened, erection of the new Theatre Royal at Liverpool began on the north side of Williamson Square in June 1771, while the company continued to play at the old Drury Lane.

Gibson never saw the new building after it was completed. He had a benefit at Covent Garden Theatre in London on 10 April 1771, and on 12 April he gave what proved to be his last performance, as Allworthy in *Tom Jones*. Although his name was in the advertisements for Sullen in *The Beaux' Stratagem* on 16 May, he was replaced by Dunstall. He was too ill to act at Liverpool in the summer and retired to

his residence at Everton, nearby, where he died on 21 August 1771, at the age of 58. He was buried on 26 August in Walton Churchyard, near the grave of the actor John Palmer. The inscription on his tomb, said to have been written by David Garrick, read:

To the memory of William Gibson, late patentee of the Theatre Royal in Liverpool, who died August 21, 1771, aged 58. If Judgment and Industry in his Profession, if a steady uprightness of Heart, if an Invariable Attachment to Truth, Honour, and Friendship, desire the praises of Mankind, no one ever had a more just title to them than he whose remains are here interr'd. A Wit's a feather, and a chief's a rod An honest Man the Noblest Work of God.

On 24 September 1771, Garrick sent Samuel Foote a copy of his epitaph on Gibson. Tongue-in-cheek, he told Foote it had been written by a young apprentice of Liverpool:

Gibson, *from Sorrow rests beneath this Stone.*
An honest Man! belov'd as soon as known:
Howe'er deficient in the Mimic Art,
In real Life he justly play'd his part,
The Noblest Character he acted well,
And Heaven applauded when ye Curtain fell.

Those same lines were used again by Garrick for William Havard's epitaph in 1778, when he changed only the name of the subject and the word "deficient" to "defective."

In his short will made at Liverpool on 12 June 1771 (and witnessed by William Barry, then the treasurer of the Liverpool theatre) Gibson left all his possessions in "Bills Bonds Public ffunds Cloaths . . . Debts Patent for playing in Liverpool and everything else belonging to me to my dear and much beloved ffriend Mrs. Elizabeth Bennett, formerly of the Theatre Royal in Drury Lane London and do hereby appoint her the sole Executrix of this my will." Contrary to the assertions of Baker in the *Biographia Dramatica* and of Gilliland, the will did not provide for any money to go to the Covent Garden Actors' Fund, either in direct bequest or after Mrs Bennet's death. The will was proved by Elizabeth Bennet at the Episcopal Registry in Chester on 4 September 1771 and at the Prerogative Court of Canterbury in London on 23 September 1771. According to Baker the legacy to her amounted to upwards of £8000. A newsclipping in the British Museum, dated 17 August 1771, claimed that Gibson had died with a fortune worth £15,000. The will itself provided no figures.

Elizabeth Bennet (1714–1791), an actress of varied but limited talents, had been in the Covent Garden company in the earlier years of Gibson's career, and she also had acted with him at Liverpool. They had lived together for many years, presumably —as one of Winston's press cuttings at the Folger Shakespeare Library claims—"in no criminal way. They paid their housekeeping share and share alike." When she died in 1791, she directed in her will: "all the Books I now have which were the property of the late Mr William Gibson at the time of his decease to be equally divided among" William Smith, Thomas King, and Richard Wroughton, all eminent actors. She also left bequests to numerous other actors, managers, and theatrical tradespeople.

The new Theatre Royal, Liverpool, opened on 5 June 1772, with a prologue, written by the elder George Colman, full of compliments to the late manager. As an actor, Gibson had served London audiences for some 32 years in a respectable manner. Despite some disparaging verses in the anonymous *Rosciad of C–v–nt G–rd–n*, published in London in 1762, to the effect that he was full of dullness as a performer, there was general testimony to Gibson's sound understanding and, according to Baker, "in a few characters of age and simplicity, he was at once natural and affect-

ing." In his *Thespis*, Hugh Kelly wrote at some length of Gibson's merits:

> *Were sterling sense, or excellence of*
>   *heart,*
> *For fame's bright goal in Thespis bound*
>   *to start;*
> *Say, above Gibson who could think to*
>   *rise,*
> *Or urge a nobler title to the prize?*
> *But fate, perhaps, when Gibson first*
>   *possest*
> *The strong conception, and the feeling*
>   *breast,*
> *Suppos'd a voice was quite below his*
>   *care,*
> *Or never once design'd him for a play'r—*
> *Yet though in parts of energy and fire,*
> *She ne'er permits him boldly to aspire;*
> *And tho' that note's harsh, dissonance*
>   *of jar*
> *With quick-soul'd sense holds ever-living*
>   *war;*
> *Still there are times, when self-created*
>   *farce*
> *Subdues even Nature in her stern-ey'd*
>   *course;*
> *And Gibson's mind too nervous for her*
>   *laws,*
> *Appeals to truth, and rises with applause—*
> *Behold in Prim, what pleasantry we trace*
> *Thro' all that sober sanctified grimace;*
> *Where rebel flesh, with countenance*
>   *demure,*
> *Serenely hot and holily impure,*
> *Betray a sly concubinary flame,*
> *And steals poor spirit into actual shame—*
> *In Old Rents too, when Hearty, kindly*
>   *wrong,*
> *Thinks gath'ring grief must vanish at*
>   *a song,*
> *Then Gibson's face so tristfully is hung,*
> *And holds such hum'rous combat with*
>   *his tongue,*
> *That ceaseless mirth will laugh herself*
>   *to tears,*
> *And quite fright the grating in her ears.*

In his younger days Gibson cut a handsome figure. Toward the end of his career he was called "King Gibson" because his person, then grown bulky and ponderous, suited him so well for the many heavy old monarchs, such as Cymbeline, whom he portrayed. In discussing death scenes on the stage, George Steevens once wrote to Garrick: "Henry the Sixth, standing still to receive the dagger of Richard, too often excites merriment. Poor Gibson was sure to convulse the audience with laughter whenever he fell in that character; and yet it is no more than justice to his memory to observe, that all who knew him were sincerely sorry when he died a natural death." At Liverpool Gibson was considered, however, to be a masterful actor, above all competition.

An inoffensive man, of respected character, Gibson dedicated himself to professional integrity. One anecdote is indicative of his disdain for the vanities of the world. In giving advice to a young tyro who had just joined the theatre, Gibson supposedly said: "let me advise you, as an old man well acquainted with life, to avoid public-houses. When you are no longer required at the theatre, go home, study any part that may be assigned to you, take a glass of small beer to refresh yourself before you go to bed, and if it happens to be the King's birth-day, the news of a great victory, or any occasion of national joy has occurred, put a little nutmeg and sugar in it."

Giffard, Mr [fl. 1759–1762], actor.

A Mr Giffard was paid £2 16s. 8d. on 15 December 1759 for working 17 days at Covent Garden Theatre beginning on 24 November. The same Giffard, identified as an actor, was working at Covent Garden on 22 September 1760 for a modest 3s. 4d. daily. We would guess that that Giffard was the one who was advertised as making his first appearance on any stage when he acted Witling in The Refusal at Covent Garden on 2 January 1761.

At some point before 21 February 1762 Giffard left Covent Garden; on that date, according to a note in the Burney papers,

"a little girl, daughter of Mr. Giffard, late of Covent Garden, burnt herself terribly and died in great agonies." She had seen feathers burned under the noses of persons fainting or in fits and had tried it on one of her dolls; the doll and the girl's clothes caught fire.

After his daughter's death, Giffard apparently remained in London but did not perform. Of his later career nothing certain is known, unless he was the "Gifford" who, with his wife, played in Halifax in September 1768. His lowly status at Covent Garden would probably rule out his having been the Giffard who led a troupe to Salford, near Manchester, in the summer of 1760. (Charles Beecher Hogan tentatively identified the Giffard who acted in The Refusal on 2 January 1761 as William, the son of Henry Giffard, but we believe that William began to perform as Master Giffard in the 1730s and that by the mid-1740s he had concluded his London career.)

Giffard, Edward [fl. 1733–1745], numberer, housekeeper, boxkeeper.

Edward Giffard's earliest notice in London theatre bills was on 16 May 1733, when he and three others shared a benefit at the Goodman's Fields Theatre, then managed by Henry Giffard, who was doubtless related in some way to Edward. On 14 May 1734 at the same house Edward shared a benefit with Excell and was identified in the playbill as a numberer. He was mentioned again in benefit bills in 1735 and 1736. The London Stage lists an "F." Giffard in the Goodman's Fields troupe in 1740–41, but that surely is a misprint for "E." Giffard, who had a solo benefit on 27 April 1741 and was cited as "Numberer and House-Keeper."

On 1 April 1742 on Miss Hippisley's benefit bill Edward's Christian name was given and his post described as boxkeeper. Three weeks later, on 27 April, Edward's own benefit bill called him the company's numberer and box bookkeeper. Tickets for Mrs. E. Giffard were accepted that night; while that reference may have been to Edward's wife (though we do not know whether or not he had one), it is more likely that Elizabeth Giffard was the woman cited.

The Giffard clan was at Lincoln's Inn Fields in 1742–43, and Edward shared a benefit there on 7 April 1743, but when the Giffards moved to Drury Lane in 1743–44, Edward was not on the roster. At Goodman's Fields on 19 March 1745 Edward received a solo benefit, after which his name disappeared from the London playbills.

Giffard, F. *See* **GIFFARD, EDWARD.**

Giffard, Henry   *1694–1772, actor, manager.*

Many eighteenth-century sources state that the actor-manager Henry Giffard was born in 1699, but Lysons's *Environs of London* cites Giffard's tombstone as evidence for 1694. His birthplace was London —in Lincoln's Inn Fields, according to some early sources—and he was the youngest of eight sons of William Giffard, of Buckinghamshire stock. Henry was educated in a private school in London, we are told, and when he was about 16 he gained a position as a clerk in the South Sea Company through the influence of his father. He held the job for three years.

Clark in *The Irish Stage in the County Towns* placed Giffard at the Smock Alley Theatre in Dublin in 1716, but Chetwood, writing in 1749 when Giffard had just completed his long London career, said that Henry, unknown to his friends, joined a troupe of actors at Bath in 1719 and there made his first stage appearance. If that is true, then the Mr Giffard who performed in London in 1717 and 1718 was another person—perhaps related to Henry (an elder brother?; we have entered him as William Giffard, fl. 1716?–1737) but surely not Henry's father, who seems to have been

opposed to Henry's theatrical interests. Company lists and playbills from Dublin collected by the late William Smith Clark make it clear that from 1720–21 through 1728–29 Henry Giffard was in the Smock Alley troupe. That would not preclude his having performed elsewhere, so some sources may be correct in saying that Henry acted at Bath for two years (that is, until 1721) and then returned to London, where he attempted unsuccessfully to be reconciled to his father. In the O. Smith papers at the British Museum it is stated that the elder Giffard died "about six months after" and Henry was "deprived of fortune, and left wholly destitute." Chetwood and other early writers claimed that Giffard joined John Rich's company at Lincoln's Inn Fields and acted there for two years before going to Ireland—but that may be a reference to the Giffard who performed in London in 1717 and 1718. *The London Stage* lists no Giffard in London in the early 1720s.

The Dublin bills for the 1720s reveal that Henry Giffard acted a number of important parts: Valentine in *Love for Love*, Courtney in *The Fatal Extravagance*, Honorio in *The Rival Generals*, Lorenzo in *The Spanish Fryar*, Sir Charles in *The Careless Husband*, Reynard in *Tunbridge Walks*, Don Carlos in *The Mistake*, Atall in *The Double Gallant*, Cunningham in *The Amorous Widow*, Percy in *Vertue Betray'd*, the King of Tidore in *The Island Princess*, Mr Tridewell in *The Northern Lass*, the title role in *Philaster*, Perez in *Rule a Wife and Have a Wife*, Archer in *The Beaux' Stratagem*, and Careless in *The Committee*.

Giffard became one of the sharers at Smock Alley and married a young woman of the company, Mary (Molly) Lyddal, the daughter of performers who acted in Dublin with their daughters Mary and Nancy from about 1716. Mary, according to O. Smith, "had given great promise of talent in her profession, was amiable in her manner, and her affection as a wife [was] truly exemplary." The Dublin bills listed a Mrs Giffard—presumably Mary—from 1720–21 through 1727–28 playing such roles as Louisa in *The Fatal Extravagance*. That does not fit with the story that before she was 21 Mary died giving birth to a daughter and that she left behind a son who had been born, according to Chetwood, in Giffard's house on the North Strand. Chetwood claimed that the son was still acting in 1749, and it seems likely that he was William Giffard. *The History of the English Stage* in 1741 reported that the son was born a year before his mother died. His birth was variously reported as taking place in 1715 (very unlikely), 1721, and 1730. If the disappearance of Mrs Giffard's name from the Dublin company lists after 1727–28 indicated her death soon afterward, then her son may have been born about 1726 or 1727 and her daughter about 1728 or 1729.

Henry Giffard married a second time— "Some Years after," said Chetwood; six years later, stated the *History*. His new wife was of the same Dublin theatre and, indeed, of the same family: Anna Marcella (Nancy) Lyddal. From evidence in Giffard's will it is probable that the wedding took place as early as 1729 (very soon after the death of Henry's first wife, if we are correct in interpreting the evidence concerning her). In any case, Anna Marcella was using Giffard's name by 1729.

By that time Henry had made his first appearance at Drury Lane in London. Hailed as from Dublin and it "being the first time of his appearing on this stage," Giffard played Hal in *1 Henry IV* on 7 May 1726. On 19 May he acted Brazen in *The Recruiting Officer*, a part essayed in 1718 by the earlier Giffard. Henry seems not to have remained in London; he did not appear there again until 1729.

The Dublin actor Thomas Odell opened the Goodman's Fields playhouse in Ayliff Street, Whitechapel, on 31 October 1729. Advertised as "from the Theatre Royal in Dublin" Henry Giffard played Plume in *The Recruiting Officer* at the opening. Henry's first full London season suggests what an extensive repertoire he had acquired by then: after Plume, he acted Archer in *The Stratagem*, Castalio in *The Orphan*, Valentine in *Love for Love*, Reynard in *Tunbridge Walks*, Hastings in *Jane Shore*, Sir George in *The Busy Body*, Lorenzo in *The Spanish Fryar*, Aboan in *Oroonoko*, Bellmour in *The Old Bachelor*, the title part in *The Gamester*, Carlos in *Love Makes a Man*, Careless in *The Committee*, Mirabel in *The Inconstant*, Altamont in *The Fair Penitent*, Sir Harry in *The Constant Couple*, Hamlet, Bevil Junior in *The Conscious Lovers*, Wilding in *The Temple Beau*, Townly in *The Provok'd Husband*, Sebastian in *The Fatal Villainy*, Sir Charles in *The Careless Husband*, Ford in *The Merry Wives of Windsor*, the title role in *The Rover*, the Copper Captain in *Rule a Wife and Have a Wife*, Loveless in *Love's Last Shift*, Faithful in *The Man's Bewitched*, Edgar in *King Lear*, Stanza in *The Widow Bewitch'd* (in which he spoke the prologue), and the title role in *Oroonoko* on 1 August at Tottenham Court. With Giffard throughout the season and often playing opposite him was his wife Anna Marcella.

Odell's venture at Goodman's Fields was an uphill struggle against much opposition, for he was trying to provide London with a third legitimate theatre. By the summer of 1731 he was ready to give up. Odell and Giffard may have quarrelled, for in early May 1731 Giffard and his wife made some appearances at the Haymarket Theatre; Giffard played Hal in *1 Henry IV* and Townly in *The Provok'd Husband*. Then, on 2 June the *Daily Advertiser* reported:

We hear that Mr. Odel, Master of the Playhouse in Goodman's Fields intends to decline to concern himself any longer with the management of that theatre and that Mr. Giffard, an eminent comedian, is about publishing proposals for the building a new one in that neighborhood and is likely to have the assistance of several reputable and wealthy Gentlemen to accomplish his design.

Two days later Odell inserted a signed advertisement in the Goodman's Fields playbill:

N.B. The article in the Daily Advertiser of Wednesday last which mentions Mr. Odell's intending to decline concerning himself any longer with the Management of Goodman's Fields Play House is a false and scandalous libel for which the Printer of that Paper will be prosecuted with the utmost severity by me.

But Odell did, in fact, give over the management to Giffard, who ran the playhouse in 1731–32 and, while doing so, laid plans for a new theatre in Ayliff Street.

Giffard proved to be a fine manager. When the new season opened on 27 September 1731, he advertised that "The House is entirely new fitted up, made more commodious and warm, and the Play [*The London Merchant*] will punctually begin at Six o'Clock." He knew his out-of-the-way playhouse would not naturally attract crowds, so he tried in various ways to lure audiences away from the patent houses. On 30 October the *Daily Post* reported that Giffard had given a party for his company in honor of the King's birthday, and their Majesties' healths were drunk. He supplied a bonfire, and "large Quantities of Liquor [were] given to the Populace on that happy Occasion." The manager repeated the celebration in 1732, providing music as well and, again, attracting publicity. He also enhanced his troupe by luring a number of new performers to Goodman's Fields, among them Josias Miller, William Havard (who was also a playwright), the son of "Jubilee Dicky" Norris (from Ireland), and Mrs Roberts (from Drury Lane). As he strengthened his company, his rivals at Drury Lane were weakened by the retirement of Colley Cibber, the deaths of Robert

Wilks and Barton Booth, and dissension in the ranks.

Giffard's major attempt to win a greater audience was his new theatre. He published proposals saying that he planned to obtain a lease for 41 years and sell shares at £60 each. As it turned out, his lease, from Sir William Leman, was for 61 years and he found 23 subscribers who put up £100 each. Giffard proposed giving each of his sharers 1s. for each acting night (they may have been paid 1s. 6d.) and providing them with passes. Edward Shepherd was hired as the architect, and the new playhouse opened with *1 Henry IV* on 2 October 1732. The theatre was intimate, with a fan-shaped seating arrangement in the pit; the capacity was estimated by Arthur Scouten in *The London Stage* as perhaps 707.

Henry acted first at the old and then the new theatres in Goodman's fields through the 1735–36 season, making sporadic appearances elsewhere. He was seen in most of his old characters plus such new ones as Othello (which he acted first on 19 October 1730; he usually played Cassio), Moneses in *Tamerlane*, Clerimont in *The Tender Husband*, Juba in *Cato*, Pedro in *The Pilgrim*, the title part in *The Fall of the Earl of Essex*, Pyrrhus in *The Distrest Mother*, Macduff in *Macbeth*, George Barnwell in *The London Merchant*, Osmyn in *The Mourning Bride*, Dudley in *Lady Jane Gray*, Harlequin in *Father Girard*, Henry VI and Buckingham in *Richard III*, Antony in *Julius Caesar*, Tom in *The Conscious Lovers*, Loveless in *The Relapse*, Camply in *The Funeral*, Henry VIII, Cassander in *The Rival Queens*, the title role in *Theodosius*, Cortez in *The Indian Emperor*, Clodio in *Love Makes a Man*, Rashly in *The Fond Husband*, Adrastus in *Oedipus*, Jaffeir in *Venice Preserv'd*, Essex in *The Unhappy Favorite*, the Dauphin in *Henry V*, and Villeroy in *The Fatal Marriage*. In September, October, and November 1733 he made appearances at Drury Lane (just after he bought Mrs Booth's share of the theatre's patent) in *The Spanish Fryar, Richard III, Henry VIII*, and *Rule a Wife and Have a Wife*. It is possible that his Drury Lane performances were designed to test his power there; nothing seems to have come of it, however.

One might suppose from the considerable number of important roles Giffard played that he was an actor of some ability, but critics of the time were not impressed. *The Comedian* in October 1732, commenting on Giffard's portrayal of Osmyn in *The Mourning Bride*, said "Would [he] endeavour to rid himself of a Sort of Snip-Snap which *Wilks* had too much of he would be a more agreeable Actor." The actor Griffin (in a manuscript diary now at the British Museum) said Giffard "was a tolerable actor himself but had a dismal voice." His strength, apparently, lay in management.

On 7 November 1733 when the city celebrated the arrival of the Prince of Orange, Giffard made his usual, well-publicized effort: "at the new Theatre in Goodman's Fields, there was a Bonfire and Beer for the Populace; the side of the Theatre was illuminated with a great number of candles and two large triumphal arches raised," according to the *Daily Post*. Giffard even managed to turn Parliament's attempts to regulate the nonpatent playhouses in 1735 into publicity sympathetic to his venture. In *The Case of Henry Giffard* he retold the story of how Odell had erected the Goodman's Fields Theatre but after a year and a half had sold his right in it to Giffard. The new manager had acted one season, he said, to raise money for a new playhouse, and into his venture he had poured all his fortune and "*applied many thousand Pounds in the Purchase of Cloaths, Scenes, Decorations, and other Necessaries for the same, and contracted Debts to a great Amount*; so that in case a Law should pass to suppress the said Theatre, it will absolutely divest the said

Giffard of his *Legal* Property, which is very large, and be the utter Ruin of him and his Family." The bill against the theatres did not at that time pass, and Giffard continued for another season at Goodman's Fields.

He took some time off in the summer of 1735, just after the playhouse bill had been defeated, to perform in Ireland. The *Dublin Evening Post* reported on 5 July 1735 that Giffard and Dennis Delane had joined the Aungier Street troupe: they had "favoured that company with their Presence, thereby to render the Diversions more agreeably pleasant to the Ladies." Then the company was reported as setting out for Cork and Carlow, and Giffard spent at least part of the summer touring the southern circuit. He returned to London for the 1735–36 season at Goodman's Fields. On 30 April 1736 he presented *The Conscious Lovers* in honor of the royal marriage and once again gained favorable publicity. The *Daily Post* reported the following day that "there was a very splendid appearance of Ladies and Gentlemen to whom Mr. Giffard had distributed Tickets. The Stage was decorated in a particular manner with several glass Lustres and the outside of the House illuminated with a great number of Candles —a large quantity of liquor was given to the populace. A Prologue by Mr. Sterling was spoke by Mr. Giffard on the happy occasion."

Henry moved his troupe to the larger Lincoln's Inn Fields Theatre for the 1736–37 season, though the *Daily Post and General Advertiser* on 13 October 1736 was "assured Mr. Giffard will very shortly open the Theatre in Goodman's-Fields, notwithstanding the many false and invidious Reports of his having intirely left that part of Town." The reports were not false at all, and one wonders what Giffard was up to. On his playbill for 13 November at his new house he printed "Proposals by Mr. Henry Giffard, Director of the Theatre Royal in Lincoln's Inn Fields, for the better carrying on of the said Theatre by Subscrip-

tion, and entertaining such persons of quality and others as shall do him the honour
to become subscribers, at half the expense
usually of attending such entertainments."

The astute Giffard suggested the following conditions:

1st no less than Twenty to be subscribed for.
2nd Each Subscriber to pay for the Box £2.10
—Pit £1.10. Gallery £1 3rd The money to
be paid upon the delivery of the said Twenty
tickets 4th In order to prevent more Tickets
coming at one time than the House will contain, the Tickets of each subscriber will be
numbered and only one Ticket will be admitted any one night on a week (Benefits
excepted) which gives the Subscriber the
choice of six nights for every Ticket. 5th
Subscribers may transfer their tickets privately
but not by any publick Advertisement, nor
will they be allow'd to be sold in the Streets
or at the doors of the said Theatre, under the
penalty of losing the Tickets so dispos'd of.
6th Mr. Giffard obliges himself to play several
reviv'd and new Plays and bring out, (at
least) one Pantomime entertainment and revive another. 7th any person may subscribe
for the Boxes, Pit or Gallery, singly or together. 8th No Subscriptions will be taken
for any other number of Tickets than Twenty,
Forty, Sixty and so on. 9th, Persons who subscribe for Twenty tickets bring in one a week;
Forty, two a week; Sixty three a week and so
on. Subscribers Tickets to be deliver'd on Saturday the 20th Nov. and to commence from
and be admitted on Monday the 22nd of the
same month. N.B. If the Subscription money
be sent to the Theatre, Tickets will be delivered pursuant to the proposals to any persons without giving in their names. Subscriptions are taken at White's Chocolate House
in St. James's St., Will's Coffee House at Lincoln's Inn backgate; Tom's and Will's Coffee
House in Cornhill; at the Angel and Crown
Tavern in Whitechapel and at the Theatre.

Giffard's subscription plan, even to the
marvellously complicated setting forth
thereof, is not unlike plans used by repertory companies to this day. We are not sure
how well Henry's plan worked; the Licensing Act of 1737 brought an end to his
Lincoln's Inn Fields venture.

During the 1736–37 season Giffard was
probably too busy managing his larger
playhouse and fighting parliamentary pressures to do much acting. He added few new
parts to his repertoire that season: Riot in
The Wife's Relief, Alvarez in *Alzira*, Addle
in *The Independent Patriot*, King Charles
in *An Historical Play (King Charles)*,
Prim in *A Bold Stroke for a Wife*, and a
few others. Occupying some of his time,
too, was a silly paper war. The *Daily Journal* of 25 December 1736 printed a notice
accusing Giffard of causing a disturbance
at a Drury Lane performance of the burlesque *Tiddi-Doll*, which was attached to
the pantomime *Harlequin Restor'd*. The ac-
cusation came from the minor Drury Lane
performer E. D. Cole, whose daughter had
a part in *Tiddi-Doll*. Giffard published a re-
joinder, backed up with affidavits, in the
31 December issue of the *Daily Post*; he
denied the charges and accused Cole of
having hired people at 2s. each to attend
Lincoln's Inn Fields and hiss *The Beggar's
Pantomime*, which was running in competition to the Drury Lane offering. Early in
January Cole published a denial, and the
paper war ended. The fact that Cole was
not given a new role at Drury Lane for the
following five months suggests that he was
probably the guilty party in the squabble.

On 3 May 1737 Giffard placed an advertisement in the *Daily Post and General
Advertiser*: "To be Sold: The Interest of
the Theatre and Materials in Goodman's
Fields. Inquire of Mr. Giffard at his House
in Grange-Court, in Cary-Street." He seems
not to have been successful in finding a
purchaser, for, as will be seen, his holdings
were auctioned off a year later. The very
month that Giffard tried to sell his Goodman's Fields property, Sir Robert Walpole
renewed his attempts to pass a licensing act.
The *Rambler's Magazine* in 1787 remembered what happened, but may have melo-
dramatized some of the story. Walpole, the

publication said, had been the butt of many lampoons and, in retaliation, had

caused a piece of two acts to be written, fraught with the most pointed sarcasms on the late king and his ministers. This little drama was styled the *Golden Rump,* and was sent to Gifford, who at that time was manager of a theatre in Goodman's Fields [*recte*, Lincoln's Inn Fields], and had made Sir Robert Walpole his enemy by representing pieces on his stage inimical to the character and interests of the minister. Gifford did not directly fall into the trap by acting the piece; but, conceiving it a fair opportunity to make Sir Robert his friend, took the copy to the minister, and, to shew his great respect for him, discovered the name and the person who delivered it to him, and who he conceived to be the author. Sir Robert . . . seemed to be highly pleased with the manager, for his very respectful and proper attention to government, and desired he would call on him in a few days. Immediately on the departure of Gifford, Sir Robert took the copy to the king, and read the whole to him.

The King reacted violently, wanting to "cut up every theatre in England by the roots." A bill was introduced into Parliament and passed in a few days. Before it passed, however, Giffard discovered Walpole's intentions and, through a friend who was a member of the House of Commons, received assurance that if his theatre was silenced, the manager would receive "an employment equal in its emoluments to 600*l.* per annum."

That promise, the *Rambler's Magazine* said, came to nothing, and Giffard was left with a theatre in which, by law, he could not produce plays. "The statute made it penal to represent plays, out of the city and liberties of Westminster, for hire, gain, or reward." Other versions of *The Golden Rump* incident had Walpole reading passages of the obscene play on the floor of the House of Commons, inciting the members to take action on the licensing bill. Henry Fielding, whose satirical jabs at Walpole

had appeared on the stage of the Haymarket Theatre, wrote in *An Apology for the Life of Mr. T..... C.....* in 1740,

Suppose, Sir, some *Golden Rump* Farce was wrote by a certain Great Man's [i.e. Walpole's] own Direction, and as much Scurrility and Treason larded in it as possible. . . . Suppose Giffard had a private Hint how to act in this affair, and was promised great Things. . . . Suppose he was promised a *separate License.*

The *Rambler's Magazine* may have picked up part of its story from Fielding's suppositions; as will be seen, Giffard was back in business in 1740–41.

The passing of the Licensing Act in the spring of 1737 brought an end, at least temporarily, to Giffard's London venture. In June he, Delane, Bridgwater, and Adam Hallam joined the Smock Alley company in Dublin. Giffard was there (still? again?) in July and August of 1738, acting Sir Charles in *The Careless Husband,* Sir Harry in *The Constant Couple,* Heartfree in *The Provok'd Wife,* Juba in *Cato,* and Hamlet. Then he performed in Carlow and, in September and October, Drogheda. Meanwhile, in London on 28 July 1738 in the *Daily Post* had appeared a notice of the sale of Giffard's theatrical goods:

To be Sold by Auction, on Wednesday, August 2 and the following Days, At the Great House the Corner of Carlisle-street, Soho-Square—A Large Quantity of Theatrical Goods, consisting of Mens and Womens Cloathes of Cloath, Velvet, and Silk embroider'd, laced, and plain, properly adapted to all the Entertainments of the Stage; as also various Sets of Scenes, with Machines, and other Decorations, belonging to several Pantomime Interludes; large Glass Lustres, rich Screens, and Velvet Chairs with Gilt Frames, a large Harpsichord, with a Quantity of Musick in Score, late the Property of Mr. Henry Giffard, with Plate, Watches &c.

Bernard Warren was the auctioneer; we do not know if the sale, which was advertised up to 7 August, was a success, nor if Giffard came over from Ireland to take part in it.

In the winter of 1738–39 Henry and a younger Giffard, identified only as Giffard Junior, led a company to Edinburgh. By 9 January 1739 they had run into trouble, for one John Morison, apparently in their employ, was jailed for "presuming to put up placerts within this City" advertising a performance of *The Careless Husband* at Carubber's Close, according to *Fragmenta Scoto-Dramatica* (1835). By 22 March Henry was back in London, acting at Drury Lane for the first time, the bill said, in 12 years (he had performed there briefly in late 1733). He acted Sir Harry in *The Constant Couple* for his wife's benefit. They were living at the time at No 4, Craven Buildings, Drury Lane.

Giffard remained at Drury Lane for the 1739–40 season, taking a benefit on 15 April 1740 and advertising his lodgings as at Mr Bolney's in Great Queen Street, near Lincoln's Inn Fields. He seems not to have played many roles at Drury Lane during his stay there; in addition to Sir Harry he acted Young Mirabel in *The Inconstant* in the spring of 1739, and during the 1739–40 season he performed infrequently and tried only one new part, John in *The Chances*. It is probable that he spent much of his time that season trying to get permission from the Lord Chamberlain to open Goodman's Fields Theatre again. Yet he acted in Dublin in the summer of 1740.

On 5 July 1740 Garrick wrote to Peter Garrick that "My Ld Chamberlain has given him [Giffard] a very hopeful Answer, & I don't doubt of his success/ he has had Several friends back his Interest." Garrick asked his brother to use his influence to aid Giffard. The effort was successful, and in the fall of 1740 Giffard was once again active as manager of Goodman's Fields. There he stayed for two seasons, adding to his list of characters such parts as Lovewell in *Love and a Bottle*, Leontes in *The Winter's Tale*, Dumont in *Jane Shore*,

Bertram in *All's Well that Ends Well*, Lothario in *The Fair Penitent*, the Drunken Man and Aesop in *Lethe*, Polydore in *The Orphan*, Belvile in *Pamela*, Heartwell in *The Old Bachelor*, and Johnson in *The Rehearsal*. Between seasons, in the summer of 1741, Giffard (presumably Henry) was in Ipswich. On 21 July at the Tankard Street playhouse there he played Young Mirabel in *The Inconstant* and Aesop in *Lethe*, two of his regular parts. In the fall he returned to London to bring before the public the young David Garrick.

The *Rambler's Magazine* recalled in 1787 that Giffard had advertised for 19 October 1741 a performance "of vocal and instrumental music, in two parts. Between the acts the audience will be entertained, gratis, with the tragedy of 'King Richard the Third.' The part of Richard by a young gentleman, being his first appearance on any stage; and this young gentleman was no less a personage than the admirable Garrick." Walpole did not attempt to stop Giffard, and, the *Rambler's Magazine* said, Henry "played on, and was so successful, that in a few years he purchased the estate which is now called Coventry-court, and is situated in the Haymarket." Garrick's debut in London was very much a Giffard affair: the manager played King Henry, his wife acted Lady Anne, and William Giffard was Tressel.

Though Giffard must have recouped his losses through Garrick's success in 1741–42 and his own acting at Smock Alley in the summer of 1742, he was again in financial straits the following season, when he operated without Garrick, once again Lincoln's Inn Fields. There he performed many of his old roles plus a few new ones: Easy in *The Careless Husband*, Heartly in *The Non-Juror*, and Wildair in *The Constant Couple*. On 8 February 1743 the *Daily Post and General Advertiser* revealed Giffard's plight:

We are inform'd that Mr. Giffard, as an expedient to recovering in some degree the loss he has sustain'd by his late undertaking in Lincoln's Inn Fields, has apply'd to the late Patentee of the Theatre Royal in Drury Lane [John Highmore] for the favour of his appearance in the character of Lothario (in which it is observable he amus'd himself some years since to a very numerous and polite audience) with which request the said Gentleman has generously comply'd.

On 8 March, for Giffard's benefit, Highmore played his old role at Lincoln's Inn Fields.

Giffard and his wife spent the late spring and summer of 1743 at the Smock Alley Theatre in Dublin. There on 12 May he played Sir Charles Easy and she acted Lady Betty Modish in *The Careless Husband*; she was incorrectly advertised as making her first appearance on that stage. During their engagement Giffard also played Loveless in *The Relapse*, Bellmour in *The Old Bachelor*, Heartly in *The Non Juror*, Dorimant in *The Man of Mode*, Castalio in *The Orphan*, Johnson in *The Rehearsal*, Bevil Junior in *The Conscious Lovers*, Sir Harry in *The Constant Couple*, Edgar in *King Lear*, Altamont in *The Fair Penitent*, King Henry in *Richard III*, Juba in *Cato*, and Cassio in *Othello*.

The Giffards in 1743–44 were at Drury Lane, where Henry remained through the 1746–47 season, having been frustrated in his attempts to establish a third legitimate theatre in London. Some of his new parts during his stay were Sempronius in *Cato*, Southampton in *The Unhappy Favorite*, Iago in *Othello* (on 10 March 1744, the only time he seems to have acted the role), Mirabel in *The Way of the World*, Sir John Brute in *The Provok'd Wife*, Wronglove in *The Lady's Last Stake*, and the King of France in *King John*. During that period he was elected, on 5 October 1745, to membership in the Sublime Society of Beefsteaks.

Giffard augmented his income, we believe, by selling liquor at his lodgings at No 11, Craven Buildings. In the *General Advertiser* of 4 November (1745?) appeared the following announcement: "Messrs

Henry and Jon Giffard sell the best Arrack, French Brandy, Jamaica Rum and all other sorts of spirituous liquors wholesale, also retale, in any quantity not less than two Gallons."

A Giffard appeared at the Capel Street Theatre in Dublin in March and April of 1747 as Fribble in *Miss in Her Teens*, Foppington in *The Careless Husband*, Colonel Britton in *A Wonder a Woman Keeps a Secret*, and Tancred in *Tancred and Sigismunda*. Henry Giffard's name appeared in the Drury Lane bills in London during those months, and though the company list compiled by Clark for the Capel Street Theatre in 1746–47 included "Henry" Giffard, that must be a mistake, and we suspect the actor who appeared in Dublin was W. Giffard. Similarly, the Mr and Mrs Giffard who played in *Tancred and Sigismunda* at Smock Alley in June 1747, described as making their first appearances on that stage, surely could not have been Henry and Anna Marcella, who were well known to Smock Alley audiences.

The Henry Giffards spent their last full season in London at Covent Garden. Henry played a fairly light season, offering some of his old parts and a few new ones: Ranger in *The Suspicious Husband*, the Ghost in *Hamlet*, Sir Charles in *The Fair Quaker of Deal*, and the Mad Scholar in *The Pilgrim*. He returned to Covent Garden in the fall of 1748 to play Lorenzo in *The Spanish Fryar* on 28 September and Aimwell in *The Stratagem* on 7 October, after which he and his wife left the London stage. The couple retired to Brentford where, according to Genest, they were much respected.

On 15 April 1757 Henry Giffard drew up his will, describing himself as of Ealing. To Sir John Chapman of Cockenhatch, Hertford, he left "twenty several messuages or tenements" in Coventry Street, Coventry Court, Haymarket, by virtue of two leases from Peter Johns to John Maidman which had been conveyed to Giffard. Chapman was to hold those properties in trust for the benefit of Henry's wife, Anna Marcella Giffard. £30 yearly was to be held out for Henry's son William ("by a former wife"), provision to be made in case of the deaths of Anna Marcella and William for William's son Joseph, who was, in April 1757, about 11 years old.

Giffard left £5 to Sir John Chapman for his troubles and asked that eventually, when Mrs Giffard thought proper, Henry's "diamond ring I usually wear and all my ffamily pictures" should go to his son William. To William also he gave his gold watch, all his wearing apparel, and all of his books except his *Tatlers, Spectators, Guardians,* nine volumes of Pope's works, and Milton's *Paradise Lost.* Finally, Giffard said:

And as well for the Love and the Affection I have for my said Wife as for and in due Consideration of the great Addition to my Purse and Estate from the various Large Sums of Mony earned and produced by her in her Business or Employments as an Actress in the Theatres during the first twenty years of our Marriage and of her frugal and prudent Managemant thereof for me and in my ffamily then and ever Since, I do hereby give and bequeath unto my said dear wife Anna Marcella all the Residue and Remainder of my personal Estate. . . .

If that statement was correct, the Giffards were married about 1728.

On 3 February 1770, after Henry's estate had grown, he added a codicil to his will. He had "become possessed of Seven hundred and fifty pounds Government Securities called the four percents of the year 1763 payable at the Bank of England." He bequeathed those, "and whatever additional sums" should be purchased, to Sir John Chapman in trust, to be divided equally among Giffard's wife Anna Marcella, his son William, and William's son Joseph. The "produce of the Rents of my Houses in the Haymarket are . . . increased in their annual Income the yearly Sum of Twenty

pounds," Henry stated, and that should be added to the annuity of £30 previously bequeathed to William Giffard. Henry added an unwitnessed memorandum on 3 February 1770 asking that "Molly Giffard who now lives with me if she continues to do so at my decease may have ten Pounds for mourning." Further, Henry Giffard, a staymaker of Kilkenny, Ireland, if living at Henry's decease, should receive £50. Henry's relationship to Molly Giffard was not made clear, though she may well have been the Mary Giffard mentioned in Anna Marcella Giffard's will.

Henry Giffard died at Ealing on 20 October 1772 and was buried at Brentford on 25 October. Lysons transcribed the inscription on Giffard's tombstone: "Beneath this stone lie the remains of Henry Giffard Esq. late of this parish, who died October 20, 1772, aged 78 years. . . ." Five years later Mrs Giffard was buried beside him. Henry's will was proved by his widow on 7 December 1772, Sir John Chapman having renounced execution thereof. Reed in his "Notitia Dramatica" recorded an unidentified clipping of 20 October 1772 that said Giffard died "in a very advanced Age, and much regretted by all." The clipping emphasized Giffard's judgment and encouragement of young actors and praised him for having introduced Garrick to the London stage. The Licensing Act had virtually ruined Giffard, the account said, and he had never received a promised indemnification and recompense, though "he continued to apply for [it] to the End of his Life." Giffard's will, however, suggests that he ended his life in comfortable circumstances.

Considering the importance of Giffard in the eighteenth century theatre, one would expect to find a number of portraits of him; according to his wife's will, he sat for an artist, but the resulting picture has not been found. In a satirical print published on 24 October 1743 by G. Foster and called *The Theatrical Contest* the figure marked "L" may have been intended to represent Giffard. Remarkably, *The Dictionary of National Biography* contains no entry for Henry Giffard or any of the other Giffards who performed in London.

Giffard, Mrs Henry the second, Anna Marcella, née Lyddal *1707–1777, actress, singer.*

Though concrete evidence is hard to come by, the second wife of the actor-manager Henry Giffard was apparently born Anna Marcella (Nancy) Lyddal in 1707, the daughter of parents who acted at the Smock Alley Theatre in Dublin from as early as 1716. Chetwood in his *General History* in 1749 claimed that Anna's mother said her daughter was born in 1711, but Lysons, in *The Environs of London*, cites Anna Marcella's tombstone, which states that she died in 1777 at the age of 70. From references in Henry Giffard's will we would guess that Anna married Henry about 1728 or 1729. Anna was evidently the sister of Henry's first wife, Mary Lyddal. Both girls acted in Dublin with their parents. Company lists and playbills collected by the late William Smith Clark for Dublin theatres show that Anna (called Nancy Lyddal or Miss Lyddal) was certainly in the Smock Alley troupe from 1720–21 through 1722–23 and presumably before and after. Her known roles were Miss Prue in *Love for Love*, Sygismunda in *The Rival Generals*, Lucinda in *The Deceit*, and Lady Betty in *The Careless Husband*.

Advertised as from the Theatre Royal, Dublin, Anna Marcella Giffard made her first appearance on the English stage on 4 November 1729 at the Goodman's Fields Theatre as Monimia in *The Orphan*. That part, and several others she played in her first London season, she continued acting for many years. During the 1729–30 season she was also seen as Jane Shore, Miranda in *The Busy Body*, the Queen in *The Spanish Fryar*, Belinda in *The Old Bachelor*, Belvidera in *Venice Preserv'd*, Angelina in *Love Makes a Man*, Ruth in *The Committee*, Bi-zarre in *The Inconstant*, the title role in *The Fair Penitent*, Lady Lurewell in *The Constant Couple*, Ophelia in *Hamlet*, Indiana in *The Conscious Lovers*, Lady Lucy Pedant in *The Temple Beau*, Lady Townly in *The Provok'd Husband*, Victoria in *Fatal Villainy* (and she spoke the epilogue), Mrs Ford in *The Merry Wives of Windsor*, Dorcas in *The Fair Quaker*, Colombine ("a Scotch Woman") in *Harlequin Turn'd Dancing Master* for her benefit on 1 April 1730, Mrs Sprightly in *The Fashionable Lady*, Angelica in *The Rover*, Estifania in *Rule a Wife and Have a Wife*, Kitty in *The What D'Ye Call It*, Amanda in *Love's Last Shift*, Mrs Sullen in *The Stratagem*, Angelica in *Love for Love*, the Countess of Rutland in *The Unhappy Favorite*, Cordelia in *King Lear*, Desdemona in *Othello*, Matilda in *The Widow Bewitch'd*, Imoinda in *Oroonoko*, and Polly in *The Beggar's Opera*. The size and range of her repertoire matched that of her husband, who acted opposite her in many plays.

Chetwood called Mrs Giffard "an amiable Person" and a "well-esteemed Actress, both in Tragedy and Comedy." *The Comedian* in October 1732 said no more than that she was not without merit. Later reports, however, gave her more attention. On 3 January 1736, for example, Thomas Gray wrote to Horace Walpole after seeing *King Arthur*:

Mrs GIFFORD is by way of Emmeline, & should be blind, but heaven knows! I would not wish to see better than she does, & seems to do; for when Philidel [an airy spirit] restores her to sight, her eyes are not at all better than before; she is led in at first, by a Creature, y^t was more like a Devil by half than Grimbald himself; she took herself for Madame la Confidente, but every body else took her to be in the Circumstances of Damnation; when Emmeline comes to her sight, she beholds this Mrs Matilda first, & cries out

Are Women all like thee? such glorious Creatures

which set the people into such a laugh, as lasted the whole Act.

Samuel Foote in *The Roman and English Comedy Considered* in 1747 said that Mrs Giffard was "unequal'd in the Character of [Lady] Macbeth," but to say that was to "but barely do her Justice." *A Letter of Complaint* the same year was similarly complimentary though restrained:

If Mrs Giffard's Manner was equal to her understanding, she wou'd compell everybody to acknowledge her a surprising Performer. In Lady Macbeth she is excellent; and Hermione was very near eclipsing a much more popular actress [probably Mrs Horton]; in short in every Part she performs, the severest of her enemies cannot but own she is more than decent.

Mrs Giffard acted at Goodman's Fields from 1729–30 through 1735–36, adding to her repertoire such parts as Arpasia and Selima in *Tamerlane*, Marcia in *Cato*, Lady Essex in *The Fall of the Earl of Essex*, Hermione and Andromache in *The Distrest Mother*, Maria in *The London Merchant* (a small role but perhaps indicative of her ability to play both youthful and mature roles), Elvira in *The Spanish Fryar*, Letitia in *The Old Bachelor*, Almeria in *The Mourning Bride*, Lady Jane Gray, Lady Anne in *Richard III*, Lady Macduff in *Macbeth*, Amanda in *The Relapse*, Biddy in *The Tender Husband*, Lady Harriet in *The Funeral*, Statira in *The Rival Queens*, Athenais in *Theodosius*, Cydaria in *The Indian Emperor*, Emilia in *The Fond Husband*, Eurydice in *Oedipus*, Lady Wealthy in *The Gamester*, Princess Catherine in *Henry V*, and Isabella in *The Fatal Marriage* and a number of prologues and epilogues. During the early 1730s Mrs Giffard also appeared at other theatres. At the Haymarket she acted Lady Percy in *1 Henry IV* on 3 May and Lady Townly in *The Provok'd Husband* on 7 May 1731. She probably played in Dublin in the summer of 1735

when her husband acted there, and on 18 June 1736 she was at the Lincoln's Inn Fields Theatre playing the title part in *Alzira*—and she also spoke the epilogue.

She was with her husband at Lincoln's Inn Fields in 1736–37, playing several of her old roles plus Emmeline in *King Arthur*, Semandra in *Mithridates*, Julia in *The Independent Patriot*, the Queen in *An Historical Play* (*King Charles*), and other new parts. She became ill during the winter. The *Daily Post* reported on 18 December 1736 that Mrs Giffard had "been dangerously ill of a fever [but] is now in a fair way of recovering." She did not act until 12 February 1737 and was then noted in the playbill as reappearing for the first time since her "late indisposition." But on 21 February it was reported that she had returned the part of Lady Betty Manly in *A Tutor for the Beaus* to Miss Hughes, finding herself still indisposed. She was doubtless in Dublin with her husband in the summer of 1737, the Licensing Act having been passed in London.

On 2 February 1738 Mrs Giffard acted Lady Townly at Drury Lane, following that with Almeria, Calista, and Lady Betty. She was at Drury Lane for the 1738–39 and 1739–40 seasons, but she carried a light schedule and was seen in few new parts: Eudocia in *The Siege of Damascus*, Emira in *Mustapha*, and the First Constantia in *The Chances*. With her husband she performed at Goodman's Fields in 1740–41 and 1741–42. There she acted more frequently and essayed such new characters as Ann Lovely in *A Bold Stroke for a Wife*, Hillaria in *Tunbridge Walks*, Hermione in *The Winter's Tale*, Charlot in *The Fatal Curiosity*, Helena in *All's Well that Ends Well*, Evandra in *Timon of Athens*, the title part in *Pamela*, Millamant in *The Way of the World*, and Melinda in *The Recruiting Officer*. She was at Lincoln's Inn Fields in 1742–43 but tried no new roles, and she completed her season in time to get to Ireland by May.

We have a fairly complete record of Mrs Giffard's roles at the Smock Alley Theatre in Dublin from 12 May to 21 July 1743: Lady Betty in *The Careless Husband*, Berinthia in *The Relapse, Laetitia* in *The Old Bachelor*, Maria in *The Non-Juror*, Loveit in *The Man of Mode*, Monimia in *The Orphan*, Indiana in *The Conscious Lovers*, Lady Lurewell in *The Constant Couple*, Cordelia in *King Lear*, Calista in *The Fair Penitent*, Queen Elizabeth in *Richard III*, Marcia in *Cato*, and Desdemona in *Othello*. Though there is a possibility that Anna Marcella performed a few years later in Dublin, we think 1743 was probably her last engagement there.

She performed at Drury Lane from 1743–44 through 1746–47, adding to her repertoire such characters as Belvedere in *Women Pleased*, Lady Macbeth (which she first played on 7 January 1744), Lady Fanciful in *The Provok'd Wife*, Cleopatra in *All for Love*, and, in quick succession in March and April 1747, just before she left Drury Lane, Mrs Winwife in *The Artful Husband*, Rosalure in *The Wild Goose Chase*, Constance in *King John*, and Alcmena in *Amphitryon*.

Anna Marcella Giffard's last full season in London was spent at Covent Garden where, in 1747–48, she acted Clarinda in *The Suspicious Husband*, Lady Sadlife in *The Double Gallant*, and several roles with which she had been identified over the years: Belvidera, Amanda, Desdemona, Elvira, Lady Harriet, Miranda, Estifania, and Hillaria. She returned to Covent Garden in the fall of 1748 for two performances: as Lady Fanciful in *The Provok'd Wife* on 21 September and 11 October, after which she left the London stage.

The Giffards were living at No 4, Craven Buildings, Drury Lane, as of 22 March 1739, when they shared a benefit. On 25 March 1740 they were at Mr Bolney's in Great Queen Street, near Lincoln's Inn Fields. By March 1744 they were living in James Street, Covent Garden, and a year later they were probably at No 11, Craven Buildings, Drury Lane.

The Giffards retired to Brentford in late 1748. Henry Giffard died in 1772, providing handsomely for his wife, his son William (by his first wife), and William's son Joseph. On 9 September 1776 Anna Marcella Giffard, still living in Brentford, wrote her will. Sir John Chapman had been Henry Giffard's executor, though he renounced in favor of Mrs Giffard; to him Mrs Giffard left 10 guineas for a ring. She left £30 to her sister Sarah Hamilton, £10 to her servant Mary Giffard (possibly the "Molly" Giffard of whom Henry Giffard spoke in his will), £10 to Mary Marshall, £10 to James Giffard, and £20 to her executor William Keasberry—presumably the proprietor of the Bath theatre. Everything else in her personal estate Mrs Giffard left to Keasberry in trust, to be placed out at interest for the benefit of Mrs Giffard's sister Sarah Hamilton for life. After Sarah's death, legacies were to be distributed as follows: £200 to Mrs Giffard's nephew William Hamilton, £50 each to William's sons John and Marlborough, £200 to her nephew Morton Hamilton, and equal proportions of £100 to each of Morton's sons who should be living after the death of Sarah Hamilton.

The rest of her estate—presumably that part left her by her husband—she wished to be used to provide £20 annually for her stepson (though she called him her son) William Giffard. After William's death the annuity was to go to William Keasberry's wife (Anna Marcella Giffard's niece) Henrietta. Should Henrietta survive her husband, she was to receive an additional £400. Mrs Giffard's niece Catherine Hamilton was to receive the produce of £400 at the rate of 5%. Mrs Giffard, so far as is known, had only one child by her husband, a daughter who died in the 1730s at the age of two—but that information came from the not always reliable *History of the English Stage* (1741).

On 18 November 1776 Mrs Giffard drew up a lengthy and very detailed codicil. In it she gave William Giffard her rights to a house in Windmill Lane (including the furniture, should he live there). She also left William sundry possessions, including her books, bookcases, pictures of Henry and Anna Marcella Giffard and, apparently, of William and his wife, and many small household items such as silver, plate, furniture, and linen. To Henrietta Keasberry she left many more of her household goods, and she remembered also Henrietta's mother (Sarah Hamilton), a Mrs Friends, Sir John Chapman, and William Keasberry.

Anna Marcella Giffard died on 21 January 1777, aged 70 years, at New Brentford where, according to Lysons, she was buried on 23 January. On 30 January James Giffard of the parish of St Paul, Covent Garden, grocer, and his wife Diana deposed as to the handwriting in Anna Marcella's will. The will was proved on 7 February 1777.

We do not know in what way Anna Marcella was related to James and Diana Giffard. The registers of St Paul, Covent Garden, contain many references to James, his first wife Anne, and their six children, and his second wife Diana Goodenough and their eight children. The eighth child of James and Diana was christened Anna Marcella on 14 November 1773, a year after Henry Giffard's death. Most of the other people mentioned in Mrs Giffard's will, on the other hand, had theatrical connections. Her sister Sarah Hamilton had a considerable career as an actress in Dublin and London and introduced two sons to the stage; Sarah's daughters Catherine and Henrietta acted, and the latter married the actor-manager William Keasberry; her son Myrton (called Morton in Mrs Giffard's will) was also an actor. Not mentioned by Mrs Giffard was a sister, whose Christian name is not known and who had a stage career as Mrs Sterling.

A Mrs Giffard was pictured in the char-acter of a queen, standing, her right hand to her breast, in an engraving by Terry which was published by J. Harrison in 1779. The late date would suggests that the picture is not of our subject unless it was drawn many years earlier.

Giffard, Mrs M. *[fl. 1733–1737]*, actress.

The identity of Mrs M. Giffard is not certain. The wills of Henry Giffard and his wife Anna Marcella mention a Molly and a Mary Giffard (possibly the same person), but there is no proof that the wills refer to the Mrs M. Giffard who acted in London from 1733 to 1737. The coincidence of the appearances in London of William Giffard and Mrs M. Giffard might suggest a relationship between the two – husband and wife, perhaps, or brother and sister – but there seems to be no evidence to clarify the matter.

Mrs M. Giffard made her first appearance on any stage at Goodman's Fields on 6 April 1733 as Calphurnia in *Julius Caesar* at William Giffard's benefit. The theatre was then managed by Henry Giffard, who may have been William's younger brother. In 1733–34 Mrs M. Giffard was cited for only one part, that of a Royal Attendant on Britannia on 11 February 1734 at Goodman's Fields in *Britannia*. In 1734–35 she was mentioned in the bills more frequently, her parts being an Attendant on Juno in *Jupiter and Io*, Gypsey in *The Stratagem*, Betty in *Woman's a Riddle*, and Mrs Topknot in *The Gamester*. The London Stage probably was in error when it listed a Mrs W. Giffard in the Goodman's Fields troupe in 1735–36, for no roles are listed for such an actress, though Mrs M. Giffard, who is not listed that season in *The London Stage*, was active with the troupe and added Ann Page in *The Merry Wives of Windsor* to her list of characters. At benefit time, on 16 April 1736, Mrs M. Giffard's tickets were accepted at the playhouse.

Mrs Giffard's last season in London was

in 1736–37 at Lincoln's Inn Fields, whence the Giffard clan had removed. There she acted several old parts plus a role in *All Alive and Merry*, Pinup in *A Tutor for the Beaus*, Flora in *The Wonder*, Mrs Snare in *The Fond Husband*, and Teramina in *The Wife's Relief*. After that season, though some Giffards remained active in London, Mrs M. Giffard, William Giffard, and Master Giffard (their nephew William, Henry's son?) left the London stage. From Mrs M. Giffard's roles one would take her to have been younger than the William Giffard who acted with her at Goodman's Fields in the 1730s, but we can guess little else about her.

Giffard, [Mrs Thomas?], Jane, later Mrs John Egleton   *d. c. 1734, actress, singer, playwright.*

On 9 November 1717 at the Lincoln's Inn Fields Theatre "a Gentlewoman who never appear'd upon the stage before" played Mary the Buxom in *2 Don Quixote*; when the play was repeated on 25 November a Mrs Giffard was assigned the part, and one can assume she was the unidentified actress of two weeks earlier. In notes kindly supplied us by Charles Beecher Hogan is the suggestion that Mrs Giffard may have been the wife of Thomas Giffard who, according to Stockwell, acted in Dublin in 1720. It is also possible, however, that she was the wife of the William Giffard who acted in London in 1717. A third possibility is that, despite her use of "Mrs" (which was not uncommon for spinsters who were of age), she was a Giffard, possibly William's sister and close to him in age. In any case, it seems most probable that she was the Jane Giffard who later married the actor John Egleton.

After her appearance as Mary the Buxom, Mrs Giffard played Patch in *The Busy Body* on 28 November 1717, Bettrice in *The Lady's Triumph* on 22 March 1718 (William Giffard and Egleton were also in the cast; *The London Stage* incorrectly as-

signs the play to Theobald instead of Settle and omits the cast that is contained in the 1718 edition), and Le Jupe in *The Coquet* on 19 April (Egleton was also in the cast). At Southwark Fair in September she acted Lucy in *Sir Richard Whittington*.

At Angel Court on 24 September 1718 Mrs Giffard played Lucy in *The Recruiting Officer* (Giffard played Brazen), after which she returned to Lincoln's Inn Fields to act Flora in *The Fair Example*, Lucy in *'Tis Well If It Takes*, and perhaps a role in *Love for Love*. The cast for *Love for Love* was not given in the bill for 7 May 1719, but the play was presented for the benefit of Mrs Giffard, Egleton, and Boheme. William Giffard did not perform in London after September 1718, nor was any male Giffard seen in London for many years thereafter.

Through the 1720–21 season Mrs Giffard continued at Lincoln's Inn Fields, playing some of her earlier parts and such others as Lady Raleigh in *Sir Walter Raleigh*, Lady Wealthy in *The Gamester*, Mrs Frail in *Love for Love*, Gertrude in *Hamlet*, Lucy in *The Recruiting Officer*, Calphurnia in *Julius Caesar*, Mrs Day in *The Committee*, the Queen in *Cymbeline*, Widow Lackit in *Oroonoko*, Mrs Termagant in *The Squire of Alsatia*, Emilia in *Othello*, Almeyda in *Don Sebastian*, Almeria and Alibech in *The Indian Emperor*, Goneril in *King Lear*, Mrs Quickly in *The Merry Wives of Windsor*, Lady Plyant in *The Double Dealer*, Mademoiselle in *The Provok'd Wife*, Tamora in *Titus Andronicus*, Andromache in *Troilus and Cressida*, and the Duchess of York and Lady Anne in *Richard III*. During that period she also appeared in the droll *Friar Bacon* at the Leigh and Hall booth at Southwark Fair on 5 September 1720.

Sometime between 29 May and 27 September 1721 Mrs Giffard (her Christian name was Jane, according to an inventory dated 12 April 1722 now at the British Museum) became Mrs John Egleton and performed under that name for the rest of her career. Except for a few performances with other groups, Mrs Egleton remained with John Rich's company at Lincoln's Inn Fields and, beginning in 1732, at Covent Garden, until the end of her career in 1733.

Among the new parts she attempted during that time were Flareit in *Love's Last Shift*, Florella in *The Orphan*, Mopsophil in *The Emperor of the Moon*, the Hostess in *1 Henry IV*, Lady Bountiful in *The Stratagem*, Lucy in *The Old Bachelor*, Abigail in *The Drummer*, Salome in *Mariamne*, Colombine in *Jupiter and Europa*, Sysigambis in *The Rival Queens*, Lady Touchwood in *The Double Dealer*, Lady Laycock in *The Amorous Widow*, Juletta in *The Pilgrim*, Mrs Trudge in *Love and a Bottle*, Kate in *The Taming of the Shrew*, Doris in *Aesop*, Mrs Amlet in *The Confederacy*, Sentry in *She Wou'd If She Cou'd*, Mrs Security in *The Gamester*, Peg in *The Cobler's Opera*, Hob's Mother in *Hob's Opera*, Lucy in *Tunbridge Walks*, the title role in *The Wife of Bath*, Dorcas in *The What D'Ye Call It*, Lucy in *The Beggar's Opera*, Parly and Lady Darling in *The Constant Couple*, Juno in *The Judgment of Paris*, Mrs Motherly in *The Provok'd Husband*, Viletta in *She Wou'd and She Wou'd Not*, a role in her own ballad opera "The Maggot" (performed on 18 April 1732 but apparently never published), Huncamunca in *The Tragedy of Tragedies*, Lady Wishfort in *The Way of the World* at the opening of Covent Garden on 7 December 1732, and Widow Blackacre in *The Plain Dealer*. Mrs Egleton sang in such works as *Macbeth*, often performed singing roles in pantomimes and ballad operas, and introduced songs within plays.

Occasionally during that period Mrs Egleton appeared elsewhere. On 22 August 1723, for example, she acted Lady Westford in the droll *The Blind Beggar of Bethnal Green* at the Pinkethman-Norris booth at Bartholomew Fair, and it is likely that she repeated the role at Richmond on 2 September, as she certainly did at Pinketh-

man's Southwark Fair booth on 25 September for her benefit with her husband. In 1727 she may have spent part of the summer acting at York; on 23 August 1729 she played Tippet in *The Hunter* at Fielding's booth at Bartholomew Fair; in August 1730 she acted at Reynolds's booth at Tottenham Court and at both London fairs; and she appeared at the fairs again, working for Hall, Hippisley, and Fielding, in August and September 1731. At the fairs, as at the patent house, she sometimes played singing roles or offered songs as entertainments between the acts.

Jane Egleton's salary as of 25 September 1724 was £1 0s. 8d., and she was granted regular benefits, usually shared with one other person, sometimes her husband. At her benefits she normally shared an average of £100 before house charges, though occasionally she did better, as on 6 April 1724 when she and her husband received £146 6s. 6d., or on 24 April 1728 when she and Hall shared £166 19s. before charges, or on 29 April 1731 when she split with Mrs Wright a gross of £146 14s.

Davies commented that Mrs Egleton was "extremely diffident" and often under the "utmost apprehension of failing to please." But, he said, she was a comic actress much admired by the best critics, and she always applied herself to the task of developing a new character. In *The Memoirs of Macklin* it was said that "She wanted prudence, however, to regulate those talents, and to secure the continuence of public approbation; for whether from herself, or from the example of her husband, like a second Ariadne, she died enamoured of Bacchus, about the year 1734."

In Hogarth's famous picture of Act III of *The Beggar's Opera*, Jane Giffard Egleton was pictured as Lucy, kneeling at the left of the picture, but, alas, her back is to the viewer.

Giffard, W. [*fl.* 1746?–1752], *actor.*
The *General Advertiser* reported on 14

September 1752 that Mr W. Giffard and Mrs Bland from the theatre in Dublin had arrived in London and would soon make their appearance at the Covent Garden Theatre. W. Giffard may well have been the Giffard who performed at the Smock Alley and Capel Street Theatres in 1746–47 and was, according to the late William Smith Clark's investigation of Irish company lists and playbills, at Smock Alley in 1747–48 and at Capel Street in 1749–50. That Giffard seems not to have been Henry. We know very little about the Dublin Giffard's roles. In March and April 1747 he played Fribble in *Miss in Her Teens*, Foppington in *The Careless Husband*, Colonel Britton in *The Wonder*, and Osmond in *Tancred and Sigismunda*—all at Capel Street. In the bills those months was a Mrs Giffard who, so far as can be determined, was not Mrs Henry Giffard or, indeed, any of the female Giffards who performed in London. At Smock Alley on 22 June 1747 the Dublin Giffards were seen as Laura and Osmond in *Tancred and Sigismunda*. A year later, on 28 April 1748 at Smock Alley, a benefit performance was held for a Mr Giffard, and again he would seem to be the Giffard who came to London in 1752.

On 29 September 1752 W. Giffard and Mrs Bland appeared at Covent Garden, with Giffard acting Zanga in *The Revenge*. The prompter Cross noted in his diary that as Zanga Giffard was indifferent. The actor was not only a newcomer to London but inexperienced as well, for Aaron Hill wrote in his prologue for Giffard's first appearance:

There, thrown too forward, into points of sight,
He trembles, conscious of th' excess of light.
Young, and untaught as yet, myself to trust,
I plead their pity, who have tastes too just.

Just how "untaught" Giffard was one cannot tell from Hill's rather traditional plea for a performer making his first appearance at a London patent house. Hill's statement would not be inconsistent with Giffard's having acted for a few years in Dublin which, judging by the newspaper notice mentioned earlier, he apparently had.

Giffard attempted King Lear on 16 October 1752, then played Townley in *The London Cuckolds*, Granger in *The Refusal*, Axalla in *Tamerlane*, and Carlos in *Love Makes a Man*. His last appearance in London may have been on 5 December; at any rate, he seems not to have performed the whole season.

W. Giffard was doubtless related to the other Giffards who performed in Great Britain in the eighteenth century, but the exact relationship is not clear. He seems to have been of a younger generation than the William Giffard who performed in London in the 1730s and 1740s and who was, we believe, Henry Giffard's son. But the fact that Aaron Hill wrote a special prologue for young W. Giffard suggests a person with good theatrical connections.

Giffard, Mrs W. *See* **GIFFARD, MRS M.**

Giffard, William ｛*fl. 1716?–1737*｝, actor.

It is difficult to distinguish correctly all the Giffards who acted in London, but it seems likely that the Mr Giffard who performed in Dublin in 1716 and in London in 1717 and 1718 was the William Giffard who appeared in London from 1728 to 1737. He was not the William Giffard who was Henry Giffard's son, but rather a member of an earlier generation—an older brother of Henry, perhaps.

Clark in *The Irish Stage in the County Towns* stated that a Mr Giffard was active at the Smock Alley Theatre in Dublin in 1716 and identified him as Henry; we take that to be incorrect, for Henry was supposed to have been born in 1699 and to have made his initial stage appearance at Bath in 1719. The Smock Alley Giffard turned up at the Lincoln's Inn Fields playhouse in London on 23 May 1717, sharing a benefit with four others. The following 14 December Giffard was a Spirit in *Mangora* (or at least he was so listed in the 1718 edition of the work). The manuscript promptbook of *The Lady's Triumph* shows that he played a Gentleman in that piece, presumably on 22 March 1718. At his shared benefit with three others on 3 May Giffard tried the title role in *The Gamester*, and the following 5 September at Southwark Fair he appeared as Supercargo in *Sir Richard Whittington*. On 24 September at Angel Court Giffard acted Brazen in *The Recruiting Officer*. In that cast was a Mrs Giffard, and she had also appeared in *The Lady's Triumph* at Lincoln's Inn Fields the previous March. Though she may have been our subject's wife, it is more likely she was Jane Giffard, who later married John Egleton (another member of *The Lady's Triumph* cast).

No Mr Giffard appeared again in London until Henry Giffard began acting there in 1726 (interestingly, in the role of Brazen, but that fact should not lead us to suppose our subject was the Giffard in London in 1726). The Giffard we have been following returned to London, we believe, in 1728. On 16 May he acted Ferret in *The Royal Merchant* at Lincoln's Inn Fields, where Mrs Egleton was performing. Giffard followed that with the Beggar in *Love and a Bottle* on 22 May, Guzman in *The Successful Strangers* on 25 June, Squib in *Tunbridge Walks* on 2 July, Bomilcar in *Sophonisba* on 5 July, Hazard in *The Wife's Relief* on 19 July, and, at the Haymarket, the title role in *The Spanish Fryar* on 9 August (the summer season at Lincoln's Inn Fields had just ended). At Bartholomew Fair on 24 August, at Hall and Miller's booth, Giffard acted Old Booth in *Bateman*.

Giffard repeated his role of Ferret at Lincoln's Inn Fields on 1 October 1728, but he did not remain with the troupe. During the 1728–29 season he acted at the Haymarket, playing Old Traffic in *The Metamorphosis* and Watchit in *The Craftsman* on 15 October 1728. He followed that appearance with his portrayals of Chamont in *The Orphan*, Tim in *The Lottery*, Gomez in *Don Carlos*, Pierre in *Venice Preserv'd*, Balance in *The Recruiting Officer*, the Miller's Man in *The Humours of Harlequin*, an unspecified character in *The Royal Captives*, Darony in *Hurlothrumbo*, Omar in *Tamerlane*, Bung in *The Smugglers*, and Sir Jolly Glee in *The Patron*.

On 26 August 1729 at the Hall and Oates booth at Bartholomew Fair Giffard played the Great Turk in *Maudlin*, and Reynolds's booth at Southwark Fair on 8 September he took part in *The Beggar's Wedding* and played the Miller's Man (again) in *The Humours of Harlequin*. On 23 September for Reynolds he acted Balance in *The Recruiting Officer*. Some of the roles just mentioned—Balance, Chamont, and Pierre—were acted the following season by "W." Giffard (William) at Goodman's Fields, thus giving us a clue to the identification of the Giffard we have been following.

The bills at Goodman's Fields in 1729–30 had to distinguish William Giffard from Henry, who, with his wife, was also in the troupe. Their roles suggest that Henry was the younger man. During William's first season at Goodman's Fields under Thomas Odell's management he acted such parts as Balance, Chamont, Pierre, and also Gibbet and Aimwell in *The Stratagem*, Scandal in *Love for Love*, the title role (again) in *The Spanish Fryar*, Burleigh in *The Unhappy Favorite*, Simon Pure in *A Bold Stroke for a Wife*, the title role in *The Old Bachelor*, Sir Thomas in *The Gamester*, the Governor in *Love Makes a Man*, Sciolto in *The Fair Penitent*, a Bravo in *The Inconstant*, Gloster in *Jane Shore*, Claudius in *Hamlet* (Henry played Hamlet), Sir John in *The Conscious Lovers*, Veromil in *The Temple Beau*,

Manly in *The Provok'd Husband*, Falstaff in *The Merry Wives of Windsor* (Henry played Ford), Abel in *The Committee*, Iago in *Othello*, and Gloucester in *King Lear* (Henry played Edgar). William's post-season activity included playing the title part in *Mad Tom of Bedlam* at Tottenham Court on 1 August 1730 and Pease Stock in *Wat Tyler and Jack Straw* at a Bartholomew Fair booth he operated with Pinkethman on 20 August and subsequent dates.

Except for a few appearances elsewhere, William Giffard played at Goodman's Fields through the 1735–36 season, adding to his London roles such parts as Clause in *The Royal Merchant*, the title role in *Cato*, Raymond in *The Spanish Fryar*, Acasto in *The Orphan*, the Governor in *Oroonoko*, the Mad Englishman in *The Pilgrim*, Morelove in *The Careless Husband*, Surly in *Sir Courtly Nice*, Careless in *The Double Gallant*, the title role in *Tamerlane*, Charles in *Love Makes a Man*, Woodcock in *Tunbridge Walks*, Macbeth (on 20 May 1731 for his shared benefit with Collett), Scipio in *Sophonisba*, Caliban in *The Tempest*, Clincher Senior in *The Constant Couple*, Falstaff in *1 Henry IV*, Cassio and later Brabantio in *Othello*, Sullen in *The Stratagem*, Gardiner in *Lady Jane Gray*, Buckingham in *Richard III*, the King in *The Mourning Bride*, Worcester in *Henry IV*, Laertes in *Hamlet* (on 24 October 1732; Hulett acted Claudius), Casca in *Julius Caesar*, Bellmour in *Jane Shore*, Apemantus in *Timon of Athens* (at Drury Lane, on 23 November 1733, though that may be an error, for Henry Giffard appeared at Drury Lane about that time), Haemon in *Oedipus*, Priuli in *Venice Preserv'd*, the Uncle in *The London Merchant*, Blunt in *The Committee*, the King of France in *Henry V*, Osmond in *King Arthur*, Baldwin in *The Fatal Marriage*, Leon in *Rule a Wife and Have a Wife*, and Sempronius in *Cato*.

William's last season in London was spent at Lincoln's Inn Fields, whence the Giffard clan had removed and where, in the spring of 1737, the Licensing Act brought an end to their efforts. In 1736–37 Giffard acted such new roles as Pyropus in *Ignoramus*, Mr Ashley in *Hymen's Triumph*, Gripeacre in *The Independent Patriot*, Ireton in *An Historical Play*, Fireball in *Sir Harry Wildair*, and Trusty in *The Funeral*. His last appearance seems to have been on 6 May 1737, when he acted Blunt in *The Committee*.

A William Giffard acted in London from 1740 to 1744, but we do not believe him to have been the William we have been following, but a member of a younger generation of Giffards, perhaps our William's nephew. It also seems probable that the later William was the Master Giffard who acted in the 1730s along with our subject and that Mrs M. Giffard, who acted from 1733 to 1737, may have been our subject's wife.

The London Stage lists in its index William Giffard as the author of *Merlin; or, The British Inchanter, and King Arthur, the British Worthy*, which was presented on 28 September 1736 at Goodman's Fields with William as Osmond and was published that year. The work, however, seems to have been Dryden's *King Arthur*, perhaps slightly altered by Giffard.

Giffard, William *1724?–1807, actor.*

If our identification is correct—and it must be taken as conjectural—the Master Giffard who acted in the 1730s was William, the son of Henry Giffard by his first wife, Mary, née Lyddal. Chetwood said that Henry's son was born in Dublin, in Henry's house on the North Strand; *The History of the English Stage* in 1741 reported that the boy was born a year before his mother died, which event dated about 1725. The boy's birth was also reported as 1715 (not very likely), 1721 (which fits well with later facts), and 1730 (most unlikely).

Master Giffard, as the playbills styled him, played Cordelio in *The Orphan* on 24 November 1731 at the Goodman's Fields playhouse, which his father Henry managed. The role was a standard one for children, as was the Prince of Wales in *Richard III*, which Master Giffard acted on 20 March 1732. In 1732–33 he played Lucius in *Julius Caesar* on 6 April 1733 at the benefit of "W. Giffard"—an elder William, possibly our subject's uncle; on that date Mrs. M. Giffard made her first stage appearance. Master Giffard repeated his role in *Richard III* on 11 April. On 10 September 1733 he played Lucius again; on 28 December he was Finisher in *Don Quixote*; and on 31 January 1734 he acted Fleance in *Macbeth*. He played Lucius again on 20 September 1734, was unnoticed in London bills for some time, and then, at Lincoln's Inn Fields on 1 March 1737, appeared as the Duke of York in Havard's piece about Charles I, *An Historical Play*. The Licensing Act of 1737 brought an end to the activity of several of the Giffards in London; the elder William Giffard, Mrs M. Giffard, and Master Giffard left the stage.

The William Giffard who appeared in London from 1740 to 1744 seems not to have been the William who acted in the 1730s with Master Giffard but a younger player, and we conjecture that he was, in fact, the Master Giffard of earlier years, now matured and acting older roles. As will be seen, some of the parts he played had been acted by the elder Giffard, who may have trained him for them.

On 28 October 1740 "W. Giffard" acted Valentine in *Love for Love* at the Goodman's Fields Theatre, a house managed by Henry Giffard. He was then seen as George Barnwell on 29 October, Fantom in *The Drummer* on 30 October, Dumont in *Jane Shore* on 3 November, Axalla in *Tamerlane* on 4 November, Garcia in *The Mourning Bride* on 12 November, Vizard in *The Constant Couple* on 13 November, Manuel in *Love Makes a Man* on 18 November, Pylades in *The Distrest Mother* on 26 November, Morelove in *The Careless Husband* on 27 November, Vernon in *1 Henry IV*

on 28 November, Worthy in *The Recruiting Officer* on 29 November, Careless in *The Double Gallant* on 1 December, Horatio in *Hamlet* on 4 December, Malcolm in *Macbeth* on 10 December, Florizel in *The Winter's Tale* on 15 January 1741, Frederick in *The Wonder* on 28 January, Horatio in *The Wife's Relief* on 2 February, Tressel in *Richard III* on 10 February, Young Wilmot in *The Fatal Curiosity* on 14 February, Frederick in *The Miser* on 16 March, and Aesop in *Lethe* and Altamont in *The Fair Penitent* on 7 April for his benefit with Crispe.

At Goodman's Fields in 1741–42 William added to his list of characters Bertran in *The Spanish Fryar*, Manly in *The Provok'd Husband*, Charles in *The Busy Body*, Blandford in *Oroonoko*, Castalio in *The Orphan*, Williams in *Pamela*, Don Juan in *Rule a Wife and Have a Wife*, Lovewell in *The Gamester*, Bellmour in *The Old Bachelor*, Fainall in *The Way of the World*, Aimwell in *The Stratagem*, Smith in *The Rehearsal*, Duart in *Love Makes a Man*, and Edmund in *King Lear*. During that season he repeated his role of Tressel on 19 October 1741 when Garrick made his London debut as Richard III.

With the other Giffards William moved to Lincoln's Inn Fields in 1742–43, playing some of his old parts and trying such new ones as Blunt in *The Committee*, Richmond in *Richard III*, Bickerstaff in *Bickerstaff's Unburied Dead*, Woodvil in *The Non-Juror*, Belmont in *Jane Shore*, Scandal in *Love for Love*, Hotspur in *1 Henry IV*, the title part in *The Lying Valet*, Standard in *The Constant Couple*, and the Player King in *Hamlet*. His last season in London, 1743–44, he spent at Drury Lane, where he added to his repertoire such parts as Portius in *Cato*, Raleigh in *The Unhappy Favorite*, Pounce in *The Tender Husband*, Oronces in *Aesop*, Lysimachus in *The Rival Queens*, Young Wou'dbe in *The Twin Rivals*, Fenton in *The Merry Wives of Windsor*, Lennox in *Macbeth*, Poins in *2 Henry IV*,

Aegeon in *Oedipus*, and Carlos in *The Fatal Marriage*. His last performance in London was at Drury Lane on 5 May 1744, when he played Scandal in *Love for Love*.

After the 1740s the career of the William Giffard we have been following is difficult to trace. He seems not to have been the W. Giffard who acted at Covent Garden in 1752 (that was clearly a young and inexperienced actor) nor the Giffard who was active at Covent Garden in 1759, 1760, and 1761 (that Giffard seems to have been a very minor actor and was advertised as making his first appearance). There was a Mr Giffard at Salford, near Manchester, in June 1760 and a "Gifford" performing in Halifax with his wife in September 1768, but there is no evidence to suggest that those references are to our subject.

The *Gentleman's Magazine* in April 1807 reported the death of William Giffard, the son of Henry, at Cockermouth on 6 March 1807. That source stated that William had introduced Garrick at Ipswich "with a company of his father's comedians." Henry Giffard was, indeed, at Ipswich in the summer of 1741, but young William could hardly have been Garrick's sponsor. The *Gentleman's Magazine* also said that William retired about 1767, though Baker's diary said William was still acting in 1770 after having left his wife and run off with the wife of another man.

William Giffard was named in Henry Giffard's will of 15 April 1757 for an annuity of £30, and Henry cited William's son, Joseph, as a child of 11 at that time. William also figured prominently in the will of his stepmother Anna Marcella Giffard, who drew up her will on 9 September 1776 and added a codicil the following 18 November. Tate Wilkinson said that the actor William Crisp(e), with whom William Giffard shared a benefit on 7 April 1741 at Goodman's Fields, was a relative of Giffard. The *Gentleman's Magazine* in February 1805 claimed that Giffard was at

that time 90 years old and living in Cornwall; that would place his birth in 1715, which does not fit with the other evidence we have.

Giffard, ₁Mrs William?₁, Elizabeth ₁*fl. 1741–1744*₁, *actress*.

On 7 April 1741 Mrs Elizabeth Giffard made her first appearance on any stage at Goodman's Fields as Lavinia in *The Fair Penitent*. The theatre was managed by Henry Giffard, who acted Lothario, and in the cast were William Giffard (1724?–1807) as Altamont (it was his shared benefit) and Mrs Henry Giffard as Calista. Elizabeth's relationship to the other Giffards is not clear, but perhaps she was the wife of William (the registers of St Paul, Covent Garden, refer to a William and Elizabeth Giffard, as we shall see). For her second stage appearance Elizabeth played Angelica in *The Constant Couple* on 14 September. Then she acted Mrs Grace in *The Provok'd Husband* on 25 September, Dorinda in *The Stratagem* on 30 September, Isabinda in *The Busy Body* on 5 October, Lady Easy in *The Careless Husband* on 7 October, Elvira in *Love Makes a Man* on 28 October, Selima in *Tamerlane* on 4 November, Lavinia again on 11 February 1742, Serina in *The Orphan* on 2 March, Maria in *George Barnwell* on 23 March, Queen Elizabeth in *Richard III* on 21 April, Beatrice in *The Anatomist* on 12 May, and Mariana in *The Miser* on 18 May.

During the season Mrs Giffard was sometimes advertised as Mrs "Eliz." Giffard and sometimes as Mrs "E." Giffard. On 29 March 1742 a benefit was held for "Mr. W. and Mrs. E. Giffard"—which certainly does not suggest a husband and wife, and at Edward Giffard's benefit on 27 April tickets sold by Mrs. E. Giffard were accepted. Though William and Elizabeth Giffard may not have been man and wife, we would take references to Mrs E. Giffard to be to Elizabeth and not to a Mrs Edward Giffard.

In 1742–43 at Lincoln's Inn Fields Elizabeth Giffard added to her repertoire Lady Graveairs in *The Careless Husband*, Chloris in *The Rehearsal*, Sylvia in *The Old Bachelor*, Regan in *King Lear*, and Alicia in *Jane Shore*. During her last season in London, 1743–44, she was at Drury Lane, but for only half the season. She acted Mariana in *The Miser*, Dorinda in *The Stratagem*, Mrs Foresight in *Love for Love*, and Isabella in *The Wonder*. On 25 January 1744 she was replaced in *The Miser* by Mrs Mills and thereafter seems not to have acted again.

Though one would suppose that, had William and Elizabeth Giffard been married, they would have been cited in playbills as Mr and Mrs W. Giffard and not (as on 29 March 1742) as "Mr. W. and Mrs. E. Giffard," a reference in the St Paul, Covent Garden, registers on 23 April 1744 (just a few months after Elizabeth's last stage appearance) might be to them: William and Elizabeth Giffard christened a daughter Harriot on that date. We know that William Giffard married at some point and had a son Joseph, who was born about 1746. The wills of Henry and Anna Marcella Giffard make no mention of William's wife, so she may have been dead by 1757, when Henry's will was made.

Gifford. *See* **GIFFARD.**

Gigli, Bernardo ⌊*fl. c. 1750*⌋, *giant.*
An engraving by J. Fougeron, after Millington, depicts the Italian giant Bernardo Gigli, who, according to the *British Museum Catalogue of Engraved British Portraits*, was exhibited in London about 1750.

Gilbert, Mr ⌊*fl. 1726–1729?*⌋, *actor.*
On 12 April 1726 at the Haymarket Theatre a Mr Gilbert shared a benefit with Miss Beswick (possibly to be identified as Lavinia Fenton). The Gilbert who acted Brazen in *The Recruiting Officer* on 23 September 1729 at Southwark Fair may have been the same person.

Gilbert, Mr *d. 1792, horn player.*
Musgrave's Obituary lists the death of a Mr Gilbert, French horn player, in February 1792. The *Gentleman's Magazine* noted that Gilbert used to play at the principal theatres in and around town but had been in retirement at Bramley, Yorkshire, for several years. It was there that he died. He was perhaps related to the horn player James Gilbert.

Gilbert, Mr ⌊*fl. 1794*⌋, *house servant?*
A Mr Gilbert, possibly a house servant, was one of many whose benefit tickets were accepted at Covent Garden on 17 June 1794.

Gilbert, Mrs ⌊*fl. 1749*⌋, *actress.*
Mrs Gilbert played Mrs Day in *The Committee* on 27 February 1749 at a benefit performance for Lewis Hallam at the New Wells, Lemon Street.

Gilbert, Mrs, formerly Mrs Norton ⌊*fl. 1796–1800*⌋, *actress, singer.*
The Mrs Gilbert who made her first Covent Garden appearance on 23 September 1796 as Lady Waitfor't in *The Dramatist* had acted during the summer of that year in Birmingham as Mrs Norton. On 19 August in Birmingham her benefit tickets were accepted; her address at that time was No 15, Navigation Street. After her debut in London the *Monthly Mirror* in September stated:

She comes, we understand, from Birmingham. Her performance we thought too broad and violent; and other faults were discernible, which must be removed before her reputation in London can be established. If *size*, however, can constitute an actress, this lady is not deficient; for by the uncertain measurement of the eye, she must be more than six foot. She would make an excellent *Glumdalca* and *Mabel Flourish.*

BERNARDO GIGLI

engraving by Fourgeron, after Millington

As will be seen, the suggested casting was followed by the Covent Garden management.

During the rest of the 1796–97 season Mrs Gilbert played the Big Woman in *Barataria* on 26 September, Marcelina in *The Follies of a Day* on 17 October, Mabel Flourish in *Love in a Camp* on 18 October, Lucy in *The Guardian* on 25 November, Mrs Sneak in *The Mayor of Garratt* on 1 December, Cecily in *The Midnight Hour* on 13 December, a Bacchante in *Comus* on 10 January 1797, Glumdalca in *Tom Thumb* on 19 April, a chorus part in *The Italian Villagers* on 25 April, Grace in *Fashionable Levities* on 6 May, Lady Godiva in *Peeping Tom* on 16 May, and Mrs Foresight in *Love for Love* on 13 June.

During the summer of 1797 Mrs Gilbert acted in Haymes's troupe at Richmond and then returned to Covent Garden for the 1797–98 season to play such new roles as Altea in *Rule a Wife and Have a Wife*, Mrs Fulmer in *The West Indian*, Gipsey in *The Beaux' Stratagem*, Lady Bab in *High Life Below Stairs*, and Tib in *Every Man in His Humour*. Her 1798 summer was spent at Birmingham, after which she came back to Covent Garden to play such parts as Mrs Highman in *The Intriguing Chambermaid*, the Landlady in *The Magic Oak*, and Mrs Muggins in *Tagg in Tribulation*.

Mrs Gilbert was in Birmingham again in the summer of 1799, then back at Covent Garden for what may have been her last season in London. She repeated some of her earlier parts and added a few new ones: Molly Brazen in *The Beggar's Opera*, Lady Pride in *Barnaby Brittle*, and the Abbess of St Claire in *Raymond and Agnes*. In 1799–1800 Mrs Gilbert was paid £1 10s. weekly, which was 10s. less than her salary the previous seasons. The Miss Gilbert who was active in 1798–99 and 1799–1800 was presumably her daughter.

Gilbert, Miss [*fl.* 1798–1800], *actress*.

Miss Gilbert, who was presumably the daughter of the Mrs Gilbert who acted in London from 1796 to 1800, acted in Birmingham in the summer of 1798 and was first noticed in the Covent Garden playbills on 8 December 1798, when she acted Charles Mortimer in *Laugh When You Can*. She had a principal role in *Albert and Adelaide* beginning 4 May 1799 and played the Duke of York in *Richard III* on 6 May. After spending the summer of 1799 in Birmingham with Mrs Gilbert, she returned to Covent Garden to act some of her old parts and also the Page in *The Orphan* and Little Bob in *The Poor Sailor*. She had an unspecified role in *Joanna* beginning 16 January 1800.

Gilbert, James [*fl.* 1794], *horn player*.

Doane's *Musical Directory* of 1794 listed James Gilbert, of Stratton Ground, Westminster, as a horn player who participated in the oratorios at Westminster Abbey and in concerts presented by the New Musical Fund.

Gilbert, John [*fl.* 1665–1670], *scenekeeper*.

A warrant in the Lord Chamberlain's accounts dated 20 February 1665 listed John Gilbert as a scenekeeper at the Bridges Street Theatre. *The London Stage* also lists Gilbert as a member of the King's Company at that playhouse in 1666–67 and 1669–70.

Gilbert, Mrs Joseph. See GOPELL, MISS.

Gilbert, Richard [*fl.* 1702–1705], *actor, manager*.

The *Post Man* on 3 October 1702 cited Richard Gilbert as one of several strolling players who were required to pay town constables 2s. daily when they performed. The same Gilbert, perhaps, was at York in 1705. The Minute Books of the York Merchant Taylors contain an entry on 23 February that year granting Gilbert and his company the use of their hall to act in, for a fee of 20s. weekly.

Giles. See also GYLES.

Giles, Mr [*fl.* 1777–1789], *wardrobe worker*.

In a memorandum to the proprietors of Drury Lane in September 1777 (?), Richard Brinsley Sheridan remarked on problems the previous year with dressers and dressing rooms. He received a complaint from Kirk the housekeeper that he had been "exceedingly distressed last Year, by our taking away the two Rooms for Mr. Giles and that he had been oblidged to let People dress in his own Room. . . ." The remark is not very clear about Giles's position in the theatre (his salary, according to the same memorandum, was £50 yearly, £10 more than Kirk's). But the Drury Lane accounts on 19 September 1789 listed Giles in the wardrobe at £1 weekly.

Giles, Miss [*fl. 1781–1794*], *concessionaire.*

Miss Giles operated the fruit concession at Drury Lane from as early as 19 May 1781 to as late as 18 July 1794—the first and last entries in the account books concerning her. She appears to have been on a regular salary of £1 weekly, though she paid the management £100 per season for the privilege of running her concession. In addition to fruits, Miss Giles (and her staff, presumably) sold playbills and books of songs for musical pieces. For example, on 13 December 1781 Miss Giles paid £31 for 1550 books of songs in *The Carnival of Venice*. The accounts indicate that she did not pay her £100 concession fee in a lump sum but in smaller portions—usually about £25—as the season progressed. That she should have been paid a regular salary seems odd, though perhaps she served some function on the theatre staff; one entry on 18 July 1794 notes that she was paid £2 for working one week before the season opened and one week after it closed.

Giles, Edward [*fl. 1732–1741*], *actor.*

Edward Giles was first mentioned in the playbills when he played Leander in *The Cheats of Scapin* at the Haymarket Theatre on 16 February 1732. He went on to act the Wandering Jew and Orsmadius in *The Blazing Comet* on 2 March, Sabatier in *The Wanton Jesuit* on 17 March, Sir Philip in *A Bold Stroke for a Wife* on 23 March, Brazen in *The Recruiting Officer* for his benefit on 31 March, Torrismond in *The Spanish Fryar* on 10 May, and George Barnwell in *The London Merchant* on 1 June. On the last date he was identified by his first name and spoke the prologue.

He seems not to have attached himself

to a single company in 1733. At Goodman's Fields from January to the middle of May he acted the third Drawer in *The Tavern Bilkers*, an Attendant in *The Amorous Sportsman*, and, for his benefit, Foppington in *The Relapse*. Tickets for his benefit, which he shared with Williams, were available at Giles's Coffee House in Pall Mall, and we may guess that acting was a sideline for him which he indulged in only part of his time. On 28 May he acted Basset in *The Provok'd Husband* at the Haymarket, and he had a role in *The Amorous Lady* there on 26 July. The next day he turned up at Covent Garden playing the second Manager in *The Stage Mutineers*, and in August at that house he acted Jack Stanmore in *Oroonoko*, Budgett in *The Fancy'd Queen*, and Scaevola in *The Tuscan Treaty*.

Giles appeared at Drury Lane for a few performances in the early part of 1734 (he seems to have avoided performing in the fall of any year). On 15 January he was Security in *The Intriguing Chambermaid*; on 19 January he played Sir Farcical in *The Author's Farce*; and on 4 February either he or Hewson acted Monsieur Quadrille in *Cupid and Psyche* (the newspapers differed in their information).

Giles acted no more in London, but a Mr Giles was playing in Norwich in 1736–37, and on 12 January 1738 a Mr Giles, cited as having acted at Drury Lane, played Foppington in *The Relapse* at the Aungier Street Theatre in Dublin. There on 26 January he was More of More Hall in *The Dragon of Wantley*. During the 1739–40 season he acted at the Smock Alley Theatre in Dublin, playing such parts as Valentine in *The Mock Lawyer* and Wellfort in *The Sharpers*. He was again at Aungier Street in 1740–41, one of his roles being Squire Gauky in *L'Arlequin Mariner; or, The Squire on an Ass*. On 27 April 1741 Giles was given a benefit at Smock Alley. The Giles who acted in Norwich and Dublin was very likely Edward.

Giles, [John?] [*fl.* 1710–1740], box-keeper.

The Mr Giles who shared a benefit with Cole at Drury Lane on 21 April 1710 and was last noticed on 29 May 1740 sharing a benefit with Boucher at Covent Garden may have been named John. On 20 May 1723 a John "Gilis" witnessed a notice John Rich sent to the managers of Drury Lane; two days before at Rich's theatre the Giles who is our subject shared a benefit. It seems very likely that Gilis and Giles were one and the same. Virtually all the citations of Giles over the years concerned benefits. After the initial one noted above he had benefits at Lincoln's Inn Fields in 1715, 1717, 1721, 1722, 1723, 1724, and 1725; the account books of the theatre make it clear that he worked there through 1729–30, that he was a boxkeeper, and that his daily salary was about 5*s.* In 1730 and 1731 he shared benefits at the Goodman's Fields Theatre; during 1735–36 the accounts at Covent Garden show that he had returned to Rich's company at 1*s.* daily; and on 29 May 1740 he shared a benefit there.

Gilham, Mr [*fl.* 1778–1779], violinist, clarinetist.

The Drury Lane accounts indicate that Mr Gilham was paid £2 weekly for playing violin and clarinet in the theatre band in 1778–79.

Gilis, John. *See* GILES, [JOHN?].

Gill, Mrs [*fl.* 1728], actress.

Mrs Gill played Betty in *The Craftsman* on 15 October 1728 and Elvira in *The Spanish Fryar* on 26 October 1728 at the Haymarket Theatre.

Gill, Andrew [*fl.* 1732], musician.

Andrew Gill, "Musician," of Mile End, Old Town, married Ann Dawson, of the same place, at St Dunstan's, Stepney, on 11 April 1732, according to the marriage registers of that church.

Gillander, Mr [*fl.* 1794–1795], carpenter.

The Covent Garden account books list Mr Gillander as a carpenter at the theatre during the 1794–95 season.

Gillatt, Charles [*fl.* 1784–1794], singer, violinist.

A Mr Gillatt was one of the tenors who sang in the Handel Memorial Concerts at Westminster Abbey and the Pantheon in May and June 1784. Doane's *Musical Directory* of 1794 listed Charles Gillat, doubtless the same musician, of No 208, Piccadilly, as a tenor and a violinist who performed for the New Musical Fund and the Portland Chapel Society.

Gilles, Mr [*fl.* 1785–1795], house servant.

The Drury Lane bills and accounts show that Mr Gilles (or Gillis) worked at the theatre as a house servant. Each year, from 21 May 1785 through 5 June 1795, his benefit tickets were accepted. The accounts did not specify his particular function in the playhouse.

Gillet, Mr [*fl.* 1757], dancer.

At the Haymarket Theatre on 22 August 1757 a Mr Gillet played the Doctor in *Harlequin's Maggot*. The work was not repeated.

Gillett, Mr [*fl.* 1790–1797], house servant?

Mr Gillett's benefit tickets were accepted at Drury Lane on 29 May 1790. A Mr Gillet, very possibly the same person, had his benefit tickets accepted at Covent Garden on 30 May 1795, 31 May 1796, and 27 May 1797. Perhaps our subject was a house servant.

Gilliard, Eustace [*fl.* 1686], trumpeter.

The Lord Chamberlain's accounts cited Eustace Gilliard as a member of the King's

Musick once: on 12 October 1686 he and three other men received silver trumpets.

Gillibrand, Mr [fl. 1734–1740], house servant?

On 12 June 1734 at the Haymarket Theatre Mr Gillibrand shared a benefit with the nephew of Robert Wilks. He may have been one of the house servants, though the benefit would suggest he held a rather important post. A year later, on 23 May 1735, his benefit tickets were accepted at Drury Lane, and through the 1739–40 season Gillibrand was apparently attached to that house. At benefit time most years his tickets were accepted, though 1737–38 is not accounted for.

Gillier. *See also* GALLIARD.

Gillier, Mons [fl. 1721–1722], manager?

A French troupe acted at the Haymarket Theatre from 4 December 1721 to 10 April 1722, sometimes calling themselves the Duke of Montagu's company, in honor of the new owner of the theatre. Monsieur Gillier was apparently the manager of the troupe. He was given permission by Montagu to take over some scenery and other effects left behind by De Grimbergue's troupe the previous season, but John Potter, who built the Haymarket, refused to give Gillier the scenery until Gillier paid him 42 guineas. The outcome of the story is not known.

Gillier's troupe performed *Andromaque*, *Phèdre*, *Mithridate*, *Britannicus*, *Le Cid*, *Les Horaces*, *Le Menteur*, *Rodogune*, *Amphitryon*, *Les Précieuses Ridicules*, *Atrée et Thyèste*, *Rhadamiste et Zénobie*, *L'Ingrat*, *Alcibiade*, *Oedipe*, *Le Chevalier à la Mode*, *Le Comte d'Essex*, *Arlequin Cartouche*, and *Arlequin Hulla*—all for the first time (in French) in London.

Gillier, Master b. c. 1734, dancer.

On 24 April 1740 Master Gillier, a six-year-old student of Muilment, made his first stage appearance in a solo *Tambourine Dance* and, with Miss Morrison, a minuet, at Drury Lane. The young pair offered their minuet at Covent Garden the following day. Master Gillier danced again at Drury Lane on 4 April 1741, but he was back at Covent Garden in 1742–43. There he appeared in a new ballet called *Le Rendez-vous gallant* on 17 December 1742 and shared a benefit on 19 April 1743 with several others. At the benefit he offered his *Tambourine Dance* and with Mlle Janneton Auretti performed *L'Aimable Vainquers*.

Gillier, Jean Claude 1667–1737, composer, violinist.

Born in Paris in 1667, Jean Claude Gillier became a prolific composer of music for comedies and vaudevilles both in France and in England. He played violin at the Comédie Française and composed for that theatre music for over 40 theatrical pieces. Most of his composing was done between 1695 and 1716, and 1724 and 1734. Between those two periods of activity Gillier turned his attention to the writing of *Recueil d'airs français sérieux & à boire . . . composé en Angleterre* (1732). It is clear that he spent some of his time in England.

Some of his songs were included in English collections as early as 1694–95, and Henry Playford published Gillier's *A Collection of New Songs* in 1698. Gillier wrote music for *The Ladies' Visiting Day*, which opened in London in 1701, and according to *Grove's Dictionary of Music and Musicians* Gillier was in London two years later and played in a concert at York Buildings in April 1703. His music for the Queen's Theatre was advertised on 16 December 1706, and the following year brought out music he composed for *The Stratagem*. Jean Claude Gillier died in Paris on 30 May 1737.

Gillier, Peter [fl. 1739–1768], string player.

Peter Gillier was one of the original subscribers to the Royal Society of Musicians when it was formed on 28 August 1739. On 1 January 1742 he was appointed to the royal band, and on 18 January he was sworn a violist in the Chapel Royal, a position he held until at least 1763. Gillier played violoncello in the *Messiah* at the Foundling Hospital in May 1754 for 10*s.* 6*d.*, and he participated in 1758 at the same fee. By 22 September 1760 he was working for 5*s.* daily at Covent Garden in the theatre band, a job he still held in 1767–68. *Mortimer's London Directory* of 1763 cited him as a violist and violinist and noted that he was living in Frith Street, Soho. An earlier Peter Gillier, possibly his father, published a collection of songs in 1698.

Gillingham, George *1768–1827?, instrumentalist.*

GEORGE GILLINGHAM

artist unknown

Among the first violins listed by Charles Burney as performing at the Handel Memorial Concerts at Westminster Abbey and the Pantheon in May and June of 1784 was a Mr Gillingham. He was, very likely, George Gillingham, who was proposed by (Robert?) Shaw for membership in the Royal Society of Musicians on 7 March 1790. It was attested at that time that he had been baptized the son of Thomas and Ann Gillingham on 11 December 1768 in the parish church of Guddington, Bedford. He was said to be married but childless. He was adept on the violin, tenor (viola), and violoncello, played "the Principle Second Violin at the Theatre Royal Covent Garden," and led "the Band in the summer at the Theatre Birmingham." Gillingham was elected to the Society by a unanimous vote on 6 June 1790. He played the violin in the concerts sponsored by the Society for the benefit of the clergy of St Paul's Cathedral in May of 1791, 1792, and 1793.

Gillingham left for Philadelphia later in 1793 apparently, for Doane's *Musical Directory*, published in London in 1794, placed him in that city. In 1794 and subsequently he was leader of the 20-member band of Wignell and Reinagle's company at their New Theatre in Chestnut Street. He was one of the directors of the Amateur and Professional Concerts of Philadelphia. After 5 December 1796 a Mrs Gillingham appeared in the company to act and sing. There is no record of her having performed in England.

At some time before 27 November 1797, when he turned up as leader of the band at the Greenwich Street Theatre, he had moved to New York, and was engaged as leader of the band at the Park Street Theatre.

Extant American playbills, and the accounts in John Durang's *Memoir*, Odell's *Annals of the New York Stage*, and Pollock's *The Philadelphia Theatre in the Eighteenth Century* provide only fleeting glimpses of the Gillinghams. She seems to have acted at Philadelphia in 1796–97, 1799–1800, and perhaps other seasons. He was evidently the leader of the Chestnut Street band for many years. They both toured to the South—Baltimore, Washington, the towns of the Eastern Shore—with the Wignell and Warren company. John Bernard, in his *Restrospections of America*, tells some amusing anecdotes involving the "worthy little fellow" Gillingham and his large and overprotective wife on such a tour in 1798.

Odell records the performance of oratorio selections in St Paul's Church in New York, on 28 and 30 May and 4 June 1816, by a group of 150 "amateurs" led by Gillingham for the benefit of Zion Church and the Orphan Asylum. That was the first of a yearly succession of spring oratorios and concerts in New York in which Gillingham was concerned. The last one known was on 13 February 1821.

A notation in the Minute Books of the Royal Society of Musicians, dated 3 May 1829, declared that G. Gillingham ("of America") had been dead for two years. His brother (no doubt the violinist John Gillingham) had been paying George's subscription to the Society.

An anonymous engraving of George Gillingham was published as a plate to A. Toedteberg's *Portraits of Actors* (1893).

A Miss L. Gillingham is reported by Odell as having sung under Gillingham's direction at St Paul's Church in New York on 7 June 1820. She was in three vocal concerts, in February, April, and May, in 1821. An undated lithograph by Imbert of a Miss E. Gillingham, vocalist, is on a music sheet, *Sweet Bird that Shun'st the Noise of Folly*, in the Harvard Theatre Collection.

Gillingham, John ₁*fl. 1794–1829?*₁, *violinist.*

A John Gillingham, violinist, was listed in Doane's *Musical Directory* in 1794 with no information as to his employment. He

was probably the Gillingham who played in the large band assembled by Dr Samuel Arnold to perform the *Messiah* for the benefit of the Choral Fund at the Haymarket Theatre on 15 January 1798. A notation in the Minute Books of the Royal Society of Musicians, dated 3 May 1829, referred to the fact that the "brother" of the violinist G[eorge] Gillingham, then two years deceased, had been paying George's subscription. He was to be reimbursed.

Gillis. *See* **GILLES.**

Gillo, Mr ₁*fl. 1714*₁, *actor.*

A Mr Gillo, possibly a son of the Restoration actor Thomas Gillow (whose name was frequently spelled Gillo), acted in Richmond in the summer of 1714 in a troupe called the Duke of Southampton and Cleaveland's Servants. They performed *Injured Virtue*. The play was given again, probably by the same company, at the King's Arms in Southwark on 1 November 1714, with Gillo as the Priest of Jupiter.

Gillow, Mr ₁*fl. 1729*₁, *actor.*

Mr Gillow acted at the Haymarket Theatre in the first half of 1729, his first recorded role having been the First Countryman in *The Humours of Harlequin* on 25 February. Following that he appeared as a character in *The Royal Captives* on 27 March, Soarethereal in *Hurlothrumbo* on 29 March, Moneses in *Tamerlane* on 2 May, Conscience in *The Smuglers* and Stout in *The Patron* (and Gillow spoke the prologue) on 7 May, Swab in *The Beggar's Wedding* on 29 May, and Dick in *Flora* on 26 July. He was granted a solo benefit on 12 May when *Hurlothrumbo* was repeated. Perhaps Gillow was a descendant of the Restoration actor Thomas Gillow.

Gillow, Thomas *d. 1687, actor.*

Thomas Gillow's first known role was Sosius in *Herod and Mariamne* at Lincoln's Inn Fields about August 1673. For the following nine years he performed with the Duke's Company, playing such parts as Lamot in *Love and Revenge* on 9 November 1674, Theinmingus in *The Conquest of China* on 28 May 1675, Polyndus in *Alcibiades* in September 1675, Muphti in *Ibrahim* in March 1676, Stanly in *Tom Essence* in August 1676, Chilax in *Antony and Cleopatra* on 12 February 1677, Isidore in *Timon of Athens* in January 1678, Phorbas in *Oedipus* in September 1678, Agamemnon in *Troilus and Cressida* in April 1679 or earlier, Metellus in *Caius Marius* in October 1679, Acasto in *The Orphan* in late February 1680, Raymond in *The Spanish Fryar* on 1 November 1680, Gloucester in *King Lear* in March 1681, and Bedamar in *Venice Preserv'd* on 9 February 1682.

Gillow's first recorded role with the United Company at Drury Lane was Melanax in *The Duke of Guise* on 28 November 1682. Thereafter he was seen as Titinius in *Julius Caesar*, Oldrents in *The Jovial Crew*, Barberino in *A Duke and No Duke*, Testimony in *Sir Courtly Nice*, Gobrias in *A King and No King*, and Bevil in *Epsom Wells*—among other parts. His last known role was the Governor in *The Island Princess*, a performance of which was presented at Court on 25 April 1687. But by that date Gillow may not have been acting, for he died in May.

The parish registers of St Bride, Fleet Street, contain several references to Gillow and his family. Mary, the daughter of Thomas and Mary "Gilloe," was baptized on 13 February 1676; their daughter Elizabeth was baptized on 10 January 1677; and their son William "Gillo" was baptized on 3 February 1678. Anne, the daughter of Thomas and Christian Gilloe, was baptized on 9 March 1681; if that entry referred to Thomas the actor, then his wife Mary had died and he had remarried. An Ann Gillo was buried at St Bride's on 29 December 1703.

Thomas Gillow's burial was also recorded in the registers at St Bride's, on 31 May 1687; another hand noted that he was from Vine Court and an actor. Gillow's age at his death is not known, though testimony given concerning the splitting of the United Company in 1694–95 cited Gillow as one of the younger actors in 1687. Judging from some of his roles, however, one would take Gillow to have been more mature by the late 1680s, and, if he was, perhaps the following baptismal record at St Giles in the Fields concerned him: Thomas the son of Thomas and Phillippa "Gillowe" was baptized on 20 December 1648. Information is too scanty, however, to be certain of the identification.

Gillow, Mrs [Thomas, Mary?] [fl. 1675–1678?], *actress.*

The Mrs Gillow who was active in the Duke's Company at the Dorset Garden playhouse from 1675 to 1677 may have been Mary, the wife of the actor Thomas Gillow. Only a few roles are known for her: Ardella in *Alcibiades* in September 1675, Garcia in *Don Carlos* on 8 June 1676, Jacinta in *The Wrangling Lovers* on 25 July 1676, Lucetta in *The Rover* on 24 March 1677, and Cleone in *The Siege of Babylon* in September 1677. It is worth noting that baptismal information in the registers of St Bride, Fleet Street, show that the children born to Thomas and Mary Gillow in 1676 and 1677 arrived at times which would not conflict with the known performances of Mrs Gillow. Mary Gillow seems to have died between 3 February 1678, when her son William was christened, and 9 March 1681, by which date her husband may have remarried.

Gilmarine, Mrs [fl. 1728], *actress.*

Mrs Gilmarine played a Countrywoman in *The Rivals* on 21 February 1728 at the Haymarket Theatre as a member of Mrs Violante's company.

Gilpin, Miss [fl. 1766], *actress.*

Advertised as a young gentlewoman

making her first appearance on any stage, Miss Gilpin played Miss Biddy in *Miss in Her Teens* at the Haymarket Theatre on 18 June 1766. On 13 August at the King's she acted the same role in her own name; on 20 August she played Lucy in *The Minor*; and on 27 August she was Jenny in *The Provok'd Husband*. Returning to the Haymarket on 2 September, she repeated the role of Lucy. Her last known appearance was on 11 September at the King's Theatre as Jenny.

Gilson, Mr [fl. 1784], *singer.*

Mr Gilson, possibly the son of the pleasure-garden singer of the 1760s, sang tenor in the Handel Memorial Concerts at Westminster Abbey and the Pantheon in May and June 1784.

Gilson, [Cornforth?] [fl. c. 1755–1770?], *singer.*

A Mr Gilson was a singer at Vauxhall from about 1755 to 1766, during which time several songs which he offered there were published. On 11 March 1765 at the Haymarket Theatre he sang in *The Choice of Apollo*, and he also entertained at London taverns. At the Huntington Library is an extra-illustrated set of *The Tavern Haunter* which contains the music for "A Bacchanalian, Sung by Mr. Gilson," dated January 1766. Perhaps the singer we have been following was Cornforth Gilson of Edinburgh. In 1759 was published *Lessons in the practice of Singing, with an addition of the Church Tunes, in four parts, and a collection of Hymns, Canons, Airs, and Catches . . . by Cornforth Gilson, teacher of music in Edinburgh.* Cornforth Gilson sang with his daughter at the concerts of the Edinburgh Musical Society in 1768, 1769, and 1770.

Giminiani. *See* GEMINIANI.

Gingell. *See* GYNGELL.

By permission of the Henry E. Huntington Library and Art Gallery

"A Bacchanalian," sung by CORNFORTH GILSON

Gioccomazzi, Signor [fl. 1768], *singer.*

Signor Gioccomazzi (or Giaccomazzi) sang a comic role in *Gli amanti ridicoli* at the King's Theatre on 5 November 1768, when the season opened. The records do not indicate what else he sang in London or whether or not he completed the season.

Giolo, Prince. *See* "PAINTED PRINCE, THE."

Giordani, Francesco [fl. 1753–1767], *singer, dancer?*

Francesco Giordani was the son of Giuseppe and Antonia Giordani and brother of Marina, Nicolina, and Tommaso Giordani. All were members of Giuseppe's small opera company.

Francesco was doubtless in the cast of his father's burletta *L'amanti gelosi* when the company opened the long run of the piece at Covent Garden on 17 December 1753. No casts were given. He sang Giandandrea in performances of *Lo studente a la moda* on 18 January 1754 and following, Leandro in *L'amore costante* on 11 February and following, and Perillox in *La cameriera accorta* on 4 March 1754 and subsequent dates.

The company was at the Haymarket on 3 February 1755 for one performance of *L'albergatrice* and at Covent Garden on 12 January 1756 for another single performance, of *La comediante fatta contatrice*. Only Nicolina, by then famous as "La Spiletta," was named in either bill as performing.

Faulkner's Dublin Journal of 27 October 1764 announced Francesco's arrival in Dublin from England, calling him a dancer. Presumably he accompanied his family to Crow Street Theatre in the season of 1766–67.

Giordani, Giuseppe [fl. 1745–1764], singer, manager, librettist.

Giuseppe Giordani was the manager of a small group of opera singers, most of them members of his immediate family, who performed on the Continent, in England, and in Ireland. Alfred Loewenberg, in Giuseppe's son Tommaso's entry in Grove, says that he and his family company "left Naples about 1745, wandering northwards and performing at the smaller Italian towns (e.g. at Sinigaglia during the fair of 1747) until they reached Graz (1748), Frankfurt o/M. (1750), Amsterdam (1752) and finally London." This Giuseppe is liable to confusion with the Giuseppe Giordani called Giordaniello (c.

1753–1798), but apparently they were not even related. He and his son Tommaso have also been confused occasionally with the violinist and composer Felice dé Giardini (1716–1796).

In December 1753 the troupe, consisting of Giuseppe Giordani, his wife Antonia, his daughters Nicolina and Marina, his son Francesco (all singers), and his son Tommaso (an instrumentalist and composer), with an unrelated seventh member, the singer Francesco Lini, came from Paris to London. Giuseppe (and probably his company) lodged "at Mr Milbourn's Grocer in James St. Covent Garden." On 17 December the newcomers opened at Covent Garden with a burletta called *Gli amanti gelosi*, the music by Cocchi and the libretto by Giordani himself. It was a great success, the daughter Nicolina winning especially fervent admiration in the part of Spiletta. Her other roles are unknown. The Giordani company performed to enthusiastic audiences three times a week through 11 March, presenting in addition *Lo studente a la moda* (from 18 January 1754), in which Giuseppe sang Palmiero, *L'amore costante* (from 11 February), in which he sang Don Bertoldo, and *La Cameriera accorta* (from 4 March), in which he sang Vanesio.

When, on 3 February 1755, the little troupe sang *L'albergatrice* at the Haymarket, it was billed as "A New Comic Opera presented by Mr Giordani, with his Company, and La Signora Spiletta." They played only one more time that season. That was on 17 February, when Giordani and his daughter, "Sga Spiletta," shared a benefit. The next news of them and the last in England is the bill of Covent Garden for 12 January 1756, when *La comediante fatta cantatrice* was advertised only as the "first appearance on the stage in two years," of "Sga Nicolina called Spiletta." Anna Bandiera and Antonio Lazzari had then joined the little company.

Whether Giordani's ensemble returned to the Continent or toured provincially is not now known, but from January 1756 until November 1764, nearly nine years, they left no record. On 23 November 1764 they presented, at Smock Alley, Dublin, the burletta which had, long before, inaugurated their first London season, *Gli amanti gelosi*. Though few casts exist, at least some members of the family troupe, with additional singers, returned to Smock Alley in the 1765–66 season and in 1766–67 went over to the Crow Street Theatre. After that, apparently only the composer-son Tommaso remained in Dublin, where he was prominent in musical circles until his death in 1806.

Giordani, Signora Giuseppe, Antonia, ₁née Ambrosini?₁ *d. 1764, singer.*

Antonia Giordani the singer was the wife of Giuseppe Giordani and the mother of the singers Francesco, Marina, and Nicolina Giordani and the composer Tommaso Giordani. Antonia came to London from Paris with the family troupe in 1753. She also certainly opened with the others at Covent Garden Theatre on 17 December in the successful burletta *Gli amanti gelosi*, though her role is not known. She sang the part of Don Saverio in *Lo studente a la moda*, which opened on 18 January 1754. She was perhaps the Antonia Ambrosini advertised in the character of Celindo in *L'amore costante* on and after 11 February. It may be that Ambrosini had been her maiden name. (Because of the uncertainty, Antonia Ambrosini is listed separately in the first volume of this dictionary.) Signora Giordani sang Silvio in *La cameriera accorta* in several performances on and after 4 March.

The next known appearance of the troupe and of Signora Giordani was at the Haymarket Theatre on 3 February 1755, when Giordani's new comic opera *L'albergatrice* was presented. No casts were given for that performance or for the company's last appearance in England, at Covent Garden on the night of 12 January 1756, in *La come-diante fatta cantatrice*. Nothing is known of the family's activities during nearly a decade following their disappearance from London. The company went to Dublin in the fall of 1764. But they had scarcely arrived when, sometime late in October, Antonia died at their lodgings in Capel Street.

Giordani, Marina ₁*fl. 1753–1767?*₁, *singer.*

The singer Marina Giordani was the daughter of Giuseppe and Antonia Giordani and sister of Nicolina, Francesco, and Tommaso Giordani. All were members of Giuseppe's small opera company.

Marina accompanied the family to London and opened at Covent Garden on 17 December 1753 in her father's burletta *L'amanti gelosi*. The cast had a long run, but Marina's part is not known. Marina took the role of Violante in the performances, on 18 January 1754 and following, of *Lo studente a la moda*; she was Emira in *L'amore costante* on 11 February and following, and she sang Leonora in *La cameriera accorta* on 4 March (her benefit) and following.

The company was at the Haymarket on 3 February 1755 for one performance of *L'albergatrice* and at Covent Garden on 12 January 1756 for another single performance, of *La comediante fatta cantatrice*. Only Nicolina, by then famous as "La Spiletta," was named in either bill as performing.

Marina was still with her father's troupe when it went to Dublin to sing at Smock Alley in 1764. She was said to have been absent from the stage for many months when she reappeared on the occasion of her brother Tommaso's benefit, at Smock Alley on 7 May 1766, singing a part unspecified in *L'eroe cinese*. Perhaps she went on singing with the troupe in Dublin through 1766–67. But there is no evidence.

Giordani, Nicolina ₁*fl. 1753–1767*₁, *singer.*

Nicolina Giordani was the daughter of Giuseppe and Antonia and sister of Francesco and Marina, both singers, and Tommaso, instrumentalist and composer.

Nicolina accompanied her father's touring opera company from Naples through northern Italy, Germany, Holland, and France, arriving with them in London in the early winter of 1753. She completely eclipsed her parents and siblings as a performer so far as the London audiences were concerned. The company opened on 17 December at Covent Garden with the burletta _Gli amanti gelosi_, libretto by Giuseppe Giordani and music by Cocchi. No other roles are recorded, but Nicolina, in the character Spiletta, was received with such approbation that she bore the designation "La Spiletta" afterward in England and Ireland. The laconic Richard Cross, in his prompter's diary wrote only: "An Italian Comic Opera by some performers just arriv'd from Paris. Went off pretty well,—a Girl greatly admir'd." But Thomas Gray looking back a decade later recalled in a letter to Count Algarotti seeing

a little troup of Buffi, that exhibited a Burletta in London, not in the Opera-House, where the audience is chiefly of the better sort, but in one of the common theatres full of all kinds of people & (I believe) the fuller from that natural aversion we bear to Foreigners: their looks & their noise made it evident, they did not come thither to hear; & on similar occasions I have known candles lighted, broken bottles, & penknives flung on the stage, the benches torn up, the scenes hurried into the street and set on fire. the curtain drew up, the musick was of Cocchi with a few airs of Pergolesi interspersed. the Singers were (as usual) deplorable, but there was one Girl (she called herself the Niccolina) with little voice & less beauty; but with the utmost justness of ear, the strongest expression of countenance, the most speaking eyes, the greatest vivacy & variety of gesture. her first appearance instantly fix'd their attention; the tumult sunk at once, or if any murmur rose, it was soon hush'd by a general cry for silence. her

first air ravish'd every body; they forgot their prejudices, they forgot, that they did not understand a word of the language; they enter'd into all the humour of the part, made her repeat all her songs, & continued their transports, their laughter, & applause to the end of the piece.

Horace Walpole, in a letter to Bentley on 19 December 1753, described her as having "more vivacity and variety of humour than ever existed in any creature." Arthur Murphy, in the _Gray's Inn Journal_, 22 December 1753, while expressing some doubts about the total performance, praised Nicolina for "such pleasing variety of action, and such variety of graceful deportment, that she is generally acknowledged to be, in that Cast of playing, an excellent comic actress." Paul Hiffernan, in _The Tuner_, No 1, gave more explicit criticism still:

She plays off with inexhaustible spirits all muscular evolutions of the face and brows; while in her eye wantons a studied archness, and pleasing malignity. Her voice has strength and scope sufficient; has neither too much of the feminine, nor an inclining to the male. Her gestures are ever varying; her transitions quick and easy. Some over-nice critics, forgetting, or not knowing the meaning of the word Burletta, cry that her manner is outré. Wou'd she not be faulty were it otherwise? The thing chargeable to her is (perhaps) too great a luxurience of comic tricks; which (an austere censor would say) border on unlaced lasciviousness, and extravagant petulance of action.

Charles Burney reported that "she was frequently encored two or three times in the same air, which she was able to vary so much by her singing and acting, that it appeared at every repetition, a new song, and she another performer."

During the rest of the winter season 1753–54, while busily retailing _Gli amanti gelosi_ the company introduced several other burlettas and comic operas: _Lo studente a la moda_ on 18 January, in which Nicolina sang Giulietta, *L'amore costante* on 11 February, in which she sang Auretta, and *La cameriera accorta* on 4 March, in which she sang Diamantina.

By 3 February 1755, when *L'albergatrice* was given at the Haymarket, she was the acknowledged star of the troupe as the bill showed: "A New Comic Opera presented by Mr. Giordani, with his Company, and La Signora Spiletta." She was perhaps also assuming some managerial functions, for a notation of 20 January 1755 among the Lord Chamberlain's records in the Public Record Office reveals the granting of a "License to Nicolina Giordani for *Burlettas* or *Italian Comedies* at the Little Theatre in Hay. during this season." She (as "Sga Spiletta") and her father shared a benefit on 17 February. The last news of the company in England was the Covent Garden bill for 12 January 1756, when *La comediante fatta cantatrice* was advertised only (and bafflingly) as the "first appearance on the stage in two years" of "Sga Nicolina called Spiletta."

For the following nine years there was no trace of the singing Giordanis. But in the fall of 1764 they began to pop up in Dublin. *Faulkner's Dublin Journal* of 27 October carried an item about the arrival in Dublin of "Francisco" Giordani. The *London Daily Advertiser* of 27 November confirmed the arrival of Francesco, Giuseppe, Marina, and Nicolina. No mention was made of the mother Antonia or the other brother Tommaso. The company opened at Smock Alley with the old favorite *Gli amanti gelosi*. They played there in 1764–65 and 1765–66, and then moved on to Crow Street in 1766–67. Spiletta sang at the King's Theatre, London, in 1774.

Giordani, Tommaso *c. 1730–1806, instrumentalist, composer.*

Tommaso Giordani was born in Naples about 1730, a son of the singer, manager, and librettist Giuseppe Giordani and his wife Antonia. Tommaso's siblings were all singers—Francesco, Marina, and the gifted Nicolina, "La Spiletta."

When Tommaso was about 15 his father left Naples and strolled up Italy and across Europe with a small opera company, apparently of shifting composition but always with the Giordani family as nucleus. They are known to have performed in Sinigaglia, Graz, Frankfurt, Amsterdam, and Paris before coming to London late in 1753, where they lodged "at Mr. Milbourn's Grocer in James St. Covent Garden."

On 17 December 1753 the Giordani company opened a season of burlettas under Rich's management at Covent Garden. Unlike the rest of the family, Tommaso did not sing, and very likely, as both W. J. Lawrence and Alfred Loewenberg have conjectured, he was playing harpsichord in the theatre band and adapting music for the troupe. The engagement at Covent Garden ended in the spring of 1754, and the company disappeared from notice until it surfaced for two performances at the Haymarket on 3 and 17 February 1755. One more performance, that of 12 January 1756, ended their London experience. In no opera bill during the entire series of London performances was Tommaso named.

The record is similarly dark as regards Tommaso for some months after Mossop brought Giuseppe Giordani's company to Smock Alley in the fall of 1764 to counter Barry's Italian musicals at the Crow Street house. But Tommaso was surely there, even though most of the attention was lavished on his glamorous sister "La Spiletta." Very likely he was performing in the band, which, Lawrence says, "had been strengthened for the burletta season, and in which the clarinet was now introduced for the first time in Ireland."

Tommaso's mother had died at the family's lodgings in Capel Street late in October 1764, but the rest of the singers, opening with Nicolina's popular vehicle *Gli amanti gelosi* on 23 November, went on nevertheless to a successful season. Tommaso's handiwork as a composer first was shown the Irish on 2 January 1765 when Ann Catley sang Polly in *The Beggar's Opera* to music which Tommaso had worked over and had Italianized out of all whooping. The irony that *The Beggar's Opera* had originally been intended as a satire on Italian opera was not lost on the Dublin critics. More fitting, they found, was Tommaso's original burletta *Don Fulminone, or the Lover with Two Mistresses* which he produced on 7 January. For 17 January he wrote music for a new spectacle, *The Enchanter, or Love and Magic*. On 26 March, Mossop brought out at Smock Alley, in opposition to a lackluster production of the opera at Crow Street, a *Maid of the Mill* with entirely new settings of songs, by Tommaso.

While in the summer of 1765 "La Spiletta" and her brother Francesco transferred their talents to Crow Street, Tommaso remained at Smock Alley. On 24 April 1766 he scored perhaps his greatest success to that point when the undergraduates of Trinity College turned out in caps and gowns *en masse* to cheer Tenducci singing the Giordani score of *Love in Disguise*, an operetta by a Trinity student. Tommaso played the harpsichord at the performance. When on 7 May 1766 he produced a new score for Metastasio's *L'eroe cinese* for his benefit, his sister Marina made her reappearance after some months' absence from the stage.

In the 1766–67 season Giordani served the Crow Street Theatre Royal, on 25 February 1767 staging there his *Phyllis at Court* adaptation of Lloyd's successful Drury Lane opera *The Capricious Lovers*. In Passion Week that spring his oratorio *Isaac* was sung at the Fishamble Street Music Hall. During most of that period he was probably living in Bachelor's Walk, where an advertisement for his harpsichord lessons placed him in 1765.

No further trace has been found of

Tomasso Giordani's activities until 1 August 1769, when his setting of the *Castle Ode* of Gorges Edmond Howard was sung in Dublin's Rotunda. Shortly afterward, he left Dublin for London.

On 6 February 1770 "A new comic opera, music entirely new" by Giordani, *Il padre e il figlio rivali*, was staged by him at the King's Theatre, the first evidence that he had entered on his duties as director of musical affairs at the King's, which was, with teaching and composing, to occupy him for the next 14 years. About 1770 also was published his overture to *The Elopement*.

For 8 March 1774 the "new serious opera" *Antigono* was advertised, with music "by Giordani and other eminent composers," and the *Artaserse* of 17 May was similarly described. Such *pasticcios*, very popular toward the end of the century, were to absorb much of his talent. On 30 May 1778 he produced Metastasio's *Il re pastore* with his own music. On 29 October 1779 he wrote songs for the original production of Sheridan's *The Critic*.

Late in the summer of 1783 Tommaso Giordani returned to Dublin to take part in a series of concerts Michael Leoni (Myer Lyon), the great Jewish-English tenor, had been giving in the Rotunda since June. His friend Gorges Edmond Howard published an ode in the *Public Register*, welcoming him back to Ireland.

Leoni and Giordani then instituted what they called the English Opera House, renting the Capel Street Theatre for the performances. It opened its doors on 15 December 1783 with two new pieces for which Giordani wrote the music, *Gibraltar* by Robert Houlton (Giordani later, on 14 June 1784, furnished music for his burletta *Orpheus and Eurydice*) and W. C. Oulton's interlude *The Haunted Castle* (Giordani on 5 May 1784 wrote the music for his interlude *The Mad House*). The season brought a number of excellent singers to the Capel Street house, notably Mrs. Bill-

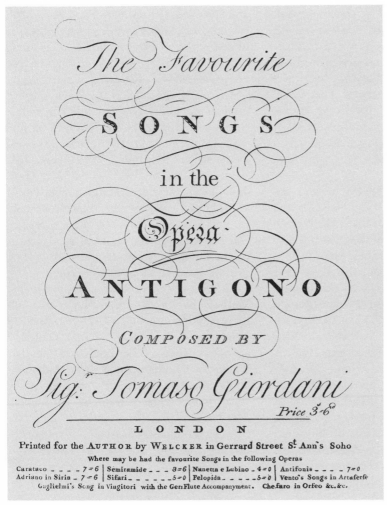

The Favourite

SONGS

in the

Opera

ANTIGONO

COMPOSED BY

Sig.ʳ Tomaso Giordani

Price 3ˢ-6ᵈ

LONDON

Printed for the AUTHOR by WELCKER in Gerrard Street Sᵗ Ann's Soho

Where may be had the favourite Songs in the following Operas

| Caratuco | _ _ _ _ 7 = 6 | Semiramide | _ _ _ 3 = 6 | Nanetta e Lubino | _ 4 = 0 | Antifonis | _ _ _ _ 7 = 0 |
| Adriano in Siria | _ 7 = 6 | Sifari | _ _ _ _ _ 5 = 0 | Pelopida | _ _ _ _ 5 = 0 | Vento's Songs in Artaferse |

Guglielmi's Song in Viagitori with the GerːFlute Accompanyment. Che faro in Orfeo &c. &c.

Folger Shakespeare Library

Title-page to *Antigono,* by GIORDANI

ington and Giordani's brilliant pupil and protégé the tenor Peter Duffey. Others of note in the company were Miall the acting manager, Egan, Glenville, Miss Palmer, and Mrs Morell and, as translator, the satirist Williams ("Anthony Pasquin"). But the auditorium was too small to allow them to recover expenses, and the proprietors were bankrupt after seven months. Before the enterprise collapsed Giordani wrote 13 musical pieces, according to W. J. Lawrence.

Pursued by bailiffs, Giordani fled to England in July 1784 with his recent bride, a daughter of Tate Wilkinson. But by the fall he had arranged a truce with his creditors and was at Smock Alley, Dublin, with Daly, in charge of musical matters. On 4 January 1785 the interlude *The Hypochondriac* (Franklin and Giordani) ·came out, with Giordani conducting the band. On 27 January Messink's pantomime masque *The Island of Saints, or the Institution of the Shamrock* carried various choruses, airs, and recitatives composed by Giordani, with all the dance music based upon Irish folk tunes. In April 1785 there was a substantial run of W. C. Oulton and Giordani's new serio-comic opera *Calypso*, with Mrs Billington starring as Eucharis. That work, except for snatches of incidental music, ended Giordani's exertions for Smock Alley. He had been living during that period at No 4, Paradise Row, where he continued to teach music.

In the winter of 1788–89 he was engaged as music director at the New Theatre Royal, Crow Street, where some say that he also played the violin. But that was possibly Felice de Giardini instead. He collaborated again with W. C. Oulton, this time in a musical prelude of two acts called *Perseverance*, 12 March 1789. In April his *Te Deum* for the recovery of King George III, sung at Francis Street Chapel, was attended by both Catholics and Protestants. On 12 February 1791 at Crow Street he contributed music to *The Distressed Knight*, an anonymous piece. He was then living at No 9, Pitt Street. During the Lenten Season of 1792 he sponsored a series of "Spiritual Concerts" in the Rotunda. Apparently his last substantial work was the composition of music for Leonard MacNally's opera *The Cottage Festival*, on 28 November 1796.

Giordani was a subscriber to the Irish Musical Fund from its earliest year, 1787. In 1794 he was elected its president. He is frequently named in the Minute Books. On 19 January 1800 he was appointed conductor of the spring commemoration concert. But by 5 March of that year his health was so poor that the Society voted him £10 for medical payments, and on 16 March "Doc[tor] Cogan and Mr. Duncan" were elected to replace him as conductor. From then on the records are replete with evidences of his slow dissolution. By 6 April 1800, when the Fund granted him two guineas a week for a month, he could not write. The allowance was continued month by month, although it was twice suspended

and then reduced until in 1803 he was receiving only half a guinea a week because of the poverty of the Fund. He died sometime in February 1806 at his house, No 201, Great Britain Street.

On 24 February 1806 the Fund paid five guineas for Giordani's funeral. His widow collected a pension from the Fund off and on until March 1814. By 13 March she had died and her "daughters" were given a half guinea a week. She was called "Mrs Giordani" until the end, although a notation of 12 July 1813 named her "Mrs Horseman, former Mrs. Giordani." A Jane Giordani and her sister were mentioned as claimants on the Fund, jointly or severally, from time to time from 1814 through 1822.

Alfred Loewenberg has recently repeated William Barclay Squire's opinion that "all the many instrumental works published in London and Paris as by 'Signor Giordani' are Tommaso's" (and not by the earlier Giuseppe "Giordaniello"). That judgment holds true also, apparently, for the many vocal works. The *Catalogue of Printed Music in the British Museum* contains 89 titles by Tommaso Giordani: of canzonets, ballads, concertos for various instruments, overtures, glees, capriccios, marches, preludes, trios, sonatinas, and harpsichord instrumentals. Grove credits Tommaso Giordani with "more than 50" operas "if all those are counted which he merely adapted or added to."

Among Giordani's notable pupils, besides Peter Duffey, were T. P. Cooke and John Field.

Giordini. *See* GIARDINI.

Giorgi, Signor *d. 1808, dancer.*
Signor Giorgi made his first appearance at Drury Lane Theatre performing with Signora Lucchi in a dance called *The Italian Peasants*, which was presented after Act II of *Macbeth* on 4 October 1757. Later that season he danced in *The Tempest* and in *Harlequin Ranger*. Subsequently he was a

featured dancer at Drury Lane every season through 1776–77 and appeared in hundreds of performances of dozens of dances, many with his wife Signora Ann Giorgi, who joined the Drury Lane company in 1759–60.

Giorgi and his wife were members of the company at the Jacob's Wells Theatre in Bristol in 1759 and 1760. They danced at Birmingham in the summer of 1762 and at Richmond in 1766. Beyond the fact that David Garrick wrote to Peter Newcombe, head of the Hackney School, on 6 March 1770, recommending Giorgi for the position of dancing master ("Mr Giorgi of our house, whose skill & probity, I will answer for"), little else can be told of him except the occasional records of his earnings and the long list of dances in which he appeared at Drury Lane and later at the Haymarket.

A selection from the numerous productions in which Giorgi danced includes (with the season of first performance) *Comus* and *Harlequin's Invasion* in 1759–60; *The Enchanter* in 1760–61; *Arcadia, Cymbeline,* and *The Genii* in 1761–62; *The Witches* in 1764–65; *Daphne and Amintor, Cymon,* and *The National Prejudice* in 1767–68; *A Trip to Scotland* in 1769–70; *The Pigmy Revels* in 1772–73; *Alfred, A Christmas Tale,* and *Florizel and Perdita* in 1773–74; *The Maid of the Oaks, Oroonoko,* and *As You Like It* in 1774–75; *The Sultan* in 1775–76; and *The Savage Hunters* in 1776–77. His salary in 1774–75 was 10s. per day.

His daughter, Miss Giorgi, made her first appearance at Drury Lane on 8 May 1767, and his son, Master Giorgi, first appeared at Covent Garden on 19 November 1774. Among the students whom Giorgi brought on at Drury Lane were Miss Collett, Master Whitlow, Miss Lings, Master and Miss Byrne, and Miss Wilkinson.

Signor Giorgi also danced at the Haymarket in the summers of 1782 and 1783, appearing in such pieces as *The Separate Maintenance* and *Harlequin Teague.* His students danced at the Haymarket in 1785, 1786, and 1787. He also appeared at the King's Theatre on 23 March 1786 (for the benefit of Vestris), 23 December 1786, 20 January 1787, 13 March 1787, and 14 June 1787.

After 1787, Signor Giorgi retired but remained in London. He had subscribed to the Drury Lane Theatrical Fund in 1766; according to James Winston's notation in the Fund Book (now at the Folger Shakespeare Library), Giorgi died in January 1808. His wife died in 1809.

Giorgi, Signora, Ann *d. 1809, dancer.*

Signora Ann Giorgi began her British career, so far as is known, at the Jacob's Wells Theatre in Bristol in 1759. Her name appeared for the first time in a London playbill on 31 December 1759, when she and her husband danced in the chorus in *Harlequin's Invasion,* at Drury Lane. She was employed there as a chorus dancer every winter season through 1773–74, but evidently she and Signor Giorgi tried their luck out of London in the summers. They were at Birmingham in the summer of 1762 and Richmond in 1766.

A selection of the numerous productions in which she danced, many times with her husband, includes (with the season of first time): Lyssa in *The Enchanter* in 1760–61; *Arcadia, Fortunatus,* and *The Genii* in 1761–62; *The Spring, The Witches,* and *As You Like It* in 1762–63; *Cymbeline* and *The Hermit* in 1764–65; *Romeo and Juliet* in 1765–66; *Cymon* and *The National Prejudice* in 1767–68; *The Jubilee* and *King Arthur* in 1770–71; *The Pigmy Revels* in 1772–73; and *A Christmas Tale* in 1773–74. Her salary in 1773–74 was 6s. 8d. per day.

Two of her children, Miss and Master Giorgi, also danced on the London stage. In 1766 Signora Giorgi had subscribed to the Drury Lane Theatrical Fund, against which she claimed in September 1794. Her husband died in 1808. According to a notation by James Winston in the Fund Book (now at the Folger Shakespeare Library), she died in 1809. On 25 March 1809 her quarterly annuity of £7 was marked "Default." In that notation her first name was given as Ann.

Giorgi, Master [fl. 1774–1787], dancer.

Master Giorgi, the son of the Drury Lane dancers Signor and Signora Giorgi, first appeared on the stage on 19 November 1774 at Covent Garden Theatre in the dancing chorus of the masque in *The Druids*, a piece which was repeated numerous times throughout the 1774–75 season. He, or a brother perhaps, danced with Miss Byrne in a new piece called *The Medley* on 28 May 1784 at the Haymarket Theatre. On 28 August at the same house he and Miss Byrne offered a turn called *Recreation*. Still called Master Giorgi (sometimes Master George), he danced specialty numbers on occasion, usually with Miss Byrne (who was a pupil of Signor Giorgi), at the Haymarket in the summers of 1785, 1786, and 1787.

Giorgi, Miss [fl. 1767], dancer.

On 8 May 1767, Miss Giorgi, the daughter of the Drury Lane dancers Signor and Signora Giorgi, made her first noticed appearance at that theatre in a minuet with Miss Collett; both young ladies were identified as scholars to Signor Giorgi. She and Miss Collett gave their minuet again on 16 and 26 May.

Giorgi, Brigitta. *See* BANTI, SIGNORA ZACCARIA.

Giorgi, Giovanni [fl. 1774], violinist.

According to van der Straeten's *History of the Violin*, Giovanni Giorgi, probably the pupil of Tartini, appeared in London as a violinist in 1774.

Giorgi, Joseph [fl. c. 1785], harpsichordist.

In the Public Record Office is a letter signed by "Joseph Giorgi Harpsichord Performer" about 1785 protesting his treatment at the hands of the Trustees of the Opera House. They had refused to engage Giorgi even though as a creditor upon the bankruptcy of William Taylor, the manager, he was entitled to preference. Presumably Giorgi had been with the King's Theatre band the previous season.

Giorgi, Peter d. 1808, musician.

In a will drawn on 3 February 1808, a musician named Peter Giorgi left his unspecified estate in trust to be shared by his six children, born out of wedlock, to Mary Cummings (by then deceased). The children, all bearing the family surname, were specified as Augustus Frederick, Rosina May, Caroline Cecilia, Leonora, Leander Anthony, and Charles Burges. A seventh child, named May Magdalen Roberts Giorgi, who may have been a legitimate child, was left his furniture and household goods, except his musical instruments and music, which were bequeathed to the son Augustus Frederick. The will was proved at London on 14 September 1808 by John Warrington Rogers, the elder, of Manchester Buildings, Westminster, the executor. Perhaps Peter Giorgi was one of the family of dancers and musicians who performed in London during the latter half of the eighteenth century.

Giorgi, Rachele D'Orta. *See* D'ORTA, RACHELE.

Giorgi-Banti, Brigitta. *See* BANTI, SIGNORA ZACCARIA.

Giornovichi, Giovanni Mane 1735?–1804, violinist, composer.

Most biographers of the Italian musician Giovanni Mane Giornovichi (sometimes called Jarnowick) have set his birth at

Palermo about 1745, but uncertainty exists concerning the year. The Abbé Robineau in *Les Caprices de la fortune* (1816) stated that when Giornovichi died in 1804 he was 69 years of age; he would thus have been born in 1735. Giornovichi's first public performance on the violin was at the Paris Concert Spirituel in 1770 when he played the sixth concerto of his master Lolli. Though not very successful at first, he soon became very popular, especially after playing his own first concerto to great applause. Giornovichi was much in fashion in Paris for some ten years, but reactions to his quarrelsome personality and his scandalous behavior eventually made it necessary for him to leave that city. When he played at Frankfurt in September 1779, he was announced as "First violinist of France and concertmeister of Prince Rohan-Guimenée." Soon after, he joined the orchestra of the King of Prussia and was also engaged at the royal chapel at Potsdam, until his quarrels with Duport forced him to leave Berlin in 1783.

After traveling about Europe, Giornovichi arrived in London by 1790, and in March of that year he was among the violinists who played in concerts at the Hanover Square Rooms organized by Dussek. (These appearances pre-date by some 14 months the concert of 4 May 1791 in which Grove and van der Straeten claim he made his debut.) Also playing violin in those same concerts was Felix Janiewicz (or Yaniewicz), with whom Giornovichi is sometimes confused.

Giornovichi remained in London until 1796, an accomplished artist but a troublesome person. In 1791 he was a musician and composer for the opera at the Pantheon. In a private concert at Mrs Cadogan's on 4 January 1792, he played delightful music all the evening, in "the highest good humour." He performed for the Oxford Musical Society on 1 May 1793, the opening day of the season in which that organization resuscitated its concerts

in the Oxford Music Room. When the new Drury Lane Theatre was inaugurated on 12 March 1794 with a gala concert of Handel's music, Giornovichi played a concerto. Giornovichi was paid £105 for playing the violin in the oratorios presented by Linley and Storace at Drury Lane in the spring of 1794, and on 15 May and 3 June 1794 he performed concertos at the King's Theatre. On the latter date, in a command performance before the King and Queen, in the last movement of his concerto, he included the melody of "Rule Britannia." That same year, in which he was living at No 10, Pall Mall, he also was granted a license to give entertainment at the Haymarket for an unstated period. On 18 May 1795, for Sga Storace's benefit at Drury Lane, after the mainpiece Giornovichi played a concerto in which he introduced "*With low suit and plaintive ditty* and *Rule Britannia.*"

About this time he quarreled with J. B. Cramer, whose challenge to a duel Giornovichi, nevertheless, would not accept. Numerous anecdotes of Giornovichi's behavior in England and on the Continent testify to his arrogance and impropriety. It is said that once he was grossly rude in the presence of the King and the Duke of York.

After playing at the King's Theatre in 1795–96, Giornovichi performed in Dublin in 1797 and then went to Hamburg, where he resided until 1802, earning a considerable income by his violin and billiards playing. He returned to Berlin for a brief time before settling at St Petersburg, where he died on 21 November 1804 of a stroke suffered during a billiards game.

It is reported that Dragonetti judged Giornovichi's playing on the violin, though lacking in power, to have been the "most elegant he ever heard before Paganini's." A fine tone, a light bow-hand, and a peculiar grace distinguished his playing.

His numerous compositions published in London and on the Continent are listed in the British Museum's *Catalogue of Printed*

Music. According to *Grove's Dictionary*, he had lived for a while at Edinburgh, where several of his compositions were published by Gow, including a single sheet titled *Mr. Jarnovichi's Reel, composed by himself* (c. 1800) and *Jarnovichi's Horn-pipe*, which appeared in Gow's *Fourth Collection of Strathspey Reels* (1800).

Giraldo, Mr ₁*fl. c. 1717–1720*₁, *violinist.*

Mr Giraldo (or Girardo, Ghirardo) played second violin and served as a waiting page at the Cannons Concerts about 1717 to 1720 for £7 10s. per quarter.

Girardeau, Isabella ₁**née Calliari?**₁ ₁*fl. 1709–1712*₁, *singer.*

Perhaps Isabella Girardeau was the Isabella Calliari who was mentioned in Quadrio's list of singers who were active between 1700 and 1720, though as Girardeau she was often styled Mademoiselle. An agreement drawn up on 24 December 1709 concerning the personnel in the company at the Queen's Theatre in the Haymarket listed "Mad^ll Girardo" as one of the opera singers. The members of the troupe agreed not to work elsewhere without permission. Two roles are known for Isabella during her first season in London: Celinda in *Almahide* on 10 January 1710 and Mandana in *Idaspe fedele* on 23 March. About 1710 she was one of several opera performers who participated in a concert at the Duchess of Shrewsbury's house in Kensington.

Isabella was paid £300 for her 1710–11 season, during which she is known to have sung Climene in *Pirro e Demetrio*, Fronima in *Etearco*, and Almirena in *Rinaldo*, Handel's first London opera. In 1711–12 she sang Oronte in *Antioco* and Veremonda in *Ambleto*.

Girardo. *See* **GIRALDO** and **GIRARDEAU.**

Giraud. *See* **GIROUX.**

Girelli Aguilar, Maria Antonia ₁*fl. 1759–1773*₁, *singer.*

The soprano Signora Maria Antonia Girelli Aguilar (sometimes Anguillar) was active in the Italian opera houses during the third quarter of the eighteenth century. Her known performances included Perillo's *Berenice* in 1759 at Venice (her name is on the printed libretto), Clelia in Gluck's *Il trionfo di Clelia* for the inaugural performance of the new Teatro Communale at Bologna on 14 May 1763, and Eurydice in the first Italian production of Gluck's *Orfeo*, under the composer's direction, at Parma on 24 August 1769 in celebration of the wedding of the Archduchess Maria Amelia to Prince Ferdinando. On 17 October 1771 at Milan she sang Silvia in Mozart's *Ascanio in Alba*, on the occasion of another Hapsburg celebration, the wedding of Princess Maria Ricciarda to Archduke Ferdinand.

Advertised as Signora Girelli, she made her debut in London at the King's Theatre on 14 November 1772 in the title role of *Sofonisba*. Of her performance Dr Burney wrote: "Her style of singing was good, but her voice was in decay, and her intonation frequently false . . . however, it was easy to imagine from what remained, that she had been better." *Sofonisba* was repeated throughout the season, as was *Artaserse* (first performance on 1 December 1772) in which she sang Mandane, the role in which she took her benefit on 18 March. On 19 January 1773, at the first performance of *Il Cid*, an opera by Antonio Sacchini, who was newly arrived in England, she sang Cimene, a role well suited to the singer's "spirited and nervous style" described by Burney. Signora Girelli Aguilar sang in a concert of vocal and instrumental music given at the King's Theatre on 5 February 1773 for the benefit of the Musicians' Fund. On 9 March she performed in *Orfeo*, and on 30 March in *Apollo ed*

Issea. On 6 May she sang Serpane in Sacchini's *Tamerlano*, which was repeated on 8, 11, 15, 22 May. Her final performance in London was given in *Il Cid* on 19 June 1773.

Gireux. *See* **GIROUX**.

Girls, Mr *d. 1780, house servant.*

The *Morning Chronicle* on 17 August 1780 reported the death on the twelfth of Mr Girls, who worked in the Drury Lane treasury office.

Gironimo, Mr [*fl. 1721*], *musician.*

On 17 April 1721 at Drury Lane Mr Gironimo, a musician, provided "A Particular Entertainment" between the acts of *The Amorous Widow*.

Giroux, Gabriel [*fl. 1785–1808?*], *dancer, choreographer.*

Oxberry, writing in his *Dramatic Biography* about the popular dancer and actress Mrs Caroline Searle, called her father Gabriel "Geroux" a ballet master and principal dancer at the Paris Opéra who "visited London, and became a member of the Italian Opera House, and commenced dancing master, by which he realized a considerable property and succeeded . . . to dance himself into the good graces of a merchant's daughter, and persuaded her" to marriage.

Giroux first came to the notice of the London public in the bill of the King's Theatre for 24 January 1786, where he was credited with composing "a new *Divertissement Sérieux*," which was danced at the end of the first act of the new comic opera *Il marchese Tulipano*. He composed divertissements for entr'acte service also on 11 March and 23 May.

Years later, on 15 September 1802 at the Haymarket Theatre, "Pupils of Mr. Giroux, Late Ballet Master of the Opera-House" danced in *The Fairies' Revels*. Master Giroux was Malcolm, Miss Giroux

was Jane, and Miss C. Giroux was Peggy. William C. Smith in *The Italian Opera . . . 1789–1820* does not cite Giroux until the 1802–3 season at the King's Theatre, when he served, not as ballet master but as one of sixteen dancers in the *corps de ballet*. That season a female Giroux, either his wife or one of his daughters, was also dancing at the King's. They returned to the company in the season which ran from 14 January through 4 August 1804. In both seasons the company lists had spelled the name "Gireux." (There is a possibility that the "Giraud" who had danced in the 1801–2 season was Giroux.)

Though no Giroux—under any spelling —was at the King's Theatre after 1804 so far as Smith's account shows, both Giroux and many of his numerous children served the ballets, pantomimes, and musical extravaganzas at the Royal Circus in St George's Fields for a number of years. Furthermore, they had, or claimed to have had, an association with the opera house for several years more. Discriminating among the members of the family is difficult, sometimes impossible. Oxberry tells us that by 1827 the junior Mr Giroux was "a celebrated dancing-master" and had been "a few years back attached to several of our theatres." He tells us also that Caroline (by then Mrs Searle) had been born in Islington in 1799 and had danced at the Royal Circus when she was three years old. And he goes on to detail her substantial career. Oxberry also mentions several other daughters of the elder Giroux.

Giroux family members were mentioned in various combinations dozens of times in surviving Royal Circus bills. They were apparently regulars there from about 1802 through 1805. One of their typical advertisements of the latter year is that for the performance of 29 April 1805 when they were in a "serio-comic divertisement" called *The Knights of the Garter*: "Principal dancers, Mr. Giroux, Miss Giroux, Miss C. Giroux, and Miss Caroline Giroux, from the Opera House. Pupils of Mr. Giroux, sen. Mr. and Miss Giroux will dance a Pas Deux, and the latter will introduce Mademoiselle Parisot's celebrated Shawl Dance. . . ." The "Mr" in that bill may have been the junior male Giroux, inasmuch as the notice for 20 May following referred to "Mr. Giroux, Miss Geroux, and Miss C. Giroux, from the Opera House, Pupils of Mr Giroux, Senior."

The entire family departed the Royal Circus—and perhaps London—after 1805. For when the spectacles in St George's Fields opened for the season on 18 April 1808, Easter Monday, Mr Giroux presented his new ballet called *Love's Artifice, or the Noble Peasant*, in which were "Lord Walpole (disguised as a Peasant) Mr. Giroux, his first appearance on this stage for three years," and "Betsey, Miss C. Giroux; Little Gipsey, Miss Caroline Giroux; and Lucy, Miss Giroux." By 1812 a Miss L. Giroux was being mentioned with the group. By 1814 a Miss F. Giroux had been added. The latest notice we have is one of 1814 (no closer dating) at the Surrey (formerly the Royal Circus), welcoming from Paris Monsieur Godeau, "the first Rope Dancer in the World," and announcing the "new Grand Serio Pantomime, called The KNIGHT of the BLACK PLUME . . . in which the Misses Giroux will dance a new Pas de Deux, composed by Mr. Giroux, jun."

By the time of Oxberry's *Memoir* (1827) two of the sisters were "teaching the art at Bath and Bristol, and netting about 1800£ per annum," and Mrs Searle, in addition to her theatrical duties, had 31 apprentices and 60 private pupils to instruct.

Girst. *See* GRIST.

Gismondi. *See* HEMPSON.

Giton. *See* GUITON.

Gitten, Mr ₁*fl. 1766*₁, *house servant.*
Egerton MS 2272 at the British Museum cites a Mr Gitten as a lobby doorkeeper at Covent Garden in 1766.

Giuliani, Cecilia, née Bianchi ₁*fl. 1787–1789*₁, *singer.*
The singer Signora Cecilia Bianchi Giuliani was named in the libretto of *Orfano Cinese* (Venice, 1787). She made her first appearance in London on 5 April 1788 at the King's Theatre singing Epponina in *Giulio Sabino*. On 8 May she was Aristea in *L'Olimpiade*. Songs she sang in both of those operas were published about 1788. For the 1788–89 season at the King's Signora Giuliani was paid £891 13*s.* 4*d.* and was granted a free benefit. For that she sang the title role in *Ifigenia in Aulide*, Adelina in *Il disertore* (at the performance on 21 March 1789 that work was presented with all parts except those of Sga Giuliani and Sg Marchesi omitted), and Cleofide in *La generosità d'Alessandro*. In March and May she was plagued with illness, and she did not return for the following season. The *Morning Chronicle* on 16 February 1789 noted that "Giuliani shone more in the recitatives as an Actress than as a Singer, though her style seems improved since last season." After leaving England Signora Giuliani sang at the Hoftheater in Vienna and later in Milan.

Giulinani, Signor ₁*fl. 1776*₁, *singer.*
Signor Giulinani sang Eupalte in *Piramo e Tisbe* at the King's Theatre in the Haymarket on 14, 17, and 21 December 1776. No other appearances are known for him.

Giupponi. *See* GUIPPONI.

Giustinelli, Signora ₁*fl. 1774*₁, *singer.*
The London Stage reports that Signora Giustinelli sang Armidoro in *La buona figliuola* at the King's Theatre on 17 March 1774.

Giustinelli, Giuseppe ₍*fl. 1763–1769*₎, *singer, oboist.*

Giuseppe Giustinelli sang Thirsis in *Orione* on 19 February 1763 at the King's Theatre in the Haymarket. On 25 April he participated in the annual benefit for indigent musicians, and on 9 June at the Haymarket Theatre he sang in a concert for Capitani's benefit (Capitani was in debtor's prison). Giustinelli was at the King's Theatre again in 1763–64, singing Olentus in *Cleonice*, Timotele in *Senocrita*, and a role in *Pellegrini*.

On 2 November 1764 Giustinelli sang in the first performance of the English opera *Almena* at Drury Lane; the work played for only six nights to thin houses. On 15 February 1765 at Drury Lane Giustinelli sang Pompy in *Pharnaces*, an opera altered from the Italian; he was the only Italian singer in the cast. His salary at Drury Lane was £7 per week.

Giustinelli was not heard from again until 5 February 1768 when he sang in *The Cure of Saul* at the King's Theatre. That night he also played a concerto on the oboe. On 2 and 23 February 1769 at the Haymarket Theatre he and Mrs Jewell sang Dryden's *Ode on the Power of Music* in *An Attic Evening's Entertainment*.

Dr Burney said that Giustinelli "had a good voice, and sufficient merit to supply the place of second man on our stage in the serious operas, for several years. . . ."

"Gizziello," stage name of Gioacchino Conti *1714–1761, singer.*

The male soprano known professionally as "Gizziello" (sometimes Egissiello or Ghizziello) was born on 28 February 1714 at Arpino, Italy, and was christened Gioacchino Conti. At the age of eight he was entered in the studio, at Naples, of Domenico Egizzio, from whom he drew his pseudonym and under whose tutelage he remained for seven years, until 1729. At the age of 16 Gizziello made his debut at the Teatro delle Dame in Rome in Vinci's

Artaserse in February 1730 and was an immediate sensation. One anecdote surrounding his debut concerned the famous singer Caffarelli, who, while at Naples and hearing of Gizziello's immense popularity, took himself to Rome, incognito, and upon hearing the lad sing cried out "Bravo! bravo! bravo Gizziello! E Cafforelli che le lo dice!" Gizziello sang at Naples in 1732 and 1733, and at Venice in 1735 he sang in *Demofoonte* and *La clemenza di Tito*.

On 13 April 1735 the London press announced that "*Signor Conti*, who is esteemed the best singer in Italy, being sent for by Mr. Handel, is expected here in a few days." Gizziello had been engaged by Handel, whose company was performing at Covent Garden Theatre, as an attraction to combat the enormous appeal of Farinelli, who was with Porpora's rival opera com-

H. R. Beard Collection, Victoria and Albert Museum

"GIZZIELLO" (Gioacchino Conti)

engraving by Van Haecken, after Lucy

pany at the King's Theatre. Handel began his campaign on 5 May 1736 with a revival of *Ariodante*, in which Gizziello made his debut in the title role. On the following morning the London *Daily Post and General Advertiser* reported that the young singer had "met with an uncommon reception; and in justice to both his voice and judgment, he may be truly esteemed one of the best performers in this kingdom." Obviously no match for Farinelli, he was described by Dr Burney as "more of promising, than mature abilities." Gizziello was a shy and modest person, uncommon for the *castrati*, who were the public's darlings and usually behaved with outrageous temperament. It was reported that when he first heard Farinelli sing, at a rehearsal, "he burst into tears, and fainted away with despondency."

Gizziello's next role was Meleager in Handel's *Atalanta*, which was given a splendid production with new scenes in the presence of the King and Queen on 12 May 1736 in honor of the marriage of the Prince of Wales, Frederick, to Princess Augusta. Gizziello's first two songs in the first act were written to take advantage of his "new, graceful, and pathetic style of singing," for according to Burney the singer had a "delicacy and tenderness" and a soprano voice higher than any of the first males for whom Handel had previously written. The opera was performed regularly until the end of the season on 9 June. In a letter to Horace Walpole on 11 June 1736, Thomas Gray wrote of the splendid scenic effects and his liking of Gizziello "excessively in everything but his mouth." In the text of the letter Gray drew a caricature which Toynbee called "a sketch of a square cavernous mouth, in outline like a knucklebone." Some six years later, Gray still remembered the ugliness of the singer's mouth: "he had a very promising Squeak with him," he wrote to Chute and Mann in July 1742, and "his Mouth, when open, made an exact Square."

Continuing with Handel's company at Covent Garden the following season, Gizziello sang Ruggiero in *Alcina* in a command performance on 6 November 1736. He sang in *Atalanta* in honor of the Prince of Wales's birthday on 27 November and was reported to have "much improved since last year." His other performances were Sigismonde in *Arminio* on 12 January 1737, Anastasio in *Justin* on 16 February, and Alessandro in *Berenice*, his last for Handel, in the presence of the Royal Family on 18 May 1737.

Upon his return to Italy, Gizziello studied at Bologna with Bernacchi. In 1739 he was a success in *Didone* at Padua. In 1743 he went to sing in Lisbon, where he remained for ten years except for occasional performances in Naples in 1747 (where he sang with Caffarelli in *Achille in Siro*), Venice in 1749, and Padua in 1751. He also was a member of the opera at Madrid from 1749 to 1752. The story that in consequence of narrowly escaping with his life from the great earthquake in Lisbon in 1756 Gizziello retreated into a monastery is without basis, since he left that city in 1753, never to return. Evidently he did retire to his native town of Arpino that year, reputedly yet at the height of his vocal powers. He soon went to Rome, where he suffered ill health and turned his mind to religious concerns.

Gizziello died at Rome on 25 October 1761. Additional details of his continental career may be found in the *Enciclopedia dello spettacolo*.

Portraits of Gizziello include a mezzotint by Van Haecken, after C. Lucy, 1736, and an engraving by C. Piotti Pirola, published at Milan in 1837. He also appears in an engraving of a large group of Italian singers done after Antonio Fedi between 1801 and 1807.

Gladeau, Mrs. *See* GREVILLE, MRS [H. F.?].

Gladwin, Thomas *(fl. c. 1730–1763)*, *harpsichordist, organist, composer.*

The earliest published song by Thomas Gladwin listed in the *Catalogue of Printed Music in the British Museum* is *By Hope possess'd*, printed about 1730. During his life he composed several other songs of a popular nature and some lessons for the harpsichord. On 25 April 1739 he played a lesson on that instrument at a concert for Lyne's benefit (reported by Latreille with no place specified), and on 28 August Gladwin became one of the original subscribers to the Royal Society of Musicians. For several years he appeared almost annually at concert halls and at the Haymarket Theatre. At Hickford's Music Room on 5 February 1741 he played the harpsichord for another benefit for Lyne; on 26 February 1741 he offered a concerto on the harpsichord at the Haymarket; and at the same playhouse on 10 March 1743 he played the organ. *Mortimer's London Directory* in 1763 listed Gladwin as an organist and teacher of the harpsichord; he was then living in South Audley Street.

Glanville, Miss, later Mrs Michael Doyle *(fl. 1758–1779)*, *singer.*

Miss Glanville (or Glenville, Granville) was one of the singers in the musical company that performed at Marylebone Gardens in the summers of 1758 through 1760 and at the Haymarket Theatre in the summer of 1761. Casts were rarely indicated, but when Miss Glanville was mentioned in the bills it was usually in such good company as Signora Seratina, Reinhold, and Kear. Each summer at Marylebone she was given a benefit, usually shared with one other, but on 20 August 1760 she had a solo benefit and was advertised as singing the Old Woman in *La serva padrona*—the short opera that was the troupe's usual offering. In 1759 the troupe varied their pattern by offering *La cicisbea alla modo;, or, The Modish Coquette*. Miss Glanville may also have performed in *La strattag-*

gema, which was given that summer.

At the Haymarket in the summer of 1761 the company performed *The Stratagem (La strattaggema*, presumably), *The Ridiculous Guardian, The Coquette (La cicisbea alla modo*, probably), *The Servant Mistress*, and *La serva padrona*, and Miss Glanville was probably involved in most of them. She was certainly in *La serva padrona*, for on 8 August she replaced, for that performance only, Signora Seratina.

Faulkner's Dublin Journal on 18 September 1779 reported that Miss Glanville had married the Irish actor Michael Doyle. She was described as from Waterford.

Glanville, Thomas *(fl. 1757)*, *singer.*

According to J. T. Smith's *A Book for a Rainy Day* (1845), Thomas Glanville sang at Marylebone Gardens in 1757. He was probably related to the Miss Glanville who performed there in subsequent years.

Glash, Mr *(fl. 1714)*, *oboist.*

Mr Glash played the hautboy at a concert given for his benefit at a tennis court (location unknown, but in London and not the one in James Street) on 4 May 1714.

Glass, William *(fl. 1739)*, *musician.*

William Glass was one of the professional London musicians who was an original subscriber to the Royal Society of Musicians when it was organized on 28 August 1739.

Glassington, Miss *(fl. 1781–1782)*, *actress.*

On 14 March 1781, "A Young Lady," identified as Miss Glassington by the *Hibernian Magazine* of that month, made her debut at the Crow Street Theatre, Dublin. A year later, on 11 April 1782, again announced as "A Young Lady," she made her first and only appearance at Drury Lane Theatre as Rosalind in *As You Like It*. No other London performances by her are known. Probably she was the daughter of the actor Joseph Glassington and the niece of the actress Elizabeth Glassington.

Glassington, Elizabeth, later Mrs Charles Charlton [*fl.* 1769–1829], *actress.*

Probably the child of an itinerant theatrical family (a Mrs Glassington was acting at York in 1727), Elizabeth Glassington was performing at Cork and at the Crow Street Theatre, Dublin, under the management of Henry Mossop in 1769–70. Announced as from Dublin, she appeared at Plymouth in the summer of 1771 and had, by 1771–72, joined the company at Norwich, where her brother Joseph Glassington (fl. 1771–1829) was also acting. On 24 August 1772 the Committee of the Norwich Theatre ordered that "Mr & Miss Glassington be continued but not to have their Salaries exceed £2.5.0 p week." She acted several times at Edinburgh in 1773–74 (where her roles included Selima in *Tamerlane* and Belvidera in *Venice Preserv'd*) and at King's Lynn in 1774. Her trial engagement with Wilkinson's company at York, where she made her debut as Jane Shore on 26 April 1777, was overshadowed by the appearance in the same company of the young Sarah Siddons, who aroused everyone's enthusiasm and approbation to the neglect of the hopeful Elizabeth.

When in 1777 Miss Glassington performed in her brother's booth at Stourbridge Fair near Cambridge, where one of her roles was Jane Shore, the *Morning Chronicle* of 15 September 1777 called her "An agreeable young actress and a distinguished favourite at Cambridge." She was with her brother again at that fair in subsequent years through 1782. In 1778 Elizabeth Glassington and her brother were members of a company consisting mainly of provincial players which performed at the China Hall, Rotherhithe, in South London, between 25 May and 26 June, her

known roles being Jane Shore on 1 June and Juliet on 10 June.

By July 1779 she had married Charles Charlton (fl. 1779–1829), a provincial actor who later became a manager at Bath. In the summer of 1779 they were members of Wilkinson's company acting at Birmingham. On 16 July 1781, the *Hampshire Chronicle* announced that Mrs Charlton and her husband, then at Portsmouth, were joining the Norwich company in 1781–82; she is known to have acted Harriet in *The Jealous Wife* when that company visited Colchester on 12 August 1782. A month later, on 13 September 1782, the Committee of the Norwich Theatre ordered Mr and Mrs Charlton discharged, but on 16 October the order was tempered:

This Committee having ordered a Dismission of Mr and Mrs Charlton, but now taking into Consideration that Mr Charlton signed an Engagement to continue with the Company for the ensuing Winter Season and Considering that it may be difficult for Mr Charlton to engage himself elsewhere as the Winter Season is so far advanced; they therefore direct that Mr Starkey writes to Mr Barret to acquaint him that it is recommended to him to offer Mr Charlton the Sum of ten Guineas if he shall leave the Company at the End of this Year's Summer Season which if accepted he is to pay out of the Proprs shares of Summer Circuit but if he declines such offer then the Manager is at Liberty to retain Mr Charlton and his Wife for the next Winter Season at Norwich.

The Charltons, it seems, remained with the Norwich Company well beyond the "next Winter Season," and until 1786. With that company she played at Gloucester in March 1788 and September 1789.

Curiously, on 14 March 1781, "A Young Lady," identified as Miss Glassington by the *Hibernian Magazine* (March 1781), had made her debut at the Crow Street Theatre, Dublin. A year later, "A Young Lady," also identified as Miss Glassington was announced as making her first appearance on the stage as Rosalind in *As You Like It* at Drury Lane on 11 April 1782. Elizabeth, of course, had been at Crow Street more than a decade earlier and she had some years of experience behind her now, including her brief engagement at the China Hall Theatre in 1778; by 1782 she was acting as Mrs Charlton, so it would seem that this Miss Glassington may have been Elizabeth's sister or even her niece, a daughter of Joseph Glassington.

In 1791–92 the Charltons joined the theatre at Bath, where they remained for many years. He became deputy manager to Dimond in 1795 and eventually (after 1805) manager of the new Theatre Royal in Beaufort Square, from which position he retired in May 1827. In June 1829 both Mr and Mrs Charlton became annuitants of the Bath Theatre Fund. Their daughter married a Mr Elwall of Bristol in May 1806.

Glassington, Joseph [*fl.* 1771–1829], *actor, manager, dancer.*

Joseph Glassington was a member of the company at the Norwich Theatre in 1771–72 with his sister Elizabeth Glassington. On 24 August 1772 the Committee of that theatre ordered that "Mr & Miss Glassington can be continued but not to have their Salaries exceed £2. 5. 0 p week." Probably they were the children of an itinerant theatrical family; a Mrs Glassington was acting at York as early as 1727. About 1776 Joseph Glassington managed a company playing at Tunbridge Wells. In 1778 he and his sister were with a troupe that performed at the China Hall, Rotherhithe, in south London between 25 May and 26 June, where Glassington's roles included Leander in *The Mock Doctor* on 8 June and Benvolio in *Romeo and Juliet* on 10 June.

Glassington had a traveling company that played at Stourbridge Fair, Cambridge, each year from 1777 to 1781, and he was a member of Mrs Baker's company in Kent

in 1785. On 2 July 1785 he acted the Irishman in a performance of *The Apprentice* at the Windsor Castle Inn, King Street, Hammersmith, by a company that was resident there between 17 June and 27 July. At Plymouth on 17 August 1789, Glassington played Sir Charles Freeman in *The Beaux' Stratagem* and danced as one of the Natives in the ballet *The Death of Captain Cook.*

In 1795–96, announced as from Liverpool, Glassington was playing at Manchester. By 1799 he was performing minor roles and serving as prompter for the Bristol Theatre, where he remained until 1801. On 21 April 1801, while traveling to Bristol from Bath, where he also worked, his coach overturned, and he suffered a broken leg; Mr Paul (the Bristol Theatre treasurer) received a dislocated shoulder, and the actresses Mrs Taylor and Mrs Summers were "much bruised."

Felix Farley's Bristol Journal of 29 August 1801 announced that Glassington had been engaged to succeed Wilde as prompter of Covent Garden Theatre in the autumn. Glassington remained in that London post until 1818. His salary in 1801–2 was £5 per week. The Covent Garden account books show that he enjoyed substantial benefit receipts over the years, taking, for example, £337 9s. 6d. on 10 June 1805, £443 7s. 6d. on 15 June 1807, £506 2s. 6d. on 26 June 1812, and £308 3s. on 11 July 1814. The last years of his life were spent at the theatre at Bath, under the management of his brother-in-law, Charles Charlton. By June 1829 he was an annuitant of the Bath Theatre Fund.

Glasson, Mlle [*fl.* 1741], *dancer.*

Mademoiselle Glasson danced one of the Women in an entertainment called *The Triumph of Britannia Over the Four Parts of the World* at Hallam's Bartholomew Fair booth on 22 August 1741.

Glaud, Mr [*fl.* 1764], *singer.*

Mr Glaud offered "The Cries of Edinburgh" at a Haymarket performance of *The Gentle Shepherd* on 9 April 1764.

Glegg. *See* CLEGG.

Glen, Ann ₍*fl.* 1755–1766₎, *actress.*
A "gentlewoman who never appeared on any stage before" played the Countess of Rutland in *The Earl of Essex* at Covent Garden on 24 February 1755; when the play was repeated on 19 April the actress was identified as Mrs (Ann) Glen. For her solo benefit on 29 April she attempted Belvidera in *Venice Preserv'd. Faulkner's Dublin Journal* on 6 December 1755 reported that Mrs Glen would make her Smock Alley debut, heralded as from Covent Garden, on 8 December. On 21 October 1756 she was back in London, playing Lady Townly in *The Provok'd Husband* for her benefit at Drury Lane. Cross commented in his diary: "Insipid."

Off she went again to Smock Alley, to play Lady Townly on 25 November 1756, Belvidera on 14 January 1757, Millamant in *The Way of the World* on 21 January, Sylvia in *The Recruiting Officer* on 18 February, and Indiana in *The Conscious Lovers* on 18 March. She returned to Drury Lane in early 1758. On 10 January she acted Zara in *The Mourning Bride* ("bad" wrote Cross); she repeated the role on 16 January ("Mrs Glen did Zara agen–oh!"). On 18 April she played Lady Townly, and on 22 June Cross noted that she had been engaged again for the following season. In 1758–59 Ann acted Anna Bullen in *Henry VIII*, Lady Macduff in *Macbeth*, Octavia in *Antony and Cleopatra*, and Lady Wronghead in *The Provok'd Husband*.

She announced that on 26 April 1760 she would, for her own benefit, play Indiana in *The Conscious Lovers* as her last appearance in London. True to her word, she headed for Norwich, where she began performing in 1760 and was still acting in 1766.

Glendening. *See* CLENDINING.

Glenn, Mr ₍*fl.* 1758–1760₎, *actor.*
Mr and Mrs Glenn acted briefly at the Haymarket Theatre with Theophilus Cibber's pickup company in January 1758. On 12 January Glenn was the Host and Mrs Glenn acted Viletta in *She Wou'd and She Wou'd Not*, and on 16 and 18 January Glenn played Sir Harry Gubbin and his wife acted Biddy in *Numps's Courtship*. Mrs Glenn made appearances at Norwich from 1759 to 1762, and Mr Glenn is known to have acted there in 1760. Perhaps they were related to Ann Glen, who was active in London and Norwich during the same period.

Glenn, Mrs ₍*fl.* 1758–1762₎, *actress.* *See* GLENN, MR.

Glenville. *See* GLANVILLE.

Glover, Henry ₍*fl.* 1666–1671₎, *machinist.*
On 21 November 1666 a draft was made (recorded in the *State Papers Domestic*) of the appointment of Henry Glover as keeper of the "Scenes, Machines, Engines, & other things to yᵉ same belonging" at the royal theatre in Whitehall. The only other record of Glover dates from June 1671 when he was reimbursed for money he had spent from his own pocket for oil, thread, and cotton for the theatre lights.

Glover, Leach *d.* 1763, *dancer, actor.*
Leach Glover, who had a dancing career that stretched from 1717 to 1741, may have been the Mr Glover who was a member of the Duke of Southampton and Cleaveland's Servants in 1714. The group acted *Injured Virtue* in Richmond during the summer and at the King's Arms Tavern in Southwark on 1 November 1714. Glover played Antonius. Advertised as never having "Danc'd in Publick," Leach

Glover performed at the King's Theatre on 16 March 1717. The playbill at Lincoln's Inn Fields for 23 April noted that Glover was a scholar of Dumirail.

Glover left London and was not seen again there until 12 February 1719, when he danced at the King's Theatre, it "being the first time of his Performance in publick since his return from the Court of Paris." At the end of the 1718–19 season he left London again. On 6 February 1722 he made his first appearance on the stage of the Haymarket Theatre; then, after another absence from London, he returned to Lincoln's Inn Fields to dance regularly during the 1723–24 season. At his benefit there on 10 April 1724 he collected a total of £121 8s. before house charges; his daily salary for that season was 10s. Glover usually appeared as an entr'acte dancer, but he was also seen during the season in pantomimes. He danced Mezzetin (Apollo) in *Jupiter and Europa* on 19 October 1723, a Mezzetin Man in *The Necromancer* on 20 December, a Fury in *Amadis* on 4 January 1724, and Mezzetin again in *The Robbers* on 2 March.

Glover danced regularly at Lincoln's Inn Fields through the 1728–29 season, offering entr'acte specialty turns and playing such new parts as the Mad Dancing Master in *The Humours of Bedlam*, Sysiphus in *Harlequin Sorcerer*, Scaramouch and a follower of Mars in *Mars and Venus*, a Sicilian in *The Rape of Proserpine*, and a Frenchman in *Apollo and Daphne*. During the mid-1720s Leach Glover's father was cited on the theatre's free list, though his Christian name was not given. The dancer's benefits at Lincoln's Inn Fields averaged £100; his daily wages seem to have risen to 15s. by 1726.

After 1727–28 Glover was gone from the London stage until 17 March 1730, when he returned to John Rich's troupe at Lincoln's Inn Fields to dance *Numidian* with Miss La Tour. Glover stayed with Rich's company at that playhouse and,

from 1732 on, at Covent Garden. Between 1730 and 1740–41 he appeared in such new roles as a Demon in *The Rape of Proserpine*, an Infernal in *Perseus and Andromeda*, Zephyrus and Apollo in *Apollo and Daphne*, a Zephyr and "Un Amour" in *The Nuptial Masque*, and Cupid and Apollo in *The Royal Chace*. He also continued offering dances and ballets between the acts of plays—such pieces as *The Masqueraders*, *The Faithful Shepherd*, a *Scots Dance*, *Grand Dance in Momus*, *Fawn*, *Grecian Sailors*, *Pastor Fido*, and many untitled pieces. During the 1730s he was living in Chandos Street and receiving £150 per season. By his final season, 1740–41, his salary was 16s. 8d. daily and he was dancing infrequently. His last benefit, on 2 April 1741, brought him £172 1s. before house charges. After leaving the public stage in 1741, Glover succeeded Anthony L'Abbé as dancing master to the Princesses Amelia and Carolina.

The parish registers of St Paul, Covent Garden, contain three entries concerning Leach Glover: on 22 February 1756 Mary Ann, the wife of Leach Glover of St Anne, Westminster, was buried; on 6 January 1762 Glover's son Thomas was buried; and on 13 January 1763 Leach Glover, still identified as from St Anne's parish, was buried. The *Gentleman's Magazine* reported the suicide in October 1784 of a Miss Glover, daughter of the dancing master—presumably Leach Glover or possibly a descendant. A copy of *The Sorrows of Werter*, probably the 1780 English edition of Goethe's work, was found under her pillow. The *Gentleman's Magazine* was anxious to spread the word of Miss Glover's suicide in order "to defeat, if possible the evil tendency of that pernicious work."

Glover, Mrs Samuel, Juliana; née Betterton *1779–1850, actress.*
Juliana Glover—so baptized, but signing herself "Julia" throughout her long career—was born on 8 February 1779 at

Harvard Theatre Collection

JULIA GLOVER

by "P. G. H."

Newry, where her parents frequently performed. Her father, Thomas William Betterton (d. 1834), a native of Dublin, had for professional reasons changed his surname Butterton to that of the great Restoration actor. Her mother, also an actress, married Betterton in Belfast on 21 December 1778. She was the widow of the actor Wingfield Palmer. (Our entry on Betterton erred in calling her the widow of James Parker.)

Brought up for the stage almost from infancy, Julia probably joined her parents in performances at Newry, where her father had built a theatre in Hill Street in 1783. After playing at Edinburgh in 1785–86, the Bettertons were with Tate Wilkinson's company on the York circuit between 1786 and 1789. It is said that at York Julia appeared as a Page in *The Orphan* and played the Duke of York to George Frederick Cooke's Richard III, but we find no confirmation of those reports. The Better-

tons were at Liverpool in the summer of 1791. They returned to Newry in the summer of 1792 to play under Dawson's management. There Julia offered entr'acte dances, sometimes with her father, sometimes alone. Her first definite notice as an actress came at Newry on 20 July 1792, when for her benefit she appeared as the young Prince Arthur in *King John*. For her father's benefit on 26 July she danced in *Wild Oats* but did not act.

The Bettertons then performed at Drogheda and at the Crow Street Theatre, Dublin, in 1792–93. Mrs Betterton died in 1793 and her widower, daughter, and son John wandered around the Irish provincial towns throughout that year. Hailed "as a ten-year-old [actually she was 14] dramatic genius engaged at a considerable expense," at Waterford in March, Julia played in scenes from *The Fair Penitent* and *Venice Preserv'd*, acted a young girl in *The Virgin Unmask'd*, and danced a minuet with her brother. A manuscript in the Folger Library dating from Waterford at that time describes her "great Powers of Voice and expression." After playing at Wexford in March and April, they were at Kilkenny in June and July, with Julia acting Moggy M'Gilpin in *The Highland Reel* on the fifth of the latter month. They then joined the company at Galway until the end of October, where Julia offered prologues, epilogues, recitations, and dances and played sparkling comedy roles such as the boyish Captain Flash in *Miss in Her Teens*. Late in 1793 they returned to Dublin, playing at the Capel Street Theatre until December and at Crow Street from January to the spring of 1794.

Leaving Ireland in the middle of 1794 the three Bettertons crossed over to join Watson's company at Hereford for a brief spell, then settled with Dimond and Keasberry's troupe at Bath and Bristol for several seasons. Julia made her first appearance at Bath on 9 May 1795 probably as Elwina in *Percy*. At Bristol in late September she acted Elwina, receiving "the warmest approbation from a brilliant though not crowded audience," according to the report of *Felix Farley's Bristol Journal* of 26 September 1795. Over the next two seasons at those twin theatres, she acted an impressive line, including Desdemona, Lady Macbeth, Cordelia, Lady Teazle, Lady Amaranth in *Wild Oats*, and Joanna in *The Deserted Daughter*—in the last role she was accounted "a charming breeches figure."

When Tate Wilkinson was "deprived of the assistance" of Miss Wallis for assize-week at York in the summer of 1797, he engaged Miss Betterton for six nights. The advertisement in the York press announced that her opening character would be Elwina in *Percy* on 31 July 1797; the young lady's abilities were confirmed by the information that though only 17 years of age, she was of "such infinite promise as to have induced Mr. Harris (manager of the theatre-royal, Covent-Garden) to engage her for five years on the following terms; fifteen, sixteen, seventeen, eighteen, and nineteen pounds per week!"

Though Julia's reputation was growing, she was hardly in a position to command such high terms. Actually Harris had offered both her and her father a combined salary of £15, or £7 10s. each, for the 1797–98 season. She made her debut at Covent Garden as Elwina on 12 October 1797. An *Occasional Address*, written by Richard Cumberland, was delivered by Holman to introduce Julia before the play. After her second appearance, on 21 October, as Charlotte Rusport in *The West Indian*, the *Monthly Mirror* in a lengthy criticism of her first two roles found her too mechanical and possessed of an impudent and unbecoming confidence. She appealed to the head, sometimes to the fancy, but never to the heart.

In any part of her elaborate *Elwina*, did she put in motion the springs of terror or of pity? Did a sigh once escape the bosom, or a tear bedew the eye of sensibility?—No; and for this reason:—the audience contemplated her performance as they did the *Fantoccini*, in the last pantomime; cast an eye on the *puppets*, took a pinch of snuff, ejaculated "vastly clever," and thought no more of it. . . .

In her performance of *Elwina* we discovered a thorough knowledge of the *machinery* of the stage; studied preparation; the most systematic arrangement; very skillful display of the *points*; and a uniform anxiety for effect; but all this proves only that she had been *brought up to the business.* . . . Of that animation which is inspired by circumstances as they arise out of the scene, of that feeling . . . there was, throughout the five acts, a most *freezing* privation.

The *Monthly Mirror* critic thought that as Charlotte Rusport she destroyed all the amiable and sentimental traits of that character by her affectation and boldness. Her father, who had made his debut as Castalio in *The Orphan* on 20 October and then played Belcour in *The West Indian* with Julia on the twenty-first, was treated with similar strictures: "This gentleman . . . has all the defects of his daughter; his *tragedy* is without passion, and his comedy is without humour."

Julia did not win the friendship or admiration of Mrs Abington (whom she resembled) or Mrs Pope, leading actresses of the company; nevertheless, for one so young she enjoyed excellent roles during her first London season. On 3 November she was scheduled to play before the Royal Family; "the indulgent King," wrote Fanny Burney, "hearing she was extremely frightened . . . desired she might choose her own part for the first exhibition in his presence." She fixed upon Portia in *The Merchant of Venice*, but the monarch's judgment of her is not known. Her other roles in 1797–98 included Miss Dorrillon in *Wives as They Were, and Maids as They Are*, Emily Fitzallon (and the epilogue) in the premiere of Cumberland's *False Impressions* on 23 November, Julia Faulkland in *The Way to Get Married*, Miranda in *The Busy Body*,

Lady Surrey in *England Preserv'd*, Lady Jane in the premiere of Holcroft's *He's Much to Blame* on 13 February, a principal part (and the epilogue) in *Curiosity*, Eleanor de Ferrars in the premiere of Cumberland's *The Eccentric Lover* on 30 April, Mrs Kitely in *Every Man in His Humour*, and Lady Amaranth in *Wild Oats*. For her benefit on 16 May 1798, when she acted Joanna in *The Deserted Daughter* and tickets could be had at her lodgings No 47,

Great Queen Street, Lincoln's Inn Fields, her receipts totaled £184 8s. 6d. less house charges.

After playing the 1798 summer season at Birmingham, Julia returned for her second year at Covent Garden at a salary raised to £8 per week. That season her engagement to James Biggs, the Covent Garden actor whom she had met at Bath, was cut short by his death on 9 December 1798. On 14 May 1799 she played Lady Macbeth

Victoria and Albert Museum

JULIA GLOVER as Ophelia and Charles M. Young as Hamlet

by Clint

to her father's Macbeth (and Master John Betterton danced a hornpipe) for their shared benefit at which they received £267 1s. 6d. less house charges.

Her father, who evidently owed his engagement at Covent Garden to a stipulation in Julia's articles, treated her brutally and seized her salary. It was said that for £1000 he had sold his daughter to Samuel Glover, the reputed scion of a large fortune, to whom she was married on 20 March 1800, during her third season at Covent Garden, when she earned £8 10s. per week. Earlier in the season she had played such roles as Mrs Sullen in *The Beaux' Stratagem* and Clarinda in *The Suspicious Husband* under her maiden name. A week after her marriage, when she acted Letitia Harding in *The Belle's Stratagem* on 27 March, she was cited as "the Late Miss Betterton." Her name continued on the bills in that form during April for Lady Henrietta in *How to Grow Rich* on the fifth, Caroline in *The Votary* on the seventeenth, Miss Richland in *The Good-Natured Man* on the twenty-second, Leonora in *Lovers' Quarrels* on the twenty-ninth, and Lady Ann Mordent in *The Deserted Daughter* on 2 May. In the *Dramatic Censor* for 5 April 1800 Thomas Dutton criticized her refusal to use her recently acquired married name:

From whatever cause it may originate, whether from prudery, affectation, or vanity, there is something sovereignly ridiculous in the singularity and mysteriousness of this Actress's announcement in the Bills. . . . As she is understood to be recently married to a very worthy gentleman of the name of GLOVER, we think Mrs. GLOVER, the late Miss BETTERTON, would be preferable to the solitary *defunct* phrase by which she is now announced.

By 10 May 1800 Julia had heeded Dutton's advice and was announced in the bills for the role of Miss Walsingham in *The School for Lovers* as Mrs Glover. She was Susan in *The Follies of a Day* on 15 May, Lydia Languish in *The Rivals* on 20 May,

Lady Flippant in *The Fashionable Levities* and Maria in *Five Thousand a Year* on 2 June, and Miranda in *The Busy Body* on 7 June.

During the summer of 1800 Mrs Glover acted again at Birmingham. She played a benefit for her father on 18 September, then returned to Covent Garden for 1800–1801 at a salary of £9 per week. After playing at Brighton in the summer of 1801, she was again at Covent Garden in 1801–2 for £10 per week, but the following season she joined Drury Lane, making her first appearance there on 21 October 1802 as Mrs Oakly in *The Jealous Wife*. She then returned to Covent Garden for four years, 1803–4 through 1806–7, at a constant £12 per week, and also appeared summers at the Haymarket. On 28 September 1810 she began to play with the Drury Lane company at the Lyceum. She was there for two years; then she moved with that troupe in 1812–13 to the newly built Drury Lane Theatre, where she remained for some ten seasons at £14 per week.

At Drury Lane Julia Glover was the original Alhadra in Coleridge's *Remorse* on 23 January 1813, the Queen to Kean's *Richard III* on 12 February 1814, and Emilia to his Othello on 5 May 1814. On 16 September 1816 she acted Andromache to Macready's Orestes at Covent Garden— his first appearance there and her first in ten years. In his *Recollections of an Actor*, Walter Donaldson remembered Mrs Glover's playing Hamlet for her benefit at the Lyceum in 1822. That year she was also with Dibdin's company at the Surrey Theatre and then returned to Drury Lane for a season but was discharged, according to Winston's *Diaries*, on 25 November 1823. On 18 December 1822 Mrs Egerton played Emilia for Mrs Glover, for Mrs Glover had for some reason been arrested. She was engaged again at Covent Garden for 1825–26 and 1826–27 at £1 6s. 8d. per night. When she acted Mrs Subtle in *Paul Pry* at Drury Lane on 27 October 1829, the bills announced that she was making her first appearance there in five years.

In the 1830s she acted at the Haymarket, the Strand, Drury Lane, and the Olympic. Among her best characters were Estifania, Mrs Malaprop, Mrs Candour, Mrs Heidelberg, Mrs Subtle, and Widow Green (in *Love Chase*); and eventually she was seen in a line of vulgar wives, old maids and aunts, and peasant women.

On the day of her sixty-sixth birthday, 8 February 1846, Webster, the Haymarket manager, presented her with a handsome silver cup in the green room to mark the anniversary and to acknowledge her "sterling talent," shown through 50 years as an actress. Early in 1850 she was still acting at the Strand, her Widow Warren in Holcroft's *The Road to Ruin* on 18 January being considered "excellent" by Henry Crabb Robinson in his *Diary*. On 12 July 1850 she was given a farewell performance at Drury Lane, but having been ill for some weeks she could scarcely speak the lines of Mrs Malaprop, her final character. She died four days later on 16 July at the age of 71 and was buried on the nineteenth in the churchyard of St George the Martyr, Queen Square, Bloomsbury, near the remains of her father, who had died in 1834, after preying on her for years. Her husband, who made her equally unhappy, died a debtor in the Marshalsea at a date unknown to us, but years prior to Julia's death. Julia's brother John Betterton died in May 1816 after an undistinguished career as a dancer.

Administration of her estate, estimated at £450 was granted on 31 July 1850 to Samuel Edmund Glover, one of her "lawful children." In the grant she was described as "Juliana Glover formerly of No. 42 Pembroke Sq. Kensington but late of No. 21 Soho Sq. in psh of St Ann Westminster widow."

Her administrator and eldest son, noticed in *The Dictionary of National Biography* as Edmund Glover (1813?–1860), acted and managed in London. He married Elizabeth Nelson Pepperell (1809–1895), an actress, at St Paul, Covent Garden, on 3 September 1833, at which time his mother signed her name as a witness "Juliana" Glover, the same form appearing in the administration grant of her estate. Edmund and Elizabeth Glover had three children who followed the profession in the nineteenth century: Samuel Glover, actor, Phyllis Glover, actress (who married the actor Thomas Powrie), and William Glover (1833–1916), scene designer and manager. The last-mentioned William's son, Harold Glover, married the actress Nellie Lupino, and their six children all became performers.

Julia Glover's second son, William Howard Glover (1819–1875), also noticed in *The Dictionary of National Biography*, became a composer and concert impresario and eventually wrote music criticism and conducted in New York, where he died in 1875.

Julia's eldest daughter, Georgina, acted in the provinces and married the actor John Bland. A second daughter, Phyllis Frances Agnes Glover, born on 7 January 1807, made her debut as Juliet at Drury Lane on 29 April 1822; a promising and clever young actress, she died on 7 November 1831. She had been married to the actor William Carpenter Evans (d. 1854). A third daughter, Mary Glover, made her debut at Covent Garden on 25 September 1826; she died in 1860, evidently unmarried.

In her middle years Julia Glover was a leading actress. Despite the claim of *The Stage* (1814–15) that her playing was "violent" and "coarse," generally she was regarded as a performer of refinement and was sometimes called in her last years "the Mother of the Stage." In 1823, Boaden thought her to be the ablest actress in London.

Of medium height, in figure she tended to plumpness; she became, according to

Leslie's *Autobiography,* "monstrously fat." Indeed pictures of her in her mature years display an ample figure, but those of her early days reveal her as slender and handsome. Portraits of Mrs Glover include:

1. By S. Drummond. Pastel drawing. In the Garrick Club.

2. By "P. G. H." Watercolor, 1802. In the Harvard Theatre Collection. Engraving by W. Ridley, published as a plate to the *Monthly Mirror,* July 1802.

3. Portrait engraving by E. Bowles. Published by the engraver, 1825.

4. Portrait engraving by H. R. Cook. Published as a plate to *Ladies' Monthly Museum,* 1818.

5. Portrait engraving by A. Cardon. Published as plates to *La Belle Assemblée* and Bell's *Weekly Messenger,* 1813.

6. Portrait engraving by Mackenzie, after Rivers. Published by Vernor & Hood, 1802.

7. As Miss Brown in *Look Before You Leap.* By unknown engraver. Published in *Theatrical Times,* 19 December 1846.

8. As Mrs Candour in *The School for Scandal.* Engraving by Rogers, after T. Wageman. Published as a plate to Oxberry's *Dramatic Biography,* 1826.

9. As Mrs Candour. Engraving by J. Rogers, after J. W. Gear. Published as a plate to *Dramatic Magazine,* March 1831.

10. As Empress Elizabeth. Engraving by J. Bailey, published by the engraver as two-pence colored.

11. As Estifania in *Rule a Wife and Have a Wife.* Engraving by T. Wright, after T. Wageman. Published as a plate to Oxberry's *New English Drama,* 1820.

12. As Eugenia in *The Foundling of the Forest.* Watercolor by S. De Wilde, 1811. In the British Museum.

13. As Lady Allworth in *A New Way to Pay Old Debts.* Watercolor by W. S. Lethbridge. In the Garrick Club. Engraving by Thomson as a plate to the *Theatrical Inquisitor,* 1818.

14. As Norma in *The Pirate.* Engraving

by H. R. Cook, after T. Wageman. Published as a plate to Oxberry's *New English Drama,* 1818.

15. As Mrs Oakly in *The Jealous Wife.* Engraving by H. R. Cook, after T. Wageman. Published as a plate to Oxberry's *New English Drama,* 1818.

16. As Mrs Oakly, with Mr Pope as Oakly. Engraving by Alais. Published by J. Roach, 1807.

17. As Ophelia, with Charles M. Young as Hamlet. Painting by George Clint, exhibited at the Royal Academy, 1831. In the Victoria and Albert Museum.

18. As Roxalana in *The Sultan.* Engraving by Schiavonetti, after De Wilde. Published as a plate to Cawthorn's *Minor Theatre,* 1806.

A painting, at one time believed to be by George Clint, of a scene showing Mrs Glover, Mrs Paton, and Macready, has been identified by Mander and Mitchenson (*The Artist and the Theatre,* No 13) as the work of Samuel De Wilde, depicting Maria Bland, Ursula Booth, and John Bannister in a scene from *The Children in the Wood,* 1793.

Glover, Thomas [*fl.* 1776–1804], *pit doorkeeper.*

Thomas Glover's name was placed on the Drury Lane paylist in 1776–77 as a pit doorkeeper at 9s. per week. He was listed for that position on a tally sheet for that theatre dated 7 January 1792. In a manuscript concerning Chancery proceedings dated 2 October 1801, his full name was given, at which time he was identified as the Drury Lane employee and also as a coal merchant. Glover was still at Drury Lane in 1803–4, earning £2 2s. per week.

Gluck, Christoph Willibald *1714– 1787, composer, instrumentalist, glass harmonica player, singer.*

Christoph Willibald Gluck was born at Erasbach, near Berching, in the Upper Palatinate, on 2 July 1714. He was the eldest son of Alexander Johannes Gluck and his wife Walpurga. His father, a forester at Erasbach, was appointed to the service of Prince Lobkowitz of Eisenberg about 1729. After receiving his early education at Kamnitz and Albersdorf, in 1732 Gluck went to study at Prague, where he played violin and cello for various dances and sang in churches. In 1736 he traveled to Vienna to become chamber musician to young Prince Lobkowitz, son of the patron of Gluck's father.

After more travel and study with several masters, and after a visit to Paris, Gluck arrived in London in the autumn of 1745 in the company of his young prince. Gluck was 31 years old and already had seen some of his commissioned operas performed at Milan, Venice, Cremona, Turin, and Bologna. Soon after his arrival in London, he was asked by Lord Middlesex, then impresario of the opera at the King's Theatre, to compose a piece in celebration of the Duke of Cumberland's recent victory at Culloden.

Harvard Theatre Collection

CHRISTOPH VON GLUCK

engraving by Walther, after Duplessis

In the presence of the victorious Duke, Gluck's *La caduta dei giganti*, to a text by Vanneschi, received its first performance on 7 January 1746. The opera enjoyed only modest success despite the report of the *Daily Advertiser* the next day that "The Performance was received and carried on with great Attention, Tranquillity, and Applause." It was performed four more times during the month.

Gluck's second London composition was *Artamene*, again to a revised text by Vanneschi. It played at the King's Theatre on 4 March 1746. Written in extreme haste, it was really a *pasticcio* taken from three of the composer's earlier works, *Tigrane*, *Sofonisbe*, and *Ipermestra*. The piece subsequently had four performances during the rest of March and another four in April. But Gluck's works, hardly measuring up to the genius of Handel's during that decade, did not excite London auditors. Handel presumably was openly critical of the young composer's deficiencies and was reported to have stated that "his own cook knew more of counterpoint than Gluck did." Handel's cook and valet at that time, it should be noted, was the professional musician Gustavus Waltz. Gluck and Handel met cordially, however, and together they attended a concert for the benefit of the Musicians' Fund given at the King's Theatre on 25 March 1746, when the works of both were played.

A month later, on 23 April 1746, for his own benefit, Gluck gave a "glass harmonica" concert at the Haymarket Theatre. According to the *General Advertiser*, he played on 26 drinking glasses, "tuned with spring water, accompanied by the whole band, being a new instrument of his own invention." (Actually Richard Pockrich, an eccentric Irishman, had given concerts on the "Armonica" as early as 3 May 1743 at the Smock Alley Theatre, Dublin.) Whose concerto Gluck played is not known, but it seems not to have been his own composition.

In November of 1746 one of Gluck's few instrumental works, a set of six sonatas for two violins and bass, was published in London by Simpson. By that time, Gluck had left London to join Mingotti's Italian opera company at Hamburg.

Gluck soon became one of the most important composers of operas for the century's leading librettists, particularly Pietro Metastasio. His operas, performed at Europe's leading opera centers, especially at Vienna, where Gluck served for many years as musical director to the Hapsburg court, won his reputation as a cosmopolitan master. Among his best known and most influential productions were *La clemenza di Tito* at Naples on 4 November 1752, *La Cinesi* at Vienna on 24 September 1754, *Antigono* at Rome on 9 February 1756, *Il re pastore* at Vienna on 8 December 1756, *Orfeo ed Euridice* at Vienna on 5 October 1762, *Alceste* at Vienna on 26 December 1767, and *Iphigénie en Tauride* at Paris on 18 May 1779.

At Vienna on 15 September 1750, Gluck married Marianna Pergin (or Perg), daughter of Joseph Pergin, a rich merchant-banker. She inherited a large fortune from her father which enabled Gluck to live comfortably for the rest of his life. In 1769 they adopted Gluck's ten-year-old niece, Marianna Helder; a child of musical promise, she filled a gap in their childless marriage, even taking her uncle's surname. She died in 1776, at the age of 17.

After passing several years of retirement in ill health, Gluck died of a stroke at Vienna on 15 November 1787, at the age of 73.

Gluck has been the subject of many articles and books, including M. Cooper, *Gluck* (London, 1935); A. Einstein, *Gluck* (London, 1936); W. Brandl, *Christoph Willibald Ritter von Gluck* (Wiesbaden, 1948); R. Tenschert, *Christoph Willibald Gluck: der grosse Reformator der Oper* (Freiburg, 1951); and *Bibliography of the Works of C. W. von Gluck* (London,

1959). A *Gluck-Jahrbuch*, edited by H. Abert, was published at Leipzig from 1914 to 1918. A complete edition of Gluck's works was begun by R. Gerber in 1951. A list of Gluck's compositions and an estimate of his genius will be found in *Grove's Dictionary*. He is also given substantial notices in the *Enciclopedia dello spettacolo* and the *Encyclopaedia Britannica*.

Numerous engravings and lithographs of Gluck are in the collections of the Hoftheater at the Hofburg, Vienna, and the Civica Raccolta delle Stampe Achille Bertarelli, Castello Sforzesco, Milan. Among them are engravings after J. Duplessis (who did several portraits of Gluck) by Artaria, Groh, Landon, Niger, Rohrbach, Sichling, and Walther. Other portrait engravings include those by Hoffman, Loeschenkohl, Saint Aubin (after Krafft), and Sasso (after Demarchi). A marble bust of Gluck by Jean Antoine Houdon is at the Paris Opéra. A terracotta bust by Houdon is at the Royal College of Music, London, and a terracotta bust by Francis (son-in-law of Houdon) is at the Royal Academy of Music, London. An engraving of the Houdon bust was done by Quenedey.

Glynne, Mary [fl. 1670–1673], actress?

The London Stage lists Mary Glynne as a member of the King's Company from 1670–71 through 1672–73. Warrants in the Lord Chamberlain's accounts dated 3 March 1671, 31 July 1671, and 3 July 1673 cited her but gave no indication of her function in the troupe. Perhaps she was a minor actress.

Goadby, Mr [fl. 1734], actor.

On 4 and 5 November 1734 at the Great Room at the Ship Tavern Mr Goadby acted Zama in *Tamerlane*.

Goble, Mr [fl. 1708], house servant.

In the Coke papers at Harvard is a salary schedule dated 8 March 1708 for the

Queen's Theatre staff. A Mr Goble is listed among the wardrobe staff at 5s. daily. He was not a dresser, for they are listed separately, and his salary would suggest that he held a post of some importance.

Godart. See CHANNOUVEAU.

Goddard, Mr [fl. 1789], fencing master.

In the spring of 1789, according to Michael Kelly's *Reminiscences*, Mr Goddard, "a noted fencing master," in the newspapers challenged the formidable duellist Chevalier de St George to fence with him at the Pantheon. A very large crowd saw to their great surprise the Chevalier defeated by Goddard, who, it was later rumored, had achieved his unexpected victory by bribing his opponent with "a large sum of money." Goddard was described in Henry Angelo's *Reminiscences* as an Englishman, but nothing more is known about him.

Goddard, Henry d. 1725, actor.

Henry Goddard was active in the Smock Alley company in Dublin about 1707–8, one of his parts there being the Governor of Barcelona in *The Spanish Wives*. By 21 February 1716 he was in London, acting the Servant to Gonsalvo in *The Perfidious Brothers* at Lincoln's Inn Fields. On the following 3 April he was in the Mob in *The Humours of Purgatory*. At Drury Lane on 9 and 12 June 1719 he acted the Gaoler in *The Bondman*. He was doubtless active at the theatres in London throughout the 1716–1725 period, though his name was rarely mentioned in the bills; he obviously played only minor roles.

His death was reported in the *Daily Journal* of 19 July 1725: "Last week Mr. Henry Norris a player at the New House, son to the celebrated Comedian of that name, had a rencounter with Mr. Goddard belonging to the old Play House in which the latter was so wounded that he died in two days after. Mr. Norris who is also much

wounded is gone, as we hear, for Ireland." Norris surrendered, was tried on 31 August, and was burned on the hand as punishment for manslaughter. The report described Goddard as an inferior player or servant at Drury Lane.

Goddard, Sophia Ann 1776–1801, actress, dancer.

Miss Sophia Ann Goddard, born in 1776, made her first stage appearance at Margate in July 1797. In August 1797 the *Monthly Mirror* reported from Margate that "A Miss Goddard, about whom the papers have been very busy, has played several characters with some promise; but her friends have certainly over-rated her talents." Announced as from Margate, she made her first appearance in London as Letitia Hardy in *The Belle's Stratagem* at Drury Lane Theatre on 10 November 1797, at which time the *Monthly Mirror* pronounced that "This young lady has fallen sacrifice to the art of puffing. She has been placed at the head of the school before she has imbibed the rudiments of knowledge." In the judgment of that journal, her talents were "not of a primary nature." Evidently the management of Drury Lane agreed, for her next performance of Letitia Hardy, on 14 November 1797, was her last appearance in a London theatre.

In December of 1798, Miss Goddard joined the theatre at Norwich, where she became a popular favorite. Her acting of Portia in *The Merchant of Venice* was well received. As Jane Shore, according to the *Norwich Mercury* of 12 January 1799, she performed "to greater advantage than we ever remember to have seen her. The last scene was given to such effect that she loses nothing by comparison with Mrs. Siddons, whom we recollect in the same character." Miss Goddard was also reported to have been a particularly graceful dancer.

After 16 months at Norwich and on the East Anglia circuit, Miss Goddard died of consumption on 15 March 1801, at the age

Courtesy of Alick Williams

SOPHIA ANN GODDARD

artist unknown

of 25. At the time of her death she was engaged to John Yallop, who later was knighted for his services as sheriff and mayor of Norwich. She was buried on 20 March in the Bolingbroke family tomb in the churchyard of St Peter Mancroft, Norwich, where the burial register identified her as a single woman, from the parish of St Stephen, and the daughter of Florimond and Sophia Goddard. The following inscription graced her tombstone.

This Stone is dedicated to the Talents and Virtues of SOPHIA ANN GODDARD, who died March 15th, 1801, aged 25.

> The former shone with superior
> Lustre and Effect
> in the great school of Morals,
> THE THEATRE
> while the latter
> Inform'd the private Circle of Life
> with Sentiment, Taste and Manners
> that still live on in the memory
> Of Friendship and Affection.

Her obituary in the *Gentleman's Magazine* of March 1801 reported that at Norwich she had much improved as an actress and had it not been for her untimely death she would have made her way to the London stage again, for she promised to succeed in a line of characters sustained by Elizabeth Farren. "Her figure was elegant, her understanding excellent, her manners were amiable," claimed the March *Monthly Mirror*, "and her character, in all respects, was highly meritorious."

A small portrait of Miss Goddard by an unknown artist was reproduced in a publication of the Church of St Peter Mancroft in the 1950s. The present location of the portrait, which perhaps at one time belonged to the Bolingbroke family, is unknown to us.

Godfrey, Mrs [*fl.* 1741], *housekeeper.*

The Covent Garden accounts show a payment of £5 11s. on 6 January 1741 to "Mrs. Godfrey, in full of her bill, for looking after the House, etc."

Godfrey, Lewis [*fl.* 1794], *singer?*

Doane's *Musical Directory* of 1794 listed Lewis Godfrey of Brick Lane, Bethnal Green, as a bass (singer, probably, though he may have been a bass viol player) who participated in the oratorio performances at Drury Lane.

Godfrey, William *d. 1785, organist.*

William Godfrey was one of the original subscribers to the Royal Society of Musicians when it was formed on 28 August 1739. *Mortimer's London Directory* of 1763 described him as an organist from Lambeth. On 6 February 1785 the Society received word that Godfrey had died, and John Hall (possibly an undertaker) was given £3 for the musician's funeral expenses.

Godwin. *See also* **GOODWIN.**

Godwin, Mr *[fl. 1702–1709], dancer, dancing master*

Mr Godwin (or Goodwin) danced an Irish Trot at Drury Lane on 20 August 1702. On 11 June 1703 he and Mrs Clark danced at a benefit concert for Mrs Boman at Lincoln's Inn Fields, and three days later at the same playhouse Godwin offered a *Venetian Dance* and a new *Whim*. He appeared at Lincoln's Inn Fields again on 23 March 1704 and at the Queen's Theatre in the Haymarket on 17 January 1706. A concert was held at Godwin's dancing school on 21 November 1709, and it is likely that there were other events there, records of which have not yet been found.

Godwin, Mr *[fl. 1726–1727], house servant?*

A Mr Godwin is mentioned in the Lincoln's Inn Fields account books in 1726–27. He was apparently one of the house servants.

Godwin, Mr *[fl. 1733–1749], puppeteer, booth operator, actor.*

Mr Godwin and Mr Plat gave puppet performances in Norwich in 1733–34, and Godwin, apparently alone, was a puppeteer in Canterbury in 1739. On 25 August 1742 at Bartholomew Fair Godwin had a booth opposite the White Hart, near Cow Lane in West Smithfield at which was performed (with puppets?) *The Intriguing Footman.* The following 31 January 1743 he had a theatrical booth in Tyburn Road opposite Duke Street, Grosvenor Square, where, according to an advertisement, every evening for a week he presented a play by waxwork figures four feet tall. The performance consisted of *Princess Elizabeth, or Rise of Judge Punch* and *The Honest Yorkshireman.*

With Adam he managed a booth at Bartholomew Fair on 23 August 1743, presenting *The Triumphant Queen of Hungary* and *The Wanton Maid* — with live actors. At May Fair on 1 May 1744 at Hal-

lam's new theatre adjoining the market place Godwin played Timothy and Mrs Godwin Leonora in *The Royal Hero*; two days later he acted Hostess Quickly and Mrs Godwin played Anglaura in a droll on Falstaff called *The Captive Prince.* With Reynolds he may have operated a booth at Bartholomew Fair in August 1747, though *The London Stage* does not record it. He had a booth at Southwark Fair on 10 September 1747 at which he presented *The Cheats of Scapin* (with puppets or live actors?). The last notice of him was dated 23 August 1749, when he and Harris operated a booth at Bartholomew Fair; they presented *The Intriguing Footman* and *Trick Upon Trick* "With the Escapes of Harlequin into a Quart Bottle" — capitalizing on the prank of the famous bottle conjurer, who drew a crowd and failed to appear at the Haymarket on 16 January 1749.

Godwin, Mrs *[fl. 1744], actress. See* **GODWIN, MR** *[fl. 1733–1749].*

Godwin, Mrs *[fl. 1758–1771], actress, singer, dancer.*

Mrs Godwin was one of the Lilliputian dancers in a production of *The Tempest* at the Smock Alley Theatre in Dublin on 11 January 1758. The following 21 April she played Lady Faulconbridge in *King John.* A Mr Godwin, doubtless related, was also at Smock Alley at the time. Mrs Godwin performed at Cork on 8 August and 4 October (and probably other dates in between); then, back at Smock Alley, she was Mrs Coaxer in *The Beggar's Opera* on 17 October and a dancing witch in Macbeth on 31 October.

She made her first London appearance on 26 September 1764 playing Lady Percy in *1 Henry IV* at Covent Garden. She acted Iris in *All for Love* on 11 April 1765 and Lady Scrape in *The Musical Lady* on 24 April. Her benefit tickets were accepted on 9 May. Mrs Godwin continued at Covent Garden for two more seasons, though the only new role for which she received billing was Isabella in *All in the Right* on 26 April 1766. In the summer of that year she performed at Richmond. The last notice of her was on 2 March 1771, when she played Gertrude in *Hamlet* at the new theatre at the Unicorn in Stratford-upon-Avon. The company there, led by Booth, performed 11 other plays in which Mrs Godwin doubtless participated.

Godwin, John d. *1707, singer.*

John Godwin, who was buried on 7 August 1707 in the South Cloister of Westminster Abbey, had been "one of the children of the Choir" in the Chapel Royal. If his name was misspelled in the Abbey registers, perhaps he was a son of John Goodwin, a member of the King's Musick who died in 1693.

Godwin, Joseph [fl. 1702], *mountebank.*

Joseph Godwin (or Godwyn) and five other mountebanks were cited in the *Post Man* of 3 October 1702 as being required to pay 2s. per day to town constables, a fee charged all strolling players. Godwin had probably been performing in London, since the newspaper notice was published there.

Goff. *See* GOUGH.

Gold. *See also* GOULD.

Gold, Mr [fl. 1744], *actor.*

At May Fair on 1 May 1744 a Mr Gold played Colonel Britain in a droll called *The Royal Hero* at Hallam's new theatre adjoining the market place.

Gold, Margaret [fl. 1729], *actress.*

As a member of the Lilliputian Company at the Lincoln's Inn Fields Theatre, young Margaret Gold played Jenny Diver in *The Beggar's Opera* on 1 January 1729.

Golden, Ruben [fl. 1672], *musician.*

Ruben Golden and four others musicians were ordered on 15 July 1672 to be apprehended for practicing music without a license.

Goldfinch, Mr [fl. 1786–1837], *actor, singer, manager.*

A Mr Goldfinch sang at Sadler's Wells in the summers of 1786 and 1787. He was probably the Goldfinch who labored as a provincial performer and manager for many years. With his wife and two young daughters Goldfinch sang at Bury from 4 November to 21 December 1796. The *Monthly Mirror* of November 1798 identified Goldfinch as the "comic and vocal hero" of Stanton's company at Lancaster. In that year Goldfinch opened a temporary theatre at Caton, near Lancaster, where, according to the *Monthly Mirror* report, the people were generous and he "closed with a snug contribution towards the support of a winter campaign." At Lancaster, the Goldfinch family "made up the comic department" of Stanton's company.

By 1826 Goldfinch was residing at Hull. In October 1837 the *Gentleman's Magazine* mentioned that he was "now or very lately living at an advanced age in Hull."

Goldfinch's daughter Louisa married the Scottish manager Corbet Ryder (d. 1839) and also performed in the northern counties. Another daughter, probably the Miss C. Goldfinch who was with the family at Bury in 1796, married the Yorkshire actor O'Callaghan; she died at the age of 31 at Headingley, near Leeds, on 8 August 1826.

Goldie, Mrs [fl. 1771], *actress.*

On 28 January 1771 at the Haymarket Theatre a Mrs Goldie played Lucilla in *The Fair Penitent.*

Golding, Daniel [fl. 1681–1682], *housekeeper.*

Daniel Golding was the housekeeper for the King's Company at the Drury Lane Theatre in 1681 and 1682. On 23 February 1681 he was named in a suit concerning

King's Company profits, and on 22 May 1682 he was involved in a suit over the troupe's costumes. The actor Philip Griffin had been taking costumes away from the playhouse for his own use, and Golding was the carrier of a letter to Griffin insisting that he bring the costumes back. When Griffin refused, Golding, on orders, locked up Drury Lane to force Griffin to return the clothes.

Golding also testified that the King's Company was in financial trouble; £400 was owed to four tradesmen, and Charles Killigrew was at law with one of the sharers, Mr Kent. Golding said, however, that the disagreements were not responsible for the dissolution of the company.

Goldsmith, Miss [fl. 1777–1778], *house servant?*

The Drury Lane accounts on 1 November 1777 and 15 June 1778 cited a Miss Goldsmith, possibly one of the house servants. Her salary was 2s., apparently daily.

Gom, Mr [fl. 1759–1760], *housekeeper?*

The Covent Garden accounts mentioned a Mr Gom frequently during 1759–60. He seems to have been the theatre housekeeper, for most payments to him were large amounts designated for the scenemen or others working under Gom. On 5 October 1759, for example, Gom was paid £6 9s. 3d. for the scenemen; on the nineteenth he received £9 4s. 2d. for the carpenters; on the following day he was paid another £12 for the carpenters; on 5 January 1760 he was paid £12 1s. for the scenemen; and on 2 August 1760 he received £1 12s. 6d. for the men who cleaned the theatre after the season was over.

In 1759–60 and in the fall of 1760 a Stephen Gom received payments: on 24 November 1759 he was paid £50 on account and described as "of Uxbridge." On 28 November another (or the same?) £50 was paid him on account; on 22 December

he was given £38 5s. to complete his bill. On 23 December 1760 £53 was paid Stephen Gom for work done since the previous 6 December 1759, apparently at Cowley. Perhaps Stephen Gom was the Mr Gom who served at the theatre, but he would appear to have been someone outside the playhouse, possibly a brother or the father of our subject, who did work for John Rich and was paid from theatre funds.

Gomery, Robert [fl. 1797–1816], *actor, singer.*

Robert Gomery played one of the Spahis in *Sadak and Kalasrade* at Sadler's Wells on 29 May 1797. That season he also appeared there as Red Beard in *Blue Beard, Black Beard, Red Beard, and Gray Beard*. In 1801–2 he was engaged at Drury Lane Theatre at a salary of about £1 per week. Gomery was in the cast of *Richard III*, the inaugural production, at the new Bath Theatre on 12 October 1805. On 17 June 1814 he made his debut at the Haymarket Theatre as Francisco in *The Tale of Mystery*, and in 1816 he was a member of the "English Opera" at the Lyceum in the Strand. Gomery's first name is found on a manuscript in the Folger Shakespeare Library.

"Gomez, Madame de." *See* **HAYWOOD, MRS VALENTINE.**

Gondeau. *See* **GONDOU.**

Gondon, [Mr?] [fl. 1747–1750], *performer?*

The Covent Garden accounts on 25 April 1747 noted that one Gondon (or is this Mrs Gondou?) was off for the rest of the season. On 29 September 1749 Gondon, who was being paid 3s. 8d. daily, was to be off after 21 April 1750.

Gondorff, Charles [fl. 1768], *singer.*

At the Haymarket Theatre on 28 April

1768 playgoers were entertained with singing by a Hungarian named Charles Gondorff. The puff said, "he mimicks three voices one and the same time, to wit the natural sound of the Base, the Bassoon and the Flagolet (the latter has the sound of a small organ) all which is performed without the least movement of the lips."

Gondou, Mrs *[fl. 1743–1757]*, *dancer.*

Mrs Gondou (or Gondeau) danced in *Les Amant volages* in *The Dragon of Wantley* at Drury Lane on 4 February 1743. On the following 11 February she was in *Comus*, and on 4 May, when her benefit tickets were accepted, she danced *A French Peasant* with Froment. An anonymous actor in the company that season commented that the troupe's dancers were "great performers but in bad taste and without grace." Mrs Gondou did not return to Drury Lane the following season.

From 1744–45 through 1756–57 she danced at Covent Garden, sharing benefits each spring, usually with two others but once with seven. Some seasons her name was not mentioned in the bills, though she was doubtless busy in the dancing chorus, working obscurely. Some of her advertised assignments over the years included a Country Lass in *Orpheus and Eurydice*; Earth, a Country Lass, and the Fifth Follower in *The Rape of Proserpine*; a Grace in *The Loves of Mars and Venus*; a Follower and a Spanish Woman in *Apollo and Daphne*; an Aerial Spirit in *Merlin's Cave*, and a Scaramouch Woman in *The Necromancer*. She also appeared in such specialty dances as *Peasant*, *The Muses Looking Glass*, *The Mouse Trap*, and a *New Masque*. On occasion she danced a minuet with Rector. Her salary in 1746–47 was 10s. weekly. After her shared benefit on 19 May 1757 Mrs Gondou seems to have left the London stage.

Perhaps related to Mrs Gondou was Leon Gondou, who on 26 May 1742 at the Por-

tuguese Embassy Chapel witnessed the marriage of John Perrault and Marie Jean du Valle.

Gooch, William *d. 1678, musician.*

According to his will, William Gooch was a citizen and "musitian of London." He wrote his will on 11 January 1678, adding a codicil the following day. To his cousin Margaret, the wife of Peter Watts, he left 50s.; to Sarah Taylor he left 10s.; he forgave Thomas Taylor a debt of 20s.; to the poor of St Katharine Cree he gave 20 dozen loaves of bread, at 12d. per dozen, to be distributed yearly on 24 June for three years; and he left 20s. to the poor of "St Margarett's Iffetshall" in Suffolk (which must be an error for Tivetshall St Margaret, which is in Norfolk). The rest of his estate Gooch left to his brother and executor, John Gooch of Barnard's Inn. The will was proved on 10 February 1678.

Gooch, Mrs William, Elizabeth Sarah, née Villa Real *[fl. 1775–1796?]*, *actress.*

The parish registers of St George, Hanover Square, contain the marriage record on 13 May 1775 of William Gooch, Esq, of Bath, and Elizabeth Sarah Villa Real of St George's, a minor who married with the consent of her mother, Elizabeth Hutchinson. A playbill at Harvard from "Scarbro" dated 24 July 1794 lists Miss Spinster in *Every One Has His Fault* as played by a Miss Gooch, who was noted as making her first appearance on that stage. It seems possible that Mrs Gooch was the actress in question; if so, she apparently had been performing elsewhere before that date. In January 1796 Mrs William Gooch was granted a license to act at the Haymarket Theatre (a warrant in the Public Record Office spelled the name "Goortz"). On 22 February Mrs Gooch appeared at that playhouse as Almeria in *The Mourning Bride* and Lady Minikin in *Bon Ton*, after which

ELIZABETH SARAH GOOCH

artist unknown

she seems to have disappeared from the London stage.

In the Harvard Theatre Collection is an engraved portrait captioned "Mrs Gooch." The print is cropped, and the artist and engraver are not mentioned. The Hall catalogue does not list the engraving. The pictured woman is, presumably, Mrs William Gooch.

Good, Mr [fl. 1703–1705?], singer.

Mr Good sang with Mason at Drury Lane on 27 December 1703. They sang again on 11 and 17 January 1704, and Good sang alone on 30 March. The late Dr Emmett Avery thought that Good may have sung the part of Delbo in Arsinoe at Drury Lane on 16 January 1705, though the printed edition of the work lists Mr Cook.

Good, Mrs [fl. 1742]. See GOULD, GRACE.

Goodall, Mr [fl. 1734], actor.

A Mr Goodall acted the role of Jack in The Lottery at the Haymarket Theatre on 7 June 1734.

Goodall, Mr [fl. 1741–1751], actor, house servant?

A Mr Goodall acted minor roles at Covent Garden Theatre from 1741–42 through 1750–51. His name first appeared in the bills on 16 October 1741 for Silvius in As You Like It, a role he continued to play whenever that work was revived over the ensuing decade. In 1741–42 he also acted Cleomines in The Winter's Tale on 11 November, Verdugo in The Pilgrim on 22 December, Cabinet in The Funeral on 8 February 1742, and Sancho in Love Makes a Man on 3 May, when he shared a benefit with Mr and Mrs James. His other roles at Covent Garden included Robert in The Mock Doctor on 31 October 1743, Cromwell in Henry VIII on 24 January 1744, the Dauphin in Henry V on 19 April 1744, Trippet in The Lying Valet on 25 April 1744, Solarino in The Merchant of Venice on 26 April 1744, and Sir John in The Country Lasses on 22 April 1746.

After 1743–44, Goodall seems to have filled supernumerary roles, for his name appeared very infrequently in the bills, and perhaps he also worked as a house servant. On 26 April 1744, 27 April 1750, and 4 May 1751, he shared benefit tickets with other minor performers and house personnel.

On 25 April 1748, Goodall was given a benefit at the Haymarket Theatre, at which time The False Friend and The Humours of Purgatory were performed, but the cast lists are unknown. The Master Goodall who danced at Drury Lane Theatre on 5 May 1761 may have been his son.

Goodall, Master *fl. 1761*, *dancer*.

A Master Goodall appeared with Master Settree and Miss Blagden in a masquerade dance at Drury Lane Theatre on 5 May 1761. Perhaps he was the son of Mr Goodall (fl. 1741–1751), an actor at Covent Garden.

Goodall, Mrs Thomas, Charlotte, née Stanton *1765–1830, actress, singer*.

Charlotte Stanton Goodall was born in 1765 to Samuel Stanton (d. 1797), a theatrical manager in the Midlands, and his first wife Elizabeth. In describing Samuel Stanton's group of strollers, the 1790 edition of *The Secret History of the Green Room* gave a tolerable description of a typical country sharing company of the latter part of the century:

The *Manager*, out of the money taken at the doors, play-bills, candles, &c., being first paid, divides the overplus equally among all the performers; excepting that the Manager is allowed four shares for the Scenery and Dresses, one share for his Trouble in superintending the Stage, one for his services as an Actor, and another for his wife; and as he is an absolute Monarch, as soon as his children can lisp out a few words, he sends them on the boards, and takes a share for each of them. The expense of Scenery and dresses, and the deficiencies of bad houses, he throws into a fund called the stock debt; and if he is an adept, he takes good care, the sum may always be large; so that when the company is successful, he is sure to pay it off.

Stanton had by these methods "amassed a tolerable fortune" and purchased much property in Staffordshire. It was in that milieu that Charlotte, her brothers Charles and John, and at least two sisters (one of whom, Elizabeth, became the first Mrs John Nunns and the other perhaps the first Mrs

George Bartley) grew up. Apparently Charlotte and her siblings performed almost from infancy.

According to *The Secret History*, Charlotte's father thought his own company too humble for her burgeoning talents and so persuaded Palmer of Bath to allow her to try out. In her first role at Bath, Rosalind in *As You Like It* on 17 April 1784, she pleased Palmer so greatly that he offered her a permanent engagement. She remained at Bath and Bristol (where she first played in May 1784) for four years, becoming a favorite especially in "breeches" parts because of her fine figure but also successfully essaying a variety of other roles, including Lady Teazle in *The School for Scandal*, Miss Hardcastle in *She Stoops to Conquer*, Mrs Page in *The Merry Wives of Windsor*, and Juliet in *Romeo and Juliet*.

In 1787 at Newcastle Charlotte married Thomas Goodall (1767–1832?) of Bristol, an adventurer and an officer in the mer-

Harvard Theatre Collection

CHARLOTTE GOODALL

artist unknown

chant marine who was also an amateur playwright. His comedy *The Counterplot* was produced at Bath about 1787.

The Secret History later retailed (but deprecated) the gossip that she had contended with Mrs Simpson at Bath over the part of Desdemona and had departed the company in a huff when Palmer decided against her. By puffing her in the papers and by the exertion of some unspecified pressures on John Philip Kemble—the rumour further ran—Stanton and Goodall had forced her acceptance at Drury Lane at £4 or £5 per week. Very likely there had been puffing—a standard practice—but she seems to have had abilities easily sufficient for the company she was entering, even though it did contain Miss Farren, Mrs Jordan, and Mrs Siddons. Kemble said of her first appearance, as Rosalind on 2 October 1788, "She is a fine woman, and was favorably received by the audience." Her pay was actually £6 per week and was raised to £7 in 1789–90. She was steadily employed at Drury Lane for the rest of the 1788–89 season, though her refusal to play Lady Anne in *Richard III* and other parts she considered below or aside from her line led to a quarrel with Kemble which was aired in the newspapers. On 30 July 1789 she made her first bow at the Haymarket, showing off the "beautiful symmetry of her person" in the breeches of Sir Harry Wildair in *The Constant Couple*. She also, on 7 July, went to Brighton to help open that theatre.

Mrs Goodall played at Drury Lane in the winters and the Haymarket in the summers every year through the summer of 1793. In the fall of 1794, the Drury Lane company being temporarily disbanded to await the completion of the new theatres she with others joined Colman at the Haymarket house for the winter season, returning briefly to help open the new Drury Lane in April. She was again at the Haymarket for the 1794 summer season, but on 20 October 1794 (according to an unattributed press clipping in the Enthoven Collection) she was said to have been discharged from the Haymarket. But she remained on display at Drury Lane through 1797–98, still drawing £7 per week. The *Monthly Mirror* for July 1798 reported that she had "left the stage" and lamented, "as the theatres are at present, she is an actress that cannot well be spared." On 19 May 1803 "after an absence of 5 years from the profession," according to a notation in the O. Smith collection in the British Museum, she returned to the Haymarket stage as Floranthe in *The Mountaineers*, but after a short run her name disappeared permanently from the bills.

Mrs Goodall evidently had more beauty than talent and more charm than beauty. But she had enough of all three to remain on the stage and hold onto some of the

Harvard Theatre Collection

CHARLOTTE GOODALL, as Sir Harry Wildair

engraving by Leney, after De Wilde

juiciest comedy roles for over a decade. Yet she was invariably placed second to Miss Farren and Mrs Jordan in their respective lines, which also happened to embrace some of her best roles. John Williams exercised his wit on her in *A Pin Basket to the Children of Thespis* (1797): "She is to Miss FARREN what GREY is to PITT— / Each would copy the whole, yet can shew but a bit." Her critics usually emphasized her beauty as did Thomas Bellamy in *The London Theatres* (1796): "a figure as graceful as ever was form'd"; and F. G. Waldron in his *Candid and Impartial Strictures* (1795): "This lady's person is remarkably well proportioned, but shewn we think to the best advantage in male habiliments, in which she excels all other females since the days of Woffington." Waldron went on to say "Her voice wants strength, and has a little of the nasal tone that disgusts—Her face is pleasing and tolerably expressive, and her deportment easy, with some grace." Some, like the anonymous author of *The Druriad* (1798) accused her of lack of animation, of being "gentle, mild and tame." Said he, "she might certainly become an actress of some merit; at present she gives us the idea of a well-constructed automaton." But William Hazlitt looked back over more than thirty years to her Rosalind, which "still haunts the glades of Arden."

Besides Rosalind, her first character, and one which she played throughout her career, Mrs Goodall acquired the following parts: Flora in *She Wou'd and She Wou'd Not*, Lady Emily in *The Heiress*, Charlotte Rusport in *The West Indian*, Clarinda in *The Double Gallant*, Marcella in *The Pannel*, Jacintha in *The Suspicious Husband*, Mrs Sullen in *The Stratagem*, both Angelica and Mrs Foresight in *Love for Love*, Millamant in *The Way of the World*, Viola in *Twelfth Night*, Lady Trifle in *Divorce*, both Clarissa and Araminta in *The Confederacy*, Adeline in *The Battle of Hexham*, Maria in *The Citizen*, Lady Townly in *The*

Provok'd Husband, Hyppolito in *The Tempest*, both Lady Minikin and Miss Titup in *Bon Ton*, Isabella in *The False Friend*, Charlotte Weldon in *Oroonoko*, Oriana in *The Inconstant*, Julia in *The Two Gentlemen of Verona*, Emily in *The Deuce is in Him*, the Countess in *The Follies of a Day*, Florinda in *Tit for Tat*, Letitia Hardy in *The Belle's Stratagem*, Bella in *The Runaway*, Nancy Lovell in *The Suicide*, Catherine in *Catherine and Petruchio*, Mrs Flurry in *Better Late than Never*, Widow Bellmour in *The Way to Keep Him*, Lydia Languish in *The Rivals*, Olivia in *The Irishman in Spain*, Mrs Cadwallader in *The Author*, Thalia in *Poor Old Drury!!*, Fatima in *Cymon,* the Widow Brady in *The Irish Widow*, Maria Sydney in *Cross Partners*, Alcmena in *The Two Sosias*, Angelina in *Love Makes a Man*, Miss Julia Wingrove in *The Fugitive*, Mrs Sneak in *The Mayor of Garratt*, Cecilia in *The Chapter of Accidents*, Violante in *The Wonder*, Miranda in *The Busy Body*, Laetitia Rayner in *The Box-Lobby Challenge*, Lady Harriet in *I'll Tell You What*, Eliza Ratcliffe in *The Jew*, Donna Violante in *The Purse*, Lady Sneerwell in *The School for Scandal*, Nerissa in *The Merchant of Venice*, the Marchioness Merida in *The Child of Nature*, Mrs Harlow in *The Old Maid*, Mrs Woodville in *The Wheel of Fortune*, Alithea in *The Country Girl*, Amanda in *A Trip to Scarborough*, Belinda in *All in the Wrong*, and Marianna in *Measure for Measure*.

Mrs Goodall's range was not wide. It was almost exclusively the territory bordered by broad farce on the one hand and sentimental comedy on the other. She was not amiss in delivering the brittle wit of Sheridan, and once or twice she approached the borders of melodrama, as when she gave the first representation of the Countess Wintersen in Benjamin Thompson's *The Stranger*. But generally she preferred, and her audiences preferred her in, jilts and flirts, hoydens and fun-loving country girls, softly pliable but humorous heroines, and fashionable ladies. She avoided tragedy and pantomime with equal determination.

Charlotte Goodall's husband Thomas evidently personally furnished the highly romantic account of his career which was printed in the *European Magazine* for May 1808 and which was the basis for the entry written by John Knox Laughton in *The Dictionary of National Biography*. Though probably exaggerated, as Laughton surmises, the main outlines which emerge of the "Admiral of Hayti," as Goodall styled himself after participating in the Haitian revolt of the rebel Christophe, can be confirmed. Successively naval cadet, merchant-adventurer, privateer, and mercenary, he was twice captured and twice escaped after naval engagements with the French. He and Charlotte had eight children together. Three of them were christened at St Paul, Covent Garden: "Elizabeth Daug^r: of Thomas Goodall by Charlotta his Wife" on 23 January 1792, "Thomas Symons Son of Thomas Goodall by Charlotte his Wife Born 27: May: 1793" on 22 June 1793, and "William Goodall of Thomas, & Charlotte," born 1 March and baptized 22 March 1797.

Goodall was away from home and out of England for long periods of time from 1790 to 1801 and from 1805 until 1808 and again between 1808 and 1812. He claimed to have remitted to his agent and attorney in England, one William Fletcher, £120,000. Fletcher was not only untrue to his trust in the matter of the money (which was probably a considerably smaller amount than Goodall asserted), but he also took advantage of his friend's frequent absences to make Charlotte his mistress. After a sensational trial on 19 July 1813 a jury awarded Goodall £5000 damages.

Charlotte Goodall died in Somers Town, London, in July 1830. An undated clipping in the British Museum states that she had been supported in her widowhood "by her son, a portrait painter of considerable tal-

ent. She has likewise left behind her a daughter, who keeps a school in the neighbourhood of London, and an elder son, who holds an important office in the Government at Montserrat."

It is probable that the Miss Goodall who sang and acted at the King's Theatre in the spring of 1818 on programs sponsored by the New Musical Fund was Mrs Thomas Goodall's daughter.

Portraits of Charlotte Goodall include:

1. By G. Hayter, painting. Present location unknown. Engraving by Hawkins, published by Bellamy and Roberts, 1789.

2. By an unknown artist, watercolor portrait. In the Harvard Theatre Collection.

3. Engraved portrait by W. Ridley. Published as a plate to Parsons's *Minor Theatre*, 1794.

4. As Adelaide in *The Battle of Hexham*. Engraving by R. Laurie. Published by R. Sayer, 1789.

5. As Frederick in *Lovers' Vows* (?). Painting by John Hoppner. At Kenwood (Iveagh Bequest). Some confusion surrounds this picture. It has been taken to be a portrait of Dorothy Jordan as Rosalind in *As You Like It*, and it was shown as such in "The Georgian Playhouse" exhibition at the Hayward Gallery in 1975. An engraving by H. Cook, titled "Lady in Character," was published by the engraver in 1832. A pencil notation on a proof copy at the British Museum identified the subject as Mrs Goodall as Frederick. Most expert opinion, however, supports the identification as Mrs Jordan.

6. As Sir Harry Wildair in *The Constant Couple*. Painting by De Wilde. In the Garrick Club. Engraving by W. Leney for *Bell's British Theatre*. An anonymous engraving was published as a plate to *British Drama* in 1817.

Goodchild, Thomas [*fl.* 1794], *bass player.*

Doane's *Musical Directory* of 1794 listed Thomas Goodchild of No 252, Fooley

Street, as a double bass player who performed at concerts sponsored by the Choral Fund.

Goode, Mr [*fl. 1708*], *gallery keeper.*
Mr Goode was one of the two gallery keepers at the Queen's Theatre in the Haymarket in 1708. On 8 March of that year, according to the Coke papers at Harvard, Goode was receiving a daily wage of 2s. 8d.

Goode, Mr [*fl. 1760–1761*], *door-keeper.*
The Covent Garden accounts on 22 September 1760 cited Mr Goode as one of the lobby doorkeepers. His daily salary was 2s. He was still working at the theatre in 1761.

Goodfellow, J. *1722–1759, actor, singer, prompter.*
On 29 June 1744 at the Haymarket Theatre Hamlet was played by a "young Gentleman, his first attempt on any stage." The new actor was J. Goodfellow, who inspired a writer to the *Daily Advertiser* of 10 July to say that "if ever a Man was born a Player, this is he." The writer said Goodfellow had a "happy musical voice" and a "natural Easiness of Action" that was remarkable for a man of 22 just beginning his career. The author of the letter signed himself "H. Buskins" and may, for all we know, have been Goodfellow himself or a close friend. Goodfellow performed at the Goodman's Fields playhouse in 1744–45 and lodged at Mrs Simpson's in Church Lane, near the Wells. On 27 November 1744 he played Hamlet again, then Macheath in *The Beggar's Opera* on 3 December, Richard III on 5 December, Torrismond in *The Spanish Fryar* on 31 December, Pierre in *Venice Preserv'd* for his benefit on 5 February 1745, Ferdinand in *The Tempest* on 14 February, Phocias in *The Siege of Damascus* on 12 March, Hotspur in *1 Henry IV* on 17 April, and King Lear on 2 May.

His rather spectacular first season at Goodman's Fields brought Goodfellow to

the attention of the Drury Lane management, and there he was lured for the 1745–46 season, making his first appearance on 8 October 1745 as the Ghost of Gaffer in *The Tragedy of Tragedies*. During the rest of the season he was similarly taken down several pegs by being assigned such parts as Hellebore in *The Mock Doctor*, Guildenstern in *Hamlet*, the Boxkeeper in *The Gamester*, the Lieutenant in *Lady Jane Gray*, Dick in *The Lying Valet*, the Surveyor and Campeius in *Henry VIII*, Nimming Ned in *The Beggar's Opera*, Silvius in *As You Like It*, Perkin Warbeck in *Henry VII*, Antonio in *The Tempest*, the Surgeon in *The Lady's Last Stake*, the Captain in *Twelfth Night*, and Blunt in *Henry IV*.

At the beginning of the 1746–47 season at Drury Lane he was allowed to play Gratiano in *Othello*, a Committeeman in *The Committee*, Stratocles in *Tamerlane*, and the Doctor in *Macbeth*, but Richard III was the only important old role he was able to act at Drury Lane, and the arrival at Drury Lane in 1746–47 of Spranger Barry effectively blocked Goodfellow from the kind of leading parts he had acted at Goodman's Fields.

Consequently, he returned to Goodman's Fields on 3 December 1746 as Hamlet. During the remainder of the season his old roles were restored to him and he was seen in a few new ones: Chamont in *The Orphan*, Myrtle in *The Conscious Lovers*, Macbeth, Tancred in *Tancred and Sigismunda*, Hardy in *The Funeral*, Biron in *The Fatal Marriage*, and Felix in *The Wonder*. But on 7 April 1747, when he played Hamlet for his benefit, he announced that his "Friends have always express'd a very great dislike of his belonging to the Stage, [so] he has Resolv'd upon taking this Benefit, to enable him to return to his former Employment." He had, he stated, been indisposed of late and promised his followers not to "trouble them in this sort" any more.

Within a few years Goodfellow had second thoughts. On 6 August 1751 at the New Wells, Lemon Street, he returned to the stage to act Richard III for his benefit. He was back again on 5 September to play Othello (for that night only) for Mrs Hallam's benefit. Those reappearances were designed to keep the wolves from his door, as a notice in the *General Advertiser* on 11 January 1752 made clear:

Mr Goodfellow begs leave to acquaint his friends that through the indisposition of two of his principal performers he is compelled to postpone his Benefit to a farther Day; Timely notice of which shall be given in this paper; Tickets deliver'd out for Monday the 13th Instant will then be admitted.—As the sole intent of this Benefit is to satisfy his creditors, who are to share the profits arising from it, he humbly hopes to meet with encouragement, and assures those ladies and Gentlemen who honour him, that the whole performance shall be carried on with the utmost decorum, and will be free from all danger of interruption.

The London Stage prints that notice as though Goodfellow planned his benefit for Drury Lane, but that was not the case; he apparently hoped to act at the New Wells, Lemon Street, but the benefit seems not to have taken place.

Goodfellow did return to the New Wells, however, on 16 November 1752 to play Othello, and he acted Richard III on 23 November, Pierre in *Venice Preserv'd* on 28 November, and Brazen in *The Recruiting Officer* on 30 November. On 20 December he was granted a benefit at Drury Lane, at which he acted Hamlet; then he left the London stage. He acted in Dublin in 1754–55 and, according to *Faulkner's Dublin Journal* of 27 April 1756, he was given a benefit that month as the prompter at Smock Alley. He received a shared benefit on 26 July as well. On 16 March 1757 he took an unnamed part in *Macbeth*, and on 26 April 1758 – the last theatrical reference to him – Goodfellow received a benefit as the Smock Alley

prompter. The *Journal* reported on 4 September 1759 that J. Goodfellow had died in Cork on 26 August.

Goodgroome, John *d. 1704, instrumentalist, singer, composer.*

John Goodgroome was probably born in the 1620s. According to Pulver's *Biographical Dictionary*, Goodgroome was born in Windsor. He became a chorister at St George's Chapel, Windsor, and by the time Playford's *Musicall Banquet* was published in 1651 Goodgroome was a teacher of "Voyce or Viole." At the Restoration he became a member of the Chapel Royal in London, replacing Thomas Purcell. On 20 August 1664 he succeeded to the elder Henry Purcell's post in the private music for lutes, viols, and voices; he also replaced Purcell as one of the composers for violins. Goodgroome's wages were £40 yearly, plus a livery allowance of £16 2s. 6d. A note in the Lord Chamberlain's accounts dated 14 April 1669 stated that Goodgroome should receive £80 12s. 6d. in livery allowances due the deceased Purcell for the years 1664 through 1668 as well as Goodgroome's own livery. But by 1670 Goodgroome still had not received payments from 1664 to 1670.

In May, June, and July 1671 he attended the King at Windsor for a fee of 8s. daily (apparently paid on time), and on 14 April 1674 he was listed as one of the countertenors waiting upon Charles II at the Chapel in Windsor. He served at Windsor again from 1 July to 11 September 1675 for 6s. daily. When James II ascended the throne he tried to pay some of his late brother's debts; on 25 February 1686 Goodgroome was cited as not having received livery payments for 1664–1667, 1670, and 1676–1684. The following 21 September he was to be paid £225 15s. Goodgroome was reappointed to the Chapel Royal under William and Mary in 1689 and continued to serve until his death on 27 June 1704.

John Goodgroome was probably the brother of Theodore Goodgroome, who taught Mrs Pepys singing, much to Samuel's dissatisfaction. The John Goodgroome who was organist at St Peter, Cornhill, about 1725 may have been our subject's son. Theodore and the younger John Goodgroome seem not to have been public performers. The elder John composed some songs which appeared in *The Treasury of Music* in 1669 and in *The Musical Companion* in 1672.

Goodgroome, William ₁*fl. 1674–1703*₁, *singer.*

William Goodgroome was one of the boy singers in the Chapel Royal who accompanied the King to Windsor from 18 May to 3 September 1674 for a salary of 3*s.* daily. With them was their master, John Blow. Young William again attended the King at Windsor in August and September 1678, after which his voice must have changed, for the Lord Chamberlain's accounts make no further mention of him. But the parish registers of St Dionis Backchurch contain three entries relating to him: on 5 May 1701 William and Anne "Goodgrome" baptized a daughter Anne; she was born on 20 April, and the burial registers show that she was buried on 7 May. Goodgroome was identified as a music master and a lodger at Dr Hicks's house. On 1 December 1703, however, Goodgroome was cited as a landlord: one John Vanomme, late a lodger at William Goodgroome's, was buried in the church.

Gooding, Mr ₁*fl. 1799–1800*₁, *house servant?*

On 3 July 1799 and 14 June 1800 benefit tickets of Mr Gooding—one of the house servants, perhaps—were accepted at Drury Lane.

Goodman, Mr ₁*fl. 1748*₁, *actor.*

At Phillips's booth at Southwark Fair on 7 September 1748 a Mr Goodman played Prospero in *The Tempest*, "taken" from Shakespeare. The following 10 October Goodman held a benefit for himself at the New Theatre, Bowling Green, Southwark; he played Lord Townly in *The Provok'd Husband* and Flash in *Miss in Her Teens.*

Goodman, Mr ₁*fl. 1782*₁, *actor.*

Mr Goodman acted a role in *The Taylors* at the Haymarket Theatre on 25 November 1782. Possibly he should be identified as the dancer Goodman who was active in London from 1789 onward.

Goodman, Mr ₁*fl. 1789–1819*₁, *dancer, actor.*

The Mr Goodman who was in the pantomime *I Don't Know What!* at the Royal Circus on 12 May 1789 may have been the actor Goodman who performed in 1782–83, but we take him to have been a different person. Our subject had a principal role in *Meadea's Kettle, or Harlequin Renovated* at Sadler's Wells on 9 April 1792 and was a Robber in *La Forêt Noire* at the Wells that same year. His association with the Wells continued during the summers through 1800, some of his parts being a French Officer in *The Honours of War*, a Sailor in *Sans Culottes*, an Officer in *William Tell*, a Sailor in *England's Glory*, Ethelwolf in *Alfred the Great*, and Beau in *Peter Wilkins.* The *Monthly Mirror* in January 1796 reported that Goodman the dancer from Sadler's Wells was then performing at Portsmouth.

At a salary of £1 5*s.* weekly Goodman danced at Drury Lane in 1798–99. He was mentioned in the playbills occasionally: a Slave in *Blue-Beard* on 6 October 1798, a part in *The Captive of Spilburg* on 14 November, a Villager in a dance called *The Scotch Ghost* on 6 December, a Vassal in *Feudal Times* on 19 January 1799, and a Peasant in the dance *Moggy and Jemmy* on 5 February. Goodman was seldom elevated to solo parts, though on 22 December 1800, for example, he danced Pantaloon in

Harlequin Amulet. Most of the time he was just a member of the dancing chorus. By 1806 he was earning £1 10*s.* weekly, but by 1811 he had dropped back to £1 5*s.* He continued at Drury Lane through the 1818–19 season.

Goodman, Mrs *[fl. 1722]*, *actress.*

Percy Fitzgerald published an inventory of players in his *New History*, dating it 12 April 1722 and citing British Museum Additional MS 2201. A Mrs Goodman, otherwise unknown and not mentioned in *The London Stage*, was cited as a member of John Rich's troupe at Lincoln's Inn Fields.

Goodman, Miss. *See* **BURNETT, MRS** [**WILLIAM?**].

Goodman, Adam *[fl. 1739–1767]*, *bassoonist.*

On 28 August 1739 when the Royal Society of Musicians was organized, Adam Goodman became one of the original subscribers. For 8*s.* in May 1754 and on 27 April 1758 he played the bassoon in the *Messiah* at the Foundling Hospital. As of 22 September 1760 he was playing in the band at Covent Garden for a salary of 3*s.* 4*d.* daily. *Mortimer's London Directory* of 1763 listed Goodman as a maker of oboe and bassoon reeds who lived in Martlet Court, Bow Street, Covent Garden. He was still playing at Covent Garden on 14 September 1767, but his daily salary had dropped to 1*s.* 3*d.*

Goodman, [Ann?] *[fl. 1793?–1819?]*, *dancer.*

On 31 August 1795 a Mrs Goodman was a Lass in *England's Glory* at Sadler's Wells. The following day she danced in *Cupid Benighted*, and on 2 August 1796 she was seen in a comic dance called *The Apple Stealers.* Perhaps she was the female Goodman earning £1 5*s.* weekly as a dancer at Drury Lane from 1815 to 1819, and possibly she was Mrs Ann Goodman, who

was cited several times in the minute books of the Royal Society of Musicians in 1793 and 1795. Ann Goodman was the mother of a Mrs Burnett, possibly the Mrs Burnett who sang and acted at Sadler's Wells and Drury Lane during the 1770s and 1780s. Ann Goodman made a claim against the Royal Society of Musicians on 3 February 1793. Her sister, a Mrs Harris of Exeter, had left £1000 to John and James Winter in trust for Ann Goodman. After Ann's death the money was to go to Mrs Burnett.

On 1 January 1795 the Society was informed that Mrs Goodman's legacy had not been paid, and they agreed to continue giving her an allowance until she received her interest from the legacy and could repay the Society. On 6 June the Society ordered that the best terms possible should be made with Major Winter of Woolwich (was he John or James?) for obtaining the money which had been improperly claimed by Mrs Goodman. Precisely what had happened is not clear, but on 5 July Major Winter agreed to repay the money obtained by Mrs Goodman, at £10 10*s.* per year during her life. The Minute Books do not indicate what happened after Major Winter made his first yearly payment.

To have been granted an allowance by the Royal Society of Musicians Mrs Goodman must have been the widow of a member.

Goodman, Cardell *b. 1653, actor.*

Cardell Goodman is one of the very few Restoration performers who have been treated to a modern biography, and this entry on him owes a debt to John Harold Wilson's *Mr. Goodman the Player* (1964).

Goodman was born in October or November 1653 in Southampton, the son of Cardell and Katherine Goodman. The elder Goodman was born about 1608, took an M.A. in 1629 and a B.D. in 1636 from Cambridge, and in 1641 was appointed rector of Freshwater and Brook on the Isle of Wight. There he became friendly with the Hooke family, a relationship that bene-fited his son in later years. Goodman re-fused to swear the oath of allegiance to Cromwell's government, lost his position in 1651, and moved to Southampton. There he died in March 1654, only a few months after the younger Cardell, his only son, was born.

Katherine Goodman moved with her child to Cambridge, where in time she placed young Cardell in Thomas Wybor-row's school. On 30 November 1666, when Cardell was only 13, he was admitted to St John's College, Cambridge (his father's college), as a pensioner—that is, he or his mother paid his way. On 4 November 1667 he was granted a scholarship. He was 17 when he took his degree in 1671. The fol-lowing year he was in London; on 29 No-vember 1672 he looked up Robert Hooke, but, as Hooke recorded in his *Diary* the following day: "Goodman here from Cam-bridge, not let in." Hooke, it seems, was not being rude but was busy with a serving girl and did not wish to be disturbed. It is prob-able that Goodman and Hooke met another time and that through Hooke Goodman gained introductions to people of impor-tance in London. One of the luminaries Goodman met was Thomas Killigrew, the manager of the King's Company, and in the spring of 1673 Goodman became an ap-prentice member of Killigrew's troupe at about 10s. weekly. (A British Museum copy of the 1691 edition of *Julius Caesar* has a manuscript cast with Goodman down for Decius Brutus; most of the cast could have been gathered about 1670–71, but Goodman's name on the list would suggest a later date.)

The first certain role we know of for Goodman was in the summer 1673 at the Lincoln's Inn Fields playhouse (where the King's Company was operating temporar-ily); he played Mariamne (a bit part) in Duffett's burlesque of *The Empress of Mo-rocco*, and in the epilogue burlesque of *Macbeth* he was Thunder. All of the char-

Harvard Theatre Collection

CARDELL GOODMAN, as Mariamne

artist unknown

acters in *The Empress of Morocco* were played by men in blackface, Goodman's role being that of a cinder wench, a bur-lesque on the character of Princess Mari-amne in Settle's work of the same name. The frontispiece to the 1673 edition of Duffett's piece pictured Mariamne and has been taken as a likeness of Cardell Good-man. If that identification is correct, Good-man leaped very quickly to prominence, which does not quite fit with the story told later by Colley Cibber that as late as 1682 Goodman was one of the younger actors still struggling for leading roles. It should also be noted that we have no record of his appearing in London casts—though he was in the King's Company—between the sum-mer of 1673 and March 1677.

Wilson suggests that Goodman went with the King's players to Oxford in the summer of 1674; the group made little money that year and created much disturbance with their raucous behavior. Perhaps during part of 1674–75 Goodman toured the provinces with John Coysh, playing, as a manuscript cast shows, Peregreen in *Sir Salomon*, the juvenile lead—though the date of that cast may be closer to 1680. Goodman was certainly in London on 20 November 1674, for Robert Hooke loaned him £1 on that date. *The London Stage* lists Cardell as a member of the King's Company in 1675–76 at the new Drury Lane playhouse, and the Lord Chamberlain's accounts confirm that he was in the group as of 8 June 1676. Wilson guesses that Goodman may have played the title role in *Julius Caesar* on 4 December 1676, for he is known to have acted it in later seasons.

Those were lean years for Goodman. On 2 January 1677 he was ordered to appear before the Lord Chamberlain in connection with a case brought against him by one Thomas Kite; on 22 January he was ordered to pay Kite 3s. weekly for 20 weeks. Perhaps it was about that time that Goodman and his fellow player Philip Griffin were sharing lodgings. Colley Cibber remembered Goodman's telling him how he and Griffin economized by "lying together in the same Bed and having but one whole Shirt between them: One of them being under the obligation of a Rendezvous with a fair Lady, insisted on his wearing it out of his Turn, which occasion'd so high a dispute that the Combat was immediately demanded, and accordingly their Pretensions to it were decided by a fair Tilt upon the spot." The story is unlikely, but their poverty may have been real.

Goodman's next known roles were in March 1677: Captain Mullineux in *The Country Innocence* and (on the seventeenth) the small part of Polyperchon in *The Rival Queens*. On 20 March Goodman was cited again in the Lord Chamberlain's accounts: John Lane of Hart Street, Covent Garden, sought payment from Goodman for "a mare hyred & spoyled by Good-

man worth above six pounds." Later, in 1681, Goodman was charged with (and pardoned for) highway robbery; perhaps that escapade took place in March 1677 when he "spoyled" that horse. Goodman was ordered on 24 April 1677 to pay Mr Lane £5 at the rate of 4s. weekly while the King's Company acted (and the actor had a salary coming in). We know Goodman was active at the theatre in the spring and summer of that year: on 5 May 1677 he acted Plautino in *Scaramouch*; in mid-June he played Antellus (the lead) in *Wits Led by the Nose*; and Wilson thinks that about July 1677 Goodman perhaps played Alexander the Great in *The Rival Queens* when the older actors refused to perform. Goodman may have been living about that time at Mrs Alice Price's in Great Russell Street, Bloomsbury. Mrs Price was possibly the mother of the actress Elizabeth Price, who was for a while Goodman's mistress.

Cardell was gradually strengthening his position in the King's Company, but the troupe was torn by dissension, and the older players clung to the best parts. On 28 September 1677 Charles Killigrew and a group holding the majority of shares in the company tried to form a new troupe with the younger players; Goodman, had the scheme worked out, would have become one of the "Master Partners or sharers."

During the 1677–78 season Goodman played the rash Ethelwold in *King Edgar and Alfreda*, Alexas in *All for Love*, the noisy Pharnaces in *Mithridates*, Trainsted in *The Man of Newmarket*, Hylas in *Trick for Trick*, and, doubtless, many other parts of which we have no record. Outside the theatre he kept running into trouble, as the Lord Chamberlain's accounts show. On 15 (or 18?) December 1677 his landlady sued him for back rent and for £5 16s. which she was foolish enough to lend him. On 4 April 1678 an order was issued to "Apprehend & take into Custody Cardell Goodman, one of his Mats Comoedians for certain abuses & misdemeanours [undescribed] by him committed." Goodman was sent to the Porter's Lodge in Whitehall, but his crime could not have been too serious, for on 31 August 1678 his certificate of membership in the King's Company was renewed. The following 23 December one Daniel Smith sued Goodman and Mrs Sarah Young, alias Goodman, for a debt of £12 16s., and on 2 January 1679 a John Dutton sued the pair for £28.

Warrant concerning CARDELL GOODMAN, JAMES GRAY, and THOMAS CLARK

Disputes within the King's Company brought acting to a halt in the spring of 1678. Those and his financial difficulties probably persuaded Goodman to join Thomas Clark and James Gray and try his chances in Edinburgh. Cardell was there from about the spring of 1679 to February 1680. After his return, on 30 July 1680, he and other young members of the King's players signed an agreement with Charles and Henry Killigrew; though the terms were later disputed, the new arrangement gave Goodman a share in the company and a chance to play some of the leading roles which had belonged to such veterans as Hart and Mohun. The theatrical records are so scarce that we cannot tell if Goodman moved then into some leading roles; we can guess he may have acted Prince Artaban in *Fatal Love* in the fall of 1680 and toured with the troupe to Oxford in March 1681—but those meagre details tell us little about his place in the company.

On 18 April 1681 Cardell was pardoned for committing highway robbery on some unspecified earlier date—perhaps in 1677. Cibber, remembering in 1740 what Goodman had told him many years before, wrote that Goodman robbed once and was caught, but the records suggest that the rascal made quite a career of it, getting off lightly because of his connections at court. In 1696 witnesses at the trial of Sir John Fenwick testified to Goodman's malpractices of earlier years. Mrs Anne Cross swore that "A-going to Salisbury Mr. Goodman robbed me. He owned it to me." Edmond Godfrey told of "Goodman's stopping him in '80 to rob him, and they fired at each other." Godfrey said a minister identified the robber as Goodman, and Godfrey later saw Goodman at a playhouse. Goodman was apparently indicted, convicted, pleaded the King's pardon, and was given his freedom.

Cardell was turning into quite a naughty fellow. In mid-October 1681 he and Betty Cox spoke a special epilogue to *Mithridates*,

which may have prompted one of the scandal mongers of the day to write:

> *Lett Lumley Coax his Mrs. Fox,*
> *And help his younger Brother;*
> *Let Goodman Pox faire Mrs. Cox,*
> *And all Six flux together*

He was also growing "intractable" at the theatre, Cibber recalled. In 1681–82, just before the King's Company was merged with the Duke's players, Goodman is known to have acted Townly in *Sir Barnaby Whigg*, Seliman in *The Loyal Brother*, and Altomar in *The Heir of Morocco*, but he was not yet playing the leading parts he thirsted for, and he probably knew that after the merger he would have little chance of taking major parts away from Thomas Betterton, the veteran of the Duke's Company. He must have grown intractable indeed when, after the companies joined in 1682, he dropped back to hireling status at £2 weekly. Of his roles during the early years of the United Company we know very little: the title role in *Julius Caesar*, Annibal in *Constantine*, and the title role in *Valentinian* in 1683–84 and, perhaps that early, Vernish in *The Plain Dealer*.

Goodman found more excitement outside the theatre. About 1684, perhaps earlier, he met Barbara Palmer, Duchess of Cleveland. By that time she was no longer the favorite mistress of Charles II. Her three sons, especially Henry, the Duke of Grafton, took umbrage at her liaison with Goodman and apparently arranged a plot to discredit him. In the summer of 1684 Goodman was arrested for highway robbery "committed some years since." He had been pardoned in April 1681 for such an offense; now he was either up to his old tricks or the charge was revived (at Grafton's urging?) despite the pardon. At any rate, into Newgate went Cardell Goodman. In July 1684 a new pardon was issued, but Goodman never got it. A trial was held, and on 2 September the Grand Jury returned a verdict of ignoramus and Goodman was set free. Rumor had it that £100 had been given to a witness for the prosecution to deny his previous testimony.

Goodman did not, it seems, rush back to the arms of his new mistress (and savior?) but went into hiding with the actor John Wiltshire "att Mr. Robert Shotterell's house in great Russel Street in Bloomsbury near Mountague house"—not far from where Goodman had been living before. Goodman soon came out of hiding only to find himself charged with hiring a mountebank named Alexander Amadei to poison his mistress's sons, the Dukes of Grafton and Northumberland. Why Goodman should have wished to antagonize his mistress by doing away with two of her sons was never made clear, and the charges were almost certainly trumped up by someone—possibly Grafton—who wanted Goodman out of the way.

On 13 October 1684 the Principal Secretary of State, the Earl of Sunderland, wrote to Lord Chief Justice Jeffreys that it was the King's pleasure that Goodman should be "seized & kept in Custody." On 20 October Goodman was taken to Newgate. Christopher Jeaffreson wrote a letter on 29 October reporting that

Yesterday Mr. Goodman, the player, was indicted for hiring a doctor to poyson the Duke of Grafton, the Duke of Northumberland, and the Lord Peterborough, with some other persons of quality. Which the said doctor proved under his hand, but Goodman denied it, and offered such bayle as was not accepted. So he was returned to Newgate. He was very fine, and talked boldly; but the Lord Chief Justice was sharp upon him, and told him he must not huff the Court. It is reported that the D—— of Cleveland keeps him.

Goodman came to trial on 7 November 1684. He was charged with

being a Person of a Wicked Mind, and of an Ungodly and devilish Disposition, and Conversation [who] did solicite, perswade, and endeavour to procure one Alexander Amydei, to prepare & procure two Flasks of Florence Wine, to be mix'd with deadly Poison, for the poisoning of the Right Noble Henry, Duke of Grafton, and George, Duke of Northumberland.

Amadei testified that Goodman had tried to get him to pay £100 to "the prosecutrs sister" to "take off the prosecution" in the highway robbery case the previous summer, but Amadei refused. Goodman also, said the Florentine, offered him £140 and maintenance for the rest of his life on the Continent to poison the two dukes.

Goodman was found guilty as charged, and on 24 November 1684 he was sentenced to pay £1000 and find securities for his good behavior for life. Since Cardell could not pay the fine, he was sent to the Marshalsea. Either Charles II on his deathbed grew lenient, or the Duchess of Cleveland pulled some strings, or Amadei was revealed as a charlatan—or perhaps all three: on 16 January 1685, three weeks before he died, the King remitted Goodman's fine (without giving him an outright pardon), and by the end of February Cardell was free. King James was persuaded by the Duchess of Cleveland to give Goodman a full pardon, which he did on 22 October 1685.

Back to the arms of the Duchess went the grateful Cardell. A satirical poem, *The Duchess of C———'s Memorial* (1707) put these words into Barbara's mouth:

*Poor Rowley [Charles II] being dead and
     gone
I howl'd and had Remorse Sir,
To comfort me scum Goodman came
     Whom I made Master Horser.*

A satirist in 1685 wrote:

*Noe reason I see
Our Goodman shou'd be,
Soe very much angry with her sonn,*

For though her estate,
Be encomber'd with debt
She allwayes was free of her person.

(The encumbered estate was that of Catherine Lucy, who married the Duke of Northumberland.) In 1686 a satirist spoke of the Duchess walking openly "with Rake-hell Goodman hand in hand," and another referred to "Mr Goodman the Player which she keeps as a Stallion." One can hardly blame the satirists for their remarks; the Duchess had appointed Goodman her Gentleman of the Horse in order to legitimatize their being together in public.

Goodman acted from time to time, according to later sources. Davies wrote that

Goodman, long before his death, was so happy in his finances, that he acted only occasionally, perhaps when his noble mistress wished to see him in a principal character; for Goodman used to say "he would not act Alexander the Great but when he was certain that the Duchess would be in the boxes to see him perform."

Possibly he acted Alexander in *The Rival Queens* when it was performed on 19 December 1685. Peregrine Bertie saw Goodman in *Mithridates* on 4 February 1686, possibly in the role of Ziphares, and Cardell may have appeared as Alexander on 27 October 1686 at court. He was certainly well known for the latter role and frequently called "Alexander" by playgoers (only Macaulay thought Goodman was nicknamed "Scum").

Dryden wrote Etherege on 16 February 1687 that "The Coffee-house stands certainly where it did, & angry men meet in the Square sometimes, as Abercomy, and Goodman lately did. where they say Alexander the Great was wounded in the arme. by which you may note, he had better have been idle." (J. H. Wilson identifies Abercomy as Duncan Abercromy, a Captain in the Duke of Grafton's first regiment of foot guards.)

The satirical poets took pains to rib Goodman about his affair with the Duchess of Cleveland and his facial resemblance to the devil. Sackville's *A Faithful Catalogue* in February 1688 enumerated Barbara's lovers:

Now (Churchill, Dover) see how they
*   are sunk*
Into her loathsome, sapless, aged trunk!
And yet remains her c———'s insatiate
*   itch,*
And there's a devil yet can hug the witch.
Pardon me, Bab, if I mistake his race,
Which is infernal, sure, for though he has
No cloven foot, he has a cloven face.

In other poems Goodman was described as having a "pock-fret" face.

But *The Session of Ladyes* in 1688 pictured Cardell as a second Adonis, much sought after by ladies of all classes and "scarcely recover'd of his Dressing Room Wounds."

Tho' such an Adonis before was not
*   known;*
He exceeded the other in Beauty &
*   Grace;*
With Age and diseases tho' impotent
*   grown,*
He resembled the other exactly in Face.

To this New Adonis, in Park, & at Plays,
Whose Eyes had the Power of Life, and
*   of Death,*
Each beautiful Lady an Altar did Raise;
But all their perfumes cou'd not sweeten
*   his Breath.*

At the conclusion of the poem Dame Venus "To Cleveland put Rakehelly Goodman to bed."

Robert Gould's revised version of *The Playhouse, a Satyr*, spoke of

Goodman himself, an Infidel profess'd,
With plays reads Cl———d nightly to
*   her Rest:*
Nay in her Coach she whirls Him up and
*   down,*

And Publishes her Passion to the Town,
As if 'twere her Delight to make it known.

Yet in the early 1690s Goodman had another mistress, a Mrs Wilson—or so she was called in Mrs Manley's *Rivella*. Mrs Manley had it that Goodman kept Mrs Wilson in grand style, though she was from the Pope's Head Tavern in Cornhill. Possibly that woman was the "wife" who was with Goodman, according to the testimony of George Marsh in Fenwick's trial, at a meeting in the early 1690s.

Not everyone pictured Goodman as a lecher or a scoundrel. Charles Gildon in 1692 edited *Miscellany Poems upon Several Occasions*, to which he attached an "Epistle Dedicatory to Mr. Cardell Goodman," in which he stated, "I will declare in Public what I know of those excellent Accomplishments, which render you so dear to all that are acquainted with you. Your Wit and your Courage are things not to be question'd, much less your Generosity, that being a vertue that never resides alone." Or was Gildon being ironic?

Cardell was drawn into a Jacobite conspiracy that developed about 1694. He was promised a captaincy in a troop of horse to be raised to overthrow William III. A meeting was held at Goodman's lodgings in Brownlow (now Betterton) Street in the spring of 1694, the subject being a proposal to kidnap the King. A year later (while the plot was still brewing) Goodman participated in a rally on 10 June 1695 at the Dog Tavern in Drury Lane, celebrating the birthday of Prince James. On 3 July a Grand Jury accused 20 Jacobites, among them Goodman, of treason. Cardell surrendered himself on 10 July; he posted bail, managed with the aid of friends to get the trial postponed, and in time the charge against him was dropped.

By 1696 the plan to kidnap King William had changed to an assassination plot. The attempt on the King was set for 15 February 1696; if it were to succeed, King James would sail from France to conquer England. Goodman seems to have been on the fringes of the plot and was not made acquainted with the "whole Scheme and Design." The attempt was unsuccessful, and Goodman wound up, again, in Newgate. The Duchess of Cleveland let it be known that he was no longer in her employ. Several of the conspirators were executed, but the Crown needed the testimony of Goodman, Captain George Porter, and one Peter Cooke to convict the leading Jacobites, most especially Sir John Fenwick.

Goodman was encouraged by Archbishop Tenison to turn King's evidence, and on 10 April 1696 he wrote to Tenison that he was willing to "satisfy you in all I know." He sent Tenison "My humble duty & my poor wifes to yr Lady." But since Goodman had not been deeply involved in the plot, he knew something of the invasion plans but nothing of the assassination scheme. His validity as a witness was also questioned in view of his history of misdeeds, but his testimony and that of Porter helped bring in a true bill against Fenwick.

On 9 June 1696 Goodman was out on bail. He was seen in theatrical circles again and about that time chatted with Colley Cibber "of several loose Passages of his younger Life." He was still not safe, however. Lord Ailesbury, Viscount Montgomery, and Fenwick wanted Goodman out of the way, for his testimony might help hang them all. Goodman was offered £500 in cash and £500 annually as a pension if he would leave the country. Consequently, on 29 October 1696 he and a Jacobite friend, William O'Brien, left for France. On 5 November the King offered a £5000 reward for Goodman's capture.

As it turned out, Goodman's testimony was not essential. Parliament passed a bill of attainder, and Sir John Fenwick was beheaded on 28 January 1697. Ailesbury and Montgomery fled to the Continent. The *Post Boy* of 8/10 February reported a rumor: " 'Tis said for certain that Mr. *Good-man* is to be brought over hither from *France* in a short time, to take his Trial." The issue of 15/18 May told of another rumor: "Mr *Goodman*, now in *France*, is closely confined in a Dungeon." Theophilus Lucas in his *Games and Gamesters* (1744) said that Goodman "died of a Fever, in the 50th Year of his Age, *Anno* 1699." Lucas was misinformed.

At some point Cardell gained his freedom. He and O'Brien stayed in Calais for a while, then went to Saint Germain, where they were received at the court of the exiled King James. Goodman's promised pension did not arrive, of course. Though he wanted to return to England, the Jacobites in France prevented him. He was apparently arrested and sent to southeastern France; his wife requested permission of the former Queen Mary to join him, and perhaps she did. Lord Aislesbury's *Memoirs* tell us that about 1713 Goodman was at Monteliman, where he was allowed a maintenance of £87 10s. annually by the French but not permitted to leave the area. No record of Goodman's death has been found.

Cardell Goodman apparently had a fair amount of acting talent. Gildon's *The Life of Mr. Tho. Betterton* (1710) stated that "in the Madness of *Alexander* the *Great*, in *Lee's* Play, Mr. Goodman always went through it with all the Force the Part requir'd, and yet made not half the Noise, as some who succeeded him; who were sure to bellow it out in such a manner, that their Voice would fail them before the End. . . ."

The frontispiece to Duffett's *The Empress of Morocco* (1673) pictures the character of Mariamne, which Goodman played, but we have no way of knowing whether it was intended to show the character or the actor in the character.

Goodman, John [*fl.* 1720–1728], *trumpeter.*

A warrant among the Lord Chamber-lain's papers in the Public Record Office authorizes payments, amounts unstated, to a Mr Goodman and a Mr Abingdon, trumpeters, and a Mr David, double bass player, for practicing and performing in a *Te Deum* before the King at St James's Palace on 15 November 1719. His first name was given as John when he and Joseph Abingdon were named in another such warrant on 20 October 1721. John Goodman was still a trumpeter in the royal establishment in 1728 under the Serjeant Trumpeter John Shore.

Goodman, Joseph [*fl.* 1714–1759?], *trumpeter.*

The Lord Chamberlain's accounts show the trumpeter Joseph Goodman to have been a member of the King's Musick from as early as 1714. He or another trumpeter of the same name also served in the third troop of horseguards. Goodman was listed among the trumpeters in the royal musical establishment until 1759, by which time he was replaced by Edward Toms. Goodman had become one of the original subscribers to the Royal Society of Musicians on 28 August 1739.

Goodsens, Francisco *d. 1741, string instrumentalist.*

A benefit concert was presented at York Buildings on 5 March 1703 for "Signor Francisco," and on the following 18 May he played at a recital in Hampstead. On 1 December 1707 he was granted special permission by the Lord Chamberlain to play at the operas at the Queen's Theatre. He was, it seems certain, Francisco Goodsens, who, about 1708, offered to play at the Queen's for £1 10s. nightly. He was listed as a violoncellist, though the records show that he was sometimes pressed into service on the bass and double bass, and he was also proficient on the violin and viola. At the opera house he settled for a daily salary of 11s. 3d., but the Lord Chamberlain's accounts show that at some point his income was up to 15s. daily or £30 for the season. He continued at the Queen's Theatre until about 1711, making occasional appearances elsewhere, one being on 14 June 1710, when he held a benefit concert at the Great Room in Peter's Court.

Goodsens (or Goodsence) augmented his income about 1710 by playing at the Duchess of Shrewsbury's house in Kensington, and by 11 September 1713 he was a liveried musician in the Queen's Musick. He continued active in the royal musical establishment until his death. At the accession of George I on 1 August 1714 Goodsens became a violist in the Chapel Royal at an annual salary of £40. Over the years he frequently attended the royal family at Windsor and Hampton Court.

On 6 June 1741 Goodsens made his will, describing himself as of the parish of St Margaret, Westminster. To his daughter Emelia he left his gold watch, tea chest, and silver teaspoons. He cancelled a five-guinea debt owed him by Francis Dowman, who was the husband of Goodsens's daughter Charlot. The rest of his estate he left to his two daughters equally. Francisco Goodsens died within a few months. John Lyne replaced him in the King's Musick on 18 November 1741, and the Goodsens girls proved their father's will two days later.

Goodshaw, Mrs [fl. 1727–1729], actress.

Mr and Mrs Goodshaw acted at York in 1727, one of Mrs Goodshaw's parts there being Leonora in *The Mourning Bride*. She was probably the Mrs Goodshaw who played a role in *Hunter* at Fielding's booth at Bartholomew Fair on 23 August 1729. Mr Goodshaw seems not to have been mentioned in any London advertisements.

Goodson, Richard 1655–1718, singer, organist, composer.

Born in 1655, Richard Goodson was at some time before 1682 a chorister at St Paul's Cathedral. Upon the death of his friend Edward Lowe in the summer of 1682 Goodson became Professor of Music at Oxford and organist of Christ Church and of New College. He received his bachelor of music degree from Oxford about the same time. He composed some odes and some songs for an opera, *Orpheus and Eurydice*. Goodson died at Great Tew on 13 January 1718 and was buried in Christ Church Cathedral, Oxford. His son Richard succeeded him as Professor of Music and organist of New College.

Goodwin. *See also* GODWIN.

Goodwin, Mr [fl. 1744–1769?], doorkeeper.

A Mr Goodwin was a doorkeeper at Drury Lane Theatre from 1744–45 through 1758–59 and probably beyond, sharing in annual benefits with other house servants. Probably he was still serving on 19 May 1769 when a Mr Goodwin shared benefit tickets with Humphreys, a doorkeeper.

Goodwin, Mr [fl. 1791–1808?], house servant?

On 1 October 1791 a Mr Goodwin and the watchman at Drury Lane Theatre were paid £1 4s. They received a similar sum on 14 January 1792, but Goodwin's function was not stated. He was, also, the only person of that name associated with Drury Lane, all other Goodwins being at Covent Garden. This Mr Goodwin continued to be paid small sums—usually about 12s. per week—through 1 November 1794. A Mr Goodwin was on the Drury Lane salary list in 1807–8 for £1 10s. per week.

Goodwin, Mr [fl. 1794–1804], dresser.

A person named Goodwin was paid 8s. per week as a men's dresser at Covent Garden Theatre in 1794–95, shared in benefit tickets in 1795 and 1797, and was employed as a dresser at the Haymarket Theatre in the summer of 1804.

Goodwin, Master *[fl. 1796–1803], singer, actor, dancer.*

The Covent Garden performers Thomas and Eleanor Goodwin had three sons. One of them, no doubt, was the Master Goodwin who sang a principal vocal part in *Harlequin and Oberon* and played a Young Devil in *A Duke and No Duke* at Covent Garden in 1796–97. The following season, 1797–98, he was one of the Indian chorus in *Ramah Droog*, a dancing Swabian Peasant in *Albert and Adelaide*, and a singer in the choruses of *The Magic Oak* and *Raymond and Agnes*. He also sang in *Joanna* in 1799–1800. On 28 November 1803 Master Goodwin danced a military hornpipe at the Royal Circus.

Goodwin, John *1662–1693, violinist, composer.*

Born in 1662, John Goodwin was appointed a violinist in the King's private music on 17 November 1682, replacing the deceased Thomas Purcell. Goodwin was the godson of John Mason, the Wokeing musician (according to Mason's will of 6 March 1672), and he was also related to other musical families: the Blagraves, the Frosts, and the Searles. The Lord Chamberlain's accounts frequently mentioned Goodwin. On 26 January 1685, for instance, he was ordered to practice for a ball at the court theatre; at the accession of James II he was reappointed to the King's Musick at £50 annually; he accompanied the King to Windsor from 19 May to 16 August and from 17 September to 11 October 1687 and he returned there from 24 July to 20 September 1688; he was reappointed as a violinist under William III but at a reduced salary of £30 a year; he accompanied William to Newmarket in early October 1689 at 3*d*. daily and journeyed with the King to Holland from 1 January to 13 April 1691; and on 24 November 1692,

the accounts show, Goodwin was suspended for using "scandalous and menacing language" to Dr Richard of the Treasury Chamber.

Goodwin was also cited in several wills during that period. When Thomas Blagrave's will was proved on 4 December 1688, Goodwin benefited to the amount of £20 and forgiveness of debts. Margaret Blagrave's will, proved on 17 October 1689, named Goodwin and his cousin Frances Frost (Mrs John Frost) as executors. Mrs Blagrave left Goodwin £100, one of her four houses in Westminster near the Cockpit, and, after the death of Frances Frost, a house and land in Teddington. Goodwin, John Blow, and Henry Frost witnessed the will of the musician Richard Hart on 26 December 1689.

Goodwin was active in musical affairs outside the court. Motteux's *Gentleman's Journal* in January 1692, reporting on the St Cecilia's Day celebration at Stationers' Hall on the previous 23 November 1691, cited Goodwin as one of the six stewards for 1691, and it is probable that he performed on such occasions.

John Goodwin died on 7 July 1693 at the age of 31. The following day Thomas Clayton replaced Goodwin in the King's Musick, and on 10 July Goodwin was buried in the north cloister of Westminster Abbey. He had made his will on 3 July 1693, describing himself as from Westminster and "sick in body." He requested burial in the cloisters of the Abbey and made the following bequests: £100 and his diamond ring to his cousin Frances Frost, £20 to his uncle Anthony Blagrave of Norwich, £10 each to his (Blagrave's?) sons Richard and John, £20 to Goodwin's brother (in law?) Ambrose Searle, £20 each to Searle's children, £20 to Willian Browne of Westminster, £5 to Mrs Mary Mills of Hampton, £5 to the musician Theophilus Fitts of Hampton, £5 to Sarah Eve, a silver watch to Harry Luppingcott, and £5 to the poor of St. Margaret, Westminster.

He left his silver tobacco box to Captain Nehemiah Arnold, a silver-headed cane to Mr Hearne, another silver-headed cane to a Mr Harris (the musician Morgan Harris?), his silver snuff box to Captain James Bringfield, £5 to the widow of China Blagrave, and £5 to Mrs Blagrave's daughter. Goodwin named Frances Frost his residuary legatee and appointed her husband John his executor. Frost proved the will on 20 July 1693.

Goodwin did some composing, one of his songs, "Since my Mistress proves Cruel," being in Playford's *Theater of Music* in 1685.

Goodwin, Peter _fl. 1785?–1838?_, music copyist, musician?

In 1794, Peter Goodwin was listed in Doane's *Musical Directory* as a music copyist, working at Covent Garden Theatre and living at No 27, Bow Street, in that area. Probably he was a practicing musician, and perhaps he was playing at the theatre. He may have been the Mr Goodwin who was paid £10 14s. by Covent Garden on 20 December 1785 for copying the music to *Omai* and who was paid £11 16s. in 1786 for music copying for the Liverpool Theatre, but that person may have been Thomas Goodwin (d. 1820).

A Mr Goodwin was employed as an "orchestra keeper" at the Haymarket Theatre in the summer of 1804. Perhaps he was the Goodwin who was paid 7s. 6d. by Drury Lane on 16 March 1816 for playing bells.

On 5 January 1834 a P. Goodwin was refused relief by the Royal Society of Musicians because he was not a claimant by the time the general meeting took place. But on 1 February 1835, 7 February 1836, 1 January 1837, and 4 February 1838, Mr Goodwin sent the Society his thanks for donations.

Goodwin, Starling _d. 1784, organist, composer._

The Mr Goodwin who died on 5 March 1784 and was identified by the *Gentleman's Magazine* as the organist of St Saviour, Southwark, and St Mary, Newington Butts, and one of the musicians belonging to Ranelagh Gardens, was no doubt the organist and composer of pleasure-garden songs, Starling Goodwin. On 7 August 1785, Mrs Elizabeth Goodwin applied to the Governors of the Royal Society of Musicians for assistance but was denied, because Mr Goodwin (Christian name not given) had neglected paying his subscription for some years before his death.

About 1750 Starling Goodwin, who by that time was already the organist at St Saviour, was the director of a musical society which gave monthly concerts at Lambeth Wells. Starling Goodwin published *A Collection of Songs with a Cantata from Anacreon . . . Sung by Mr. Champness at Ranelagh. To which is added two favourite Songs for two Voices* (1764); the song *Fly, fly, false Man* (1760); *Twelve Voluntarys for the Organ or Harpsichord . . . Book 1* (1770?); and *The Complete Organist's Pocket Companion, containing a choice Collection of Psalm-Tunes with their Givings-Out, and Interludes* (1775?). *A Collection of Songs, No. 6*, by S. Goodwin, was published about 1790.

The "Celebrated Song from *Anacreon*," set by Starling Goodwin, was sung by Mr A. Small at the Grotto Gardens, St George's Fields, on 30 August 1771.

Goodwin, Thomas _fl. 1784–1801?_, actor, dancer.

Thomas Goodwin was an obscure performer at Covent Garden Theatre who spent his modest career dancing in the choruses of musical pieces. He was probably the Mr Goodwin who shared benefit tickets with other minor personnel on 15 May 1784, 1 June 1792, 4 June 1794, 30 May 1795, 27 May 1797, 31 May 1798, 4 June 1799, and 10 June 1800. In 1793–94 his salary seems to have been £2 2s.

per week. Goodwin's name seldom appeared in the bills, but he was noticed as an Infernal in *Joan of Arc* in 1797–98 and a Sailor in *The Death of Captain Cook* in 1799–1800. He was probably the Goodwin who acted Tom in *The Jealous Wife* at the Haymarket Theatre on 29 April 1788 and may have been the Goodwin who acted at the Haymarket in 1801.

On 7 February 1784 Thomas Goodwin had married the dancer Eleanor Byrn at St Andrew, Holborn. As Mrs Goodwin, she continued to perform at Covent Garden through 1790–91. One of their children, mentioned in her entry, was perhaps the Master Goodwin who performed at the same theatre from 1796–97 through 1799–1800.

Goodwin, Mrs Thomas, Eleanor, née Byrn [fl. 1772–1810?], dancer.

Eleanor Byrn was the daughter of Ann Byrn, whose burial notice on 8 February 1793 specified her parish as St Martin-in-the-Fields, where, probably, Eleanor was born. Her father's first name is not known. She was the sister, perhaps elder, of the dancer and choreographer James Byrn (1756–1845), with whom the earliest part of her stage career was linked.

Her first appearance was on 5 May 1772 at Drury Lane Theatre with her brother and Miss Wilkinson in a *New Tambourine Dance*; all three young people were advertised as scholars of Signor Giorgi. Eleanor appeared with her brother in minuets and allemandes at Drury Lane in 1773–74 and then joined Foote's summer company at the Haymarket. For the following few years he seems not to have been as active a performer as Master James, but when she did appear it was usually with him. In the summers of 1778 and 1779 at the Haymarket she danced in such pieces as a *Provencal Dance, The Merry Lasses, The Gardeners*, and a *Tambourine Dance*. In 1779–80 she danced at Bristol and at Cambridge and then returned to the Haymarket, where she appeared in the summers regularly

through 1783 dancing as Creusa in *Medea and Jason*, in *The Italian Peasants, The Nosegay Lovers*, and other specialties.

In the autumn of 1782 she and her brother (now styled "Mr" Byrn) were engaged at Covent Garden. Her weekly salary of £2 per week at that time exceeded her brother's £1 10s., although eventually he was to become the more famous performer. They appeared in *Diversion-à-la-Mode* and *The Rival Nymphs* but were rarely cited in their first seasons at the winter house, although they probably labored regularly in the choruses.

At St Andrew, Holborn, on 7 February 1784 Eleanor married Thomas Goodwin (fl. 1784–1801?), a sometime minor actor at the Haymarket and Covent Garden. On 18 March 1784, when she danced in *The Rival Nymphs*, she was advertised as Mrs Goodwin. Earning a constant £2 per week through 1789–90 at Covent Garden, she appeared as Colombine in *Harlequin Rambler* and *Aladin*. She also played similar roles at the Haymarket (in *Here and There and Every Where* and *Harlequin Teague*) every summer from 1784 through 1791, with the exception of 1788. In the Harvard Theatre Collection is her signed receipt, dated 15 June 1790, acknowledging payment of £66 6s. 8d. for dancing 199 nights, at 6s. 8d. per night, in 1789–90.

During her last season at Covent Garden, 1790–91, she performed a principal character in *The Provocation*, danced *The Jockies* with Ratchford, Platt, and Jackson, and appeared in *The Woodman*. By then her salary had been reduced to £1 10s. per week.

Her last recorded London engagement was at the Haymarket in the summer of 1791; on 17 June she danced a triple hornpipe with her brother James and Miss De Camp, and on 1 July, with those two and Platt, she appeared in a new dance, *The Kiss; or Give and Take*. The latter piece was repeated on 26 July, evidently her last performance.

Three children of Eleanor Goodwin, by

her husband Thomas, were baptized at St Paul, Covent Garden: Edward Thomas on 12 June 1785, John on 25 March 1787, and William Henry (about four months old) on 2 November 1789. One of them, perhaps the eldest, may have been the Master Goodwin (fl. 1796–1803) who sang and danced at Covent Garden in the last years of the century. Her husband Thomas Goodwin may have continued as a performer at least until then, as well. The Miss Goodwin who performed at Drury Lane in 1806–7 may have been their daughter. A Mrs Goodwin was paid £2 2s. per week at Covent Garden from 1800–1801 through 1809–10, but we do not know if that person was our subject.

Goodwin, Thomas *d. 1820, violist, music copyist, arranger, music librarian.*

In 1794 Thomas Goodwin, of No 1, Little Court, Castle Street, Leicester Square, was listed in Doane's *Musical Directory* as a violist, subscriber to the New Musical Fund, a participant in the Handelian concerts at Westminster Abbey, and a copyist at Covent Garden Theatre. He was probably the Mr Goodwin who was paid £10 14s. by that theatre on 20 December 1785 for copying out music to *Omai* and who received £11 16s. from the Liverpool Theatre in 1786 for similar work. He compiled from contemporary composers the music for *Harlequin's Museum* at Covent Garden on 20 December 1792 and arranged the music for *Hartford Bridge* on 23 March 1793. He also arranged the music for *Mago and Dago* at the same theatre on 26 December 1794. *The Overtures, Songs, Dances, &c. in . . . Harlequin's Museum* as compiled by him was published in 1792, as was *The Overture, Songs, &c. in . . . Mago & Dago* in 1794.

Thomas Goodwin's name continued to appear in the Covent Garden account books during the first decade of the nineteenth century. On 19 February 1801 he was paid £167 18s. 6d., his bill for copying in the previous season, and on 10 November 1801 and 25 January 1803 he was also entered for music copying. In 1805 he was a subscriber to the New Musical Fund.

In the second decade of the nineteenth century Goodwin served in the important post of music librarian at Covent Garden Theatre. He was, no doubt, the Thomas Goodwin (husband of Sarah), musician, of No 55, Great Queen Street, who died in 1820.

One of Thomas's sons, William Goodwin, born in 1797, was appointed librarian of the Royal Academy of Music upon its establishment in 1823 and was well known in musical circles for his concerts at Crystal Palace; he died on 1 April 1876. Another son, Thomas Goodwin, born at London in 1799, went to New York in 1827, where he became a music librarian and historian before he died in that city on 28 June 1886. His chatty *Sketches and impressions, musical, theatrical, and social* was published the year after his death.

Goodwin, William [fl. 1770?–1775?], *composer, musician?*

The composer William Goodwin who wrote songs which were published as having been sung at Ranelagh Gardens was probably also a musician there. His published music included *A Pastoral from Mr Cunningham's Collection. Sung by Mr. Hudson at Ranelagh* (1770?); *Kate of the Green. Sung by Mr Hudson at Ranelagh* (1770?); *The Triumph of Bacchus*, a song, 1772; and a series of three lessons for the harpsichord and piano (1775?).

Goold. See GOLD and GOULD.

Goortz. See GOOCH.

Goostree, Joseph *1732–1812, machinist, singer, dancer?*

The Mr Goostree who appeared as a chorus singer at Sadler's Wells on 12 and 14 May 1783 was no doubt Joseph Goostree, who during the 1790s was a machinist at Covent Garden Theatre. By 1793–94 he was functioning in that latter capacity at Covent Garden with a salary of £2 per week.

Goostree made machines for such productions as *Windsor Castle* in April 1795, *Merry Sherwood* in December 1795 (when he also arranged for the hiring and keeping of the horses required); *The Round Tower, Harlequin and Quixotte, Joan of Arc,* and *Harlequin's Return* in 1797–98; *Ramah Droog* and *The Magic Oak* in 1798–99; and *The Volcano* in December 1799. In March 1797 he, Mrs Egan, and Mr Dick were credited with the dresses and decorations for *Raymond and Agnes*. By 1797–98 his son Samuel, who seems to have been primarily a dancer, also began to arrange machinery. Probably it was Joseph, however, who worked at the Birmingham Theatre in the summers of 1797 and 1798. It is also possible that some of the stage appearances credited by us to the son may have been made by the father.

The elder Goostree's name continued to be listed in the Covent Garden accounts from 1800–1801 through 1811–12 at a constant salary of £2 10*s.* per week. On 24 June 1801 he, Sloper, and Hill were paid £103 for some work at Covent Garden. He was employed for 1812–13 but his last salary payment came on 5 December 1812. About that time he died.

Joseph Goostree, described as from "Pancras Parish," was buried at St Paul, Covent Garden, on 9 December 1812, at the age of 80. In his will, signed on 9 April 1800, in which he styled himself a "gentleman," of Covent Garden Theatre, he left his unspecified estate to his wife Joan, sole executrix, who proved the will on 16 December 1812. The Elizabeth Goostree who was buried at St Paul, Covent Garden, on 13 February 1799, aged 64, may have been his first wife or his sister. The James Goostree, Esq., of Great Pulteney Street, whose marriage to Miss Hartman of Leicester Fields on 16 August 1771 was announced in the *Gentleman's Magazine* of that month, may have been related.

Goostree, Samuel (*fl.* 1785–1806), *dancer, actor, machinist.*

Samuel Goostree, the son of the Covent Garden machinist Joseph Goostree (1732–1812), appeared as a Running Footman in the pantomime *Here There and Every Where* at the Haymarket Theatre on 31 August 1785. Advertised as Master Goostree, he performed his modest role nine other times in September and five more in the following summer of 1786, but after that time his theatrical activities seem to have ceased for some eight years. In 1795–96 he reappeared on the Covent Garden stage as a dancer at £3 per week. His father also may have been put into service as a supernumerary in the pantomimes in the 1790s, so the careers of the two Goostrees cannot always be separated with certainty. We assume it was Samuel who between 1794–95 and 1800 filled such roles as a Female Savage in *The Shipwreck*, an Arab and a Persian in *Harlequin's Treasure*, a Danish Chief in *The Round Tower*, and a Servant in *Raymond and Agnes*. At the Haymarket in the summer of 1800 he played a Negro Robber in *Obi*.

As a dancer the younger Goostree earned £3 per week in 1795–96, £2 10*s.* in 1796–97 and 1797–98; the next two seasons his salary was £4. By 1797–98 he began to assist his father as a machinist as well. The name of Goostree Junior continued to appear, along with his father's, in the Covent Garden account lists at least through 1805–6, at £4 per week. On 10 July 1801 he was paid £20 by the Haymarket for his machine tricks prepared that month for the pantomime *The Corsair*.

Goosetree, Stephen (*fl.* 1740s), *pugilist.*

Stephen Goosetree was a pugilist who engaged in noonday bouts, frequently in a booth in Tottenham Court and sometimes at the Haymarket Theatre, in the 1740s. The press carried notices of his challenges: "A severe Trial of Manhood between the following Champions: I Stephen Goosetree, celebrated for my strength and agility well known for my superior strength and skill who never appear'd on any Stage before . . . do challenge the Norwich Butcher."

Gope, Mr [fl. 1783], *musician.*
A Mr Gope (Cope?) was a musician at the King's Theatre in the Haymarket in 1783.

Gopell, Miss, later Mrs Joseph Gilbert [fl. 1790–1798], *actress, singer.*
Miss Gopell sang in a concert at the Assembly Rooms in Bristol on 21 October 1790 and made her first appearance as an actress in Bristol playing Rosetta in *Love in a Village* on 27 February 1792. *Felix Farley's Bristol Journal* thought she sang with "great chastity and taste." On 2 April Miss Gopell sang with Incledon and Master Welsh at a concert at No 19, Bridge Street, Bristol. On 5 August 1793, shortly before her London debut, it was reported that Miss Gopell would sing the title role in *Rosina* and that she was a pupil of the celebrated Mrs Miles of Bath. That apparently led to some confusion, for the *European Magazine* in 1793 thought Miss Gopell had performed under the name of Mrs Miles or Miss Guest (Mrs Miles's maiden name).

Hailed as from Bath, Miss Gopell did, indeed, sing the lead in *Rosina* at the Haymarket Theatre, on 16 August 1793, and she introduced into her part the song "Sweet Echo." As luck would have it, the playbill listed her as Miss "Copell." The *European Magazine* said

She has for some time performed at Bath with applause [the Bath and Bristol companies were virtually identical], and possesses no small talents for the Theatre. Her figure is small and her voice not wanting in harmony, though it seemed to be barely of sufficient compass for the Theatre in London. It is probable a further trial will be made of her powers before she is returned to a provincial Playhouse.

A further trial was scheduled, for 29 August 1793 at the Haymarket, but Miss Gopell was indisposed, and her appearance as the Lady in *Comus* was postponed until 2 September. After that performance she was returned to the provinces as predicted.

She was heard in a concert at the Assembly Rooms in Bristol on 22 January 1796, and the following 19 July she sang at a benefit for the Charity Schools held at St George's Church, Gloucestershire. She acted in Bristol through 1797–98. On 2 August 1798 at St Stephen's she married Joseph Gilbert, a wholesale linendraper. The *Bristol Journal* of 11 October that year announced that Mrs Gilbert had been engaged by the Drury Lane Theatre in London, but she apparently never returned to the capital. The Mrs Gilbert who acted and sang in London from 1796 to 1800 was clearly a different woman.

Gordom. *See* JORDAN.

Gordon, Mrs. *See* GONDOU, MRS, and LYON, MISS.

Gordon, Miss [fl. 1770], *actress.*
Miss Gordon played Jenny in *The Gentle Shepherd* at the Haymarket Theatre on 19 March 1770.

Gordon, Alexander *d. c. 1754, singer, antiquarian, composer.*
Alexander Gordon was born before 1692 in Scotland (in Aberdeen, some sources say) and took an M.A. at Aberdeen University. He became in time an accomplished linguist and antiquary, traveled widely, published several scholarly books, painted, taught languages and music, and became a singer in London music rooms and at the opera. About 1710, after he completed his degree, "Singing Sandy," as his countrymen called him, journeyed to France, Germany, and Italy. He settled for some time in Italy and made there what

may have been his first appearance in an opera: in 1716 in Messina he sang in *La principessa fedele*; the libretto listed him as "Alessandro Gordon, Britannico." In 1717–18 he sang at the Teatro di San Bartolomeo in Naples.

On 7 December 1719, hailed as "lately arriv'd from Italy," Gordon sang at Lincoln's Inn Fields Theatre at a concert held for his benefit. He was again advertised as recently returned from Italy on 19 January 1720 when he sang at the same theatre. He reappeared there on 5 and 10 February, singing in Italian; then, on 2 April at the King's Theatre he sang the title role in *Numitor*. On 27 April he appeared as Tiridate in *Radamisto*, and on 30 May he was Aristeo in *Narciso*. The following year he held a benefit at York Buildings on 6 February 1721; then, after the passage of another year, he held another benefit at the Haymarket Theatre on 26 January 1722. In 1722 he tried, according to Martin's *Allan Ramsay*, to establish a pastoral opera in Edinburgh, but the venture may not have been successful, for he was back in London for the 1722–23 opera season at the King's Theatre. Perhaps he participated in *Muzio Scevola*, *Ciro*, *Floridante*, and *Crispo*, though the only roles known for him are Azzio Tullo in *Coriolano* on 19 February 1723 and Ugone in *Flavio* on 14 June. His musical career in London may have ended temporarily after that, but his fame as a singer lingered on. In the *Session of Musicians* in May 1724 the musician William Corbett was encouraged by Apollo

> to cleanly Edinburgh repair,
> And from ten Stories high breathe
>   Northern Air;
> With tuneful G[o]rd[o]n join, and thus
>   unite,
> Rough Italy with Scotland the polite.

And in 1730 Malcolm's *Treatise of Musick* contained a poem in praise of Gordon:

> With Gordon's brave ambition fired,
> Beyond the towering Alps, untired
>   To tune my voice to his sweet notes,
>   I'd roam;
> Or search the Magazines of Sound
> Where Musick's treasures lay profound.

Gordon's desertion of the London musical scene was caused by his increased involvement in his antiquarian pursuits. About 1720 he had become interested in studying the Roman antiquities of his native Scotland, and he had made several trips to various parts of the country. After his musical activity in London ended, he returned to Scotland, and in 1726 was published his *Itinerarium Septentrionale*. He then engaged himself in a scheme to cut a canal between the Firths of Clyde and Forth, but the government was unwilling to supply the necessary funds. Then Gordon is said to have joined the bookseller John Wilcox in London for a while, but he was not suited to a trade, and poverty sometimes made him dishonest in his transactions. In 1729 he published *The Lives of Pope Alexander VI and his son Caesar Borgia*, and in 1730 he brought out his translation of Maffei's *De gli Anfiteatri* under the title *A Compleat History of the Ancient Amphitheatres*. He tried his hand at writing a comedy, *Lupone*, which was acted at the Haymarket Theatre in London on 15 and 16 March 1731. He turned out a supplement to his *Itinerarium Septentrionale* in 1732.

Gordon was one of the original members of the Sublime Society of Beefsteaks when it was formed in 1735, and in 1736 he was appointed to secretarial posts in the Society for the Encouragement of Learning, the Society of Antiquaries, and the Egyptian Club. The following year he published a study of Egyptian mummies in England which was illustrated, as were many of his works, by himself.

Perhaps it was in order to pay his debts and to finance a trip to America that Gordon returned briefly to the concert stage.

On 17 December 1739 at Covent Garden he performed for his own benefit, and on 4 April 1741 at the same house another benefit brought him more than £100 before house charges. In the latter year he brought out a history of ancient Egypt. He was by that time married and, as usual, in debt. He was dismissed from the Society for the Encouragement of Learning, and his effects were seized, whereupon, in August 1741, Gordon left England for South Carolina.

His position there was secretary to the new governor, and in the colonies he did very well for himself, accumulating land in Charleston and Ansonborough. He continued his antiquarian interests, sending back to the Royal Society a description of the natural history of South Carolina, but that was not read until after Gordon's death. Sick and weak, he wrote his will on 22 August 1754 at Charleston. He left his son Alexander his self-portrait and some other pictures and asked him to publish an essay he had in manuscript about the history of Egypt (which the younger Alexander did not do). To his son and to his daughter Frances Charlotte he left his land in South Carolina. Gordon's wife must have died before 1754, for the will made no mention of her. Alexander Gordon died some time before 23 July 1755, when a conveyance of his land was executed by his beneficiaries.

The Dictionary of National Biography contains details of Gordon's nontheatrical career but almost nothing on his musical life. In 1965 Carl Morey wrote an article on Gordon in *Music and Letters* that supplied many missing details.

Gordon, John [*fl. 1744–1773*], *violinist, violoncellist, proprietor?*

John Gordon's first notice in London playbills was on 6 April 1744, when he played a concerto on the violin at Drury Lane. The following 5 November at Theophilus Cibber's "Academy" at the Hay-market Theatre he offered a concerto on the violoncello, and it was as a cellist that he appeared sporadically at concerts for the ensuing 20 years. He played at Mr Snow's in the parish of St Margaret, Westminster, some time in 1750 for Master Snow's benefit; at the King's Theatre on 24 March 1757 for the aid of "decay'd" musicians; at the music room in Dean Street, Soho, on 1 April 1758 when *Acis and Galatea* was performed and on 28 January 1761 for Tenducci's benefit; and at the King's again on 11 May 1762 for the benefit of indigent musicians. *Mortimer's London Directory* of 1763 gave Gordon's address as Nassau Street (now Gerrard Place), Soho. Mortimer supplied Gordon's Christian name and noted that the musician was in the King's and Queen's bands. Nalbach in *The King's Theatre* states that Gordon was a member of the opera orchestra at that playhouse.

After 1763 Gordon was not mentioned in concert bills, but a Mr Gordon, almost certainly John, joined Peter Crawford and T. Vincent in 1764–65 in the management of the King's Theatre. O'Reilly's *An Authentic Narrative of the Principal Circumstances Relating to the Opera House in the Hay-Market* (1791) states that the triumvirate paid £14,000 for the rights to the opera, and the Duchess of Northumberland noted in her diary that the trio spent £26,000 altering the auditorium and repainting and relining the boxes—but did nothing about the "Old & Dirty" scenery and costumes.

Crawford withdrew from the management on 9 May 1767 (according to *The London Stage*; in August 1766 according to Nalbach) and was replaced by Mr Drummond, a banker who had been involved in opera proprietorship as early as 1738–39. The new trio remained in control until 1769, losing money in the venture. George Hobart took over the management of the opera in 1769–70, keeping Gordon on as a recruiter. John's new duties took him to the Continent frequently. On 11 January 1771, describing himself as a musician in ordinary to the King and a resident in the parish of St Anne, Soho, Gordon empowered his wife Elizabeth to receive any moneys owed him. It is likely that he was out of England shortly after that, as he was most certainly in 1773, when the King's Theatre announced on 23 October that Gordon had recently spent two months in Italy and had made two trips to Paris recruiting singers and dancers.

But the opera management changed again in November 1773: Hobart gave up the venture and, since nothing more was heard of Gordon, it is probable he dropped out of theatrical affairs, too. Dr Burney said John Gordon was the son of a Norfolk clergyman and that he was a good cellist.

Gore, Mrs _(fl. 1786–1803?)_, _actress._
Mrs Gore played Penelope in _The Natural Son_ at the Windsor Castle Inn, King Street, Hammersmith, on 5 August 1786. Years later, on 19 June 1795 at the White Lion Inn in Wych Street (the former south continuation of Drury Lane), Mrs Gore acted the Marchioness Merida in _The Child of Nature._ An undated bill in Lysons's "Collectanea" at the Folger Shakespeare Library (arranged with other bills dated September 1795) listed Mrs Gore as Serina in a performance of _The Orphan_ at the Assembly House, Kentish Town. She appeared at Tunbridge Wells beginning 3 October 1795, and at the theatre in Worthing on 29 September 1796 Mrs Gore played Alinda in _The Noble Pilgrim_ and Daphne in _Midas._ She was probably the Mrs Gore who performed at Plymouth on 9 May 1803 (a Mr Gore acted at Plymouth in 1801 and 1804 and was possibly there in 1803 as well).

Gore, Israel _b. 1759, singer._
Born in 1759, Israel Gore of Windsor was one of the countertenors in the Handel performances at Westminster Abbey and

the Pantheon in May and June 1784. During 1787–88 he was earning £21 per season singing for the Academy of Ancient Music, and on 4 December 1788 he was recommended for membership in the Royal Society of Musicians. His sponsor in the Society, J. Dupuis, reported that Gore, then thirty years old and single, had studied music under Mr Porter of Canterbury for seven years (not as apprentice), had practiced music as a livelihood for another seven, and was a Gentleman of the Chapel Royal and a member of the choirs at Windsor and Eton. He was unanimously elected to the Society on 1 March 1789.

On 19 February 1790 Gore was one of the principal singers in the _Messiah_ at Covent Garden. He did not participate in other oratorios at Covent Garden in February and March, but he sang (with the chorus) "Bless the true Church" from _Athalia_ at Drury Lane on 17 March. On 3 June 1792 he was proposed as one of the governors of the Royal Society of Musicians, but the Minute Books contain no reference to the actual election.

Doane's _Musical Directory_ of 1794 listed Israel Gore as a resident in King Street, Covent Garden, and a principal alto in the Royal Society of Musicians, the Chapel Royal, St Paul's, and the choirs of Westminster Abbey and Windsor. Perhaps the Francis Gore who died at the age of eight months on 26 December 1798 and was buried in Westminster Abbey on 31 December was Israel's son.

Gori, Signor. _See_ CORRI, SIGNORA DOMENICO.

Gorman, Mr _(fl. 1795–1798)_, _house servant._
Mr Gorman (or Gormon) was cited in the Drury Lane accounts on 25 April 1795. His salary was apparently 1s. daily. The accounts listed him among the house personnel in 1798, and on 16 June of that

year he was one of many whose benefit tickets were accepted at the theatre.

Gorselli, Signor (*fl. 1794*), *musician.*

A Signor Gorselli was listed in Doane's *Musical Directory* in 1794, but with no additional information. Perhaps that listing was a confusion with Fausto Borselli (fl. 1789–1790), a singer at the King's Theatre.

Gorsuch, Mrs (*fl. 1728*), *singer.*

Mrs Gorsuch sang Minerva in *Penelope* on 8 May 1728 at the Haymarket Theatre.

Gorton, William (*fl. 1694–1702*), *violinist.*

The Lord Chamberlain's accounts cited William Gorton regularly for livery payments from 30 November 1694 to April 1702. He was one of the instrumentalists in the King's Musick at a salary of £40 annually. He was usually listed with other members of the band of 24 violinists who played for William and Mary.

Gosley, Mr (*fl. 1757–1762*), *dancer.*

Mr Gosley (or Gosly) was first mentioned in the Covent Garden playbills on 10 December 1757 when he danced in *Macbeth*. His only other citations during the 1757–58 season concerned his participation as a dancer in *The Prophetess*, beginning on 1 February 1758, and in a comic ballet that was offered first on 28 April. Through 1761–62 Gosley appeared at Covent Garden in minor dancing assignments: in a dance called *The Threshers*, as a Satyr in the pantomime ballet *The Feast of Bacchus*, in *The Fair* and *Comus*, as a Gardener, Earth, a Demon, and a Country Lad in *The Rape of Proserpine*, as a Hussar in a dance entitled *The Hungarian Gambols*, and as Scaramouch in *Apollo and Daphne*. His daily salary in 1760–61 was 5s., next to the bottom of the scale; his annual income in 1761–62 was £43. Once, on 14 October 1758, the printers were not even sure who he was and spelled his name

"Goslin" in the bill. After the 1761–62 season he seems to have left the London stage.

Goslin. *See* GOSLEY, GOSLING, GOSTLING.

Gosling, Mr (*fl. 1794–1801*), *boxkeeper.*

The Drury Lane accounts show that on 3 May 1794 Mr Gosling the boxkeeper was raised 6d. per day, but no indication of his previous or new salary was given. On 13 March 1798 and 4 March 1799 he was paid arrears in salary, and in 1801 he was cited as receiving 15s. weekly for his work.

Gosnell, Winifred (*fl. 1662–c. 1697*), *actress, singer, dancer.*

Samuel Pepys met Winifred Gosnell on 12 November 1662:

At noon dined home with my wife, and by and by, by my wife's appointment, come two young ladies, sisters, acquaintances of my wife's brother [Balty], who are desirous to wait upon some ladies, and proffer their service to my wife. The youngest [Winifred], indeed, hath a good voice, and sings very well, besides other good qualitys; but I fear hath been bred up with too great liberty for my family, and I fear greater inconveniences of expenses, and my wife's liberty will follow, which I must study to avoid till I have a better purse; though I confess, the gentlewoman, being pretty handsome, and singing, makes me have a good mind to her.

Pepys could not help interviewing Winifred further, of course, and on 17 November she was at his home again, singing. Then, "there being no coach to be got, by water to White Hall; but Gosnell not being willing to go through [the] bridge, we were forced to land and take water again, and put her and her sister ashore at the Temple. I am mightily pleased with her humour and singing." But Winifred would not take employment with the Pepyses until "she hears from her mother," but "I am so fond of her that I am loth now not to have her. . . ."

By 22 November Pepys had so excited himself that he bought a book of country dances, "against my wife's woman Gosnell comes, who dances finely. . . ." And by 29 November he and his wife had found a nickname for Miss Gosnell—"Marmotte"—and Pepys was waiting impatiently for her to join the household. Finally, on 5 December 1662 his palpitations ended; Winifred Gosnell came to serve as a companion to Mrs Pepys.

On 8 December Pepys took Winifred to Temple Bar,

she going about business of hers today. By the way she was telling me how Balty did tell her that my wife did go every day in the week to Court and plays, and that she should have liberty of going abroad as often as she pleased, and many other lies, which I am vexed at, and I doubt the wench did come in some expectation of, which troubles me.

The following day, having employed Winifred only since the fifth, Pepys talked things over with his wife and Miss Gosnell left their service.

Later that month, on 26 December 1662 at the Lincoln's Inn Fields Theatre Pepys saw "Gosnell and her sister at a distance, and could have found it in my heart to have accosted them, but thought not prudent. But I watched their going out and found that they came, she, her sister and another woman, alone, without any man, and did go over the fields a foot."

By March 1663 Winifred had become a member of the Duke's Company at that very theatre. She probably had a walk-on in *Hamlet* when it was played on 9 March 1663, and Pepys rediscovered her on 28 May when he saw that play: "Who should come upon the stage but Gosnell, my wife's maid? but neither spoke, danced, nor sung;

which I was sorry for." Yet, "she becomes the stage very well." To ogle Winifred again, Pepys returned to the theatre the following day and saw *The Slighted Maid*, "wherein Gosnell acted Pyramena, a great part, and did it very well, and I believe will do it better and better, and prove a good actor." Since that role was normally taken by Mrs Betterton, historians have suggested that perhaps Winifred Gosnell was that actress's understudy.

In August 1663 Winifred sang "Ah, love is a delicate thing" in *The Playhouse to Be Let*—the only time she was named in a printed cast. On 10 September 1664 Pepys saw her in Davenant's *The Rivals*: there was "good acting in it; especially Gosnell comes and sings and dances finely, but, for all that, fell out of key, so that the musique could not play to her afterwards, and so did [Henry] Harris also go out of the tune to agree with her." Her role in that play was Celania (the prompter Downes later remembered it, incorrectly, as Celia), a part later taken by Moll Davis.

Miss Gosnell must have risen to a respectable position in the acting company. On 31 May 1668 Pepys noted "that Mrs Davis is quite gone from the Duke of York's [play]house and Gosnell comes in her room, which I am glad of." But his hopes were dashed; though the rumor was true, when Pepys went to hear Winifred sing in *The Slighted Maid* on 28 July 1668 he was crushed to discover that she had "become very homely, and sings meanly, I think." The following 21 January 1669 Pepys saw *The Tempest* with one role "ill done by Gosnell, in lieu of Moll Davis." The role, as Sybil Rosenfeld has suggested, may have been Ariel, which Mrs Davis had played.

Pepys was not the only person to observe that Winifred Gosnell was deteriorating. In *Poems on Affairs of State* is Scroope's "In Defense of Satire" (1677), which seems to link Winifred with John Sheffield, the third Earl of Mulgrave:

Grandio thinks himself a beau garçon,
Goggles his eyes, writes letters up and
*   down,*
And with his saucy love plagues all the
*   town,*
Whilst pleas'd to have his vanity thus
*   fed,*
He's caught with Gosnell, that old hag,
*   abed.*

The last reference that has been found
to Winifred Gosnell is a petition from her
to Charles, Earl of Dorset, when he was
Lord Chamberlain—which dates the document between 1689 and 1697:

The humble Peticion of Winifred Gosnold
Sheweth

That your Pet^r has belonged to their Ma^{ts}
Playe [house] ever since it was a Company,
and spent her youth in their service by Acting there, made herselfe incapable of getting
b[re]ad, in another place or way; she formerly
might have disposed of her selfe elsewhere,
and had other maintenance, but then they
would not part with her, now they have hired
other singers and Discharged her from what
she has and can plead right to, from the first,
without any misdemeanour or want of voice,
she being as Capable as ever of serveing them,
sh[e] has no hopes of releife, but your Lord^{pps}
favour and Goodnesse. Your Pet^r therefore
[m]ost humbly prays, that your Lord^{pp}. will
be pleased out [of your] great Goodness and
Inclination to Acts of Justice to [Comm]and
the Masters to reinstate her as formerly, or
to g[ive] her Sallary to support her from
want.

If Winifred was successful in her plea the
records do not show it.

Goss, Mr [fl. 1776], actor.

A Mr Goss acted Ramilie in *The Miser*
at the Haymarket Theatre on 18 September
1776.

Goss, The Masters [fl. 1794], singers.
See GOSS, JOHN JEREMIAH.

Goss, John Jeremiah 1770–1817, singer.

John Jeremiah Goss, an alto singer, was
born in 1770 at Salisbury, where he became a chorister of the Cathedral and
eventually a lay vicar. In 1794 Doane's
Musical Directory listed him as a member
of the New Musical Fund and a participant
in the Handelian commemorative performances in Westminster Abbey. Doane listed
three other singers who were probably
Goss's sons or younger brothers, all of Salisbury and all participants in the Handelian
concerts at Westminster Abbey; they were
cited as "Goss, Junr.," "Goss, Master," and
"Goss, Master Junr."

Appointed a Gentleman of the Chapel
Royal in London on 30 November 1808,
Goss also held the positions of vicar choral
of St Paul's Cathedral and lay vicar of
Westminster. A principal singer at the
concerts of the Three Choirs for many
years, his voice, according to Grove, "was
a pure alto of beautiful quality and his
skill and taste in part-singing remarkable."

Goss died in London on 25 April 1817.
At the meeting of the Governors of the
Royal Society of Musicians on 7 December
1817, it was proposed that Miss Goss, age
15 and presumably his daughter, should
be allowed "an annuity of £52 . . . for
the sum of 600 pounds," but the motion
did not carry.

At Salisbury in 1776 the dramatic pastoral *Edward and Egwina* (*sic*); *or, The
Feast of Ceres* was published with music by
a Mr Goss. That composer could not have
been John Jeremiah, who was only six at
the time, but perhaps he was his father. The
musician Sir John Goss (1800–1880), the
son of Joseph Goss, organist of Fareham,
evidently was no relation to John Jeremiah
Goss.

Gossett, Benjamin [fl. 1714–1740], trumpeter.

Benjamin Gossett was a trumpeter in the
King's Musick by 1714, according to docu-

ments in the Public Record Office. In 1740 he was replaced by Frederick Smith. Gossett was listed as one of the original subscribers to the Royal Society of Musicians in the "Declaration of Trust" which established that organization on 28 August 1739.

Gostling, John c. 1650–1733, singer, viola da gamba player.

John Gostling was born in East Malling, Kent, about 1650, the son of Isaac Gostling, a mercer. John went to Rochester School, then entered St John's College, Cambridge, in October 1668 and took his degree in 1672. On 27 February 1675 he married Elizabeth Turner, a spinster about 22 years old, from Maidstone, Kent, with the consent of her mother, Mrs Turner, alias Rutton. Gostling gave his age as about 24 and his home at that time as Woldham, Kent.

When John Gostling was appointed to the Chapel Royal on 25 February 1679, his position carried no fee, but three days later he was given a salaried post left vacant by the death of William Tucker. Gostling was described as a bass singer from Canterbury and a Master of Arts. Charles II heard Gostling at Canterbury one day and, according to Roger North, the King said "all the rest sang like Geese to him." Evelyn called him "That stupendous Base Gosling." Gostling and Purcell were good friends, and for the singer's rich voice Purcell wrote a number of anthems, most notable among them being "They that go down to the sea in ships." In addition to his singing ability, Gostling, according to Hawkins, was proficient on the viola da gamba.

In 1683 Gostling was made a minor canon at St Paul's in London, a post he held until 1690. He succeeded John Harding as Clerk of the Chapel Royal; from 1689 until his death Gostling was prebendary of Lincoln; by 1718 he was subdean at St Paul's; and he also held the post of vicar of Littlebourne. His annual salary as a member of the King's Musick was £30 under William and Mary (it had doubtless been higher under Charles and James). Gostling was named to accompany William III to Holland in January 1691, for which service he was surely paid an extra fee. In 1697 he was to have been paid £120 in arrears in liveries for 1689 to 1696—which probably accounts for his having made John Blow his attorney on 19 July 1691; many Restoration musicians found themselves in financial straits because of erratic livery payments from the Crown.

By the 1720s Gostling was spending more and more time in Canterbury. On 22 November 1727 excuses had to be made for his inability to come to London to be newly appointed to the Chapel Royal at the accession of George II:

This is to remember, that on account of the great age and infirmities of the Rev^d Mr. John Gostling, Priest in ordinary of his Maj. Royal Chapell, living at Canterbury (being a Minor Canon of that Metropolitan Church), whereby he was altogether unable to perform a journey up to London in order to be sworn and admitted into the Chappell Royal as newly confirm'd by his Maj. King George the Second, I [Edward Aspinwall, subdean of the Chapel] did, with the approbation of the Rt. Revd Edmund Lord Bishop of London, Dean of the said Chappel Royal, commission the Rev^d Dr. Elias Sydall, Prebendary of the Church of Canterbury, in residence there, to administer the oath of admission into the Chappel to the said Mr. John Gostling. . . .

Gostling had become a minor canon at Canterbury Cathedral as early as 1674, and the registers there contain many entries concerning the musician and his family. John and his wife baptized a son John on 13 February 1676; their daughter Elizabeth was baptized on 1 December 1678, shortly before John Gostling became a Gentleman of the Chapel Royal in London. Their other children were Thomas, baptized on 23 March 1680; a second John (the first having died), baptized on 7 July 1682; Katherine, baptized on 16 August 1783; and Mary, baptized on 11 July 1684. Gostling's wife died sometime during the ten years following Mary's birth, and John married again, his second wife's name being Dorothy. Their son William was baptized on 30 January 1696. William grew up to marry a woman named Hester, by whom he had several children who were baptized at Canterbury. Like his father, William became a minor canon of the Cathedral, as did William's son John. William died in 1777.

John Gostling died on 17 July 1733 and was buried in the cloisters of Canterbury Cathedral on 21 July.

Gotfred, Mrs James. *See* **FERRARI, SIGNORA GIACOMO GOTIFREDO.**

Gotini, Mr [*fl.* 1799], *scene painter.*
On 13 May 1799 Mr Gotini was paid £2 9s. and on 18 May £3 17s. by Covent Garden Theatre for painting scenes, along with Marinari, Greenwood the younger, Demaria, and others, for Sheridan's *Pizarro*, which had its first performance on 24 May 1799.

Gotlieb, Mons [*fl.* 1791–1796], *costume designer.*
The advertisement for the musical piece *The King and the Cobbler* at Astley's Amphitheatre on 6 May 1791 announced "the dresses, in character by Mons Gotlieb" and Mr Clary. Gotlieb was also credited for the costumes of *Harlequin in His Element* at the same theatre on 8 September 1794. With Clary and Bates he costumed *The Magician of the Rocks* there on 16 May 1796.

Goudain, Mons [*fl.* 1728], *dancer.*
Monsieur Goudain played a Devil in Mrs Violante's "Dramatick Entertainment of Dancing in Grotesque Characters" called *The Rivals* at the Haymarket Theatre on 21 February 1728. The performances ran through 6 May.

Gouge, Mr [*fl.* 1698–1730?], *singer, composer.*
Mr Gouge (sometimes George or Goudge) was a member of Thomas Betterton's company at the Lincoln's Inn Fields Theatre in 1698–99 and perhaps the following two seasons. He is known to have shared a benefit with Miss Bradshaw on 8 May 1700 at York Buildings and to have sung at Lincoln's Inn Fields on the following 5 July. He composed a number of light songs, among them *While Sighing at your Feet I lye*, separately published about 1700 and sung by Gouge at Lincoln's Inn Fields; "Free from Troubles," "How happy Sylvia," "When, when you malicious Planets," "Pastora was the Fairest," and " 'Tis said the War's over"—all published in *Mercurius Musicus* in 1699 and 1700; *Alexis shun'd his Fellow Swains*, separately published about 1720; and *Jockey and Jenny*, published about 1730. It is not known whether or not Gouge was still alive when the 1720 and 1730 publications came out; most of his activity dates from 1698 to about 1703.

Published songs tell us not only of some pieces Gouge set to music but of several popular songs by others which he sang either at the theatre or in concerts at music rooms. Eccles's *The Jolly, Jolly Breeze* from *Rinaldo and Armida* and *Belinda's pretty, pleasing Form* from *Women Will Have Their Wills* were published in 1700 with Gouge named as the singer. *Rinaldo* had been performed in November 1698 by Betterton's troupe, but the cast list in the first edition did not mention Gouge. The second work was never published but was performed on 24 February 1713 (as *A Woman Will Have Her Will*) according to *The London Stage* (Robert Hume and Judy Milhous suggest about spring 1700 as its premiere). Gouge was also cited as having sung Wilford's *Tell me dear charmer* at Lincoln's Inn Fields; the song was published about 1700. The January 1703 issue of *Mercurius Musicus* contained another Eccles song from *Rinaldo and Armida,* "Ah! Queen, ah! Queen, ah!", described as sung by Mr Gouge.

Gough, Mr [*fl.* 1791–1792], *animal trainer.*

On 23 January 1792, Mr Gough was paid £5 19s. 6d. by the Drury Lane company playing at the King's Theatre for the use of his greyhounds and "his attendance" in *Cymon* on 31 December 1791. He received additional payments of £5 4s. on 24 March 1792 and £3 5s. on 4 July 1792 for the greyhounds in subsequent performances of *Cymon.*

Gough, Catherine, later Mrs P. Galindo *1765–1829, actress.*

Harvard Theatre Collection

CATHERINE GOUGH, as Zenobia

engraving by Leney, after Graham

According to her autobiographical sketch in *Mrs Galindo's Letter to Mrs. Siddons* (1809) Catherine Gough was born in Ireland in 1765. Her father's poor management and improvident habits, according to her story, dissipated a considerable estate and forced her to go upon the stage. She had, she said, developed her abilities in Jones's genteel amateur theatricals in Fishamble Street, Dublin, in 1793. That account may have been true, but it sounds like many others told by actresses, and by some actors, to justify taking up a profession still stigmatized as not quite respectable.

In any event, Catherine seems not to have acted professionally in Ireland prior to her debut at Covent Garden Theatre in London on 22 October 1795 as Alicia in *Jane Shore.* One of her two sisters, Ann Gough, also went upon the stage, acted in Ireland and Shrewsbury (not in London), and married the actor Thomas Huddart. A notation on a manuscript now at the Folger Shakespeare Library, dating from about seven weeks prior to Catherine's debut, described her as resembling "in her Person & Talents" Mrs Siddons, "tho of a less heroic Cast." That puffing notice in later years assumed a bitter irony, in view of the bizarre relationship which developed between the two women.

After repeating Alicia on 29 October, Miss Gough played Calista in *The Fair Penitent* on 6 November and Hermione in *The Distrest Mother* for her benefit on 15 December. The Covent Garden treasury paid her £36 10s. 6d. on 22 December "to cash Benefit Ballance."

Though the critic in the *Monthly Mirror* of December 1795 judged her an intelligent actress, he found that the transition from the rarified and somewhat elegant environment of the private theatre in Dublin to the vastness of a London house was "by no means favourable" to her. Her voice did not carry, largely because she pitched it too low. Except for her oriental-turban headdress her taste in dress was praised as elegant. She had, the critic said, a wonderful face and graceful deportment, "with the single abatement of a strange inclination of the arms forming an angle from the elbow," a fault brought on by stage fright, since it was "scarcely perceptible after the first night." In *A Pin Basket to the Children of Thespis* (1797), John Williams praised her as "Full of loveliness, elegant, gorgeous, and gay" in person and manner, but he was less enthusiastic about her acting:

> In Alicia *her phrenzy was ably sustain'd*
> *But where she's not mad she declaim'd*
> *and she pain'd*
> . . . .
> Her Calista *was rather endur'd than enjoy'd.* . . .

In his assessment of Miss Gough, the critic of the *Monthly Mirror* had ended with the advice that she should continue with her efforts in the public theatre, since she required practice "to rear her talents to maturity." That practice, however, was not to be on the London stage. The management of Covent Garden, according to a story in the *Thespian Dictionary* (1805), told her that her applause had "proceeded from the good nature of the audience"—to which she had replied "she was much surprised they did not extend that good-nature to others in the company, who stood in greater need of it." They had sent her packing back to Ireland nevertheless.

At Belfast on 21 April 1796 Miss Gough acted Calista at the Arthur Street Theatre. During her engagement there she also performed Mrs Beverly in *The Gamester* on 25 April, Alicia on 27 April, Hermione on 29 April, and Isabella in *The Fatal Marriage*, for the first time, on 2 May. During the summer she acted at Fishamble Street and Crow Street, Dublin; she played Lady Teazle in *The School for Scandal* on 15 August 1796. She made her

first appearance at Edinburgh on 17 January 1797 as Lady Randolph in *Douglas*. Her notices for the season at Edinburgh were very complimentary. As the Queen in *Richard III* she did the part "great justice," especially in the parting scene in the Tower. She was commendable as Arpasia in *Tamerlane*, but her Lady Macbeth was wanting: "She cannot assume that determined firmness of look and deportment, which is characteristic of the part." That season she also acted Hermione, Lady Miniken in *Bon Ton*, Mrs Beverly, Oriana in *The Inconstant*, Ormisinda in *Alonzo*, and Julia Faulkland in *The Rivals*. When she returned to Edinburgh in 1798 and 1799, she continued to show herself an actress of promise and a person of "genteel and graceful" manner, playing Angelina in *Love Makes a Man*, Calista, Mrs Page in *The Merry Wives of Windsor*, Lady Jane in *He's Much to Blame*, Miss Wooburn in *Everyone Has His Fault*, and Evelina in *The Castle Spectre*. As Jane Shore on 23 April 1799 she "shone conspicuous." She also played at Hull for five nights in January 1799.

During the 1798–99 season Miss Gough was also a member of the company in Bristol and at the Orchard Street Theatre in Bath. It was at Bath that she first met Mrs Siddons, as well as a fencing master and sometime actor by the name of Galindo. Galindo had been acting minor roles at Bristol from 1793–94 through 1798–99, and he was also acting in Bath in 1798–99. In 1798 a Miss Galindo was playing children's roles at Bristol, which strongly suggests that Galindo himself was either married or a widower. During his years at Bristol, Galindo advertised his Fencing Academy in Shannon Court, off Corn Street.

During her winter engagement at Dublin in 1799–1800, Miss Gough became reacquainted with Galindo, who was then in that city as well. They were married sometime between 24 June and 4 November

1801; after the latter date, Miss Gough began to appear as Mrs Galindo. Her husband's first name is not known, but his first initial "P" is on correspondence now in the Folger Shakespeare Library.

As Mrs Galindo she acted at Crow Street in 1801–2 and 1802–3 but was not especially successful, being handicapped by "a most disgusting whine" in her voice. When she played Andromache to Mrs Siddons's Hermione in *The Distrest Mother* on 14 June 1802, her whining was "wretched." But by January 1803, having enjoyed the advantage of instruction from Mrs Siddons, she was "much improved."

In 1802 began an enthusiastic friendship between the Galindos and Mrs Siddons, who was performing in Ireland that summer. Also begun was a bizarre episode in Mrs Siddons's life, all the more extraordinary because of the great actress's usual image of uprightness, piety, and freedom from scandal.

In *Mrs Galindo's Letter to Mrs. Siddons*, an eight-page pamphlet written in a florid manner and with much bombast and pathos, Mrs Galindo published her accusations that Mrs Siddons had infatuated her husband, monopolized his time, ensnared his affections, and indulged in a physical affair with him, while all the time she pretended to be a bosom friend of Mrs Galindo. The threesome traveled together, and so great was Catherine's early trust in Mrs Siddons that the great actress was made godmother of a daughter born to the Galindos in July 1803. Later that year Mrs Siddons persuaded Harris, the manager at Covent Garden, to engage Galindo, but when her brother John Philip Kemble heard of the arrangement he became so furious—obviously embarrassed by his sister's improprieties—that he forced Harris to withdraw the offer. In February 1804 Galindo came to London, nevertheless, to be near Sarah, leaving Catherine in Dublin, to follow seven months later. Catherine complained that she had to support herself

and her family, yet she seemed ignorant of the affair at the time and, indeed, had another child, presumably by her husband. The Galindos stayed in London for three years, until about 1808, when the fencing master borrowed £1000 from Sarah Siddons in order to enter into a partnership with William Macready for the lease of the Manchester Theatre. The venture failed, and when Galindo was unable to repay Mrs Siddons he also lost his interest in her. Mrs Galindo's charge, and her purpose in writing her pamphlet, was that Sarah was taking her revenge by demanding repayment immediately, thereby threatening to ruin him, Catherine, and their three children. Sarah never recovered her money. (But the Galindos' oldest child, Johnny, was referred to with affection several times in Mrs Siddons's letters.)

We do not know what happened to the Galindos after 1809. Several documents in the Prerogative Court of Canterbury may refer to Galindo's brothers or other relatives. On 2 May 1807 the administration of the estate of Samuel Galindo, late ensign in the 29th Regiment of Foot on the Island of St Vincent's, bachelor, was granted to his father James Galindo. In a will drawn on 11 May 1814 at Woolwich, George Galindo, of the Navy Office and of No 12, Marshmont Street, Russell Square, left his estate to his brother Richard Miles Galindo, of No 9, Ely Place, Holborn, with the stipulation that "he must give to my dearly beloved Mother my two dearly beloved Sisters and my four dearly beloved Brothers a Mourning Ring." The will was proved in London on 2 June 1814 by Richard Miles Galindo, brother and executor.

Catherine Galindo died on 18 January 1829, aged 64, and was buried at St Anne's, Dublin. During the height of her career in Dublin, between 1800 and 1804, she had been a promising actress, although she hardly deserved to be puffed, as she was by one provincial manager, as "a second Mrs Siddons." Ironically enough, the same theatrical advertisement, quoted by Winston in *The Theatric Tourist* (1804), predicted that when Mrs Siddons retired from the stage Miss Gough would replace her in London—"*but two stars cannot move in one sphere.*" Verses in *Familiar Epistles to Frederick J———s, Esq; on the Present State of the Irish Stage* (1804) provide some details of her merits and defects:

> *Away—for sad G–li–do room—!*
> *Living momento of the tomb; —*
> *Upon her dark unalter'd brow,*
> *Sits one eternal cloud of woe,*
> *And from her throat a voice she heaves*
> *Like winds that moan thro' ruin'd caves;*
> *The trembling stage she passes o'er,*
> *As if she stepp'd knee deep in gore;*
> *And every dismal glance she scowls,*
> *Seems cast at daggers, racks, and bowls.*
> *But this is error; —sternest grief*
> *Bars not the soul from all relief;*
> *And human feelings ne'er remain*
> *Stretch'd on the unceasing rack of pain.—*
> *Poor Shore, some rays of hope beguile,*
> *And Denmark's queen must sometimes*
> *   smile;*
> *Maternal joy, in Constance, speaks*
> *And lives on Lady Randolph's cheeks.*
> . . . .
> *Could but our fair one, learn to bear*
> *An easier look, and lighter air,*
> *Give more emotion to her face,*
> *And to her shape a* varying *grace;*
> *With so much feeling, so much sense,*
> *We'd own our claim to eminence*
> *Confess her easily the queen*
> *Of all that sweep our tragic scene.*

An engraved portrait by W. Sedgewick of Miss Gough, "Of the Private Theatre Fishamble Street," was published in the *Hibernian Magazine* in March 1796. An engraving of her as Zenobia, by W. Leney, after J. Graham, was published as plates to *Bell's British Theatre* (1796) and Cawthorn's *British Library* (1796).

Gough, Daniel [*fl.* 1709?–1751], *impresario, actor?, singer?*

On 19 September 1709 a concert was presented at a new playhouse in Hampstead operated by a Mr Goff. The presentation consisted of songs and comic dialogues, and Goff assured the public that the concert would be "perform'd with much better Decorum than before." The *Post Boy* of 13/15 September had reported that the Justices of Middlesex had issued an order silencing the Hampstead players. What was indecorous about the earlier performance was not reported. Years later, on 28 November 1730, a Mr Goff (the same person?) sang at the Goodman's Fields playhouse.

A Mr Gough performed at the Smock Alley Theatre in Dublin in 1732–33 and is known to have acted the title role in *The Cheats of Scapin* on 3 May 1733. He was at Smock Alley again in 1733–34 and at the Ransford Street playhouse in 1734–35, after which Dublin references to the performer ceased.

It is possible that the above references concern Daniel Gough, the proprietor of the Rose Tavern and its gardens in 1737. The gardens had been open without charge to the public before Gough took over, but Daniel began charging an entrance fee. On 12 July 1738 he advertised the opening of "Marybone" Gardens. There one could hear a band of musicians from the opera house and legitimate theatres playing concertos, overtures, and airs. Gough built a large garden orchestra and charged, in 1738–39, 12*s.* for the season. In 1740 he installed an organ by Bridges in the garden orchestra and built a great room for balls and suppers. John Trusler succeeded to the management in 1751.

Gough, Henry [*fl.* 1784–1794], *bassoonist.*

Henry Gough was named by Dr Burney as one of the bassoonists in the Handel Memorial Concerts at Westminster Abbey and the Pantheon in May and June 1784. In 1794 he was listed in Doane's *Musical Directory* as a bassoonist, a member of the

New Musical Fund and the Academy of Ancient Music, a participant in the performances at Westminster Abbey, and then residing at No 8, Red Lion Court, Spitalfields Market. Perhaps he was related to the George Gough who was a member of the Irish Musical Fund in Dublin between 1798 and 1800 and to the Mr Gough who was a violinist in the Haymarket Theatre band in 1815 and 1816.

Gould, Grace d. c. 1766, wardrobe keeper.

Grace Gould was a dresser at Covent Garden in 1735–36, working for 1s. 8d. nightly and occasionally supplying the theatre with feathers and perhaps other materials, certainly for a fee. The following season she was mentioned in the accounts as having received 12s. for a widow's scarf and three hoods and £7 17s. 6d. for a black velvet gown and coat. It is likely that she augmented her dresser's salary by work as a seamstress throughout her career.

Perhaps Mrs Gould (or Good, Goold, Gold) worked regularly at Covent Garden until her death about 1766, but some seasons are not accounted for: 1736–37, 1738–39, 1739–40, 1742–43 through 1754–55, 1761–62, and 1764–65. Otherwise she was regularly mentioned at benefit time. By 1760–61 she had advanced to wardrobe keeper at 3s. 4d. daily. Grace Gould probably died in late 1766. Her last mention at benefit time was on 15 May of that year, when her tickets were accepted; on 13 January 1767 the theatre management paid £4 8s. for Mrs Gould's funeral.

Goulding, George [fl. c. 1786–1834], musician, music seller.

From about 1786 to 1834 George Goulding was active in London as a music seller, publisher, and musical instrument maker, and Doane's *Musical Directory* of 1794 informs us that Goulding was also a musician who participated in the Handelian performances at Westminster Abbey. His business career is outlined in Humphries and Smith's *Music Publishing in the British Isles*. Goulding was in business for himself from about 1786 to 1787 at No 25, James Street, Covent Garden, and from about 1787 to 1798 at The Haydn's Head, No 6, James Street, Covent Garden. He had an additional shop at No 17, Great Turnstile, Holborn, in 1787 and an agency for the sale of pianos and organs at No 113, Bishopsgate Street Within in 1788. He published catalogues of new music in 1791 and 1792.

From 1798 to about 1810 Goulding was in partnership with Phipps and D'Almaine. They had a shop at No 45, Pall Mall, from 1798 to about 1804 and additional premises at No 76, St James's Street, from 1800 to 1804, and a shop at No 117, New Bond Street from about 1804 to 1808, and No 124, New Bond Street from about 1808 to 1810. Goulding had a branch shop in Dublin at No 7, Westmoreland Street from about 1803 to 1810 called Goulding, Knevett, and Company until about 1806 and then Goulding, Phipps, D'Almaine and Company. The London firm became Goulding, D'Almaine, Potter, and Company in 1810. The partnership operated at No 124, New Bond Street until 1811, then at No 20, Soho Square until 1823. They maintained their Dublin branch at No 7, Westmoreland Street until 1816, when it was taken over by Isaac Willis. The London firm went under various names until about 1823, when it became Goulding and D'Almaine, music sellers and publishers, at No 20, Soho Square, until 1834. Over the years Goulding and his colleagues brought out several catalogues of instrumental and vocal music.

A number of entries in the parish registers of St Paul, Covent Garden, doubtless concern our subject. On 16 July 1789 George Goulding, bachelor, married Sarah Clark Dennis Goulding, spinster. They were, perhaps, cousins, and on the following 15 November their first child, Jane, was christened. A George Goulding, perhaps our subject's father, had been buried just a week and a half before, on 6 November. George and Sarah Goulding buried a stillborn child on 20 May 1792. Their daughter Georgina was christened on 7 September 1794 and buried on the thirteenth. On 1 November 1795 they christened their daughter Mary, but she too died in infancy and was buried four days later. This sad history ended when the Gouldings buried another stillborn child, a girl, on 28 August 1797.

Goupy, Joseph *c. 1678–c. 1768, scene painter, landscape painter.*

Accounts of Joseph Goupy given in *Bryan's Dictionary of Painters and Engravers* and in *The Dictionary of National Biography* suggest that he was born at Nevers, France, about the beginning of the eighteenth century and that when he was quite young he came to London to settle with his uncle, Lewis Goupy (d. 1747), who was a painter well placed under the patronage of Lord Burlington. But documents in the Public Record Office relating to a legal action brought against Goupy in 1738 imply that he was born in England, and the testimony of Mrs Dorothy Chabeny, one of his pupils, on 12 September 1739, that she "had been informed that he had exercised his trade for forty years or thereabouts" would place the beginning of his career about 1699. Assuming that Goupy had completed an apprenticeship at the usual age of 21, his year of birth would have been about 1678. The miniaturist Bernhard Goupy, who was also resident in England during the period of Joseph's life-

National Portrait Gallery

"An Artists' Club in 1735," showing JOSEPH GOUPY, standing behind seated figure center

by G. Hamilton

time, has been called his brother but may have been an uncle.

In 1711 Joseph was a subscriber with his uncle Lewis to the new academy of painting in Great Queen Street begun under Sir Godfrey Kneller. By his own assertion, after a long period of study and having "for many years together travelled to Rome and abroad to improve himself in the said studies," Goupy was by 1717 "esteemed a complete master" in the arts of drawing and painting. So great was his reputation by that date that Goupy claimed "he could with the greatest ease get £600 a year and upwards." By then he had copied the seven Raphael cartoons at Hampton Court in watercolors for Baron Kielmannsegge, receiving 220 guineas; they were later bought by the Duke of Chandos for 50 guineas each and then passed into the possession of the Rt Hon W. E. Gladstone.

About 1719 he became associated with the artists Sir James Thornhill and Michael Dahl. Dahl drew Goupy's portrait and gave him 15 guineas in exchange for a picture by Goupy. Dahl valued Goupy's work as worth double his own and claimed that "Goupy was the best hand in England at his trade."

Through his friendship with Handel, Goupy became an occasional scene painter for the operas. With Peter Tillemans he did scenes for the King's Theatre in 1724, possibly for *Tamerlano* and *Giulio Cesare*, and in 1725, possibly for *Rodelinda*. He probably designed scenes for *Admeto* on 31 January 1727, and he and Tillemans did the decorations for *Riccardo I* on 11 November 1727. Goupy's painting of "Mutius Scaevola burning his hand in the presence of Porsena" was no doubt inspired by the production of the opera *Muzio Scevola* in 1721. (The painting was done at the behest of Goupy's patron John Hedges, a man of wealth and position and a British envoy. Hedges's estate eventually sued the artist in 1738 for sums advanced to the artist but not repaid. The case seems finally

to have been settled out of court.) Goupy then did an etching (1726) of the "Mutius Scaevola" which he dedicated to his friend, the well known mathematician, Dr Brook Taylor (d. 1731).

By 1736 Goupy was living in a house in Saville Street. Through his friendship with Taylor, Goupy became the drawing master of Frederick, the Prince of Wales, worked for him at Kew and Cliveden, and in 1736 was appointed his "cabinet-painter." Among his pupils for painting were the aforesaid Mrs Dorothy Chabeney, who paid him four guineas per month for tuition over a period of at least 20 years, probably Matthew Robinson, and John Hedges himself, as well as the Princess of Wales.

Goupy enjoyed the patronage of his Prince for some years. In 1749 he was sent on a mission to Paris by Frederick. When the latter died in 1751, Goupy's public notice diminished. Upon the accession of George III, Goupy received the modest pension of a guinea per week. He did not die in 1763, as reported in *The Dictionary of National Biography*, for his name was entered in the catalogue of the first exhibition of the Society of Artists in 1765 for contributing a watercolor of "La Penserosa e l'amor" and a copy of the "Mutius Scaevola," at which time he was put down as living "at Kensington." On 3 May 1765 he was elected a Fellow of the Society of Artists and signed the Roll on 7 January 1765. His name also appeared in 1766 on the "Roll Declaration of the Incorporated Society of Artists" and on the "List of Non-Exhibitors" drawn up by the Society's secretary for the years 1766, 1767, and 1768, a circumstance which suggests that the officials of the Society assumed him to be still alive.

Goupy was a good miniature-painter in watercolor and a skillful copyist of Italian masters. In the *Dictionary of Engravers*, his contemporary Strutt called him "a man of genius" and stated that in his "very spirited plates," only a few of his own conception, he adopted the style of Salvator Rosa and "particularly excelled in landscapes, which he executed with great taste and in a masterly manner." The artist John Wootton called him "a very ingenious man at painting and drawing."

Collections of Goupy's work were sold at auction in March 1765 and by Langford & Son on 3 April 1770. Drawings and watercolors by him can be found in the British Museum. He, and not Laguerre as commonly believed, was responsible for the bad restoration of four of the nine panels of Montegna's "Triumph of Julius Caesar" at Hampton Court, for which he received £200 from Cooke, King William's vice-chamberlain. He also copied works for William, third Duke of Devonshire, John, second Duke of Rutland, William, second Earl Cowper, and for many other noblemen.

One of Goupy's best-known engravings is a caricature of Cuzzoni, Farinelli, and Heidegger made in 1730 from a sketch provided by the Italian artist Mario Ricci in 1729. That famous print is sometimes attributed in error to Hogarth and has caused some confusion because there are actually three states of the etching. The first is without names under the characters. The second bears the name of the Countess of Burlington, Faustina's patroness, at the lower left in a place where the artist's name would normally be found, and the persons are identified as Cuzzoni, Farinelli, and Heidegger. The third state has the name of Senesino below Farinelli's, but that seems to have been a later addition, and the figure itself seems originally intended for Farinelli. The matter is further complicated by the fact that in his original sketch, Ricci had pictured only two persons, Cuzzoni and Farinelli, and Goupy or the Countess had added the seated Heidegger.

Goupy also did a well known caricature of Handel seated at the organ, with a large wig and enormous tusks on his boarlike head. The original colored drawing once belonged to Horace Walpole; it was sold at Messrs Puttick and Simpson's and passed into the hands of Edward F. Rimbault, who wrote a most informative article on it in *Notes and Queries* in April 1876. Prints of it were engraved in 1730 and in 1754. The drawing, now in the Fitzwilliam Museum, Cambridge, is reproduced with the notice of Handel in this dictionary.

A portrait of Goupy, holding a small picture of a landscape, was painted by Michael Dahl. He was also painted by Huyssing and by his uncle Lewis Goupy, and he appears in the painting by Gawen Hamilton of "An Artists' Club in 1735," which is now in the National Portrait Gallery. A bust of Goupy, from life, was done by Rysbrack.

Gourdon. *See* GAURON.

Gouret. *See* GOURIET.

Gouriet, Mr ₁*fl. 1798–1802₁, *dancer, choreographer.*

Mr Gouriet (or Gouret, Gourriet, Gourlier) danced in the pastoral ballet *Elisa* on 10 May 1798 at the King's Theatre. On 17 April 1799 his comic ballet *Le Tintamarre* was presented at Sadler's Wells, and the following 8 July he was one of the dancers in another of his works, *La Fête du Serrail.* He served as a choreographer and dancer at the Wells in 1800 and continued appearing there in the summers of 1801 and 1802. Gouriet also worked at Drury Lane in 1800–1801 at a salary of 5*s.* 6*d.* daily. There on 6 May 1801 he danced the character of Don Pedro in *Alonzo the Brave, and the Fair Imogine*, a ballet. In 1801–2 he was a dancer at the King's Theatre.

Gourion. *See* GAURON.

Gourriet. *See* GOURIET.

Gourroin, Mons ₁*fl. 1728₁, *dancer.*
On 21 February 1728 at the Haymarket

Theatre Monsieur Gourroin played a Countryman in Mrs Violante's "Entertainment of Dancing" called *The Rivals*.

"Governess General of the Kentish Drama, The." *See* BAKER, SARAH, NÉE WAKELIN.

Gow, Andrew *1760–1794, violinist, violist.*

Andrew Gow, one of the sons of Neil and Margaret Urquhart Gow, was a violinist and violist, according to Doane's *Musical Directory* of 1794, a member of the New Musical Fund (and on that society's committee in 1794), and a participant in the Handel performances at Westminster Abbey. In London he lived at No 60, King Street, Golden Square, though when he died on 7 July 1794 he was, evidently, at the Gow family home at Inver, near Dunkeld, Scotland. Humphries and Smith's *Music Publishing in the British Isles* states that Andrew and his brother John were music sellers in London and agents for the compositions of their father Neil and brother Nathaniel from about 1787. They place Andrew's death in 1803, which is certainly incorrect. Farmer's *History of Music in Scotland* gives Andrew's birth as 1760.

Gow, John *1764–1827?, violinist, violist.*

John Gow was one of the sons of the Scottish musician Neil Gow and his wife Margaret, née Urquhart. About 1787 John and his brother Andrew set up shop at No 60, King Street, Golden Square, as music sellers, dealing especially in the compositions of their father Neil and their brother Nathaniel. Doane's *Musical Directory* of 1794 cited John as a violinist and violist and a member of the New Musical Fund. He was on the Court of Assistants of that society that year and again (or still) in 1805 and 1815. John participated in the Handel performances at Westminster Abbey.

After Andrew Gow's death in 1794 John moved his premises to No 31, Carnaby Street, where he remained until 1815. Then he moved to No 31, Great Marlborough Street. He was joined in business by his son John about 1823, and they set up at No 162, Regent Street. Humphries and Smith's *Music Publishing in the British Isles* gives John Gow's death as 1827; Farmer's *History of Music in Scotland* gives his death as 1826 and states that John was born in 1764. A letter written by John from Carnaby Street to his brother Nathaniel in Edinburgh on 28 November 1797 (now at the National Library of Scotland) indicates that John's wife was named Augusta.

Goyon, Mons [*fl. 1783?–1792*], *dancer.*

The dancer Goyon who appeared in London in 1786–87 may have been the dancer of that name mentioned in Fuchs's *Lexique* as having performed in Bordeaux from 1783 to 1785. On 23 December 1786, hailed as from the Opéra at Paris, Monsieur Goyon danced *Le Chercheuse d'esprit* at the King's Theatre for his first appearance in England. During the rest of the 1786–87 season he danced in *Le Berger inconstant*, a *Divertissement*, the ballets *L'Heureux Événement* and *La Bergère capricieuse*, a *pas de trois* with Mlle Mozon and Mme Perignon in the ballet *Sylvie*, *Le Divertissement Asiatique*, and *Le Cossac jaloux*. The *Petit almanach des grands spectacles de Paris* in 1792 cited Monsieur Goyon as a dancer at the Opéra that year.

Grabu, Louis [*fl. 1659–1695*], *violinist, composer, producer.*

The violinist Louis Grabu was in France in 1659, may have come to England at the Restoration the following year, and was certainly in London by 31 March 1665 when, according to the Lord Chamberlain's accounts, he was appointed to the King's Musick as a composer replacing Nicholas Lanier. At the Chapel Royal, St James, on 2 April 1665 "Ludovicus Grabeu of Shalon in Catalunnia" married Catherine Deluss (or, as she signed herself, de Loes) of Paris. Our guess is that Grabu was from San Celoní, in the northeast corner of Spain. On 12 November 1666 an order was issued to John Banister and the King's band of 24 violinists to "from tyme to tyme, obey the directions of Louis Grabu." Banister had been playing fast and loose with his powers and with his musicians' money, so the King put Grabu in his place as "our Director in Ordinary, as master of our English Chamber Musicke." Grabu also received Banister's arrears in pay—or was supposed to have done so.

On 1 October 1667 Samuel Pepys heard Grabu rehearsing "An English Song upon Peace" with his violinists and some singers: "But, God forgive me! I never was so little pleased with a concert of musick in my life. The manner of setting of words and repeating them out of order, and that with a number of voices, makes me sick, the whole design of vocall musick being lost by it." Yet, "the instrumental musick he had brought by practice to play very just." The English musician Pelham Humphrey, fresh from a visit to France, was greatly disturbed at Grabu's rapid rise at court. On 15 November 1667 Pepys reported Humphrey as saying "that Grebus, the Frenchman, the King's master of the musick . . . understands nothing, nor can play on any instrument, and so cannot compose; and that he [Humphrey] will give him a lift out of his place; and that he and the King are mighty great! and that he hath already spoke to the King of Grebus would make a man piss."

Pepys had invited Grabu and some other musicians to dinner that day. They played some music, and Pepys confided to his diary: "nor do I see that this Frenchman do so much wonders on the theorbo, but without question he is a good musician, but his vanity do offend me." On 15 April 1668 at Whitehall Pepys listened to "the fiddling-concert, and heard a practice mighty good of Grebus."

Despite Pelham Humphrey's cocky prediction, Grabu remained in favor with the King. On 17 April 1668 he was paid (over and above his usual salary and livery) £165 9s. 6d. for writing music for Charles II from 4 November 1666 to 25 March 1668. That covered not only his compositions but expenses associated with composing, such as paper and candles. It is not likely that Grabu was paid on schedule, however, for the King was often years behind in payments to court musicians. On 9 January 1669, for instance, Grabu was owed £200 by the King; on 11 March 1672 he was to have been paid £117 4s. 6d. for work done in December 1668 and February 1669. Like many other court musicians, Grabu ran into debt and had to assign money due him to his creditors; one instance was on 23 May 1673, when he assigned £137 4s. 6d. in arrears from April 1668 to a London merchant named Walter Lapp. Had Grabu received all his fees on time he probably would have been well off, for in addition to serving as master of the King's Musick and composer, he was responsible for the teaching of two boys, probably Children of the Chapel Royal.

In 1674 Grabu busied himself with the production of his opera *Ariadne, or The Marriage of Bacchus*. He and Pierre Perin, the librettist, had collaborated on the work in France in 1659. For the London production the new Drury Lane Theatre in Bridges Street was used instead of Whitehall. A warrant dated 27 March 1674 directed Christopher Wren to have some scenery from Whitehall moved to Bridges Street for the French opera; Grabu would, the order claimed, return it after two weeks. The opera was presented by the "Royal Academy of Music" on 9 April 1674 but seems not to have caused a stir in musical circles.

There was a misunderstanding concerning some of the French dancers in Grabu's opera, for in May 1674 the Drury Lane people—Thomas Killigrew, Charles Hart, and John Lacy—complained that six dancers they thought were to perform for their troupe now said they had a previous agreement with Grabu. Details of the case are lacking, but apparently Grabu had ţalked his countrymen into quitting Drury Lane for some reason, even though they were paid 5*s.* daily to dance there after the opera production was over. The dancers were ordered to continue at Drury Lane. The controversy seems petty, but it may have been a partial reason for Grabu's being replaced as master of the chamber music at court on 29 January 1675 by Nicholas Staggins.

Grabu was owed what was then a great amount of money. When he left his court post his salary was £675 in arrears. On 5 May 1677 Grabu was still trying to get his back pay. The Lord Chamberlain reported on 5 June that the musician was owed £450 out of the Exchequer, £145 4*s.* 6*d.* out of the Treasury, and £32 5*s.* out of the Great Wardrobe. Grabu was found "to be very poor and miserable," said the Lord Chamberlain, and deserved payment of his back salary as soon as possible. Grabu probably got his money eventually, but to keep body and soul together he sold music to the public theatres. He wrote some of the music for Shadwell's version of *Timon of Athens*, and his setting of "Hark how the songsters" was printed in Playford's *Choice Ayres* in 1679. Grabu also composed a song for *Squire Oldsapp*, which was performed about June 1678. But he was clearly making little headway in England; on 31 March 1679 he was issued a passport for France and returned to his native land.

On 12 September 1683 Lord Preston wrote from Paris to the Duke of York, speaking of a Mr Grahme, who seems almost certainly to have been Grabu:

I should not have presumed to give your Highness the trouble of this if something of charity had not induced me to it. I do it at the instance of a poor servant of his Majesty's, who some time since was obliged by a mis-

fortune to leave England. It is Mr Grahme, sir, whom perhaps your Highness may remember. Mr Betterton coming hither some weeks since by his Majesty's command, to endeavour to carry over the Opera, and finding that impracticable, did treat with Mnsr Grahme to go over with him to endeavour to represent something at least like an Opera in England for his Majesty's diversion. He hath also assured him of a pension from the House [i.e., playhouse], and finds him very willing and ready to go over. He only desireth his Majesty's protection when he is there, and what encouragement his Majesty shall be pleased to give him if he finds that he deserves it.

Grabu returned to England in the fall of 1683. The "something at least like an opera" turned out to be Dryden's *Albion and Albanius,* a spectacle which included, among other treats, a huge peacock whose open tail filled the Dorset Garden Theatre proscenium opening. The work, with music by Louis Grabu, opened on 5 June 1685. Roger North, writing about 1726, remembered that "The first full opera that was made and prepared for the stage, was the *Albanio* of Mr Grabue, in English, but of a French genius. It is printed in full score, but proved the ruin of the poor man, for the King's death supplanted all his hopes, and so it dyed." King Charles had heard at least portions of the work before his death in February 1685. Dryden wrote in his preface that the King "had been pleas'd twice or thrice to command, that it shou'd be practis'd before him, especially the first and third Acts of it; and publickly declar'd more than once, That the composition and Chorus's were more Just, and more Beautiful, than any he had heard in England." Those rehearsals, according to a letter written by Edward Bedingfield, took place at the Duchess of Portsmouth's (she was Louise de Kéroualle, one of the King's mistresses) where the music by "Grabunche" "pleaseth mightily."

But the death of King Charles dampened Grabu's hopes; then the news of the Duke of Monmouth's rebellion reached London on the sixth night of the run of *Albion and Albanius* and was a major factor in closing the production. Modern critics have declared both the play and the music wretched and suggested that that was why the opera failed. Nor was contemporary response favorable. A satirical poem called "The Raree-show, from Father HOPKINS" came out in 1685 ridiculing Dryden (Bayes), Grabu, and the show generally:

> *From Father* Hopkins, *whose Vein did inspire him,*
>> *Bays sends this Raree-show publick to view;*
> *Prentices, Fops and their Footmen admire him,*
>> *Thanks Patron, Painter, and Monsieur* Grabu.
>
> *Each Actor on the Stage his luck bewailing,*
>> *Finds that his loss is Infallibly true;*
> Smith, Nokes, *and* Leigh *in a Feaver with railing,*
>> *Curse Poet, Painter, and Monsieur* Grabu.
>
> Betterton, Betterton, *thy Decorations,*
>> *And the Machines were well written we knew;*
> *But all the Words were such stuff we want Patience,*
>> *And little better is Monsieur* Grabu.
>
> D—— *me says* Underhill, *I'm out two hundred,*
>> *Hoping that Rain-bows and Peacocks would do;*
> *Who thought infallible* Tom *could have blunder'd,*
>> *A Plague upon him and Monsieur* Grabu.
>
> Lane *thou has no Applause for thy Capers,*
>> *Tho' all without thee would make a Man spew;*
> *And a Month hence will not pay for the Tapers,*
>> *Spite of* Jack Laureat *and Monsieur* Grabu.
>
> Bays *thou would have thy Skill thought universal,*

> *Tho' thy dull Ear be to Musick untrue;*
> *Then whilst we strive to confute the* Rehearsal,
>> *Prithee learn thrashing of Monsieur* Grabu.

And so on.

Though there was public criticism of Grabu's music, Dryden was extravagant in his praise of Grabu. In the preface to *Albion and Albanius* he spoke of the Frenchman's

extraordinary Tallent, in diversifying the Recitative, the Lyrical part, and the Chorus: In all which, (not to attribute any thing to my own Opinion) the best Judges and those too of the best Quality, who have honor'd his Rehearsals with their Presence, have no less commended the happiness of his Genius than his Skill. And let me have the liberty to add one thing; that he has so exactly express'd my Sence, in all places, where I intended to move the Passions, that he seems to have enter'd into my thoughts, and to have been the Poet as well as the Composer. This I say, not to flatter him, but to do him right; because amongst some *English* Musicians, and their Scholars, (who are sure to judge after them,) the imputation of being a *French-man,* is enough to make a Party, who maliciously endeavour to decry him. But the knowledge of *Latin* and *Italian* Poets, both which he possesses, besides his skill in Musick, and his being acquainted with all the performances of the *French Opera*'s, adding to these the good Sence to which he is Born, have rais'd him to a degree above any Man, who shall pretend to be his Rival on our Stage. When any of our Country-men excel him, I shall be glad for the sake of old *England,* to be shewn my error: in the mean time, let Vertue be commended, though in the Person of a Stranger.

Despite all that, Dryden did not use Grabu again but turned to the young Henry Purcell, who soon became London's leading opera composer.

His hopes dashed by the death of King Charles and the failure of *Albion and Albanius*, Grabu returned to Paris on 3 December 1685. He may have returned to

England in 1687, for music by him was used in Waller's alteration of *The Maid's Tragedy* on 6 April of that year, and on the following 8 December Grabu was paid his arrears in salary even though he was no longer in the royal service. After 1687 Grabu is hard to trace. Zimmerman, in his biography of Purcell, reports a concert advertised by Grabu on 15 November 1694, but that seems to be the last notice of him.

Grace, Mrs (*fl. 1721–1726?*), *dancer, actress?*

On 26 April 1721 a Mrs Grace danced at Lincoln's Inn Fields. She was not mentioned again in that theatre's bills, though she may have performed the remainder of the season. Perhaps she was the Mrs Grace who acted at the Smock Alley Theatre in Dublin from 1721–22 through 1725–26. Some of that woman's known roles there were Jenny in *Love for Love*, Eugenia in *The Rival Generals*, Dolly in *The Deceit*, Teresa in *The Spanish Fryar*, Miss Flirt in *A Wife and No Wife*, Penelope in *Tunbridge Walks*, Prudence in *The Amorous Widow*, Situp in *The Double Gallant*, Constance Holdup in *The Northern Lass*, and Panura in *The Island Princess*.

Grace, Master (*fl. 1733*), *dancer.*

On 31 March 1733 at Drury Lane "Young Grace" danced the little negro Pompey in *The Harlot's Progress*. The Mrs Grace who married Charles Macklin was also in the company, so perhaps Master Grace was her son.

Grace, Miss. *See* BARRE, MRS.

Grace, Ann. *See* MACKLIN, MRS CHARLES THE FIRST.

Grace, Elizabeth. *See* ELRINGTON, MRS. RICHARD.

Grace, (*G.?*) (*fl. 1787–1796*), *actor.*

At the Royalty Theatre in November 1787 a Mr Grace played the Old Man in *Harlequin Mungo*. At the Haymarket Theatre on 9 April 1788 he appeared as Captain O'Cutter in *The Jealous Wife* and Thomas in *The Irish Widow*. The following September at the same house Grace acted the title role in *Barnaby Brittle* and Quildrive in *The Citizen*. At Portsmouth on 29 April 1789 Grace played Staff in *Fashionable Levities* and Friar Tuck in *Robin Hood*. Perhaps the actor we have been following was the G. Grace who, on 3 October 1791, was paid £5 5s. as a gift in lieu of an engagement at Drury Lane; he was probably assured of a position that never materialized and had to settle for a consolation prize.

Mr Grace, probably the same actor, played at the Crow Street Theatre in Dublin in 1791 and then at Kilkenny in February and May 1792 and Newry the following July. Grace (or Grase) was a member of the company at Richmond, Surrey, in the summer of 1795, and he was hailed as from there when he made his Manchester debut on 27 November of that year. The January 1796 *Monthly Mirror* confirmed that Grace was in Ward's troupe in Manchester during the 1795–96 season.

"Gradelin" or **"Gradellino."** *See* CONSTANTINI, CONSTANTINO.

Gradwell, Thomas (*fl. 1661–c. 1673*), *actor.*

The Restoration actor Thomas Gradwell may have been related to Henry and Richard Gradwell, who were active in the London theatre in the 1630s. A warrant dated 17 December 1661 in the Lord Chamberlain's accounts listed Thomas as a member of the King's Company at the Vere Street Theatre. Later warrants mentioned Gradwell as a continuing member of the troupe receiving annual livery as one of the King's servants. His last mention in the accounts was on 2 October 1669, though he may have been working in the company long after that.

Very few roles are known for Gradwell. The prompter John Downes said in 1708 that Gradwell had played "The Uncle" (that is, Miramont, the title role) in *The Elder Brother*; the King's Company is known to have performed that work on 23 November 1660, on 6 September 1661, and toward the end of 1662. Gradwell had a role in *Catiline* on 18 December 1668 and several subsequent dates at the Bridges Street Theatre, and a manuscript cast in a British Museum copy of the 1691 edition of *Julius Caesar* lists Gradwell as *Trebonius* in a production that may have dated about 1670–1673.

Graeff, Johann Georg *b. c. 1762, violinist, flutist, pianist, composer.*

Johann Georg Graeff was born about the year 1762 at Mentz, where his father held a government post. Though intended for the clergy, his interest in music brought him under the instruction of Abel and Haydn, and he left his native city for Basle and then went to Berne and Lausanne. After five years in Switzerland Graeff went to Paris, and in 1784 he came to England. He was an accomplished pianist, violinist, and flutist and on the last instrument played in the Salomon concerts in 1791 and 1792. Doane's *Musical Directory* of 1794 gave "John George" Graeff's address as No 57, Upper John Street, Fitzroy Chapel, and noted that he performed for the New Musical Fund. He was a member of the Court of Assistants for that society in 1794 and 1805 and perhaps other years as well. According to the testimony submitted to Sainsbury for his dictionary, Graeff was the composer of "about 21 or 22 Operas."

Graf, Friedrich Hartmann *1727–1795, flutist, drummer, composer.*

Born in Rudolstadt in 1727, Friedrich Hartmann Graf (or Graff, De Graeff) was the youngest son of Johann Graf (d. c. 1745), the German violinist and composer. He served as a kettle drummer in the Netherlandish campaign, according to Grove, and was wounded. In Hamburg in 1759 he gave concerts on the flute, and from 1761 he offered subscription concerts. Graf toured as a flute virtuoso until 1772 and then settled for a while in Augsburg as Kappelmeister. He was invited to Vienna in 1779 to write an opera for the German theatre there.

The *Morning Herald* in London on 23 November 1782 reported that Graf had arrived and that Haydn was expected "hourly." They would compose for the Hanover Square concerts. But the same paper on 6 February 1783 admitted that "Neither Haydn nor Graaf, the musical composers for the new concert, are yet arrived, though they have been expected for more than a month past. . . ." Graf finally appeared on 17 February, two days before the first concert, and the series of 12 concerts was presented with no new works by Haydn (though the maestro was represented by some older works at every concert) and a number of works by Graf. Graf supervised the concerts.

While in England Graf composed an opera, *Andromeda*, according to Grove, though Sonneck lists no such work, and perhaps Grove is in error; an opera *Andromeda* was produced in 1788 on the Continent, with music by Reichardt, who had visited London about 1785. Oxford gave Graf a doctorate in music on 15 October 1789. Graf died in Augsburg on 19 August 1795.

Graham, Mr *d. 1761, actor.*

The burial registers at Richmond, Surrey, contain a notice on 15 November 1761 that one "Graham, player" was buried that day. Graham is otherwise unknown, though he may have been a performer at the Richmond theatre whose name never appeared in the bills.

Graham, Mr [*fl. 1768–1786?*], *actor.*

A Mr Graham, not to be confused with

George Graham (fl. 1769–1819), was a member of Foote's summer company at the Haymarket in 1768, when he performed a role in *The Devil Upon Two Sticks* on 30 May for his first appearance and then during the season played Hounslow in *The Stratagem,* Wat Dreary in *The Beggar's Opera,* the Physician in *The Rehearsal,* and Corydon in *Damon and Phillida.* His wife was also a member of the company. In the spring of 1769 the Grahams were playing at Edinburgh, where he acted Constant in *The Constant Couple* on 23 March. On 7 November 1769, announced as from the Haymarket, Graham made his debut at the Smock Alley Theatre, Dublin, where he was engaged at least through 1770–71. He was probably the Graham who returned to the Haymarket on 20 September 1771 to act Launcelot in *The Merchant of Venice.* With Mrs Graham he acted at Brighton in 1774 and 1775.

In the summer of 1777, Graham, his wife, and their son George Graham were all members of the company playing at the China Hall, Rotherhithe, in south London. The elder Mr Graham was in the bills for Puff in *Miss in her Teens,* Sir Francis Gripe in *The Busy Body,* Heeltap in *The Mayor of Garratt,* the Nurse in *Polly Honeycombe,* Sir Jasper in *The Mock Doctor,* Gibby in *The Wonder,* the Uncle in *George Barnwell,* Hardcastle in *She Stoops to Conquer,* Brabantio in *Othello,* and a part in *All the World's a Stage.*

Probably he was the Graham who acted in Worcestershire in 1778, at Cork in 1781 and 1782, and at Liverpool in 1786.

Graham, Mrs ₁*fl. 1748*₁, *actress.*

A Mrs Graham played Mrs Idle in *The Consequences of Industry and Idleness* at Yates's booth, facing the Hospital Gate, on 24 August 1748, at Bartholomew Fair.

Graham, Mrs ₁*fl. 1768–1786?*₁, *actress.*

Mrs Graham, the wife of the actor Mr Graham (fl. 1768–1786), was a member of Foote's summer company at the Haymarket Theatre in 1768, making her first appearance as Jenny in *The Commissary* on 14 July and then playing during the season Mrs Sullen in *The Stratagem,* Lettice in *The School Boy,* Mrs Coaxer in *The Beggar's Opera,* Alithea in *The Country Wife,* Leonora in *The Spanish Fryar,* and Chloris in *The Rehearsal.*

The Grahams played at Edinburgh in the spring of 1769 when her roles included Mrs Oakly in *The Jealous Wife* and Mrs Junket in *The Absent Man.* On 8 November 1769, with her husband, Mrs Graham began an engagement, which presumably lasted for two years, at the Smock Alley Theatre, Dublin. With her husband and son George, she acted at Brighton in 1774 and 1775. The three of them were with the company which performed at the China Hall, Rotherhithe, south London, in the summer of 1777; her roles included Miranda in *The Busy Body,* Clarinda in *The Suspicious Husband,* Donna Violante in *The Wonder,* Millwood in *George Barnwell,* Emilia in *Othello,* and a character in *All the World's a Stage.* A Mrs Graham acted at Chester in September 1779. Probably she and her husband were the Grahams who acted at Liverpool in 1786.

Graham, Miss ₁*fl. 1770–1778?*₁, *actress.*

A Miss Graham, probably from Scotland, acted Peggy in the annual performance of *The Gentle Shepherd* at the Haymarket Theatre on 19 March 1770. A Miss Graham played at Waterford, Ireland, in the autumn of 1778.

Graham, Aaron? ₁*fl. 1799–1813*₁, *doorkeeper, messenger.*

An A. Graham was on the Drury Lane paylists by 1799, when he was paid £2 2s. for messenger work and expenses. In 1801–2 he was listed as an assistant doorkeeper; in 1802–3 he earned £1 per week. Larger sums of money were paid to a Mr Graham (£50 in January 1801, £13 13s. travel expenses in 1804–5, and as early as 1790–91 £105 9s. for an end-of-season expense list), but that recipient was no doubt Aaron Graham, the elder (1753–1818), a magistrate and a trustee of Drury Lane Theatre, who as a friend of Richard B. Sheridan dedicated his time to the theatre's financial affairs.

In 1813, in an undated letter to R. B. Peake, Sheridan remarked that his previous letter, which Peake never received, had been sent with "Graham junr," presumably a reference to Aaron Graham's son, who may have been the messenger and assistant doorkeeper of the turn of the century.

Graham, George [fl. 1769–1819?], actor.

George Graham was the Master Graham who was acting at Crow Street, Dublin, in 1769–70 and 1770–71 with his parents. When they all played at Brighton in 1774 and Edinburgh in 1775–76, George was styled as Mr Graham, indicating his maturity. The three Grahams were in the company that played in the summer of 1777 at the China Hall, Rotherhithe, south London, where George acted Altamont in *The Fair Penitent* on 18 June and then was seen as Sir George Airy in *The Busy Body*, Franklin in *The Suspicious Husband*, Scribble in *Polly Honeycombe*, Ratcliffe in *Jane Shore*, Briton in *The Wonder*, Chapeau in *Cross Purposes*, Young Marlow in *She Stoops to Conquer*, Cassio in *Othello*, a part in *All the World's a Stage*, and Freeman in *A Bold Stroke for a Wife*. Those roles, mostly, are those of younger men, compared to the more elderly characters played in the same casts by George's father.

George was acting in Worcestershire in 1778. At Edinburgh in 1780 and 1781 he played among other roles Faulkland in *The Rivals*, Finder in *The Double Gallant*, Hastings in *She Stoops to Conquer*, Or-

lando in *As You Like It*, Hotspur in *1 Henry IV*, and Sir Brilliant Fashion in *The Way to Keep Him*. He made his debut on 1 November 1781 at Smock Alley, Dublin, where he remained for two years. About that time Graham eloped with Mary O'Keeffe (1757–1813), the daughter of the popular Irish actor Tottenham Heaphy. She had married the actor and dramatist John O'Keeffe (1747–1833) in 1774 and had borne several of his children. With her husband she had acted at Crow Street in the late 1770s through 1780–81, during which time she must have taken up with Graham. In a fit of jealousy O'Keeffe beat her brutally and left for London to establish himself as a dramatist. O'Keeffe omitted any references to the matter in his *Recollections*.

Graham and Mrs O'Keeffe then lived together for many years in the north of England. The peripatetic Graham turned up at Norwich in 1784, arriving about the second week of January. On 7 February the press reported that he had appeared as Belcour in *The West Indian* on the previous Wednesday and that with an "elegant" figure and good voice he promised "to be an acquisition" to the theatre. But in the summer of 1785 he was at Brighton and in 1787 at Scarborough. By 1795 he was acting at Tunbridge Wells. He was perhaps the Graham who played Sydenham in *The Wheel of Fortune* at South Shields, near Newcastle on Tyne, on 15 July 1795.

Announced as from the Theatre Royal, Edinburgh, where he had acted in the first half of 1796, Graham appeared again in London, evidently for the first time in 21 years, on 28 April 1798, when he acted the role of an Old Woman in *Hooly and Fairly* at Covent Garden Theatre. The *Monthly Mirror* in June 1798 reported that he appeared to possess "some humour," but his character did not allow the critic "to judge properly of his merit." He did not appear again in that season.

George Graham was perhaps the Graham who was still acting at the Theatre Royal, Edinburgh, in 1818–19. Mary O'Keeffe had died on 1 January 1813 at Dalkeith, Scotland.

Graham, James *1745–1794, quack doctor, lecturer, exhibitor.*

James Graham was born in the Cowgate, Edinburgh, on 23 June 1745, the son of a saddler. Although he studied medicine at the University of Edinburgh, he seems not to have qualified. Nevertheless he later styled himself "Dr Graham." After living for a time at Pontefract, where in 1770 he married Miss Mary Pickering of that city,

by whom he had three children, Graham traveled to America. He lived for several years in Philadelphia, advertising himself as an oculist and aurist and making the acquaintance of Benjamin Franklin. He returned to England in 1774, settled for a while at Bath and Bristol, offering wonderful cures, and then moved to Pall Mall, near St James's Palace. He also practiced at Bath again in 1777, where he had as a patient Catharine Macauley, who married his younger brother William Graham.

Graham demanded large fees for his treatments; these involved balsamic medicines, milk baths, dry frictions, and the

By permission of the Trustees of the British Museum

JAMES GRAHAM, lecturing

by J. Kay

placing of his patients on a "magnetic throne" through which electrical currents would pass. At Paris in the summer of 1779 he visited Franklin and went to Aix-la-Chapelle, where he enjoyed testimonies from wealthy patients, including the Duchess of Devonshire.

Now established as a fashionable quack, in the autumn of 1779 Graham bought one of the three centre houses in the Royal Terrace, the Adelphi; the others were owned by Robert Adam, the architect of the terrace, and David Garrick's widow. There at the cost of some £10,000 he created an elaborate setting for the sale of his nostrums and the treatment of his patients. Trappings of his house included an entrance hall decorated with crutches discarded by cured patients and upper rooms full of exotic electrical apparatus, sculpture, paintings, music, perfumes, and curiosities. The entire establishment was called the Temple of Health, and in the "great Apollo apartment" he gave lectures at very high prices, promising, among other miracles, relief from sterility to persons who slept on the "celestial bed," a device made by Mr Denton, a skillful mechanic. Gigantic footmen distributed his handbills:

Temple of Health Adelphi
To their Excellencies the Foreign Ambassadors,
To the Nobility, Gentry, and Persons of Learning and Taste.
This Evening exactly at eight o'clock
The Celestial Brilliancy of the Medico-Electrical Apparatus in all the Apartments of the Temple,
Will be exhibited by Dr Graham himself.
Admission by night 5s., in the day 2s. 6d.

A session on the Celestial Bed figured at £100 per night, the Magno-electric at £50, the Elixir of Light at £100, and the Earth Bath at a modest £1 1s.

In the *Morning Post* of 1 June 1780, Graham advertised for a Temple Goddess:

Wanted, a genteel, most decent young woman; she must be agreeable, blooming, healthy and sweet-tempered, and well recommended for modesty, good sense and steadiness. She is to live in a Physician's family, to be daily dressed in white robes, with a rich rose-coloured girdle (emblematical of innocence and health) to wait on ladies at public exhibitions and give lectures on electricity. If she can sing, play on the harpsichord or speak French, greater wages will be given. A good performer on the Harmonica or Musical Glasses is likewise wanted. Enquire of Dr. Graham, centre of the Adelphi Terrace.

It has been commonly believed that the "Goddess Vestina" was Emma Hart, later Lady Hamilton (1761?–1815), the notorious and beautiful wife of Sir William Hamilton, and that the Goddess performed nude. But no real evidence has been found to verify either anecdote. According to the dramatist Frederic Reynolds, who knew Graham well, the Goddess, whoever she was, died in the doctor's service.

In a letter dated 23 August 1780, Walpole described a visit to the Temple of Health:

It is the most impudent puppet-show of imposition I ever saw, and the mountebank himself the dullest of his profession, except that he makes the spectators pay a crown apiece. We were eighteen. . . . A woman, invisible, warbled to clarinets on the stairs. The decorations are pretty and odd, and the apothecary, who comes up a trap-door, for no purpose, since he might as well come upstairs, is a novelty. The electrical experiments are nothing at all singular, and a poor air-pump that only bursts a bladder, pieces out the farce. . . .

On 2 September 1780 at the Haymarket Theatre, Colman produced a pantomime satirizing Graham, *The Genius of Nonsense*, in which John Bannister portrayed the Vocal and Rhetorical Harlequin and the Emperor of Quacks. The piece had 11 performances that season and 17 the next.

In May 1781 Graham moved his establishment to Schomberg House, Pall Mall, calling it the Temple of Health and of Hymen. Gainsborough was an uncomfortable neighbor. Graham's property was seized for debt on 25 November 1782, and at the auctions in December he managed to buy back some of his apparatus. He continued his quackeries; in March 1783 the "High Priestess" at his temple read lectures to the ladies, assisted by the "rosy, athletic, and truly gigantic goddess of Health and of Hymen, on the celestial throne."

His lectures at Mary's Chapel in Edinburgh in July 1783 brought prohibitions, so he repeated them in his own rooms and published *An Appeal to the Public*, which libeled the magistrates and got him committed to the Tolbooth, where he preached to the prisoners and published *A Full Circumstantial and most Candid State of Dr Graham's Case*, "giving an account of Proceedings, Persecutions, and Imprisonments, more cruel and more shocking to the laws of both God and man than any of those on record of the Portuguese Inquisition." He was bailed on 19 August and convicted and fined £20 on 22 August 1783, whereupon he departed Edinburgh.

By the autumn of 1783 he sponsored lectures at his house in London on the state and influence of women in society, which were delivered by Ann Curtis, Mrs Siddons's youngest sister; he also advertised he had the secret of living to at least 150 years of age.

After travels to Paris, Newcastle, the Isle of Man, and other places, he settled at Edinburgh in the late 1780s. He was now a religious enthusiast, styling himself as "the Servant of the Lord O.W.L." (Oh, Wonderful Love). In 1787 he founded the New Jerusalem Church, whence he issued publications, in the last of which on 3 April 1793 he swore he had from 31 December 1792 to 15 January 1793 taken no food nor drink except cold water and had sustained his life by applications of turf to his naked body. (Earlier in 1790 he had been earth-bathing, naked, for eight successive days of six hours' duration and a ninth day of 12 hours.) His last days were passed as a lunatic. Southey, in his *Commonplace Book*, described Graham's maddening himself with opium and rushing into the streets to "stripe himself to clothe the first beggar he met."

Graham died at his house opposite Archers' Hall, Edinburgh, on 23 June 1794.

A list of his pamphlets on diseases, prayer, and curing can be found in *The Dictionary of National Biography*.

A print of a portrait of Graham was reported in 1824 to have been in the collection of William Wadd. In his *Edinburgh Portraits*, J. Kay provided two engravings: one of Graham at a funeral in 1786 and another of him lecturing to a crowd.

Graham, Mary Ann. *See* YATES, MRS RICHARD THE SECOND 1728–1787.

Grahme, Mr. *See* GRABU, LOUIS.

Grainer, Abraham [*fl.* 1793], *musician.*

Abraham Grainer was a member of the King's Musick in 1793, according to documents in the Public Record Office.

Grainger. *See also* GRANGER.

Grainger, Mr [*fl.* 1724–1729], *tailor.*

A Mr Grainger, "House Taylor" at Lincoln's Inn Fields Theatre, received payments on account of £4 8s. (for the remainder of a bill of £9 6s.) on 6 November 1724, £10 on 11 March 1725, and £2 2s. on 3 October 1726. In the account books his name, and that of Mrs Grainger, were on the free list for tickets in 1726–27 and 1728–29. Perhaps the Mrs Grainger who acted occasionally at the Haymarket and Covent Garden between 1732 and 1735 was his wife.

Grainger, Mrs (*fl. 1726–1735*), *actress.*

A Mrs Grainger, announced as making her first appearance on any stage, acted Silvia in *The Recruiting Officer* at the Haymarket Theatre on 6 April 1732, for her own benefit, "at the particular Desire of several Ladies of Quality." When the play was repeated on 27 April, another person, Mrs Talbot, played the role. Mrs Grainger, again announced as making her first appearance on any stage, acted the title role in *The School Boy* at Covent Garden Theatre on 17 January 1735. Perhaps she was the wife of the Mr Grainger (fl. 1724–1729) who was a house tailor at Lincoln's Inn Fields Theatre. Mr and Mrs Grainger's names were on the free list for tickets at Lincoln's Inn Fields Theatre in 1726–27 and 1728–29.

Gramont, Mons (*fl. 1748*), *dancer.*
On 7 September 1748 at Phillips's booth at Southwark Fair Monsieur Gramont participated in a *Grand Dance of Furies.*

"Grand Saut du Trampolin, Le." *See* LAWRENCE, JOSEPH.

"Grand Turk." *See* CARATTA.

Grandchamps, Mons (*fl. 1749–1754*), *dancer.*
A dancer named Grandchamps, previously a performer with the Théâtre Italien in the French provinces, made his debut in England on 24 October 1749 when he danced at Drury Lane Theatre in a new grand comic ballet called *The Venetian Gardeners.* He appeared throughout the season in numerous performances of rural dances and in the choruses of such pieces as *The Chaplet, Acis and Galatea,* and *The Tempest.* After a second season at Drury Lane in similar assignments, Grandchamps was engaged at Covent Garden Theatre where on 20 November 1751 he first danced as a Fury in *The Necromancer.* On

4 December he appeared in a grand ballet at the conclusion of *Apollo and Daphne* and then occasionally danced in *Pyramus and Thisbe* and *The Miller Outwitted.* On 13 February 1752 he appeared with Cook, Mlle Camargo, and Mlle Hilliard in *Harlequin Sorcerer* (the bills for the day did not list the cast but Bonnell Thornton's review provided the names). No doubt he was the Mons Grandchamps who danced for his own benefit at the Jacob's Wells Theatre, Bristol, on 22 July 1752.

Grandchamps continued at Covent Garden in 1752–53 and 1753–54 in such assignments as an Aerial Spirit in *Merlin's Cave* and a dancer in *Harlequin Sorcerer.* He seems to have made little impact on the public. Presumably he left England at the end of 1753–54.

"Grand Hercule, Le." *See* PORTE, LOUIS.

Grande, Signor (*fl. 1687–1688*), *musician.*
According to the *Calendar of Treasury Books,* Signor Grande received an annual salary of £110 as a member of the Chapel Royal; only the master, Signor Fede, received more. A warrant on 19 December 1687 directed payment to Grande and other musicians of 3s. daily for attendance on the King at Windsor and Hampton Court from 19 May to 16 August and from 17 September to 11 October 1687. Grande made a similar trip to Windsor from 24 July to 20 September 1688 for which he was paid 6s. daily on 20 October.

Grandis, Signora (*fl. 1757*), *singer.*
In the benefit concert for indigent musicians on 24 March 1757 at the King's Theatre Signora Grandis sang Galuppi's *Nocchiero s'abbandona* and Jomelli's *Se amor provasti mei.* At the same theatre on 31 May she sang Learco in *Euristeo.* The opera was performed through 14 June.

Grange. *See* LA GRANGE and LE
GRANGE.

Granger. *See also* DE GRANGER and
GRAINGER.

Granger, Mr *[fl. 1779–1780]*, *tumbler.*
A Mr Granger was listed on Sadler's
Wells bills for tumbling on 5 and 15 April
1779 and 30 March 1780.

Granger, Mrs *[fl. 1709–1711]*, *actress, dancer.*
Mrs Granger was listed as a member of
the company at the Queen's Theatre in the
Haymarket on 24 December 1709, though
the first record of her appearance was on
15 June 1710 at Pinkethman's theatre at
Greenwich, when she acted Angelina in
Love Makes a Man. The following 27 July
she and Le Sac danced the *Dutch Skipper*
and *French Peasant.* At the Queen's on 2
May 1711 Mrs Granger danced with Thurmond, and on 9 August 1711 at Greenwich she danced with an unidentified young
gentleman. Emmett Avery reported to us
that Mrs Granger's salary in 1710–11
was £15.

Granger, Mrs Elizabeth. *See* WALLACK, MRS WILLIAM H.

Granger, James *d. 1763, actor?*
In the manuscript account book of the
Drury Lane Theatrical Fund (now at the
Garrick Club) is the notation that James
Granger died on 20 March 1763. His function at the theatre, if any, is not known
to us.

Granger, Julia, sometimes Mrs Edward, later Mrs Robert Jones *1782–1806, actress, singer.*
Born in 1782, Julia Granger was the
daughter of the actress Elizabeth Granger
(née Field) by a Dr Granger. Julia's

mother later married the elder William
Wallack (1760–1850) on 8 July 1787,
and at least four children by him became
performers or married into the profession.
Julia was raised by her maternal grandmother, Ursula Agnes Booth (1740–
1803), a London actress, who was married
to John Booth, a tailor at Drury Lane Theatre between 1780 and 1796.

At the age of four, Julia Granger made
her stage debut at Drury Lane as the Child
in *Cleone* on 22 November 1786. She repeated the role two days later, and, although she may have appeared at other
times that season, her name was not found
again on a London bill until 21 April
1794, when at the age of 12 she performed
as one of the chorus of witches and spirits
in *Macbeth* at Drury Lane. On 9 June
1794 she was in the chorus of captives in
the first performance of John Philip Kemble's melodrama *Lodoiska*, which ran 20
performances into the summer. On 10 May
1794 her name was put on the paylist at
3s. 4d. per day.

Miss Granger continued to be engaged
at Drury Lane from 1794–95 through
1796–97, at a salary of £1 per week, appearing regularly in the choruses of such
pieces as *Lodoiska, The Mountaineers, The
Cherokee, Alexander the Great, The Pirates, The Iron Chest,* and *Harlequin Captive.* Her other roles included Psyche in
Jack of Newbury on 6 May 1795, an
Italian Girl in *The Critic* on 13 April
1796, Sabina in *Celadon and Florimel* on
23 May 1796, Juba (a breeches part) in
The Prize on 18 October 1796, the Prince
of Wales in *Richard III* on 9 November
1796, Ariel in *The Tempest* on 18 March
1797, Oberon in *The Fairy Festival* on 13
May 1797, and Nelly in *No Song No Supper* on 10 June 1797. As a member of
Colman's summer company at the Haymarket Theatre in 1795 and 1796, she
played a vocal part in *Zorinske,* a Peasant
in *The Mountaineers,* Nelly in *No Song
No Supper,* Juba in *The Prize,* Prince John

Courtesy of the National Theatre, London

SARAH SIDDONS as Cleone and JULIA GRANGER as the Child

by W. Hamilton

in *1 Henry IV*, and a Girl in *The Iron Chest*.

Sometime in 1796, Mrs Booth, determined to forward her granddaughter's interests at all costs, encouraged Julia Granger to begin an affair with the dancing master J. E. Burghall, whose wife Sally was the niece of Mrs Booth's husband. An account of Mrs Booth's duplicity and of Burghall's ultimate separation from his wife without gaining Julia was given by the dancing master in a sixteen-page pamphlet entitled *A Statement of Facts* which he published in February 1797. For details of the affair see the entry of J. E. Burghall

(fl. 1778–1797). Perhaps because of the embarrassment caused by the public scandal, when Julia appeared at the Haymarket in the summer of 1797 (she was no longer engaged at Drury Lane), she acted under the name of Mrs Edward, making her first appearance on 12 June 1797 as Arabella in *The Author* and Zapphira in *A Mogul Tale*. She played the Maid in *The Deaf Lover* on 15 June, Charlotte in *My Grandmother* on 17 June, Narcissa in *Inkle and Yarico* on 21 June, and throughout the summer continued in a similar line. As Mrs Edward, she acted again at the Haymarket in the summers of 1798 and 1799, playing, among other roles in 1798, Jenny in *The Beggar's Opera*, Laura in *The Agreeable Surprise*, Eliza in *The Flitch of Bacon*, the Player Queen in *Hamlet*, Ismene in *The Sultan*; and in 1799 Miss Nancy in *Fortune's Frolic*, Mrs Trippet in *The Lying Valet*, and Lady Bab's Maid in *High Life Below Stairs*.

In 1800, now the wife of the actor Robert Jones (d. 1806), she and her husband were recruited by Charles C. Whitlock for his Federal Street Theatre company in Boston, Massachusetts, where she made her debut on the opening bill of the season on 27 October 1800 as Susan Ashfield in *Speed the Plough* and in the title role of Frances Brooke's comic opera *Rosina*. A brief interruption in her career was occasioned by pregnancy and the birth on 4 November of her daughter Julia Elizabeth Jones, the first of her four children by Jones. Mrs Jones was back on the Boston stage by 3 December, however, when she played Peggy in *The Country Girl* and Leonora in *The Padlock*.

Enjoying in America more opportunity than was her lot in London, Mrs Jones experienced modest success in the theatrical centers of the eastern seaboard. Ireland wrote that she was "still youthful [18], *petite* in person, with a pleasing and expressive face, an exceedingly sprightly and *piquant* actress in light comedy, and a very charming vocalist." In 1801–2 and 1802–3 she was engaged with her husband at the Chestnut Street Theatre, Philadelphia, and was described by Durang as "a little nonpareil" in comedy and singing roles. She was back in Boston in 1803–4, during which season her husband left her, evidently going to Charleston. After an engagement in the South, she was hired for the Park Theatre in New York, making her debut there on 27 November 1805 as Albina Mandeville in *The Will* and as Leonora in *The Padlock*. Her success during this season was great, and the management at one time had to hide her away in

Hackensack, New Jersey, according to Dunlap, to prevent Robert Treat Paine from luring her back to the Boston company. Mrs Jones's beauty earned her the soubriquet "the Jordan of America." It was said by the wife of the actor Thomas A. Cooper that Mrs Jones had become the mistress of William Coleman, editor of the *New York Evening Post*. Although she was re-engaged at the Park Theatre for 1806–7, after a lingering illness she died on 11 November 1806, at the age of 24, leaving four orphans for whom the theatres in New York, Boston, Philadelphia, and elsewhere gave benefit performances. (Julia Granger Jones should not be confused with Mrs Edward Jones, who acted at Charleston during this period.)

One of the daughters of Julia Jones, Julia Elizabeth Jones (1800–1870), on 9 March 1820 married the actor Edmund Simpson (1784–1848), by whom she had four children; by their subsequent marriages they produced a large number of American theatrical persons. Another daughter, Mary Anne Jones, married a Mr Bancker about 1822 and became a popular American actress before she died in New York on 8 October 1825.

William Hamilton's painting of Julia at the age of four as the Child, with Mrs Siddons as Cleone, in *Cleone* is at the National Theatre, London. An engraving by Thornthwaite, after Hamilton, was published in *Bell's British Theatre*, 1792. Julia Granger Jones's portrait was painted in America by the actor-manager William Dunlap.

Granger, Samuel *[fl. 1761–1777],* *actor.*

Samuel Granger acted at York about 1761 and at Edinburgh in 1762 and 1763 before he made his first appearance at the Haymarket Theatre as Dactyl in *The Patron* on 13 June 1764, as a member of Foote's summer company. He acted Old Philpot in *The Citizen* on 13 July, the

Irishman in *The Apprentice* on 23 July, a Fisherman in *The Rehearsal* on 20 August, and Old Knowell in *Every Man in His Humour* on 1 September 1764. Granger's wife was a member of the same company.

Engaged at Drury Lane Theatre for 1764–65 at 5s. 10d. per day or £1 15s. per week, Granger made his debut there on 20 September 1764 as Sharp in *The Lying Valet*. He acted Periwinkle in *A Bold Stroke for a Wife* on 25 September, a Miser in *The Witches* on 16 October, a Carrier in *1 Henry IV* on 17 October, Foresight in *Love for Love* on 20 October, and Davy in *2 Henry IV* on 9 November. On 16 May 1765 he shared a benefit with Adcock, Preston, and Keen. Evidently after that season he returned to the provinces. He acted at Edinburgh in 1775, 1776, and 1777. The Miss Granger who acted at Edinburgh in 1771 and 1772 was probably his daughter. Another child, described as the daughter of the "player" Samuel Granger, was buried at Holy Trinity Church in York on 26 August 1761.

Granger, Mrs Samuel [*fl.* 1761–1772], *actress.*

Mrs Granger acted with her husband Samuel Granger in Foote's summer company at the Haymarket Theatre in 1764. Probably she had acted previously at York, where a daughter was buried on 26 August 1761. She made her first appearance at the Haymarket on 13 June 1764 as Juliet in *The Patron*, advertised as "A Young Gentlewoman." For the eleventh performance of the piece on 13 July her name was given for the role. That night she also acted Maria in *The Citizen*. On 20 August she played Parthenope in *The Rehearsal* and on 1 September 1764 Bridget in *Every Man in His Humour*.

Again at the Haymarket for the summer of 1765, Mrs Granger acted Jenny in *The Commissary*, Trifle in *The Old Maid*, Mrs Bruin in *The Mayor of Garratt*, Tag in *Miss in her Teens*, and Parthenope in *The*

Rehearsal. Her name was not again found in the London bills until she returned to the Haymarket in 1771 (evidently without her husband) to act Miss Biddy in *Miss in her Teens* on 15 May. During that summer she acted, among other roles, Jacinta in *The Wrangling Lovers*, Isabinda in *The Busy Body*, a role in *The Lame Love*, Betty in *A Bold Stroke for a Wife*, Lucy in *The West Indian*, and Jessica in *The Merchant of Venice* (her last known London performance, on 20 September 1771). In 1771 and 1772 Mrs Granger acted at Edinburgh. In the same company there was a Miss Granger, probably her daughter.

Granier. *See also* GRENIER.

Granier, Mr [*fl.* 1734–1748?], *dancer.*

Mr Granier arrived in England in the autumn of 1734 with a company of French comedians under the direction of Francisque Moylin which performed comedies and farcical afterpieces at the Haymarket Theatre between 26 October 1734 and 3 June 1735. Presumably Granier was accompanied by his wife and three children, Joseph, Jack, and Polly, all of whom eventually performed in London. Moylin's company also played at Goodman's Fields on 23 May and 4 June 1735.

Settling in England with his family, Granier became a member of Henry Giffard's company at Lincoln's Inn Fields in 1736–37, making his first appearance on that stage on 19 January 1737 in a new dance called *La Caprice*. In the summer of 1739 he performed at Hallam's booth at Bartholomew Fair, two of his known roles being a Sailor and Neptune in the afterpiece *The Sailor's Wedding*. In the summer of 1740 he was again with Hallam at Bartholomew Fair, this time with his wife and three children also performing. After a third summer with Hallam, the Graniers joined Giffard at Goodman's Fields in 1741–42. On 9 October 1741 he and his children danced in a pantomime called *The Imprisonment, Release, Stratagems, and Marriage of Harlequin: with the Triumphs of Love*. His children danced on the evening of 19 October 1741, the night on which Garrick made his debut at that theatre as Richard III.

The Graniers accompanied Giffard in his move to Lincoln's Inn Fields in 1742–43, where Granier danced regularly in numerous performances of *The Imprisonment of Harlequin*.

By 1744–45 Granier was dancing again at Goodman's Fields in such roles as Old Dame Setebos and Time in *The Tempest*. In April 1746 he and his three children were performing at Sadler's Wells. In 1746–47 he was at Covent Garden Theatre; on 27 December 1746 he was paid £5 5s. for his children's performances (according to British Museum MS Egerton 2268, although *The London Stage* states the payment was for Granier's "Christmas performance"); and on 29 May 1747 he received another £10 10s. in behalf of his children.

Possibly it was the elder Granier who danced Pluto in *The Royal Chace* at Covent Garden during 1747–48, but by that season it seems that Granier had retired from the stage; and the listings of "Mr Granier" in subsequent London bills over the next two decades refer to his son, Joseph Granier (fl. 1734–1764), who up to 1747 was billed as one of the Masters Granier.

Granier, Mr ₁fl. 1756₁, *dancer.*

On 1 March 1756 a "Granier Jun" danced with Mlle Capdeville at Covent Garden. That billing may have been intended for Joseph Granier who was a member of the company at that time but who was by then regularly billed as Mr Granier. Possibly this dancer could have been Joseph's son, but if so he would have been barely six years old and more likely would have been billed as Master. Or the billing

may have been intended for Jack Granier, younger brother of Joseph, who was usually found at Drury Lane during that period.

Granier, Mrs ₁fl. 1734–1747₁, *dancer.*

Mrs Granier no doubt came to England in the autumn of 1734 with her husband as a member of the company of French comedians who performed at the Haymarket Theatre between 26 October 1734 and 3 June 1735. The extent of her professional activities seems to have been limited. She was a dancer at Lincoln's Inn Fields in 1742–43 and at Covent Garden in 1746–47. On 29 October 1747 the latter theatre paid a Mrs Irwin 14s. "for a Hoop Petty Coat for Mrs Granier." Perhaps Mrs Granier also performed in some of the pieces mentioned in the entry of her husband Mr Granier (fl. 1734–1748?).

Notices in the bills of a Mrs Granier after 1747 refer to Aleda Granier (née Vandersluys), who was the wife of Joseph Granier (fl. 1734–1764) and the daughter-in-law of the elder Mrs Granier.

Granier, The Masters. *See* GRANIER, JACK, and GRANIER, JOSEPH.

Granier, Miss ₁fl. 1763₁, *dancer.*

On 15 April 1763 a Miss Granier made her first (and perhaps only) appearance on the London stage dancing the role of Madam Catherina in a new pantomime ballet *The Savoyards, or Madam Catherina* at Covent Garden Theatre. Probably she was a daughter of Joseph Granier, who danced in the same piece, and his wife Aleda Granier, also a dancer.

Granier, Miss ₁fl. 1768₁, *dancer.*

At the end of Act II of *The Suspicious Husband* at Drury Lane Theatre on 4 May 1768, a Miss Granier, apprentice to Tassoni, danced a minuet with her master. The dance was repeated on 7 May. Perhaps she was the daughter of Jack Granier (fl. 1734–1775), a dancer at Drury Lane.

Granier, Jack ₁fl. 1734–1775₁, dancer.

Jack Granier was the younger brother of Joseph Granier, under whose name will be found the information on Jack's early activities as one of the two Masters Granier.

By 1746 his brother Joseph was being advertised as Mr Granier, but Jack continued to be called Master Granier until 1753. He danced at Covent Garden in 1747–48 and 1748–49, at the King's Theatre in 1749–50, and at Drury Lane in 1752–53. When he offered a hornpipe at Drury Lane on 15 December 1752 he was still called Master Granier, but when he repeated the dance on 12 May 1753, for a benefit he shared with Roger, Shawford, and the Widow Reinhold, his name appeared as Mr Granier. Either he or his brother Joseph performed at Sadler's Wells from 1753 to 1755 and in 1762.

Jack Granier was a member of the dancing chorus at Drury Lane from 1753–54 through 1756–57, appearing in such pieces as *The Oracle*, *The Genii*, and *The Chinese Festival*, the ill-fated ballet by Noverre which caused a riot at its premiere on 8 November 1755. On occasion he was assigned a specialty such as *The Pierrot's Dance* with Denison on 4 May 1754.

Although Granier's name was omitted from Drury Lane bills after 1756–57, it appeared some ten years later on a Drury Lane paylist in which he was put down for 5s. per day as a dancer in 1766–67; also on 7 March 1767 the theatre treasury advanced him £4 2s. 10d. on a note. Seven years later, on 1 October 1774, Drury Lane paid "Mr Granier for last week 12s. 6d." In 1775 Mr Granier subscribed 10s. 6d. to the Drury Lane Theatrical Fund, but according to James Winston's notation in the Fund Book (at the Folger Library) he thereafter neglected the payment.

The Miss Granier who danced a minuet with her teacher Tassoni at Drury Lane on 4 May 1768 may have been his daughter. Perhaps she was the dancer Sophia Granier, who is entered in these volumes under her married name, Mrs William Parker.

Granier, Mrs ₁Jack?₁ ₁fl. 1755?–1786?₁, dancer.

According to *The London Stage*, a Mrs Granier was dancing at Drury Lane Theatre in 1755–56, but her name was not in the bills. In 1764–65, however, a Mrs Granier was on the Drury Lane paylist at 5s. per day or £1 10s. per week. Probably she was the wife of the Drury Lane dancer Jack Granier. In the Drury Lane Fund Book at the Folger Library is a notation by James Winston saying that Mrs Granier paid her subscription of 10s. 6d. from 1771, claimed on the fund in 1781, but "returned to business" in 1786. No Mrs Granier was named in the Drury Lane bills or paylists after 1764–65, however, although mesdemoiselles named Grenier danced at the King's Theatre in 1771–72 and 1787–88.

Granier, Joseph ₁fl. 1734?–1764₁, dancer.

When a young boy, Joseph Granier was brought to England with his brother Jack and sister Polly in the autumn of 1734 by his father Mr Granier (fl. 1734–1748?) and mother (fl. 1734–1747). Both parents were dancers in Francisque Moylin's company of French comedians which played at the Haymarket Theatre in 1734–35. The Granier children made their first known appearances on the stage dancing at Hallam's booth during Bartholomew Fair in August 1740. Since the two boys were usually advertised as the Masters Granier during the early years of their careers, it is difficult to discriminate any individual performances, but for the most part they appeared together in the same pieces. They danced at Bartholomew Fair again in 1741 and then with their father in Giffard's company at Goodman's Fields in 1741–42, making their first appearance in that theatre on 14 September 1741 in *Les Muniers amoureux de la coquette*. In that season the three children danced as dwarfs in *The Imprisonment of Harlequin,* and they were dancing in the entertainments given on 19 October 1741 when Garrick made his famous debut in *Richard III.*

The Granier children danced at Lincoln's Inn Fields throughout 1742–43, at the New Wells, Lemon Street, in March 1743, and by 1745–46 they were regular performers at Goodman's Fields Theatre again. In April 1746 they danced at Sadler's Wells. In 1746–47 they joined the company at Covent Garden. By then Joseph, evidently the eldest child, had matured sufficiently to be styled Mr Joseph Granier, and his name was entered in the Covent Garden paylist for 5s. per night. Probably he was the Mr Granier who danced Pluto in numerous performances of *The Royal Chace* in 1747–48. On 4 April 1748 he and his brother and sister were performing in entertainments at the New Wells, Lemon Street.

After 1748–49 at Covent Garden Joseph Granier went to Dublin to join the Smock Alley Theatre, where on 2 October 1749 he made his debut in a dance with Miss Aleda Vandersluys, who also had been a performer at Covent Garden between 1745 and 1749. On 29 October 1750, during his second season at Smock Alley, Granier married Miss Vandersluys, who now began to perform under her married name.

Joseph and his wife were with a troupe of dancers who offered entertainments at Burrell's Hall in Glasgow on 30 September 1751. He was again at Smock Alley in 1751–52. Either he or his brother Jack danced a hornpipe in Act III of *The Beggar's Opera* at Drury Lane at a benefit shared with Roger, Shawford, and the Widow Reinhold on 12 May 1753. One of them also danced at Sadler's Wells in 1753, 1754, 1755, and 1762.

In the season of 1753–54, Joseph appeared occasionally at Covent Garden, making his first appearance there in five years on 20 November 1753 in *The Italian Peasant.* On 22 December he substituted for Grandchamp as the Aerial Spirit in *Harlequin Skeleton,* and on 4 May 1754 he again danced *The Italian Peasant.* On the same night his brother Jack Granier was dancing at Drury Lane with Denison in *The Pierrot's Dance,* a circumstance which assists in distinguishing between the two Graniers during that and subsequent seasons. It was Jack, presumably, who was in the Drury Lane company from 1753–54 through 1766–67 and Joseph who remained a regular performer at Covent Garden through 1763–64. In 1761–62 Joseph's salary was £83 for the season. The dances in which he appeared, with season of first performance, include: (1755–56) *Les Paysans gallants*; (1756–57) *Colombine Courtezan, Merlin's Cave*; (1757–58) *The Prophetess*; (1759–60) *The Fair, The Rape of Proserpine, Comus*; (1760–61) *The Chaplet, Romeo and Juliet, Florizel and Perdita*; (1762–63) *Harlequin Sorcerer, Love in a Village*; and (1763–64) *Perseus and Andromeda.*

Granier's wife also was a dancer at Covent Garden through 1762–63. The Miss Granier who made her debut at Covent Garden on 15 April 1763 was probably their daughter. Perhaps she was the dancer Sophia Granier who married William Parker and is entered in these volumes under her married name.

Granier, Mrs Joseph, Aleda, née Vandersluys [fl. 1745–1764], *dancer, singer, actress.*

Aleda Vandersluys, whose father was a dancer at Covent Garden Theatre between 1745 and 1748, made her first appearance at that theatre on 14 November 1745 dancing as one of the Followers of Proserpine and in the personification of Air in *The Rape of Proserpine.* She next danced as one of the Country Lasses in *Orpheus and Eurydice* on 25 November and in *The Peasants* and *The Drunken Tyroleze* on 5 April 1746; then for three years, through 1748–49, she remained a minor figure in the chorus. In the autumn of 1748 she went to Dublin, making her debut at the Smock Alley Theatre on 2 October dancing with young Joseph Granier (fl. 1734–1764) whom she had met at Covent Garden. Towards the end of the season at Smock Alley, on 23 April 1750, she played Polly in *The Beggar's Opera*, "being the first Time of her acting any Part on the Stage." She returned to Smock Alley in 1750–51 and on 29 October 1750 married Joseph Granier; thereafter she appeared professionally as Mme or Mrs Granier. In addition to her usual dancing, she acted Biddy in *Miss in Her Teens* on 28 March 1751.

After leaving Dublin at the end of 1750–51, Mrs Granier and her husband appeared with a company of dancers who gave entertainments at Burrell's Hall in Glasgow on 30 September 1751. In 1754–55 she was engaged with her husband at Covent Garden, where her name continued to appear in the bills for chorus dancing through 1762–63 in such pieces as *Harlequin Skeleton*, *The Prophetess*, *The Fair*, *The Chaplet*, and *Florizel and Perdita*. Probably she was the Mrs Granier who danced at the Jacob's Wells Theatre, Bristol, in 1754, 1758, 1763, and 1764, and at Sadler's Wells in 1762.

Granier, Polly ₁fl. 1734?–1749₁, *dancer.*

Polly Granier was probably brought to London as a child in the autumn of 1734 by her parents Mr Granier (fl. 1734–1748?) and Mrs Granier (fl. 1734–1747), who were dancers in Francisque Moylin's company of French comedians which played at the Haymarket Theatre in 1734–35. But possibly she was not born until after her parents settled in England. By 1740 Polly was performing with the rest of her family

at Hallam's booth at Bartholomew Fair, where she also appeared in the summer of 1741. On 14 September 1741 she and her brothers, Joseph and Jack, made their first appearances at Goodman's Fields Theatre in a dance called *Les Muniers amoureux de la coquette*. She continued to dance regularly on that stage throughout 1741–42 and then was at Lincoln's Inn Fields in 1742–43, making her debut there on 26 November 1742 in a *New Peasant Dance* with her brothers and father. When she danced with her brothers at the New Wells, Lemon Street, on 14 March 1743, her name was given in the advertisements as Polly Granier.

After appearing at Goodman's Fields Theatre in 1744–45 and 1745–46, and at Sadler's Wells in April 1746, she and her family joined Covent Garden Theatre in 1746–47, where she danced for three seasons through 1748–49, many times as a Frenchwoman in *Apollo and Daphne*. On 14 March 1748 she danced in *The Muses Looking Glass*. On 4 April 1748 she and her brothers danced at the New Wells, Clerkenwell.

Granier, Sophia. *See* PARKER, MRS WILLIAM THE SECOND, SOPHIA.

Grano, Giovanni Battista ₁fl. c. 1710–1730₁, *trumpeter, flutist, composer.*

Giovanni Battista Grano (or Granio, Granom, Gronon) was a trumpeter in the band which played a concert at the Duchess of Shrewsbury's in Kensington about 1710. Nothing is known of his background, though he was clearly of Italian ancestry. By 23 June 1712, when Grano signed a salary receipt (now in the Coke papers at Harvard), he was called John, and since the Coke papers relate chiefly to the opera, Grano was probably playing at the Queen's Theatre. At the Lincoln's Inn Fields playhouse on 22 October 1715 he accompanied Mrs Fletcher in a song; he played at Stationers' Hall and James Street in 1717–18; and on 23 December 1718 he played the German flute at a concert at Stationers' Hall. Between those appearances that we know of he may have been away from England, as he is known to have been before he appeared at Lincoln's Inn Fields on 12 March 1720 to play a concerto on the German flute. He was then advertised as making his first public appearance since his arrival in England. On 24 March he accompanied Mrs Fletcher again in a "Trumpet Song," and on 1 April he played the flute at a York Buildings concert. At Drury Lane on 24 May playgoers were entertained between the acts "By Mr Grano on the Trumpet and German Flute."

Grano played trumpet at a concert at Hickford's Music Room on 1 March 1721 and a year later, on 14 March 1722 at Drury Lane, presented a "Concerto with Trumpets composed and performed by Grano" and "A Concerto on Two Trumpets by Grano." He was not mentioned again, so far as surviving bills show, until 27 May 1725, when a benefit for him was held at Stationers' Hall. On 15 April 1729 at Lincoln's Inn Fields he played a solo on the German flute; then on 30 April at Hickford's he and Lewis Granom (Grano?) performed. A benefit for John Grano was held on 12 December 1729 at Stationers' Hall, after which his performing career seems to have ended. About 1730 *Grano's Solos for a German Flute, a Hoboy or Violin, with a Thorough Bass for the Harpsichord or Bass Violin and a ballad, Young Damon once the happiest Swain* was published.

The above account of John Grano's appearances in London in the 1720s should be treated cautiously, for Lewis Granom, who was also a trumpeter and flutist and whose name was frequently spelled Grano, just as Grano's was spelled Granom, was also active. The contemporary advertisements were not always careful to distinguish between the two musicians.

Granom, Lewis Christian Austin ₁*fl. 1722–1763₁, trumpeter, flutist.*

At the Haymarket Theatre on 11 May 1722 a benefit concert was held for "L. Grano"—probably Lewis Christian Austin Granom. The audience was entertained with "A Trumpet Concerto by Grano," "A Solo on the German Flute by Grano," and "A Concerto on the Little Flute by Grano." One assumes that the performer was the L. Grano whose benefit that was, but the identification could be incorrect, for the trumpeter and flutist John Grano was active in London at the same time.

Not until 4 January 1729 was Lewis Granom mentioned again in the London papers. On that date he began weekly concerts at Hickford's Music Room. He played a "Trumpet Song" at Lincoln's Inn Fields on 15 April; at the same performance "M. Granom"—probably John Grano, the "M." being not an initial but an abbreviation for Monsieur—played on the German flute. That conjecture is supported by the bill for a concert on 30 April at Hickford's where "J. Granom and L. Granom" played a concerto for trumpets. Since Grano's name was often spelled Granom, perhaps these two musicians were, as Grove suggests, related: John the father and Lewis the son, perhaps. It was not uncommon for the younger generations of foreign-born families to alter the spelling of their surnames.

Lewis Granom's performing seems to have ended about 1729, as did John Grano's. But Lewis had an extensive career as a composer, beginning in 1741 with the publication of his *Twelve Sonatas or Solos for the German Flute*. As the *Catalogue of Printed Music in the British Museum* indicates, Granom wrote a number of songs, many of them popular at such pleasure gardens as Cuper's, as well as several works for flute. Oddly, though a trumpeter himself, he did not compose much for that instrument.

He was very likely the Lewis Granom of St Paul, Covent Garden, whose daughter

Elizabeth was buried on 9 January 1735. *Mortimer's London Directory* of 1763 listed Granom as a teacher of the German flute living at No 1, Coney Court, Gray's Inn.

Grant. *See also* **RAYMOND, JAMES GRANT.**

Grant, Mr *[fl. 1744]*, *actor.*
Mr Grant played Sparkle in *The Miser* at the Haymarket Theatre on 10 May 1744.

Grant, Mr *[fl. 1758]*, *actor?*
Patie and Roger was performed on 13 March 1758 at the Haymarket Theatre for the benefit of McLean and Grant. No cast was listed, but perhaps Grant was one of the actors.

Grant, D. *[fl. 1754]*, *musician?*
"Mrs Midnight" (i.e., the eccentric poet Christopher Smart) engaged the Haymarket Theatre on 25 April 1754 for "her" *Concert* supplemented by *The Adventures of Fribble*. The night's performance was for the benefit of Joseph Woodbridge and D. Grant. The occasional performances of Smart's troupe, often under the title *The Old Woman's Oratory*, were carried on by singers under such pseudonyms as "Signora Gapatoona" or dancers like "Timbertoe." Very likely Woodbridge, a kettle-drummer, and Grant, probably also a musician, on less serious occasions also wore pseudonyms. But they did not do so on their benefit night.

Grant, George *[fl. 1783–1785]*, *box-keeper, lobby keeper.*
George Grant, listed in Lord Chamberlain's records as "Box & Lobby keeper" at the King's Theatre in 1784–85, had been a boxkeeper there in 1783–84 or earlier. He was, indeed, high in the favor of William Taylor, the proprietor of the theatre, who, being himself in confinement for debt, on 17 July 1783 appointed six trustees to administer the perplexed affairs of the house.

Grant was one of the trustees, along with Michael Novosielski, Simon Slingsby, John Siscott, Leopoldo de Micheli, and James Sutton, all cronies or dependents of Taylor. The arrangement collapsed in June 1785, and Taylor sold his interest to Giovanni Gallini.

Grantham, Miss. *See* **JEFFERIES, MRS** *[fl. 1762–1778]*.

Granthony. *See* **GANTHONY.**

Grantom, Miss. *See* **JEFFERIES, MRS** *[fl. 1762–1778]*.

Granum. *See* **GRANOM.**

Granville. *See also* **GLANVILLE** and **GRENVILLE.**

Granville, W. *[fl. 1784]*, *singer.*
W. Granville was one of the bass singers at the Handel Memorial Concerts at Westminster Abbey and the Pantheon in May and June 1784.

Grariani. *See* **GRAZIANI.**

Grase. *See* **GRACE.**

Grasetti, Maria *[fl. 1717]*, *singer.*
Signora Maria Grasetti (or Grassetti) sang Deidamia in *Piro e Demetrio* at the King's Theatre on 2 February 1717. She was advertised as lately arrived in London. When the opera was repeated on 2 March it was announced that she would sing only "Part of the Recitativo, without Songs, to shorten the Opera."

Grass, Miss *[fl. 1767]*. *See* **GRASSI, CECILIA.**

Grassetti. *See* **GRASETTI.**

Grassi, Cecilia, later Mrs Johann Christian Bach *b. c. 1740, singer.*

Born about 1740, Cecilia Grassi first appeared as "Cecilia Grassi di Napoli" in the role of Sabina in Galuppi's *Adriano in Siria* at the Teatro di San Salvatore in Venice early in 1760. From Venice she toured to Bologna and other cities in Italy. She sang again in Venice in 1765.

Signorina Grassi was engaged by Gordon at the King's Theatre in London for the season 1766–67 as *prima donna seria* in a troupe which included Guarducci and Morigi and Signoras Piatti, Ponce, Guadagni, and Maggiore. On 1 November 1766 Signorina Grassi and Guarducci made their debut in a "serious pasticcio" called *Trakebarne Gran Mogul*, "without," wrote Burney, "impressing the public with very favorable ideas of their talents." On 20 December she sang in the *pasticcio Ezio*. In the spring following she and Guarducci "excited more attention, and acquired more applause, than had been bestowed on them before Christmas." They starred in J. C. Bach's *Carattaco* on 14 February and Vento's *La Conquista del Messico* on 4 April. Sylas Neville heard Miss "Grass" at Ranelagh Gardens on 29 June 1767. That summer Signorina Grassi returned to Italy.

Her movements for the next year or so are obscure. On 12 January 1769 she sang in the cantata *Ercole ed Acheloo* at the Teatro di San Carlo in Naples and then returned to London, with a stopover in Venice.

Engaged once more for the opera at the King's Theatre, Signorina Grassi sang Fulvia in *Ezio* on 13 January 1770, Aristea in *Olimpiade* on 1 February and following, a part in the oratorio *La Passione* on 1, 3, and 15 March, and Eurydice in *Orfeo* on 7 April.

On 10 January 1771 she had a part in J. C. Bach's oratorio *Gioas re di Giuda*. She sang the title role in *Semiramide reconosciuta* on 9 February and was heard twice more in *La Passione*, on 28 February and 7 March.

Signorina Grassi was probably Cleonice

in Guglielmi's *Demetrio* at the King's Theatre on 3 and 5 June 1772, and she was heard in concert at the Haymarket on 23 March and 27 April of that year. She also sang Diana in J. C. Bach's serenata *Endimion* at that theatre on 6 April. Her name then disappeared from the bills for a season. Her last appearance under her maiden name was at a concert of vocal and instrumental music given for the benefit of Pinto and Eichner at the Haymarket on 19 April 1773.

She sang only once more in public, after her marriage (probably in 1774) to Johann Christian Bach. That was on the occasion of the performance of an unnamed cantata by her husband at his Hanover Square concert on 26 April 1776.

Cecilia Grassi Bach was, in Charles Burney's estimation "inanimate on the stage, and far from beautiful in her person; but there was a truth of intonation, with a plaintive sweetness of voice, and innocence of expression, that gave great pleasure to all hearers who did not expect or want to be surprised."

Hester Lynch Thrale had noted in her diary: "Grassi the Old Singing Woman was married to Bach the Harpsichord Player, but says Burney she will bring no children." The prophecy was correct. Johann Christian Bach died in London on 1 January 1782. His will, drawn the previous November, left everything he owned to Cecilia. But he also left debts of over £4000. Queen Charlotte assisted Cecilia with two gifts of money, and a performance of *I viaggiatori ridicoli* was given at the King's Theatre on 27 May 1782 for "the benefit of Mrs. Bach." The proceeds were enough to take Cecilia home to Italy. The place and date of her death are unknown.

Graupner, Johann Christian Gottlieb

1767–1836, oboist, double-bass player, composer, music publisher.

Johann Christian Gottlieb Graupner was

born on 6 October 1767, the seventh child of Johann Georg and Anna Maria Schoenhagen Graupner, at Verden, Hanover, in Prussia. Like his father, he became a regimental musician, making the oboe his specialty, although he acquired proficiency on several other instruments.

After his discharge from his regiment on 8 April 1788, he came to London. When, in 1791, Franz Joseph Haydn assembled a theatre orchestra Graupner was first oboist. Haydn left London in 1793, and Graupner sailed for Prince Edward Island. Why he chose to go to a place so remote and culturally deprived is mysterious, for it had no use for his talents.

In 1795 he went to Charleston, South Carolina, and joined the orchestra of the theatrical company under the management of John J. L. Sollée at the Church Street Theatre. There he met and, sometime before the playbill of 7 April 1796, married the actress and singer Mrs Catherine Comerford Hillyer. (She was described by Fannie L. Gwinner Cole, in her entry on Graupner in *The Dictionary of American Biography*, as "a distinguished English opera-singer, daughter of a London attorney." That seems to be an error, for there is no record of her British distinction, or, indeed none of her performance. There were both Comerfords and Hillyers on the British stage, mostly provincial and all minor figures. It is possible that Mrs Graupner had sung in London, but if she had done so, it had been in circumstances less than distinguished, since neither under her maiden name nor that of her first marriage did she appear on a playbill. Nevertheless she may have "walked on" anonymously. When on 18 August 1797 Sollée brought a company composed of Boston and Charleston players to New York's John Street Theatre for two nights, the extensive bill boasted the provenance and perambulation of each player. Mrs Graupner was said to be "from the theatre royal, Drury Lane, Being her first appearance here. . . .")

At the close of Charleston's 1795–96 season the Graupners went to Boston, where Mrs Graupner had made her American debut in 1794. She joined the acting company at the Federal Street Theatre, and he joined the band as oboist. Surviving accounts in the Boston Public Library show him as earning $14 and her as earning $12 per week in November 1798.

Graupner was a restlessly energetic man, and it was not long before he had opened a music store, advertised to give lessons, and become the proprietor of a music hall. Soon he was busy organizing and presiding over the Phil-harmonic Society. By about 1810 the orchestra of the Society, which Graupner directed while playing the double bass, was holding concerts Saturday evenings at his hall.

Graupner and his wife performed in concert often. With Thomas Smith Webb and Asa Peabody, Graupner called for the formation of the Handel and Haydn Society on 30 March 1815, and he trained its orchestra of 12 players. He published *Rudiments of the Art of Playing on the Pianoforte*, and engraved and published music which he sold at his shop. He and Mrs Graupner had several children, all of them musical.

Johann Graupner died at Boston on 16 April 1836.

Gravel, Guy [fl. 1773], *musician.*
Guy Gravel, who lived "near the Church" in Newington Butts, was made a freeman of the Worshipfull Company of Musicians on 3 December 1773.

Graven, Mr [fl. 1749], *actor, singer.*
Mr Graven played Jemmy Twitcher in *The Beggar's Opera* at Twickenham on 26 September 1749. There is a good possibility that his name was Craven, not Graven; a Mr Craven acted at the New Wells, Lemon Street on 27 February 1749 and appeared as Jacques in a French version of *The Beg-*

gar's *Opera* called *L'Opéra du gueux* at the Haymarket between 29 April and 29 May 1749.

Graves, Benjamin [fl. 1794], violinist.

Doane's *Musical Directory* of 1794 listed Benjamin Graves, of No 262, "Boro' " (Borough High Street?), as a violinist who played for the Handelian and Cecilian societies.

Graves, James [fl. 1696–1726], instrumentalist, composer.

James Graves, stated the *Flying Post* in its 17/19 November 1696 issue, was a teacher of violin, flute, and oboe living in Fauloon Court, Lothbury. He advertised for sale his collection, *Military Musick*. By April 1702 Graves was a member of the royal musical establishment, but his salary (unspecified in the Lord Chamberlain's accounts) was paid by the Hon Spencer Compton. Some of Graves's compositions were included in *The 4th Book of the Compleat Flute Master* in 1707, but the bulk of his pieces were light songs, many of them listed in *The Catalogue of Printed Music in the British Museum*. Almost all his songs were published about 1720.

Graves was given a benefit concert at Couch's Drawing Room on 24 February 1710 and another at Punch's Theatre (probably the theatre at the upper end of St Martin's Lane near Litchfield Street) on 1 March 1711. He served in the Prince of Denmark's music at least from October 1714 to 24 June 1716, according to the *Calendar of Treasury Books*, and he received extra pay in July 1718 for attending the installation of Prince Frederick and the Duke of York. On 18 July 1726 he was paid for attending the installation at Windsor of the Duke of Richmond and Sir Robert Walpole.

Gray. *See also* GREY.

Gray, Mr [fl. 1784–1785?], horn player. *See* GRAY, MR [fl. 1784–1785?], oboist.

Gray, Mr [fl. 1784–1785?], oboist.

A Mr Gray was listed by Charles Burney as a second "hautbois" among the instrumentalists assembled for the Handel Memorial Concerts at Westminster Abbey and the Pantheon in May and June 1784. Another Mr Gray was numbered among the "horns." It is not known which of these performers (if either) was the Mr Gray who was on the Minute Books of the Royal Society of Musicians on 6 February and 6 March 1785 as a member of the Society's Court of Assistants.

Gray, Mr [fl. 1785], actor.

A Mr Gray played Oliver Cromwell in *King Charles I* in a special performance at the Haymarket on 31 January 1785.

Gray, Mr [fl. 1794], singer.

A Mr Gray, "bass" (singer, probably) of James Street, Covent Garden, was cited in Doane's *Musical Directory* (1794) as a participant, in some year or years unspecified, in the Handelian memorial performances in Westminster Abbey.

Gray, Mr [fl. 1794–1797], boxkeeper.

A Mr Gray (or Grey) was one of the house personnel at Drury Lane Theatre when he shared benefit tickets with 24 fellow house servants on 5 June 1795. He had therefore probably served throughout the 1794–95 season, and perhaps earlier. He appeared on the company roster again in 1795–96 and 1796–97. He was among 13 boxkeepers sharing a benefit on 16 June 1797.

Gray, Mrs [fl. 1735–1736], charwoman?

A manuscript paylist for Covent Garden Theatre shows a Mrs Gray, "Chair woman" at that playhouse, was "allow'd 179 days at 12^d" per day. Though she may have attended to sedan chairs in front of the theatre, it is more likely she was a charwoman.

Gray, Master _[fl. 1786?–1800]_, singer.

A volume of James Hook's songs which had been sung at Vauxhall by Master Gray and other singers was published in 1799, and another of that sort came out in 1800. A number of individual songs as sung by Master Gray are listed in the _Catalogue of Printed Music in the British Museum_ tentatively dated 1800.

When on 27 March 1800 Raimondi led "an assemblage of musical excellence" (to quote the _Monthly Mirror's_ account) at Mrs Franklin's concert, Willis's Rooms, "Master Gray, from Bath" was one of the singers "happy in their respective airs." A Master Gray sang a song after the mainpiece at Covent Garden Theatre on 15 May 1800. Presumably, all of those notices refer to the same singer.

The Master Gray who had sung with Incledon, Wordsworth, and other London and Bath singers for "Mr. Cantelo's Annual Night" at Bath on 26 April 1786 was conceivably the same. But, if so, he was both very young in 1786 and about ready to give up the juvenile designation "master" in 1800.

Gray, Miss _b. 1765?, dancer._

A "Miss Gray, scholar of Tassoni" performed "A New Dance" at Drury Lane Theatre on 10 May 1773. She was almost certainly the female "Child seven years old," Tassoni's scholar, who had made her first appearance on the stage dancing a hornpipe at Drury Lane on 6 May 1772, her second appearance on 13 May following, and her third (when she danced both with "others" and alone) on 3 April 1773.

Gray, James _[fl. 1674–1684]_, actor, treasurer, manager, boxkeeper?

A warrant in the Lord Chamberlain's accounts dated 11 September 1674 listed James Gray as an actor in the King's Company at the new Drury Lane playhouse. His name was marked discharged, but the discharge was cancelled. No roles are known for him. By 1678 he was serving as the company treasurer, but there was such dissension between Henry and Charles Killigrew and the other sharers in the troupe's patent that playing ceased at some point in 1678 or 1679, whereupon Gray and some other players were lured to Edinburgh.

Thomas Sydserf, who had a company playing in the tennis court of Holyrood House, offered to make Gray the "Master or Principal of the Company of His Majesty's Comedians or Actors." Gray arrived in Edinburgh in the spring of 1679, but by February 1680 he was back in London, enticed by assurances from the Killigrews that the company troubles had been solved, that his traveling expenses would be paid for, and that his treasurer's position in the King's Company would be restored to him. But his expenses were not paid, and he was not reappointed treasurer until the middle of 1681. All that information came out in a law suit brought in Chancery by Gray in 1682. He also charged the Killigrews and Thomas Morley with secretly mortgaging the stock of the theatre for £300. The Killigrews and Morley testified that they had never made offers to Gray of travel expenses and the return of his treasurer's post, but after much litigation, on 8 February 1684, the Lord Chamberlain found for Gray. He was to be paid his expenses, but as of the following 8 December he had received nothing. Perhaps he finally received his money and then left the theatre, for no further mention of him has been found.

There is a possibility that James Gray was the "James" cited as a boxkeeper at Drury Lane (the King's Company playhouse) in a document reported in _The Theatrical Inquisitor and Monthly Mirror_ in July 1816 – a source that must be approached with caution. That James is entered in this dictionary as Mr James, but since the supposed accounts for two performances in December 1677 list "James's boxes" whereas all other employees are called Mr or Mrs ("Mr. Kent's pit," "Mr. Mohun's boxes"), perhaps James should be taken as a Christian name. If so, it is certainly possible that James Gray served as a boxkeeper before becoming the company treasurer in 1678.

Gray, James ₁*fl. 1730?–1761*₁, *actor, singer, dancer, constable?*

An actor named Gray (or Grey) played occasionally at Drury Lane Theatre late in the season of 1729–30. He was a Follower of Actaeon in *Diana and Actaeon* on 23 April 1730, Pluto in *Bayes's Opera* on 23 July, and a Coachman in *The Devil to Pay* on 6 August 1731. On the latter date he also had an undesignated role in *The What D'Ye Call It*.

Those small roles presaged Gray's professional fate during the 24 winter seasons he appeared in the bills of Drury Lane between 1729–30 and 1760–61. There is no evidence for his presence at Drury Lane in 1737–38, 1740–41, 1747–1749, 1750–1752, and 1753–1755. But he was nevertheless probably drudging in one of his humble capacities in some if not all of those seasons. He acted at the Haymarket Theatre in February 1734 and in the summers of 1734 and 1735, and in May 1734 he played at Lincoln's Inn Fields. At Bartholomew Fair on 22 August 1732 he acted an undisclosed role at the Fielding-Hippisley booth at the George Inn, West Smithfield. He was probably the "Grey" who was one of the Masqueraders in *The Ridotto al'-Fresco* at Bartholomew Fair in August 1733. On 24 August 1734 and 23 August 1736 he returned to the Fielding-Hippisley booth, first as the Constable in *The Comical Humours of Monsieur Ragout* and then in an unspecified part in *The Cheats of Scapin.*

Apparently he was satisfactory in his round of Ghosts, Gypsies, Coachmen, Soldiers, Countrymen, Fiddlers, Drawers, Fryars, and Guards, in farce, sentimental drama, comic opera, and pantomime. In *The Beggar's Opera* alone he from time to time sustained the characters of Wat, the Drawer, Paddington, and Lockit. He achieved the following specified characters and played most of them repeatedly: both Dumb and Quack in *Chrononhotonthologos*, Pluto in *Bayes's Opera*, Poundage in *The Provok'd Husband*, both James and Robert in *The Mock Doctor*, Ernesto in *The Orphan*, the Taylor in *John Cockle at Court*, Bawble in *Robin Goodfellow*, the Egg Woman in *Harlequin Shipwreck'd*, Don Uric in *Britons Strike Home*, the Apothecary in *The Double Gallant*, Deadset in *Tom Thumb*, Sattin in *The Miser*, Security in *The Intriguing Chambermaid*, Tom in *The Schoolboy*, the Porter in *Love's Last Shift*, the Sheriff in *1 Henry IV*, the Tobaccoman in *The Scornful Lady*, Hercules in *Perseus and Andromeda*, a Satyr in *Cupid and Psyche*, a Coffin Maker in *The Plot*, a Chinese Guard in *Harlequin Grand Volgi*, and Bullcalf in *2 Henry IV*. In many of his pantomime parts Gray danced; other parts apparently required him to sing.

In the British Museum in the hand of James Winston is the record of a benefit for "Mr. Gray, Constable," on 3 May 1750, in which he "entreats the Favour of his Friends to send for Tickets to his Punch-House in Russel-Court, Drury Lane." *The London Stage* does not give that information, only listing Ray, Marr, and Shawford as sharers with "Gray" on a benefit evening on which Ray played Mat-o-Mint, Marr was Filch, and Gray was Harry Paddington in *The Beggar's Opera*. If Winston's identification was correct, then minor actor and constable were one and the same.

On 22 November 1744, three days after the riots at Drury Lane Theatre against Fleetwood's pantomimes and advanced prices, one James Gray had signed himself

"Constable of Drury Lane playhouse" under an affidavit published in the *Daily Advertiser*. It certified that Fleetwood had had nothing to do with the arrest, by Gray, of one of the rioters, who had been carried before the magistrate Sir Thomas De Veil. On 3 May 1746 Gray shared a benefit with the old actor Ray, and Dunbar, a boxkeeper. "I Hope," Gray said on the playbill, "my diligence as a constable, in preserving ladies from the insults of pickpockets . . . may entitle me to some small indulgence at my benefit." On 4 May 1747, sharing his night with the actor Simpson and Plummer, a boxkeeper, Gray begged "the Favour of those Gentlemen and Ladies that intend to honour him with their Company, to be at the Theatre by Four o'clock, that he may be able to accommodate them with good places." He shared his benefit with five other house servants on 9 May 1748, but without remark. By 1750 Gray had gone into business and was advertising in the benefit bill quoted above.

"Gray, James" [*fl. 1748*]. *See* SNELL, HANNAH.

Gray, Jonathan [Thomas?] *d. 1768, clown.*

Opposite the date 24 August 1768 in Isaac Reed's "Notitia Dramatica" in the British Museum is the following notation: "About this time died near 100 Jonathan Gray a famous Jack Pudding who performed at Cov: Gard[n]. in the Pant. of The Fair and at most of the Fairs in and about Lond°." Another British Museum manuscript (BM 11826R) reproduces an item, presumably from a newspaper, opposite the date 1 September 1768: "Last week died Jonathan Gray, aged near 100, the famous Jack Pudding or Merry Andrew, who formerly exhibited at all *the Fairs* in and about London and gained great applause by his performances at C. G. T. in the entertainment called *Bartholomew Fair*."

The Era Almanac of 1883 calls him

Thomas Gray and dates his death 28 January 1768.

Gray, Sarah Jane, later Mrs Nathan Egerton Garrick *1784–1859, singer, actress.*

The Miss Gray who sang Polly in the comic opera *The Woodman* at Covent Garden Theatre on 17 October 1796 was identified in the *Pocket Magazine* of that month as the daughter of Thomas Brabazon Gray, and her age was given as 12. On 19 December she was Oberon in the elaborate new pantomime *Harlequin and Oberon*, which enjoyed an initial run of 24 nights. She did chorus singing during the rest of that season in those pieces and in the new but slighter *Italian Villagers*, which opened on 25 April 1797, and *The Village Fête*, which opened on 18 May. She was doubtless employed in the same fashion in 1797–98, though she seems to have been

Harvard Theatre Collection

SARAH JANE GRAY

engraving by Thomson, after Drummond

named in one playbill only, that of 18 December 1797, when she was one of a numerous "Chorus of Country Girls" in *The Mysteries of the Castle*.

On 10 November 1798 Miss Gray figured among many others as an Indian in the first performance of Cobb's elaborate comic opera *Ramah Droog*. On 29 January 1799 T. J. Dibdin's new long pantomime *The Magic Oak* came out. Miss Gray had an unspecified part for its month-long initial run and after that dropped out of the bills for a while. She earned £1 per week in each of her first three seasons.

The *Authentic Memoirs of the Green Room* in 1798 called her "young and promising," and the *Memoirs* and *The Thespian Dictionary* in 1805 both asserted that she had first appeared at the Royal Circus and that she had sung at the Lyceum. But she was evidently only an occasional singer at the Circus once she went to Covent Garden. Among the Circus's scattered remaining notices is one for 12 November 1798 – "Positively the Last Night but Three of Performing Previous to the Company's Departure for Scotland" – when Miss Gray was featured in "A favourite Hunting Song" after the ballet. Another notice, a clipping from a newspaper hand-dated by James Winston only 1798, placed her at Simpson's benefit in the character of Leofric the Minstrel in the spectacle *The Knights of Malta*.

Winston's notations in the Harvard Theatre Collection carry the information that she married "David Garrick's nephew" (Nathan Egerton Garrick, son of George, David's brother) when she was still very young. Mrs Garrick remained on the stage, at Covent Garden and elsewhere, many years into the nineteenth century. She may have been the Miss Gray whom Clark in *The Irish Stage in the County Towns* placed at Cork in 1800. A further notation at Harvard, attached to a portrait engraving, informs us that she was married in 1802 and then retired from the stage "but owing

to financial difficulties was obliged to return to her professional duties and in 1809 was at Manchester Th[eatre] Roy[al]; she later went to Bath for 2 years and then to Bath in 1812." R. W. Elliston recalled in his *Memoirs* that the Mrs Garrick who was "formerly Miss Gray" played the part of Polly in *The Beggar's Opera* on the reopening of the Royal Circus on Easter Monday, 1810.

The *Theatrical Inquisitor and Monthly Mirror* of August 1818 mentioned that "Mrs. Garrick, of Covent-Garden Theatre, has been performing at York, where she made her debut on the twenty-second of July, as Catherine, in 'The Exile.' " James Dibdin in his *Annals of the Edinburgh Stage* placed her in the company at Edinburgh, "from Liverpool," on 30 November 1819, playing Lucy Bertram in *Guy Mannering*. She continued there through May 1820, according to the research of Norma Armstrong, playing an unnamed character in *The Comedy of Errors*, Clorinda in *Robin Hood*, Diana Vernon in *Rob Roy Macgregor*, Jenny in *The Highland Reel*, Rosalind in *The Conquest of Taranto*, and the title role in *Rosina*. After that her record of travel and performance is silent. Her husband's full name and her first name were furnished in her obituary in the *Gentleman's Magazine* of March 1859. She died on 3 February of that year.

Several songs were published in 1795, 1799, and 1800 "as sung by" Miss Gray. She was pictured in an engraved portrait by Thomson, after R. E. Drummond, which was published by John Bell as a plate to *La Belle Assemblée* in 1818. A variant, after Drummond, was engraved by T. Woolnoth and published as a plate to the *Ladies' Monthly Museum* in 1820.

Gray, Thomas *d. 1790, musician.*

The *Gentleman's Magazine* reported that (Thomas) Gray (or Grey), a musician who had been employed at the Covent Garden and Haymarket theatres, died suddenly on 11 September 1790. A petition to the Governors of the Royal Society of Musicians was addressed on 4 October by "Mrs Sarah Gray, widow of the late Thomas Gray, late a member." She was subsequently paid £8 for his funeral expenses and two guineas a month maintenance. She must have been the Mrs Gray (for the Minute Books of the Society mention no other) who was granted £1 for "medical relief" on 1 August 1819, received (among other widows of members) a grant of £6 "for being above 70 years old" on 3 March 1822, and obtained payments of two guineas on 3 June 1827 and 6 September 1829, being ill. On 7 March 1830 £8 was voted for her funeral expenses. All of the Society records directly bearing on Thomas Gray himself have been lost.

Gray, Thomas Brabazon ₁*fl. 1785?–1799*₁, *singer, actor.*

A Mr Gray sang with fifteen others in an entertainment called *The Incas of Peru* at Sadler's Wells on 12 April 1790. It was said to be his first performance at any theatre. There is little doubt that he was the same Mr Gray who sang one of the background "Principal Vocal Parts" when Garrick's "Ode to Shakespeare" was recited at Covent Garden on 30 May 1791. He was listed last among the male singers in a chorus which also contained such names as Incledon, Blanchard, and Mrs Martyr. That was the first occasion on which his name was carried in the Drury Lane playbill. But he had probably done choral singing at the theatre in 1785–86, 1787–88, and 1788–89, notwithstanding the claim on the Sadler's Wells bill, for in each of those seasons a Gray had shared benefits or tickets with minor actors, dancers, members of the band, and house servants. He was at the Wells again on 3 October 1791 singing in the chorus to *The Magic Grot*.

Gray (or Grey) was thrust into greater prominence at Covent Garden in 1791–92,

when, listed now as an actor, he earned £2 10*s*. a week and sang not only in several choruses, but also in the title part of the dramatic opera *Artaxerxes*, Bob in the comic opera *The Woodman*, Haggard in *Blue-Beard*, Hymen in *Orpheus and Euridice*, William in *Marian*, a "Musical Character" in *The Maid of the Oaks*, and Allen a' Dale in *Robin Hood*. He served also in special vocal and spectacular effects such as the masquerade in Act II of Cymbeline, in which "Hark! the Lark at Heaven's Gate sings" was warbled by Gray, Incledon, Marshall, Darley, Linton, Mrs Mountain, and Mrs Martyr. Gray shared benefit tickets on 29 May 1792, again with a mixed bag of concessionaires, doorkeepers, boxkeepers, and singers. He continued in his general line through 1792–93 and the first months –September through November–of the new season 1793–94.

In the Folger Library's manuscript paylist Gray is shown as receiving £3 per six-day week from the Covent Garden season's beginning through 16 November 1793. But his name was no longer on the roster after 23 November. He sang at Sadler's Wells on 22 April 1794 for the first time "these three years," and on 12 July sang there again. He did not serve again at Covent Garden, so far as the bills show, until he sang some unassigned role in the musical afterpiece *Arrived at Portsmouth* on 30 October 1794. In the 1794–95 season his salary at Covent Garden diminished to £1 10*s*. per week though he served often in choruses and took part in the oratorios in the spring.

Gray had sung at the Lyceum several times in 1794. He was at Sadler's Wells playing the Steward in *Momus's Gift* in April 1795. He was Ben Bobstay in *England's Glory* on 31 August and 1 September and, at some date undetermined, Jupiter in *Pandora's Box*. He came back to Covent Garden in the fall, earning again £1 10*s*. a week in 1795–96 and being raised to £2 in the season of 1796–97. He played a Necromantic Hag in *The Talisman* at Sadler's Wells on 29 March 1796.

Characters besides those named which he acquired during his career were the Serjeant of Marines in *To Arms*, Philippo in *The Castle of Andalusia*, Antonio in *The Duenna*, a Sailor in *Lock and Key*, the Gardener in *Barataria*, Jimmy Twitcher in *The Beggar's Opera*, Frederick in *No Song, No Supper*, Asmodius in *Harlequin and Faustus*, and Rundy in *The Farmer*.

The Authentic Memoirs of the Green Room (1799) declared that he had "sprung from a musical family" and that "having sung with applause in concerts, societies, &c. was employed at Sadler's Wells for some time; but, unfortunately losing his hearing, he became latterly incapable of performing: he is, notwithstanding, serviceable to the theatre, in filling trifling characters and joining in chorusses." The judgment was just. The bills listed him in a great number of "Glees and Chorusses," and he was oftenest one of the Recruits, Servants, Sailors, Huntsmen, Choristers, Lawyers, Farmers, Gypsies and the like which populated musical farce and pastoral opera. His named characters, as we have seen, were generally inconsiderable, but he often entertained in entr'acte singing.

The crisis in his hearing must have occurred near the end of Gray's 1796–97 season, for when he signed on the next season at Covent Garden he was often in walk-on characters and minor speaking parts—the Farmer in *Oscar and Malvina*, one of the Gypsies in *Harlequin and Oberon*—and often in groups, where, no doubt, he could be keyed and supported by other voices, but he seems not to have sung again in solo parts. He was given £2 10*s.* per week in 1797–98 and was dropped again to £2 in 1798–99, the last season he was recorded as employed.

Gray was a tenor. His full name, Thomas Brabazon Gray, is attached to a number of sentimental and martial songs which were published undated but were printed at various times between 1790 and 1800: *As Blushing Phoebus, Come true loyal Britains* (*sic*), *The Death of Maria, The Dying Lover, Fill a Bumper to Bacchus*, and so on. Two works of special interest are *McPherson's Collection of Ancient Music, in the Poems & Songs of Ossian*, "Adapted by T. B. Gray," and Gray's composition *The Quarrelling Duett. Sung . . . by Mr. Johannot and Mr. Decastro, in the Pantomime of Harlequin Invincible . . . at Mr. Astley's Theatre of Arts.*

Gray had a wife who was a singer at Covent Garden during part of the period that he was there and who also sang at least once at Sadler's Wells. He also had a daughter Sarah who was a singer and who married David Garrick's nephew, Nathan Egerton Garrick.

Gray, Mrs Thomas Brabazon [*fl.* *1785–1798*], *singer, actress.*

Mrs Thomas Brabazon Gray was a singer paid £1 per week at Covent Garden Theatre in the 1785–86 season. She first appeared in the bills on 23 September as one of eight "Bacchants" (*sic*) in *Comus*. On 17 October 1785 she sang, along with 17 others, in "a Grand Chorus" which was for some reason inserted in Act V of *Catherine and Petruchio*. On 14 November she figured, with 16 others, in "Juliet's Funeral Procession with the *Solemn Dirge.*" Service in such extravaganzas was to be a major part of her duty as chorus singer for the next few years, along with assorted characters like one of the Fishwomen in *Harlequin's Chaplet* or a Female Prisoner in *The Crusade*. In 1791 she was permitted to try Widow Giggle in *Blue-Beard* and in 1792 she was given, briefly, Eurydice in *Orpheus and Eurydice*. In 1792 she was also at Sadler's Wells singing Madelon in *The Honours of War*, Pandora in *Pandora's Box*, and Fanny in *The Prize of Industry*.

Mrs Gray was at Covent Garden, where her husband also sang and acted, in the season of 1785–86 and from 1787–88 through 1792–93. In 1791–92 she was still earning only £1 per week. The "Mme" Gray listed among the "Female Bards" when *Oscar and Malvina* was sung at Covent Garden in 1798 appears also to have been Mrs Thomas Brabazon Gray. Her husband sang in that new production.

Gray, William ₍*fl.* 1794–1799?₎, *singer.*

Doane's *Musical Directory* of 1794 listed William Gray, of No 16, White Lion Street, Islington, as a principal tenor and alto (countertenor) at the Covent Garden Theatre. One might guess that Doane meant Thomas Brabazon Gray, who was a popular tenor at that playhouse, but the subscription list of New Musical Fund members in 1794 also cited a William Gray. *A Selection of favourite catches, glees, etc.* published at Bath in 1799 listed a Mr Gray as a soprano. Perhaps he was William Gray.

Graydon, Mr ₍*fl.* 1668–1670₎, *actor.*

Mr Graydon was a member of the King's Company playing at the Bridges Street Theatre in the late 1660s. He acted Longino in *The Sisters* at some time in 1668–69 and Syana in *The Island Princess* on 6 November 1668 and subsequent dates. No other parts are known for him, but a Lord Chamberlain's warrant dated 2 October 1669 granted Graydon livery for the period 1668–1670.

Grayton, Mr ₍*fl.* 1795–1796₎, *house servant?*

Mr Grayton was on the company list at Drury Lane in 1795–96. Possibly he was one of the house servants. He is not cited in *The London Stage.*

Graziani, Clementina ₍*fl.* 1788–1789₎, *singer.*

Signora Clementina Graziani (misspelled "Grariani" in the *World* on 16 December 1788) was hired to sing serious female roles at the King's Theatre in 1789 for £200 plus a benefit. She may not have earned her keep, for she sang only one role that was important enough to be mentioned in the bills: the Queen of Spain in *La cosa rara*, which opened on 10 January 1789. On 2 May she was replaced by Signora Sestini, and there is no record of Signora Graziani having received her promised benefit.

"Great Devil, The." *See* LAWRENCE, JOSEPH, and NEVIT, MR.

Greatorex, Anthony ₍*fl.* 1758–1794₎, *singer, bassoonist.*

Anthony Greatorex was, no doubt, the Mr Greatorex Senior of Burton-upon-Trent, who was among the bass singers in the original Handel Memorial Concerts at Westminster Abbey and the Pantheon in May and June 1784. In his *Musical Directory* of 1794, Doane gave Greatorex's full name and identified him as a bass singer and a bassoonist living at Burton, a subscriber to the New Musical Fund, and a participant in the Handelian concerts at the Abbey.

We believe that Anthony Greatorex to have been the father, by his wife Ann, of the more famous musician, Thomas Greatorex (1758–1831). If so, Anthony was also the father of Martha Greatorex, an organist at St Martin's, Leicester.

The Greatorex family, with roots in Derbyshire for upwards of five centuries, descended from the Greatrakes family of Callow. Their numerous members and lines, listed in *The Reliquary* (IV, 220ff), are very difficult to distinguish because of the frequent use of the same Christian names, but it seems clear that our subject was the Anthony Greatorex of Riber Hall, Matlock. His father was Daniel Greatorex, son of William, son of Daniel (b. c. 1638). Another line of the family descended from Anthony Greatorex, the elder brother of the last-named Daniel (b. c. 1638). That Anthony was the father of Anthony (1693–

1778), who was the father of William (1726–1782), who was the father of another Daniel. The last-mentioned Daniel was our subject Anthony Greatorex's distant cousin.

Greatorex, Thomas   *1758–1831, instrumentalist, conductor, composer.*

Thomas Greatorex was born on 5 October 1758 and baptized on 22 October at North Winfield, near Chesterfield, Derbyshire. He was the son of Ann and Anthony Greatorex of Riber Hall, Matlock. Descended from the Greatrakes family of Callow, the family had roots in Derbyshire for upwards of five centuries. Thomas's father, Anthony, although a nailer by trade, taught himself music, and it was said that at the age of 70 he built an organ. We believe Anthony Greatorex to have been the Mr Greatorex Senior, of Burton upon Trent, who sang in the Handel Memorial Concerts at London in 1784. Another Anthony Greatorex, who died at London in 1808, we believe to have been a cousin of Thomas's father.

At the age of eight Thomas Greatorex moved with his family to Leicester, and although he possessed a "strong bias to mathematical pursuits," according to Gardiner in *Music and Friends*, "living in a musical family, his ear was imperceptibly drawn to the study of musical sounds." At 14, in 1772, he went to study music with Benjamin Cooke in London, and in 1774, when attending a concert of sacred music at St Martin's, Leicester, where his eldest sister Martha Greatorex was organist, he met the Earl of Sandwich and the conductor Joah Bates. The former took him into his household, both town and country, and between 1774 and 1776 Greatorex assisted Bates in the Christmas oratorios which were presented at Huntingdon. According to *The Dictionary of National Biography*, for a short time Greatorex succeeded Bates as the Earl's musical director. By that early association with Bates,

Greatorex not only enjoyed a fine opportunity to watch intimately a most skillful conductor, but he also cultivated a friendship which became most advantageous at several stages of his career. When in 1776 Bates initiated his scheme for the Concerts of Ancient Music, Greatorex sang in the chorus. He continued as a performer there until, according to Sainsbury, "he was advised to try a northern air for the reestablishment of his health."

In 1780 or 1781 he accepted an appointment as organist of Carlisle Cathedral, where for some four years he delighted in the study of music and science and regular evening discussions in the select society of Dr Percy (then Dean of Carlisle), Dr Law, and Archdeacon Paley.

In 1784 Greatorex resigned from Carlisle for Newcastle. In May and June of that year he was among the bass singers in the Handel Memorial Concerts given at Westminster Abbey and the Pantheon (listed in Burney's *Account* as Greatorex Junior of Newcastle). Between 1786 and 1788 Greatorex traveled abroad, taking instruction from Signor Santarelli, the celebrated singing master at Rome, and from Pleyel at Strasburg. In Rome he was introduced to the pretender, Prince Charles Edward Stuart, who later bequeathed to him a valuable collection of music manuscripts.

After visiting the principal cities of Italy, Greatorex traveled through Switzerland, then to Cologne, and, passing through the Netherlands, he returned to England in late 1788 to set himself up as a teacher of music. He attracted many pupils and earned large sums of money. It was reported that in one week alone he gave 84 singing lessons at a guinea each. When Bates retired in 1793 as conductor of the Ancient Concerts, Greatorex was appointed to the post by the directors without submitting an application. He retained that position for 39 years, during which period, it was said, he was never absent or more than five minutes late for any rehearsal, performance, or meeting.

Greatorex was recommended for membership in the Royal Society of Musicians by Dupuis on 7 March 1790, at which time he was described as a harpsichordist, a single man 31 years of age, and with "a great way of business" in the teaching of singing. He was unanimously elected to the Society on 6 June 1790, but not until 1 May 1791 did he attend and sign the membership book. On 3 June 1792 the Governors of the Society ordered that he be summoned to the general meeting to explain why he should not be expelled for non-attendance "lest yr at St. Margarets." Evidently the explanation was satisfactory, but Greatorex does not seem to have been very active in the Society, his name appearing only once on the list (as a violinist) for the annual concert at St Paul's in May 1795.

His performances in the London theatre also were few. At Covent Garden on 20 March 1789 he played a concerto by Handel on the organ. At the same theatre on 30 April 1789 the evening concluded with "God Save the King," accompanied by Greatorex at the organ. He also played in the Covent Garden oratorios in 1790, 1791, 1792, and 1794. On 17 March 1790 was presented *Miserere Mei Deus*, composed by Gregorio Allegri in 1650 and sung from an authentic copy brought from Italy by Greatorex. Pohl, in *Mozart and Haydn in London*, recalled Greatorex's accompaniment on the glockenspiel of a chorus in *Saul* at the Haymarket in 1792. And on 15 May 1794 for the oratorio at the King's Theatre he played the new organ built by Green for the new Subscription Room. In 1794 he was listed in Doane's *Musical Directory* as living at George Street, Hanover Square.

By 1801 Greatorex enjoyed a reputation as "the head of the English school." In that year, in association with James Bartleman, Samuel Harrison, and the elder Charles Knyvett, he revived the Vocal Concerts at

Willis's Rooms. In 1806 he played the organ and piano and conducted the Chester Music Festival. From 1807 to 1812 he, Bartleman, and Harrison were granted licenses to present nine subscription concerts each spring at the Hanover Square Rooms. During his career he also conducted the festivals at Birmingham, York, and Derby. The climax of his success was his appointment, succeeding George Ebenezer Williams, as organist at Westminster Abbey in 1819. He also became a member of the board of the Royal Academy of Music upon its establishment in 1822 and was a chief professor of organ and piano there. Other professional activities included membership in the Madrigal Society and the Catch Club (1789 to 1798). He had long cultivated his interest in chemistry, astronomy, mathematics, architecture, and painting; his development of a new technique for measuring the altitude of mountains brought him a Fellowship in the Royal Society. He was also a member of the Linnaean Society.

Greatorex's busy life evidently was in harmony with his temperament and free from extraordinary unpleasantness or incident. He had a town house at No 70, Upper Norton Street (now Bolsover Street), Portland Place, and a country house on the banks of the Trent. In later years he suffered from gout and fatigue. He died at Hampton, on 18 July 1831, aged 74, of a cold caught while fishing, and was buried in the west cloister of Westminster Abbey, near Dr Cooke, on 25 July. At his funeral Croft's "Burial Service" and Greene's "Lord let me know mine end" were heard by a great congregation of mourners.

Greatorex was survived by his widow Elizabeth, six sons, and a daughter, all of whom were named in his will, made on 12 August 1830 and proved by his executors Charles Knyvett and his son William Anthony on 30 July 1831. To his sons Thomas, James, and William Anthony he left £700 in three-percent annuities, and to the last-named he also bequeathed all his harmonized glees and any benefits which should arise from his *Parochial Psalmody.* To his remaining four children, evidently minors—Anne Martha, Henry Wellington, Arthur, and Edward—he left in trust £2800 in annuities, equally divided. He ordered that his musical library, bookcases, and scientific effects be converted into money to be invested for his estate (his Handel bookcase and contents brought 115 guineas). The rest of his personal and real estate he put in trust for the interest of his wife Elizabeth Greatorex. Little is known to us concerning the subsequent activities of his children. His son Thomas Greatorex, who was born on 22 September 1800 and baptized at St Pancras on 22 December 1805, sang in the Vocal Concerts in 1811 and was by 1822 the organist of St James's Chapel. On 30 June 1822 he was recommended for membership in the Royal Society of Musicians and was admitted on 7 July 1822.

Thomas Greatorex's distant cousin, Anthony Greatorex, may have been a practicing musician in London during the eighteenth century, but we have no evidence. On 15 October 1808, describing himself as Anthony Greatorex of St Albans Street, St James's, Westminster, he drew his will which was proved on 7 November 1808 by his son John Anthony Greatorex, executor, to whom the estate was left. That son, John Anthony, of Upper Ruport Street, St James's, made his will on 30 July 1829, in which he mentioned four children: William Anthony, Charlotte Sarah, Anthony, and William; another Greatorex, named Edward, was the co-executor who proved the will on 28 June 1831.

The style of Thomas Greatorex's organ-playing was "massive," wrote Gardiner; "he was like Briareus with a hundred hands, grasping so many keys at once that surges of sound rolled from his instrument in awful grandeur." Although he was a masterful performer and a sound musician, he ap-peared to Gardiner never "to have a musical mind; he was more a matter-of-fact man than one endowed with imagination." But he was an "admirable" teacher and a cool and judicious conductor. A conservative in taste, he believed that "the style of Haydn's 'Creation' was too theatrical for England" and feigned not to be able to play it because "it was so unlike anything he had seen."

Over his long career he created little original work. He was primarily an arranger. He published psalms, harmonized by himself for four voices, and adapted ballads and songs as glees which were well received at the Vocal Concerts. His *Parochial Psalmody* was published in 1825, and his *Twelve Glees from English, Irish, and Scotch Melodies* was printed posthumously in 1833. Many of his arrangements for the Ancient and Vocal concerts were never printed.

Despite his eminence, no painting or engraving of Thomas Greatorex seems to have been done.

Greaves. *See* **GRIEVE.**

"Greber's Peg." *See* **DE L'ÉPINE.**

Green. *See also* **GREENE.**

Green, Mr [*fl.* 1725?–1729], *actor.*
A Mr Green played Maiden in *Tunbridge Walks* on 29 November 1729 in a company headed by Tony Aston "At the Front Long Room, next to the Opera-House in the Hay-Market." He was Foigard in *The Stratagem* on 1 December. Though Aston advertised "As we perform only on Mondays, Wednesdays, and Fridays, any Gentleman, &c. may here have a Room[y] Building, Clothes, and Scenes for a private Play for four Guineas, on other nights," no further performances at the Front Long Room are known.

The Green in the Aston company in 1729 could have been the Green who was at the Norwich theatre from 1725 to 1728. That actor's wife was also at Norwich, in 1727 and 1728.

Green, Mr *(fl. 1731)*, *prompter.*

The bills of the Haymarket summer theatre for 2 June 1731 announced *The Fall of Mortimer* and *The Welch Opera* and also that "Tickets deliver'd out for the Tragedy of Tragedies, with an opera call'd *The City Apprentice Turn'd Beau, or Love in a Hamper* which was to have been perform'd this Day, for the Benefit of Mr. Green, Prompter, will be taken at this Play."

Green, Mr *(fl. 1736–1737)*, *dancer.*

A Mr Green was on the Drury Lane Theatre company list as a dancer in the 1736–37 season.

Green, Mr *(fl. 1741)*, *actor.*

Mr Green, "A Citizen of London," played Torrismond for his own benefit, supported by Giffard's company at Goodman's Fields Theatre on 22 January 1741. He repeated the part on 12 February, when the bills announced "Benefit a Tradesman." What induced Giffard to offer his theatre for Green's relief is not known.

Green, Mr *(fl. 1747)*, *actor? house servant?*

A Mr Green was granted a benefit at Drury Lane on 18 May 1747, jointly with six other obscure figures, two of whom were minor performers and the rest apparently house servants.

Green, Mr *(fl. 1749–1770?)*, *singer.*

A Mr Green sang "The Song of *Robin Hood* in character" at Drury Lane Theatre on 2 May 1755. Green was said to be then making his "first appearance on any stage." But he may nevertheless have been the same Mr Green who had sung a song at the "End of Droll" on 10 and 15 May 1749 at the New Wells, Shepherd's Mar-

ket, May Fair. He sang at Sadler's Wells for Warner's benefit on 2 October 1756. He was probably referred to when the song *John and Nell*, "as sung by Mr. Green," was published at London in 1757. That Green may also have been the one who sang the song *Thank God at Last* published at London about 1770.

Green, Mr *(fl. 1768?–1772?)*, *house servant?*

Preparatory to the lawsuit between Colman and Harris culminating in 1770, James Medlicott Flack deposed that on 31 August 1768 he and John Palmer, attorney for Harris, inspected various articles entered into by Covent Garden performers and house servants. Among them were provisions that a Green and a Mrs Green were to be hired for four years, Green to receive £3 each year (presumably in lieu of benefit tickets) plus 11s. 4d. each night during the first year, 13s. 6d. per night the second year, and 14s. 4d. per night the third and fourth years. Mrs Green's terms were the same, except that she was to receive 16s. each night the fourth year, and she was allowed a benefit on 2 June each year. The Greens were probably house servants.

Green, Mr *(fl. 1784)*, *singer.*

A Mr Green was listed by Charles Burney as a countertenor among the vocal performers at the Handel Memorial Concerts in Westminster Abbey and the Pantheon in May and June 1784.

Green, Mr *(fl. 1785)*, *actor.*

A Mr Green walked on as a Messenger in *'Tis Well It's No Worse* with a pickup company in a specially licensed performance at the Haymarket Theatre on 25 April 1785.

Green, Mrs *(fl. 1732)*, *actress.*

A Mrs Green played Mrs Pincushion in *The Mock Doctor* on 4 August 1732 at "the Great Theatrical Booth in the Cherry-

Tree Garden near the Mote," during Tottenham Court Fair.

Green, Mrs (fl. 1768–1772?), *house servant? See* GREEN, MR (fl. 1768–1772?).

Green, Mrs (fl. 1780–1784), *actress.*
On 31 October 1780 "A Lady" who was said to be making her first appearance on any stage played Mrs Oakly in *The Jealous Wife* at Covent Garden Theatre. She was identified on a playbill in the Kemble Collection at the Huntington Library as a Mrs Green. She was in the company through 22 May 1781 earning £2 per week.

She had succeeded hard on the heels of Mrs Henry Green, the great exemplar of chambermaids and various comic eccentrics at Covent Garden who had retired at the end of the 1779–80 season after 45 years' service. Some of this Mrs Green's roles were in the same general lines as those of her predecessor. But she was not so good an actress, and Harris made little use of her talents. During the winter and spring of 1780–81 she played Pulcheria in *Theodosius,* Gertrude in *Hamlet,* Adriana in *The Comedy of Errors,* and Mrs Bromley in *Know Your Own Mind.* Curiously, she was not allowed to share a benefit until the end of the following season.

Mrs Green may (or may not) have played Maria in *The Man's Bewitch'd* in a special winter performance at the Haymarket Theatre on 8 March 1784. The *Morning Chronicle* cast disagrees with that in the *Gazetteer,* which names her.

Green, Mrs (fl. 1782–1786?), *house servant?*
Two widely separated notices may nevertheless refer to the same individual: the Covent Garden playbill of 15 May 1782 announced "tickets delivered by Mrs. Green and the Performers in the Orchestra will be admitted this Evening." She cannot have gained much; receipts, before house charges, were only £208 5s. On 1 June 1786 Mrs Green was one of a mixed crew of 13 carpenters, scene-shifters, and humbler servants of the Covent Garden house who shared (before charges) receipts of £224 11s. 6d.

Green, Master (fl. 1735–1741). *See* GREEN, HENRY.

Green, Master (fl. 1770–1774), *trumpeter, singer.*
At Marylebone Gardens on 21 August 1770, ten-year-old Master Green "(Mr. Jones's scholar)" joined Master Rogers "of Bath (Mr. Leander's scholar)," 12 years old, in a "New French Horn and Trumpet Concerto" composed by Barthélemon. He was next noticed as playing a concerto on the trumpet during a performance at Covent Garden Theatre on 15 May 1771. He played also at Finch's Grotto Gardens on 30 August and on 3 and 9 September 1771 and at Covent Garden on 9 April 1772. At Marylebone Gardens on 3 September 1773 he apparently sang in a chorus at a performance of *Ambarvalia.* He went back to the trumpet to play a duo with "Serjeant Jr.," another of Jones's scholars, at the Haymarket on 25 March 1774. All performances but the last were benefit offerings for actors or musicians.

Green, Miss (fl. 1735), *actress.*
A Miss Green played the title role in *Flora* at "the Great Booth on the Bowling Green" at Southwark Fair on 7 April 1735.

Green, Miss (fl. 1760–1761?), *actress.*
Although a Miss Green was set down for 10s. per diem salary as an actress in the British Museum's Covent Garden Theatre account book for the season 1760–61, there are no records of her having performed at Covent Garden that season. She may have been the "Young Gentlewoman," identified in *Faulkner's Dublin Journal* as

a Miss Green, who made her debut at Smock Alley Theatre, Dublin, on 27 November 1760 and remained in that company during the season.

Green, Miss [fl. 1777–1782], actress, singer.

Miss Green, perhaps the daughter of Mrs Jane Hippisley Green, began assuming minor roles in the Covent Garden company on 8 January 1777 as Francisca in *Measure for Measure*. She earned £1 per week that season but appeared in the bills only as the First Beggar Woman in *The Jovial Crew* on 11 January. She was active at Liverpool from 2 June through late September and there received a guinea a week.

The next season, on 29 September 1777, she reappeared at Covent Garden (again earning £1 per week) as one of many voices of the chorus singing the usual "Solemn Dirge" in Juliet's funeral procession. Miss Green remained at Covent Garden through the 1779–80 season only, playing, infrequently, as Arante in *King Lear*, Iras in *All for Love*, Mrs Bruin in *The Mayor of Garratt*, Elisa in *Alfred*, a Female Slave in *Barbarossa*, Miss Skylight in *Illumination*, Night in *Amphitryon*, a Sicilian in the first staging of Charles Dibdin's *The Mirror*, a Lady in the first offering of Frederick Pilon's *The Deaf Lover*, and an unspecified part in *The Widow of Delphi*. Except for 22 January 1781, when she played Marilla ("with a song") in *A Wife to be Let* in a special winter performance at the Haymarket, and 21 January 1782, when she was Mrs Crossbite in *An Adventure in St James's Park* on a similar occasion, she was seen no more in the bills.

Green, Charles [fl. 1685–1693], musician.

Charles Green was one of the clerks of the choir of Westminster at the coronation of James II on 23 April 1685. On 2 January 1693 he was sworn a Gentleman of the Chapel Royal extraordinary—that is, without fee until a salaried position should become available. Since he was not cited again in the Lord Chamberlain's accounts, perhaps no post materialized.

Green, Henry d. 1772? actor.

In all likelihood the "Master Green" who was first seen delivering the prologue and playing the title role in a children's performance of *George Barnwell* at the little James Street Theatre on 24 May 1734 was Henry Green. Master Green also played Sir John in the afterpiece *The Devil to Pay*. A younger brother, Master W. Green, was also concerned in the performance that night but does not seem to have made a career of the stage.

In December 1734 or earlier the Master Green of the James Street performance joined the Drury Lane company and performed Robin in *The Merry Wives of Windsor* eight times through 13 February 1735. On 22 May he and Miss Cole spoke a "New Epilogue" together. In July and August he was with the summer theatre in the Haymarket playing Slango in *The Honest Yorkshireman,* Richard in *The Provok'd Husband,* and (on 12 August) Mrs Slammekin in *The Beggar's Opera*—odd casting for a small boy. The next season at Drury Lane he appeared in the bills only twice, on 25 October 1735 as Prince Edward in *Richard III* and on 21 November 1735 as Simple in *The Merry Wives of Windsor*. He was Townly in *The Provok'd Husband* on 29 June 1735. On 22 May he had shared in benefit tickets.

Master Green returned to Drury Lane in the season of 1736–37 and 1737–38 playing only Simple, so far as the bills show, and that very infrequently. He had one performance in the part on 13 October 1739, and then "Master Green" gave way in the Drury Lane playbills in favor of "Mr Green." He remained steadily at the house through June 1745, sharing in benefit tickets each season, playing a wide array of parts. The British Museum's Additional Manuscript 18586 identifies the "Young Master Green" who played "Robin MW" with the Green of 1744–45 and adds: "He became a prominent actor." But his prominence while he was at Drury Lane was of the kind gained from the audience's frequent glimpses of him in tertiary parts and walk-ons, though occasionally he was given a role of some importance. His parts were, in order of assumption: Phaeton in *The Fall of Phaeton*, Blunt in *The Defeat of Apollo* (at the Haymarket, summer, 1737), a Forester in *The King and the Miller of Mansfield*, Orestes in *Agamemnon*, Parisatis in *The Rival Queens*, Horatio in *The Man of Taste*, Thomas in *The Virgin Unmask'd*, a "Gipsy" in *The Fortune Tellers*, Alonzo in *Rule a Wife and Have a Wife*, Doodle in *The Tragedy of Tragedies*, Selim in *The Mourning Bride*, the Marquis of Lindsay in *An Historical Play*, Jack in *The Committee*, Curio in *Twelfth Night*, Silvius in *As You Like It*, Hippolito in *The Tempest*, Mendlegs in *The Relapse*, Guildenstern in *Hamlet*, a Haymaker in *Harlequin Shipwreck'd*, Bombardinion in *Chrononhotonthologos*, Dr Hellebore in *The Mock Doctor*, Sparkle in *The Miser*, Philip in *The Rival Queens*, Puff in *The Intriguing Chambermaid*, Sir Thomas in *The What D'Ye Call It*, Tom Errand in *The Constant Couple*, Haly in *Tamerlane*, a Clerk in *Women Pleased*, Buckram in *Love for Love*, Friendly in *The School Boy*, Jaques in *Love Makes a Man*, Young Gerald in *The Anatomist*, Eliot in *Venice Preserv'd*, Barnaby in *The Old Bachelor*, Daniel in *The Conscious Lovers*, Oxford in *Richard III*, Dapper in *The Alchemist*, Scaurus in *Regulus*, Dymas in *Oedipus, King of Thebes*, Razor in *The Provok'd Wife*, Ali in *Mahomet*, Sly in *Love's Last Shift*, and Galloon in *The Gamester*.

Green's movements after he left Drury Lane are obscure. He had gone to Bristol, to the Jacob's Wells Theatre from 8 June through 3 September 1741, and he returned there at least in the summers of 1743, 1744, 1749, 1750, 1751, 1752, and 1754, and probably oftener. He acted some of his old parts at Phillips's booth at Bartholomew Fair in August 1749, including Mustachio in a burlesque *Tempest* on 23 August, an evening during which the gallery seats collapsed, killing two and injuring many. Penley in *The Bath Stage* lists a Green, doubtless Henry, in the Bath company (usually identical with that of Bristol) from 1750 through 1755. He made his Dublin debut on 29 November 1752, according to *Faulkner's Dublin Journal*, and signed his full name to a letter in the same paper on 16 March 1754.

In June 1747 Henry Green had married the well-known London comedienne Jane Hippisley, whose father had kept the Jacob's Wells Theatre in Bristol. She had made her Dublin debut at Smock Alley on 1 November 1752. In her obituary in the *Bristol Journal* in August 1791 it was stated that she "was married to Henry Green, Esq. who died some few years since, Purser of the *Namur*, a ninety-gun ship." One Henry Green was buried at St Paul's, Covent Garden, on 18 March 1772. Jane Green evidently had at least three sons by Henry Green.

Green, Mrs Henry, Jane, née Hippisley *1719–1791, actress, dancer, singer.*

Jane Hippisley was born in 1719, a daughter of the excellent comedian John Hippisley and his wife Elizabeth. Jane had at least two sisters, both actresses and both probably younger. They were Elizabeth, who performed in London, and a Miss Hippisley whose first name is not known but who acted as Mrs Fitzmaurice at York, Bath, and Edinburgh. A half brother, John, son of Hippisley's mistress, Mary Charley, also took to the stage.

On the night of her father's benefit, 18 March 1735, an actress cited only as "Hippisley's Daughter" made what the playbill called her first appearance, playing Cherry in *The Stratagem* at Covent Garden Theatre. Isaac Reed in his manuscript "Notitia Dramatica" in the British Museum identified her as the Hippisley daughter who became Mrs Green—that is, Jane. At John Hippisley's benefit the following season, on 22 March 1736, a Miss Hippisley played Rose in *The Recruiting Officer*. Nearly four years later, on 11 January 1740, "Miss Jenny" Hippisley, playing Rose at Drury Lane, was advertised as then appearing for the first time on any stage. It is impossible now to decide whether or not the statement was true.

In any case, Jane Hippisley did not then pursue her career at Drury Lane, and in 1740–41 she became an active member of the Goodman's Fields troupe under Henry Giffard. She began with Rose in *The Recruiting Officer* on 22 October 1740 and followed that with Prue in *Love for Love* on 28 October, Jenny in *The Provok'd Husband* on 31 October, Ann Page in *The Merry Wives of Windsor* on 15 November, Lucy in *The Virgin Unmask'd* on 22 November, Cleone in *The Distrest Mother* on 26 November, Situp in *The Double Gallant* on 1 December, Ophelia in *Hamlet* on 4 December, Penelope in *Tunbridge Walks* on 5 December, Hoyden in *The Relapse* on 8 December, a Follower of Hymen in *The Imprisonment, Release, Adventures, and Marriage of Harlequin* on 15 December, Perdita in *The Winter's Tale* on 15 January, Cherry in *The Stratagem* on 20 January, Mrs Vixen in *The Beggar's Opera* on 27 January, Angelina in *Love Makes a Man* on 5 February, Beatrice in *The Anatomist* on 14 February, Matilda in *King Arthur* on 19 February, Colombine in *Harlequin Student* on 3 March, Diana in *All's Well that Ends Well* on 7 March, Harriet in *The Miser* on 16 March, Cloe in *Timon of Athens* on 19 March, Lucy in *Lethe* on 7 April, and Lappet in *The Miser* (along with Lucy and an epilogue) for her benefit, shared with Blakes, on 15 April.

Harvard Theatre Collection

JANE GREEN, as the Duenna

by J. H. Green

Either Jane or another Miss Hippisley was in Ipswich in the summer of 1741; she shared a benefit with Marr on 21 July, when she played Bisarre in *The Inconstant* and Lucy in *Lethe* and spoke the epilogue. The 1741–42 season found Jane again at Goodman's Fields. But so, too, was her sister Elizabeth, and they had similar lines, making the distinguishing of their respective careers difficult whenever the bills do not provide their initials. In 1741–42, carried in the bills as Miss Hippisley, Jane played Lucy in *The Virgin Unmask'd*, Inis in *The Wonder*, Jenny in *The Provok'd Husband*, Diana in *All's Well*, Cherry in *The Stratagem*, Maria in *George Barnwell*, Patch in *The Busy Body*, Edging in *The Careless Husband*, Prince Edward in *Richard III* (on 19 October, when Garrick made his debut), Angelina in *Love Makes a Man*, Serina in *The Orphan*, Jane in *Pamela*, Kitty Pry in *The Lying Valet*, Lavinia in *The Fair Penitent*, Ophelia in *Hamlet*, Lappet in *The Miser*, Rose in *The*

Recruiting Officer, Sylvia in *The Old Bachelor*, Beatrice in *The Anatomist*, Lucy in *Lethe*, Foible in *The Way of the World* (on 27 January, when her sister played Mincing and was advertised as Miss E. Hippisley), Arante in *King Lear*, and Kitty in *The Lying Valet* for her solo benefit on 1 April. After Elizabeth joined the troupe in January, Jane appears to have acted less frequently, and some of her parts—Arante, Prue, and Silvia, for instance—she gave to her sister.

In 1742–43 Elizabeth moved to Covent Garden Theatre where her father was a member of the company, and Jane stayed with Giffard's troupe for their ill-fated season at Lincoln's Inn Fields. There Jane played Mrs Vixen on 14 February 1743, possibly Prue and Kitty on 18 February at Southwark (the bill and the *Daily Advertiser* differ), then, at Lincoln's Inn Fields again, Lucilla in *The Fair Penitent* on 8 March and Wheedle in *The Miser* on 4 April.

A Miss Hippisley acted at John Hippisley's Jacob's Wells summer theatre in Bristol in 1743, 1748, and 1751 through 1756. Inasmuch as Jane Hippisley became Mrs Henry Green in June 1747, either Elizabeth or a third Miss Hippisley was the actress at Bristol from 1748 on; Jane probably performed there in the summer of 1743, though identification is difficult. Indeed, she probably there met Henry Green, who was at Bristol in the summers of 1741, 1743, and 1744, at least. (The Miss Hippisley who became Mrs Fitzmaurice was active at Bath in the early fifties and other cities later; the Bath company was usually identical with the Bristol troupe.)

On 23 December 1745 a Miss Hippisley, presumably Jane, played Cherry in *The Stratagem* at Goodman's Fields and was hailed as making her first appearance on that stage. (Cherry had been acted on 13 November by a "Gentlewoman new to the stage.") On 2 January 1746 Miss Hippisley played Rose in *The Recruiting Officer*.

Jane Green was among the company, 70 strong, assembled by Garrick in his first season of managing dramatic affairs at Drury Lane in 1747–48. Her competition for the roles which were to make her notable was Kitty Clive, who was of course unbeatable. Yet, astonishingly, there seem to have been few conflicts with the blunt-tongued Clive. Perhaps Kitty remained placid because at first Jane filled in at Kitty's pleasure and in the smaller parts only. Perhaps she was flattered that Jane took her—or so the critics charged—as a model. In the next four seasons, 1747–48 through 1750–51, in addition to some ingenue and secondary parts already in her repertoire, Jane Green performed the following, in order: Mrs Pincushion in *The Mock Doctor*, Armelina in *Albumazar*, Florella in *The Orphan*, Lucetta in *The Suspicious Husband*, Mrs Slammekin in *The Beggar's Opera*, Dorinda in *The Tempest*, Lettice in *The School Boy*, Corinna in *The Confederacy*, Flora in *She Wou'd and She Wou'd Not*, Peggy in *The Miller of Mansfield*, Margaret in *A New Way to Pay Old Debts*, Mopsophil in *The Emperour of the Moon*, Mrs Fardingale in *The Funeral*, Mrs Tatoo in *Lethe*, Cleone in *The Distrest Mother*, Ismene in *Merope*, Lucy in *The London Merchant*, Foible in *The Way of the World*, Dorcas in *The Mock Doctor*, and Maria in *Twelfth Night*.

Jane refused to return to Drury Lane in 1751–52. The prompter Cross noted in his diary on 26 September 1751 "Mrs. Green went to Bath to play & left us—O fool." Very likely Jane's defection had something to do with her husband's commitments. He was, off and on during the forties and fifties, at Bristol in the summer and probably at Bath as well. Jane had also gone to Bristol to play at Jacob's Wells (the theatre founded by her father John Hippisley in 1729) during the summers of 1747, 1748, and 1750. Her father had died on 12 February 1748, leaving his Bristol dwelling and playhouse and the contiguous buildings to "my beloved consort M^{rs}. Mary Charley with whom I cohabit and dwell and whom I acknowledge and Esteem my Wife," though his own wife Elizabeth, he noted, was still alive. Residuary legatees were his son John "whom I had by her and called John Hippisley" and "my dear Jane now the wife of Henry Green." (It may be, though, that Jane had assumed some managerial responsibilities. Certainly she occupied her father's dwelling, which had been an inn called the Horse and Groom, during her Bristol summers and, after her retirement, until she died. She continued to act at Bristol every summer from 1756 through 1772, first at Jacob's Wells and, after 1766, at King Street. She finally fell out with the King Street manager, James Dodd, scolded him in a published letter for making her "whole summer disagreeable by your rude Behaviour," and never went back. She had been connected with the Bristol theatre for 29 years, first to last.)

In the early fall of 1751, then, Jane joined the company of the Orchard Street Theatre in Bath, for what can have been only a few nights. Her movements between September 1751 and 1 November 1752, when she turned up at Dublin's Smock Alley Theatre, are not known. On 29 November her husband Henry made his Dublin debut.

When, in the fall of 1754, Jane (and perhaps Henry, though this is unknown) returned to London, it was to Covent Garden, where Jane's father, old John Hippisley, had been so popular. There her chief competitor was Ann Pitt, not nearly so formidable as the great Clive but good enough to extend Jane's talents. And though some friction was inevitable, little was reported. A clipping hand-dated 1773 in the British Museum's Burney Collection said that

a pitched battle [was] fought in the green-room, between Mrs. Green and Mrs. Pitt, about the part of Juliet; the former of whom

it seems has often played the part in the country, but upon Colman's promising her the part of Monimia in *The Orphan,* and which he assured her should be played as soon as Mr. Cushing could get ready in Castalio, she instantly smiled consent, and the affair ended in perfect harmony.

Juliet had, indeed, been one of Jane's best parts at the time, 1752, when she first came to Covent Garden. A Bristol admirer had that year published ten decidedly unheroic couplets "*To Mrs.* Green, *in the Character of* JULIET. . . ." But she did not play the part in London. Mrs Pitt had been a noted Nurse from as early as 1753. Jane Green was 54 in 1773, and Ann Pitt was about the same age. The story is rather incredible if the dating is correct, not much less so if it should be, say, 1767, when the ladies would have been 48, and the earliest date at which they and Colman and Cushing all were at Covent Garden.

Jane remained at Covent Garden until the end of the 1779–80 season, adding, year by year, the following parts: Lady Dove in *The Brothers,* Mrs Cross in *Man and Wife,* Flippanta in *The Confederacy,* Mrs Cadwallader in *The Author,* Ursula in *The Padlock,* Old Lady Lambert in *The Hypocrite,* Lucinda in *The Englishman Returned from Paris,* Mrs Heidelberg in *The Clandestine Marriage,* Filagree in *A Trip to Scotland,* Johayma in *Don Sebastian, King of Portugal,* Mrs Grub in *Cross Purposes,* Lady Wrangle in *The Refusal,* Lady Froth in *The Double Dealer,* Lady Strangeways in *The Romance of an Hour,* Miss Harlow in *The Old Maid,* Tag in *Miss in Her Teens,* Margery in *Love in a Village,* Dorcas in *Thomas and Sally,* Mrs Sneak in *The Mayor of Garratt,* the Mother in *The Chances,* and Lucetta in *The Suspicious Husband.*

She was the original Mrs Malaprop in Sheridan's *The Rivals* on 17 January 1775 and sang in the first performance the title part in his comic opera *The Duenna* the following 21 November. She was the first

EDWARD SHUTER as Mr Hardcastle, JANE GREEN as Mrs Hardcastle, and JOHN QUICK as Tony Lumpkin

engraving by Humphrey, after Parkinson

Mrs Hardcastle in Goldsmith's *She Stoops to Conquer* and the first Mrs Garnet in his *The Good-Natured Man*. Among other parts she sustained in first performance were Mrs Markam in Elizabeth Griffith's *A Wife in the Right*, Mrs Western in Joseph Reed's *Tom Jones*, Catherine Rouge in Frederick Pilon's *The Invasion*, and Lady Bauble in William Kenrick's *The Duellist*. Her last performance was as Mrs Hardcastle, on 26 May 1780. Her last bows were taken in a week that also saw the final departure from Covent Garden's stage of Elizabeth Hartley and George Anne Bellamy.

Mrs Green had moved from a total salary of £158 in 1761–62 to £236 for the 1777–78 season, when she also received £84 "allowance in lieu of her Night," according to the Covent Garden accounts. In her final season she received £8 per week plus her benefit. Her lodgings had been at the Green Canister in Great Shire Lane, Carey Street, Lincoln's Inn Fields, at the time of her benefit in 1748. She lived in Broad Court, Bow Street, Covent Garden, in 1749, 1750, and 1751. She maintained a house in King Street, Covent Garden, by 5 May 1772 and still lived there in the winter of 1780.

Jane Green's 45 years on the stage spanned the entire Garrick era. By the time she left the stage she had accumulated several generations of appreciators of her conspiratorial chambermaids, eccentric maiden ladies, and silly hostesses. Though she began in the sweet-voiced Lucys and Peggys of ballad opera, early corpulence pushed her first into hoydenish country girls, then into important domestics. By 1750 the "cunning look and . . . ready volubility of tongue" which John Hill in *The Actor* thought the *sine qua non* of the stage chambermaid he "found in . . . utmost perfection in Mrs. Green." By 1757 *The Theatrical Examiner* was speaking nostalgically of "the time her figure was girlish" when she "was an agreeable sprightly actress" and "something to recall." In 1758 *The Theatrical Review* gave extensive expression to the view that her style was derivative from that of Kitty Clive:

Mrs. Green is a second edition of Mrs. Clive, but much less than the first in bulk, merit and contents; yet not entirely made up of repetitions, nor without alterations, a few for the better, and some for the worse.

It is a sort of misfortune for this actress, that we have not yet adopted the French custom of making important characters of the chamber-maids. She is possessed in an eminent degree of all the requisites necessary to excel in that province, where her great humour, spirits, smart lively voice, and agreeable pertness would be most luckily placed. She is perhaps a little too affected; but that which is a fault in some of the characters she now acts, would become a perfection, if those parts of chamber-maids were numerous enough to take up intirely an actress, so as to dispense her from meddling with any other parts; her excess of affectation would suit very well the exhibition of the second-hand airs that are proper to that class of women. . . . [But] in general affectation is the bane of her performance; that, and no inconsiderable mixture of imitation, have greatly cramped the growth of her talents and fame; yet, as both proceed from the desire of pleasing, she will soon get rid of them, if she can be once sensible, that Nature had put it absolutely in her power to be a most agreeable original without any foreign aids.

As long as Mrs Clive was on the boards Mrs Green was never completely free of the imputation of imitation. But she seems to have tried to be original, and gradually critical attention shifted to the contrast between the styles of Jane Green and Ann Pitt. This passage from *The Rosciad of C–v–nt G–rd–n*, (1762) illustrates:

Next G—N, and P–TT, a laughing plotting pair;
Their claims as romping chambermaids declare:
Who can, like P–TT, so happily express
The saucy manner, and the pert address?
Like Her, in unaffected airs excel,
Or act the favour'd servant half so well?
Or who, O GR—N! of all the female throng,
Can match thy volubility of tongue?
With so much ease you art and nature mix,
Provoke our laughter, and our judgment fix,
That ev'ry candid hearer must confess,
E'vn sprightly CL–VE, herself, has charm'd us less.

To *The Rational Rosciad* (1767) she had hardly faded at all in 33 years: "Gayly polite the sprightly, blooming Green/Can fill with grace a mediocre scene."

Francis Gentleman in *The Dramatic Censor* (1770) gave her excellent marks for several of her efforts. Lucetta in *The Suspicious Husband* "is a short, unimportant chambermaid, yet well drawn, and useful to the play; Mrs. GREEN made every line of her tell . . ." and Mrs Cross in *Man and Wife* "received considerable animation from that correctness and vivacity which always distinguishes Mrs Green's performance." She even edged out Mrs Pitt in some parts: Patch in *The Busy Body* "should always be in the hands of Mrs. GREEN, though we have seen Mrs. Pitt shew acting merit in the character." But in Lady Wronghead in *The Provok'd Husband* Mrs Clive "is closely traced by Mrs. Green." Mrs Blackacre in *The Plain Dealer* is gone with Mrs Clive to Strawberry Hill and won't return until "Mrs. GREEN takes her by the hand." In his summary judgment Gentleman wrote: "Mrs. Green, a very good substitute for Mrs. Clive."

The *Macaroni and Savoir Vivre Magazine* (1773) went all the way back to

1758, plagiarizing the views and whole sentences of *The Theatrical Review*—she was a second edition of Clive, her line was limited, her voice was affected. The *Covent Garden Magazine* (1773) spoke for the first time of a diminution of her powers, of a "continuous smile" and a "disagreeable mode of using her arms," and saw her merely as "useful," a word by which the ineffectual or fading veteran was habitually depreciated. But the reviewer was either spleenful or out of touch with common opinion. As late as 6 February 1778, when the York manager Tate Wilkinson was acting for his benefit the last night of a short special engagement at Covent Garden Theatre, he recalled: "I had a very brilliant audience. . . . I acted . . . Cadwallader in *The Author*——The applause was so strong in the second act of the farce, that we were obliged to stop for some time; but note, reader, that Mrs. Green was the Mrs. Cadwallader, and no wonder the audience were to a degree satisfied. She was a charming actress." At Covent Garden she was, said Wilkinson, "held in universal and deserved estimation."

The esteem in which she was held did not keep gossip from her, however. As early as 1772, in the course of a "memoir" which gives practically no information about Mrs Green except that she played chambermaids, the author of *Theatrical Biography* spoke of her having acquaintance with Garrick and continued:

The very great care and attention this skilful director took in the cultivation of her talents, might very well account for her progress; nor is it to be wondered at, when it is said that there were still stronger reasons for attentions than mere managerical regard. . . . The lady *could* not be . . . cruel; sensible of the mischiefs she had done to Garrick's heart, she repaired them by good-nature—a chopping boy bore witness to their loves—whose death is since to be lamented, both on a private and public account; on the former, as it was the *only* child our English Roscius ever

had; on the latter, as posterity may possibly be deprived of one day *seeing the father blazoned in the son.*

Several early biographical sources—*The Secret History of the Green Room* (1795) and successive editions of *The Thespian Dictionary*—suggest that Samuel Cautherley the actor was David Garrick's son. And in the brief biography of the actor Bensley in *Theatrical Biography* the supposition is obliquely hinted at. Whether or not there was a liaison between Garrick and Miss Hippisley which produced a child and, if so, whether Samuel Cautherley was that child and the author of Mrs Green's memoir in *Theatrical Biography* was misinformed about the "chopping boy" being dead cannot now be determined.

But Jane Green had children, supposedly by Henry Green. She died at five o'clock Sunday morning 21 August 1791 at her house at Jacob's Wells, Bristol, "carried off by a mortification in her limbs" after a painful struggle of eight weeks, according to her obituary in the *Bristol Journal*. She was buried at Clifton Church. She had been preceded in death "some few years since" by Henry Green, who had at some point become "Purser of the Namur, a ninety-gun ship." Administration of her property was granted on 12 September to three sons of whom she spoke in her will— Charles, John Hippisley, and Henry—and to whom she left "all that my Messuage and Tenement and the Garden thereunto adjoining and belonging situate at Jacobs Wells within the . . . Parish of Clifton which I hold under the Incorporated Society of Merchants Venturers of the City of Bristol which I hold for the term of my Life" and the lives of the sons. Besides those properties and her furniture, plate, linen, and china, there were unspecified amounts "invested in the ffunds of Great Britain Commonly called the ffive per cents" which were to be divided among the sons. Her eldest son, said in the Bristol obituary to be in 1791 a Captain of Marines, had been on the Bristol stage as a child, dancing a minuet with little Miss Pitt at Jacobs Wells on 8 September 1759 and making his debut at the new King Street Theatre as Dick in *The Apprentice* on 8 September 1766. There is a possibility that the Miss Green who was at Covent Garden from 1777 to 1780 was Jane's daughter. If so, she may have died before her mother's will was made on 20 November 1786.

A manuscript note in the Bristol Library reads:

Mrs. Green's Monument was removed from the Old to the New Church at Clifton.

Sacred to the Memory of Mrs. Jane Green, as a comedian, she was many years deservedly admired in Public, while in Private Life her Virtues gained her distinguished Esteem. She retired 1780; and died August the 21st, [no year given] Aged 72 years. As a Tribute of filial Respect this Monument was designed and erected by her Son John Hippisley.

Mrs Green was depicted as Mrs Cadwallader in *The Author* in an engraving published by J. H. Green in 1803 after a pencil drawing by J. Roberts, now in the Harvard Theatre Collection. Green also made an engraving of her as the title character in *The Duenna.* An engraving by W. Humphrey, after T. Parkinson, shows Mrs Green as Mrs Hardcastle, Shuter as Mr Hardcastle, and Quick as Tony Lumpkin in *She Stoops to Conquer*; it was published by Carrington Bowles in 1775, and a copy by an unknown engraver was published by Sayer in 1776.

Green, James [*fl.* 1784], *singer.*
James Green was listed by Charles Burney among the bass vocalists in the Handel memorial performances in Westminster Abbey and the Pantheon in May and June 1784.

JOHN and ROBERT GREEN
engraving by van Assen, after Parry

Green, John [*fl.* 1794–1804?], *singer, instrumentalist?*
Doane's *Musical Directory* of 1794 listed John Green, of No 1, Baker's Row, Walworth, Surrey, as a bass singer who was a member of the Choral Fund, the Longacre Society, the Handelian Society, and the Surrey Chapel Society. He also sang in the oratorios at Drury Lane Theatre and Westminster Abbey. Possibly he was the John Green pictured with Robert Green in an engraving by A. van Assen, after J. Parry, published by Parry in 1804. The two men were called itinerant musicians, and one was shown playing a violin and the other a pipe and tambourine.

Green, Jonathan [*d.* 1794], *boxkeeper, lobbykeeper.*
Jonathan Green was a boxkeeper at Covent Garden Theatre continuously from the season of 1748–49 until his death near the end of the season of 1793–94. He was also, perhaps, the box- and lobby-

keeper at the King's Theatre in 1783–84 and 1784–85. His address in 1779–80 and 1780–81 was "the corner of Norris St., No 55 Haymarket," according to his benefit bills.

Green earned a salary of 2s. per night in 1760–61. It was from 1776–77 through 1793–94 still only 12s. per five-day week. But boxkeepers shared annual benefits and they were strategically placed to ingratiate their clientele all season long, so that their nights were usually well attended. (For example, Green, Condell, and Vaughan split among them £238 9s. on 16 May 1760.) Not infrequently, also, boxkeepers had lucrative outside interests. In Green's case, according to the *Scottish Register*, it was stockbroking.

Certainly, as his will shows, he died a wealthy man—on 31 May 1794, said the *Scottish Register*. His will, however, was proved on 3 May. He had made it on 10 December 1793, "being advanced in years and at times afflicted with a dizziness in the head and ffaintness [and] wishing to settle my worldly Estate and Affairs to prevent all disputes and differences amongst my relations and friends after my decease. . . ." To his wife Mary (who was his second wife) he left two dwelling houses in South Street, Grosvenor Square, "and also all the several sums of Money Stocks or Securities for two thousand pounds three pounds per Centum per Annum Consolidated Annuities now standing in my own name in the Books of the Governor and Company of the Bank of England" which he had "some time ago" transferred jointly to his wife and his friend and executor James Bright Slann. In addition, Mary Green was to receive the horse, chaise, and household effects, "the annual Interest Dividends and Proceed [sic] of the Sum of ffive hundred pounds Stock of the . . . Bank of England commonly called Bank Stock" and interest on £1200 "due to me from Audley Wade of the Island of Barbadoes." Wade had married Mary Green's

granddaughter Mary, who was at her grandmother's death to receive the principal sum of £1200 if Wade had paid the interest regularly. The residuary legatee of Green's £500 in Bank Stock was his natural daughter "Elizabeth Wooley an Infant whom I had by Ann Woolley of the Queen's Court Great Queen Street Lincoln's Inn Fields . . . now deceased. . . ." In addition, Green left the child £500 for her education.

There were several Greens in several capacities at Covent Garden during Jonathan Green's tenure there, but his relationship to them (if any) is not understood.

Green, Mrs P. [*fl.* 1773–1774], *actress.*

Mrs P. Green played the Queen in *Cymbeline* five times between 12 November 1773, when she was first introduced to Covent Garden audiences simply as "A Lady," and 6 December. For the rest of the season she had a busy, though royal, time playing once each as the Duchess of York in *Richard III,* the Queen in *Cymbeline,* Queen Elizabeth in *The Earl of Essex,* the Duchess of Suffolk in *Lady Jane Grey,* and Paulina in *The Winter's Tale,* as well as Mrs Sullen in *The Stratagem.* She repeated Sysigambis in *The Rival Queens* three times. Mrs P. Green was evidently a quick and willing study, but she disappeared from view in London after 20 May 1774, when she shared a benefit with Hussey and Morris.

Green, Robert *b.* 1758?, *violist, trumpeter, violinist.*

A Mr Green was on the Drury Lane company list in the season of 1778–79, receiving £1 15s. per week for playing viola and trumpet in the band. He was perhaps the Robert Green who was recommended by one Evans as a prospective member of the Royal Society of Musicians on 6 February 1780 who was said to be 22 years old, single, a musical performer at Drury Lane, and in the band of the second regiment of Guards. He was certified to be a specialist on "trumpet, tenor viola, and Violin." Robert and John Green were pictured in an engraving by A. van Assen, after J. Parry, which was published by Parry in 1804. The two men were called itinerant musicians, and one was shown playing a violin and the other a pipe and tambourine. There is a possibility that our subject was the Robert Green in the picture.

Green, Thomas [fl. 1784], singer.

Thomas Green was listed by Charles Burney as among the bass vocalists in the Handel memorial performances in Westminster Abbey and the Pantheon in May and June 1784. He was said to be from Birmingham.

Green, W. [fl. 1734–1745], actor.

Master W. Green came into view first as Blunt in George Barnwell, with other youngsters in a "Lilliputian" performance at the little James Street Theatre on 24 May 1734. His elder brother, who was very likely Henry Green, was in the title part.

The James Street performance was evidently sufficiently obscure for the Haymarket Theatre to advertise that "Master Green Jr" was making his first appearance "on any stage" when he played Richard in The Provok'd Husband on 29 July 1736. After that date there is no certain record of any activity by him, though some of the performances credited to his older brother may have been his. (Fifty years later—around 1785—a William Green was manager of the theatre at Lincoln.)

Green, William [fl. 1694], violinist.

William Green was apparently a court violinist. A warrant in the Lord Chamberlain's accounts dated 13 June 1694 records that William Pink, "drugster," sued William Green, "violyn," for £20.

Greene. See also GREEN.

Greene, Henry d. 1741, musician.

Henry Greene was one of the original subscribers to the Royal Society of Musicians when it was formed on 28 August 1739. Musgrave's Obituary cited Greene as a "Master of Musick" who had been blind for many years. Greene died on 25 September 1741.

Greene, James [fl. 1674–1676], singer.

James Greene was one of the Children of the Chapel Royal at some time before 24 June 1674; by that time his voice had changed, and the following September he was granted two suits and an allowance of £30 annually. He was given other allowances in the years that followed, the last being on 26 April 1676. By that time he had become a page of the Chapel, but he seems not to have remained in the royal service.

Greene, Mrs Jonas. See HITCHCOCK, MARY ANNE.

Greene, Maurice 1695–1775, organist, composer.

Maurice Greene was born in London in 1695, the son of the Rev Thomas Greene, vicar of the united parishes of St Olave, Jewry, and St Martin Pomary. Young Maurice was a chorister at St Paul's Cathedral under Charles King; then, when his voice changed, he was apprenticed in 1710 to the organist of St Paul's, Richard Brind. In 1716 he was made organist of St Dunstan's in the West, an appointment, Grove notes, probably engineered by Maurice's uncle Serjeant Greene. After the death of Daniel Purcell in 1717 Greene succeeded to the post of organist of St Andrew, Holborn. He gave up that position and his St Dunstan's post in 1718, when he was appointed organist of St Paul's, succeeding Brind.

The Session of Musicians in May 1724 satirized most of the musicians in London,

National Portrait Gallery

MAURICE GREENE (seated), with J. Hoadley

by Hayman

and Greene was not excepted. In the poem, Apollo calls before him all the musicians to decide who should get the laurel:

> Gr[een]n, C[ro]fts, and some of the
>   Cathedral Taste,
> Their Compliments in Form to Phoebus
>   past;
> Whilst the whole Choir sung Anthems in
>   their Praise,
> Thinking to chant the God out of the
>   Bays;
> Who, far from being pleas'd, stamp'd,
>   fum'd, and swore,
> Such Musick he had never heard before;
> Vowing he'd leave the Laurel in the
>   lurch,
> Rather than place it in an English
>   Church.

Handel, of course, won the contest.

After the death of William Croft on 14 August 1727 Greene became second organist and composer to the Chapel Royal. The following year Greene made the mistake of favoring both Handel and his rival Bononcini, which turned Handel against him. He also blundered in helping to promote a madrigal by Bononcini which turned out to be the work of Lotti. The discovery of the true authorship brought disgrace to Bononcini and expulsion from the Academy of Ancient Music; Greene, because he had been implicated, withdrew voluntarily from the Academy, taking with him his choristers from St Paul's. In 1731 he founded the Apollo Society Concerts at the Devil Tavern, Temple Bar, and performed with his

St Paul's boys there for a few years, in opposition to the Academy concerts.

Greene was given a doctorate in music by Cambridge and succeeded to Tudway's post there as Professor of Music. For his exercise he set Pope's revised version of his *Ode on St Cecilia's Day*, which was performed on 6 July 1730. In 1735 Greene succeeded to John Eccles's post as Master of the King's Musick at an annual salary of £200 (to match Handel's salary as Music Master to the princesses; Eccles had received £250 annually). As composer to the Chapel Royal Greene wrote regularly for the court, especially for the King's birthday and New Year's Day each year. On 28 August 1739 he became one of the original subscribers to the newly founded Royal Society of Musicians, which he had had a hand in organizing on 19 April 1738.

When Greene came into an inheritance from his cousin (the natural son of his uncle Serjeant Greene) of Bois Hall in Essex, worth £700 yearly, he began collecting, reducing to score, and collating the best in cathedral music, but he did not live to see the project completed. By his death in 1755 he had published many works of his own, lists of which may be found in Grove, *The Dictionary of National Biography*, and the *Catalogue of Printed Music in the British Museum*. These included not only anthems, services, voluntaries, and a *Te Deum*, but two oratorios, three dramatic pastorals (*Love's Revenge*, also called *Florimel*, in 1734, *The Judgment of Hercules* in 1740, and *Phoebe* in 1748), and many songs, cantatas, catches, lessons, and overtures.

Maurice Greene died at the age of 60 on 1 December 1755 at his lodgings in Beaufort Buildings. His will, written on 26 July 1752 with a codicil dated 23 April 1755, was proved on 22 December 1755. He asked to be buried at St Olave, Jewry, where his father and mother had been buried. To his wife Mary (née Dillingham,

of Hampton, Middlesex) he left all his property in the parish of Havestock; Greene had evidently settled his property on her by an agreement before his death, for his will indicated that because of that settlement, Mary Greene should have no further claim on his estate. Anything which Mary did not want was to go to their daughter Katharine Festing, the wife of Michael Festing (the son of Michael Christian Festing the violinist).

Greene left £600 to a Mrs Dorothy Prince and his musical instruments, plate, and other goods to Thomas King of Waybridge, Surrey, Dr Benjamin Hoadly (who had written the libretti for Greene's dramatic pastorals), Peter Davall of the Middle Temple, and to John Jackson of Great Queen Street—those four to serve as executors and dispose of Greene's lands for the benefit of his daughter Katharine Festing. Greene left to Dr William Boyce his collection of manuscript and printed music and books on music. Boyce had previously agreed *not* to publish any of Greene's works, the will stated, though Grove has it that Greene requested in his will that Boyce carry on Greene's cathedral music project. *The Dictionary of National Biography* says Boyce agreed to take over Greene's project before Greene died. The codicil to the will provided for an additional £400 for Dorothy Prince.

In his will Greene described himself as late of Bois Hall in Havestock, Essex. He was buried as requested at St Olave, Jewry, on 10 December 1755, but on 18 May 1888 his remains were moved to St Paul's Cathedral and placed beside those of Boyce. Greene was described in Sainsbury's dictionary as "below the common size, and he had the misfortune to be very much deformed; yet his address and exterior manners were those of a man of the world, mild, attentive, and wellbred."

The Dictionary of National Biography says that a portrait by Hayman of Greene and his friend Dr Hoadly was in the possession of J. E. Street; it was purchased by the National Portrait Gallery in 1925. Henry Festing of Bois Hall, Addlestone, Surrey, had a portrait of Greene in May 1895; that was probably the portrait of Greene by an unknown artist which was given to the National Portrait Gallery by A. Garrett Anderson in 1925.

Greenleaf, Miss *[fl. 1785], actress.*
Miss Greenleaf played the Queen in *King Charles I* at the Haymarket Theatre on 31 January 1785.

Greenleaf, William *d. 1774, violinist.*
The parish registers of St Paul, Deptford, record the burial of William Greenleaf, "Fidler" of Church Street, on 27 September 1774. His wife Mary had been buried just four days before. Greenleaf's previous wife, Ann, had died in 1767.

Greenup, Mrs *[fl. 1769–1771], actress.*
Mrs Greenup (or Greenop) was a member of the cast of *The Harlot's Progress* at Sadler's Wells in September 1769 and appeared there in the summer of 1771 in *The Imprisonment of Harlequin.*

Greenwood, Mrs *[fl. 1749], actress.*
Mrs Greenwood played Mrs Constant in *The Fair Lunatick* at the Cross-Bridges booth at Bartholomew Fair on 23 August 1749.

Greenwood, Master *[fl. 1771], singer.*
A Master Greenwood sang at Sadler's Wells on 21 May 1771. Perhaps he was related to the scene painter, Thomas Greenwood (d. 1797), who was working at Drury Lane by 1771 and at Sadler's Wells by 1778.

Greenwood, Thomas *d. 1797, scene painter.*
Thomas Greenwood the elder was a scene painter at Drury Lane Theatre from 1771 and at Sadler's Wells from 1778 until his death in 1797. He was not, as has been reported, the son of the engraver and painter John Greenwood (1727–1792). Possibly he was the son of either Thomas Greenwood and Mrs Margaret Cheshire of St Martin-in-the-Fields, who were married at St George's Chapel, Hyde Park Corner, on 1 January 1747, or of Thomas Greenwood and Mrs Elizabeth Jolly, who were married at the same place on 3 February 1747. Greenwood was a common name in the eighteenth century.

The first payment to Greenwood at Drury Lane was £9 10s. on 26 November 1771, probably for work on *The Institution of the Garter*, a spectacular masque afterpiece which had opened on 28 October. He was paid eight guineas on 24 February 1772, and his name was not again entered in the account books until 5 October 1776, when he received £21, but he is known to have painted scenes designed by De Loutherbourg for *The Maid of the Oaks* on 5 November 1774 and *Queen Mab* on 11 November 1775. After 1776 he continued to receive numerous payments for salary and accounts rendered. On 9 January 1778 he was paid £22 10s.

Victoria and Albert Museum

Scene design by THOMAS GREENWOOD, the elder

for 21 days, and in 1778–79 he received £110 10s. during October and November for work done the previous season, and another £50 during November and December. He was paid £50 in 1779–80, £144 19s. 7d. in 1780–81, and £220 1s. in 1781–82; in 1782–83 he was paid £10 per week. In 1784–85 he earned £400, and in February 1792 his salary was raised to £20 per week, an increase which brought him a total of £550 16s. that season, during the rebuilding of Drury Lane Theatre, but his salary seems to have reverted to £10 per week after the new theatre opened.

During 1777–78 Greenwood also did some painting with Carver and Garvey for Covent Garden Theatre in connection with *The Norwood Gipsies*, which had its first performance on 25 November 1777, for which he was paid £60 on 10 February 1778. Perhaps he had also worked on a masque, similarly called *Norwood Gipsies* which was produced at Sadler's Wells on 31 March 1777, though it is not known if the two productions had anything in common. Greenwood's first known works for Sadler's Wells were for *Oriental Magic*, produced on 20 April 1778, and *Whim Wham* in the same season; he was the first scene painter whose name can be associated with that stage.

Before the 1782–83 season began, Greenwood and William Capon had redecorated Drury Lane: "the boxes neatly papered with a light pea green," reported Gilliland in *The Dramatic Mirror* (1808), "and ornamented with crimson curtains to all the doors; the seats were covered with baize of the same colour. His Majesty's box and the opposite one were rather more advanced than before, and the side scene lights were much increased." In April 1784 Greenwood received £43 16s. for gilding the theatre.

In 1778–79 he painted De Loutherbourg's scenes for *The Camp*, which was first performed on 15 October 1778. His scenery for *The Triumph of Mirth; or,*

Harlequin's Wedding on 26 December 1782 included a "Grand View of the Cumberland Fleet sailing for the Cup." For *Harlequin Junior* on 7 January 1784 he designed and executed new scenes, the last being "a Representation of the Repulse of the Spaniards before the Rock of Gibraltar" (an event which had occurred on 13 September 1782). His work in 1785–86 included scenes for *The Strangers at Home* on 8 December 1785, *Hurley-Burley* on 26 December, *Harlequin's Voyage, or, The Magic Mirror* ("a Splendid Representation of a Fairy's Palace") on 29 December, and *The Heiress* on 14 January 1786. In 1786–87 he painted for *Richard Coeur de Lion* on 24 October 1786, and in 1789–90 he did *The Island of St Marguerite* on 13 November 1789, *The Haunted Tower* on 24 November, and *Harlequin's Frolicks* on 26 December. The following season he designed and executed the scenery for *Don Juan* on 26 October 1790, *Better Late Than Never* on 17 November, *The Fairy Favour* on 27 December, and *The Siege of Belgrade* on 1 January 1791.

At the King's Theatre, where the Drury Lane company played in 1791–92 and 1792–93 while awaiting the completion of their new theatre, Greenwood designed the scenery for a revival of *Cymon* on 31 December 1791, a production which included a grand procession of over 100 people, a tournament on horse and foot, and Edmund Kean, at the age of four, making his first stage appearance as a Cupid lying in Cymon and Sylvia's chariot—all called by the *Morning Post* (3 January 1792) "by far the grandest spectacle ever seen upon the stage." On 23 May 1792 *Dido Queen of Carthage* was produced with scenes and machines designed by Greenwood and executed by himself and his pupils. He created the new scenes for *The Prisoner* on 18 October 1792 and for *The Pirates* on 21 November 1792, the latter showing views of the Bay of Naples and the eruption of Mount Vesuvius.

When *Macbeth* was produced as the first dramatic event at the new Drury Lane on 21 April 1794, Greenwood contributed scenes along with Malton, Edwards, Catton, and Capon. His work for that production included the blasted heath scene with a bridge; the inner apartment of Macbeth's castle; the outside view of the castle (with Catton); the cave, with moonlight and an eclipse, in which he used a transparency (he had used them as early as 1779 at Sadler's Wells); and a park and lawn and Birnam Wood (with Catton). Also during that first season in the new theatre he designed the scenes for Acts I and III of Kemble's *Lodoiska*, which was first presented on 9 June 1794.

During the remainder of the 1790s Greenwood was kept busy, along with Capon, Demaria, and Marinari, meeting the demands for spectacle created by the larger stage and house of the new theatre. In 1794–95 he worked on *Emilia Galotti* for 28 October 1794, *The Mountaineers* for 31 October, *The Cherokee* for 26 December (all the scenes designed and executed by him except for the view of the new settlement by Capon), and *Jack of Newbury* for 6 May 1795. That year he was paid £731 7s., perhaps including sums for materials. In 1795–96, when his salary was £10 10s. per week, his scenes for *Harlequin Captive* on 18 January 1796 were "remarkable for their brilliancy and effects" and consisted of:

A view of the interior part of Ormanthine's Castle; An Hermitage in the Enchanted Garden; Massy Rocks, which open and display a ship of great magnitude at sea, sailing from the audience, and diminishing according as it proceeds, and increasing in a like proportion when it tacks about; A seaport, with a view of Hurst Castle; The Waterfall of Lodore; A Park, with a large Oak Tree, which vegetates and withers on the Stage; An Enchanted Island; An Enchanted Castle and Garden, with a Magic Fountain; and The Palace of Minerva.

He and Capon were responsible for the scenes for *The Iron Chest* on 12 March 1796, and the two of them enjoyed the dubious distinction of providing the scenery for Kemble's production of Ireland's forgery of *Vortigern*, which was laid upon an indignant and unaccepting public on 2 April 1796 as a newly discovered play by Shakespeare.

The following season with Marinari he created the scenery for *Robinson Crusoe; or, Harlequin Friday*, which was first performed at Drury Lane on 26 December 1796. During that season Greenwood also designed scenery for the King's Theatre, where he provided new settings for the opera *Elvira* on 10 January 1797 and for several ballets. *L'Amour et Psiché* on 13 December 1796, *Pizarre* on 7 February 1797, and *Sapho et Phaon* on 6 April.

Certainly Greenwood was the busiest scene painter in London in the last quarter of the century. In addition to a heavy workload at Drury Lane and his occasional work at Covent Garden and the King's, from 1778 onwards he was a designer and scene painter at Sadler's Wells during the summer seasons. As mentioned above, his first known work for the Islington house was *Oriental Magic* in 1778, followed by *Whim Wham*. In 1779 he painted for *The Nymph of the Grotto* and *Harlequin's Trip*, as well as for *The Prophecy; or, Queen Elizabeth at Tilbury*, which was produced on 9 August 1779 with a variety of scenes by him including "an Emblematical Frontispiece, at the top of which, in a small Transparency," was presented the destruction of the Armada; the view through the frontispiece was closed "by a Moving Perspective representing the present Grand Fleet." That scene, described in detail by Sybil Rosenfeld in *Theatre Notebook* (XIX), is on an engraving, a copy of which is in the British Museum.

His creations for Sadler's Wells in the 1780s included a revival of *The Prophecy* in 1780; *Regions of Fancy* and *Huzza for*

Old England in 1782; *The Blazing Comet*
and *The Enchanted Wood* in 1783; *Mother
Redcap* in 1785; *The Restoration of Hymen* and *Combat* in 1786; *Victorious Rod-
ney, A Sketch of the Wells, The Follies of
a Night,* and *Shipwreck* in 1787; and
Quatre Fils Hemond (with a town and
drawbridge which came down to allow
troops to pass over it) and *The New
Scotch Reel* in 1788. Also in 1788 he designed what were described as magnificently
realistic scenes for the pantomime *The
Witch of the Lake,* which included Fingal's
Cave, the New Town of Edinburgh, a
moonlit glen, Cumberland lakes, a cataract
—"a chef-d'oeuvre of stage effect"—and
Newcastle Moors with coal pits. In 1789
he designed an illumination scene for *Mandarin; or, Harlequin Widower,* and "bril-
liantly painted" scenes for *Gallic Freedom,
or, Vive la Liberté,* especially a scene of
the subterranean dungeons. The settings
were advertised as drawn on the spot, and
by the testimony of the *Public Advertiser*
on 28 September 1789, "finer scenes of
greater effect have not been produced at
any theatre for many years."

At Sadler's Wells in 1790 he designed
for *Ceinture* (a "new species of Scenic
Picture Veluti in Speculum") and *Champ
de Mars* ("correctly drawn from the actual
observation of proper persons appointed to
attend at Paris for the purpose"); *The Son
of Neptune, Neptune's Levée,* and *Tippoo
Sahib* in 1791; *Medea's Kettle, The Fourth
of June, Mars's Holiday* (an encampment
"painted from correct Drawing purposely
taken on the Spot"), and *Savages* in 1792;
a revival of *Mandarin; or, Harlequin China*
with Andrews and *Penmaenmawr* (from
drawings by Andrews in Wales) in 1794;
Pandora's Box and *Baron Munchausen*
(with Andrews) in 1795; and *Fairy Favours* and *The Castle Spectre* in 1797.

Greenwood also painted with Dixon
three sets of wings and other scenes in
1794 for the new Theatre Royal, Birmingham, which opened in May 1795. Earlier,

Victoria and Albert Museum

Scene design by THOMAS GREENWOOD,
the elder

in 1788, he had decorated the Duke of
Richmond's private theatre at Privy Garden
and provided three scenes for *Theodosius*
and three for *The Way to Keep Him.* In
October of the same year he had been paid
for scenery he painted for theatricals at
Blenheim Palace: 5 guineas for a frontispiece with pilasters, curtains, and cornices;
2 guineas for two busts in circular frames;
and 10 guineas for an architectural scene-
drop with a view of a garden through the
arch.

The last scenes that Greenwood designed were for *The Castle Spectre,* which
had its premiere at Drury Lane on 14 December 1797. The designer had died, however, on 1 November 1797, and the execution of the work was carried out by his
son, the younger Thomas Greenwood (c.
1779–1832), and Charles Pugh.

In his will drawn on 8 April 1796,
Greenwood described himself as a gentleman of the parish of St James, Clerkenwell, but then residing in Charles Street,
Covent Garden. He left all his household
goods, furniture, other effects, clothes, pictures, and stocks and funds to his spinster
daughter Elizabeth Ann Greenwood, to
whom administration was granted as sole
executrix on 11 November 1797. Curiously, the younger Thomas Greenwood,

presumably then only about 18 years old, was not mentioned in the will.

At his death, Greenwood was owed a considerable amount of money by Richard Brinsley Sheridan, who was a notorious mismanager of Drury Lane's finances. Several sums were paid to Greenwood's daughter (£5 5s. on 11 June 1798, £30 on 12 March 1799, £20 on 13 October 1800), but the executrix's attorneys finally had to secure a judgment against the theatre. On 9 March 1805 the estate was paid £256, "By a judgment," and five installments of £36 each were paid before the end of June 1805, making a total of £400. From October 1806 through January 1807 a total of another £204 in smaller payments was made because of "Greenwood's Judgment" and on 14 October 1807 yet another £18 (the last noted). During this entire period the younger Thomas Greenwood remained on the payroll.

A picture, now lost, of the Sadler's Wells Club, painted by Hayman in 1754 for Rosomon, is said to have included Greenwood. But Greenwood's age in 1754 makes his presence in the group doubtful. While he may have been working for some years before we first notice him at Drury Lane in 1771 (some 17 years after Hayman's painting), his son was not born until about 1779. If the elder Greenwood was actually old enough to have been included in the Sadler's Wells group in 1754, then his son was sired during his maturer years. In *The Story of Sadler's Wells*, Denis Arundell suggests the possibility that the Greenwood in the Hayman painting was the elder Thomas's father.

Two watercolor sketches of Gothic exteriors by Greenwood at the Victoria and Albert Museum are called designs for scenes at "Covent Garden 1777" on the information of their one-time owner, Samuel Phelps, the actor-manager of Sadler's Wells in the middle of the nineteenth century. In addition to the engraving of his scene for *The Prophecy* (mentioned above), other engravings of Greenwood's scenes appear on the printed scores of *Lodoiska*, *The Pirates*, *The Haunted Tower*, and *The Siege of Belgrade*.

Greenwood, Thomas c. 1779–1832, scene painter.

Thomas Greenwood, sometimes called the "younger" or "junior," was born about 1779 if he was 19 years old (as T. J. Dibdin said he was) when he began to work at the Royal Circus in 1797–98. He was the son of Thomas Greenwood (d. 1797), the busy scene painter at Drury Lane and Sadler's Wells in the last quarter of the eighteenth century. The younger Greenwood's first notice as a theatrical professional was the appearance of his name in the bills—as "Greenwood, Jun"—for scenery at the Royal Circus for *Julia of Louvain* on 15 May 1797. The following autumn he was put on the paylist of Drury Lane Theatre beginning 23 September 1797 at £3 3s. per week. After the elder Greenwood died on 1 November 1797, young Thomas (with Pugh) completed execution of his father's designs for *The Castle Spectre*, which had its first performance at Drury Lane Theatre on 14 December 1797. Curiously, he was not mentioned in his father's will, proved on 11 November 1797, by which the deceased left his estate to his daughter Elizabeth Ann Greenwood.

Greenwood was regularly employed in the Drury Lane scene shop, seemingly without interruption, through 1818–19. In 1798–99 his salary was raised to £3 13s. 6d. per week; by 1800–1801 it was £4 14s. 6d.; by 1802–3, £5 15s. 6d., at which level it remained through 1804–5; then £6 6s. in 1805–6; £7 in 1806–7 £8 8s. from 1807–8 through 1815–16 (during which period he was entered as "Master Painter, superintd. of dept."); and £10 per week from 1816–17. He also received sums of £81 18s. and £95 11s. for work done at Drury Lane in the summers of 1806 and 1807, respectively.

Folger Shakespeare Library

Scene design by THOMAS GREENWOOD, the younger?

His eighteenth-century work at Drury Lane included design and execution (with Chalmers and others) of the new scenes for *Blue-Beard* on 16 January 1798; for *Feudal Times* on 19 January 1799 (including boats, a castle, a gallery, and a drawbridge blown up by a mine); for *Pizarro* on 24 May 1799 (with Marinari, Demaria, Banks, and Blackmore); for *The Egyptian Festival* on 11 March 1800 (his designs, assisted in execution by Banks); and *De Montfort* on 29 April 1800 (designed with Capon and executed by them with Banks).

During the summers Greenwood designed scenery at the Royal Circus from 1797 to 1803. Productions for which he is known to have painted include the above-cited *Julia of Louvain* on 15 May 1797; *Blackbeard; or, The Captive Princess* in 1798; *Cora; or, The Virgin of the Sun* and *Almoran and Hamet* in 1799; *The Mine or Black Forest of Istria* (according to the *Monthly Mirror* of May 1800, "the inventive powers of Mr. Greenwood were never more happily displayed than in the internal view of the robbers cavern; the transparent lake and temple of Charity; the quick-silver mine at Istria; and the chrystalling palace of the Queen of the Gnomes") and *Sir Francis Drake and Iron Arm* (a naval spectacle) in 1800; *Rinaldo Rinaldini, The Fire King*, and *Halloween* in 1801; *The Golden Farmer, The Conquest of Granada, Zamor and Zamora*, and *The Enchanted Harp* in 1802; and *Louisa of Lombardy, The Rival Statues*, and *Number Nip* in 1803. He was at the Royal Circus again in 1809, when he and Marchbanks provided scenery for Elliston's burletta production of *Macbeth*.

At the end of the eighteenth century,

with Banks, he painted the scenery for Richardson's traveling theatre. At Drury Lane he designed the settings for *Actaeon and Diana* in 1800–1801, *Artaxerxes* in 1801–2, and *Furiband; or, Harlequin Negro* in 1807–8. In 1807 he painted the scenery for *Peep Into the Past* for the New Road Theatre in Brighton, and in 1814 he and Latilla were in charge of the decorations of the Temple of Concord fireworks machine which was built in Green Park for the peace celebration. Greenwood was also the designer of much of the scenery for Edmund Kean's first performances at Drury Lane in 1814–15, including *Macbeth* on 5 November 1814.

At the end of 1818–19 Greenwood's connections with Drury Lane terminated over a disagreement he had with Elliston, who was to become the new proprietor in 1819–20. He left London to engage as designer at the Theatre Royal, Birmingham. On 24 September 1820 he wrote from Birmingham a long letter to Glossop of the Royal Coburg Theatre in London asking for the position in the painting room left vacant by the retirement of Serrez—"With respect to my qualifications for such a task *I beg to* remind you that I had the honor to conduct the Painting-Department at DL Theatre for upwards of Twenty Years! and where I shou'd have been at this period but for an unfortunate disagreement with Mr. Elliston *previous* to his becoming the Proprietor of that Concern." The letter is worth quoting at length, for it confirms some of Greenwood's professional experience and attitudes:

The great and continued demand for novelty renders it necessary at this period that every department of the Theatre should be govern'd and expedited with the greatest facility and I believe it will be found on enquiry that I am quite as rapid probably more so as any other artist in the profession.

With respect to terms I am aware that Œconomy is the order of the day, and I am sure if you think it proper to make me an offer it will be such as I ought to acceed to. It may be necessary to state . . . [that] for many years at DL Theatre I never had less than Eight Guineas latterly I had Ten Pounds Ten Years ago at the Surry Theatre Mr Elliston paid me Six Guineas, as did Mr Arnold for two seasons at the Lyceum, and here [at Birmingham] I have *Six Pounds* and am paid for my Sundays and other extra hours. I think my name and long experience *and* rapidity would be valuable to you. And if we can come to terms I not only pledge myself for a continuance of that zeal and assiduity which has so many years afforded me the applause of the public & the approbation of my employers, but also to produce *with reasonable time* proper material and assistants scenery which shall be quite as effective as at any other Theatre in the Kingdom for my fund of material for Scenic Design is *almost* inexhaustible. . . .

In 1821–22 Greenwood was employed not by the Royal Coburg but by Sadler's Wells, where his efforts included scenery for Jerrold's *The Chieftain's Oath* in August 1821. At the time of his death on 22 March 1832 he was a claimant on the Drury Lane Fund.

Greenwood's son, Thomas Longden Greenwood, became a playwright and served as Phelps's co-lessee and acting manager for 16 years at Sadler's Wells in the middle of the nineteenth century.

Greeting, Edward [*fl.* 1685–1689], *singer.*

Edward Greeting may have been the son of the Restoration violinist Thomas Greeting. Edward was appointed a countertenor in the private music of James II on 31 August 1685, the entry in the Lord Chamberlain's accounts noting that his father had drowned at sea. From 19 May to 16 August and 13 September to 11 October 1687 Edward Greeting attended the King at Windsor for 3*s*. daily in addition to his regular annual salary of £30. Greeting was still in the King's Musick on 25 March 1689 under William III.

Greeting, Thomas *d. 1682, violinist, flutist, sackbut player.*

Thomas Greeting was appointed a musician in ordinary (but without fee) in the King's private music on 15 December 1662. The Lord Chamberlain's accounts made no further mention of Greeting until 1668, and it is likely that he gave up his unsalaried post and earned a living outside the court. Indeed, we know he was a teacher in 1667 and later.

Samuel Pepys hired Greeting on 28 February 1667 for £4 to teach Mrs Pepys to play the flageolet. After she had had several lessons, Pepys also became Greeting's pupil; by 27 May Pepys was referring to Thomas as his "flagelette master." But by 12 July Pepys was getting exasperated: "how like a fool he goes about to give me direction would make a man mad." On 26 August the diarist paid the musician off, for he felt Greeting had taught "as much as he can teach us." Shortly before Greeting left Pepys, on 23 August, he brought Pepys "a tune for two flageolets, which we played, and is a tune played at the King's playhouse, which goes so well that I will have more of them. . . ." Greeting, then, may have been associated with the Bridges Street Theatre. Pepys had hired him back by 13 August 1668 to give Mrs Pepys further instruction, and on 2 March 1669 Pepys held a party at his office at which Greeting and another musician performed.

As early as 29 April 1668, when he was still busy teaching, Greeting became one of the 24 violinists in the King's Musick. During the 1670s the Lord Chamberlain's accounts made occasional references to him: on 7 October 1673 he was paid £12 for a violin; on 7 February 1674 he replaced William Saunders as a violinist in the King's Musick (a second position, apparently) and began receiving Saunders's fees; he attended the King at Windsor

THOMAS GREETING

artist unknown

in the summer of 1674; on 15 February 1675 he played violin in the court masque *Calisto*; he was at Windsor again in the summer of 1675; in 1677 he was a musician to Lady Anne in the Duke of York's household; and for 10s. daily he served at Windsor in the summer of 1679. In the Chapel Royal Greeting played both violin and sackbut. In 1673 Greeting published *The Pleasant Companion*, a collection of works by various composers, intended as lessons for the flageolet.

Details of Greeting's family are revealed in London parish registers. Joyce Greeting, the daughter of Thomas and his wife Joyce, was christened at St Clement Danes on 13 August 1661, a year before Thomas joined the King's Musick. The Greetings changed their residence, for references to them in the 1670s are in the registers of St Martin-in-the-Fields. A second daughter named Joyce (the first having died) was born on 7 October 1671 and christened at St Martin's on the sixteenth. A daughter Elizabeth was born on 24 September 1673, christened on 5 October, and buried on 6 September 1674. A daughter Catherine was christened on 12 May 1676.

Thomas Greeting died in the summer of 1682. On 5 July John Crouch replaced him in the King's Musick. On 3 April 1688

"Joyce, Widdo. of Thomas Greeting, dec'ed, one of the musitians to K. Charles the Second" was granted a bounty by King James of £10, a portion of an annual bounty of £40.

Perhaps the countertenor Edward Greeting was Thomas's son; when Edward was sworn a musician to the King in 1685 he stated that "his father drowned at sea." That fact would probably not have been recorded in the Lord Chamberlain's accounts unless Edward's father had been in the royal service.

In an extra-illustrated volume of Granger's *Biographical History of England* at the Huntington Library is an anonymously engraved portrait of Thomas Greeting. He is shown playing the flageolet, and in an eighteenth-century hand is the inscription, "Thomas Greeting, from his lessons for the Flagellet. 1678."

Gregory, Henry [*fl.* 1662–1694?], violinist, wind instrumentalist.

On one document in the Lord Chamberlain's accounts, dating from the early 1660s, Henry Gregory was listed among the violinists in the King's Musick, but his official admission on 13 March 1662 cited him as a wind instrumentalist; he was doubtless proficient on several instruments. Henry was appointed without fee as an assistant to his father, William Gregory; upon William's death Henry was to be given a regular position with a salary. During his waiting period he was granted £60 annually for life for teaching two boys music, especially flute and cornet. Though Henry still did not have a salaried post in 1662 he was granted a livery allowance of £16 2s. 6d.

William Gregory died on 20 August 1663, making Henry his residuary legatee and executor. Henry proved his father's will on 15 September and the following day was appointed to his father's place at court at a daily wage of 1s. 8d. plus livery. The appointment was in the wind instru-

ments, though a warrant dated 12 November 1663 listed Henry as a violinist, so he was serving in both musical units.

Over the years the accounts cited Henry Gregory regularly, often in connection with pension and livery payments, which he rarely received on time. In 1667, for instance, he was still owed money from as early as 1664, and in 1674 he still had money due him from 1671. His fee for teaching his boys was sometimes as much as seven years in arrears. But on 21 September 1686 King James ordered £139 4s. 5d. paid to Gregory for his teaching, and apparently the money was actually given him. The accounts also tell us that as a wind player Gregory earned a salary of £46 10s. 10d. annually (which was apparently paid on schedule; the arrears concerned his livery and teaching fees). Once, in 1682, Gregory is reported to have attended the royal family at Windsor, for which he was paid an extra £11 12s. 8½d.

The last mention of Henry Gregory in the accounts was at Michaelmas 1692, and he may have left the royal service after that. The will of Catherine, Lady Heath, which was written on 9 March 1694 and proved the following 20 June, left bequests to a niece Anne, wife of a Henry Gregory, and their son Richard. Perhaps that Henry Gregory was the musician, but we have no way of knowing.

From the will of William Gregory in 1663 we learn that Henry's mother was named Mary, that he had sisters named Elizabeth Starke and Mary Gregory, and that he was married (but his wife's name is not known).

Gregory, John [*fl.* 1738–1759?], musician.

John Gregory was listed in the Lord Chamberlain's accounts as a member of the royal musical establishment as early as 1738, when he was cited as a replacement for Jonathan Ayleworth. The establishment list for 1759 noted that Peter Benell had replaced Gregory, but no specific date for the replacement was given.

Gregory, Mrs John. *See* FITZHENRY, MRS EDWARD.

Gregory, Prince   *d. 1755?, musician.*

Prince Gregory was sworn a Gentleman of the Chapel Royal on 4 April 1740, replacing Dr William Turner. Rimbault, in *The Old Cheque Book of the Chapel Royal*, guessed that Prince was probably a descendant of the Restoration court musician William Gregory the elder and that Prince probably died late in 1755, since on 24 December of that year William Coster succeeded to his place.

Gregory, William   *d. 1663, instrumentalist, singer, composer.*

The elder William Gregory was in the King's Musick as early as 1625, when he was listed as a member of the "windy instruments" at the funeral of James I. A warrant in the Lord Chamberlain's accounts dated 15 July 1628 listed him as a flutist, and he was cited periodically through 1641 as a wind instrumentalist. His salary, in 1626, was 1s. 8d. daily, plus an annual livery allowance of £16 2s. 6d. Playford's *Musicall Banquet* in 1651 listed Gregory as a teacher of voice or viola in London. One of his pupils was the musical prodigy Susannah Perwich. Batchiler's *The Virgin's Pattern*, a biography of Susannah, called Gregory "eminently skilful at the Lyra Viol" and said that he taught Miss Perwich "all varieties of rare tunings." On 19 February 1657 Gregory and four other musicians petitioned the Committee for Advancement of Musicke to establish a "Corporacion or Colledge of Musitians" in London, but their proposal was not accepted. Gregory also busied himself during the Commonwealth period by serving in Cromwell's small group of court musicians.

At the Restoration in 1660 Gregory was appointed a violist in the King's private

Courtesy of the Faculty of Music, Oxford

WILLIAM GREGORY

artist unknown

music, and the Lord Chamberlain's accounts once again made frequent mention of him. But they also made frequent mention of a second, younger William Gregory, a relative but apparently not a son of our subject, who likewise was a wind instrumentalist. One document dating about 1660 listed "Wm. Gregory" under the lutes, voices, theorboes, and virginals and "William Gregory" under the wind instruments; one is tempted to take the first citation to concern the elder Gregory and the second the younger, but one cannot be certain. To confuse matters further, both references may have been to the same person, for many court musicians of the time held double posts.

Another warrant dating about 1660 listed William Gregory as a replacement for Daniel Ferrand in the lutes, viols, and voices. The elder Gregory would seem to be referred to here, for Ferrand (or Farrant) was a violist and a member of the King's Musick as early as 1625, and court musicians often arranged for their positions to go to friends when they retired or died. A warrant dated 12 April 1661 listed one William Gregory as a violinist and the other as a wind instrumentalist at the coronation of Charles II; either reference could have been to either man. Once the records distinguished between the two musicians: a warrant dated Lady Day 1662 (25 March 1662–63 presumably) calls William "sen'" a wind instrumentalist; the junior Gregory was on that warrant simply called one of the "Musicions."

In 1662 the elder Gregory's *Courtly Masquing Ayres* was published. Most of his compositions were glees, songs, short airs, or dances, some of which have survived in manuscript and are in the British Museum. On 13 March 1662 William's son Henry was admitted to the King's Musick as an unpaid instrumentalist; he was made an assistant to his father and assured of a salaried post when his father died. Such statements in the records almost invariably indicate advanced age and physical decline in the musician in question, and by 1662 the elder William Gregory must have been well along in years. Yet on 13 September 1662 Gregory was granted £60 annually for life to teach two boys music (Henry also received such a fee). Gregory was also paid £29 16s. 8d. every six months for the boys' maintenance and educational expenses.

On 31 January 1663 the Corporation of Music required Gregory, Locke, and Gibbons – three of the most eminent of the older musicians – to pay £10, probably for licenses to practice music as a profession, or show cause to the contrary. One might guess that the older men may have been reluctant to lay out money if their working days were numbered, as Gregory's surely were.

On 20 August 1663 William Gregory died. He had drawn up his will on the day of his death, describing himself as "sicke in body." He asked to be buried in the churchyard of St Martin-in-the-Fields. His "onely [estate] consists," he said, "of wages due me out of the Treasury chamber at Whitehall as servant to the Kings Ma:^tie in the consort of Wind-Musick." To his wife Mary he left 10s. for a mourning ring; to his daughter-in-law (unnamed; she was Henry Gregory's wife) he left 5s.; to his daughter Elizabeth Starke, 5s.; to his daughter Mary Gregory, 5s.; and to his grandchild Anne Smith, 10s. for a ring. Everything else, including any wages due him, he left to his son Henry toward payment of a bond or obligation dated 20 February 1662 for £54. The poor man was even in debt to his son. Henry Gregory, as executor, proved the will on 15 September 1663. The following day Henry was appointed to his father's place in the wind instruments and was granted his father's salary: 1s. 8d. daily plus livery – exactly what his father had been earning as far back as 1626.

Grove speaks of the elder William Gregory as a singer and composer. A portrait of Gregory by an unknown artist is at the Faculty of Music, Oxford.

Gregory, William [fl. c. 1660?–1687], *instrumentalist.*

The younger William Gregory – not a son but probably a relative of the elder man of that name – seems to have been a member of the King's Musick from about 1660. Between 1660 and the elder Gregory's death in August 1663 references to the two men in the Lord Chamberlain's accounts are often confusing; a group of such references is discussed in the elder Gregory's entry and need not be repeated here. It is clear, though, that both men played wind instruments, that both were proficient on the viola, but that only the younger Gregory was a bass viol player. Once during the early 1660s the accounts clarified matters by calling our subject "Wm Gregory, iun."

We may be fairly certain that it was the younger Gregory who was cited in a warrant dated 30 April 1663 concerning attendance at St George's Feast in Windsor. Gregory and Thomas Bates were to be paid £3 for their service, £2 for lodgings, and an extra £1 10s. for "carrying the Instruments that were for performance of the Musicke there." The elder Gregory was too old by 1663 to have performed such services. References to a William Gregory in later years, except for a very few instances, concern the younger man; by 1665 all references to the elder Gregory ceased.

On 7 February 1665 our William Gregory was to be paid £12 for a "base viol." For many years after that date there are entries in the accounts concerning arrears in livery payments. In 1666, for example, Gregory was still owed livery fees of £16 2s. 6d. annually for 1663 and 1664; on 28 August 1673 he was to be paid £80 12s. 6d. for liveries due as far back as 1666; on 13 February 1675 he assigned livery arrears from 1665–1667 and 1670 to William Parkes, and he appointed Parkes his lawful attorney; on 15 September 1679 Dr William Child, another court musician, assigned *his* livery arrears to Gregory; and finally on 21 September 1686 King James tried to clear up some of his late brother's debts by paying Gregory £96 15s. The accounts also tell us that Gregory's annual salary (usually paid on time) was £46, that in 1669 he and some of his colleagues came to the financial aid of the musician John Hingeston, and that Gregory served the King at Windsor in the summers of 1671, 1674, and 1675.

A warrant dated 17 May 1678 directed that Gregory should be made a musician in ordinary on the viola in the King's private music (a second post for him, apparently) after the death of his fellow musician Thomas Bates. When Bates died Gregory was to receive £50 annually in regular wages plus an additional £40 annually which Bates had received over the years for a second post he held. That rather ghoulish arrangement was quite common at the time. Bates was doubtless in ill health, and an amicable arrangement was worked out to dispose of his positions after his death.

When John Hingeston died in 1684 he left Gregory his "great double Basse," in remembrance, perhaps of Gregory's help in 1669. The last mention of Gregory in the Lord Chamberlain's accounts was dated 24 January 1687; he appointed Thomas Whitefield of St Martin-in-the-Fields his lawful attorney.

The name William Gregory was too common in the late seventeenth century for us to be able to identify the musician in parish registers with any certainty. One reference, however, may have concerned our man: Katherine Gregory, spinster, about 23 years old, daughter of William Gregory of St Giles in the Fields, Gentleman (which our subject would have been styled), married Henry Rogers (there was a musician of that name) of St Margaret, Westminster, bachelor, 23 years old, on 20 December 1672.

Gregson, Mr *d. 1798, house servant.*

A Mr Gregson was employed as a house servant, perhaps as a ticket taker, at Drury Lane Theatre from as early as 1790–91, for on 31 May 1791 he shared in benefit tickets with a large group of house personnel. He shared in similar benefits on 31 May 1793, 11 June 1796, and 10 June 1797. An entry in the Drury Lane account books for 3 May 1798 informs us that Gregson had died, and the list was reduced by 3s. 4d.; presumably his widow shared in the benefit tickets for which his name was included in the bills of 2 June 1798.

Gregson's wife was also a house servant at the same theatre from as early as 1790–91. She was listed among the house personnel in 1797–98, and in June 1801 she shared in benefit tickets. Presumably she was the Gregson who was listed as a ticket taker at Drury Lane in 1805–6. Gregson's son performed at that theatre between 1788 and 1803.

Gregson, Mrs [*fl.* *1790–1806*], *ticket taker? See* **GREGSON, MR** *d. 1798.*

Gregson, Mr [*fl. 1788–1803*], *actor, dancer, singer?*

Advertised as Master Gregson, the son of the Drury Lane Theatre house servants Mr and Mrs Gregson made his first stage appearance at that theatre on 29 March 1788 as Carlos in the first performance of Bertie Greatheed's new tragedy *The Regent*, which was played a total of nine times by the end of the season. The following season the lad played the same role once, on 17 March 1789. But the next season, 1789–90, his theatrical assignments increased considerably. On 1 October 1789 he played a Boy in *Henry V*, a play which had not been acted at Drury Lane for 41 years. According to a notation on a copy of the bill now in the Enthoven Collection, Master Gregson "went through the Boy with great spirit and acuteness." During the season he played the role some nine times and also performed a chorus role in *Harlequin's Frolicks* 22 times and Antonio's Page in *Love in Many Masks* eight times. On 29 May 1790 he shared benefit tickets with a group of minor performers and house personnel.

Still called Master Gregson, in 1790–91 he appeared a few times in the above-mentioned roles; in 1791–92 he played Cupid in numerous performances of *Cymon* at the King's Theatre, where the Drury Lane company was temporarily housed. In the latter season he also acted Fleance in *Macbeth*, the Black Boy in *The Irish Widow*, Carlos in *The Regent*, and a principal role in *The Village Coquette*, and he shared in benefit tickets on 13 June 1792. At the Haymarket Theatre on 25 July

1792 he played Cymbriel in *The Enchanted Wood*.

Over the next five seasons Master Gregson continued to fill similar parts in a series of musical pieces in which he also probably was called upon to sing and dance in choruses. His salary in 1793–94 was £1 per week, at which figure it remained as late as 1797–98. During the fall of the latter season, his name began to appear as Mr Gregson, but despite his new status the insignificance of his chorus roles did not alter, for he served regularly as a Sailor in *Robinson Crusoe* and a Peasant in *Blue-Beard*. Again he shared in benefit tickets on 2 July 1799 and 13 June 1800. In 1802–3 Gregson was still a minor member of the Drury Lane company.

Gremont. *See* **DE GREMONT.**

Grenier. *See also* **GRANIER** and **PARKER, MRS WILLIAM, SOPHIA, NÉE GRANIER.**

Grenier, Mlle [*fl. 1772–1773*], *dancer.*

A Mlle Grenier (sometimes Granier) was a featured dancer at the King's Theatre in 1772–73, making her first known appearance dancing with Slingsby on 14 November 1772. On 21 November she performed a new grand dance with Slingsby, Leppie, and Sga Crespi. Throughout the season she appeared in a variety of serious and pastoral ballet numbers. Perhaps she was related to the Graniers, a family of dancers which flourished in London from 1734 into the 1770s.

Grenier, Mlle [*fl. 1787–1788*], *dancer.*

A Mlle Grenier danced with Didelot, Vestris, Coulon, and the Simonet sisters in the ballet *Les Offrandes à l'amour* on 8 December 1787 and 21 additional times at the King's Theatre during 1787–88. Perhaps she was related to the Graniers, a family of dancers which flourished in London from 1734 into the 1770s.

Greniere. *See* GRANIER.

Grenoust, Mr *(fl. 1715)*, *trumpeter.*
On 13 May 1715 at the Lincoln's Inn Fields Theatre, Mr Grenoust accompanied the singer Mr Rawlins in a "Trumpet Song."

Grenville. *See also* GREVILLE.

Grenville, Thomas *(fl. c. 1787–1794)*, *organist.*
Thomas Grenville (or Greville, Granville) was the blind organist at the Foundling Hospital where the Royal Society of Musicians regularly performed the *Messiah.* He was a teacher, one of his students being John Purkis, another blind organist, who began lessons with Grenville about 1787. Doane's *Musical Directory* of 1794 listed Grenville as a resident at No 40, Devonshire Street, Queen Square.

Gresbach. *See* GRIESBACH.

Gresham, John *(fl. 1794)*, *violinist, bass player.*
Doane's *Musical Directory* of 1794 listed John Gresham, of No 4, Duke Street, Bloomsbury, as a violinist and bass player who performed at Choral Fund concerts. Possibly he was John Fanner Gresham of Tottenham who was buried at the age of 69 at St Paul, Covent Garden, on 9 January 1839, but there is not sufficient evidence to make a certain identification.

Greve, James *(fl. 1794)*, *instrumentalist.*
Doane's *Musical Directory* of 1794 listed James Greve (or Grieve), from the Guards Third Regiment, Strutton Ground, Westminster, as a performer at concerts sponsored by the New Musical Fund. Greve was

accomplished on the bassoon, clarinet, flute, and drums.

Grevelle, William *(fl. 1761)*, *drummer.*
The Drury Lane manuscript accounts in the Folger Library list a William Grevelle on 20 October 1761 as receiving 2s. for playing the "side drum in *Oroonoko.*" On 17 November he received the same amount for "side drum used in the play." There are similar notations on 18, 19, 20, 21, 23, 24, 25, and 26 November.

Greville. *See also* GRENVILLE.

Greville, [H. F.?] *(fl. 1771–1811?)*, *actor, impresario.*
Mr and Mrs Greville were acting in the Edinburgh company in 1771–72, according to James Dibdin in his *Annals.* Mrs Greville went on to achieve some reputation as comedienne and singer in London, but her husband's name can be found in only one London bill before 1800, that of a specially licensed benefit performance put on by a pickup company at the Haymarket on 31 January 1785. On that night he joined Ryder and Mrs Hudson "After the Imitations" in *A Comic Sketch of the Times.*

Greville and his wife may have separated early in their marriage, for George Anne Bellamy, Mrs Greville's friend, in her *Apology* charges him with cruel treatment, and man and wife do not seem to have acted in the same companies at the same time after the season in Edinburgh. Mrs Greville died in 1802.

In May 1792 the *Thespian Magazine* reported a Mr Greville, perhaps our man, under the management of Johnson in a company acting at the Town Hall, "which has been converted into a Theatre" at Barking, Essex.

In 1806 the Lord Chamberlain granted to a Mr Greville a "licence for Plays & Entertainments Performed by Children under 17 yrs. of Age & for Music & Dancing at

[the] Theatre in Leicester Place, Leicester Sq. (late Dibdin's) for One Year from 1[st] March." In 1807, now identified as "H. F. Greville, Esq.," he was granted a similar license for juvenile performances of "Burlettas, music & dancing also Dr[amatic] Ent[ertainment]s" at "Argyll Rooms for One Year from 30 July." He was granted licenses for subscription masquerades at Argyll Rooms on 23 May and 28 June 1808, 14 June 1809, and 4 May 1810, in addition to his annual licenses for burlettas, music, and dancing in those years and in 1811. A pencilled notation opposite the Lord Chamberlain's Licenser's memorandum granting H. F. Greville his license in 1810 reads: "In consequence of his Dramatic Licenses being used at the Lyceum."

Greville, Mrs [H. F.?], Susan   d. 1802, actress, singer.

It is likely that James Winston was correct in conjecturing that the "young gentlewoman" who sang Rosetta in *Love in a Village* ("her first appearance") at Covent Garden Theatre on 17 January 1770 and who was identified as "Mrs Gladeau" ("who performed some time since in Dublin") in the *Town and Country Magazine* was really Mrs Susan Greville. (In reviewing Mrs Greville's Drury Lane debut— again anonymous—in 1773, the *Covent Garden Magazine's* correspondent remarked that she had "previously" appeared in *Love in a Village* at Covent Garden.) The *Town and Country Magazine* thought, at any rate, that the young debutante of 1770 had "a pleasing voice and an agreeable figure and will probably be a valuable acquisition to the stage."

On 9 June 1770 Mrs Greville appeared on the Richmond stage for the first time, advertised only as "A Lady." She made her second bow there as Mrs "Grenville" on 11 June, but the rest of the season she appeared under her name properly spelled: Greville. Her husband does not seem to have been of the Richmond company that

Harvard Theatre Collection

SUSAN GREVILLE, as Sir Harry Wildair

engraving by Thornthwaite, after De Wilde

summer; and neither he nor she left any record in 1770–71. But both were in the Edinburgh company during at least part of the 1771–72 season. There in March and April Mrs Greville acted Miss Rusport in *The West Indian*, Mrs Strickland in *The Suspicious Husband*, and Queen Elizabeth in *The Albion Queens*. On the last night of the Haymarket summer season in London, 18 September 1772, she again sang Rosetta in *Love in a Village*.

Mrs Greville acted again at Richmond during the early summer of 1773, and she was said to be "from the Theatre Royal in Richmond" when she returned to the Haymarket on 18 September to take a part unspecified in *The Modish Wife* and play "(with *Epilogue* song in character") the Widow Brady in *The Irish Widow*. The Widow was the part chosen for her when she stepped upon the stage at Drury Lane for the first time on 1 November 1773. She was then again veiled under the designation "A Gentlewoman" in the playbill, but the prompter Hopkins identified her as Mrs Greville in his diary and judged her presentation of the Widow only "So, So." It was a part, nevertheless, which she repeated in several successive seasons, and on the basis of her first patent-house performance of it the *Covent Garden Magazine* decided that she had many requisites for the stage:

a smart figure, a lively countenance, a very pleasing voice, and an easy manner. These qualifications have been hitherto somewhat eclipsed by a carelessness in her action, and too great a rapidity in her delivery. . . . She is an excellent breeches figure and played with uncommon life and spirit throughout the character.

P. Lewis in *Miscellaneous Pieces in Verse* in 1774 wrote "An Extempore to Mrs. GREVILLE:"

> Tho' much provok'd, unbend that brow,
>   And bid resentment die;
> The graces mildly tell you how,
>   And reason tells you why.

Mrs Greville's grimness may have stemmed from her unfortunate marriage, as will be seen.

In the seasons from 1773–74 through 1776–77 at Drury Lane she played the following parts: Mrs Tempest in Kelly's new comedy *The School for Wives*, Arabella Zeal in *The Fair Quaker*, Sophia in *The Male Coquette*, Mrs Cheverley in Cumberland's new farce *The Note of Hand*, Emmeline in *Edgar and Emmeline*, Statira in *Alexander the Great*, Lady Lambert in *The Hypocrite*, Lady Anne in *Richard III*, Belinda in *The Provok'd Wife*, Alithea in *The*

Country Girl, Violetta in *The Brothers*, Octavia in *All for Love*, Melinda in *The Recruiting Officer*, Mrs Kitely in *Every Man in His Humour*, Mrs Fainall in *The Way of the World*, Miss Sterling in *The Clandestine Marriage*, Flora in *She Wou'd and She Wou'd Not*, Olivia in *The Plain Dealer*, Lady Constant in *The Way to Keep Him*, Sir Harry Wildair in *The Constant Couple* (but "very bad" wrote the prompter Hopkins), Indiana in *The Conscious Lovers*, Ann Lovely in *A Bold Stroke for a Wife*, and Millwood in *George Barnwell*. At the Haymarket in the summer of 1776 she sang in *The Beggar's Opera*, and there in the summer of 1778, she played one of the two Daughters in the first London revival since 1723 of Beaumont and Fletcher's *Bonduca* (with certain alterations by Colman). She also added Lady Brute in *The Provok'd Wife*. The Folger Drury Lane account books show her making £2 10s. per week during all that period. She was paid £5 9s. "for cloaths in *Irish Widow*" on 20 January 1776.

With this much variety—comedy, farce, tragedy, singing, breeches parts, prologue speaking—and so many excellent leads and supporting parts, why did Mrs Greville disappear from the London bills after the summer of 1778? At least one of her friends wondered about that. George Anne Bellamy, with her usual vagueness in chronology, said in her *Apology* that "About this time" (evidently soon after George Anne's Covent Garden benefit of 1 June 1780),

I renewed an intimacy which had formerly subsisted between Mrs. Greville and myself; a lady whom my mother had known, and been partial to from a child. This lady had been rendered unfortunate by her union with a man that treated her with the greatest barbarity: she had endeavored, by the most unremitted industry, to manage a trifling income left by her sister Lady Diemar. For, notwithstanding her theatrical talents are universally allowed, from some strange circumstances, she has been unemployed for several seasons. It is a mystery I could never unravel, why this lady should be thrown by, while others, with not half her merit, have engagements. The goodness of her heart prevailed over her scanty circumstances, and she chearfully offered me the little assistance she could spare.

Perhaps Mrs Greville grew careless professionally. The *Middlesex Journal* of 7–9 October 1775, reviewing her performance of Mrs Fainall in *The Way of the World*, said: "Mrs. Greville, to convince the town that she could keep a secret, whispered it to only a few friends in the Pit. . . . [H]er indifference is intolerable, and should be noticed by her employer." Whether or not Garrick took the cue, it is hard to imagine Frances Abington, the Millamant of that performance, tolerating such behavior for very long. Mrs Greville was evidently no respecter of persons. Dr Thomas Augustine Arne wrote Garrick on 21 August 1775 complaining that, though Garrick had extended permission to members of the Drury Lane company "to perform in the intended new Comedy at the Opera-House" for Arne's "advantage," he, Arne, was "unluckily and indeed ungenteely cut out of, at least, a clear 100 *l.* by Mrs. Greville's accepting and promising to perform the principal comic character, and (after keeping it near three weeks when it was too late to substitute another) returning the part with frivolous excuses." On 24 August Garrick regretted that Mrs Greville "should behave so ill to you" but did not offer to involve himself in the dispute.

In 1775 William Hawkins, in *Miscellanies in Prose and Verse*, praised her "very pleasing comic abilities . . . and were she to attempt tragedy, I am apt to think she would be equally applauded, having seen her in the country in several capital parts with great success, particularly Monimia in the Orphan, Juliet, Imogen, etc." She acted at Richmond in the summers of 1775 and 1776, but she also popped up at Foote's

Haymarket in September 1776 to sing Lucy in *The Beggar's Opera* and to cavort once more in *The Irish Widow*.

Mrs Greville went back to the Richmond Theatre in the summer of 1777, and there on 15 August she made her first appearance as Beatrice in *Much Ado About Nothing*. Though absent from the winter patent theatres in 1777–78, she reappeared at the Haymarket the following summer from 18 May through 14 September. After she figured as Belinda in *The Female Chevalier* on 18 May 1778 she drew both praise and instruction from the *Morning Chronicle* of the following day: "Mrs Greville . . . has real qualifications to figure as a first rate comic actress, but is too apt to be nerveless in her manner, and to substitute archness for ease, and an outré stile of acting for theatrical spirit."

Susan Greville showed up in Cork in July and September 1779, was under Joseph Glassington's management at Stourbridge Fair, Cambridge, in 1780 and at Richmond again in the summer of 1781. She received a benefit at Richmond on 6 August 1781. She shared a benefit with Williams at the Haymarket on 14 January 1782, sang Lucy for Mrs Pinto's benefit at the same theatre on 15 March 1785, and fell back once more on the Widow Brady with the epilogue song for her own benefit on 26 April 1785.

Only one more performance can be found in which Mrs Greville participated. That was at Covent Garden on 6 June 1795, when she played the Widow Brady one final time, for Mrs Clendining's benefit. In the bill she was called "late of the Theatre Royal, Drury Lane." She died at Kentish Town in 1802, according to the *Monthly Mirror* of October 1802. She was buried at Hampstead.

The Miss Greville who performed at the Haymarket and Royal Circus and in Bath early in the nineteenth century may have been Susan Greville's daughter. Mrs Greville's husband, who seems to have dropped out of her life early, was very likely the H. F. Greville granted licenses for burletta performances yearly from 1805 until 1811.

An engraving by Thornthwaite, after J. Roberts, of Mrs Greville as Sir Harry Wildair in *The Constant Couple*, was published as a plate to *Bell's British Theatre* in 1777.

Grey. *See also* **GRAY.**

Grey, Mr (fl. 1767), *instrumentalist.*
Arthur Murphy's list of the company at Covent Garden Theatre as of 14 September 1767 contains a list of musicians in the theatre's band. Among them is a Mr Grey, whose instrument was unspecified.

Grey, Mr (fl. 1770), *actor.*
A Mr Grey played the walk-on part of the Bailiff in *Tom Thumb the Great*, the afterpiece of a specially licensed performance at the Haymarket Theatre of a pickup company of obscure performers on 19 December 1771.

Grey, William (fl. 1794), *violist, clarinetist, horn player.*
A William Grey was listed in Doane's *Musical Directory* (1794) as proficient on "Viola, Clarinet, Horn." He was said to have participated in some one or more of the Handelian celebrations in Westminster Abbey and to belong to the New Musical Fund. He was said to be in Philadelphia in 1794.

Gricourt, Mons (fl. 1786–1787), *dancer.*
Monsieur Gricourt was named in the King's Theatre bills as a dancer in a few offerings in the 1786–87 season: a *Divertissement* and *La Chercheuse d'esprit* on 23 December 1786, *L'Heureux Événement* on 20 January 1787 (but by 13 March he was omitted from that ballet), the ballet *Zemira and Azor*, in which he danced the

character of Dervis, on 13 February, and the ballet *Sylvie* on 22 March.

Gridland. *See* **CRIDLAND.**

Griesbach, Charles (fl. 1794–1799), *violinist.*
In 1794 Charles Griesbach was listed ("C. Gresbach") in Doane's *Musical Directory* as a violinist, a player in the Concerts of Ancient Music and the Handelian commemorations at Westminster Abbey, and as living at Buckingham House in the service of the Queen's Band. Charles Griesbach was one of the sons of the German musician Johann Heinrich Griesbach and his wife Sophia Elizabeth, née Herschel. His four brothers are entered separately. Their uncle, the famous astronomer Sir William Herschel (1738–1822), took Dr Burney to a concert at Windsor Castle on 22 July 1799 in which all five of his Griesbach nephews played.

By his wife Sarah, Charles Griesbach had at least three sons. One, Charles James Griesbach, was born on 27 September 1797 and as a professional pianist and violinist was admitted to the Royal Society of Musicians on 5 March 1827, at which time he was married and had three children. Charles James died in 1853, when he was described as a "Professor of Music," of No 11, Westbourne Place, Bishop's Road, Paddington, and in his will left bequests to his daughter Rosalie Frances and his son Charles Frederick William. He named as executor his brother, the Rev William Robert Griesbach. In a letter to Sainsbury in 1823, Charles James had mentioned that a Mr A. Griesbach was no longer living with him.

Griesbach, Frederick. *See* **GRIESBACH, JOHANN FRIEDRICH ALEXANDER.**

Griesbach, George Ludolph Jacob *1757–1824, violinist.*

George Ludolph Jacob Griesbach was born at Hanover, Germany, on 10 October 1757 and was baptized in the Garrison Church of that city on 13 October. He was the eldest son of Johann Heinrich Griesbach who was a musician in the Royal Regiment of Guards of the Hanoverian court and the patriarch of a large musical family. Johann Heinrich's wife and George's mother was Sophia Elizabeth Herschel Griesbach, one of the ten children of Isaac Herschel (d. 1767), an oboist in the band of the Hanoverian Guards, by his wife Anna Ilse Moritzen. One of Sophia Elizabeth's brothers, Jacob Herschel, was also a member of the band and had at least two of his compositions printed in London. Two other brothers, Alexander and Frederick William, eventually became musicians in the Bath orchestra. William, the younger one (1738–1822), much later became the most distinguished astronomer of his generation and was knighted for his services to science. In a letter to his daughter Fanny on 23 July 1799, Dr Burney reported attending a concert in the Music Room at Windsor Castle on the previous evening with Dr Herschel, whose five nephews formed a principal part of the band.

Although his parents evidently did not travel to London, George Ludolph Jacob Griesbach and his four brothers (all of whom are entered separately) emigrated in the 1770s. He was placed by the English Hanoverian King George III under the instruction of Cramer for the violin and under Abel for harmony. In time he became the leader of the royal band. He was listed by Dr Burney as one of the second violinists in the Handel Memorial Concerts at Westminster Abbey and the Pantheon in May and June 1784. In 1794 he was listed in Doane's *Musical Directory* as a member of the New Musical Fund; his address was Buckingham House.

In recommending George to membership in the Royal Society of Musicians on 5 August 1804, his brother John Frederick Alexander Griesbach (1769–1825), commonly known as Frederick, testified that "It was my brother's wish to become a Member in the year 1788, but understanding he would not succeed, he became a member of the New Musical Fund, from which he is going to retire, it being his Majesty's particular wish he should become a Member of this Society, he has led their Majestys Concerts nearly twenty seven years, teaches the pianoforte." The king's "particular wish" was not denied; on 4 November 1804 George was elected to the Society, by 14 yeas and one rebellious nay, and was admitted on 6 January 1805. He played at the Society's annual concert at St Paul's in 1806 but in subsequent years he was allowed to send a deputy in his place.

George was married, by license, to Mary Wright Smith at the New Windsor Church on 31 October 1786. By her he had at least seven children: Zepporah Sophia, born 12 September 1787; Mary Ann, born 28 December 1788; Caroline Amilia, born 13 June 1791; Frances Mary, born 27 September 1793; Charlotte Elizabeth, born 26 February 1797; George Adolphus, born 24 June 1801; and Elizabeth Ann, born 23 December 1803.

Soon after George Griesbach's death in December 1824, ten members of the Royal Society of Musicians petitioned to the Governors on 2 January 1825 for the "immediate relief" of his widow Mary, and on that date she was granted £12 for the expenses of her husband's funeral. George's will, to which he signed his full name on 23 August 1791 without witnesses, was proved on 15 April 1825 by his brother Justus Heinrich Christian Griesbach (1762–1832), commonly called Henry, and George's son, George Adolphus Griesbach (1801–1875). Administration of the unspecified estate was granted to the widow Mary Griesbach on 20 April 1825.

On 4 September 1826 Mary Griesbach

wrote from Germany to the Governors of the Society requesting assistance in placing her son George Adolphus in an engagement in the musical profession. She was again in England by 3 August 1828 when her full widow's allowance was restored, her other financial resources having been depleted. On 6 August 1837 the Governors were informed by A. W. Griesbach, a nephew, of Yorkshire, that Mary Griesbach had died, and £8 was granted for her funeral.

George Ludolph Jacob Griesbach's son, George Adolphus Griesbach, became a member of the Royal Society of Musicians on 5 September 1824, and during the nineteenth century he played the violin at the opera and at concerts and also taught. He was probably the Mr Griesbach of "the orchestra of the Theatre Royal of the Italian Opera" who was bequeathed a violin in the will of Domenico Dragonetti in May 1846. He had three children by his wife Emma Taylor Griesbach (d. 1926), whom he married on 3 July 1864. George Adolphus died in 1875.

Griesbach, Henry. *See* GRIESBACH, JUSTUS HEINRICH CHRISTIAN.

Griesbach, Johann Friedrich Alexander *1769–1825, oboist, violoncellist, violist, violinist.*

Johann Friedrich Alexander Griesbach, commonly called Frederick Griesbach, was born at Coppenbrügge, Hanover, on 2 June 1769, the second son of the Hanoverian musician Johann Heinrich Griesbach and his wife Sophia Elizabeth, née Herschel. Information on his parents can be found in the entry of George Ludolph Jacob Griesbach (1757–1824), the eldest brother of the subject of this entry. J. F. A. Griesbach's other brothers are also entered separately.

With his two elder brothers, Johann Friedrich Alexander, hereinafter called Frederick, came to London in the late 1770s, and after being instructed on the oboe by Fischer he became a principal player in the Queen's band. He was listed by Dr Burney (as Griesbach Jr) as one of the second violinists in the Handel Memorial Concerts at Westminster Abbey and the Pantheon in May and June 1784. When proposed on 2 June 1793 for membership in the Royal Society of Musicians he was described as a married man with no children, 24 years of age, engaged in the Queen's band, and a performer on the oboe, violoncello, violin, and viola. He was unanimously elected on 6 October 1793, and on 5 January 1794 he signed the book of membership as "J. F. A. Griesbach." In 1794 he was listed in Doane's *Musical Directory* as F. Griesbach, of Buckingham House, member of the Queen's band, a player in the Handel concerts at the Abbey and in the Concerts of Ancient Music.

In 1800 Frederick served as a Governor of the Royal Society of Musicians. He also played the oboe in the Society's annual concerts at St Paul's regularly from 1794 through 1804. His name was on the list of the band of the King's Theatre in 1817 and 1818, and he also probably played there in other years. He was an oboist with the Philharmonic Society from 1813 to 1821, but ill health overtook him. On 4 May 1823 the Society granted him 10 guineas for medical aid, and on 1 June 1823 Mr Horsley petitioned the Governors on his behalf for more aid, but the request was refused since Griesbach was "in the receipt of a weekly salary." Several months later, however, on 3 August he was given another 10 guineas, followed by grants of 6 guineas on 2 November 1823, 7 December 1823, and 4 January 1824. In the archives of the Society is a letter from him, signed Frederick Griesbach, written from No 15, Elizabeth Street, Hans Place, Brompton, and dated "December 6th" (probably 1824), which presented his sad situation:

I have had the hope of being enabled to resume my professional duties this Season, but am now too fatally convinced of the fallibility of such a flattering idea; and having had a numerous family to provide for, has proved an undeniable obstacle towards the possibility of making any reserve for so unfortunate an event, which places me under the painful compulsion of becoming a Claimant on the Society.

I now beg leave to offer my sincere and grateful acknowledgment for former favors, which my long and expensive illness compelled me to solicit and can with truth assure the Society it was my full intention to refund, had my health permitted me to have attended all the Autumn Meetings, but unfortunately from anxiety and the fatigue of the journey to Gloucester had such an unfavourable effect on my health, as to totally incapacitate me from fulfilling the remainder of my engagements, and I was therefore obliged to return to Town very little benefited for the extreme fatigue I experienced, and since which period my health has been materially worse. Under the above unfortunate circumstances I trust you will consider my case worthy your attention and remain Gentlemen your obliged. . . .

Also in 1824, a letter signed by ten members of the Society recommended that Griesbach be given immediate relief: "he is 54 years of age, has been afflicted with a general debility of constriction which renders him unable to follow his profession."

Frederick died soon after, early in 1825, and on 6 February 1825 his widow Frances Mary Wybrow Griesbach, whom he had married at St Martin-in-the-Fields on 16 October 1792, was granted £12 for his funeral expenses. On 5 June 1825, Mrs Griesbach informed the Governors of the Society that she was leaving London to join her family in Germany, and the Governors agreed to consider any eligible master whom she would suggest for her son Henry Dougan Dickenson, who had been born on 21 January 1811 and baptized at St George, Hanover Square, on 4 June 1814. On 3 January 1830, evidently returned from Germany, Frances Griesbach's allowance from the Society was reduced to £10 for that

year because of other income she enjoyed, but on 3 July 1831, her full allowance was granted. On 2 July 1837, Mrs Griesbach sent a medical certificate to the Society, because she was too sick to attend and make her declaration for continuing assistance. Presumably she died soon after, for her name was not again mentioned in the Minute Books of the Society.

An article in *The Harmonicon* for 1830, cited in *Grove's Dictionary* (under "Oboe"), suggested that J. F. A. Griesbach "was probably the last of the outstanding players in England to use the old broad 'fishtail' reed" and praised him for his clear and powerful tone.

Griesbach, Johann Wilhelm *b. 1772, violinist, violist, violoncellist.*

Johann Wilhelm Griesbach, commonly known as John William Griesbach and sometimes William Griesbach, was born at Coppenbrügge, Hanover, on 10 January 1772, the fourth son of the Hanoverian musician Johann Heinrich Griesbach and his wife Sophia Elizabeth, née Herschel. Information on his parents can be found in the entry of George Ludolph Jacob Griesbach (1757–1824), the eldest brother of the subject of this entry. Johann Wilhelm's other brothers are also entered separately.

Somewhat younger than three of his brothers, he perhaps did not accompany them to England when they emigrated from Germany in the late 1770s and early 1780s, but he was in London by the 1790s. When he was proposed by Charles Ashley for membership in the Royal Society of Musicians on 5 April 1801, J. W. Griesbach was described as 29 years of age. He had been a professional musician for at least seven years, was a player on the violin, viola, and violoncello, a member of the Queen's band, had played in the Concerts of Ancient Music, and was a teacher. He was elected on 5 July 1801 by 11 yeas and one nay, and on 4 April 1802 he signed the book of admission as "William" Griesbach. He played in the Society's annual concerts at St Paul's in 1804, 1806, 1811, and 1812, but in 1802 and 1809 he was granted permission to send a deputy. He also played first violin in the band of the King's Theatre in the Haymarket in 1817 and 1818.

His career seems to have been less active than those of his brothers. On 20 February 1824, he wrote from Windsor to Sainsbury that "my Musical Career is of so uninteresting a nature [as to be] not worthy of recording" in Sainsbury's new biographical dictionary of musicians. Prior to his recent move to Windsor, Griesbach had lived at No 124, Jermyn Street, in central London.

Griesbach, John or John William. *See* GRIESBACH, JOHANN WILHELM.

Griesbach, Justus Heinrich Christian
1762–1832, violoncellist, horn player.
Justus Heinrich Christian Griesbach, commonly called Henry, was christened at Coppenbrügge, Hanover, on 26 April 1762, the second son of the Hanoverian musician Johann Heinrich Griesbach by his wife Sophia Elizabeth, née Herschel. Information on his parents can be found in the entry of George Ludolph Jacob Griesbach (1757–1824), the eldest brother of the subject of this entry. His other brothers are also entered separately.

In 1780 J. H. C. Griesbach came to England at the request of George III, and after instruction by John Crosdill he was appointed about 1783 first violoncello in Queen Charlotte's band. In May and June 1784, he played among the violoncellos in the Handel Memorial Concerts at Westminster Abbey and the Pantheon. On 6 February 1791 he was recommended by William Dance for membership in the Royal Society of Musicians, at which time he was described as a married man with no children, a member of the Queen's band, and a performer on the French horn as well

as the violoncello. When unanimously elected on 1 May 1791 (the first of the family to be so admitted), he signed the membership register as Henry Griesbach, the name he continued to use throughout the remainder of his career and with which he signed his will on 4 June 1831.

In 1794 he was listed in Doane's *Musical Directory* as H. "Griesback," of Buckingham House, and as a member of the Concerts of Ancient Music as well as associations already mentioned. He played regularly at the concerts given annually in May by the Royal Society of Musicians at St Paul's between 1792 and 1799 and in 1803 and 1812; but in 1813 he sent a deputy in his stead. In 1827 he was a Governor of the Society.

Henry Griesbach probably died in January 1832. By his will, signed on 4 June 1831, he left £1000 in bank annuities to Mary Blumfield, who resided with him at that time. By a codicil of 14 October 1831, he stated that he had now married her and confirmed his previous bequest. His will was proved in London on 19 February 1832 by the executors, his sons by his first wife (also named Mary), John Henry Griesbach and John William Griesbach, who were granted the residue of the estate.

Henry Griesbach's elder son, John Henry Griesbach, had been born at Windsor on 20 June 1798 and was baptized two days later. On 6 October 1819 he married Miriam Corby of Windsor at St George, Hanover Square. By her he had five daughters and one son. Two of the daughters, Mira Mary, born on 3 September 1822, and Ellen, born on 10 December 1824, and the son Henry Julius Frederick, born on 4 July 1820, were named in his recommendation to the Royal Society of Musicians on 31 December 1826 (he was admitted on 7 January 1827). John Henry Griesbach became a cellist and composer of reputation during the nineteenth century and is noticed in *Grove's Dictionary*. He died after a long and painful illness at the University

College Hospital in St Pancras, London, on 9 January 1875, at which time his residence was No 23, Holland Street, Kensington, His will was proved in London on 27 January 1875 by his widow Miriam Griesbach (b. 1798). In February 1875, giving her age as 76 (as of 2 October 1874), she petitioned the Royal Society of Musicians for assistance, her husband's subscription having been paid to 1875.

Griesbach, William. *See* **GRIESBACH, JOHANN WILHELM.**

Grieve. *See also* **GREVE.**

Grieve, John Henderson *1770–1845, scene painter.*

Born in 1770, John Henderson Grieve began working as a scene painter in London in the 1790s, but most of his career of 50 years at Covent Garden Theatre belongs to the nineteenth century and is closely interwoven with those of his sons, Thomas Grieve (1799–1882) and William Grieve (1800–1844), with whom he collaborated from 1817 until his death.

The earliest reference to John Henderson Grieve's work for the theatre occurred on 7 October 1794, when he was paid £7 6s. 6d. for painting the halls at Drury Lane. With Whitmore, Seward, and Spitzer he painted scenes for productions of *The Reasonable Wife* and *Harlequin Invincible* at Astley's Amphitheatre on 22 May 1795, and he contributed scenes to *The Magician of the Rocks* at Sadler's Wells on 16 May 1796. By then he was also employed at Covent Garden. Grieve designed and splendidly painted the lavish interiors of Astley's third amphitheatre, which opened on Easter Monday 1804. With Capon, Marchbanks, and the younger Thomas French he painted scenery for the production of *Rich-*

Courtesy of the University of London Library

Scene design for the ballet *Kenilworth,* 1831, by the GRIEVE family

ard III which opened the new Beaufort Square Theatre at Bath in October 1805. He designed scenery for Didelot's ballet *La Reine de Golconde* at the King's Theatre in June 1812; and he and his son William assisted Pyett in the design and execution of scenery for the Edinburgh Theatre in 1818.

By 1814 Grieve was assisting Andrews at Sadler's Wells with the heavy work demanded by Dibdin's productions; he was paid by the piece, and his finished work was transported from his painting shop in Lambeth by wagon to Islington. Grieve worked for Dibdin until 1818, being at the same time employed at Covent Garden. A number of watercolor copies of his designs for Sadler's Wells are in an album owned by the Garrick Club and are described by Sybil Rosenfeld in *Theatre Notebook* (v and xv).

Grieve was a member of a large cadre of scene painters at Covent Garden which included Hodgins, Hollogan, Phillips, Pugh, and Whitmore. As the others left, Grieve, joined by his son Thomas in 1817 and his other son William in 1819, became, as Miss Rosenfeld has written, "responsible for most of the scenery at Covent Garden and made that theatre celebrated for its scenic effects." The name of an I. Grieve, presumably another son, appeared on the playbills in 1818–19, but was not seen again.

John Grieve remained at Covent Garden until his death, of apoplexy, at the age of 75 on 16 April 1845. In his will, drawn on 24 October 1843, he described himself as a gentleman, of King Edward Street, Southwark, and left bequests to his sons Thomas and William and to his daughters Hannah Sarah Grieve and Ann Wilson. The will was proved at London on 26 May 1845 by Thomas Grieve, the surviving executor, the other named executor William Grieve having died at South Lambeth on 12 November 1844.

In their work at Covent Garden during the nineteenth century the Grieves carried on the tradition of romantic illusionistic spectacle inherited from De Loutherbourg as they exploited all the technical devices known to their times, including especially gas lighting which John H. Grieve saw introduced at Covent Garden in 1817. They designed for opera as well as for drama and ballet, providing scenery for some of the first productions in England of works by Mozart, Rossini, and von Weber. The most illustrious of the Grieves was Thomas, who became the leading painter for Charles Kean's famous productions and continued to work in collaboration with his son Thomas Walford Grieve (b. 1841) until he died at Lambeth on 16 April 1882. More than 600 designs by the family are at the University of London Library and more than 100 are at the Victoria and Albert Museum and the British Museum. An assessment of their style is provided by Sybil Rosenfeld in *A Short History of Scene Design in Great Britain* (1973):

It ran the gamut of the romantic picturesque: mountains and torrents, ruins by moonlight, burning forests, oriental temples and palaces, Gothic abbeys, and illuminated cities, gardens and ballrooms. Their colouring could be both brilliant and subtle; they were masters of perspective and of light and shade. Edward Fitzgerald accounted them 'the most perfect scene painters in the world as a combination' and they raised the standard both of design and execution. . . .

In the British Museum is a sketch of a tent scene for *Pizarro*, first played at Drury Lane on 24 May 1799, now attributed to J. H. Grieve, although he was not listed as one of the painters for that production.

Thomas and William Grieve are noticed in *The Dictionary of National Biography*. An excellent account, with illustrations, of the work of the Grieves in the nineteenth century is in Sybil Rosenfeld's "The Grieve Family," in *The Anatomy of an Illusion*

(International Federation for Theatre Research, 1969).

Griffen. *See* GRIFFIN.

Griffes, Mr [fl. 1791]. *See* GRIFFITHS, JOHN.

Griffin. *See also* GRIFFITH and GRIFFITHS.

Griffin, Mr [fl. 1729]. *See* GRIFFITH, THOMAS.

Griffin, Mr [fl. 1751? 1755?], *puppeteer.*

A Mr Griffin, of Tyburn Road, was the proprietor of a puppet show during the 1750s, and presumably was the person who started young Nancy Dawson (d. 1767) on her dancing career. The story is told that one day Griffin sent "Jack Pudding" into the streets of St Giles's to announce that *Jane Shore*, complete with the humors of Punch and Joan, would be presented at the King's Head Tavern in Oxford Market. Jack Pudding returned with Nancy, whom he had picked up in the streets. During the performance Griffin stole away behind the scenes with her, and Jack revealed them to Griffin's wife, who attacked them. Griffin left his wife and took Nancy with him. The incident supposedly took place when Nancy was 16, either in 1751 or 1755, depending on which year of birth for Nancy is correct, if either.

Griffin, Mr [fl. 1767–1796?], *actor, singer.*

A Mr Griffin who had played small parts and singing roles at Bath and Bristol from as early as 1767 acted Hastings in *She Stoops to Conquer* at the Haymarket Theatre on 1 July 1778. The *Morning Chronicle* of the following day said "Mr. Griffin is a good personable figure, & though not quite so handsome a man, puts us in mind of Mr. Brereton. . . . He shews some want

of judgment." During his summer engagement at the Haymarket, Griffin also acted Mervin in *The Maid of the Mill*, Drusius in *Bonduca*, Clarin in *The Gypsies*, and Mat o' the Mint in *The Beggar's Opera*. After the mainpiece on 21 August 1778 he sang a hunting song.

In 1778 Griffin also served in Joseph Glassington's strolling troupe and played at Stourbridge Fair in Cambridge. In 1779 and 1780 he was again in Bristol, and in 1781–82 he sang at Portsmouth. A clipping at the Guildhall dated 3 September 1789 stated that a Mr "Griffen" was one of the performers in *The Recruiting Serjeant* when it was presented at a theatre at the first gateway from Hosier Lane at Bartholomew Fair. Perhaps our man was the Griffin who acted at Drogheda in Ireland in August 1796.

The Master Griffin who played children's roles at Bristol in 1780–81 was probably our subject's son.

Griffin, Mrs [fl. 1729]. *See* GRIFFITH, MRS THOMAS THE FIRST.

Griffin, Benjamin *1680?–1740, actor, singer, playwright.*

If we can believe a notice in the Burney Collection at the British Museum, Benjamin Griffin was born in 1680 in Oxnead, Norfolk, the son of the Reverend Benjamin Griffin, Rector of Buxton and Oxnead and Chaplain to Sir Robert Paston, Earl of Yarmouth. Most of those details are very likely true, though the birthdate may be a decade too early. Young Benjamin was educated at the Free School of North Walsham in Norfolk, after which his father apprenticed him to a glazier in Norwich. Not caring for that trade, the story goes, Benjamin ran off with a troupe of strolling players, the Duke of Norfolk's Company; they performed at the Duke's palace in Norwich during the 1711–12 season. If Benjamin left his apprenticeship at that time, he surely must have been born later than 1680—or he began his apprenticeship very late.

In the summer of 1714 Griffin acted with the Duke of Southampton and Cleaveland's Servants at Richmond. The group offered his first play, *Injured Virtue*, an adaptation of Dekker and Massinger's *The Virgin Martyr*. The play was repeated by the troupe at the King's Arms Tavern in Southwark on 1 November 1714, with Griffin playing Sapritius—his first recorded part. The play was published in 1715. *The History of the English Stage* (1741) had little good to say of the work or of Griffin's other attempts at playwriting: "By mistaking his Talents he attempted to commence Dramatic-Poet, by vamping up an old Play or 2 of *Massinger* and *Dekker* and *scribbling* a few Farces, all which met with the deserved Contempt of such Trifling Performances."

John Rich engaged Griffin at the new Lincoln's Inn Fields Theatre, where Griffin appeared in the first half of 1715 in four premieres: Sterling in *The Perplexed Couple* on 16 February, Ezekial Prim in *The City Ramble* on 2 June, Sir Arthur Addlepate in his own *Love in a Sack* on 14 June, and Choleric in *The Doating Lovers* on 23 June. On 17 August he acted Sebastian in *The False Count*. In 1715 Griffin is said to have written, with Lewis Theobald, *The Complete Key to the last new Farce, the What-d'ye-Call-it* (by Gay). Griffin is also said to have been the author of what is now Egerton manuscript 2320 at the British Museum, a diary of plays acted at Lincoln's Inn Fields from September 1715 to June 1721, at Drury Lane from September 1721 to May 1733, at the Haymarket from September 1733 to March 1734, and at Drury Lane from March 1734 to November 1736. Griffin was, indeed, at those playhouses during those periods. The diary was continued by another hand beginning September 1737, when Griffin was in Rotterdam.

Under Rich at Lincoln's Inn Fields Griffin acted from 1715 to the end of the

Harvard Theatre Collection

JOE MILLER, BENJAMIN GRIFFIN (in long wig), JOHN HARPER, THEOPHILUS CIBBER, MARY HERON and JOHN HIGHMORE

detail from "The Stage Mutiny" by Laguerre

1720–21 season. Short and slight of build, according to Chetwood, Griffin established himself quickly as a low comedian, specializing in testy old men and skirts parts. Some of his roles at Lincoln's Inn Fields were Charino in *Love Makes a Man*, Sir William Wisewood in *Love's Last Shift*, Gerrard in *The Lucky Prodigal*, Mother Griffin in *The Woman's Revenge*, Scruple in *The Fair Quaker*, the Beggar in *The Royal Merchant*, Dorcas Guzzle in *The Cobler of Preston*, Don Lopez in his own *The Humours of Purgatory* (premiered on 3 April 1716; published that year), Gripe in *The Woman Captain*, Tickletext in *The Feign'd Curtizans*, Fernando in *The Fatal Marriage*, Polonius in *Hamlet* (on 2 February 1717), Ogle in his own *The Masquerade* (premiered on 16 May 1717; published that year), Shylock in *The Jew of Venice*, Barnaby Muckland in *The Lady's Triumph*, Pierrot in *The Jealous Doctor*, Simon Pure in *A Bold Stroke for a Wife*,

Day in *The Committee,* Gomez in *The Spanish Fryar,* a Carrier in *1 Henry IV,* Gripe in *The Busy Body,* a Witch in *Macbeth,* Dorante in *The Gamester,* Foresight in *Love for Love,* Alphonso in *The Pilgrim,* Sir John Indolent in his own *Whig and Tory* (premiered on 26 January 1720; published that year), Scrapeall in *The Squire of Alsatia,* Sir Hugh in *The Merry Wives of Windsor,* Sir Paul in *The Double Dealer,* and Nitt the Tailor in *Coriolanus.*

During that same period he put in an appearance at Bartholomew Fair: on 24 August 1719 he acted Signor Diego Fizgiggo in the droll *The Constant Lovers.* The booth was that of the Widow Leigh and Griffin's comic partner at the theatre, William Bullock. For his benefit on All Fools Day in 1721 Griffin wrote to *Mist's Weekly Journal* asking for the kind of support the *Tatler* had always given the theatrical profession. Mist, for reasons that are now obscure, responded with a puff that offended someone, for *Appleby's Weekly Journal* on 17 June reported that "Mr Griffin of the New Play House has been under examination before the Committee for seditious Libels, on account of Mr. Mist's paper." The benefit, which featured Griffin as Alphonso in *The Pilgrim,* brought the actor a respectable £129 10s. 6d., presumably before house charges.

According to Griffin's "Humble Appeal to the Publick," published in the *Daily Post* on 11 June 1733, Griffin had worked before 1721 quite contentedly at Lincoln's Inn Fields under John Rich. That year, he said, he was approached by the elder Thurmond and by Shaw, spokesmen for the Drury Lane managers, asking him to change companies. Griffin at first refused, but Stede the prompter finally persuaded him to join the Drury Lane company. His contract there was for three years at a weekly wage of £4 and a benefit each year before 15 April with £40 house charges. He was assured of advancement. Then, just after Griffin moved to Drury Lane, the

managers of both patent houses agreed not to allow actors to change companies without a private agreement; Griffin, like it or not, was trapped at Drury Lane. When his contract expired in 1724 he received a note from Castleman, the treasurer, offering him a renewal but at £3 weekly, a benefit in May, and £50 house charges at his benefit. Unable to return to Lincoln's Inn Fields, Griffin continued at Drury Lane at a reduced income until 1729. When Norris died, Griffin was raised to £4 weekly, but no change was made in his benefit arrangements. Suddenly, on 4 June 1733, he was discharged without notice or explanation.

All that must have rankled, yet Griffin's performance record shows that he appeared in a number of new and often very good roles during his stay at Drury Lane, and he kept many of his old parts. From September 1721 until the fall of 1733 Griffin tried such new characters as Abel in *The Committee,* Tribulation in *The Alchemist,* Gripus in *Amphitryon* (previously Norris's part), Manuel in *She Wou'd and She Wou'd Not,* Cimberton in *The Conscious Lovers,* Plausible in *The Plain Dealer,* the Doctor in *Apollo and Daphne,* Subtleman in *The Twin Rivals,* Calianax in *The Maid's Tragedy,* Taylor in *The Provok'd Wife,* Isander and Cleon in *Timon of Athens,* Sir William Freeman in *The Village Opera,* Aminadab Prim in *The Lover's Opera,* Silence in *2 Henry IV,* Mrs Fardingale in *The Funeral,* Justice Clack in *The Jovial Crew,* Trapland in *Love for Love,* the Surgeon in *The Relapse,* Sir Politick in *Volpone,* Busy in *Bartholomew Fair,* Scrub in *The Stratagem,* Sands in *Henry VIII,* Tipkin in *The Tender Husband,* Sir Oliver in *She Wou'd If She Cou'd,* Sir Toby in *The Comical Revenge,* Old Wilfull in *The Double Gallant,* Peachum in *The Beggar's Opera,* the Old Woman in *Rule a Wife and Have a Wife,* and Lovegold in *The Miser*—one of his most popular roles.

Griffin of Drury Lane seems not to have been the Griffin who, with his wife, appeared on 29 November 1729 at the Front Long Room next to the Haymarket Theatre with a group headed by Tony Aston. On that date that Mr Griffin acted Loveworth in *Tunbridge Walks*, and on 1 December he played Sullen in *The Stratagem*. Benjamin Griffin's schedule at Drury Lane, so far as the bills show, would have allowed him to appear in these pieces, but the roles seem not to be in his line, and so far as we know Benjamin Griffin never married. We take the Griffin who acted with Aston to have been (perhaps) Thomas Griffith.

Though Griffin's roles at Drury Lane would suggest that he was prospering there, his complaints in 1733 show that he was not. Indeed, by the early 1730s the situation behind the scenes at Drury Lane was growing increasingly unstable; through death and retirement the management of the theatre was changing, and the years of relative peace and prosperity were at an end. Whether by his own choice or not, Griffin was not acting as frequently as before. *The Comedian* in 1732 said that there was not anyone who frequented Drury Lane who "does not wish that Griffin acted oftener than he does." In the spring of 1733 things came to a head. The management had fallen into the hands of Mary Wilks, Hester Booth, John Ellis, and John Highmore; Theophilus Cibber, the scapegrace son of Colley, had expected to inherit a share in the management when his father retired, but that was not to be. Disgruntled, and surrounded by many other Drury Lane performers who were unhappy, Theophilus petitioned the Lord Chamberlain. Griffin was one of Cibber's group of malcontents, and when the theatre managers discharged him on 4 June 1733, he wrote his *Humble Appeal*, describing his financial status at Drury Lane since 1721.

The managers tried to defend themselves by boasting that they had given Griffin a present of 10 guineas. Cibber, presumably with the cooperation of Griffin, brought out a windy rebuff which cited, among other

things, Griffin's diligence. Griffin, Cibber said, was a very popular attraction and had played the taxing role of Lovegold in *The Miser* some 20 to 30 times during the previous season. In September 1733 Cibber led his followers to the Haymarket Theatre, leaving Drury Lane, with a much weakened company, in the hands of John Highmore.

Griffin played Lovegold on 23 August 1733 and Shallow in *Sir John Falstaff* on 4 September at a Bartholomew Fair booth which he operated in partnership with Cibber, Bullock, and Hallam. Then he joined Cibber's rebels at the Haymarket to appear as Trapland in *Love for Love* on 26 September. At the Haymarket between then and March 1734 Griffin tried such new roles as Sir Francis in *The Provok'd Husband*, Fondlewife in *The Old Bachelor*, Barnaby in *The Amorous Widow*, Roger in *The Scornful Lady*, and Sir Credulous in *The Mother in Law*. When Highmore capitulated, Cibber's players returned to Drury Lane, and on 12 March 1734 Griffin acted Sir Credulous there. For the rest of his career Griffin played at that house, trying, among other new roles, Butts in *Henry VIII*, Sir Jasper Fidget in *The Country Wife*, Moneytrap in *The Confederacy*, and Learchus in *Aesop*. Little is known of his activity outside the playhouse during the late 1730s, though he was in Rotterdam on 30 August 1737 for some reason. The trip seems not to have been extensive, however, for he was back at Drury Lane by 10 September.

The *Daily Advertiser* on 19 February 1740 reported that "Yesterday died of an Astmatick Disorder, at his Chambers in Clement's Inn, Mr Benjamin Griffin, a celebrated Comedian, belonging to Drury-Lane Theatre." A clipping at the British Museum claims Griffin was 60 years of age. He had acted right up to the end: on the previous 12 February he had appeared as Day in *The Committee*. The *Daily Post* lamented Griffin's death, calling him "a

Harvard Theatre Collection

BENJAMIN GRIFFIN as Tribulation, and
BENJAMIN JOHNSON as Ananias

by van Bleeck

kind good natur'd worthy Friend, always
ready to do good offices; a facetious companion and one whom everybody lov'd. By
his death the whole Town will have an
irreparable loss." On the following 4 March
administration of the goods, chattels, and
credits of Benjamin Griffin, late of the
parish of St Clement Danes, bachelor, was
granted to his sister and next of kin, Helen
Dalton, widow.

About 1747 *A Clear Stage and No Favour* recalled that "While *Griffin* liv'd the
British Stage cou'd boast,/ What *France*
long since in her *Moliere* had lost." The
prompter Chetwood in 1749 called Griffin
"not only a good actor, but a pleasing poet."
And Thomas Davies in his *Dramatic Miscellanies* (1784) said that Griffin and Ben
Johnson

were much admired for their just representation of the canting puritanical preacher and
his solemn deacon and botcher [in *The Alchemist*]; there was an affected softness in the
former which was finely contrasted by the
fanatical fury of the other.—Griffin's features
seemed ready to be relaxed into a smile, while
the stiff muscles and fierce eye of the other
admitted of no suppleness or compliance.
There is still to be seen a fine print of them in
these characters, from a painting of Vanbleek;
they are very striking resemblances of both
comedians.

The Peter van Bleeck work referred to
was completed in 1738 and is now in the
Garrick Club. The artist engraved it in reverse in 1748. The reproduction of the engraving in Mander and Mitchenson's *Picture History of the British Stage* incorrectly
identifies Johnson as playing Tribulation
and Griffin as Ananias; the roles should be
reversed. Benjamin Griffin was also pictured by John Laguerre in his satirical print,
"The Stage Mutiny," which depicts Theophilus Cibber's revolt from Drury Lane in
1733. Griffin is shown wearing a huge wig
and a large three-cornered hat.

Griffin, J. [*fl.* 1796], *equestrian. See*
GRIFFITHS, J. [*fl.* 1772–1796].

Griffin, Philip [*fl.* 1670?–1708], *actor.*

A manuscript cast in a 1691 edition of
Julius Caesar listed Philip Griffin in the
role of Casca; the cast may date from as
early as the 1670–71 season. Griffin was
certainly acting for the King's Company at
the Bridges Street Theatre in 1671–72, for
a warrant dated 27 December 1671 ordered Griffin and other players apprehended for performing without a license.

Roles Griffin is known to have played
with the King's Company before its merger
with the Duke's players in 1682 included
Sanchez in *The Spanish Rogue* in March
1673 at the Lincoln's Inn Fields playhouse,
where the King's troupe acted temporarily,

Laula the hostess in Duffett's farce *The Empress of Morocco* in the summer of 1673 at the same house, and then, at Drury Lane from 1674 to 1682: Caligula's Ghost in *Nero*, Gratiano in *Othello*, Menander in *Sophonisba* (a role he also played at Oxford, in 1681), Grimani in *Love in the Dark*, Maecenas in *Gloriana*, Vernish in *The Plain Dealer*, Rash in *The Country Innocence*, Lysimachus in *The Rival Queens*, the title role in *Scaramouch*, Durzo in *King Edgar and Alfreda*, Serapion in *All for Love*, Archelaus in *Mithridates*, Bowser in *The Man of Newmarket*, Valentine in *Trick for Trick*, Southampton in *The Unhappy Favorite*, Captain Porpuss in *Sir Barnaby Whigg*, Arbanes in *The Loyal Brother*, and King Albuzeiden in *The Heir of Morocco*.

Colley Cibber, years later, said that Griffin and Cardell Goodman were so poor in those days that they not only shared the same bed but also the same shirt—a fanciful tale, though it is probably true that the young actors were in financial straits.

Griffin figured in a few controversial theatrical matters during his days with the King's Company. On 28 September 1677, following a petition to the King by the disgruntled younger players in the troupe, the manager, Charles Killigrew, planned to reconstitute the group, bringing a number of the younger actors, including Griffin, into positions as "Master Partners or sharers." The chief complaint of the performers had been the impossibility of their rising in the company, because the older actors, especially Charles Hart and Michael Mohun, controlled the company and appropriated the best roles. But the new arrangement worked out by Killigrew brought little to the younger players, for the company finances were in a bad state and the proprietors were constantly wrangling. Indeed, in 1678 the troupe almost fell apart, and playing ceased. Some of the actors, including Griffin, went off to Edinburgh.

Griffin and the other deserters were lured back to London by promises of travel expenses (which were not paid). During their absence Charles Killigrew mortgaged the company's stock (costumes, scenery, and properties chiefly) to pay the troupe's debts. The whole miserable affair ended in a Chancery suit in 1682 in which Griffin submitted evidence against Killigrew. He chose the right side, for on 8 February 1684 the Lord Chamberlain found against Killigrew. The surviving records give only a muddled picture of what happened, but it seems that when Griffin and other younger members of the King's Company were made sharers, they put up £1000 to buy the stock of the company. When they accused Charles Killigrew of seizing the stock to pay the troupe's debts, Killigrew denied the charge and, in fact, induced the company's wardrobekeeper, Andrew Perryman, to testify that it was Griffin who had seized the stock of costumes. Apparently he had done so, arguing that they were safer in his hands than in Killigrew's. With such dissension within the company, it is little wonder that a merger with the stronger Duke's players became inevitable.

Though Griffin was not in a sharing position in the new United Company when it was formed in 1682, he seems to have succeeded to some larger roles and to have established himself as an important member of the troupe. The first part we know of for him in the United Company was Dalmatius in *Constantine* on 12 November 1683 at Drury Lane. Between then and 1695, when the troupe split, he is known to have acted Autum Mort in *The Jovial Crew*, Pontius in *Valentinian*, Casca in *Julius Caesar*, Captain Anville in *The Northern Lass*, Latorch in *The Bloody Brother*, Surly in *Sir Courtly Nice*, Du Pier in *The Commonwealth of Women*, Mardonius in *A King and No King* (Mohun's old role), Captain Leon in *The Banditti*, Sir Richard Lovemore in *The Devil of a Wife*, Rui Diaz in *The Island Princess*, Ghinotto in *The Injur'd Lovers*, and Sir

Edward Belfond in the first production of *The Squire of Alsatia*. From manuscript casts we know that he also played Manly and Vernish in *The Plain Dealer*. Writing in 1708, the prompter John Downes said, quaintly, that Griffin "so Excell'd in Surly, Sir Edward Belfond [and] The Plain Dealer, [that] none succeeding in the 2 former have Equall'd him, except his Predecessor Mr. Hart in the latter."

One of Griffin's good friends, first in the King's Company and then in the United Company, was "Orange Moll"—Mary Meggs, the concessionnaire at the Drury Lane Theatre. When she drew up her will on 24 April 1682, she named her "very loving friend" Philip Griffin, of St Martin-in-the-Fields, her executor and residuary legatee. Mrs Meggs died in 1691, and Griffin proved the will on 2 December of that year. He became owner of her fruit-selling license, which was worth between £150 and £200 (annually, one assumes). A picture of Griffin (now lost) was among her effects which Griffin claimed.

Thomas Betterton led most of the older players from the United Company at Drury Lane to the old converted tennis court theatre in Lincoln's Inn Fields in 1695, and London once again had rival acting troupes. Griffin elected to stay at Drury Lane under the wily Christopher Rich, and he seems for a while to have become Rich's manager of acting. He was, at any rate, in a position of some importance and witnessed articles of agreement with such actors as Verbruggen, Bullock, and Doggett. Then, some time between April 1696 and June 1698, he left the stage to join the military service.

On 2 June 1698 the *Post Boy* announced that

This Day at the Theatre in Drury-Lane will be Acted a Play, called, The Plain Dealer, upon a very charitable account, the Profits of the Play being given for the Release of a distressed Gentleman from Prison; and the chief Part is acted by Capt. Griffin, formerly a

famous Actor, and lately Captain of a Company of Foot in His Majesty's Service, through the Wars in Ireland.

Curiously, two days later the same newspaper reported that "One Mrs. Griffin, wife to Captain *Griffin*, who is at St. *Germains* with the late King James, is taken into Custody here, she having lately come over from *France* without a pass." Surely a different Captain Griffin was being referred to, though the report is a strange coincidence.

Philip Griffin is known to have gone to Ireland again in August 1699. He stayed in Dublin until 1700, acting at the Smock Alley Theatre. He was in London by the summer of 1700, for he and other players were reported to have performed at Drury Lane the "obscene" play *The Fox* and *Sir Courtly Nice*, on 24 June. *The London Stage* does not cite the latter performance. The players, caught in the middle of growing attacks on the immorality and profaneness of the English stage, were acquitted, as were their rivals at Lincoln's Inn Fields, who were similarly cited.

The 8/11 November 1700 issue of the *English Post* reported a full house at Drury Lane, "but Capt Griffin, who was chief actor therein [in *The Old Bachelor*], being taken ill, they were dismissed all having their money returned."

At Drury Lane between 1700–1701 and the fall of 1707 Griffin played the Duke of Britannie in *The Unhappy Favorite*, Ulysses in *The Virgin Prophetess*, Lord Lovechace in *The Bath*, Gonzalvo in *The Generous Conqueror*, Ulysses in *Cassandra*, Don Felix in *The False Friend*, Rimini in *The Patriot*, Henry VIII in *Vertue Betray'd* (a part he chose for his benefit on 9 June 1703—one of the few benefits recorded for Griffin), his old role of Manly in *The Plain Dealer*, the title part in *The Old Bachelor*, Old Bookwit in *The Lying Lover*, Algernoon in *Love the Leveller*, Ozmin in *The Faithful Bride*, possibly Cecil in *The Albion Queens* (a prompt copy trace cited him, though the cast list did not), probably a role in *Volpone* (which he chose for his benefit on 5 June 1705), Putsky in *The Loyal Subject*, Sir Thomas Freegood in *The Fashionable Lover*, Ballance in *The Recruiting Officer*, the Governor in *Love Makes a Man*, and, on 29 October 1707, the last new role recorded for him, Apemantus in *Timon of Athens*. Griffin seems not to have acted beyond December 1707, though, curiously, on 13 January 1708 he was paid £2 2s. for materials for operas, so he was still in the Drury Lane company.

Theatrical records reveal no more about Philip Griffin, which suggests that he had left the stage. Interestingly, a Captain Griffin was buried at St Paul, Covent Garden, on 11 August 1709. That Griffin was probably the "Phillip Griffith" described in an estate administration of 8 August 1709 — probably immediately after his death — as late of the service "in Nave Regia." Administration was granted to George Orton, a creditor of the deceased, Elizabeth Ruscall, widow, mother of Captain "Griffith," renouncing. That does not sound like our Philip Griffin but rather a younger man, but it is, once more, a strange coincidence. Another parish register entry may also be of interest: a Philip Griffin, Esq, and his wife Elizabeth baptized a daughter at St Giles in the Fields on 29 November 1691.

Hall's catalogue of dramatic portraits at Harvard cites, under Mr Griffin (i.e., Philip), a picture of Griffin as the Queen Mother in Duffett's *The Empress of Morocco*; the character's actual name was Laula. But the picture, if it shows any actor at all, probably depicts Cardell Goodman as Mariamne the cinder wench, as John Harold Wilson conjectures in his biography of that actor.

Griffin, Samuel [fl. 1794], singer.

Samuel Griffin, residing at No 2, Chapel Street, Holywell Street, was listed in Doane's *Musical Directory* in 1794 as a tenor, a member of the Choral Fund and the Cecilian Society, and a participant in the Handelian commemorative concerts in Westminster Abbey.

"Griffinhoof, Arthur, Esq." *See* COLMAN, GEORGE 1762–1836.

Griffith. *See also* GRIFFIN and GRIFFITHS.

Griffith, Mr [fl. 1725], dancing master.

Mr Griffith and Mrs Wall danced a "Serious Dance" at Lincoln's Inn Fields Theatre on 5 May 1725 for Griffith's benefit. Griffith was advertised as a dancing master who had never appeared on that stage before. He is not known to have danced elsewhere in London, but he clearly had a sizeable following, for the total income for the evening came to £204 19s. — twice the average during that period.

Griffith, Mrs [fl. 1752–1755], actress.

A Mrs Griffith (sometimes Griffiths) acted occasionally at Covent Garden Theatre for three seasons, 1752–53 through 1754–55. The roles for which she was named in the bills included Mrs Vixen in *The Beggar's Opera* on 30 November 1752 (also on 12 September 1753 and 16 September 1754), Cleone in *The Distrest Mother* on 26 March 1753, Eugenia in *Philoclea* on 22 January 1754, Cloris in *The Rehearsal* on 30 December 1754, Mrs Sealand in *The Conscious Lovers* on 22 March 1755, Lady Grace in *The Provok'd Husband* on 9 May 1755, and Teresa in *The Spanish Fryar* on 13 May 1755.

The possibility should be noted that this Mrs Griffith may have been Ursula Griffith, the widow and second wife of the actor Thomas Griffith (1680–1744). Elizabeth Griffith was the daughter of Thomas Griffith by his first wife. On the evening that Mrs Griffith acted Eugenia in the premiere

What passion cannot Music raise & quell
When C ...... struck his corded shell
The listning Drunkards stood around
And wondring on their faces fell
"vide Dry' Ode to S. Cecillias Night
Pub.d for the Benifit of decayed Musicians

Courtesy of the Henry E. Huntington Library and Art Gallery

CHARLEY GRIFFITH

artist unknown

of MacNamara Morgan's tragedy *Philoclea* at Covent Garden on 22 January 1754, the role of Pamela was taken by Elizabeth Griffith, who was using the stage name of Miss Kennedy. If she was not Ursula Griffith, then this Mrs Griffith may have been the aunt, mentioned in Elizabeth Griffith's letter to her husband, who in the spring of 1751 was preparing to leave Ireland for England.

Griffith, Charley [*fl.* 1759?–1792?], *organist.*

Charley Griffith entertained the customers who came to drink the chalybeate waters at Bagnigge Wells by playing the organ in the Long Room of Bagnigge House. The dates between which he flourished are not known. The Wells were opened at least as early as April 1759; and a picture of Griffith "THE BAGNIGGE ORGANFIST" (*sic*) at his console was published about 1792 "for the benefit of decayed musicians."

Griffith, Humphry *d. 1708, singer.*

On 2 April 1699 the singer Humphry Griffith was sworn a Gentleman of the Chapel Royal extraordinary and waited for a salaried position to become vacant. When Nathaniel Vestment died in August 1702 Griffith and John Freeman were sworn jointly to the vacant post, and when Moses Snow died the following December Griffith and Freeman were both sworn to full positions. Humphry Griffith died on 14 September 1708, according to *The Old Cheque Book of the Chapel Royal*. He apparently left no will. On 9 December 1708 administration of his estate was granted William Hall for Mary Griffith, Humphry's minor widow. Within a few months Mary must have reached her majority, for administration of the estate was granted her on 17 May 1709. The administrations described Griffith as of the parish of St Margaret, Westminster.

Griffith, Richard *d. c. 1799, actor, manager.*

Richard Griffith, whose theatrical career was spent primarily with the Theatre Royal, Norwich, was the son of the Irish actor Thomas Griffith (1680–1744), by his first wife, who also may have performed in Ireland. Richard's sister was the dramatist and novelist, Elizabeth Griffith (1727–1793); she married a writer also named Richard Griffith (b. 1725), and she acted, under the stage name of Miss Kennedy, in Dublin between 1749 and 1759 and at Covent Garden, London, in 1753–54. Information about the family will be found in the notices of Thomas Griffith (1680–1744) and Mrs Richard Griffith (1727–1793).

The date of Richard Griffith's birth, probably in Dublin, is not known, but he was, it seems, older than his sister Elizabeth who was born in 1727. With the performers and house servants of the Smock Alley Theatre, he signed a petition to the Lord Lieutenant to open that house after the Kelly riot in 1747. At that time Griffith may have been a house servant, not a performer.

Announced as a gentleman who never appeared on any stage before, he acted Barnwell in *The London Merchant* at Drury Lane Theatre on 18 September 1750. The prompter, Richard Cross, identified him in his diary as "Mr Griffith (Son of Griffith an Actor in Ireland)" and judged him tolerable. About a month later, on 13 October, announced as "the gentleman who had played Barnwell," Griffith acted the First Spirit in *Comus* and then was not seen again in London for another five years.

Announced as from Drury Lane, Griffith joined the Bath company in 1750–51. After an engagement at Edinburgh from 1753 to 1755, he then had another opportunity in London when he played Archer in *The Beaux' Stratagem* at Covent Garden Theatre on 24 October 1755. The impact he made this time on a London audience is not recorded, but back to the provinces he went immediately, playing at Bath between 1756 and 1760. With Keasberry, also of the Bath company, he built a temporary theatre at Winchester in 1760 "in consequence of a Camp consisting of eight regiments," according to James Winston, "that was formed in the neighbourhood, where they performed twelve weeks."

In 1760–61 and 1761–62 Griffith was engaged at Smock Alley. He was also at Edinburgh in 1761, 1762, and 1763, acting a line of fops and fine gentlemen. On 23 May 1763 he made his debut at Norwich.

Once more Griffith ventured into London, this time enjoying at least a somewhat longer trial than on the previous two occasions. At Drury Lane on 18 September 1764 he appeared in his familiar role of Archer and then acted Lord Foppington in *The Careless Husband* on 29 September, followed by Lord Trinket in *The Jealous Wife* on 13 October, the Gentleman Usher in *King Lear* on 5 January 1765, Sir Harry Wilmot in *The Platonic Wife* on 24 January, Jack Meggot in *The Suspicious Husband* on 13 February, and Young Clackit in *The Guardian* on 6 May for his benefit shared with Moody. Save the first two, those were not capital roles, designed to launch an actor into prominence. In this instance, they seemed to have launched Griffith back to the provinces, this time for good. Had David Garrick not been abroad on his grand tour at the time, Griffith would never have been engaged at Drury Lane, even at the modest 8s. 4d. per day (£2 10s. per week) he received in salary for the season. From Paris on 27 January 1765, Garrick wrote to the actor James Love that having seen Griffith perform once he had pronounced that he could never be an actor —"it is one of my never failing rules in Management, not to engage a Man or Woman, who should be marked with that blackest of all Sins against Nature, *Affectation*."

Griffith returned to Norwich to act in 1765–66 and to become manager in November 1766, a position he retained until 1780. His name appeared often in the *Committee Books* of that theatre, in regular attendance at their meetings and in connection with the business of management. On 5 August 1773 his contract with the proprietors was renewed for five years, and on 13 August 1777 they ordered articles drawn up with Mr Griffith "for engaging him as Manager & performer for the Term of three years commencing from the 31st of May last on such Terms as set forth in the former Agreement with him. . . . The penalty in Mr Griffith's Article to be £100. . . ."

When Griffith took his Norwich company to play at Bungay in June 1777, Hannah More saw their performance of *The Clandestine Marriage* and wrote to Garrick on 16 June that, as Lord Ogleby, Griffith "was rather languid than elegant, and mistook a feebleness of exertion for a refinement of breeding; yet, in my poor judgment, he rather did it deficiently than falsely."

Although Griffith's articles were renewed by the Norwich proprietors on 28 May 1779 ("Commencing from the Expiration of the present Article"), on 11 August 1780 he resigned from the management "on Account of the increasing Ill State of his Health" but remained on as an actor. He replaced Pearson as prompter in 1782, a position he held until 29 May 1783 when he was followed by Harwood. Evidently under Griffith's management over 14 years the company had enjoyed success, and according to Jackson's *History of the Scottish Stage* he had supported it "with much credit."

Little is known of Richard Griffith's last years. The year of his death has been given variously as 1798, 1799, and 1805. The last date given perhaps reflects a confusion with the supposed date of the death of the actor and prompter John Griffiths, which was stated in some sources as 1805; but John Griffiths actually died in 1801.

Griffith, Mrs Richard, Elizabeth, née Griffith, stage name Miss Kennedy
1727–1793, playwright, novelist, actress.

Elizabeth Griffith, the daughter of the Irish actor Thomas Griffith (1680–1744) by his first wife, was born on 11 October 1727, probably in Dublin, and not in Glamorganshire as has sometimes been stated,

Harvard Theatre Collection

ELIZABETH GRIFFITH

artist unknown

although her father was reputed to have been a gentleman descended from an ancient family of Wales. She was the sister of Richard Griffith (d. c. 1799), who acted and managed in Ireland and Norwich and had several engagements in London.

Little is known of Elizabeth's early education and life, although her theatrical heritage seems to have determined her for the stage. Announced as "a young Lady" who had never appeared before on any stage, she made her debut at Smock Alley Theatre on 13 October 1749 as Juliet to Thomas Sheridan's Romeo. After playing Juliet again on 20 October, she acted Alinda in *The Loyal Subject* on 10 November ("the third time of her appearing on any stage") and then played Juliet again on 1 December. On 16 December she acted Cordelia to Digges's King Lear. Performances as Cordelia and Juliet followed on 26 January 1750 and 8 February, respectively.

On 10 February the Aungier Street Theatre was opened for a brief season with *Comus,* in which Miss Griffith played the Lady, a role she repeated there on 17 and 24 February. Back at Smock Alley on 9 and 10 March 1750 she acted Andromache in *The Distrest Mother.* The play was scheduled again for her benefit on 23 March, but *The Fair Penitent,* in which she acted Calista for the first time to Sheridan's Horatio, was substituted; tickets could be had of Miss Griffith next to the Green Man in Dame Street. Her other appearances in her debut season at Dublin included Laura in *Tancred and Sigismunda* on 30 March, Andromache again on 17 April, Marcia in *Cato* on 27 April, the Countess of Nottingham in *The Earl of Essex* on 7, 18, and 24 May, and Cordelia again on 22 May. Her last appearance of the season seems to have been as the Lady in *Comus* at Aungier Street on 25 May 1750.

In her second season at Smock Alley in 1750–51, Miss Griffith, whom Hitchcock in *An Historical View of the Irish Stage* (1788) called "a tolerable actress," played Cordelia on 1 October, 17 January, and 22 March; Sylvia in *The Double Gallant,* her first appearance in comedy, on 8 October and then on 2 January and 10 May; Juliet on 29 October and 26 November; the Countess of Nottingham on 31 October and seven other times; Andromache on 5 November and 4 January and Lady Macduff in *Macbeth* on 9 November and perhaps on 9 May. She also appeared as Ismene in the popular *Phaedra and Hippolitus* on 30 November and again on 5 and 12 December, 13 February and 2 March, as well as Leonora in *The Spanish Fryar* on 8 March and 30 April, Pulcheria in *Theodosius* on 9 March, and Lucinda in *The Conscious*

Lovers on 2 May. For her benefit on 19 March 1751, when tickets could be had at her lodgings "at Mrs. Walsh's next door to the Beam and Scales in Fishamble Street," she performed the title role, for the first time, in *Jane Shore.* Her final appearances of the season were as Ismene in *Merope* on 11 and 18 May 1751.

The day after her first appearance as Ismene in *Merope,* she married Richard Griffith (1716–1788) in Dublin on 12 May 1751 in a private ceremony witnessed by her confidante Margaret Hamilton, the Lady Orrery. The marriage was the culmination of a long courtship which had begun in 1746. In 1757, with the assistance of her husband, she published anonymously what purported to be the correspondence of their courtship, in the first two volumes of *A Series of Genuine Letters between Henry and Frances,* her first effort as an author. Written in the sentimental vein, the *Letters* met with great success. Litigation and other pressures on her husband's family necessitated maintaining the secrecy of their marriage for some time, even after the birth of their son Richard in Dublin on 10 June 1752. At the time, Elizabeth lived with her aunt in Abbey Street, Dublin, and then spent the winter at Castle Carbery. Her husband suffered a severe business setback in 1753 when a linen mill that he had set up in Ireland failed, and perhaps for that reason Elizabeth decided to return to the stage, but under an assumed name, and not in Ireland but in England.

Evidently in 1753 Mrs Griffith, leaving her husband behind, journeyed to the Hot Wells, near Bristol, because of "a complaint of the breast." Thence she went to London where on 10 December 1753, announced as "A Gentlewoman from Bath (who never appeared here before)," she acted Clarinda in *The Suspicious Husband* at Covent Garden Theatre. In his "Diary" the Drury Lane prompter Richard Cross identified her as "Miss Kennedy from Bath." On 22 January 1754 she acted Pamela in the premiere of

MacNamara Morgan's tragedy *Philoclea*. The bills did not list roles for the performers, but the cast lists published with the London and Dublin editions of *Philoclea* in 1754 specified that Pamela was played at Covent Garden by Miss Kennedy. The role of the dowager Eugenia was acted by Mrs Griffith (fl. 1752–1755), an actress who perhaps was Elizabeth's stepmother or aunt.

Philoclea, a dull tale mercilessly attacked by Hiffernan in the *Tuner* on 21 January 1754, ran another eight nights through 4 February. The only other mention of Miss Kennedy's name in the bills that season was when she acted Ophelia in *Hamlet* on 19 April 1754 for a benefit she shared with Bencraft.

Soon she returned to Dublin, where she settled with her son Richard and a second child Catherine, living in uncertainty and in circumstances which often kept her husband apart from her. Those were "trying years for Elizabeth," according to Dorothy Eshelman's biographical and critical study *Elizabeth Griffith* (1949). She evidently had given up acting. (According to Genest, after leaving London she went to Dublin, where she acted regularly until 1757 as Miss Kennedy. However, the Miss Kennedy who performed at Smock Alley between 1754–55 and 1758–59 was not Elizabeth but was possibly the sister of Lawrence Kennedy, who with his wife was acting in that company.)

The Griffiths settled in London about 1756. In 1757 appeared the first two volumes of the *Genuine Letters*. Elizabeth's professional writing career flourished until 1782 and resulted in some 24 works, including novels, poems, plays, essays, and translations, some done in collaboration with her husband. The second edition of the *Genuine Letters* appeared in December 1761. The same month she published, anonymously, her translation in two volumes of *The Memoirs of Ninon L'Enclos with her Letters to Monsieur de St. Evre-*

mond, and to the Marquise de Sevigne. The work was dedicated to the Duchess of Bedford, whose husband in 1760 had given Richard Griffith a customs post. The effort was found to be "an innocent amusement" by the critic in the *Critical Review* and "entertaining" by the *London Magazine*. The *Monthly Review* judged her *Ninon* superior to a previous translation and pointed out that "where talents are not inadequate, a female Translator will ever do most justice to a female Original." Her name appeared on the title page of later editions of *Ninon* published in Dublin in 1778 and at Philadelphia in 1806. In 1764 Mrs Griffith published *Amana, a Dramatic Poem*, designed to "show the folly of human wishes." It was so severely criticized that she never published another poem.

Mrs Griffith then turned to writing for the theatre. Her comedy *The Platonic Wife* was produced at Drury Lane on 24 January 1765 while Garrick was away on his two-year continental tour. Described as "new," it was actually an adaptation of Marmontel's *L'Heureux Divorcé*. Not well received on the first night, *The Platonic Wife* was revised and improved by the second performance on 25 January and then ran for a total of six nights, with Mrs Griffith taking her author's benefits on 26 January (when the play was also published) and on 31 January, the last night. Although Victor in his *History of the Theatres* judged the piece "not without Merit in the Stile, Sentiment, and Moral," most critics found it wanting. The *London Chronicle* of 26 January laid its main faults to the author's inexperience:

In a word, want of knowledge of the business of the stage, and of conduct in the piece, seem to be the greatest faults of the female author, who has nevertheless shewn herself a great mistress of sensibility and of agreeable dialogue.

The *Critical Review* of February 1765 was gallantly patronizing: "As this comedy is wrote by a Lady, it shall pass uncensured by the Critical Reviewers." But the *Monthly Review* was less gallant:

The town was so candid and indulgent as to bear with the imperfections they could not but discern, in the unfortunate production of a female pen, during a run of six nights. We will not shew ourselves less courteous to the ingenious Lady, by too rigid an examination of a performance she may wish to forget. Let the curtain therefore descend, and all deficiencies of plot, character, sentiment, language, and moral, be forever veiled from the idea of Criticism.

By 3 March 1765 Garrick had been able to read a copy of the play and wrote from Paris to James Love: "I don't like the *platonick Wife.*"

Undaunted by the critical reception of her first play but perhaps heartened by her benefit receipts (for which figures are unavailable), Mrs Griffith worked up another piece within a year. On 9 January 1766 her comedy *The Double Mistake* was premiered at Covent Garden and ran with moderate success for a total of 15 nights. It was published on 14 January 1766 and again a week later in a corrected edition on 23 January. The *Critical Review* of that month pointed out that the play was not a new comedy but was "little more than an alteration of an old play called *Elvira, or The worst was not always true,* which stands the first in the 12th volume of Dodsley's collection." (George Digby's *Elvira* had been produced at Lincoln's Inn Fields Theatre in November 1664.) A paragraph by "Censor Dramaticus" in the *Public Advertiser* on 11 January, the day of the author's benefit night, puffed the piece:

It is chaste, sententious and genteel in its dialogue, interesting in its plot, the characters all of consequence, strongly marked and happily kept up, and even the virtuoso entertaining without being tiresome. I heartily wish it

success, and congratulate the author on such a production, which shows that virtuous principles in high life render the persons that possess them doubly charming, and add real grace and dignity to their appearance in public life. . . . I hope I may be believed when I say I have not the most distant knowledge of the author, and that impartiality shall ever be, and ever was my constant plan in observations of this kind.

Emboldened by the success of her second play, Mrs Griffith wrote to Garrick on 31 May 1766 about another play she hoped he would produce. Garrick replied that previous commitments would prevent his doing it the following winter, but he offered his congratulations for the recent success of *The Double Mistake,* his opinion of which, confided to another correspondent, had not been favorable. Perhaps the play which Garrick rejected was *Dorval, or the Test of Virtue,* a translation of Diderot's *Le Fils naturel.* Unproduced, *Dorval* was published anonymously by Dodsley in 1767. It has been suggested that Garrick's influence helped Mrs Griffith with its publication.

Garrick soon found himself the regular recipient over the next 12 years of irksome letters from Mrs Griffith, to which he tried to respond with patience and civility. In 1768 he suggested that Mrs Griffith busy herself with a translation of *Eugenié* and provided her with the Beaumarchais text. The play opened at Drury Lane 4 February 1769 under the title of *The School for Rakes* with new scenes, costumes, and decorations. The previous December Mrs Griffith had annoyed Garrick by trying to dictate the casting. On 6 December 1768 the manager rebuked her and she apologized. As doctored by Garrick, *The School for Rakes* enjoyed considerable success for 13 performances, ten of them in February, until its momentum was interrupted by the beginning of the actors' benefit nights. The role of Mrs Winifred was acted by Mrs Clive, who had postponed her retirement to launch the piece until she was replaced by Mrs Hopkins on 4 May 1769. Although he did not act in it, Garrick provided the epilogue spoken by Mrs Clive.

In her dedication of the published play to Garrick, Mrs Griffith wrote a graceful appreciation of the manager's assistance, a gesture which Benjamin Victor in the *History of the Theatres* considered most appropriate in view of "the great Services he did her, in surmounting those Difficulties she met with in her Fable!" Much of the credit continued to go to Garrick. The *Critical Review* of March 1769 found the play not "unworthy of the great dramatic genius, who lent his assistance in adapting it to the English stage." The notices were mixed. A long analysis by Francis Gentleman in *The Dramatic Censor*, after pointing out many faults and shortcomings, concluded that:

the *School for Rakes,* from its moral tendency, and the excellent sentiments with which in several places it is sprinkled, may be recommended as a comedy more deserving of attention, both in public and private, than many other pieces of much greater critical merit; virtue is patronized and inculcated through the whole, without being once put to the blush, or in the least degree sacrificed to applause-catching humour.

The first edition of *The School for Rakes* was published on 13 February 1769. Two other editions appeared in 1769, two in Dublin in 1770 and 1795, and another in London in 1797, after Mrs Griffith's death.

In June of 1769 was published *Two Novels in Letters*, dedicated to the Duke of Bedford, the first part of which, in two volumes, consisted of *The Delicate Distress* by Mrs Griffith; the second part, in another two volumes, contained *The Gordian Knot,* by her husband. In 1770 she published her translation of the *Memoirs, Anecdotes, and Character of the Court of Lewis XIV*, in two volumes. In 1771 appeared her second novel *The History of Lady Barton* and another translation, *The*

Shipwreck and Adventures of Mons. Pierre Viaud.

New plays about which Mrs Griffith had corresponded with Garrick in September 1769 and February 1770 did not come to fruition. The management of Covent Garden, however, took her comedy *A Wife in the Right* and scheduled it for its first performance on 5 March 1772. Shuter, who had played Belmont in *The Double Mistake* in 1766, paid little attention to the preparation of his role of Governor Anderson in *A Wife in the Right* and was drunk during the rehearsals he managed to attend. When he arrived drunk at the theatre on the day originally intended for the opening, the premiere was necessarily postponed until 9 March.

According to Mrs Griffith's preface to the published work, when Shuter made his first entrance the hissing of the audience called him to account for his negligence; he addressed them with an admission of his drunkenness and begged their pardon. The circumstance so rattled Shuter that he was unable to recover sufficiently to play with authority: "in the hurry of his spirits the actor not only forgot his part, the deficiency of which he endeavoured to supply with his own dialect, but also seemed to lose all idea of the character . . . and made the Governor appear in a light which the author never intended: that of a mean, ridiculous buffoon." Further antagonized, the audience threw coins and apples, breaking a chandelier, and would not suffer the play to be given out again for the following night.

Never repeated, *A Wife in the Right* was damned by the *Town and Country Magazine* (March 1772) whose critic did not give particulars, "being unwilling to disturb the ashes of the dead." On 12 March 1772 the *London Chronicle* printed the epilogue and a week later the prologue, the latter written by George Colman. Nevertheless, on 12 June 1772, the play was "Beautifully printed on fine Royal Paper" at five shillings, for the author at No 2, Hyde Street, Bloomsbury, with an impressive list of more than 500 subscribers, including Mr and Mrs Garrick, Edmund Burke, James Boswell, the Duchess of Bedford, the Earl of Chesterfield, Charles Fox, Mrs Montagu, Horace Walpole, Kitty Clive, Jane Pope, and Isaac Bickerstaff. In a letter dated 27 March 1772 (in the Huntington Library), Mrs J. H. Pye wrote to Edward Jerningham: "Well, my dear Sir, you find I was but too much in the right concerning the success of poor Mrs. Griffith's Play. I hope I have not taken an unwarrantable liberty in gracing her List of Subscribers with your name. I am sure you have such a share of Benevolence in your Disposition that you would gladly contribute to soften the Distress of a Fellow Creature, & that a Female!"

In December 1776 Mrs Griffith published her translation of *The Barber of Seville*, with an address to Richard B. Sheridan, but the work was never produced. Sheridan, however, did produce *The Times*, her final play, at Drury Lane on 2 December 1779. Another suggestion by Garrick, *The Times* was an adaptation of Goldoni's *Le Bourru Bienfaisant*. Six years earlier, Mrs Griffith had tried to interest Garrick in the play in a letter of 28 May 1773, but the manager remained aloof, as he did again in May 1775, when she wrote him for assistance in retrieving her dramatic fame, and also in November 1778, about three months before his death. With an epilogue provided by Horace Walpole, *The Times* was a modest success, running nine nights and bringing the author £146 5s. 6d., £105 15s. 6d., and £186 5s. (but less house charges of £105 in each instance) at her benefits on 6 and 9 December 1779 and 21 February 1780. Oulton in his *History of the Theatre in London* (1796) called the piece "more a *sentimental novel* than a Comedy," an observation following the comment of the *Monthly Review* (March 1780) that the genius of the writer

"seems to delight in touches of sentiment rather than strokes of humor." The *London Packet* (1/3 December 1779) reported that on opening night "Many persons appeared in the house determined to injure the piece by hissing on every trifling occasion — an inhumanity, where there was so much merit, and so few faults, deserves the severest censure, if not chastisement."

Other works by Mrs Griffith included *The Morality of Shakespeare's Drama Illustrated*, her only critical study, published in 1775 and dedicated to Garrick; *The Fatal Effects of Inconstancy*, 1774; *The Story of Lady Juliana Harley*, 1776; *A Letter from Mons. Desenfons*, 1777; *The Princess of Cleves*, 1777; *A Collection of Novels*, edited in three volumes consisting of works by Mrs Behn, Mrs Aubin, Eliza Haywood, and some translations, 1777; *Novelettes Selected for the Use of Young Ladies and Gentlemen; written by Dr. Goldsmith, Mrs Griffith, &c.*, 1780; *Zayde, a Spanish History*, 1780; and *Essays, Addressed to Young Married Women*, 1782. The publication titled *Letters Addressed to Young Married Women*, which was issued in Philadelphia by John Turner in 1796, three years after her death, was evidently not written by Mrs Griffith, despite the accompaniment of her biographical sketch copied from the *European Magazine and London Review*, 1782.

When Mrs Griffith relinquished her London life is not known for certain. Probably by the early 1780s she and her husband had returned to Ireland to live at Millicent, Nass, in County Kildare, on the estate acquired by their son Richard who, having made his fortune in East India trade, became a member of the Irish Parliament in 1783. Her daughter Catherine had married the Rev John Buck, rector of Desertcreat.

In one of her letters, Anna Seward gossiped that Elizabeth and her husband Richard Griffith had separated because of his seduction of a young heiress, but there seems to be no evidence to substantiate the story. Richard Griffith, who is noticed in *The Dictionary of National Biography*, died at Millicent on 11 February 1788. Five years later, also at Millicent, Elizabeth Griffith died on 5 January 1793. Her obituary in the *Gentleman's Magazine* for that month read: "At Millicent, in Ireland, Mrs. Griffith, relict of Richard Griffith, Esq., and joint author, with him of the Letters between Henry and Frances. A late poet characterized her excellence in composition, intended to reach the heart, by calling her 'A second Sappho, with a purer flame.'"

Elizabeth Griffith has been characterized "among the first in the second rank of novelists of the century," whose works, in the view of her contemporaries, were "unexceptional and entertaining." For a critical and biographical assessment of her works, the reader should consult Dorothy Eshelman's *Elizabeth Griffith* (1949).

Portraits of Mrs Griffith were engraved by MacKenzie, after J. Thomas, as a plate to *Lady's Monthly Museum*, 1801, and by an unknown engraver (n.d.).

Griffith, Thomas [George?] 1680–1744, *actor, singer, manager, poet.*

Thomas Griffith was born in Dublin in 1680 of a respectable Welsh family. Thomas was given a liberal education and then apprenticed to a mathematical-instrument maker—about 1694, we can assume. Before he had served three years of his apprenticeship he married, and his father had to buy the remaining four years of Thomas's time. Young Griffith's wife is said to have been an actress, and perhaps through her he became interested in the stage.

Joseph Ashbury, the manager of the Smock Alley Theatre in Dublin, engaged Griffith at a low salary, probably about 1698, as Clark in *The Early Irish Stage* suggests (and surely not in 1692 as stated in Gilbert's *History of the City of Dublin*). The young actor became friendly with Robert Wilks during the 1698–99 season, and it was very likely Wilks who was responsible for Griffith's coming to London. Of Griffith's roles at Smock Alley in 1698–99 we know little; years later Griffith told the prompter Chetwood that he had acted Rakehell in *She Wou'd If She Cou'd* and Sir Fopling Flutter in *The Man of Mode*, but though he may well have played those parts in later years, one might question if a fledgling of about 18 would have attempted them.

Chetwood tells us that in 1699 Griffith left for London with the Wilkses, the Norrises, and Bowen. Wilks supposedly arranged for Griffith to be taken on at Drury Lane for a small salary. London theatrical records contain no trace of Griffith that early, and historians may have confused Griffith with the London actor Philip Griffin, who was in and out of London about that time. Most of Griffith's stage career was passed in Dublin, though he made occasional appearances in London. On 31 December 1702, for example, he acted Count Pirro in *The Heiress* at Lincoln's Inn Fields, according to the cast list in the 1703 edition of Mrs Centlivre's play. That theatre was managed by Thomas Betterton; Griffith's friend Robert Wilks, it should be noted, acted at the rival Drury Lane playhouse. Chetwood later told the story that Wilks introduced Griffith to the prompter at Lincoln's Inn Fields, John Downes. Downes permitted Griffith to act the small role of Pizarro in *The Indian Emperor* without Betterton's knowing it. When the veteran actor-manager found out, he cried, "Zounds, Downs! What sucking Scaramouch have you sent on there?" After that, said Chetwood, Griffith stuck to comedy. It is a pleasant tale, but there is no record of Griffith's having acted that role at Lincoln's Inn Fields; the play was given during the 1702–3 season, however.

Griffith was back in Dublin for the 1703–4 season. *The London Stage* lists both a Griffin and a Griffith at Drury Lane in 1704–5, but the one role noted for Griffith—Manly in *The Plain Dealer* on 6 February 1705—was one of Philip Griffin's regular parts, and we take the "Griffith" to be an error. In Dublin in 1709 Griffith wrote a commendatory poem for Tony Aston's *The Coy Shepherdess* when it was given its first production. The following year Griffith was given a lucrative post in the revenue by Lord Southwell; the actor held the position until his death.

Thomas came back to London in the spring of 1712 to act Teague in *The Committee* on 12 April and Ned Blunt in *The Rover* on 3 May at Drury Lane; he was hailed in the bills as "from Ireland." But Griffith had too many irons in the fire in Ireland to spend much time in London. Early in 1713 a lease was granted to Griffith, John Evans, Francis Elrington, and Joseph Ashbury on a second-floor room measuring 105 feet by 21 feet in a building just off the Great Street in Cork. The group seems to have made use of the room as a theatre, on a rental basis, some years previously. About 1713, too, Griffith had an interest in the theatre near the Blackfriars Abbey in Waterford. At Smock Alley in Dublin on 16 June 1713, Griffith is known to have spoken a prologue he had written.

In the fall of 1714 Thomas returned to London to act once more at Drury Lane. He played Ben in *Love for Love* on 30 November and his old role of Teague in *The Committee* on 6 December. With him that season in London were his friends Elrington and Evans, both of whom acted more frequently than did Griffith; they were granted benefits in the spring of 1715, but Griffith was not, and, indeed, he may not have remained in London for the full season. Years later Colley Cibber remembered in his *Apology* two "uncelebrated Actors" who came over from Dublin about 1713–14 (they were identified as Griffith and Elrington in *The Laureat*). Cibber said Wilks had hired the pair without consulting his co-managers, Cibber and Thomas Doggett. Wilks had passed himself off as the sole manager of Drury Lane and had

proposed to give the Irish players benefits (or one shared benefit). When Doggett heard of that he "bounc'd and grew almost as untractable as *Wilks*," but Cibber managed to smooth things over, and the pair were given their benefit, which, said Cibber, did not do well. Cibber made no mention of Evans, nor did *The Laureat*, so the story is somewhat muddled. In any case, Griffith was back in Dublin before the end of 1715, for in that year he is known to have acted the Poet in *Timon of Athens* and his favorite role of Teague.

Thanks to the research of the late W. S. Clark, a number of Griffith's Dublin roles from 1720–21 through 1735–36 are known: Captain Novite in *Wexford Wells*, Ben in *Love for Love*, Ned Brand in *The Rover*, Gomez in *The Spanish Fryar*, Razor in *The Provok'd Wife*, Humphrey in *The Tender Husband*, Barnaby Brittle in *The Amorous Widow*, Foppington in *The Careless Husband*, Roderigo in *Othello*, Fernando in *The Fatal Marriage*, Scrub in *The Stratagem*, Snap in *Love's Last Shift*, Tom in *The Conscious Lovers*, Daniel in *Oroonoko*, Antonio in *Venice Preserv'd*, Don Cholerick in *Love Makes a Man*, Falstaff in *1 Henry IV*, Marplot in *The Busy Body*, the Gravedigger in *Hamlet*, Trappanti in *She Wou'd and She Wou'd Not*, Mr Nonsense in *The Northern Lass*, Townsman in *The Island Princess*, Pharamond in *Philaster*, the title role in *Hob*, Teague in *The Committee*, Justice Clark in *The Jovial Crew*, Hecate in *Macbeth*, Lopez in *All Vows Kept*, and Jacomo in *Don John*. All except the last, which Griffith acted in 1735–36 at the Aungier Street Theatre, were performed at Smock Alley.

On 14 or 16 September 1721 Griffith (called George in one newspaper; perhaps that was his middle name) was appointed Master of the Revels in Ireland. (Lepper and Crossle in their *History of . . . Masons in Ireland* say Griffith was made Deputy Master of the Lodge.) When the appointment was announced Griffith was described as the chief manager of the Smock Alley Theatre; he, Elrington, and Evans ran the playhouse for a number of years. Griffith kept the Revels position until 1729, when he was succeeded by Thomas Elrington. Griffith also held the post of Tide Waiter to the Port of Dublin, discharging his duties, it was said, with great courage. He was small in stature, but despite his size he stood up to armed men who tried to smuggle contraband or leave Ireland illegally. Griffith poked fun at his stature; whenever the mock tragedy *Alexander* was to be played, he advertised that "The part of Alexander the Great [would be] performed by Little Griffith."

An active Mason, Thomas Griffith probably held the position of Grand Secretary of the Irish Masons from 1725; he was the first to hold the post, his principal duty being the installation of the Grand Officers. Griffith's brother Masons usually walked in procession to the theatre for his benefits, which were always well attended because of their support. A good singer, Griffith sometimes entertained his audiences with Masonic songs, one occasion being on 24 June 1725 at Smock Alley when he sang the Mason's apprentice song.

During the 1732–33 Smock Alley season Griffith busied himself with some real estate transactions. On 21 February 1733 the rival Rainsford Street Theatre opened, so on 28 February Griffith and his colleagues leased some land in Aungier Street from Samuel Taylor and from David Digges Latouch. On 8 May the first stone was laid, and on 9 March 1734 the Aungier Street playhouse opened for business. For the opening "a new Prologue proper to the Occasion was spoke by Mr. Griffith, one of the Managers; and received with Universal Applause."

By that time Griffith had remarried. We are not certain what happened to his first wife, and of her we know little beyond the report that she was an actress. Possibly she and Thomas were the Mr and Mrs "Griffin" (Benjamin Griffin does not qualify) who, on 29 November 1729 in London at the Front Long Room next to the Haymarket Theatre, performed with a group led by Thomas Griffith's old friend Tony Aston. In *Tunbridge Walks* on that date "Griffin" played Loveworth and his wife acted Penelope; on 2 December in *The Stratagem* he was Sullen and she Dorinda. It is significant that Thomas Griffith, hailed, as usual, as from Dublin, was in London the following spring, playing at Drury Lane. On 2 April 1730 he acted Gomez in *The Spanish Fryar*; on 30 April for his benefit he appeared as Cholerick in *Love Makes a Man*; and on 12 May he was Ben in *Love for Love*. In any case, by 1733 Griffith had taken a second wife: Ursula, the daughter of Rev Richard Foxcroft of Portarlington, Ireland. She subscribed, as Mrs Ursula Griffith, to the comedy *All Vows Kept*, which was published in Dublin in 1733.

On 4 March 1735 for his benefit in Dublin (theatre not known) Griffith chose *The Country Wife*. His brethren in the Grand Lodge attended in force, as usual, but the Dublin *Evening Post* on 8 March deplored the choice of play and hoped the Masons would in the future discourage Griffith from producing such a vile and obscene work. But Griffith in the mid-1730s had more serious problems. From Jervis Quay on 8 February 1736 Griffith wrote to Dean Swift:

NOTHING but the last extremity, and your humanity, can plead my excuse for troubling you with the many misfortunes that at present attend me, having defended myself from merciless creditors as long as my circumstances could possibly protect me, but now they all fall upon me with determined cruelty, and resolve to undo me, though I am willing to divide the last shilling of my late benefit play amongst them, but that is not sufficient by forty or fifty pounds to answer their demands; my good friend Counsellor B—— having pursued me with implacable malice, and run me to such expense at law that each original debt is doubled, and executions taken out against me, and no hopes to save me and my poor helpless family from ruin unless your charitable known goodness interposes. Therefore, dear Sir, my last and only hope is fixed on your generous disposition, [I hope you] who saved a whole unhappy nation from destruction, will lend your supporting hand to defend me and my little state from misery and misfortune, and I will with utmost gratitude repay it at my next benefit, or in such other manner as you shall please to direct. . . .

We do not know if Swift obliged with aid, but the finances of the Aungier Street Theatre continued unstable for several years.

In the 17 July 1736 issue of *Faulkner's Dublin Journal* Griffith published one of his love songs and stated that many of his songs were in Allen Ramsay's collection. "Mr Griffith is going to publish by subscription all his Poems in one volume octavo," the notice said, but there is no indication that he ever did.

Griffith's performing activity during the late 1730s is only partly documented. From 1736–37 to 1743–44 at Aungier Street he is known to have acted Pearmain in *The Recruiting Officer*, Shorthose in *Wit Without Money*, and Teague in *The Committee*. On 11 October 1736 he spoke a prologue on the anniversary of their Majesties's coronation; he held a benefit which was puffed by the Masons in the 17 November 1736 issue of *Hamilton's Dublin Daily Advertiser*; on 24 May 1737 he shared a benefit with two others when *The Jew of Venice* and *The Virgin Unmask'd* were performed; he spoke a prologue on 16 September 1737; and he had a benefit on 26 January 1738. Though he continued receiving benefits, Griffith seems not to have acted too frequently during his last years. In January 1743 he wrote a special prologue for the Prince of Wales's birthday, but Bardin, not Griffith, spoke it.

Faulkner's Dublin Journal reported that

Thomas Griffith died on 23 January 1744 at the age of 63. He was, the paper said,

a most entertaining and humerous Comedian, who formerly entertained the Town in the most agreeable manner. As he was a pleasant, facetious, good-natured Companion, and generous to Persons in Distress, it is not doubted, but the public will favour his Widow with their presence next Thursday at her Benefit, the Gentlemen Proprietors of the Theatres having generously given her a benefit on this occasion.

Thomas Griffith left a daughter Elizabeth, whom he had had by his first wife. She acted as Miss Kennedy in 1754 when a Mrs Griffith—possibly Thomas's widow Ursula—also performed. Elizabeth's career was chiefly as an author. She is separately entered in this dictionary as Mrs Richard Griffith. Thomas Griffith also left a son, Richard, who became a provincial manager, acted in London in the mid-eighteenth century, and died about 1799.

Griffith, Mrs Thomas the first [*fl. c. 1697–1729*], *actress.*

Thomas Griffith, before he had served three years of his apprenticeship to a mathematical-instrument maker in Ireland, married an actress. The date of the marriage is not known, but Thomas was born in 1680 and would have been apprenticed at the age of 14, so perhaps he married about 1697. His wife may have been responsible for interesting Thomas in the stage, but we know virtually nothing about her. Perhaps she and Thomas were the Mr and Mrs "Griffin" who acted for Thomas's friend Tony Aston at the Front Long Room next to the Haymarket Theatre in London in 1729; no other performers named Griffith or Griffin seem to qualify. On 29 November Mrs "Griffin" played Penelope in *Tunbridge Walks*, and on 2 December she was Dorinda in *The Stratagem*. By 1733 Thomas had married a second time; we do not know what happened to his first wife.

The first Mrs Thomas Griffith was the mother of Elizabeth Griffith (Mrs Richard Griffith), who was born in 1727, and of Richard Griffith, who died about 1799.

Griffiths. *See also* **GRIFFIN** and **GRIFFITH.**

Griffiths, Mr ₁*fl. 1788–1793*₁, *actor.*
Mr Griffiths acted Captain Flash in *Miss in her Teens* on 29 April 1788 and the same role and Clodpole in *Barnaby Brittle* on 30 September 1788, at the Haymarket Theatre. He also acted the Starved Friar in *Harlequin's Museum* at Covent Garden Theatre during the Christmas season of 1792–93. Perhaps he was John Griffiths (d. 1801), the sometime Drury Lane actor.

Griffiths, Mr ₁*fl. 1789–1791*₁, *singer.*
A Mr Griffiths sang in the spring oratorios at Covent Garden Theatre from 1789 through 1791. He also sang in the Academy of Ancient Music concerts in Tottenham Street in 1789 and in the concerts directed by Ashley at the Crown and Anchor Tavern, the Strand, in June 1789.

Griffiths, Mr ₁*fl. 1794–1796*₁, *boxkeeper.*
A Mr Griffiths was a boxkeeper at Drury Lane Theatre in 1794–95 and 1795–96. On 29 January 1796 he was paid £7 4s. for 96 nights. With numerous house servants he shared in benefits on 6 June 1795 and 13 June 1796.

Griffiths, Mr ₁*fl. 1799–1800*₁, *dancer.*
A Mr Griffiths danced as a pantomime character in 29 performances of *The Volcano* at Covent Garden in 1799–1800.

Griffiths, Mrs ₁*fl. 1794–1795*₁, *wardrobe keeper.*
A Mrs Griffiths was paid 10s. per week for working in the women's wardrobe at Covent Garden Theatre in 1794–95.

Griffiths, Master ₁*fl. 1770–1771*₁, *equestrian. See* **GRIFFITHS, J.** ₁*fl. 1772–1796*₁.

Griffiths, Master ₁*fl. 1797*₁, *actor.*
A Master Griffiths played a Young Devil in a single performance of *A Duke and No Duke* at Covent Garden Theatre on 8 April 1797.

Griffiths, Miss *b. 1783. See* **STEWART, MRS JAMES R.**

Griffiths, Miss ₁*fl. 1792*₁, *dancer.*
A Miss Griffiths was a dancer in the summer company at Richmond, Surrey, in 1792. Among the dances she appeared in was *The Rustic Villagers* on 13 July 1792.

Griffiths, J. ₁*fl. 1772–1796*₁, *equestrian.*
J. Griffiths (sometimes Griffith or Griffin) performed feats of horsemanship at Astley's Amphitheatre regularly between 1772 and 1789. He was probably the equestrian "Griffin" whose name was listed with Astley and his son for exhibitions on Durdham Down at Bristol during October 1772. He also performed with the Astleys at Birmingham in 1776.

In May of 1792 Griffiths was at Bristol as a member of Handy and Franklin's Troop, by which time he had established a riding school in Limekiln Lane. He continued to operate his school in that city at least until 23 May 1796—when he was called "J. Griffin" in his advertisements—and probably beyond.

A Mrs Griffiths, no doubt his wife, also performed feats of horsemanship and tumbling at Astley's in London between 1772 and 1782. "Master Griffith," probably their son, announced as an apprentice to Astley, exhibited "several pleasing performances on 2 horses" at Astley's in London on 16 July 1770 and then throughout the remainder of the month; the boy also performed there, sometimes on as many as four horses, in June 1771.

A Griffiths family, according to Arthur Saxon, was active at both Astley's and the Royal Circus during the early nineteenth century. A Miss Margaret Griffith, a lady rider of Liverpool, became the first wife of the equestrian Andrew Ducrow in 1818; she died in 1837.

Griffiths, Mrs J. [fl. 1772–1782], *equestrienne. See* **GRIFFITHS, J.** [fl. 1772–1796].

Griffiths, John d. 1801, actor, prompter.

John Griffiths (often Griffith) passed some 24 years on the London stage, yet little is known of his career beyond the numerous minor roles he performed, usually in light comedy, farce, or pantomime. Though he may have appeared earlier, as a supernumerary in London or the provinces, his first notice in the bills was for an unspecified role in *The Devil Upon Two Sticks* on 16 May 1770 at the Haymarket Theatre under Samuel Foote's management. That summer with Foote, Griffiths filled about 20 different roles, albeit modest ones, a circumstance which suggests considerable prior experience. These included, among others, Francisco in *Hamlet*, an Officer in *Venice Preserv'd*, Bruin in *The Mayor of Garratt*, the Physician in *King Lear*, Austria in *King John*, Arcas in *Damon and Phillida*, Bridoun in *The Commissary*, Jupiter in *Midas*, and the Prompter in *Taste*.

Every summer between 1770 and 1777, except 1773, Griffiths acted at the Haymarket. At some time during that period he also became the prompter there, in which capacity he took a benefit on 19 September 1774. The roles he played would not have prevented him, it would seem, from being the prompter, as they were usually of the walk-on or supernumerary variety: Gibbet in *The Beaux' Stratagem*, Governor in *The Author*, Subtle in *The Tobacconist*, Heeltap in *The Mayor of Garratt*, Barberino in *A Duke and No Duke*, Robin in *The Knights*, and unspecified small roles.

In 1771–72 Griffiths began a winter engagement with Drury Lane Theatre which extended for 11 seasons. On 12 October 1771 at that theatre he and Atkins were paid £1 5s. "to make up salary," and on 11 November 1771 Griffiths played Sattin in *The Miser*, followed by Francisco in *The Tempest* on 2 December, Hortensius in *Timon of Athens* on 4 December, and the Priest in *Twelfth Night* on 10 December. Over the years at Drury Lane Griffiths's line seldom varied from his accustomed roles at the Haymarket and included, in addition, a Fryar in *The Witches*, Jarvis in *The Fashionable Lover*, Sir Jasper in *The Citizen*, and numerous servants and supernumeraries in such pieces as *The Irish Widow*, *Harlequin's Invasion*, *The Pigmy Revels*, *The School for Wives*, and *The Earl of Warwick*.

In 1775 Griffiths subscribed to the Drury Lane Fund. His salary in 1775–76 was £1 5s. per week, but it was raised to £1 10s. the following season. On 18 May 1779 he shared benefit receipts of £146 16s. with Chaplin, Holcroft, and Miss Field. He was probably the Mr "Griffith" who, by desire of the Noble Order of Bucks, enjoyed a specially licensed benefit at the Haymarket on 20 December 1779, when *Jane Shore* was played and he acted Belmour.

After 1781–82, Griffiths no longer acted at Drury Lane or at least did not appear in the bills. According to the *Thespian Dictionary* (1805) he had become a prompter at that theatre, but the author confused Griffiths's service in that capacity at the Haymarket with his tenure at Drury Lane. Griffiths subsequently acted in London only on occasion. On 31 January 1785 at the Haymarket he was Mat o' th' Mint in *The Beggar's Opera*. For his benefit on 6 March 1786, by permission of the Lord Chamberlain, he acted Major Sturgeon in *The Mayor of Garratt* at the Haymarket; that night "some of the principal performers in London" supported the singing program. Three months later, on 5 June 1786, he acted Sir Charles Marlow in *She Stoops to Conquer* and Justice Guttle in *The Lying Valet* with a company which played at the Windsor Castle Inn, King Street, Hammersmith, for 17 nights that summer. In September he performed at Richmond, Surrey. At the Haymarket in 1786–87 he acted Justice Guttle in *The Lying Valet* on 18 December, the Devil in *The Devil Upon Two Sticks* for the benefit of Harwood (the Drury Lane prompter) on 8 January, and Cadwallader in *The Author* on 12 March 1787 for his own benefit, when tickets could be had of him at No 3, Southampton Buildings, Holborn, and numerous places about town.

When the Royalty Theatre in Well Street was opened by his former Drury Lane colleague John Palmer on 20 June 1787, Griffiths was its prompter, but his tenure was aborted by the short life of the venture. Supposedly he later became prompter at the Royal Circus in St George's Fields. Probably he was the Mr "Griffes," of No 19, Greville Street, Hatton Garden, who shared a benefit with Mr Tanns at the Royal Circus on 31 August 1791. He may have been the Griffiths who performed at Manchester in 1783, 1790, and 1792.

According to John Philip Kemble's notation on a manuscript now in the British Museum, John Griffiths died on 21 November 1801. In his *Itinerant* Samuel W. Ryley indicated that Griffiths died at Shrewsbury in 1799, an old man; but there is no record of his burial at either of the city's churches, St Chad or St Mary. The Miss Griffiths who was a great favorite as a singer at the Manchester theatre between 1799 and 1805 may have been his daughter.

Griffiths, Nehemiah ₁*fl. 1794*₁, *violinist, violist.*

Nehemiah Griffiths, of No 10, Adam's Place, Borough, was listed in Doane's *Musical Directory* in 1794 as a violinist and violist and a member of the Surrey Chapel Society.

Griffiths, Sarah ₁*fl. 1746–1771*₁, *house servant.*

Mrs Sarah Griffiths was a house servant at Covent Garden Theatre for some 25 years, from 1746–1747 through 1770–71. Probably she worked with the wardrobe or properties. The theatre paid her on 11 February 1758 for "Flowers, a sash, and work for the dancers £4 15*s.*" and on 6 January 1768 16*s.* for green wreaths. Each spring she shared in benefit tickets with numerous other house personnel, usually taking as her portion a very modest amount, as for example: £1 4*s.* 6*d.* on 22 May 1747, £1 9*s.* on 19 May 1760, and £2 18*s.* 6*d.* on 19 May 1769.

"Grim." *See* **GRIMALDI, GIUSEPPE.**

Grim. *See* **QUIN.**

"Grimacier, The." *See* **"CELEBRATED GRIMACIER, THE."**

Grimaesse, Mr ₁*fl. 1729*₁, *dancer.*

When *Italian Jealousy* was performed at Lincoln's Inn Fields on 8 April 1729, the role of Scaramouch was taken by Newhouse, according to the *Daily Courant*, or by Grimaesse, according to the *Daily Journal*. Grimaesse sounds suspiciously like a pseudonym.

Grimaldi, Miss ₁*fl. 1778–1781*₁, *dancer.*

Miss Grimaldi, one of the daughters of Giuseppe Grimaldi (d. 1788), performed a comic dance with Master Mills at Drury Lane on 26 September 1778. For her father's benefit on 5 May 1779 she danced with him, Master Mills, and others in *The Tempest*. On 19 April 1781 a Miss Grimaldi danced with her brother Joe in *The*

Wizard of the Rocks when he made his first appearance on the Sadler's Wells stage. They danced again at the Wells on 18 May 1781 and probably many times thereafter during the following several seasons. In *Grimaldi, King of Clowns*, Richard Findlater stated that the Miss Grimaldi who danced with Joe at the Wells was Mary, eldest daughter of Giuseppe. Findlater mistakenly believed Mary to have been about 12 years old in 1781, but actually she was about 18 and was then Mrs Williamson, having married the pantomime actor James Williamson at St George, Bloomsbury, on 24 January 1779, when both were minors. Therefore, the Miss Grimaldi who danced at Drury Lane and Sadler's Wells between 1778 and 1781 was one of Giuseppe's three younger daughters—Isabella Louisa (b. 1764), Margaret Charlotta (b. 1765), or Catherine (b. 1767). Information about these children will be found in their father's notice.

Grimaldi, Alexander [fl. 1706–1729], doorkeeper.

Alexander Grimaldi was a stage doorkeeper at Lincoln's Inn Fields Theatre by 1721–22, and perhaps earlier, through at least 1728–29. On 4 May 1722, when he had a benefit, £18 2s. in money and £44 19s. in tickets was taken in receipts. A payment of £10 10s. was made to him on 29 January 1724, and additional payments, on account, of £10 each were made on 23 February and 9 December 1726. His name was found on the theatre's free list for tickets from 1726–27 through 1728–29.

He was no doubt the Alexander Grimaldi who with his wife Dorcas baptized the following children at St Martin-in-the-Fields: Elizabeth Grimaldi, born on 10 December, baptized on 15 December 1706; Alexander Grimaldi, born on 28 December 1707, baptized on 4 January 1708 (buried on 31 May 1708); Mary Grimaldi, born on 20 November, baptized on 10 December 1710 (buried on 21 December 1711);

By permission of the Trustees of the British Museum

ALEXANDER GRIMALDI

artist unknown

Alexander Grimaldi, born on 5 November, baptized on 28 November 1714; Charles Grimaldi, born on 5 April, baptized on 12 April 1716. Another child, Arabella Grimaldi, was baptized at St Paul, Covent Garden, on 25 August 1709.

Probably his wife was the Mrs Grimaldi who, announced as making her first appearance on the stage, sang in Italian and English with two other novices, Mrs Davis and Mrs Forsythe, at Lincoln's Inn Fields on 16 May 1726.

A vignette of Alexander Grimaldi, by an unknown engraver, is in the British Museum. A manuscript notation on the bottom of the print informs us that Grimaldi was a Venetian, the stage doorkeeper at Lincoln's Inn Fields, and "much employd in workes of gold ornaments on looking glass, borders, sconces, &c."

Grimaldi, Mrs [Alexander, Dorcas?] [fl. 1706–1726], singer.

A Mrs Grimaldi, Mrs Davis, and Mrs Forsythe—"being the first Time of their respective appearances on the Stage,"—sang in Italian and English at Lincoln's Inn Fields Theatre on 6 May 1726. Probably she was Dorcas Grimaldi, wife of Alexander Grimaldi (fl. 1706–1729), doorkeeper at that theatre, whose children are noted in his entry.

1837), was a member of a dynasty of Italian performers which stretched through western Europe and across the Channel, but there is little basis to the claims that there was a royal pedigree in the family with lineage to the Prince of Monaco. We find no evident connection between the theatrical Grimaldis and the English miniature painter William Grimaldi (1751–1830),

GRIMALDI GENEALOGY

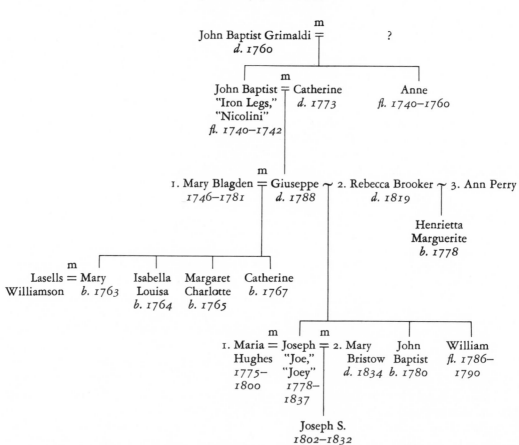

Grimaldi, Anne [fl. 1740–1760],
dancer. See GRIMALDI, JOHN BAPTIST
[fl. 1740–1742].

Grimaldi, Giuseppe d. 1788, dancer,
ballet master, dentist.

Giuseppe Grimaldi, the father of the famous clown Joseph Grimaldi (1778–

who was born in Shoreditch and did have lineage to the noble Genoese family of Grimaldi. Although often called by his Anglicized name of Joseph, as it is found in most of the English legal documents, we use for our subject his given name of Giuseppe to distinguish him from his son Joseph with the least confusion. Most of the time in London he was referred to as Signor Grimaldi.

Typical of many contradictions about him, the year of Giuseppe's birth is problematical: at the time of his death in 1788 he was, according to Charles Dickens (the early biographer of Joe), aged 78, making his year of birth 1710; the newspaper obituaries reported him variously as 72 (1716) and 73 (1715); and the parish burial register of Northampton Chapel in Exmouth Market, Clerkenwell, states 75 (1713). His son claimed him to have been Genoese. But perhaps he was born at Malta, the native place of his grandfather. Given the family's peregrinations, he could have been born in any one of dozens of European locales.

Considerable confusion has also characterized conjectures about his early activities and identity. He was not, as has sometimes been stated, the dancer originally known as "Gamba di Ferro" or "Iron Legs," for that person we believe to have been his father John Baptist Grimaldi (fl. 1740–1742), called also Nicolini, in whose separate entry on these pages will be found a more detailed explanation of the family line. His grandfather was also named John Baptist Grimaldi (d. 1760); he seems to have spent a number of years in London as a dancer and dentist and is also entered separately.

When and in what capacity Signor Grimaldi came to England are also questions which defy definitive answers. He was certainly performing in London before 1760, the date given by Joe in his *Memoirs* as the year of his father's migration. Without a doubt, Giuseppe Grimaldi practiced some dentistry; it was a family tradition. But his son's claim that he immigrated with an appointment of dentist to Queen Charlotte was probably another legend, perhaps spread by Giuseppe himself. He had been a resident of London at least some four years before Charlotte Sophia married George III in 1761. But his notoriety included the story that he had been dismissed from the Hanoverian Court when without ceremony he thrust his thumb and finger into the King's mouth and pulled out a loose tooth. The extraction and expulsion were charges denied by Joe, who declared in his *Memoirs* rather that his father had resigned his royal appointment to resume his theatrical life.

It has also been suggested that Giuseppe Grimaldi was the person of that name who made his first appearance on the English stage on 1 November 1742 dancing at Covent Garden Theatre, but that dancer was his father John Baptist (Nicolini) Grimaldi. While Giuseppe may have performed earlier in London, or elsewhere in England, the earliest date we find is 10 January 1758, when he was named as one of the "Ballerini" in the new dances at the King's Theatre. He was accorded similar billing on the final night of that month and perhaps also appeared on other nights during the opera season. On 12 October of that year, announced as making his first appearance on that stage, Grimaldi performed at Drury Lane with Mrs Preston and Mrs Vernon in *The Millers*, a dance repeated throughout the season, as was the pantomime dance *The Swiss*, in which he first appeared on 2 November. He was injured in a jump in the latter dance on 2 December but was back in that piece a week later, on the ninth. On 4 January 1759 he joined with Giorgi, Noverre, Sga Lucchi, and Mrs Vernon in a new comic dance called *The Flemish Feast*, which concluded the pantomime *Fortunatus*. In his *Grimaldi King of Clowns*, Richard Findlater has suggested that Signor Grimaldi was the deviser of *The Millers*; the reviewer in the *London Chronicle* did not name the choreographer but called him a "man of genius" and also specially described Grimaldi's vigorous dancing:

Grimaldi is a man of great strength and agility: he indeed treads the air. If he has any fault, he is too comical; and from some feats of his performing, which I have been witness to . . . those spectators will see him . . . with most pleasure, who are least solicitous whether he breaks his neck, or not. . . .

In the summer of 1760 Grimaldi was at Liverpool, where he advertised his skill "to draw teeth, or stumps without giving the least uneasiness in the operation" at his lodgings with Mrs Davis in the old churchyard.

Grimaldi enjoyed regular employment at Drury Lane for 27 consecutive seasons (except 1777–78) through 1785–86, almost up to the time of his death. His name

Folger Shakespeare Library

Playbill, Drury Lane Theatre, 2 December 1758

GIUSEPPE GRIMALDI in *The Swiss*

can be found in the bills for numerous dancing roles, but he became best known as Pantaloon in the harlequinades, a role he had assumed at least by 3 January 1763 in *The Magic of the Mountain*. The piece was devised by Guerini, whose name appeared in the bills for Pierrot (although in his *History of the Theatres* Victor stated that Guerini played the Pantaloon). As a pantaloon, Grimaldi was also seen in numerous performances of such pieces as *The Rites of Hecate, Queen Mab, The Hermit, The Elopement, The Pigmy Revels, Harlequin's Jacket,* and *Harlequin's Invasion*. By 1764–65 he was a ballet master at Drury Lane and as such took a benefit on 1 May 1765. Earlier benefits had been shared with Vincent on 24 April 1762 and with Aldridge on 25 April 1763 and 4 May 1764; at the last one he and Aldridge suffered a deficit of £10 6s.

As ballet master Grimaldi composed and appeared in dozens of specialty numbers that were performed as separate ballet pieces or were included in mainpieces (the dance of the slaves in *Oroonoko*, the dance of fantastic spirits in *The Tempest*, the dances in *Florizel and Perdita*). Although his salary was not enormous, it was respectable in comparison with most of the Drury Lane performers. In 1764–65 he was paid £6 per week (the salary, it seems, also included the services of his first wife), and by 1774–75 he received £4 per week (with his wife being paid separately). His net benefit income was equally respectable; for example: £164 16s. shared with Messink and Georgi on 5 May 1772; £185 18s. with Hurst on 4 May 1773; £177 1s. 6d. with Hurst on 28 April 1774; £95 17s. with Hurst on 6 May 1775; £152 with Hurst on 26 April 1777 (tickets from Grimaldi at the Little Piazza, Covent Garden); £106 with Lamash on 5 May 1779 (tickets from Grimaldi at his house, No 125, Holborn); and £46 with Delpini on 14 May 1781.

The association of the Grimaldis with Sadler's Wells Theatre, where later Joe and his family became household names in the Pentonville community, seems to have begun about 1763. Signor Grimaldi was found regularly there in the summers from that year through 1769, playing Pantaloon and serving as ballet master. Earlier, in August 1761, he had joined with Shuter and Nancy Dawson in Lee's company which played for several weeks in Winchester.

In September 1769 he assisted in the Jubilee at Stratford; in an impudent letter to Garrick in 1771 he claimed he still had money owing him for those services. Sometime in May 1771 from Paris he had requested a letter of credit from Garrick, who refused. The manager assumed that Grimaldi had been paid for the "Stratford Business" long ago and wrote to his brother George Garrick to settle the matter immediately, adding of Grimaldi: "I only know he was ye worst behav'd Man in ye Whole Company & Shd have had a horse Whip." Grimaldi had a gusty, indelicate sense of humor, which on one occasion, according to Oxberry, resulted in his persuading a fellow performer to paint a face upon his own buttocks and then exhibit it to Garrick. One time in 1777 he had a terrible tragicomical quarrel with De Loutherbourg, the Drury Lane scene designer, which ended with the Signor, this time, the butt of the joke: "Signor de Grimaldi drew his fiddle stick upon Monsieur de Loutherbourg," reported the press, "upon which the last, with a brush of red oaker, gave a diagonal line across Pantaloon's face, which looked as if he had cut his head into two parts—the Frenchman retired and left the Italian with his mouth open, as we have often seen him in a Pantomime."

At the Bristol Theatre Royal in the summer of 1774 Grimaldi produced the pantomime *Love's Magic*, which played ten times in 30 nights. During his stay in Bristol he advertised his services as a "'Surgeon-

Dentist" at Mrs Thomson's in Prince's Street, the same address given for obtaining tickets for his benefits, and stated that after his return to London he could be consulted at his "House under the Little Piazza, Covent Garden." Upon his return to Bristol in August 1775 he again advertised that "Grimaldi, Surgeon-Dentist, who has had the Honour of attending her MAJESTY, the Prince of Wales, and the Prince and Princess of Brunswic [sic], and the Happiness of having his Applications crown'd with Success. Will practise in Bristol at Mrs M'Ardle's, at the corner with King Street."

Signor Grimaldi's only known appearance at Covent Garden Theatre occurred on 29 April 1778, when he played the Clown in *Mother Shipton*, announced as for that night only.

Harvard Theatre Collection

GIUSEPPE GRIMALDI as Clown, and JOSEPH GRIMALDI as Monkey

by G. Cruikshank

The Gordon Riots of June 1780 gave rise to one of the anecdotes in the Grimaldi apocrypha. To prevent violence upon themselves from the anti-Catholics, citizens were posting "No Popery" signs on their doors. As Henry Angelo told the story, at that time Grimaldi resided in a front room on a second floor in Holborn, near Red Lion Square (other versions say opposite the gateway to Sadler's Wells or in Little Russell Street):

the mob passing by the house, and Grimaldi being a foreigner, they thought he must be a papist; on hearing that he lived there, they all stopped, and there was a general shouting. A cry of "No Popery!" was raised, and they were just going to assail the house, when Grimaldi . . . put his head out of the window, from the second floor; making comical gestures, he called out, "Genteelmen, in dis hose dere be no religion at all." Laughing at their mistake, they proceeded on, first giving him three huzzas, though his house, unlike all the others, had not written on the door "No Popery."

When the Royal Circus was opened in St George's Fields, Lambeth, under the management of Charles Hughes and the elder Charles Dibdin on 7 November 1782, Signor Grimaldi was the ballet master. His association, as described by Dibdin, and summarized by Findlater, was one "from which he hoped to win new wealth and influence, and which throws some light upon his character." He had been put in charge of a company of 60 children, including about 20 apprentices bound to him at substantial fees, whom he was to train in the Academy to perform "exercises in music, dancing, oratory, etc." in the productions. According to Dibdin, Grimaldi "performed his duty, perhaps, better than any other could have done," but ignoring Dibdin's authority and conspiring behind his back, he managed to persuade the proprietors to sell him a half share in the enterprise. All the time, however, "he made a parade of declaring, that he conceived himself under the highest obligations to me," wrote Dibdin, "that I had given him his bread at the Circus, and he would rather die, than do anything that could militate against my interest."

Dibdin understandably was incensed at the intrigue of "the grovelling Italian." When, however, the parents of Grimaldi's apprentices brought petitions against his supervision of the children, "Criminal accusations were preferred, addressed to religious lords; the magistrates interfered, and a complete investigation into the morals and conduct of the place was ordered." Grimaldi escaped without evident penalty, but his enterprise there was aborted when the Surrey magistrates closed down the Royal Circus within a month of its opening for lack of a proper license. When it reopened in March 1783 Grimaldi and Dibdin were no longer associated with the venture.

In view of what we know about Grimaldi's idiosyncratic personality, the charges brought against him by the apprentices' parents were no doubt true. It was said that this harsh teacher was not above putting a fledgling dancer into a small cage and hauling it to the flies of the theatre, where it remained until the Signor saw fit to lower it and release the captive. Anthony Pasquin (John Williams) wrote:

What monster is this, who alarms the beholders,
Full folly and infamy perch'd on his shoulders,
Whom hallow'd religion is conspiring to save
Ere sin and disease goad the wretch to his grave?
'Tis Grimaldi! Alas, nature starts at the name
And trembles with horror, and reddens with shame!
In the hate of his principles all are agreeing
And the fruit of his loins curse the cause of their being.

With a pestilent curse he infects their sad times
A vile abstract of hell and Italia's crimes.

In his last years at Drury Lane, Grimaldi, now in his seventies, tried to maintain a vigorous schedule but was being overtaken by poor health. In 1783–84 he appeared in numerous performances as the Clown in *Fortunatus* and *Harlequin Junior* until on 13 January 1784 he became "extremely ill" and it was uncertain when he could play again. Within several weeks, however, he rallied; on 3 February he returned to *Harlequin Junior* to play the role 18 times before the end of the season. In 1784–85 he played the Clown often in the same piece and in *The Caldron*. In the autumn of 1785–86 he again performed regularly in *The Caldron*. On 26 December 1785 he appeared as Clodpate in the premiere of *Hurly Burly*. On the twenty-ninth and thirty-first he repeated Clodpate, his last performances at Drury Lane, for on 2 January 1786 he was replaced in the role by Williamson, his son-in-law. Two months later, on 25 February 1786, Grimaldi made his will.

Sufficiently recovered from his ailments by summer, old Grimaldi resumed playing, not at Drury Lane, but at the Haymarket, where on 3 July 1786, announced as making his first appearance on that stage, he performed Pierrot in *Here, and There, and Every Where*. After another four performances of that piece, he appeared as the Clown in *Harlequin Teague* on 4 September, a role he played again on the sixth, the eleventh, and then on the thirteenth of September 1786 for his final London performance of record.

A year and a half later, on 14 March 1788, Signor Grimaldi died of dropsy. One press report gave his lodgings in Covent Garden as his place of death; De Castro in his *Memoirs* claimed he died at lodgings in Theatre Court, Lambeth. He was buried at the Northampton Chapel in Exmouth

Street, Islington, on 23 March. Though he was not buried "at the Pantheon between the Windows" as requested in his will, a most extraordinary directive in his will had been complied with: "I desire Mary Grimaldi now Williamson to see me put into my coffin and the day that I am buried to sever my head from my body. . . ." Mary had a surgeon do the macabre task, "she touching the instrument at the time." (He had also specified that the whole expense of his funeral and the head stone should not exceed £10.)

That bizarre final gesture was merely the climax of a lifetime obsession with death. Old Grimaldi seemed haunted by it, and Joe related stories of accompanying "Old Grim," as his father was sometimes called, on walks through the graveyards of local churches. Joe Miller's resting place in Portugal Street was his favorite spot for melancholy reflections. He often read aloud to the children from *The Uncertainty of the Signs of Death*. His anxiety about death was heightened, if we are to believe his son, on the fourteenth of every month. "At its appearance, he was always nervous, disquieted, and anxious; directly it had passed, he was another man again, and invariably exclaimed in his broken English, 'Ah! now I am safe for anoder month'." Indeed, his death had come on the fourteenth of the month, but Joe's claim that "he was born, christened and married on the 14th of the month" was a fiction, at least in respect to the last. Presumably a recurrent nightmare had made him fear the appearance of the Devil on the first Friday of every month.

In a cruel joke, he once feigned being dead, as Joe related the event, in order to know what the reaction of his sons might be at his real death. Having been brought into a darkened room by a servant to find the father laid out, young Joe quickly saw through the hoax and immediately played the part of the griefstricken son to the hilt. But the younger John was taken in and, "perceiving in his father's death nothing but a relief from flogging and books . . . and the immediate possession of all the plate in the dining-room, skipped about the room, indulging in various snatches of song, and, snapping his fingers, declared he was glad to hear it." Whereupon Grimaldi leaped from the bier to beat the younger lad unmercifully.

In his son's *Memoirs*, the Signor was characterized as

a very honest man, and a very charitable one, never turning a deaf ear to the entreaties of the distressed, but always willing, by every means in his power, to relieve the numerous reduced and wretched persons who applied to him for assistance. It may be added—and his son always mentioned it with pride—that he was never known to be inebriated. . . .

But as Findlater neatly comments, "Filial piety, rather than historical accuracy, prompts this and other tributes." On the contrary, Signor Grimaldi was a difficult and sometimes despicable person, thoroughly libertine in his habits and, even allowing for the exaggeration of the record, somewhat unfeeling toward the plight of his women and children. Described as a "Batchelor," he had married Mary Blagden at St Paul, Covent Garden, on 13 April 1762. In the marriage register he was listed as "Joseph Grimaldy of this Parish" and she as "Mary Blagden of the same parish, spinster & minor." Because she was only 16 (Grimaldi was thrice her age) the marriage required the consent of her father, William Blagden, who was probably one (or all) of the Blagdens, dancers and dressers, noticed in the second volume of this dictionary. Mary had been dancing in the Drury Lane chorus since 1759–60, and her brother, Master Blagden, had been with that theatre as early as 1755–56.

Within five years of their marriage the Grimaldis had four daughters: Mary, baptized at St Paul, Covent Garden, on 19 January 1763; Isabella Louisa, baptized at the same church on 14 October 1764; Margaret Charlotta, born in 1765; and Catherine, born in 1767. A Catherine Grimaldi was buried at St Paul, Covent Garden, on 24 May 1773, but she was no doubt the Signor's mother.

The lurid story of Giuseppe and Mary's married life is revealed in Mary's application for divorce in 1779, which was discovered by Findlater at County Hall and related in his notes to a modern edition of Dickens's *Memoirs of Joseph Grimaldi* (London, 1968). "Very soon" after the marriage, Grimaldi "began to behave cruelly towards her" and soon after the birth of their first child, Mary, took to beating his wife unmercifully. His abuse included the hurling of knives and plates at her, cutting and bruising her; on one occasion the beating was so severe she was unable to perform at the theatre for three weeks. She deposed that Grimaldi

spent the greater part of his time in the company of men of bad character and abandoned women and frequented notorious brothels or bawdy houses and frequently stayed at such houses until four or five in the morning and then returned home to the said Mary Grimaldi his wife and told her of the several acts of debauchery he had on the preceding nights been guilty of and would then without the least provocation very much abuse and ill-treat her.

In the 1760s Grimaldi publicly carried on affairs with the three young Wilkinson sisters, dancers and rope-walkers at Sadler's Wells. As Findlater continues his account of Mrs Grimaldi's grievances:

He "spent the greater part of his time with them" and with another girl-dancer, and "for months successively did not return to his bed until four or five o'clock in the morning." When the unfortunate wife reproached him, the elderly Italian threatened to bring his teenage mistresses back home and "keep" them publicly. Although she was pregnant, he would—when he returned—turn her out of bed and make her sleep with the children, or

order her to sit up all night by her bedside.

About 1767 Grimaldi contracted syphilis—probably from Carolina Wilkinson—but he insisted on having intercourse with his wife, although she was pregnant, and she caught the disease in a virulent form. In 1770, he set up house separately in Chelsea, leaving her without any money. Grimaldi visited the house twice a week and ordered a dinner for himself and the servant only. When he had gone, the leftovers were taken to Mrs Grimaldi, "who chiefly lived in the kitchen of the said house, by reason . . . he constantly locked up and took with him the keys of the several other rooms. . . ." On another occasion, five years later, he locked her in her room for six weeks, forbade anyone to speak or correspond with her, and set his mother, Catherine, to guard the room with a brace of loaded pistols. . . .

Finally in 1775 Grimaldi and his wife stopped living together, he moving in with his next unfortunate victim, Rebecca Brooker, and Mary going to live with her mother. In 1779 Mary sued for divorce, but when she was buried at St Paul, Covent Garden, two years later on 13 July 1781 she was nevertheless entered in the burial register as "Mary Wife of Joseph Grimalde [*sic*]."

At the time his first wife died, in 1781, Grimaldi had been living for some six years with Rebecca Brooker, another of his pupils and a hard-working dancer at Drury Lane. She was the younger daughter—her age was between 18 and 22—of a Holborn butcher named Zachariah Brooker who owned a shop and house in Parker's Lane. Grimaldi never married her but sometimes lived under the same roof with her somewhere in Stanhope Street, Clare Market, where Joe Grimaldi was born to her on 18 December 1778 and was baptized on 28 December at St Clement Danes: "Joseph Grimaldi, of Joseph and Rebecca." At the time of Joe's birth, however, Signor Grimaldi lived at No 125, High Holborn. During that same period the sexually vigorous old Grimaldi was having an affair of some endurance with one Ann Perry, by whom he had another illegitimate child, Henrietta Marguerite, in December 1778, the same month of Joe's birth. Later Ann Perry lived with him at his house in High Holborn and adopted the name Grimaldi. Findlater suggests that another son, the William Grimaldi mentioned in the Signor's will as his "dearly beloved" was also by Ann Perry, but we believe him to have been the child of Rebecca Brooker as was John (Jean) Baptist Grimaldi.

In addition to the above-mentioned directives in his will, proved at London on 20 March 1788 a week after his death and three days before his burial, Grimaldi wanted his estate, in order "to avoid all disputes," to be formed by the sale of his possessions and the gathering of monies owed him on notes for benefit tickets and "for the Teeth," to be "put out to the best advantage in behalf of" Mary, now Williamson, his eldest daughter, and his sons Joseph, Jean Baptist, and William, each to share equally one-fourth. But "for their bad behaviours" he cut off his daughters Margaret Farmer and Catherine Grimaldi without a shilling. The will contains no references to his daughters Isabella Louisa or Henrietta, nor to Rebecca Brooker nor Ann Perry.

Joe's recollection that the family had lived in some luxury, with four servants, including a Negro footman, was undoubtedly inflated. It is unlikely that the Signor's income from wages and benefits, even supplemented by teaching and dentistry, would have allowed him to accumulate the estate in excess of £15,000 that his son claimed Giuseppe possessed at the time of his death. By 1783 the town house at High Holborn was no longer in his possession—or at least he was no longer a Holborn rate-payer—and he was living in rooms at No 5, Princes Street. Moreover, his subsequent changes of address, some five in six years, would "scarcely indicate," in Findlater's view, a "state of settled comfort."

Whatever estate old Grimaldi left his children they were cheated of it, according to Joe. Thomas King, the eminent comedian of Drury Lane Theatre and a manager of Sadler's Wells from 1771 to 1782, was named by Grimaldi as a co-executor but refused the responsibility. The other executor, Joseph Hopwood, a lace manufacturer in Longacre, went bankrupt within a year, fled England, and by Joe's account was never heard of again. The directories, however, reveal that Hopwood was back in London in 1791.

Rebecca Brooker, Signor Grimaldi's second "wife," continued to perform on the London stage as Mrs Brooker through 1809–10. She claimed on the Drury Lane Fund in 1810, and she died 23 October 1819. Information on her career can be found in her notice as Mrs Giuseppe Grimaldi the second (d. 1819). His first wife is also entered separately as Mrs Giuseppi Grimaldi the first (1746–1781). We know nothing more about his mistress, Ann Perry.

Giuseppe Grimaldi's eldest daughter Mary married the pantomime actor James Williamson at St George, Bloomsbury, on 24 January 1779. Of Giuseppe's other three daughters by his first wife Mary, little is known. Isabella Louisa Grimaldi, who was baptized on 14 October 1764, perhaps became the Mrs Goodwin mentioned in one of Joe Grimaldi's obituaries. Margaret Charlotta, who was born in 1765 and became Mrs Farmer, and Catherine, who was born in 1767, were both alive in 1788 when they were disinherited by their father. One of the three younger daughters—Isabella, Margaret, or Catherine—performed with brother Joe in his first Sadler's Wells appearance on 19 April 1781.

The famous Joseph Grimaldi, Giuseppe's first son by Rebecca Brooker, is entered separately. He appeared at Sadler's Wells in 1781, at the age of three, with his half sister Mary. In 1789, after the Signor's death, three young Grimaldis performed in

Harlequin's Frolicks, the Christmas pantomime at Drury Lane which opened on 26 December. Joe was one of them. We believe the other two to have been his younger brothers John Baptist and William, also sons of Rebecca Brooker, who that season was dancing at Drury Lane. It seems unlikely that she would have been caring at that time for any of the Signor's children by Mary Blagden Grimaldi or Ann Perry. John soon ran off to sea and, except for a mysterious reappearance for several hours some years later, was never heard from again. Beyond his mention in his father's will and the appearance at Drury Lane in 1789, William remains a mystery, never acknowledged by Joe in the *Memoirs*. Both John Baptist and William Grimaldi are also separately entered.

Henrietta Marguerite, Signor Grimaldi's daughter by Ann Perry, born in the same month as Joe, was not mentioned in her father's will nor in her half-brother's *Memoirs*. After Joe's death in 1837, his executor Richard Hughes received a letter from a Jane Taylor, who claimed to be the great clown's sister and hoped she had been remembered in his will. But when Hughes replied that Joe had never brought up her name or existence in any fashion, she was not heard from again.

Many years after Giuseppe's death, the *New Monthly Magazine* (July 1839) recalled him as "a low humorist; and, in those days of practical jokes, thought a very clever fellow." His cruder, more boisterous style, stemming from the traditions of the fair booths of the Continent, was perhaps ultimately too broad for English taste. Willson Disher credited him with being "the founder—and, in several cases, tutor—of a new school of pantomime." But as Findlater has indicated, despite his numerous pupils, there is no real evidence which points to his training of a new school. How much influence he exerted upon the creation of Joey the Clown is conjectural, although clearly his son owed his very early

training to him. Yet Giuseppe died when Joe was only ten years old. The father had a substantial reputation as a pantaloon, but did not play the clown character until 11 May 1779 in *The Elopement*, a piece in which he had for some years previously appeared as Pantaloon.

Grimaldi, Mrs Giuseppe the first, Mary, née Blagden   *1746–1781, dancer.*

The first wife of the ballet master Giuseppe Grimaldi (d. 1788) was born Mary Blagden in 1746, the daughter of William Blagden, who was probably one (or all) of the Blagdens, dancers and dressers, entered in Volume II of this dictionary. Mary's mother may also have been employed at Drury Lane Theatre, as was Mary's dancing brother, Master Blagden (fl. 1755–1759).

The early career of Mary Blagden has been noticed in Volume II, published before we became aware of her first name and her subsequent marriage to Signor Grimaldi, but we repeat that information here for convenience. Miss Blagden was first mentioned in the bills on 12 December 1759 when she participated at Drury Lane in a *Dutch Dance* on an occasion in which Master Blagden also appeared. Her only other notice that season was on 19 June 1760 when the Richmond company performed at Drury Lane, and she was again in the *Dutch Dance*. Her name reappeared in the bills on 21 April 1762 in a louvre and minuet with her teacher Settree.

At the age of 16, and described in the register as "Mary Blagden . . . spinster & minor," she married the pantomime dancer Giuseppe Grimaldi at St Paul, Covent Garden, on 13 April 1762, by license and by consent of her father.

As she subsequently had four children by Grimaldi within the first five years of her marriage, she obviously was spared little time for professional pursuits. In 1764–65, however, Signor Grimaldi and his wife were being paid a total of £1 per night, or £6 per week, for their services to Drury Lane. In 1765–66 she was one of the witches in *The Witches*, a role typical of her lower station in the chorus. The following season she and Grimaldi together were paid 16s. 8d. per night or £5 per week. They were still receiving that combined salary in 1772–73. In 1766 she had subscribed 10s. 6d. to the Drury Lane Fund, and according to a subsequent notation in the fund book her salary in 1775 was 4s. 2d. per night, or £1 5s. per week, an amount she was still being paid in 1776–77.

Information about her children and the details of her marriage tribulations are given in her husband's entry. She separated from him about 1775 and sued for divorce in 1779. When she was buried at St Paul, Covent Garden, on 13 July 1781, she was registered as "Mary Wife of Joseph Grimalde [*sic*]."

Grimaldi, Mrs Giuseppe the second, Rebecca, née Brooker *d. 1819, dancer, singer.*

Although Rebecca Brooker was the mother of Joseph Grimaldi, the most famous pantomime clown in theatrical history, little is known about the details of her life. She was born probably sometime between 1753 and 1757, for when she began to live with Giuseppe Grimaldi about 1775, her age seems to have been between 18 and 22. Her father was Zachariah Brooker, a butcher who had a family shop in Parker's Lane, Holborn (not in Newton Street as her son's *Memoirs* state).

She had been employed since childhood at Drury Lane Theatre, where Garrick, it is said, rented her from her father as an occasional fairy in the afterpieces. She also may have worked as a youngster at Sadler's Wells. Her name appeared in the Drury Lane account books in 1776–77, when she earned £1 per week as a utility dancer. Although she remained regularly employed for many years at that theatre, it was not, as far as we can determine, until 26 October

1790 that her name appeared on a bill: she was noticed as one of the chorus dancers in the afterpiece *Don Juan*. In that instance she was called Mrs Brooker, the designation usually given in the subsequent bills and accounts, although on a few occasions it was given as Miss Brooker.

About 1775 she began to live under the same roof with Giuseppe Grimaldi, her dancing master. She never married him, even after his first wife Mary died in 1781. At Rebecca's lodgings in Stanhope Street, Clare Market, their son Joseph was born on 18 December 1778; he was baptized on 28 December at St Clement Danes, "Joseph Grimaldi, of Joseph and Rebecca." By that time, however, Giuseppe was living at No 125, High Holborn, and was having an affair with an Anne Perry who gave birth to his child Henrietta Marguerite the very month in which Joseph was born.

Mrs Brooker seems to have been spared the vicious cruelties which had been heaped upon Mary Grimaldi, Giuseppe's first wife. Her life with the Signor, however, could hardly have been idyllic. Yet she had at least two subsequent sons by him, John Baptist in 1780 and William by 1786. Both are noticed separately in these volumes.

According to Richard Findlater's *Grimaldi, King of Clowns* (1955) Rebecca was "a short, dark-haired, sallow-skinned London girl, brought up in a hard school, with a sharp tongue and a talent for comic acting." When Giuseppe died in 1788, he failed to mention her in his will. She then took her three sons into rooms in Great Wild Street, not far from Clare Market. John soon ran off to sea, and William we lose track of after his appearances with his brothers at Drury Lane in 1789–90. Joseph lived with her as a youngster, and because she needed his wages at the theatre to supplement her own modest income, she refused an offer from the Putney schoolmaster Mr Ford to adopt Joe and continue his education.

From 1790–91 through 1809–10, the

last year of her performing, her salary at Drury Lane remained a constant £1 5s. per week. No doubt she received support from Joe after his career blossomed at the beginning of the nineteenth century. From about that time they shared a large house in Penton Place, Pentonville, with Mr and Mrs William Lewis of Sadler's Wells. The *Memoirs* imply, by the repeated references to Joe's mother coming to visit or holding afternoon tea parties, that in her later years she lodged separately from her son's family.

Mrs Brooker's duties at Drury Lane included dancing and singing in such afterpieces as *The American Heroine* in 1791–92, *Harlequin's Invasion* in 1792–93, *The Pirates* in 1793–94, *The Cherokee* in 1794–95, *Robinson Crusoe* and *The Triumph of Love* 1796–97, and *Blue-Beard* in 1797–98. In the summers she performed at Sadler's Wells, where she is known to have danced a Country Lass in *England's Glory* on 31 August 1795.

Mrs Brooker had been one of the original subscribers in 1775 to the Drury Lane Theatrical Fund, against which she claimed in 1810. According to a notation in Winston's fund book she died on 23 October 1819. Joe Grimaldi mentioned her infrequently in the *Memoirs*, although they seem to have enjoyed a warm relationship and she no doubt had been some considerable influence on his adolescence.

Grimaldi [John Baptist?] *d. 1760?, dancer, dentist.*

A Mr Grimaldi performed Pantaloon in the pantomime *Orpheus and Eurydice* at Covent Garden Theatre on 12 February 1740 and continued to appear in numerous performances of the piece that season and in 1740–41 and 1741–42.

That person was not the Mr Grimaldi, called "Gamba di Ferro" ("Iron Legs"), who danced at the same theatre in 1742–43. When that latter person made his debut on 1 November 1742, he was announced as making his first appearance on the English stage. Although the bills were some-

times cavalier in respect to such announcements, in that instance it would seem that the public would have remembered a Grimaldi who had been appearing regularly at the same theatre over the previous three seasons. Moreover, the subject of this entry was busy on the Covent Garden stage during the times that "Iron Legs" was, according to Campardon, performing in specifically named ballets at the Paris fairs between 1740 and 1742. There has been considerable confusion over the Grimaldi lineage. The famous clown Joe Grimaldi himself, in a letter dated 6 May 1810, claimed that his grandfather was John Baptist, a native of Italy, and most biographers have identified him with "Iron Legs" yet have been puzzled by Campardon's calling his Christian name Nicolini; but we take "Nicolini" to have been a stage name not unfamiliar in the Italian tradition. There was also *another* Nicolini, whose real name was Nicola Grimaldi (1673–1732), a famous male contralto, but we find no connection between him and the dancing Grimaldis.

We believe that the dancing Nicolini was indeed John Baptist Grimaldi, Joe's grandfather, and that an elder John Baptist, the subject of this entry, was the father of Nicolini (or "Iron Legs").

Our conviction is strengthened by a will, found in the Public Record Office, dated 11 March 1760, of one John Baptist Grimaldi, "a Native of Malta," but obviously living in the area of Covent Garden at that time, in which the estate was left to "my Grandson Joseph Grimaldi and Anne Grimaldi my daughter." The grandson Joseph Grimaldi could not have been the famous Joe, who was not born until 1778. Therefore he was the elder Joseph (Giuseppe), the father of Joe. "Nicolini" or the younger John Baptist, the father of Giuseppe, is not mentioned in the will and was presumably dead. But Anne Grimaldi, probably Giuseppe's aunt, was no doubt the sister of "Nicolini," and thus the will serves to clarify the identity of the Sga Grimaldi who danced with "Iron Legs" at London in 1742. (See the entry of John Baptist Grimaldi, the younger, called Nicolini, fl. 1740–1742, for additional discussion.)

The elder John Baptist Grimaldi's will, which was proved at London on 17 March 1760 and for which administration was granted to Joseph Grimaldi (Giuseppe) and Ann Grimaldi, "Spinster," also directed them to "Prosecute Capt. Jeremy Balfour for my Effects he took from me when he was in the Latitude of Cape ffinestre to the Value of two thousand Guineas." The will had been witnessed by John Neale, a grocer in Panton Street, John Capitani of Suffolk Street (probably the singer at the King's Theatre), and William Wotton, of Bow Street, Covent Garden.

Most likely our subject was the Mr Grimaldi who had advertised as early as 1737 "Signor Grimaldi's Dentifrice" as having been in use "for years past." It is also very possible that he was (or was related to) the "Signor Grimaldo Francolino of Malta" (noticed separately under Francolino) who danced and performed feats of strength at the King's Theatre in London in 1726–27. The facts that Francolino was from Malta and was an "Operator for the Teeth" make it likely that there was a connection.

Grimaldi, John Baptist, called "Nicolini" and "Gamba di Ferro" [fl. 1740–1742], *dancer*.

On 1 November 1742 at Covent Garden Theatre, a Signor Grimaldi, called "Gamba di Ferro" (Iron Legs), danced in his first appearance on the English stage. We believe that person to have been John Baptist Grimaldi, the father of Giuseppe Grimaldi (d. 1788) and the grandfather of the famous Joe Grimaldi (1778–1837). Considerable confusion has existed over the Grimaldi lineage. The great clown Joe claimed that his grandfather's name was John Baptist. In his *Spectacles de la Foire*, Campardon named the grandfather Nicolini Grimaldi ("*dit Jambe de fer*"), but we

believe "Nicolini" to have been a stage name. We also believe that John Baptist Grimaldi, or "Nicolini," was the son and namesake of the dancer who died in 1760 and who is noticed above in this dictionary. Our conviction is strengthened by the will described in the elder John Baptist Grimaldi's notice. The Grimaldi of this notice, John Baptist the younger, known as "Iron Legs" or "Nicolini," was of Italian origin.

In 1742 Nicolini was one of the dancers of the Opéra-Comique. At the Saint Germain fair about that time he was dancing in a piece entitled *Le Prix de Cythère*, when the oft-related incident which testified to his iron legs occurred. One of his leaps took him so high that he broke one of the chandeliers above the stage, shattering glass over the face of Nehemet Effendi, ambassador of the Sublime Port, so enraging the Turk that he ordered Nicolini to be beaten if he did not make a public apology. Nicolini complied and soon (according to Joe Grimaldi's *Memoirs*) verses commemorating the prodigious leap appeared:

> Hail Iron Legs! immortal pair,
>   Agile, firm knit, and peerless,
> That skim the earth, or vault in air,
>   Aspiring high, and fearless,
> Glory of Paris! outdoing compeers,
>   Brave pair! may nothing hurt ye;
> Scatter at will our chandeliers,
>   And tweak the nose of Turkey.

At the Opéra-Comique, Nicolini danced Scaramouche in *L'Antiquaire* on 7 July 1742. Soon after, he must have departed for London. His debut at Covent Garden was on 1 November in a dance unnamed in the bills. The following night he performed a *Chinese Dance* with Mlle August and appeared in *The Peasants* with others. The latter dance was repeated on 4 and 6 November; on 9 November he danced *La Folie*. On the twentieth he appeared with a Sga Grimaldi in two pieces, *Les Bouffons de cour* and *Les Jardiniers Suédois*. That night Sga Grimaldi was making her first appearance on the English stage. Her identity has also been a matter of conjecture: "Iron Legs had for a partner either his wife, his sister, or his daughter," wrote Thomas Dibdin:

for so equivocal was the lady's character, that no one has been able to ascertain the precise degree of relationship. The nymph was thought to be his sister or his daughter, for she was remarkably like him; being a squat, thick, strong figure, and endowed with as much agility and strength, that she could break chandeliers almost as well as himself.

Campardon's identification of Nicolini's dancing partner as his sister would appear correct. She was, we believe, the Anne Grimaldi described as the daughter of the elder John Baptist Grimaldi in his will made at London on 11 March 1760; and therefore she was the sister of Nicolini, the aunt of Giuseppe Grimaldi (d. 1788), and the great-aunt of Joe. Her father left his estate to her and his grandson Giuseppe; on 17 March 1760 those two legatees proved the will in London. Anne Grimaldi also had been attached to the Grande Troupe Étrangère and the Opéra-Comique in 1742 when she was advertised as "sister" to the dancer Grimaldi.

Nicolini and his sister danced regularly in *Les Bouffons de cour* and *Les Jardiniers Suédois* at Covent Garden through 4 December 1742. The fact that their names disappeared from the bills after that date gives credence to the story told by Henry Angelo of Nicolini's duping of the manager John Rich:

Rich . . . listened with rapture to Grimaldi; who proposed an extraordinary new dance; such a singular dance that would astonish and fill the house every night, but it could not be got up without some previous expense, as it was an invention entirely of his own contrivance. There must be no rehearsal, all must be secret before the grand display in, and the exhibition on, the first night. Rich directly

advanced a sum to Grimaldi and waited the result with impatience. The *maître de ballet* took care to keep up his expectations, so far letting him into the secret that it was to be a dance on horse shoes, that it would surpass anything before seen, and as much superior to all the dancing that was ever seen in pumps. The newspapers were all puffed for a wonderful performance that was to take place on a certain evening. The house was crowded, all noise and impatience—no Grimaldi—no excuse; at last an apology was made. The grand promotor of this wonderful, unprecedented dance had been absent over six hours, having danced away on four horseshoes to Dover and taken French leave.

So far as we know, Nicolini did not return to England, though his father and son continued to reside there, as well as his sister and wife. Nicolini's wife was named Catherine. Reference was made by Mary Grimaldi, the first wife of Giuseppe, in a divorce action against her husband in the 1770s, to her husband's mother Catherine, who was sometimes posted as a guard to prevent her leaving her room. Catherine may have been the Madame Grimaldi who danced Colombine in *Harlequin Triumphant* at Bence's booth in September 1752, during Southwark Fair, though that performer may have been Anne, her sister-in-law. Catherine was buried at St Paul, Covent Garden, on 24 May 1773, having been, it seems, estranged from Nicolini for many years.

Since Nicolini was not mentioned in his father's will in 1760, we assume he was dead by that year. In her recent study entitled *The Pre-Romantic Ballet* (1974), Marian Hannah Winter provides some details of the career of one Nicolini Grimaldi, the leader of a famous pantomime troupe on the Continent known as *Les enfants hollandais*, who was a theatrical impresario in Germany during the 1760s. That Nicolini, whose wife was the widow of a member of an important Dutch family of dancers named Oploo, does not seem to have been our subject, though perhaps he was related.

Grimaldi, Mrs John Baptist, Catherine d. 1773, dancer? See GRIMALDI, JOHN BAPTIST [fl. 1740–1742].

Grimaldi, John Baptist b. 1780, dancer.

John Baptist Grimaldi, the son of Giuseppe Grimaldi (d. 1788) by his second wife Rebecca Brooker, was born on 13 September 1780, probably in Miss Brooker's lodgings in Stanhope Street, Clare Market; he was baptized at St Margaret, Westminster, on 24 August 1784. John was the only brother mentioned by Joe Grimaldi in his *Memoirs*. In his father's will, made on 25 February 1786 and proved on 20 March 1788, he was named (as Jean Baptist) as one of the four children, with Mary (Mrs Williamson), Joe, and William, to share equally in the estate.

Probably John was one of the three young Grimaldis (the others being Joe and William) who performed in the premiere of *Harlequin's Frolicks* at Drury Lane on 26 December 1789 and 21 additional times that season. His mother was a member of the theatre's dancing chorus at that time and was caring for her three children by Giuseppe Grimaldi at lodgings in Great Wild Street. John probably had performed at an even earlier date at Sadler's Wells.

Despite, or perhaps because of, his exposure to stage life at so tender an age, John could not be "prevailed upon to accept any regular engagement, for he thought and dreamt of nothing but going to sea and evinced the utmost detestation of the stage." Sometimes he filled in as a fairy or animal in the Drury Lane pantomimes, according to Joe's *Memoirs*, but several years after his father's death, when John was only 12 to 14 years of age, he persuaded Richard Wroughton, then manager of the Wells, to obtain for him a berth on an East Indiaman. Wroughton outfitted

him for the sea at a cost of £50, and the lad boarded. But he found that the ship would not sail for another ten days, so leaving behind his expensive gear, he swam to another vessel just setting sail, signed on as a cabin boy, and disappeared, according to Joe, for some 14 years.

The *Memoirs* contain a long account of John's sudden reappearance backstage at Drury Lane in November 1803. After a joyous meeting with him, Joe went on stage, believing that John would wait until after the performance when both brothers would go together to join their mother. But when Joe appeared dressed after the performance, John was not to be found in the theatre or in the streets, though Joe frantically searched. Subsequently, the efforts of the police and the Admiralty failed to turn up a clue. Several explanations were posited. John had been carrying a bag full of coins and was accompanied to the theatre by a man whom Joe assumed to be a friend; possibly he was a recent acquaintance and had done John in for the money. Another theory was that John had been robbed and murdered in some infamous London den. No corpse, however, turned up. The third theory may have been the closest to the truth: that having decided to set off to see his mother without waiting for Joe, John had been picked up by a press gang and was subsequently slain in a naval engagement; that no information to that effect was ever forthcoming was explained by the belief that John had gone under an assumed name since leaving London as a boy.

For additional information on his parents and siblings, see the entry of Giuseppe Grimaldi (d. 1788).

Grimaldi, Joseph 1778–1837, dancer, actor, singer, manager.

The "King of Clowns," Joseph Grimaldi, known more familiarly in the days of his triumphs as "Joe" or "Joey," was born on 18 December 1778 in Stanhope Street,

Clare Market, at the lodgings of his mother, Rebecca Brooker (d. 1819). She was a utility dancer at Drury Lane Theatre and the daughter of Zachariah Brooker, a butcher of Parker Lane, Holborn. Joe's father was Signor Giuseppe Grimaldi (d. 1788), ballet master at Drury Lane and Sadler's Wells, who in his own time won a reputation as an eccentric and unprincipled libertine. Through his father, Joe descended from an international dynasty of dancers who also practiced a little dentistry.

Joe's grandfather was John Baptist Grimaldi (fl. 1740–1742) called "Nicolini" and "Iron Legs," a dancer at the Paris fairs and the Opéra-Comique who performed in London in 1742 with a woman who was probably his sister Anne Grimaldi (d. 1781). "Iron Legs," in turn, was the son of the elder John Baptist Grimaldi, a dancer and dental practitioner in London, where he died in 1760, leaving a will which has provided the key to unlocking some of the mysteries of the Grimaldi lineage. Details of Joe's family background, including full and half siblings, will be found primarily in the notices in these pages of his father Giuseppe Grimaldi and his grandfather John Baptist Grimaldi but also in those of the other Grimaldis mentioned above, all of whom, with the possible exception of Joe's grandmother, Catherine, had theatrical careers of varying lengths in London.

His father Giuseppe had begun to live with his pupil, the young dancer Rebecca Brooker, by about 1775, although he was at the time still married to Mary Grimaldi (d. 1781), the mother of at least four children by him. He never married Rebecca, and while she seems to have been spared the vicious cruelties suffered by the Signor's first wife, her cohabitation with him could hardly have been idyllic. When Giuseppe died in 1788 he failed to mention her in his will.

By 1778, Giuseppe was living separately from Mrs Brooker in his house at No 125, High Holborn, and was keeping

National Portrait Gallery

JOSEPH GRIMALDI

by Cawse

yet another woman, named Anne Perry, who had his child Henrietta Marguerite the very same month in which Joe was born. Although Anne Perry seems to have become a permanent fixture in High Holborn, where she went to live with the Signor and assumed his name, he continued to allot time enough to Mrs Brooker for her to produce two more of his sons, John Baptist in 1780 and William before 1786, both full brothers of Joe (and also noticed separately on these pages).

The future great Clown was given religious legitimacy, at least, by baptism on 28 December 1778 at St Clement Danes ("Joseph Grimaldi, of Joseph and Rebecca"). From Joe's *Memoirs*, written by himself but later put into the third person and published by Charles Dickens, it seems that Joe spent the first ten years of his life in the area of Clare Market. Joe—prompted by "Filial piety, rather than historical accuracy" (in the words of Richard Findlater in his modern edition of the *Memoirs*, 1968)–characterized his father as "a very honest man, a very charitable one," but the evidence points in a different direction. The Signor had not been nicknamed "Old Grim" without reason. How his father divided his time between his two abodes is not clear, but certainly the *Memoirs* suggest that he lived with young Joe and his brother and that he was an extraordinary influence, positive and negative. The *Memoirs* relate Giuseppe's eccentricities, especially in respect to his superstitious and morbid preoccupation with death.

Probably a more steadying influence on Joe's childhood was his mother, characterized by Findlater in *Grimaldi King of Clowns* (to whom this notice is much indebted) as "a short, dark-haired, sallow-skinned London girl, brought up in a hard school, with a sharp tongue and a talent for comic dancing."

Though his father was a harsh parent, Joe owed to him his very earliest education in the tricks and skills of his theatrical trade. Few others in London could have been a better teacher than this sixtyish pantaloon of the harlequinades. Joe made his first stage appearance while still a toddler, but when and where are matters of disagreement. Findlater and *The Dictionary of National Biography* give the date as Easter Monday, 16 April 1781, at Sadler's Wells, when at the age of 28 months Joe danced with one of his sisters in the pantomime *The Wizard of the Rocks; or, Harlequin's Release*. In the *Memoirs*, however, it was stated that Joe had made his debut at the age of 23 months at Drury Lane as the Little Clown in *Robinson Crusoe*. But Joe had his own year of birth wrong, believing it to have been 1779, instead of 1778, so presumably the time intended in the *Memoirs* for the Drury Lane debut was about November 1781. Indeed Sheridan's pantomime *Robinson Crusoe* was played frequently at Drury Lane in the winter of

1781–82, but its premiere had occurred in the previous season, on 29 January 1781, a date which did fall 25 months after Joe's birth and before the Sadler's Wells debut. Acceptance of testimony in the *Memoirs* must be tempered with skepticism. In his farewell address at Sadler's Wells on 17 March 1828, Joe persisted in the belief that he had been born in 1779 and then told the audience, "At the early age of 3 years I was introduced to the Public by my Father at this Theatre. . . ."

Findlater also suggests that after his presumed debut at the Wells on 16 April 1781, Joe did not appear at Drury Lane until December 1782, in *The Triumph of Mirth; or, Harlequin's Wedding*, in which his father played the Clown at its premiere on the twenty-sixth.

During the 1780s, as Master Grimaldi, Joe evidently performed a number of sprites and fairies on the stages of Sadler's Wells and Drury Lane, probably in many of the productions in which his mother and father appeared. Sometimes he worked in a bear or monkey skin. The story is told in the *Memoirs* about the night in 1782 when he performed as a monkey side-kick to his father's Clown:

In one of the scenes, the clown used to lead him by a chain attached to his waist, and with this chain he would swing him round and round at arm's length, with utmost velocity. One evening . . . the chain broke and he was hurled a considerable distance into the pit, fortunately without sustaining the slightest injury; for he was flung by a miracle into the very arms of an old gentleman who was sitting gazing at the stage with intense interest.

In the romantic ballet *Adelaide de Brabant; or, The Triumph of Virtue*, which was performed at the end of Act II of the mainpiece *The Double Gallant* at Drury Lane on 8 May 1784, young Joe, then six, danced "in an astonishing manner," according to the *Gazetteer* of 12 May.

Joe's father died on 14 March 1788. In

his grotesque will (in which he asked to have his head severed from his corpse), Giuseppe ordered that his possessions be converted into money "to be put out to the best advantage of" his eldest daughter Mary (then Mrs Williamson) and his three sons Joseph, John Baptist, and William, all four to share equally. Because of their "bad behaviour" he cut off his other daughters Margaret Charlotte and Catherine Grimaldi, and he made no reference whatever to his other children, Isabella Louisa and Henrietta, or to Rebecca Brooker and Anne Perry. While Joe's claim that his father's estate was worth in excess of £15,000 was no doubt much exaggerated, the children were cheated out of it, whatever its value, by the co-executor Joseph Hopwood, who went bankrupt and fled England within the year.

Soon after his father's death, Joe and his two brothers were taken by their mother Rebecca Brooker to rooms in Great Wild Street, not far from Clare Market, where they struggled on her slight salary from Drury Lane and on whatever the children could contribute by their work. Joe played a Daemon in *Harlequin Junior* at Drury Lane on 10 and 13 November 1788, and on 17 February 1789 he acted Young Marcius in Kemble's adaptation of *Coriolanus* which had a total of seven performances before the end of the season.

In the 1789–90 season Master Grimaldi's name was found on the Drury Lane paylist for £1 5s. per week. With his brothers he danced in the premiere of *Harlequin's Frolicks* on 26 December 1789 and 21 additional times that season. He played Helena's Page in the premiere of Kemble's *Love in Many Masks* on 8 March 1790 and in subsequent performances and on 15 May again appeared in *Harlequin Junior*. About that time his brother John ran off to sea and his brother William disappeared from all accounts, leaving Joe and his mother to get along by themselves.

From time to time, when not at the theatres, Joe attended school at a Putney academy run by Mr Ford. One of the Grimaldi legends is that Ford offered to adopt Joe and continue his tuition, but Mrs Brooker could not sacrifice the boy's income at the theatres. Joe also began to breed pigeons, collect insects, and form his extraordinary collection of flies which ultimately included, it is said, some 4000 specimens. Among the most idyllic parts of the *Memoirs* are those which describe Joe's early-morning expeditions to find Dartford Blues.

In 1790–91, still being paid £1 5s. per week (a salary he received regularly at Drury Lane through 1797–98) and now billed as Young Grimaldi, he appeared as a Mandarine in numerous performances of *The Fairy Favour*, which had its premiere on 27 December 1790. On 4 February 1794 he acted a Page in *Lodoiska*.

During those years he also performed regularly at Sadler's Wells, where he formed lifelong friendships with Richard Lawrence, Bob Fairbrother, Jack Bologna, and Jack Richer, all performers and sons of performers, and with Jean Baptiste Dubois, a tumbler and dancer from whom Joe may have learned much. Some nights in the spring and fall Joe worked both houses, exhausting himself by running back and forth from one to the other. At the Wells his performances included a Dwarf in *The Savages* and Jacky Suds in *The Master's Holiday* in 1792, the title role in *The Sans Culottes* in 1793, a Lacquey in *The Mandarin* and the Dwarf in *Valentine and Orson* in 1794, Slang in *The Spirit of the Grotto*, and the Old Woman in *Venus's Girdle* in 1796. Earlier, in 1790, he had also danced at the Dog and Duck, in St George's Fields.

Sometime in the mid-1790s Joe and his mother moved into a house in Penton Place, Pentonville, which they shared with their friends and fellow performers, Mr and Mrs William Lewis. The combined winter income of the Grimaldis at that time was

£2 10s. per week. Fortunately, it was supplemented by summer employment at the Wells. Joe's comic abilities had attracted some attention, but he had not yet created any great stir in his profession, although he was very well received as Hag Morad in Dibdin's pantomime *The Talisman* at Sadler's Wells on Easter Monday 1796.

At Drury Lane in 1796–97 he began to appear in small acting parts as well as to dance in pantomimes and specialty numbers. Now old enough for his name to appear in the bills as Mr Grimaldi, he acted Aminadab in *A Bold Stroke for a Wife* on 19 October and Dick in *The Belle's Stratagem* on 25 October, one of the Spouters in *The Apprentice* on 18 November, and Jessamy in *The Confederacy* on 24 November, and on 1 February 1797 he played a female role, the Maid in *Rule a Wife and Have a Wife.*

But his talent lay not in the drama. Although an "admirable" actor, Joe was a "bad study" and even experienced difficulty, it is said, in learning the few speeches sometimes required of him in the harlequinades. He was bred and trained for pantomime, and in that season of 1796–97, he enjoyed his first real opportunity to capture attention. On 9 November 1796 he played the modest role of Ormandine's Servant in *Harlequin Captive.* When the pantomime was given two nights later, Banks was in that part and Joe took over the Clown from Dubois, a role he repeated on 15 and 19 November. On 12 November he assumed the role of Glaude in the dance *The Scotch Ghost.* He also was one of the Goatherds in *The Mountaineers* on 26 November. A month later, on 26 December, he took the role of Pero in the revival of the Christmas pantomime *Robinson Crusoe,* in which his mother served as one of the dancing savages in the Indian Festival dance performed upon Friday's return to his island. On 20 January 1797, on a night when *Robinson Crusoe* was played again, Grimaldi also sang in the mainpiece *Theo-*

dosius, the first performance of that tragedy in 23 years, in which J. P. Kemble acted Varanes and Mrs Siddons Athenais. That extraordinarily active season for Grimaldi also included his appearance as Camazin, the Tartar chief, in *Lodoiska* on 16 February. In that role he won some celebrity for his acrobatic swordsmanship; his so-called crawling fight became a model for Kean's portrayal of the final scene in *Richard III.* On 6 March, Grimaldi performed Robert in the ballet *The Labyrinth.*

During the last several seasons of the century, however, his career at Drury Lane advanced little, even though his salary was raised to £1 10s. in 1798–99 and to £2 10s. in 1799–1800. He still acted his modest dramatic roles and, except when playing Camazin, remained in the background in the pantomimes and spectacles. His new assignments included: in 1797–98, Cymon in *All the World's a Stage,* a Servant in *The Deaf Lover,* a Peasant in *Richard Coeur de Lion,* the Chimney Sweeper in *A Trip to the Nore,* Pedro in *Catherine and Petruchio,* Roger in *The Mayor of Garratt,* a Peasant in *Blue-Beard,* a Countryman in *The Country Girl,* and a featured role as Scaramouch in *Sylvester Daggerwood,* for the first time on 11 May 1798; in 1798–99, a character in *Feudal Times* and Bauldi in the ballet *Moggy and Jemmy;* and in 1799–1800, Lopez in *Love Makes a Man,* a Countryman in *A Trip to Scarbrough,* a character in *The Egyptian Festival,* and a role in the ballet *The Lucky Escape.*

At the minor summer house prospects were more promising. At the Wells on Easter Monday, 9 April 1798, his reputation had been increased considerably by his performance in the new pantomime *The Monster of the Cave; or, Harlequin and the Fairy.* That summer he also played the villain Oscitel in the "Historical Ballet of Action," *Alfred the Great, or, the Patriot King,* and probably appeared also in *The Prisoners; or, an Escape from France.*

On 11 May 1799 Grimaldi married

Maria Hughes (1775–1800) at St George, Hanover Square, and they moved into a rented house at No 37 (now No 44), Penton Street. She was the eldest daughter of Richard Hughes (d. 1814), then the manager of Sadler's Wells, by his wife Lucy (née Williams) Hughes (1748–1838). By all accounts, especially Joe's in the *Memoirs*, the newlyweds enjoyed an idyllic and devoted relationship.

At Sadler's Wells, his new father-in-law, anxious to see Joe advance, brought his talents to the attention of Charles Isaac Mungo Dibdin, who in 1800 became a co-manager and house writer. "Mr. Hughes had told me that I should find him a very clever lad," wrote Dibdin in his *Professional & Literary Memoirs*, "and begged that I would cultivate his talents as much as I possibly could; in consequence of which I used to watch him at rehearsals, while he was exhibiting his 'Monkey Tricks' to the Performers; and noted down any peculiar whimsicality I saw in him."

Dibdin's pantomime *Peter Wilkins, or, Harlequin in the Flying World* was on the program for the opening of the Wells on 14 April 1800, in which was introduced the innovation of two Clowns—Gobble, the Eating Clown, performed by Dubois, and Guzzle, the Drinking Clown, performed by Grimaldi. It would be a mere quibble to contradict the assertions of Grimaldi's biographers that that was his first appearance as the Clown—he had, as noted above, played the part at Drury Lane in *Harlequin Captive* several times in November 1796—for if it was not the first, it was certainly the

Harvard Theatre Collection

JOSEPH GRIMALDI, as Clown in *Harlequin and Asmodeus*

engraving after Norman

significant beginning of his development of the character in which his genius would spread joy to thousands over three decades. The event was additionally important (despite the fact that it was all but ignored by the press), because in the production both Clowns wore costumes "more extravagant than it had been for such characters to wear"; Dibdin had designed the two new dresses—"the Costume of the Clown was completely changed; and a whimsical mixture of colours and compositions invariably studied. . . ." The traditional make-up of a red-faced, rustic booby was abandoned by Joe for the red half-moons painted on the cheeks. The crowds and clowns from the two patent houses, hearing of Grimaldi's new style of clowning, flocked to the Wells. Young Joe was hailed as successor to Dubois (whom Dibdin called "Goliath of clowns"). "I never saw anything equal to him," wrote Dibdin, "there was so much *mind* in everything that he did." When Garrick played a drunken man, it was said that he was "all over drunk"—Grimaldi was "all over Clown."

The last theatrical season of the eighteenth century ended in a triumph for Joe Grimaldi, then not quite 22 years of age. The first season of the new century brought a cruel challenge to the Clown's spirit. In the autumn of 1800 Grimaldi returned to his small roles at Drury Lane, but now with increased prestige and the expectation of a revival of the Christmas pantomime at that theatre after a three-year hiatus. On St Luke's Day, 18 October 1800, his wife Maria died in childbirth, with the child. (She had experienced a difficult pregnancy from its onset, so one must wonder why she had danced in the ballet *The Lucky Escape* on 2 June 1800 in the previous season.) After her burial in her father's family vault at St James, Clerkenwell, Joe tried to bury his enormous sorrow under a heap of work, appearing, ironically, within two days of her death as the Second Gravedigger in *Hamlet*, his first Shakespearean

part. Abandoning the honeymoon house in Penton Street, he moved to No 4, Baynes Row, across Coppice Row.

The new pantomime at Drury Lane in 1800–1801 was *Harlequin Amulet*, staged by the new ballet master James Byrn (1757–1845), a performer from the Royal Circus who had recently returned to London after four years in America and Jamaica. He played Harlequin and Joe played Punch (and changed into Clown after the sixth scene). With that pantomime, which ran 33 nights, Byrn made innovations in Harlequin, striking vigorous new attitudes and startling the audience by running up a wall and over the side of a house "with such amazing velocity that it was impossible to detect the means by which he was assisted." Instead of the loose jacket and trousers in which Harlequin traditionally had been garbed, Byrn appeared in a costume which "consisted of a white silk shape fitting without a wrinkle, and into this the variegated silk patches were woven, the whole being profusely covered with spangles and presenting a very sparkling appearance." In his own arduous part Grimaldi exhausted himself. According to the *Memoirs*:

he had to perform Punch, and to change afterwards to Clown. He was so successful in the first-mentioned part, that Mr Sheridan wished him to preserve the character throughout—a suggestion which he was compelled resolutely to oppose. His reason for doing so . . . was that his personal decoration consisted of a large and heavy hump on his chest, and a ditto, ditto, on his back; a high sugar-loaf cap, a long-nosed mask, and heavy wooden shoes; the weight of the whole dress, and of the humps, nose, and shoes especially, being exceedingly great. Having to exercise all his strength in this costume, and to perform a vast quantity of comic business, Grimaldi was compelled by fatigue at the end of the sixth scene to assume the Clown's dress, and so relieve himself from the immense weight. . . .

At Sadler's Wells in the summer of 1801 Grimaldi appeared as Clown in Dibdin's pantomimes *Harlequin Benedick, Harlequin Alchymist*, and *The Great Devil*. In the last piece he severely burned his foot when his stage pistol went off as he was withdrawing it from his boot. At the end of the season, Dubois, who was performing the other Clown, grew discontented with the increasing popularity of Grimaldi and an unsatisfactory salary and left the Wells for Covent Garden. Now, as Dibdin put it, Grimaldi was "*Solus* as Clown at the Wells; and has stood *solus*, in point of merit, as *the* Clown ever since."

He did not return immediately to Drury Lane in the autumn of 1801, for he had quarreled with Kemble the previous spring over his assignment to the Easter pantomime—contrary to Grimaldi's articles—and had been dismissed in a letter from the prompter. Instead he went to play in Richard Hughes's theatre at Exeter for £4 per week and also appeared for several performances in Mrs Baker's company at Rochester. When Sheridan, who did not pay much attention to his theatre, finally missed Grimaldi at Drury Lane he enquired after the cause, grew enraged, and summoned his Clown back by December 1801.

On the twenty-fourth of that month Grimaldi married young Mary Bristow, a small-part actress at Sadler's Wells and Drury Lane and the daughter of the provincial actor Bristow and his wife (fl. 1797–1804). Her mother had sung at Drury Lane in the spring of 1800. In December 1803, after her husband's death, she became Mrs Robert Skinner, under which name she acted at Edinburgh. Mary's sister Louisa Maria Bristow acted at Covent Garden between 1805 and 1810; she married the harlequin-friend of Grimaldi, John Bologna, in June 1818. A Maria Bristow, who also acted at Covent Garden in the early part of the nineteenth century and who received £75 by the will of Grimaldi

in 1837, was probably another sister. Mary's brother George Bristow acted at London and Edinburgh in the first two decades of the nineteenth century.

Mary Bristow herself had not performed in London in the eighteenth century. She appeared among the vocalists in *Harlequin Amulet* and *Pizarro* at Drury Lane in the autumn of 1800 and continued in obscurity—even when her husband had become a household name—in the Drury Lane chorus at £1 10s. per week through 1805–6 and then at Covent Garden, at a similar salary, through 1821–22. The *Memoirs* say little about her beyond the statement that Grimaldi had lived with her "very happily for more than thirty years when she died"—in 1834. Their only child Joseph S. Grimaldi was born on 21 November 1802.

With Dibdin over the next four summers at Sadler's Wells, Grimaldi prospered, earning about £6 per week plus his benefits. His engagement there was renewed in 1803, "at a high and rising salary" according to Dibdin, for which he "performed in every line." That year he played Sir John Bull in *New Brooms*, the Giant's Dwarf in *Jack and the Beanstalk*, Clown in *Fire and Spirit; or, a Holiday Harlequin*, the title role in *Philip Quarll* (in which the hero lived among monkeys), Clown in *Goody Two Shoes; or, Harlequin Alabaster*, and Gorthmund, Prince of the Assassins, in *The Old Man of the Mountains*. The last piece had a sensational ending when the besieged Gorthmund was killed by a fall into a cauldron of fire. In 1804 Grimaldi was seen in a number of shows, for which Dibdin equipped the Wells with a tank, including *The Siege of Gibraltar* and *Anthony and Cleopatra; or, Harlequin Nilus*. "Grimaldi and the Water," wrote Dibdin, "were the Alpha and Omega." In 1806 he performed a famous dance of vegetables in *Harlequin and the Water Kelpie* and a grand combat in *The Invisible Ring; or, the Water Monster and Fire Spectre*. Grimaldi had also played on the Kent circuit in

March 1802, taking home about £300.

At Drury Lane, however, during those years Grimaldi's talents were being undervalued by a management unsympathetic to pantomime. He appeared as Punch in *Cinderella* in January 1804 and in *Old Harlequin's Fireside* in 1804–5. Again he played the Second Gravedigger when Master Betty acted Hamlet that latter season. Although he began the season of 1805–6 at Drury Lane, Grimaldi soon broke his engagement, making his final appearance at that theatre on 7 November 1805 as Pan in *Terpsichore's Return*. Later in his *Memoirs*, Grimaldi called his departure the result of a "very trifling misunderstanding." At the beginning of the season his salary of £5 per week had been supplemented by a £2 bonus in compensation for his taking over temporarily the duties of ballet master, made vacant by the defection of Byrn to Covent Garden, while the company awaited the arrival of the new appointee to that position, James D'Egville. Grimaldi had agreed to that responsibility, subject to the proviso that the £2 bonus would become a permanent increase; according to the *Memoirs*, Aaron Graham, then assisting Sheridan with the theatre's financial affairs, ratified that condition. But soon after D'Egville arrived, Graham reduced Grimaldi's salary, provoking his resignation.

The dispute over the bonus no doubt gave Grimaldi the excuse he was seeking to leave Drury Lane. Certainly by the seventh of November, the date of his last performance there, he had agreed to join an adventure in Dublin, where Charles Dibdin had leased Astley's Amphitheatre on Peter Street from 9 November 1805 to 14 February 1806. Dibdin had articled him at the attractive salary of 12 guineas per week and his wife Mary at two guineas. Moreover, a more appreciative management at Covent Garden had offered him an engagement for the ensuing season at £6 per week, to be raised to £7 for the following two seasons, and to £8 for the

fourth and fifth. According to his *Memoirs*, Joe had agreed to the terms before leaving for Ireland, but Charles Dibdin, whose brother Tom had urged the arrangement upon the Covent Garden proprietor Thomas Harris, claimed that the negotiations did not occur until after Grimaldi returned.

In any event, the Dublin season proved to be a disaster for Dibdin. Not even Grimaldi, who arrived by the third week to play in *Harlequin Aesop*—"As it was performed at the Aquatic Theatre, Sadler's Wells . . . three months to nightly overflowing houses"—could turn the tide, bringing only a house of £24 on his opening. Dibdin's account differs somewhat from Grimaldi's, who claimed to have taken £197 19*s*. at his own benefit and stated that the season was eminently successful until bad weather set in.

On 9 October 1806, as Orson in Tom Dibdin's *Valentine and Orson*, Grimaldi made his debut at Covent Garden. Valentine was played by Charles Farley (1772–1859), the producer of pantomimes and melodramas at Covent Garden, who became a dear and important friend. It was Farley, according to the *Memoirs*, who was Joe's real master, "as he not only took infinite pains to instruct him in the character of Orson, but afterwards gave him very valuable advice and assistance in getting up many other parts." The role of Orson was considered by Grimaldi the most difficult he ever played: "the multitude of passions requiring to be portrayed, and the rapid succession involving an unusual share of both mental and physical exertion upon the part of the performer." The *Memoirs* are replete with stories of physical exhaustion; perhaps they were prompted by Dickens's technique of constantly foreshadowing Grimaldi's premature collapse. But by his account, after every performance of the first act Grimaldi would sink into an armchair. "He would sob and cry aloud, and suffer so much from violent and agonizing spasms," but he always recovered by the end of the interval to return to the stage for the next act. Dickens wrote:

The effect produced on the audience by Grimaldi's personification of this character was intense: it enhanced his reputation greatly, bringing him before the public in quite a new line. The compliments and congratulations which he received from persons ranking high in his profession, in literature, and in the fine arts, bore high testimony to the merit and striking character of this singular performance.

An even greater triumph for Grimaldi occurred two months later, on 26 December 1806, with *Harlequin and Mother Goose; or, The Golden Egg*. Written by Tom Dibdin and composed by Ware, with Jack Bologna as Harlequin, Luigi Bologna as Avaro the pantaloon, Miss Searle as Colinette the columbine, Samuel Simmons as Mother Goose, and Grimaldi as Clown, the piece ran for 92 nights to deafening applause. It became the most famous Christmas entertainment in the history of English pantomime and the greatest success of Grimaldi's career.

Grimaldi was a sensation in *Mother Goose*. The picture conjured up by Findlater of the Clown waiting in the wings for his first entrance captures the excitement and the color:

He wears a red shirt, frilled and decorated with blue and white facings, which is cut away at the chest and waist to reveal an ornamented shirt beneath; his blue-and-white-striped breeches end above the knee with a red-white-and blue ribbon, which is repeated at his wrists; and beneath his blue-crested wig, his whitened face is daubed with red triangles on either cheek. He is a very English Clown. . . .

The *Monthly Mirror* wrote that "of all the whimsical beings that, by their contortions and vulgarities in pantomime, set the young, ay, and old folks too, in a roar, the

Harvard Theatre Collection

JOSEPH GRIMALDI, as Clown in *Harlequin and Mother Goose*

by De Wilde

clown of Grimaldi is the most surprising, diverting and effective. We can in no way describe what he does. . . . He must be seen." Lord Eldon, the Lord Chancellor, who saw *Mother Goose* a total of 12 nights, exclaimed, "Never, never did I see a leg of mutton stolen with such superhumanly sublime impudence as by that man." Among the numerous street ballads and broadsides which appeared in tribute to the production was:

> *Come all ye who love mirth and fun,*
> *   No matter who ye may be,*
> *To Covent Garden all must run,*
> *   Who merry would, and wise be:*
> *You'll of your time find no abuse,*
> *   Since for your cash, i' fegs, sirs,*
> *Your old acquaintance, Mother Goose,*
> *   Will give you Golden Eggs, sirs.*

Eventually, *Mother Goose* reputedly brought Covent Garden a profit of £20,000. At the end of the 1806–7 season, Grimaldi signed a pay sheet (now in the Harvard Theatre Collection) to acknowledge receipt of £51 10*s*. as his salary for the season; that was a comparative pittance, but on the eighty-eighth night of *Mother Goose,* 9 June 1807, he and Bologna took more than £604, a sizable sum, in shared benefit receipts. Although he continued to be hailed in and to profit largely from revivals of *Mother Goose,* Grimaldi thought little of the pantomime and declared "his own part to be one of the worst he ever played; nor was there a trick or situation in the piece to which he had not been well accustomed for many years before."

During the following 16 winter seasons at Covent Garden, through 1822–23, and 12 summers at Sadler's Wells, through 1819, Grimaldi had no equal as the Clown in numerous pantomimes and melodramas. At Covent Garden (and the Haymarket and Lyceum between 1809 and 1812 while the fire-gutted Covent Garden was being built anew) his performances included *Harlequin in his Element,* Baptist in *Raymond and Agnes,* Skirmish in *The Deserter of Naples* in 1807–8; *Don Juan* in 1809–10; *Harlequin and Asmodeus* in 1810–11; *Harlequin and the Red Dwarf* in 1812–13; *Harlequin Hoax* in 1814; *Harlequin Gulliver* in 1817–18; *Harlequin Munchausen* —when the press observed that "Grimaldi, though as comic, is not as active as he used to be"—in 1818–19; and *Harlequin and Don Quixote* and *Harlequin and Cinderella* in 1819–20.

At Sadler's Wells in 1807 he starred in *Jan Ben Jan; or, Harlequin and the Forty Virgins,* an Oriental tale, in which his comic song "Me and my Neddy" became so popular that watch faces were painted with his countenance on them, singing it. On one night in July, according to a far-fetched anecdote in the *Memoirs,* a deaf-and-dumb sailor was so convulsed by Grimaldi's antics that he suddenly regained his speech, previously lost by sunstroke, and cried out "What a d——d funny fellow!"

In 1808 at the Wells, Grimaldi performed in *Harlequin Highflyer; or, Off she goes* in which he sang "Oh! my dreary!" and "A Bull in a China Shop." In *Thirty Thousand; or, Harlequin's Lottery* he offered "Smithfield Bargain, or Will Putty." Other songs during the season were "Odd Fish," "Whip Club," and "Looney's Lamentation for Miss Margery Muggins." His most outstanding performance came in *The Wild Man, or Water Pageant,* in which Charles Dibdin included a scene "representing the powerful influences of Music over even the Savage Mind; which as the flute player varied his Measure, drew from Grimaldi, a very impressive exhibition, in action, of all the various passions of the natural mind; and so popular did this Scene become," according to Dibdin's testimony, "that the incident, as a Scene, has been perpetually introduced as an attractive feature on Benefit Nights, at almost every Theatre in Town, and many in the Country; under the Title of 'The Power of Music.' " His portrayal of the Wild Man was a tragic dumb show of such rare excellence that many in the audience were brought to tears. In *The Old Playgoer,* William Robson described this "very height of pantomimic action" performed to the accompaniment of a single small flute:

As a wild man . . . he is about to tear a child to pieces, whose father, destitute of other means of conquering him, tried the power of music. The first fierce glance and start, as the sound struck upon his ear, were natural and fine—the hands hung as if arrested, the purpose was at pause.

As the plaintive air of the flageolet continued, it was really wonderful to watch . . . when at length, the savage heart became so softened that his whole frame shook convulsively, and he clasped his hands to his face in an agony of tears, he never failed to elicit the

Harvard Theatre Collection

JOSEPH GRIMALDI, as Clown in *Harlequin and the Red Dwarf*

engraving after Norman

proudest triumph of the actor's art—the sympathetic drops from the eye of every spectator. And, when the measure was changed to a livelier strain, the picture became almost frightful, for his mirth was in as great an extreme as his grief—he danced like a fury!

I have seen him play this a dozen times at least, and was as much affected by the last exhibition as the first.

His rendering of the songs in *Bang Up; or Harlequin Prime* contributed to the success of that piece at the Wells in 1810. With his performance in *Harlequin and Blue Beard* in 1811 he caricatured Maria De Camp's singing in Kelly's *Blue-Beard*. Other productions included *Whang Fong; or, Harlequin in China* in 1812, *London; or, Harlequin and Time* in 1813, the aquadrama *Kaloc* in 1815, and *Barissa; or, the Hermit Robber* in 1816.

In the spring of 1817 an extraordinary circumstance occurred: Sadler's Wells opened the season without Joseph Grimaldi. According to Dibdin, the management could not accede to Grimaldi's demand for a higher salary and his request to be excused from his duties for a time in order to make a provincial tour. On the other hand, according to Grimaldi's *Memoirs*, his only request was that his salary of £12 per week—which he had been receiving since 1812—be raised to 12 guineas. The proprietors agreed but then took from him one of the two benefits he was accustomed to having each summer. Grimaldi relied heavily on those benefits, usually taking a minimum of £150 each (in 1812 he took £225 at one). When Paulo substituted as the Clown in *Forget me not; or, the Flowers of Waterloo*, the house was slim and placards appeared throughout Islington—"No Paulo!" and "Joey for ever!" The Wells reputedly lost £2534 that season.

Joe, however, went with his son to Birmingham in April 1817 to earn £210 for six nights. (He had been there previously in the spring of 1808.) He then played at Liverpool, Worcester, Preston, Hereford, Berwick, Glasgow, Edinburgh, and Brighton. At Birmingham again in October 1817 he performed for Elliston's benefit and then was at Leicester. In about 46 nights away from London he earned some £1750.

In 1818 Grimaldi returned to Sadler's Wells on his own terms at the behest of Mrs Hughes, the main shareholder and his first mother-in-law. The terms no doubt included the right to make a provincial tour each year. He was now a proprietor, having bought at an unknown price five shares (an eighth part). The other proprietors included Mrs Hughes with 14 shares, Charles Dibdin and the businessman T. Barfoot each with seven, and Mrs Jones, daughter of the late composer William Reeve, with five. The return of Grimaldi was "hailed with shouts of applause." But the season, according to both Dibdin and Grimaldi, was not a success. They dropped the curtain at the season's end "chopfallen," wrote the former. Grimaldi claimed that each shareholder lost £333 13s., but Charles Whitehead, the editor of the 1846 edition of the *Memoirs*, claimed to have seen the treasurer's books which showed a profit in the seasons of 1818, 1819, and 1820.

When, as the result of a dispute with the other proprietors, Charles Dibdin resigned as manager of Sadler's Wells soon after the 1819 season began, Grimaldi was appointed to the position. According to the Grimaldi *Memoirs*, Dibdin had resigned ten days before the opening on 12 April but had been persuaded to stay on till Whitsun. On opening night a fourteen-year-old lad, John Meeking, was trampled to death in the gallery rush and it was Grimaldi who came before the curtain to calm the audience. That was the night on which

Grimaldi introduced the most famous of his songs, "Hot Codlins," in Dibdin's *The Talking Bird*:

> A litle old woman her living she got
> By selling codlins [*i.e., apples*], hot, hot, hot;
> And this little old woman, who codlins sold,
> Tho' her codlins were hot, she felt herself cold;
> So, to keep herself warm, she thought it no sin
> To fetch for herself a quartern of . . .

at which point the audience shouted out "Gin!"—and in shocked amazement Grimaldi would respond, "Oh for shame!" There were at least three additional verses, each inviting the obvious rhyme from the audience, and each followed by a nonsense chorus of: "Ri tol iddy, iddy, iddy,/ Ri tol, iddy, iddy, ri tol lay." That season Grimaldi also produced a pantomime of his own concoction, *The Fates; or Harlequin's Holy Day*, which he claimed saved the season financially.

During the season of 1819–20 at Covent Garden, having "a few nights to spare," Grimaldi earned £160 by playing four nights in March at King's Lynn in Norfolk. He must have done so after *Harlequin and Don Quixote* closed in mid-February after 39 performances and before 4 March 1820 when he wrote to Joseph Munden from his house at No 8, Exmouth Street, Spa Fields, Clerkenwell: "Time presses upon me fast as after this week I shall be excessive busy at the Wells therefore mention a Day I may expect you will take *Pot-luck* with me—" (MS in Harvard Theatre Collection). On 3 April 1820 he opened as Baroness Pompsini in *Harlequin and Cinderella; or, The Little Glass Slipper* at Covent Garden. Within a few weeks he began the season at Sadler's Wells, where the American actor-manager John Howard Payne had taken over as manager. That summer Joe's son, who had made his debut with success as Friday in *Mother Goose* back in 1814, appeared with him in *The Yellow Dwarf; or, Harlequin of the Golden Mimes.* At the end of the season, for Payne's benefit on 2 October 1820, Grimaldi offered a program called *Scraps: or, Fun for the Gallery,* which consisted of bits and pieces of earlier triumphs including his "Typitywitchet" song and the famous pas de deux with Jack Bologna from *Mother Goose.* Everyone in the boxes and pit was given, gratis, an engraved portrait of Grimaldi, after Wageman. But the evening was marred when a stray spark from a candle or lamp on the stage provoked a near panic.

The *Memoirs* stated that, with special permission to be absent from Covent Garden, Grimaldi went with his son and Ellar to perform for Henry Harris at the Dublin Pavilion in September 1820. It would have been a neat trick, since he appeared at Sadler's Wells for Payne's benefit on 2 October and, according to the contradictory *Memoirs,* had been acting at Covent Garden since it opened on 20 September.

In 1820–21 at Covent Garden Grimaldi played Kasrac in *Aladdin* until the new Christmas pantomime was brought on. Called *Harlequin and Friar Bacon; or, The Brazen Head,* it proved to be very successful for 52 nights. His son Joseph played the Lover in the harlequinade, and Joe himself was the Clown. Making his first visit in years to Covent Garden, George IV caught "Joey" at the top of his form — including his dagger scene from Macbeth in Clown costume and a hilarious scene in which as a chimney sweep he inadvertently spread soot throughout the white boudoir of a fashionable lady — and the King was so convulsed with laughter, the unlikely story goes, that his stays burst. Although onstage he seemed at the height of his vigor, Joe was beginning to tire. Within a week of his opening in the Easter pantomime *Undine; or, The Spirit of the Waters,* he gave to his son his part of Gyblin.

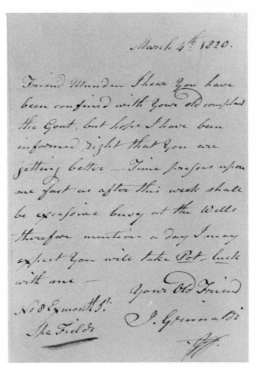

Harvard Theatre Collection

Letter by JOSEPH GRIMALDI to JOSEPH MUNDEN

4 March 1820

The previous summer, indeed, had been his final season at the Wells, for in the spring of 1821 he quarreled with Daniel Egerton (1771–1835), the new lessee, over his contract and refused to return to the Islington house. Grimaldi should have welcomed the summer lay-off to gather his strength for another planned excursion, to Dublin in the autumn, with his son and Ellar. The *Memoirs* fail to mention that Grimaldi played 20 nights in July 1821 at Birmingham at a salary of £20 per week (and £9 for his son) and half a clear benefit. At Birmingham he had his portrait drawn by Raven on six large oval papier-maché boxes, which he distributed to friends. Later in Dublin on the eighteenth night of *Friar Bacon* he became very ill — "with an agony of mind perfectly indescribable, Grimaldi found his health giving way by alarming degrees beneath the ravages of old age" (*Memoirs*) — and was unable to play for a week. He then dragged himself through the rest of the thirty-two-night engagement, departed Ireland on 6 December 1821, and rushed back to Covent Garden in time to begin rehearsals for the Christmas pantomime, *The Yellow Dwarf*, which ran 42 nights. At Easter, *Cherry and the Fair Star* was revived.

Grimaldi seemed driven to continue performing, despite the infirmity of his once seemingly indestructible frame. In the early summer of 1822 he played six weeks at the Coburg "at a considerable sum per week and a free benefit," but his "continued and dangerous indisposition" forced cancellation of several performances. He received £150 for 12 nights in August at Cheltenham, where he had originally gone to drink the waters.

He seemed almost himself again in 54 performances of *Harlequin and the Ogress; or, The Sleeping Beauty*, the Covent Garden Christmas pantomime in 1822–23. At the end of March he began to play Tycobac in Farley's new Easter melodrama *The Vision of the Sun; or, The Orphan of Peru*. Grimaldi's herculean efforts to go on with the show are effectively described in the *Memoirs*:

even during the earlier nights of its very successful representation he could scarcely struggle through his part. His frame was weak and debilitated, his joints stiff, and his muscles relaxed; every effort he made was followed by cramps and spasms of the most agonizing nature. Men were obliged to be kept waiting at the side-scenes, who caught him in their arms when he staggered from the stage and supported him while others chafed his limbs — which was obliged to be done incessantly until he was called for the next scene, or he could not have appeared again. Every time he came off his sinews were gathered up into huge knots by the cramps that followed his exertions, which could only be reduced by

violent rubbing, and even that frequntly failed to produce the desired effect. The spectators, who were convulsed with laughter while he was on stage, little thought that while their applause was resounding through the house he was suffering the most excruciating and horrible pains. . . .

By 26 April he was playing again in *Harlequin and the Ogress*. As the Clown in that piece on 3 May 1823 — "it was only with the most extreme difficulty and by dint of extraordinary physical exertion and agony that he could conclude the performance" — he gave his last performance at Covent Garden. On 5 May, when the melodrama *The Vision of the Sun* was brought back, the role of Tycobac was filled by his son.

Grimaldi returned to Cheltenham to recuperate. In August 1823 he traveled from the watering place to Birmingham, where he played, according to the *Memoirs*, a pantomime of his own, *Puck and the Pudding*, for three nights, taking £186 12*s.* as his share of the profits. A notation in a manuscript at the National Library of Ireland (MS 4292) claimed he worked four nights, accompanied by his son. Three or four, they were his last professional appearances. A local critic in the *Birmingham Reporter* of 4 September 1823 liked the performances but wrote "Mr G. seems much the worse for wear: indeed, the introduction of his son on the boards contemporary with himself indicates that we must take him as an apology for loss of agility in the parent."

Although he had agreed to return to Cheltenham to play one night, for £100, in *Valentine and Orson* with his son and his friend Colonel Berkeley — "to amuse the people" — a relapse prevented him. Upon arriving at Cheltenham from Birmingham "he was attacked by a severe and alarming illness," which confined him to bed for a month and left him a cripple for life. Findlater's speculation that he had suffered an attack of poliomyelitis perhaps is correct. At the least, the crippled Clown had been humbled, it would seem, by a severe and permanent rheumatoid arthritis. It was a most cruel destiny for the son, now only 45, of a vigorous acrobat who had sired him at the age of about 65 and the grandson of a mountebank called Iron Legs.

Except for a brief venture into co-management in the Wells in 1824, Old Joe passed his last years in morose and quiet retirement, estranged from his son, who had plunged himself into habits so unstable that not even Joe's influence could compensate for the fellow's notorious professional reputation. (The son came to his end, probably of delerium tremens, at No 24, Pitt Street, on 11 December 1832 at the age of 30.)

Grimaldi intended to make a return to Sadler's Wells in the summer of 1827, but his performances announced for the Wells that season never occurred: "poor old Joey Grimaldi was dragged from a sick bed, with a view to prop the falling fortunes of this former scene of his early fame," reported the *Weekly Dramatic Register* on 2 June, "but alas! all would not do—for Joey . . . broke down under the accumulated pressure of *mental* and *bodily* infirmity."

The following year more than 2000 people packed the Wells on St Patrick's Day, 17 March 1828, to bid farewell to Grimaldi. It was, of course, a scene packed as well with high emotion. The burletta *Humphrey Clinker* was given, Campbell sang, Miss Searle danced, Payne juggled, and Joe Junior and Ellar performed the pas de deux from *Mother Goose*. With the greatest difficulty Joe himself played the drunken sailor Hock in Tom Dibdin's *The Sixes; or, The Fiends*, and sang a duet with his son. Some five hours after the evening had begun, dressed in black with white waistcoat and gloves and with all the other performers standing behind him, Grimaldi came forward to address the audience:

Ladies and Gentlemen,—I appear before you this evening for the last time in this theatre. Doubtless, there are many persons present who think I am a very aged man: I have now an opportunity of convincing them to the contrary. I was born on the 18th of December 1779 [actually 1778] and, consequently, on the 18th of last December attained the age of forty-eight.

At a very early age—before that of three years, I was introduced to the public by my father at this theatre; and ever since that period have I held a situation in this establishment. Yes, ladies and gentlemen, I have been engaged at this theatre for five-and-forty years.

By strict attention, perseverance, and exertion, did I arrive at the height of my profession, and, proud I am to acknowledge, have ofttimes been honoured with your smiles, approbation, and support. It is now three years since I have taken a regular engagement, owing to extreme and dangerous indisposition: with patience have I waited in hope my health might once more be re-established, and I again meet your smiles as before;—but, I regret to say, there is little or, in fact, no improvement perceivable, and it would therefore now be folly in me ever to think of again returning to my professional duties. I could not, however, leave this theatre without returning my grateful thanks to my friends and patrons, and the public; and now do I venture to offer them, secure in the conviction that they will not be slighted or deemed utterly unworthy of acceptance.

To the proprietors of the theatre, the performers, the gentlemen of the band—in fact, to every individual connected with it, I likewise owe and offer my sincere thanks for their assistance this evening. And now, ladies and gentlemen, it only remains for me to utter one dreadful word, ere I depart—Farewell!—God bless you all! may you and your families ever enjoy the blessings of health and happiness.— Farewell!

The Sadler's Wells farewell brought him £315 and an ordeal from which he did not recover "for some days." When a stuffy and chary management refused him a night at Covent Garden, where he had

JOSEPH GRIMALDI's "Last Song"

by G. Gruikshank

no longer wear the motley! Four years ago I jumped my last jump, filched my last custard, and ate my last sausage. I cannot describe the pleasure I felt on once more assuming my cap and bells tonight—that dress in which I have so often been made happy in your applause; and as I stripped them off, I fancied that they seemed to cleave to me. I am not so rich a man as I was when I was basking in your favour formerly, for then I had always a fowl in one pocket and sauce for it in the other. [Laughter and applause from the audience.] I thank you for the benevolence which has brought you here to assist your old and faithful servant in his premature decline. Eight-and-forty years have not yet passed over my head, and I am sinking fast. I now stand worse on my legs than I used to do on my head. But I suppose I am paying the penalty of the cause I pursued all my life; my desire and anxiety to merit your favour has excited me to more exertion than my constitution would bear, and, like vaulting ambition, I have over-leaped myself. Ladies and Gentleman, I must hasten to bid you farewell; but the pain I feel in doing so is assuaged by seeing before me a disproof of the old adage, that favourites have no friends. Ladies and Gentlemen, may you and yours ever enjoy the blessings of health is the fervent prayer of Joseph Grimaldi—*Farewell! farewell!*

Although he was required to pay the Drury Lane house charges of £210, when the private gifts were added, Grimaldi received £580 from this benefit. Over the years, indeed, his benefits had paid him well: £238 at Covent Garden on 23 May 1809; £423 on 26 June 1810; £423 on 25 June 1811; £394 on 24 June 1812; £331 on 1 July 1813; £426, shared with Bologna, on 29 June 1814. At the Wells he had regularly enjoyed two benefits per season, which usually brought him a minimum of £150 each. In his later professional years his weekly salary, as well, at both houses had been respectable if not spectacular. In 1828 he began to receive an annuity of £100 from the Drury Lane Theatrical Fund. There are no indications in the *Memoirs* that in his years of retire-

played for 16 years, Stephen Price, the American manager at Drury Lane, where he had played from the age of two through 27, gave him that theatre on 27 June 1828 for a second farewell. The vast Drury Lane, perhaps twice the size of the Wells, was thronged to pay homage. Sitting on a chair center stage, Joe played a barber shop scene from *The Magic Fire.* "Hot Codlins" evoked the familiar refrains from his audience. All the clowns and harlequins in London then performed, and finally their King of Clowns addressed the assembly, not in the speech prepared for him by Thomas Hood (printed in the *Memoirs*) but in his own words (cited by Findlater):

Ladies and Gentlemen, I appear before you for the last time. I need not assure you of the sad regret with which I say it; but sickness and infirmity have come upon me, and I can ment he found himself in financial jeopardy, although many of his colleagues died in humiliating poverty.

From 1820, and perhaps earlier, Grimaldi had lived at No 8, Exmouth Street, Spa Fields, in Clerkenwell, until about April 1832, when he took a smaller house several hundred yards away at No 23, Garnault Place. He left that residence at Michaelmas 1832 for another small place at No 6, Prospect Row, Woolwich (now No 11, Prospect Vale), and then moved to Bowling Green Row in 1834. His wife Mary suffered a paralytic stroke about 1832 and required Joe's constant nursing until her death in 1834, after which he moved to No 31, George Street, Woolwich. In June 1835, he returned to Clerkenwell, to a house at No 33, Southampton Street, off the Pentonville Road, where he resided with a housekeeper, Susannah Hill. He used to frequent the public house the Marquis of Cornwall, whose proprietor George Cooke carried him the few yards back and forth on his back.

In the Lilly Library at Indiana University is an autograph letter from Grimaldi dated "Dec 5th, [from] Arlington St. nr Sadlers Wells," addressed to a "Dear Old Friend"—a variant copy is in the Harvard Theatre Collection—which reveals his mood during retirement:

I shall not be able to come—Poor Joey's laid up in lavender, This cold weather and will never again make Christmas folk grin with his anticks, his buffooneries and his quips and cranks. no more concealment of sausages in his capacious breeches pockets— no more bottles stowed away—no more merry songs and sayings and gibes. O! my heart grieves! Well, there must be an end to everything mortal and as poor Palmer said when he stood on the stage (his last words) "There is another and a better world," I wonder if I shall be able to "clown" it there. Well, Adsum [?], would I could come to your Son's benefit and give him the advantage of my pranks and humour. But I can't go—impossible. I am

"hipped." I will, however, put my mite down, which will not be a "mighty one," I tell you, for I am far from a millionaire. Oh! that pain —it is coursing on again, and I must drop the pen that quivers in my hand—

Come and see poor Joey—come dear Friend and talk to me as of yore. The sight of your jolly rubicund mug will mayhap ease me and drive for the nonce "dull care away."

Your as ever,
Joey Grimaldi
("Grim-all-day")
Joking to the last you see

Joe Grimaldi died the night of 31 May 1837 at his house in Southampton Street. On Monday 5 June (not 6 June as given in *The Dictionary of National Biography*) he was buried in the graveyard of St James on Pentonville Hill, with a private ceremony, next to the grave of Charles Isaac Mungo Dibdin, who had died in 1833. A simple memorial placed in the churchyard reads:

Sacred
to the Memory of
Mr Joseph Grimaldi
Who Departed This Life
May 31st, 1837
Aged 58 Years

In his will, signed on 3 September 1836, in which he described himself as a "Comedian," Grimaldi left bequests amounting to some £500 to his surviving in-laws and friends. In the will he provided the full name of his late second wife, Mary Anne Catherine, and left to her sisters various amounts in New 3½% investments and other items: to the eldest, Louisa Maria Bristow, £74; to the "second sister," Mrs Charlotte Christiana Bryan, £100 and all his household goods and chattels except his plate and jewels; to the "third sister," Mrs Maria Susannah Neville, £50. To his housekeeper Mrs Mary Arthur he gave £100. His plate and plated goods "together with two patchwork quilts the larg-

est made by my first wife, poor dear Maria
the smaller one by her sister Julia now
Mrs Bennett . . . Which I hope will be
received out of respect to her dear Memory," he left to his niece Mrs Elizabeth Eye
(Gye?), the eldest daughter of his brother-
in-law Richard Hughes the younger. To
Mr Dayus, treasurer of Sadler's Wells, he
bequeathed £25 for "his kind attentions to
me and my dear Wife upon all occasions."
He also left £25 each to his dear friends of
long attachment Richard Henry Norman,
of No 5, Melina Place, Westminster Road,
and James Banister of No 20, Union Street,
Deptford, and £50 to his servant Susannah Hill. To his brother-in-law Richard
Hughes, of Finchley, the proprietor of
Vauxhall Gardens, Grimaldi left his share
in Sadler's Wells Theatre and appointed
him executor. Hughes proved the will on
22 July 1837.

A year after Grimaldi's death, H. D.
Miles labeled him the "Pan of Pantomime"
and wrote in his *Life of Joseph Grimaldi*
that "in a low deportment [*sic*] of art, he
was the most wonderful creature of his day,
and far more unapproachable in his excellence than Kean and Kemble in theirs." In
"Some Recollections of Grimaldi" which
appeared in "The Manager's Note-book" is
a lengthy but very revealing account of the
great Clown at work:

. . . His eyes, large, globular, and sparkling,
rolled in a riot of joy; his mouth, capacious,
yet with a never-ending power of extension,
could convey all sorts of physical enjoyment
and distaste; his nose was not the mere bow-
sprit appendage we find that respectable feature to be in general: it was a vivacious
excrescence capable of exhibiting disdain,
fear, anger, even joy. We think we see him
now screwing it on one side; his eyes, nearly
closed, but twinkling forth his rapture; and
his tongue a little extended in the fulness of
his enjoyment; his chin he had a power of
lowering, we will not say to what button of
his waistcoat, but certainly the drop was an
alarming one.

It always appeared to us that Grimaldi
moved his ears; and this, anatomically speaking, is not an impossibility. Be it as it may,
the way in which he drew down his lower
jaw on any sudden surprise gave this effect to
the auricular organs. Speech would have been
thrown away in his performance of Clown;
every limb of him had a language. What eloquent legs were his! Look at him approaching
that cottage of gentility; THE man is changed:
see how he stands looking at the window, at
which hangs a bonnet: his back is toward
you; but it tells the tale, the lady within is to
be won. Look how he bends towards the balcony—Romeo in red and white: see how
mincingly he puts forth his foot, and passes
his hand over his garments; he must woo in
another shape; he turns round in utter be-
wilderment; anon a boy passes—he plays at
marbles with him, first for money, then for
his jacket; he wins it: a dandy passes—he ab-
stracts his coat tails: a miller—he steals a
sack: he has stolen yonder chimney-pot, and
made a hat; taken that dandizette's shawl, and
converted it into a waistcoat: the sack becomes white ducks; the tails render the jacket
a coat; a cellar-door iron ring forms an eyeglass; and he moves, an admirable caricature
of the prevailing fashion of the day.

Then, was there ever such a coach-builder?
Go to school, Mr. Houlditch; for, with a coal-
scuttle and a few cheeses, Grimaldi would
construct you a vehicle at a moment's notice.
Is his vegetable man unforgotten? He was no
paltry humorist who conceived the notion of
making a melon into a head, and turnips and
radishes do the duty of hands and fingers. His
love-making—what infinite variety in his ap-
proaches! His boisterous freedom with the
London fish-dealer; his sailor-like jollity at
Portsmouth; his exquisite nonchalant air
when attired as a dandy; and his undeniable
all-overishness when, as Clown, he meant to
impress, being suddenly smitten by the beauty
of his fair enslaver. It was all what we had an
hundred times seen, without the innate ridicu-
lousness of the things being made apparent
to us. Grimaldi had looked on the follies of
humanity, and fairly turned the seamy side
without. Then his treatment of that old man
villainous, "yclept Pantaloon," whom, old and
infirm as he is, no one pities at all, though he

is treated by all the persons of the medley drama in a way that no elderly gentleman should be expected to endure. We applauded and rejoiced in those vices in Grimaldi that we hated in the Pantaloon; here is a bone for your metaphysicians to pick: we were quite blind to the moral delinquency of Mons. Clown's habits; he was a thief—we loved him, nevertheless; a coward, a most detestable coward—still we loved him: he was cruel, treacherous, unmanly, ungenerous, greedy, and the truth was not in him—yet, for all this, multiplied up to murder, if you would, we loved him, and rejoiced in his successes. . . .

Grimaldi finished writing his reminiscences on his birthday in 1836, but arrangements for their publication by Thomas Egerton Wilks who was to revise the manuscript were aborted by Joe's death the following year. They were published in February 1838 as *The Memoirs of Joseph Grimaldi*, edited by "Boz"—Charles Dickens—with 12 engravings by George Cruikshank and an engraved portrait, after Raven. In 1846 a new edition was brought out by Charles Whitehead, with more plates. Richard Findlater published a modern edition with an introductory essay and very important annotations in 1968. Grimaldi's original manuscript remained for some years in the possession of Richard Hughes, his brother-in-law. In 1874 it was sold at London for 100 guineas, bound in red morocco and extra-illustrated with numerous playbills and pictures; perhaps it was purchased then by the Henry Stevens who owned it when Grimaldi's notice for *The Dictionary of National Biography* was written. When Findlater prepared his edition in 1968 the manuscript still existed, but its whereabouts would not be revealed to him by Sacheverell Sitwell, who presumably knew. For additional information on Grimaldi's life, private character, and technique, the reader should consult Findlater's excellent *Grimaldi King of Clowns* (1955). A comprehensive description of pantomimes is

Harvard Theatre Collection

JOSEPH GRIMALDI

engraving by Blood, after Wageman

provided by David Mayer in *Harlequin in his Element, the English Pantomime, 1806–1836* (1969).

"If to be loved by a whole nation in his lifetime and to live in all men's fancies a hundred years after is a true sign of greatness," eulogized Willson Disher, "then Joseph Grimaldi has a right to be reckoned among our famous men." On 30 May 1937 a Centenary Memorial Service for Grimaldi was held at St James, Pentonville. Six years earlier, in January 1931, a gathering of clowns from the Olympia Circus in London and others from all over Europe made a pilgrimage to lay a wreath on his grave. On a less reverent note, large colored posters depicting Grimaldi in his various roles and tying him in with the House of Whitbread, Brewers, were stuck up in the London Underground system in 1959.

We make no claim of comprehensiveness for the following list of portraits of

Joseph Grimaldi. Because there are various versions of some of the engravings especially, for convenience we have placed in a parenthesis the number of the description, when applicable, in the *Catalogue of Engraved Dramatic Portraits in the Harvard Theatre Collection.*

1. By John Cawse, painting. Purchased by the National Portrait Gallery in 1889. On loan to Sadler's Wells Theatre.

2. By George Cruikshank, pencil sketch. Lying down, with feet to front. In the British Museum.

3. By George Cruikshank, two pen and ink sketches of head on single sheet. In the British Museum.

4. By J. E. T. Robinson, watercolor drawing, 1819. In the Garrick Club.

5. By unknown artist, painting. In the Garrick Club.

6. By unknown artist, watercolor, at age 58. In the Beard Collection, Victoria and Albert Museum.

7. In dancing attitude, cruet statuette, by unknown sculptor. In the Beard Collection, Victoria and Albert Museum.

8. Portrait engraving by T. Blood, after T. Wageman. Published by C. Westmacott, 1820.

9. Portrait engraving by H. Brown (member of Sadler's Wells orchestra). Published by the engraver.

10. Portrait engraving by W. Greatbach, after T. Raven. Published as frontispiece to the *Memoirs*, 1846.

11. Portrait engraving by J. Rogers, after T. Wageman. Published as a plate to *Oxberry's Dramatic Biography* by C. Virtue, 1827.

12. Portrait engraving (within oval wreath), by unknown artist.

13. As Clown. Engraving by J. Brandard. (12)

14. As Clown, with Ellar as Harlequin, and Barnes as Pantaloon. Watercolor by H. Brown. In the British Museum. Another version of this watercolor by Brown is in the Percival Sadler's Wells Collection.

15. As Clown. Engraving by H. Brown. Published as a plate with *West's New Pantomimical Characters*, 26 July 1811. (11)

16. As Clown. Engraving by H. Brown. Published as a plate with *West's New Pantomimical Characters*, 1811. (8)

17. As Clown, "as he appeared when he took his farewell Benefit at Drury Lane Theatre on the 27th of June, 1828." Seated, holding tub of water on his lap. Engraving by H. Brown, 1828. (5)

18. As Clown. Engraving by R. Cooper. Published as a plate to the *Drama*, by T. & I. Elvey, 1822. (31)

19. As Clown. Painting by S. De Wilde, 1820. In the Harvard Theatre Collection.

20. As Clown, with title "I shall sing 'Hot Codlins in the Car.'" Engraving by Dorrington. (21)

21. As Clown. Watercolor by T. M. Grimshaw. In the London Museum.

22. As Clown, with title "The Spirit overcoming the Flesh, or the Downfall of my Deary." Engraving by F. W. Pailthorpe, after G. Cruikshank. (22)

23. As Clown, with title "Clown up Grimaldi." Engraving by W. Wells, after G. Cruikshank. (19)

24. As Clown. Watercolor by unknown artist. In the London Museum.

25. As Clown. Watercolor by unknown artist. In the Harvard Theatre Collection. This drawing is a variant of the engraving, by unknown engraver, published by J. K. Green, 1833. (27) Three other variant engravings of the same picture are also in the Harvard Theatre Collection. (28, 29, 30)

26. As Clown, with his Pretty Deary. Engraving by unknown artist. Published on title page of Fairburn's *Laughable Song Book*, 1813. (23) Another copy was published with the title "The Nearer the Bone, the Sweeter the Flesh." (24)

27. As Clown, with Pantaloon, Columbine, and Harlequin. Engraving by unknown engraver, after Cruikshank. (20)

28. As Clown. "Drawn from life by permission," by unknown engraver. Published by C. E. Pritchard, 1818. (6)

29. As Clown. Engraving by unknown artist. Published by Hodgson & Co., 1822. (7)

30. As Clown, with row of performers behind. At his Drury Lane Farewell, 1828. Engraving by unknown artist. In the Enthoven Collection, Victoria and Albert Museum.

31. As Clown. Engraving by unknown artist. Published as a plate to Scales's edition of *Harlequin in his Element*. (25)

32. As Clown. Engraving by unknown artist. (26)

With the following items we depart from our usual practice of listing pictures alphabetically by the role and provide them by *title of production*, a procedure which we believe in this case to be more convenient to the reader.

33. In *Aladdin; or, The Wonderful Lamp*. As Kazrac the Chinese Slave. By unknown engraver. Published by W. West, 1813. (53)

34. In *Fashion's Fools*. As the Coachman-Clown, singing the "Whip Club." Watercolor by T. M. Grimshaw, 1809. In the London Museum.

35. In *Gnomes and Fairies*. As Clown. By unknown engraver. (32)

36. In *Harlequin and Asmodeus*. As Clown. By unknown engraver, after Norman. Published by R. Ackermann, 1811. (38) A reproduction of this engraving, on a plate with other characters, was published by W. West, 1811. (39)

37. In *Harlequin and Asmodeus*. As Clown, with title "Grimaldi's Lobster Minuet." By unknown engraver. (40)

38. In *Harlequin in his Element*. As the Drunken Watchman, on a plate with several others. By unknown engraver. Published 26 July, 1811. (62)

39. In *Harlequin and Friar Bacon*. Engraving by I. R. Cruikshank. Published as a plate to *British Stage*, February 1811. (41) A copy was engraved by F. W. Pailthorpe, after Cruikshank. (42)

40. In *Harlequin and the Golden Fish*. As Clown. A drawing by unknown artist. In the Harvard Theatre Collection.

41. In *Harlequin and the Golden Fish*. As Clown, with title "Grimaldi's Bang-up." Engraving by W. Heath. Published by Palser, 1812. (33)

42. In *Harlequin and the Golden Fish*. As Clown, with title "Grimaldi's Tandem." Engraving by W. Heath. Published by Palser. (34) A copy was engraved by F. W. Pailthorpe, after Heath. (35)

43. In *Harlequin and the Golden Fish*. As Clown. By unknown engraver, after Norman. (36)

44. In *Harlequin and the Golden Fish*. As Clown, two portraits on one sheet, one feeding frog and the other playing leapfrog. Engraving by W. Heath. Published by Palser, 1812. (37)

45. In *Harlequin Gulliver*. As Clown, seated, with Master Longhurst as the Canary Bird, singing comic duet. By unknown engraver. (43)

46. In *Harlequin Gulliver*. As Clown, with open arms, with Master Longhurst as the Canary Bird. By unknown engraver. Published by W. West, 1818.

47. In *Harlequin Hurry-Scurry*. As Clown. Engraving by C. Tomkins. Published by W. Love, 1823. (44)

48. In *Harlequin Jubilee*. As Clown, exercising his Recruits. By unknown engraver, 1814.

49. In *Harlequin and Mother Goose*. As Clown, with John Bologna as Harlequin, Miss Searle as Columbine, Luigi Bologna as Pantaloon, and Samuel Simmons as Mother Goose. Watercolor by T. M. Grimshaw, 1808. In the London Museum. Reproduced in Vol. II, p. 190, of this dictionary.

50. In *Harlequin and Mother Goose*. As Clown. Watercolor by De Wilde. In the

Garrick Club. An etching in color by De Wilde was published in 1807. (15) A larger engraving by De Wilde was also published. (13) An engraving by Harris, after De Wilde, was published by R. Bentley as a plate to the *Memoirs*, 1846. (14)

51. In *Harlequin and Mother Goose*. As Clown, with Bologna as Columbine, titled "The Comic Dance in Mother Goose." By unknown engraver. Published by A. Neil.

52. In *Harlequin and Mother Goose*. As Clown, with Bologna as Columbine held in air, titled "Trick in the Comic Dance in Mother Goose." By unknown engraver. Published by A. Neil.

53. In *Harlequin and Mother Goose*. As Clown, with Bologna as Columbine. By unknown engraver. Published by R. Ackermann, 1807. Reproduced in Vol. II, p. 192, of this dictionary (but incorrectly identifying Bologna as the male dancer; he is the columbine). (16) The same picture was published by W. West, 1811. (17) Another copy, of Grimaldi only, was also published on a plate with seven other portraits by West. (18)

54. In *Harlequin and Mother Goose*. As Clown, standing, with broom and kettle. By unknown engraver. Published by A. Neil.

55. In *Harlequin Munchausen*. As My Lord Humpty Dumpty. By unknown engraver. Published by J. Sidebethen, 1819. (45)

56. In *Harlequin and the Ogress*. As Clown. By unknown engraver. Published by J. Allen, 1823. (48)

57. In *Harlequin's Olio*. As Clown. Watercolor by T. M. Grimshaw, 1816. In the London Museum.

58. In *Harlequin and Padmanaba*. As Clown, standing, holding small keg, on plate 3d with other characters. By unknown engraver. Published by W. West, 1812. (46)

59. In *Harlequin and Padmanaba*. As Clown, seated in basket carriage, drawn by dog, with title "Grimaldi's Bang-Up." By unknown engraver. Published by W. West, 1812. (47)

60. In *Harlequin and Padmanaba*. As Clown, with Pantaloon, Harlequin, and Columbine. A toy theatre sheet, published by H. Burtenshaw, 1812.

61. In *Harlequin and Padmanaba*. As Clown, in burlesque of Romeo Coates's curricle, on basket coach, pulled by two dogs, whip in hand, trumpet in mouth. Engraving by W. Heath, 1811.

62. In *Harlequin and Padmanaba*. As Clown, with Norman, in Persian dress. By unknown engraver (after Norman?). Published by W. West, 1812.

63. In *Harlequin and the Red Dwarf*. As the Bold Dragoon, with the Pantaloon. By unknown engraver. (54)

64. In *Harlequin and the Red Dwarf*. As Clown, with the Nondescript. By unknown engraver. (58)

65. In *Harlequin and the Red Dwarf*. With Norman, in the Epping Hunt scene. By unknown engraver. (57)

66. In *Harlequin and the Red Dwarf*. Riding at the Epping Hunt. Engraving by G. Cruikshank. Published as a plate to *Fairburn's Dashing Song Book*, 1813. (56)

67. In *Harlequin and the Red Dwarf*. In Hussar burlesque, throwing Napoleon to a Russian Bear. Engraving by G. Cruikshank. Published as a plate to *Fairburn's Dashing Song Book*, 1813. (55)

68. In *Harlequin and the Red Dwarf*. With another figure and the Alpaca. Engraving after Norman. Published by R. Ackermann, 1813. (59)

69. In *Harlequin and the Red Dwarf*. In Hussar uniform. By unknown engraver. Published by W. Heath, 1813.

70. In *Harlequin and the Red Dwarf*. In "Big Head" costume for Queen Rodabellyana. Also shows Grimaldi as Clown. Toy theatre sheet, published by W. West, 1818.

71. In *Jack and Jill*. As Clown. By unknown engraver. Published by W. West,

1812. (49) The performer is not Grimaldi, however, but James Kirby.

72. In *The Ogre and Little Thumb.* As Scamperini, with Charles Farley as the Ogre. By unknown engraver. Published as a plate to the edition of the play, by T. & R. Hughes, 1807. (60)

73. In *The Rival Genii.* As Clown in the dance of "Fun and Physic." Watercolor by T. M. Grimshaw, 1814. In the London Museum.

74. In *The Sixes.* As Hock, "As he appeared in that character at Sadler's Wells on the 17th of March, 1828, when he took his farewell benefit at that theatre." Engraving by H. Brown. (50)

75. In *Valentine and Orson.* As Orson, with Frank Hartland as Valentine and Miss Gladhill as the Child. As performed at Sadler's Wells. By unknown engraver. In Harvard Theatre Collection, but not listed in catalogue.

76. In *Whang Fong; or, Harlequin in China.* As Whang Fong. By unknown engraver.

77. In *The Wild Man.* As the Wild Man, with man playing flute, and small child. By unknown engraver. In the Enthoven Collection, Victoria and Albert Museum.

78. In *The Wild Man.* As the Wild Man. Watercolor by T. M. Grimshaw, 1809. In the London Museum.

Various other engravings of Grimaldi, in "characters" or "situations" also appeared:

79. As a Servant, on a plate with others. By unknown engraver. Published in *West's New Pantomimical Characters,* 1811. (61)

80. Singing "All the World's in Paris." Engraving by G. Cruikshank. A copy, with words of the song below, was published by J. Pitts. (63, 64, 65)

81. Singing "Pretty Betty Brill." With woman handing him an oyster, and words of song below. Published by J. Pitts. (66)

82. As Joey Grim, in "Joey Grim's

Capers." Standing on sidewalk in front of picture shop. Engraving by Cruikshank. (51)

83. As Joe Grim the Grocer. Standing in front of grocer shop. By unknown engraver. (52)

84. On a donkey, with title "Joe Grim and his Neddy." With words of song. By unknown engraver. Published by J. Cole.

85. In a burlesque of gentlemen jockies, on hobby horse. Engraving by Cruikshank, 1810.

86. In clown costume, with lobster, sausages, and other accessories; cottage and trees in background. By unknown engraver, 1829.

87. Being carried home by Mr Cook of the Marquis of Cornwall. Engraving by F. W. Pailthorpe, 1846.

The following pictures of Grimaldi, engraved by Cruikshank, were published as plates to Dickens's first edition of the *Memoirs* in 1838:

88. "Debut into the Pit at Sadler's Wells." As monkey, with his father (?).

89. "Appearing in Public." In carriage, followed by crowd.

90. "Live Properties." With geese, vegetables, and other props.

91. "Mr Mackintosh's Covey." Duck hunting.

92. "A Startling Effect." As Grave Digger in *Hamlet.*

93. "Master Joey going to visit his Godparents."

94. "The Barber Shop." Last appearance?

95. "The Last Song." In chair, center stage. Clown costume. With view of stage boxes and band. In the British Museum is a pencil sketch by Cruikshank of Grimaldi, seated for his last song, face indistinguishable, probably a study for the engraving.

Grimaldi, Mrs Joseph the first, Maria, née Hughes *1775–1800, dancer.*

Maria Hughes was born in 1775, the

eldest daughter of Richard Hughes (d. 1814), a proprietor of Sadler's Wells and a manager of provincial theatres, by his wife Lucy, née Williams (1748–1838).

On 11 May 1799 Maria married Joseph Grimaldi (1778–1837) at St George, Hanover Square, and went to live with him at No 37, Penton Street, Pentonville. While she may have performed as Miss Hughes at Sadler's Wells under her father's management, the only performance by her known to us was at Drury Lane on 2 June 1800, when, advertised as Mrs Grimaldi, she was a chorus dancer in the ballet *The Lucky Escape*. At that time she was about five months pregnant and was experiencing a difficult term. She died in childbirth (as did her child) on St Luke's Day, 18 October 1800, at the age of 25, and was buried in her father's family vault at St James, Clerkenwell. Her epitaph consisted of the pencilled lines found in her pocket-book:

Earth walks on Earth like glittering gold;
Earth says to Earth, We are but mould:
Earth builds on Earth, castles and towers;
Earth says to Earth, All shall be ours.

Joe Grimaldi never forgot this tender love of his youthful days. In his will, made 36 years later, after the death of his second wife in 1834, Joe left to his niece, Mrs Elizabeth Eye (Gye?) the daughter of the younger Richard Hughes: "two patchworked quilts the largest made by my first wife, poor dear Maria the smaller one by her sister Julia now Mrs Bennett . . . Which I hope will be received out of respect to her dear Memory."

Grimaldi, Mary *b. 1763. See* **WILLIAMSON, MRS JAMES.**

Grimaldi, Nicola. *See* **"NICOLINI."**

Grimaldi, William [*fl. 1786–1790*], *dancer.*
William Grimaldi was the third son of Giuseppe Grimaldi, probably by his second "wife" Rebecca Brooker, but possibly by his mistress Ann Perry. William was born after his brothers Joe in 1778 and John in 1780.

In his will made on 25 February 1786 and proved on 20 March 1788, Giuseppe Grimaldi named William as one of the four children, with Mary Williamson, Joe, and John Baptist, to share equally in the estate, and he alone was specifically referred to as "my dearly beloved."

William was, we believe, one of the three young Grimaldis (the other two being Joe and John) who danced in the premiere of *Harlequin's Frolicks* at Drury Lane on 26 December 1789 and 21 additional times that season, at a time when Mrs Brooker was a member of the dancing chorus in that theater.

Nothing else is known of William. Joe Grimaldi never mentioned him in his *Memoirs*.

Grimaldo, Francolino. *See* **FRANCOLINO, GRIMALDO.**

Grimberg, Grimberghs, Grimberque. *See* **DE GRIMBERGUE.**

Grimwood, Mr [*fl. 1750*], *actor.*
At the Yeates-Warner booth at Southwark Fair on 7 September 1750 Mr Grimwood played the High Priest and Mrs Grimwood Princess Miriam in *Jeptha's Rash Vow*.

Grimwood, Mrs [*fl. 1750*], *actress.* *See* **GRIMWOOD, MR.**

Grist, Mr [*fl. 1796*], *proprietor.*
In 1796 Mr Grist opened a pleasure garden called the Temple of Flora on the south side of Westminster Bridge. Soon he was indicted for "keeping a disorderly house." At the Surrey assizes on 30 May 1796 he was sentenced to six months in the King's Bench Prison and, as reported in

Bell's Weekly Messenger for 5 June 1796,
"to give security for his good behavior for
five years, himself in 500 *l.*, and two others
in 250 *l.* each." There was no evident connection between this person and the actor
Thomas Grist (d. 1808).

Grist, Harriet, later Mrs Berry, then Mrs Thomas Ludford Bellamy *b. 1777?, actress.*

Harriet Grist, the daughter of the actor
Thomas Grist, began her career as a child
actress in the provinces, where her father
had developed his career after leaving London in 1777. Her first known performance
was as Jenny Diver in *The Beggar's Opera*
on 19 January 1792 at Edinburgh. There
she played Annette in *Robin Hood* on
25 January and Narcissa in *Inkle and
Yarico* on 4 and 8 February. In March
1792 she was acting at Newcastle, where
the *Newcastle Courant* described her as a
child of 15. She returned to Edinburgh that
spring to perform a Villager in *Richard
Coeur de Lion* on 7 and 9 April and Sophia
in *The Road to Ruin* on 23 April. In the
summer of 1792 she was engaged to play
at the Theatre Royal, Margate.

On 11 October 1792 Miss Grist made
her first appearance at Covent Garden
Theatre as Sophia in Holcroft's comedy
The Road to Ruin. "The young lady, allowing for the drawback of having to combat the difficulty of following such a good
performance as Mrs. Merry," reported the
European Magazine, "made a good substitute for her predecessor in Sophia . . .
and throughout evinced such a portion of
vivacity as must render her extremely
serviceable where youthful gaiety is a leading trait." During that season Miss Grist
played Sophia a total of 18 times. On 29
January 1793 she acted the boy role of
Edward in the first performance of Mrs
Inchbald's comedy *Every One Has His
Fault*, a role she played a total of 32 times
before the season's end. She also acted
Aurelia in *Such Things Are* on 24 April

Harvard Theatre Collection

HARRIET GRIST as Sophia, and SARAH
HARLOWE as Jenny in *The Road to Ruin*

engraving by Barlow

1793 and Roxalana in *The Sultan* on 1
June.

In the summer of 1793 young Harriet
was with the company at Richmond, Surrey, where she is known to have acted
Sophia in *The Road to Ruin* and Little
Pickle in *The Spoil'd Child* for her benefit
on 9 September. She returned to Covent
Garden for 1793–94, at a salary of £2 per
week, first appearing again on 1 October
in Edward, followed by Sophia on 3 October, Nancy in *Three Weeks After Marriage*
on 9 October, Miss Jenny in *The Provok'd
Husband* on 22 October, and Dora in *The
Little Hunchback* on 30 October. In November she played Edward again on the
seventh, Belinda in *Modern Antiques* on
the ninth and twentieth, and Catalina in
The Castle of Andalusia on the twelfth.
She repeated Belinda on 7 December and
acted Marianne in *The Dramatist* on 18

December. After a performance as Catalina on 21 December her name disappeared from the bills and the paylist, for she deserted the theatre to run off "with a Gentleman," presumably the Mr Berry whose name she assumed by marriage or otherwise soon after. In the Harvard Theatre Collection is a Covent Garden pay sheet which she signed as Harriet Grist in receipt of £27 6s. 8d. from 21 September through 28 December 1793.

As Mrs Berry, Harriet acted at Richmond in the summer of 1794, at Edinburgh in August 1795, and at Margate in August 1796. On 10 May 1797 she played Zelinda in a specially licensed performance of *The Romance of an Hour* at the Haymarket Theatre for the "Benefit of the Unfortunate Sufferers in the Glorious Action between Sir John Jervis, and the Spanish Fleet, off Cape St. Vincent [on 14 February 1797]."

In the winter season of 1797–98 she went to act in Dublin, making her debut at the Fishamble Street Theatre on 29 November. She remained in Ireland through 1801, enjoying success and great applause, according to the *Monthly Mirror*. In May 1799 she had married Thomas Ludford Bellamy (1771–1843), who had sung in the London oratorios in the early 1790s and who was now a popular singer in Dublin as well as stage manager of the Crow Street Theatre. When her husband became a proprietor of the theatre in Manchester at the beginning of the nineteenth century, she joined that company, remaining in Manchester until Bellamy gave up the management in the middle of 1805. The critic in *The Townsman* was regularly enthusiastic about her Manchester performances: her Rosalind in *As You Like It* had "great merit," her Stella in *The Maid of Bristol* was "beautiful simplicity," her Estifania in *Rule a Wife and Have a Wife* was "excellent." Of her Miss Hoyden in *A Trip to Scarborough* in February 1804, the critic wrote "She is the best representative of the part I ever saw on *these* boards." Although she was not so successful playing Emma in *Speed the Plough*, her Imogen in *Cymbeline* was "as conspicuous as I ever remember to have seen it here." The critic of another Manchester journal, the *Theatrical Inquisitor* (1804), complained of her indecent costume in *Barbarossa*, which was "not only offending the delicacy of her own sex, but absolutely disgusting to the whole audience."

After leaving Manchester, Mrs Bellamy acted at Belfast, where her husband was proprietor of the Arthur Street Theatre. When he returned to London in 1807 to take up an engagement at Covent Garden, Mrs Bellamy joined the Haymarket company for the summer of 1808, under the management of James Winston. Her Angela in *The Castle Spectre* was received with reservation; for although her voice and figure were still good and her manner clever, she proved "*un peu passée*," and her double chin was not suitable for youthful parts. Her playing of Mrs Haller in *The Stranger* was criticized for artfulness at the expense of honesty.

Presumably Mrs Bellamy remained in London with her husband during the rest of his long career until his death on 3 January 1843, at which time their residence was at No 50, Judd Street, Brunswick Square. Administration of his estate was granted to "Harriet Bellamy widow the relict & universal legatee" on 29 March 1843, a circumstance which refutes Winston's notation in a Folger manuscript that she died at Maida Hill in February 1833.

Barlow's engraving of her as Sophia, with Sarah Harlowe as Jenny, in *The Road to Ruin* was published by J. Roach in 1793.

Grist, Thomas *d. 1808, actor.*
Sometime in the early summer of 1775 a Mr Lawrence wrote to David Garrick to recommend a young man's talents, and Garrick respectfully replied on 14 July that

"I wish to see & hear him with my own Eyes & Ears—if You are not too Sanguine (from Y^r knowledge of Y^e Young Man, or from Y^e fairness of his private Character) by Your Account I shall be Able to make the Men Stare & the Ladies cry at him. . . ." If an audition could be arranged, and if he should prove to have talent, Garrick promised to "foster 'Em provided that his behaviour answers half of Y^r Encomium."

No doubt the Young man was Thomas Grist of Nottingham, who, announced in the Drury Lane bills as a young gentleman making his first appearance on any stage, acted Othello on 17 October 1775. William Hopkins in his prompter's diary identified him by name and added: "his figure is well enough, a good Voice and powerful, when he knows how to manage it—he is Awkward—but it was a very good first appearance, and if there is proper care taken of him, he may make an Actor." The next morning, one of the newspapers (press clipping in Enthoven Collection) reported his success, oddly mistaking his name:

Harvard Theatre Collection

THOMAS GRIST, as Edgar

engraving by Martin, after Needham

A young gentleman, whose name we hear is Firsk, made his appearance last night at this theatre in Othello. Considering it as his first essay, the performance was a very capital one: his conception of his author, was in general correct; and his voice, which is of a vast compass, he happily modulated to the various trying scenes which compose this great, and singular character. He was universally applauded by a numerous audience, particularly through the third act, where he discovered great powers and judgment.

His stage deportment does not betray, that he has at present 'sacrificed to the graces';— the blundering rascal of a taylor, took infinite pains to embarrass him, by lacing him up in the vilest made suit of cloaths we ever beheld: We would advise this young Gentleman, not to black his face so unmercifully in future, for last night it resembled the bottom of an old boiler.

To sum up our opinion of him in a few words, he strikes us, as a rough, unpolish'd

jewel, which, when it has received the soft touches and masterly finishing of the *Little Dramatic Jeweller*, will prove a diamond of no contemptible water.

Presumably Grist was receiving instruction from David Garrick himself, but the great actor, now in the last feverish season of his career, probably had little time for him. When Grist repeated Othello two nights later on 19 October, Hopkins wrote: "Mr Grist did not play better than the first night." A month later, on 21 November 1775, Grist made another attempt in a capital role, when, still advertised as a young gentleman, he acted Osmyn in *The Mourning Bride*. He had not improved: "Some part of it very well he was not quite perfect—few Hisses," wrote Hopkins. On 22 November he was paid £10, and on 24 November £6 6s. He repeated Othello on

28 December and Osmyn on 30 December but played no other roles for the remainder of the season. On 1 January 1776 the theatre paid him £20, by order of Garrick, and on 12 April 1776 another £10.

On 29 January 1776, having left London, Grist wrote to Garrick from Norwich (where he was now acting) to express his regrets at hearing the announcement of the great actor's intention to retire and to ask him to put in a good word for him with the new managers: "If by your interest, Sir, I could procure an engagement in Drurylane on such terms as you think I deserve, it would make me happy." Garrick's influence helped, for Grist was reengaged at Drury Lane in 1776–77 at a salary of £2 10s. per week. When he acted Axalla in *Tamerlane* on 4 November 1776, he was hissed. He gained little advantage in his performances of Lenox in *Macbeth* on 25 November, Tybalt in *Romeo and Juliet* on 10 December, Mithranes in *Semiramis* (the premiere of Ascough's tragedy) on 14 December, and Sir John Bevil in *The Conscious Lovers* on 17 December. At his benefit on 15 May 1777, he shared net receipts of some £89 with Messink and Blurton. On 30 May he acted Gonzalez in *The Tempest*. After subscribing 10s. 6d. to the Drury Lane Theatrical Fund, he left that theatre, never again to perform in London.

Despite his failure in London, Grist was to enjoy a useful and respectable career as a provincial actor over the ensuing three decades. In the early part of the 1780s he was, according to the *Thespian Dictionary* (1805), one of the "principal tragedians" at the Smock Alley Theatre, Dublin, under Daly's management. In the winter season of 1783 he was at Edinburgh, playing Othello on 1 January and Hamlet to Mrs Bellamy's fading Ophelia on 5 February. At the end of that year he joined the theatre at Manchester, appearing in *The Castle of Andalusia* on 10 December 1783, as Othello on 31 December, as well as Hamlet, Hotspur, Iachimo, Lord Hastings in *Jane Shore*, and several comic roles. His acting as Richard was greatly admired by G. C. Küttner, a German visitor to the Manchester theatre:

I have seen the part excellently performed; the actor understood perfectly the strange spirit of this character with all his peculiarities; he shows the character as fully as Shakespeare and history represent him, and takes on all the different poses into which this hypocrite used to cast himself.

Grist soon became a favorite at Manchester, returning regularly to play there. He acted there in 1784–85 and 1785–86 and in 1787 and 1788. In May 1788, effusive verses on "Mr. Grist, Comedian, Formerly a Tradesman in Salisbury" were published in the *Salisbury Country Magazine*, which praised his "Voice that modulates to every key" and his "graceful action." Early in 1789, Grist was with Masterman's company at Swansea and then returned to Manchester, where he advertised on his benefit bill on 9 March 1789 that he had agreed "To perform twelve Nights without Salary, or any other Kind of Emolument, but what may arise from the Receipts to his Benefit Night, after deducting the Managers charges of 31 l. 10s., together with extra Painting &c." At the time he was living at Mrs Byers's, Fountain Street. He then joined Wilkinson's York circuit for 1789, 1790, and 1791. In his *Wandering Patentee*, Wilkinson wrote generously of him: "Mr. Grist has received much fame in almost every provincial theatre. He is social in every town with many of the most creditable inhabitants, and is entertaining without recourse to scandal; is in general master of his bottle, and the bottle not master of him—More than I can say of many I wish well."

Grist no doubt was in Edinburgh early in 1792, for his daughter Harriet Grist, still a young girl, acted Jenny Diver in *The Beggar's Opera* there on 19 January of that year.

In July 1791 he was playing at Birmingham, in 1792 he was with Stephen Kemble's company at Sheffield, and early in 1793 he returned to play at Manchester. In *The Thespian Mirror . . . of the Theatres Royal Manchester, Liverpool, and Chester* (1793), Grist was well praised:

So piercing his eye and expressive his look,
We see in his face what's writ in the book
. . . .
Conceptions refresh'd in the fountain of learning,
Were also display'd with a judgment discerning.

After playing at Derby in 1794, Grist rejoined Wilkinson's company for 1796 and 1797, playing the circuit of York, Wakefield, Hull, Pontefract, Doncaster, and Leeds. In 1800 he returned to Manchester for the remainder of his career. By 1804 the critic of *The Townsman* was less approving of his performances, finding his Looney Macwolter "really shocking" and his Cymbeline only "respectable." As Major O'Flaherty in *The West Indian*, Grist deserved no compliment ("When shall we have an *Irishman*?"), and as Kilmallock in *The Mountaineers* he proved no singer. When he played Saville in *The Belle's Stratagem* in March 1804, he hardly looked the age of 23 and "might well have been mistaken for Saville's Father."

Grist died at Nottingham on 12 November 1808. His daughter, entered here as Harriet Grist, made her debut at Covent Garden on 11 October 1792; subsequently she became Mrs Berry and then married the singer and Manchester manager, Thomas Ludford Bellamy (1771–1843).

An engraving of Thomas Grist as Edgar in *King Lear*, by Needham, after Martin, was published by Gales & Martin, 1786. An engraving by an anonymous artist of Grist as Othello was published by R. Crutwell, J. Hodson & Co, 1775.

Griswold, Mrs ₁*fl. 1735–1736₁, *house servant.*
The Covent Garden accounts listed Mrs Griswold as a house attendant earning 1s. 4d. daily for 179 days during the 1735–36 season.

Grizziello. *See* "GIZZIELLO."

Groath, Mrs ₁*fl. 1765–1777₁, *dresser.*
On 9 February 1765 the Drury Lane staff included among the women dressers Mrs Groath; she was paid 1s. 6d. daily or 9s. weekly. The "Grouth" designated as a dresser at the same salary in 1776–77 was very likely the same woman. The theatre accounts from 1771 to 1776 also contain entries concerned with a yearly rent of £30 which Mrs Groath paid to the theatre, but what she was renting from Drury Lane was not stated.

Groce, Miss. *See* BARRE, MRS.

Grognet, Marie ₁*fl. 1724–1736₁, *dancer, actress.*
Fuchs's *Lexique* states that Marie Grognet made her debut as a dancer at the Opéra Comique, danced in the troupe of Pontau and de Vienne at the St Laurent fair in 1724–25, and then performed in the provinces and in Italy with the Duke of Modena's company. On 12 October 1733 Mademoiselle Grognet, advertised as from the Opéra at Paris, made her first appearance on an English stage at Drury Lane in the ballet *La Badine*. She also offered a solo tambourin. Despite the dissension in the ranks at Drury Lane and the secession of Theophilus Cibber and many of the performers, Mlle Grognet stayed at Drury Lane throughout the 1733–34 season. She was seen as the Petit Maître in *The Harlot's Progress* on 24 October 1733, Phoebe in the afterpiece *The Country Revels* on 5 December, La Coutillion in *The Harlot's Progress* on 13 December, the Marquis de Quelque Chose in *The In-*

triguing *Chambermaid* on 15 January 1734, and a Nymph in *Cupid and Psyche* on 4 February. On 18 March she put on boy's clothes to dance a minuet with Miss Robinson, and she danced a minuet with Mrs Anderson on 1 April at Lincoln's Inn Fields and with Mrs Sanderson on 31 May at the James Street Theatre.

During 1734–35 she was in the troupe managed by Francisque Moylin at the Haymarket Theatre, where she had a benefit on 5 May 1735 at which she donned her boy's clothes again to perform a minuet and *The Wedding* with Mimi Verneuil. Mlle Grognet had also appeared at Covent Garden that season, dancing the Petit Maître in *Perseus and Andromeda* on 13 February 1735, performing in a number called *Fawns* on 24 April, and, on 20 May, appearing in *Les Bergères champêtres* and a minuet in boy's clothes with Miss Baston.

Mlle Grognet returned to Paris, where she was seen dancing in the comic opera *Gage touché* on 18 March 1736. She performed with the Opéra Comique and then appeared in the provinces and outside of France as the leading *danseuse* in the troupe of the Duke of Modena.

Gronoman, Miss. *See* **"SYBILLA, SIGNORA."**

Groombridge, Mr ₁*fl. 1784*₁, *singer.* Mr Groombridge sang bass in the Handel performances at Westminster Abbey and the Pantheon in May and June 1784.

Groombridge, Mr ₁*fl. 1794*₁, *singer.* Doane's *Musical Directory* of 1794 listed Mr Groombridge of West Smithfield as a tenor who sang for the Madrigal Society.

Groome, Richard ₁*fl. 1763–1775*₁, *musician.* The register of the Worshipfull Company of Musicians shows that Richard Groome, of No 16, Fleet Street, became a freeman on 26 October 1763 and was admitted to livery on 25 July 1770. He was fined an unspecified amount for an unexplained action in October 1775.

Gross. *See* **CROSS.**

Grossi. *See* **"SIFACE."**

Grossman, ₁**John Joseph?**₁ ₁*fl. 1743–1758*₁, *violinist, viola d'amore player.* Mr Grossman played a solo on the viola d'amore at Lincoln's Inn Fields on 15 March 1743. He was very likely the Grossman who played violin in the *Messiah* at the Foundling Hospital on 27 April 1758 for a fee of 10*s.* Otto Deutsch in his *Handel* suggests that Grossman's full name may have been John Joseph Grossman.

Grossmith, Mr ₁*fl. c. 1783*₁ *treasurer.* James De Castro in his *Memoirs* (1824) identified the treasurer of the Royal Circus about 1783 as Mr Grossmith.

Grother, Henry ₁*fl. 1794*₁, *singer?* Doane's *Musical Directory* of 1794 listed Henry Grother, of No 16, New Montague Street, Spittal Fields, as an alto (singer, presumably) who participated in the oratorios at Drury Lane and Westminster Abbey.

Grouth. *See* **GROATH.**

Grove, Henry *d. 1691, trumpeter.* The Henry Grove who was one of several musicians ordered apprehended on 2 October 1672 for practicing music without a license was very possibly Henry Grove (or Groves) of the parish of St George, Southwark, a marine trumpeter. He was the executor and apparently the heir of Thomas Martindale, a fellow marine trumpeter who made his will on 23 November 1676; Grove proved the will on 30 August 1680. When Grove was bound for sea on the *Charles* on 28 December 1676, he made a power of attorney and will in favor of his wife Clemence. Grove apparently died on board the *Princess Anne of Denmark*; his widow proved his will on 25 November 1691.

Groves, Mr, stage name of Mr Chambers *b. 1760 or 1764, singer, actor.*

Mr Chambers, who acted under the name of Groves, was born either in 1760 or 1764 (the newspapers in 1799 when he married reported his age variously as 35 and 39). On 23 May 1781 Groves made his first public appearance singing "The Early Horn" at Drury Lane Theatre. He did not appear there again, but he was at the Haymarket Theatre on 14 January 1782 singing "How sweet are the Woodlands" with, appropriately, Mr Forrest. A Mr "Grove" played Neptune in the pantomime *What You Please* at the Royal Circus on 23 August 1788, and a Mr "Grover" was a principal character in the musical *The What Is It?* at the Circus on 12 May 1789. Our subject was probably the performer in both instances.

Groves left London and, according to the *Morning Chronicle* of 28 August 1799, performed with various strolling companies. We take it, therefore, that he was probably the Groves who appeared on 25 July 1793 at the Town Hall in Abergavenny as a member of a troupe that probably came from Liverpool. On 19 August 1799 at Holywell Groves married a Miss Davis, aged 76. He was, the *Morning Chronicle* pointed out, 35 years old. The Stamford *Mercury* on 23 August said that the wedding took place on 11 August, that the bride's name was Miss Louisa Davies, aged 76, and that Chambers, alias Groves, was 39.

Groves, Mr ₁*fl. 1770–1779*₁, *actor, singer.*

A Mr "Grove" acted at the Theatre Royal, Edinburgh, in November 1770, playing Security in *The Intriguing Chambermaid* on the nineteenth and an unnamed character in *The Devil Upon Two Sticks* on the twenty-eighth. He was surely that Mr Groves who came with Samuel Foote to London for Foote's summer season of 1771 at the Haymarket Theatre. Groves acted one of the Mob in *The Mayor of Garratt* on 22 May and then played a Watchman in *The Upholsterer*, a Footman in *The Devil to Pay*, a part in the comic opera *Dido*, a role in *Madrigal and Truletta*, and a Servant in *The Busy Body*. He rejoined Foote in the summer of 1772 to perform unknown parts in *The Nabob* and *The Rehearsal*. Groves must have been in the company at Drury Lane or the King's Theatre in the fall of 1779, for a letter from Sheridan to the company prompter or secretary dated 29 October said curtly: "Scratch out Grove."

Grubb, John ₁*fl. c. 1793–1841*₁, *manager, author, actor.*

John Grubb, whom John Williams in *A Pin Basket to the Children of Thespis* (1796) described as "a cropt, stupid, good-natured fellow," had the good fortune to possess a father of means, who had earned his living as a clerk to the Fishmongers' Company for many years and as a successful attorney. Young Grubb, as he liked to be called, lived well off his father's considerable property. He also followed the law, but his penchant for involvement in theatrical affairs drained away whatever money his legal success brought. By about 1793 Grubb purchased Mate's share in the theatre at Margate for £2200, and as well as taking some active share in its management, he also acted there, since, as Williams put it, no one could prevent him. At Margate, where he was dubbed the "play mad" proprietor, he is known to have acted at one time in Cumberland's version of *Timon*. He also played Sir Toby Belch in a performance of *Twelfth Night* given at the Margravine of Anspach's private theatre in January 1796.

At the end of the 1794–95 season Grubb, along with Joseph Richardson, bought Thomas Linley's shares in the proprietorship of Drury Lane, and it did not take long for him to sink into the morass of Sheridan's ill management. On 17 August 1795 he took a bond for £1000 from Sheridan, and on 19 September 1795 Sheridan signed a memorandum authorizing Grubb and Richardson to act with him in management, really as his surrogates. Grubb was allotted one-seventh of the net profits, and it was stipulated that if either Grubb or Richardson should withdraw he would forfeit £500 and Sheridan would then be bound to repurchase the shares. From April 1796 to the end of the season Grubb served as acting manager of Drury Lane and thereafter as an active proprietor through 1799–1800. On 17 May 1796 a comic extravaganza of his own composition, *Alive and Merry*, was produced, the critics finding it to possess laughable incidents but to be on the whole "awkwardly managed." That farce, sometimes attributed to Brown, can be found in Larpent MS 70 at the Huntington Library.

Grubb's house in Great Queen Street, Lincoln's Inn Fields, had been conveyed on 30 November 1796 as security to the bankers when he became a partner in the theatre; by 1797 Grubb was living at No 14, Store Street, Bedford Square. In December 1799 the Great Queen Street house was put up for sale to settle Drury Lane's debts. Grubb found himself not only in daily frustration with Sheridan's helter-skelter notes and demands but also in serious financial peril. It is not easy to follow Sheridan's manipulations, but on 16 November 1801 Grubb found it necessary to empower his attorneys to recover his shares in Drury Lane from Sheridan. On 15 September 1802 Sheridan served notice of his dissolution of the partnership, the theatre

having paid Grubb £251 2s. 7d. on 14 April 1801 in execution of his debt. But Grubb continued by order of the Lord Chancellor to serve in the management at a salary of £9 per week from the season of 1802–3 until the theatre burned after the season of 1807–8. Thereafter, Grubb's involvement in the financial affairs of Drury Lane Theatre property is reflected in several documents, including a note dated 24 May 1823 by which the proprietors agreed to pay John Grubb, "late of Horsendon House in the County of Bucks, but now of Southampton in the County of Hants.," the sum of £1500. An agreement dated 3 March 1841 permitted Grubb to sell shares in Drury Lane to the value of £1000 to Abraham Willand.

A patent for the Margate Theatre was issued from 15 June 1807 to John Grubb and others for a period of 21 years but performances were allowed only from 15 June to 31 October each year.

Guaccini, Pietro ₁*fl. 1713–1719₁, *singer.*

Pietro Guaccini (or Guarini) was advertised as newly arrived from Italy when he sang Vitiges in *Ernelinda* at the Queen's Theatre in the Haymarket on 28 March 1713. A benefit concert was held for him on 19 December 1719 at York Buildings, at which time he was called "Servant to his Highness the Duke of Brunswick and Lunenburg."

Guadagni, Signora ₁Signora **Felice Alessandri**₁ ₁*fl. 1767?–1771₁, *singer.*

Dr Burney said that Signora Guadagni had sung Cecchina in *La buona figliuola* in Italy with success before appearing in England. She was the wife of the opera composer Felice Alessandri, who resided in England with her from the fall of 1767 to 1771, using Guadagni (her maiden name?) as a stage name. The 1767 edition of *La schiava* lists her as a singer, and we know she sang the title role in that opera later in the season, so perhaps she appeared in it when it was presented at the King's Theatre on 7 November 1767. She was ill during much of December, and the comic opera had to be postponed several times. The casts for most of the operas, especially the comic pieces, were rarely listed in the bills.

In 1769–70, after an absence (at least from the bills) for a season, Signora Guadagni was again engaged at the opera as the first woman; her name in the announcement of the company roster on 5 September 1769 was spelled "Guadini." Singing first man in the troupe was Gaetano Guadagni, who was very probably related to her, perhaps her brother. Signora Guadagni sang Fiorina in *Le contadini bizzarre* on 7 November to open her season and was also heard in the title part in *La schiava*, a principal but unnamed character (certainly La Marchesa) in *I viaggiatori ridicoli*, and the title role in *La buona figliuola*. Though Grove, under Alessandri's entry, says that the composer and his wife left London in 1770, Signora Guadagni was cited in the bills in the spring of 1771. On 1 March at Covent Garden she sang an Italian song between sections of *Samson*, unless that was a mistaken reference to Gaetano Guadagni.

Guadagni, Gaetano   *c. 1725–1792, singer.*

The *castrato* Gaetano Guadagni was born about 1725 in Lodi, near Milan, according to Grove. (Burney said the singer was born in Vicenza.) He evidently had little musical training in his early years but had a fine appearance and excellent potential in his contralto voice. He made his debut in Parma in 1747 just before coming to England as the first man in an Italian burletta troupe managed by John Francis Croza. The company opened their London engagement at the King's Theatre on 8 November 1748, with Guadagni singing Celindo in *La commedia in commedia*,

advertised as "the first of this Species of Musical Drama ever exhibited in England." The troupe had a sufficient following to perform through 10 June 1749, but the bills did not usually mention the casts, and critical commentators were silent on Guadagni. He is known during the season to have sung at the King's Theatre March benefit for indigent musicians and their families, and he was probably the "Guadanno" who sang at a Haymarket benefit for Margarita Giacomazzi on 17 April 1749 (a performance not listed in *The London Stage*). Dean in *Handel's Dramatic Oratorios and Masques* says Guadagni sang at the Foundling Hospital on 27 May.

The burletta company performed again in 1749–50 but was not as successful, and Croza ended his season on 28 April 1750 and departed, leaving behind a number of debts. Guadagni's roles in Croza's presentations that season were not mentioned in the bills, but he had gained favor in London musical circles; and he sang Didimus in

Civica Raccolta delle Stampe Achille Bertarelli, Castello Sforzesco, Milan

GIOVANNI MANZUOLI and GAETANO GUADAGNI

detail from engraving after Fedi

Handel's oratorio *Theodora* on 16 March 1750 at Covent Garden. On 31 March at the King's Theatre he sang Prenesto in *Il trionfo di Camilla*. He also sang again at the annual benefit for "decay'd" musicians at the King's. He journeyed to Bristol to participate in the St Cecilia Day concert on 22 November 1750 at the Assembly Rooms at St Augustine's Back, and on 27 April 1751 he held a benefit for the profit of Signora Cuzzoni at the Haymarket. Guadagni spent all or a portion of the 1751–52 season in Dublin.

In 1752–53 he was presumably still in England, though the bills show only his participation in the King's Theatre annual benefit on 30 April 1753. But Dean states that Guadagni was more active in Handel performances in the early 1750s than the bills show: he sang in *Judas Maccabaeus* in 1750, 1751, and possibly 1753 as an Israelite Man and a Messenger; in *Samson* in 1750 and 1753 as Micah; probably in *Belshazzar* in 1751 as Cyrus; probably in *The Choice of Hercules* in 1751 and 1753 as Hercules; in *Esther* in 1751 as Ahasuerus; and possibly in *Jephtha* in 1753 as Hamor.

A new burletta company performed at Covent Garden from 18 November 1754 to February 1755 but met with little success; one of the singers was Guadagni, who on the opening night sang Giacinto in *L'Arcadia in Brenta*. During that season Guadagni participated in Garrick's production of *The Fairies* at Drury Lane. That adaptation of *A Midsummer Night's Dream* opened on 3 February 1755 with the bills showing Curioni as Leander, but the prompter Cross and the first edition of the work cited Guadagni in the role. He is said to have received acting instruction from Garrick. In the spring of 1755 Guadagni again participated in the King's Theatre benefit for indigent musicians. Dean suggests that in 1754 or 1755 Guadagni sang in *L'Allegro ed il Penseroso* as well as in a number of revivals of the *Messiah*. Burney said that during his first visit to England Guadagni "was more noticed for his singing in English than Italian" and was a particular success in *The Fairies* (yet Burney incorrectly had the singer leaving England in 1753).

The story had been handed down that after singing in Paris and Versailles in 1755 Guadagni went to Lisbon to sing under Gizziello and narrowly missed being killed in the earthquake; then the terrified Gizziello went into a monastery and persuaded Guadagni to join him there and receive musical instruction. In *The Castrati in Opera* Angus Heriot doubts seriously if Guadagni ever went to Portugal, and Gizziello is known to have left there in 1753 in any case. That Guadagni received instruction from Gizziello, however, seems to have been true.

In 1760 Guadagni sang in Parma; in 1762 he was the original Orfeo in Gluck's opera; and that composer wrote the title part in *Telemacco* for him in 1765. When Guadagni returned to England in 1769 Dr Burney wrote:

[A]s an actor, he seems to have had no equal on any stage in Europe: his figure was uncommonly elegant and noble; his countenance replete with beauty, intelligence and dignity; and his attitudes and gestures were so full of grace and propriety, that they would have been excellent studies for a statuary. But though his manner of singing was perfectly delicate, polished, and refined, his voice seemed at first to disappoint every hearer. Those who remembered it when he was in England before, found it comparatively thin and feeble. For he had now changed it to a soprano, and extended its compass from six or seven notes, to fourteen or fifteen.

In the spring of 1769 Guadagni, for his benefit on 16 March at the King's Theatre, sang (presumably) in *Le moglie fedele*. Burney analyzed his singing:

The Music he sung was the most simple imaginable; a few notes with frequent pauses, and opportunities of being liberated from the composer and the band, were all he wanted.

And in these seemingly extemporaneous effusions, he proved the inherent power of melody totally divorced from harmony and unassisted by unisonous accompaniment. Surprised at such great effects from causes apparently so small, I frequently tried to analize the pleasure he communicated to the audience, and found it chiefly arose from his artful manner of diminishing the tones of his voice, like the dying notes of the Æolian harp. Most other singers captivate by a swell or *messa di voce*; but Guadagni, after beginning a note or passage with all the force he could safely exert, fined it off to a thread, and gave it all the effect of extreme distance. And though neither his voice nor execution contributed much to charm or excite admiration, he had a strong party in England of enthusiastic friends and adherents, of whom, by personal quarrels and native caprice, he contrived to diminish the number very considerably before his departure. He had strong resentments and high notions of his own importance and profession, which revolted many of his warmest friends, and augmented the malice of his enemies.

The extravagant Mrs Cornelys made Guadagni her festival and concert director for 6 June 1769, when she celebrated the King's birthday with a soirée at Carlisle House. In 1769–70 Guadagni was busy at Drury Lane, the King's Theatre, and the Haymarket, singing in operas and in between parts of oratorios. Among his appearances were those in the title part of *Gioas re di Giuda* and participation in Jomelli's *La Passione* and Handel's *Judas Maccabaeus*. The following season he sang in the *Messiah* at Covent Garden and in *Ruth* at the Chapel of Lock Hospital; at the King's he sang the title role in an *Orfeo* made up of music by various composers augmenting Gluck.

But his behavior became increasingly irritating to his audience. He had received applause for his singing of Orfeo, but, as Burney reported,

in the midst of the utmost public favour, his private difference with the Hon. Mr. Hobart, the patentee [of the King's Theatre] at that time, concerning an imagined affront put

upon his sister in favour of Zamparini, together with his determined spirit of supporting the dignity and propriety of his dramatic character, by not bowing acknowledgment, when applauded, or destroying all theatrical illusion by returning to repeat an air, if encored at the termination of an interesting scene, he so much offended individuals, and the opera audience in general, that, at length, he never appeared without being hissed.

Guadagni evidently continued working with Mrs Cornelys at her harmonic meetings and at some point sang in *Artaserse* at one of her gatherings while still under contract to the King's Theatre. He was fined £50 for that, and at the trial it was revealed that at the King's Guadagni had been paid £1150, apparently for the 1770–71 season and had demanded £1600 for 1771–72 and been refused. Because of that, according to the report of the trial in the Burney clippings (hand dated 15 February 1771), Guadagni left England in a huff.

In 1772 he sang in Verona; then he accompanied the Electress Dowager of Saxony to Munich, where he lived until 1776. He appeared that year for the last time in Venice and then retired to a sumptuous villa in Padua. According to Heriot, Burney had found Guadagni in Padua earlier, in 1770 during a period when the singer was not needed in London and wrote that "for taste, expression, figure, and action [Guadagni] is at the head of his profession." At Padua he earned 400 ducats yearly for participating in four festivals. Mount-Edgcumbe also saw Guadagni at Padua, but much later, in 1784: he sang an anthem, and "his voice was still full and well toned." Guadagni also entertained the English visitor by showing him his puppet stage and puppets. Michael Kelly was also treated to a puppet show by Guadagni, who had his figures perform *Orfeo*, with Guadagni singing the leading role. Guadagni died in Padua in November 1792, his wealth dissipated.

An engraving after a design by A. Fedi, published between 1801 and 1807, shows Guadagni in a large group of singers.

Guadanno or **Guadini.** *See* GUA-DAGNI.

Gualandi. *See* "CAMPIOLI."

Guard, William *d. 1788, carpenter, actor.*

William Guard began working as a scenekeeper at the Covent Garden Theatre in 1759. On 27 May 1764 he witnessed the will of Thomas Thorne, the stage carpenter, and perhaps by then and certainly within a few years, Guard himself served as a carpenter. But he augmented his income by serving as a supernumerary and by working inside fabricated stage animals. On 8 October 1767, for example, he was paid 7s. for performing "on" a horse and "in" a lion in *Perseus and Andromeda* (the "on" may have been an error for "in"). Similarly, in the 1769–70 season the accounts show that Guard (often spelled Gard) was paid £1 10s. on 10 February 1770 for working 12 nights in the "Lyon" in *Harlequin's Jubilee*. His partner in the lion was Mr Singleton; we are not told who took which end of the beast. On 12 January 1773 Guard was paid for performing for 14 nights in the ostrich in *Harlequin Sorcerer* at 2s. 6d. nightly. He was also in the ostrich in *The Fair* the following December.

By the 1777–78 season Guard's position backstage had risen to the responsible post of master carpenter, and he gave up serving inside stage animals. The accounts from 1777–78 through 1787–88 frequently named Guard as the recipient of money for the scenemen working under him—amounts ranging from £10 18s. 6d. to over £100. Between 8 June and 21 September 1782 he received nine payments totalling approximately £900. Throughout the years

Guard shared benefits, usually with two or three others.

The last mention of Guard in the Covent Garden accounts was on 24 November 1787. On 11 April 1788 he made his will, describing himself as a carpenter in Bow Street, Covent Garden, just steps from the theatre. He indicated in his will that he had already invested in some stock, and he asked his executors to sell whatever of his effects they should choose and invest in 3% consolidated bank annuities. He said the yearly interest and dividend should amount to £30, and the interest should go to his wife Susannah, then, after her death, to their daughters Hannah Proctor and Betty Pitts equally. To his sister Sarah, a widow, Guard left 10 guineas. He appointed his wife and his son-in-law Joseph Pitts his executors.

Guard wrote his will on 11 April, it was proved on 13 April, and he was buried at St Paul, Covent Garden, on 27 April 1788. The haste to prove the will was not then unusual, and the delay of the burial for two weeks may have been a fulfillment of Guard's wishes if he feared, as many then did, burial alive. A manuscript in the British Museum indicates that Guard's executors were paid £100 on 26 September 1788.

Guardani. *See* GUADAGNI.

Guarducci Toscano, Tommaso *b. c. 1720, singer.*

Tommaso Guarducci was born about 1720 in Montefiascone, in the province of Viterbo. He studied singing under Bernacchi in Bologna and then, beginning about 1745, sang at most of the important theatres in Italy. In 1758–59 and in 1762 he sang at the Teatro San Carlo in Venice, but not with as much success as he found in England.

He was engaged in the *Prima uomo* (male soprano) in serious opera at the King's Theatre for the 1766–67 season. An indisposition plagued him in late December 1766, and the playbills did not mention him until his solo benefit on 5 March 1767 when, for that night only, he sang in *Siface*. On 2 May he sang Montezuma in *La conquista del Messico*. Grove states that Guarducci also sang in *Caratacco* in the spring of 1767; *The London Stage* lists performances of that work beginning on 14 February, but, as with most of the opera bills that season, no cast was listed.

Guarducci probably sang far more in 1767–68, too, than the bills reveal. He is known to have appeared in *Tigrane* on 27 October 1767, and he sang Sesostris in *Sesostri* on 10 March 1768. At Covent Garden he had participated in the oratorio performances in February. Despite the paucity of references to him, Guarducci apparently created a sensation in England; he certainly drew high praise from Dr Burney:

Tommaso Guarducci Toscano, a scholar of Bernacchi, was tall and aukward in figure, inanimate as an actor, and in countenance illfavoured and morbid; but with all these disadvantages, he was a man of great probity and worth in his private character, and one of the most correct singers I ever heard. He was unfortunate in arriving here so soon after Manzoli, the impressions of whose great voice and majestic manner of singing had not been effaced by his immediate successor, Elisi. Guarducci's voice, though of much less volume than Manzoli's, was clear, sweet, and flexible. His shake and intonations were perfect, and by long study and practice he had vanquished all the difficulties of his art, and possessed himself of every refinement of his particular school.

Though prejudice ran high against him on his first arrival in London, his merit at length made its way, and his highly polished manner of singing was very much approved and felt by the principal professors and persons of taste and discernment who heard him. He soon discovered that a singer could not captivate the English by tricks or instrumental execution, and told me some years after, at Montefiascone in Italy, that the gravity of our

Civica Raccolta delle Stampe Achille Bertarelli, Castello Sforzesco, Milan

TOMMASO GUARDUCCI

engraving by Gregori, after Macpherson

taste had been of great use to him. "The English," says he, "are such friends to the composer, and to simplicity, that they like to hear a melody in its primitive state, undisguised by change or embellishment. Or, if when repeated, *riffioramenti* are necessary, the notes must be few and well slected, to be honoured with approbation." Indeed, Guarducci was the plainest and most simple singer, of the first class, I ever heard. All his effects were produced by expression and high finishing, nor did he ever aim at execution. He sung in the English oratorios upon short notice, with very little knowledge of our language, and still less practice in pronouncing it. However, he was well received and well paid, for he had £600 for twelve oratorios, a larger sum than was ever given on a like occasion, till the time of Miss Linley.

Guarducci left England in 1769. Dr Burney visited him in his native town in 1770. For his semi-retirement the singer had built himself a fine house and furnished it in the English manner. He sang for Burney.

His voice, I think, is more powerful than when he was in England, and his taste and expression seem to have received every possible degree of selection and refinement. He is a very chaste performer, and adds but few notes; those few notes, however, are so well chosen that they produce great effect, and leave the ear thoroughly satisfied. . . . In Rome they still speak of his performance in Piccinni's "Didone abbandonata" with rapture.

Guarducci continued making stage appearances, but he was plagued for 40 years of his life with an inflammation of the chest which gave him much trouble in his later years.

Guarducci was pictured in an engraving by F. Gregori, after J. Macpherson, and in a group of musical persons by Antonio Fedi, engraved between 1801 and 1807.

Guarini. *See* GUACCINI.

Guaxandi. *See* "CAMPIOLI."

Guerin. *See also* GAURON.

Guerin, Mrs ₁*fl. 1758*₁, *dancer. See* GUERIN, ₁ETIENNE?₁.

Guerin, Master ₁*fl. 1756*₁, *dancer. See* GUERIN, ₁ETIENNE?₁.

Guerin, ₁Etienne?₁ ₁*fl. 1749?–1762?*₁, *dancer, dancing master?*
The Mr Guerin who danced at Covent Garden in 1755–56 and 1757–58 may have been the dancer of that name who performed in the Mangot troupe in Lyon in 1749–50 in *Les Eléments, Ajax, Les Indes galantes, Les Fêtes de Polymnie,* and *Omphale.* The Mr Guerin who came to London made his first appearance on the English stage at Covent Garden on 1 No-

vember 1775 dancing with Mlle Capdeville. He danced throughout the 1755–56 season, though the bills seldom named the pieces in which he participated. On 2 January 1756 Guerin Junior made his first appearance on stage, dancing, as his father had earlier in the season, with Mlle Capdeville. The younger Guerin seems to have made relatively few appearances and did not, it seems, complete the season. The senior Guerin danced with Mlle Capdeville in the ballet *Les Statues animées* on 2 March and shared a benefit on 22 April.

Guerin did not return to Covent Garden the following season, but he was there again in 1757–58, as was, briefly, Mme Guerin. On 21 September 1757 Guerin was given a £50 advance on his salary; then he danced during the season in the ballet *The Jovial Coopers,* in a minuet with Miss Hilliard in *Romeo and Juliet,* in *The Savoyards,* and in an untitled comic ballet. Mme Guerin danced in *The Prophetess* on 1 February 1758 and, with her husband, in the comic ballet on 28 April.

The same Guerin, perhaps, was the Monsieur Guerin who served as principal dancer of the Norwich company and operated a successful dancing school in the Haymarket, Norwich, in 1759 and 1760. There is also a good possibility that the Guerin we have been following was Etienne, a dancing master who baptized a daughter at St Pierre (France?) on 25 March 1762. Etienne Guerin was very likely the Guerin who danced at Lyons in 1749–50.

Guering, Mr. *See* GUERINI, FRANCESCO.

Guerini. *See also* GURRINI.

Guerini, Signor ₁*fl. 1763*₁, *dancer, choreographer.*
The Magician of the Mountain, "A New Pantomimic Entertainment of Italian Grotesque Characters," was performed at

Drury Lane on 3, 4, and 5 January 1763. The piece was contrived by Signor Guerini, who made his first appearance on the English stage dancing Pierrot at the first two performances; he was replaced by Ackman on 5 January. The *Biographia Dramatica* said, "The good sense of the audience condemned this piece to oblivion, after, we think, two representations."

Guerini, Francesco *c. 1710–1780, violinist.*

According to van der Straeten in *The History of the Violin*, Francesco Guerini was born in Naples about 1710. The Mr Guering who played the violin on 15 April 1730 at Hickford's Music Room for his own benefit was probably Francesco; he was advertised as a virtuoso who had recently come from the Continent with the Duke of Hamilton. From 1740 to 1760 Guerini served in the chapel of the Prince of Orange at the Hague, after which he returned to London, where he died in 1780. He composed a number of works for violin, violoncello, and harpsichord. Perhaps the violinist Vincenzio Guerini was a son of Francesco. Vincenzio was the leader of the band at the Naples opera house for many years, according to Ita Hogan's *Anglo-Irish Music*. He played in the band at the Crow Street Theatre in Dublin in 1804, then moved to Belfast in 1806, where he conducted the choir at St George's Church, opened a music shop, and taught music. He founded the Anacreontic Society there in 1814. Vincenzio Guerini left Belfast in 1839.

Guest, George *1771–1831, organist, singer, composer.*

George Guest was born on 1 May 1771 at Bury St Edmunds, the second son of the organist and composer Ralph Guest (1742–1830). His father had been born in 1742 at Brosely in Shropshire and, after serving as leader of the choir in that parish during his late youth, at the age of 21 went

to London to take up work as a cabinet maker. Ralph Guest's great interest in music was further stimulated by concerts at the Portland Chapel, which he joined; after five years he became assistant in a music business in Bury St Edmunds, where he also became a member of the choir of St Mary's in 1795. Eventually he was the organist of that church from 1805 to 1822. Intended for music from his earliest days, young George Guest was instructed by his father and by the age of two, according to his own claim, he was able to practice the scales and sing "God Save the King." At the age of five he sang Handel's "He shall feed his flock" at St James's Church in Bury, accompanied by a full band.

At the age of seven he began to play the organ and attracted the attention of Taylor, organist at Chelmsford, who recommended the lad to Dr Nares. After the latter heard him sing some songs of Handel, George was accepted into the Chapel Royal at St James's, London, where he so distinguished himself that Stanley, Nares's successor, and Linley brought him forward to sing two songs in the oratorios; according to Guest's own account given in his manuscript autobiography to Sainsbury in January 1824 (and now in the Glasgow University Library), so impressed was the King upon hearing him that he commanded Stanley to have the boy "always sing two songs in the succeeding Oratorios." No doubt the event referred to was his appearance as Master Guest to sing in *Judas Maccabaeus* at Drury Lane on 19 March 1784. George sang in the Handel Memorial Concerts given at Westminster Abbey and the Pantheon in May and June 1784. He performed in *Samson* on 11 March 1785 at Drury Lane and probably in other pieces during that oratorio season and the one in 1786. Probably he was the Master Guest who had sung in the *Messiah* and other pieces during the Hereford musical festival of 1783.

In 1787 Guest left the Chapel Royal to

accept the post of organist at Eye, Suffolk, which he held for two years before being awarded a similar post at St Peter's, Wisbech, Cambridgeshire, a situation he retained until his death. At Wisbech he taught and composed as well. His publications include *Fugues and Voluntaries for the Organ*; *An Anthem for Christmas Day, inscribed to Dr Clarke*; *A Set of Hymns for the Service of the Church*; *Six Grand pieces for a full Military band;* as well as quartets for flute and strings, duets for violoncellos, and glees and songs.

Guest died at Wisbech after a long illness on 10 or 11 September 1831, at the age of 60. No doubt the music master John Guest (fl. 1795) of Bury was his relative, perhaps his older brother. There seems to have been no connection between the Guests of Bury St Edmunds and Jane Mary Guest (later Mrs Miles).

Guest, Jane Mary, later Mrs Abram Allen Miles [fl. 1782–1824], *pianist, composer, teacher.*

Born in Bath, the daughter of a tailor of that city, Jane Mary Guest began to study music by the time she was four and a half years of age. Evidently Rauzzini was her teacher for some time. At the age of 14 she came to London to study under Johann Christian Bach, who died in January 1782, and in 1783 she had six subscription nights performing on the piano at the Festino Rooms (described by the *European Magazine* as "late Bach & Abel's"). In 1784, when the *European Magazine* praised her "fleetness and facility of finger, expression of touch, diversity of grace, and general mastery upon the instrument," Miss Guest enjoyed the patronage of the Queen, the Prince of Wales, Princess Augusta, Princess Elizabeth, and the Duke of Cumberland. On 4 August 1785 she played a concerto on the pianoforte in a concert given in Foreman's Long Room, Bristol Hot Wells.

On 29 August 1789 she married Abram Allen Miles at St George, Hanover Square.

Soon she numbered among her many pupils Hester Thrale, daughter of Hester Thrale Piozzi. In 1806 she became the teacher of Princess Charlotte. Mrs Miles performed some of her unpublished concertos in the Bath concerts directed by Rauzzini. She was still alive when Sainsbury was preparing his *Dictionary of Musicians* in 1824.

The publication of *Six Sonatas for the Harpsichord, or Piano-Forte; with an Accompaniment for a Violin or German Flute . . . Opera Prima* by Jane Mary Guest was announced in the *European Magazine* of July 1784.

Guest, Ralph 1742–1830, *organist, composer.*

Ralph Guest was born in 1742 at Brosely in Shropshire, according to the manuscript memoir he provided for Sainsbury in 1823 and which is now in the Glasgow University Library. At the age of six "he began to discover a powerful propensity to Music" which he satisfied in the choir of his parish church. At the age of 14 he was apprenticed to a cabinet maker, but continuing his musical interests he also became the leader of his church choir. Upon the completion of his articles at the age of 21, Guest moved to London to work for a leading cabinet manufacturer. Stimulated by concerts at the Portland Chapel, he joined that excellent choir, in which he sang for five years.

Departing London about 1768, Guest established a cabinet business in Bury St Edmunds, where under Frost he took instruction in the organ. About 1795 he gave up his business to take up an appointment as director of the choir and organist to St Mary's Church in that city, positions he held for many years. Guest also taught private pupils. His publications included *The Psalms of David*, arranged for every day in the month, with an introduction on singing and thorough bass; *Hymns and Psalms*, the music to which he adapted and composed; and many songs, some of which appeared in the *Ladies' Monthly Museum.* He died in 1830.

Ralph Guest's second son, George Guest (1771–1831), became an organist, composer, and singer at the Chapel Royal and in London oratorios. The music master John Guest (fl. 1795) of Bury was probably Ralph's older son.

Guglielmi, Pietro, called "Pier Alessandro" *1728–1804, composer, conductor.*

Pietro Guglielmi, called "Pier Alessandro," was born on 9 December 1728 at Massa di Carrara, the son of the musician Jacopo Guglielmi, from whom he received some of his musical instruction. He also studied under Durante at Naples, and his first opera was performed there in 1757. He turned out about 100 operas in his lifetime, mostly comic pieces, many of which achieved considerable popularity in his day everywhere in Europe. Two especially, *Il ratto della sposa*, which received its premiere in Venice in 1765, and *La sposa fidele*, first given at the same city two years later, were great favorites.

In 1767–68 Guglielmi and Felice Alessandri were engaged as composers to the King's Theatre in London, Guglielmi serving also as conductor of the orchestra. He made his London debut conducting the *pasticcio Tigrano*, to which he contributed part of the music, on 27 October 1767. His additions to *Siface* were heard in December, his new serious opera *Ifigenia in Aulide* in January 1768, his *Sesostro* on 10 March for his benefit, *Il ratto della sposa*—perhaps with some revisions in the last act—later in March, and *I viaggiatori ridicolo tornati in Italia* in May. Burney found the last work "exceedingly pretty."

Before Guglielmi left London in 1772 he also produced (and supposedly conducted) *Ezio*, the *pasticcio L'Olimpiade*, *La costanza di Rosinella* (*La sposa fedele* under a new title), *Il disertore*, *Le pazzie*

Civica Raccolta delle Stampe Achille Bertarelli, Castello Sforzesco, Milan

Francesco Gasparini and PIETRO ALESSANDRO GUGLIELMI

detail from engraving after Scotti

d'Orlando, Il carnevale di Venezia, L'assemblea, and *Demetrio.* Guglielmi, with J. C. Bach produced Gluck's *Orfeo* in London for the first time, but with additions to flesh out the evening's performance. Two airs were contributed by Guglielmi, whose wife sang them. Guglielmi and his wife shared benefits in March 1771 and March 1772.

They left England in the summer of 1772 for Italy, where the composer discovered that his popularity had waned in the face of the competition of Paisiello and Cimarosa, two young composers who had gained fame while he was gone. Guglielmi continued turning out operas, his last dating 1802. But perhaps only *La pastorella nobile* of 1788 and *La bella pescatrice* of 1789 came up to some of his previous efforts. He also held the post of *maestro di cappella* of San Pietro in Vaticano, which was given him in 1793. In addition to his stage works, Guglielmi also composed a number of oratorios, cantatas, and some chamber music, most of the latter composed during his London years. A list of his output and details of his continental career are in the *Enciclopedia dello spettacolo*.

Pietro Guglielmi died in Rome on 18 November 1804, according to Grove; the *Enciclopedia* gives 19 November. Pietro Carlo Guglielmi (c. 1763–1817) was the son of our subject and had a similar but less prolific career as a composer and conductor in the nineteenth century.

An engraving after a design by L. Scotti, published between 1801 and 1807, shows Guglielmi in a large group of composers.

Guglielmi, Signora Pietro, Lelia, née Achiapati ₁*fl. 1770–1772₁, singer.*

Signora Guglielmi, the wife of the composer-conductor Pietro Guglielmi, was born Lelia Achiapati. Guglielmi came to London in the fall of 1767 but his wife was not heard there until she sang in his new opera *Ezio* on 13 January 1770. She was engaged at the King's Theatre as a second woman. The following 1 February she sang a principal part in *L'Olimpiade* and the following day sang in the theatre's benefit concert for indigent musicians and their families. On 1 March she sang in Jomelli's *La Passione*; on 22 March she was Atalia in *Gioas re di Giuda*; on 29 March she offered an entr'acte song, accompanied by Duport; and on 19 May she sang Rosetta in *Il disertore*. During the following two seasons she was heard as Angelica in *Le passie d'Orlando* and the title role in *La buona figliuola* and in other roles not cited in the bills. She and her husband left England in the summer of 1772.

Guiardele, [Signora Favre?] ₁*fl. 1793–1802₁, dancer.*

"Mlle Favre Guiardele" danced at the King's Theatre on 1 June 1793 in the ballet *Le Jaloux puni* and in a new divertissement on 8 June. Also in the former piece was Favre Guiardele, probably her husband but perhaps her father. The following season she danced in *Les Ruses de l'amour* and *Le Bon Prince* as well as in several specialty numbers.

After an absence of four years she reappeared at the King's on 16 May 1798, for that night only, in a pas seul incidental to the ballet *Kitty and Jemmy*. Two years later at the same house she danced with D'Egville in *Télémaque* on 21 June 1800, in *Laura and Lenza* on 28 June, and in *Hyppomène et Atalante* on 19 July. She was also on the King's company list in 1800–1801 and 1801–2.

Guiardele, Favre ₁*fl. 1775?–1802₁, dancer, ballet master.*

Perhaps Favre Guiardele was the dancer mentioned by Noverre in a letter written from Milan on 8 December 1775 to Greville concerning prospective performers for Drury Lane: "finally I have one named Guiardel who is young, tall, and who has talent." At that time Guiardele was earning 500 guineas per season at Milan and wanted 300 guineas, plus travel expenses, to engage at London.

At the end of the opera *Alessandro nell' Indie* at the King's Theatre in London on 27 November 1779, Guiardele, recently engaged as ballet master at the opera, made his first appearance in England in a "new Serious Ballet" of his own composing. The theatre announced on 14 December that Guiardele having arrived at London too late "to compose all the first Dances," the ballet for that evening, *Il Desertore*, was made ready by Zuchelli. On occasion Guiardele's name was given in the bills as "Gardel," but there seems to have been no relationship between him and the Gardel family of dancers at the Paris Opéra. During the season of 1779–80, Guiardele danced a minuet with Mme Simonet and also a new grand ballet on 14 December, appeared in a grand chaconne and in the ballet *La Bergère coquette* on 22 January, in the *Chaconne of Jomelli's* on 1 April, and in *La Serenata Spagnola interrota* on 9 April. On 22 April three new ballets by him were offered: *The Rural Sports, La Fête pastorale,* and a *Serious Ballet.*

His whereabouts for the ensuing 12 seasons are unknown to us, but in 1792–93, accompanied by Mlle Favre Guiardele (perhaps his daughter, but probably his wife), he returned to the King's Theatre as a principal dancer. In the spring of 1793 he danced in *Le Jaloux puni,* a court minuet with Mlle Millard, and as Achilles in *Iphigenia in Aulide.* The following season he appeared in *Adelaide* on 1 February 1794, in the dances in the opera *Il Capriccio drammatico* on 1 March, in *Les Ruses de l'amour* on 1 April, and in *Le Bon Prince* on 31 May.

Guiardele's name was not seen on the bills again until the turn of the century; he and Mlle Guiardele were on the company list of dancers at the King's Theatre in 1800–1801 and 1801–2.

Guichard. *See* GUISHARD.

Guidetti, Giovanni [*fl. 1752–1768*], dancer, choreographer.

Giovanni Guidetti, a Florentine, was a *primo ballerino* at the San Samuele and San Cassiano theatres in Venice in 1752 and 1753; at the latter theatre he served as choreographer in 1754. In 1759 he was dancing at the Burgtheater, Vienna, where Hilverding was in charge of ballet. The following year he was at the Teatro di via del Cocomero, Florence, and then in 1761 he performed for a while at the Teatro San Salvatore, Venice.

Though evidently Guidetti was in Paris in 1766, his name is found on no surviving theatre lists. Early that year, however, negotiations between Jean Monnet at the Paris Opéra and David Garrick for the purpose of bringing Giovanni Guidetti to Drury Lane Theatre must have been underway. On 14 August 1766 Monnet wrote to Garrick that arrangements were now completed and that Guidetti would leave for England on 1 September. The dancer's terms at Drury Lane Theatre included a salary of 150 guineas per year, plus "300 Livres argent de France" for traveling expenses. Guidetti was to be the "*Premier Danseur* and the composer of Ballets," and he was not to dance at any other London theatre without Garrick's permission.

After agreeing to the terms, Garrick suffered second thoughts. He had already been warned by George Colman who had been at Guidetti's debut in Paris and had written to Garrick on 27 July 1766 that he was among the worst dancers he had ever seen—"A little grotesque pantomime at first, but no execution as a dancer . . . and damned thick-winded." On 4 September 1766 Garrick wrote to his friend Domenico Angelo, then in Paris, to find out from Monnet "what we are to Expect from *Guidetti*—if he has comic execution, he will

Biblioteca, Museo Teatrale Burcardo, Rome

GIOVANNI GUIDETTI

artist unknown

succeed with Us—but if he is worn out, & feeble, We shall be disappointed."

The Drury Lane account books show that Guidetti was paid at a rate of 17s. 6d. per day, or six guineas per week. He made his debut on 11 October 1766, when at the end of Act II of *Venice Preserv'd* he danced with Signora Giorgi in a new comic dance called *The Vintage*; at the end of the play he appeared with Mrs King in a dance called *The Italian Bakers*. These pieces were repeated throughout the early half of the season. He also danced in *Cymon*, first on 2 January 1767 and then regularly during the remainder of the season. On 23 March 1767 the treasury repaid Garrick £21 which he had advanced to Monnet for Guidetti, presumably for the dancer to travel to England, and on 9 April Guidetti received £33 5s. to complete his salary "in full" to that date. A Mr Larbor was paid £2 2s. on 1 June 1767 "for attending Guidetti" in some unknown capacity.

There are no extant critical reactions to Guidetti's performances at London, but perhaps Garrick's apprehension proved justified, since the dancer was not reengaged. In 1768 he resumed his Italian career. An unsigned watercolor of him in a gardener's dance from *Il Muzio Scevola* at Florence in 1760 is in the Museo Teatrale Burcardo, Rome.

Guidi, Antonia, later Sga Vincenzo Galeotti *c. 1735–1780, dancer.*

The beautiful ballerina Antonia Guidi was born about 1735 and began her career in Copenhagen in 1754. Although married to the dancer and choreographer Vincenzo Galeotti in the 1750s, she continued to carry out her professional career under her maiden name. She was engaged as a member of Noverre's company at Stuttgart on 3 September 1762 for one year to June 1763, at a salary of 1000 florins and 200 florins journey money. After engagements in Venice and Turin during the 1760s, she and her husband joined the King's Theatre

in London for 1769–70. She made her debut on 6 February 1770 dancing with Slingsby in a new dance composed by Galeotti. She danced again on 22 February, this time with her husband, and on 19 May she appeared as a principal dancer in *Il disertore*. She and Galeotti had their benefit on 24 May.

For her first appearance at the King's the following season she performed a new hornpipe "on skates" with Galeotti, on 12 March 1771. She did not dance again until 1 April, when it was announced that she had now sufficiently recovered "from her indisposition" to return to the stage. At her benefit on 23 May, Signora Guidi offered a selection of various dances, including *The Dutch Dance on Skates* and *The Statue*. The latter was repeated on 15 June.

During her third and final season at the King's Theatre, 1771–72, Signora Guidi danced with Galeotti and four other dancers in *A Venetian Dance* which was introduced into the opera *Carnevale di Venezia* on 14 January 1772. Her performance of *The Statue* was offered frequently throughout the spring, and for her benefit on 14 May she danced as a Shepherdess in a new ballet called *Le Jaloux sans un rival*. In her last performance at London, on 11 June 1772, she danced a *provenzale* with Slingsby and a new pas de trois *"en Berger Gallante"* with him and Signora Crispi.

The Galeottis returned to Venice in 1772–73. Eventually they settled at Copenhagen where she died in June 1780. Information on her continental career may be found in the entry of Vincenzo Galeotti in the *Enciclopedia dello spettacolo*.

Guigaut, Eldner [fl. 1663], musician.

On 19 October 1663 Eldner Guigaut (or Elenor Guigant) was sworn one of the King's French musicians in ordinary.

Guilford, Mr [fl. 1792], actor.

Mr Guilford acted Selim in *The Mourn-*

ing Bride and the Watchman in *The Apprentice* at the Haymarket Theatre on 26 November 1792.

Guimard, Marie Madeleine, later Mme Jean Etienne Despréaux *1743– 1816, dancer.*

Marie Madeleine Guimard, one of the most famous French dancers of the last half of the eighteenth century, was born at a house in the Rue de Bourbon-Villeneuve, Paris, on 27 December 1743, the natural daughter of Fabien Guimard, an inspector of cloth manufactories at Voiron (Isère), and Marie Anna Bernard. In December 1765, she received *lettres de légitimation* by special grant of Louis XV. At about the age of 16, either at the end of 1758 or the beginning of 1759, she joined the *corps de ballet* at the Comédie Française, having obtained the position through the influence of M. d'Harnoncourt and the Président de Saint-Lubin, "two gentlemen of somewhat doubtful reputation," who had taken a special interest in her, according to Cyril Beaumont.

Guimard remained at the Comédie until the end of 1761. While there she was described as being "well formed and already endowed with the prettiest neck in the world, passable features—and particularly roguish eyes." Despite her mother's careful supervision over her at that time she had managed to become clandestinely involved with Léger, a dancer at the Opéra.

Early in 1762 Mlle Guimard signed on at the Opéra (l'Académie royale de musique) as a dancer and understudy to Mlle Allard. She made her debut in *Les Caractères de la danse* with success. On 9 May 1762, Mlle Allard having suffered an injury to her foot, Mlle Guimard appeared in the principal role of Terpsichore in the prologue of Fuzelier's ballet *Les Fêtes grecques et romaines*. Bachaumont, in *Mémoires secrètes*, was impressed by her lightness, but noted an occasional lack of "more rounded grace."

Harvard Theatre Collection

MARIE MADELEINE GUIMARD

engraving after Fragonard

By 1763 she had attained the rank of *première danseuse noble* at the Opéra. She was by then the mistress of Jean Benjamin de la Borde, first *valet de chambre* of Louis XV. Before the Court at Fontainebleau in 1764 she triumphed dancing the role of Eglé in Rameau's opera *Castor et Pollux* (in which she also attempted, unsuccessfully, to sing). Between then and 1788 she became the darling of Paris, dancing in numerous ballets to the unflagging applause of an adoring public. Among her most notable performances were those in *Les Triomphe des arts* (1764), *Ninette à la cour* (1778), *Les Caprices de Galatée* (1776), *La Chercheuse d'esprit* (1778), and *Le Déserteur* (1788). Noverre, in whose ballets she often appeared, wrote of her dancing: "Mlle. Guimard . . . never courted difficulties, a noble simplicity dominated her dancing. She danced tastefully and put expression and feeling into all her movements." Baron Grimm described her performance in *La Chercheuse d'esprit*:

All her *pas*, all her movements, were distinguished by their softness and harmony, a sure and picturesque combination. Her simplicity is artless without being foolish. . . . How animated she becomes under the soft rays of feeling! She resembles a rose-bud which is seen to open, escape from the fettering tendrils, tremble, and flower. We have seen nothing so delightful and so perfect in this style of mime.

On 26 February 1789 the *Morning Post* announced that Mlle Guimard had been engaged to dance at the King's Theatre, London, on terms that included remuneration for the expenses of her journey, a courier to attend her, board and lodging, a free benefit, and a carriage for her journey and the time she would be in London. Addi-

Harvard Theatre Collection

MARIE MADELEINE GUIMARD, in *Per Navigateur*

engraving by Janinet, after Dutertre

tionally, Signor Ravelli, assistant manager of the theatre, was obliged to be at Dover to receive her. She made her debut at the King's Theatre on 28 April 1789, dancing with Didelot in the "celebrated *Minuet* of Iphigenia" at the end of Act I of Noverre's ballet *Admète*. Although 46 years old, "the grandmother of the graces skipped about with much elegance," reported the *Morning Post* (13 May). She danced in *Les Jalousies du Sérail* on 2 May. On 7 May, her benefit, when tickets could be had of her at No 10, Pall Mall, and at which she cleared the impressive sum of £735, she performed a pas de deux Russe with Nivelon and danced Galatée in *Les Caprices de Galatée*, the ballet that Noverre had created for her at Paris in 1776. On 14 May she danced Ninette in *Ninette à la cour*, repeated Galatée on 23 May, and on 9 June danced Annette in *Annette et Lubin*. For Didelot's benefit on 15 June she danced in *Le Tuteur trompé* with the *Minuet de la cour* as well as in *Les Folies d' Espagne*.

In a spectacular fire on 17 June 1789 the King's Theatre burned to the ground. Extensive property was lost by the performers but Mlle Guimard suffered only "the loss of one of her slippers." In order to play out its season the opera company moved to Covent Garden Theatre, where on 2 July 1789 Mlle Guimard gave her last London performance, performing the same dances as on 15 June. For her appearances over less than two months she had been paid, according to Dancourt's *La Guimard*, a total of £538 6s. 8d., plus the free benefit.

Soon after Guimard's return to Paris she married on 14 August 1789 the choreographer Jean-Etienne Despréaux (d. 1820) and retired from the Opéra on a pension of 5400 livres. Despréaux seems to have been the last of a string of lovers which had included de la Borde, the Prince de Sourbise, and Monseigneur de Jarente, Bishop of Orleans. With Despréaux she moved to a modest house in Montmartre, the Revolution having swept away the elegance and extravagances which had always marked her style. Previously she had owned, in the Parisian suburb of Pantin, a country house which had been sumptuously decorated by Fragonard and included a miniature theatre where once the society of Paris had gathered to watch private and often titillating performances. When she had tired of Pantin she built herself the "Temple of Terpsichore" in the Rue Chaussée d'Antin, which she was obliged to dispose of by lottery in 1785.

With Despréaux she lived out the remainder of her life in comparative quiet, moving to the Rue des Ménars in 1807, where she died on 14 May 1816. The details of her continental career may be found in the *Enciclopedia dello spettacolo*, in Campardon's *Académie royale* and *Les Comédiens du Roi*, and in Cyril Beaumont's *Three French Dancers of the Eighteenth Century*, to all of which this notice is heavily indebted.

Portraits of Mlle Guimard include:

1. Painting by Jean Fragonard, showing her dancing. A caricature engraving was published by E. Humphrey at London on 26 March 1789.

2. Painting by Fragonard, showing her seated.

3. Marble bust, by F. Merchi. In the Musée de l'Opéra, Paris.

4. Engraved portrait by Desmaisons, after Guérard, "La pastorale," showing her dancing.

5. Engraved portrait by Jaminet, after Dutertre, showing her dancing.

6. Engraved portrait by Prud'hon, after a drawing by Coeuré, in Bergère costume.

7. In *Le Premier navigateur*. Engraving by Delpech, after Le Comte.

8. In a *pas de trois*, with Marie Allard and Jean D'Auberval. Anonymous engraving, dated 1779.

9. Engraving by le Campion, after Testard, of Guimard's monument on the Rue de la Chaussée d'Antin.

10. Engraved portrait by E. Gervais, after F. Boucher. Printed by F. Chardon, Paris; another impression printed by Lemercie & Cie, Paris.

Guin. *See* **GWINN, GWYN, GWYNN, QUIN.**

Guind, Mr [*fl. 1784–1785*], *musician.*

According to a document in the Public Record Office a Mr Guind, otherwise unknown, was a performer at the King's Theatre during the 1784–85 season at a salary of £80.

Guipponi, John [*fl. 1670–1674*], *machinist.*

The London Stage lists John Guipponi as a member of the King's Company in the 1670–71 and 1673–74 seasons. The Lord Chamberlain's accounts on 10 April 1671 and 27 September 1673 show Guipponi to have been a machinist in the troupe. He would have worked at the Bridges Street Theatre until the fire in 1672 and then at Lincoln's Inn Fields, where the company took up temporary residence until 1674.

Guisbach. *See* **GRIESBACH.**

Guise, George *d. 1740, boxkeeper?, treasurer.*

The London Stage lists Mr Guise as a boxkeeper at Covent Garden and notes that he shared a benefit with two others on 20 May 1735. Paul Sawyer, after an investigation of some Chancery documents at the Public Record office concerning litigation between the Covent Garden manager John Rich and Guise's wife Mary, informs us that Guise's first name was George, that he was appointed a deputy or under treasurer at Covent Garden about November 1736, and that he served in that capacity until or almost until his death on 31 July 1740.

Guise was of the parish of St Clement Danes, though he was living in Greenwich at the time of his death. The accounts for Covent Garden show that in 1735–36 he worked 172 days at 2s. daily and shared a respectable income (before house charges, probably) of £146 6s. 6d. with two others at benefit time. By May 1739 he was sharing a benefit with only one other co-worker, but his last recorded benefit, on 16 May 1740, was shared with two others.

Guise, John ɪ*fl. 1784–1794*ɪ, *singer.*
John Guise of Windsor sang tenor in the Handel performances at Westminster Abbey and the Pantheon in May and June 1784. Doane's *Musical Directory* of 1794 listed him as John Guise, M.B., of No 12, Dartmouth Street, Westminster, and of Windsor. He sang for the Chapel Royal, St Paul's, and at the Handelian performances at Westminster Abbey, and he was the master of the "West[minster] Boys."

Guishard, John ɪ*fl. 1784–1805*ɪ, *singer.*
John Guishard (or Guichard) was one of the countertenors who sang in the Handelian concerts at Westminster Abbey and the Pantheon in May and June 1784. He was a member of the Academy of Ancient Music, but during the 1787–88 season he was replaced by J. Danby. On 11 August 1789 and subsequent dates through the middle of September he sang in the chorus in *The Battle of Hexham* at the Haymarket Theatre. The following summer he was in the chorus of Indians in *New Spain* at the Haymarket from 16 July through 14 August 1790. On 15 October 1791 the Drury Lane company performed *The Cave of Trophonius* at the King's Theatre, their temporary home, and the playbill listed Guishard as one of the Priests. One of John Philip Kemble's notes for the 1791–92 season, however, says that "Walker came into the Chorus instead of Guichard, who never attended the Theatre."
Doane's *Musical Directory* of 1794 listed Guishard, of No 4, Stephen Street, Rathbone Place, as an alto who participated in

concerts presented by the New Musical Fund, the Academy of Ancient Music, and the Anacreontic Society. He also sang in the oratorios at Westminster Abbey. On the list of subscribers to the New Musical Fund in both 1794 and 1805 Guishard was cited as a member of the Court of Assistants of that society.

Guistinelli. *See* GIUSTINELLI.

Guiton, Peter ɪ*fl. 1675–1678*ɪ, *oboist, recorder player.*
On 15 February 1675 when the masque *Calisto* was performed at court, Peter Guiton played either the oboe or recorder or both (there are two different lists among the Lord Chamberlain's papers). On 27 May 1675 he was listed among the French oboists, and a certificate dated 8 June 1678 identified him as a member of the Chapel Royal.

Gulick, Mrs ɪ*fl. 1718–1724*ɪ, *actress.*
Mrs Gulick's earliest mention in the bills was on 15 October 1718, when she played Florinda in *The Fair Example* at Lincoln's Inn Fields. The following 25 May 1719 she shared a benefit with three others at that playhouse, so it is certain that she was busy during the season even if her name rarely appeared in the bills. During the 1719–20 season she was noticed more frequently. Her first part was Alicia in Beckingham's *Henry IV* on 7 November 1719, after which she acted Mrs Foresight in *Love for Love*, Betty in *The Pretenders*, Clarinna in *Cymbeline*, Charlotte in *Whig and Tory*, Lucy in *Oroonoko*, Miranda in *Woman's a Riddle*, Justina in *The Imperial Captives*, Lady Macbeth (on 17 March 1720), Jenny in *The Fair Quaker of Deal*, Olympia in *Sir Walter Raleigh* (for her shared benefit with Mrs Knapp), and Nottingham in *The Unhappy Favorite*. On 23 August at Bullock and Widow Leigh's booth at Bartholomew Fair Mrs Gulick played the Queen in *Love's Triumph*.
She remained at Lincoln's Inn Fields for

the 1720–21 and 1721–22 seasons, adding to her repertoire such roles as Mrs Overdone in *Measure for Measure*, Alinda in *The Pilgrim*, Double Diligence (normally a man's role) in *The Cheats*, Jiltup in *The Fair Quaker*, the Aunt in *The London Cuckolds*, and Mrs Chat in *The Committee*. Between the two seasons she acted Melissa in *The Noble Englishman* at Lee's booth at Southwark Fair on 8 September 1721. After her shared benefit with two others at Lincoln's Inn Fields on 16 May 1722 (total profits £104 8s., probably before house charges) Mrs Gulick left the company. She is not known to have acted again until 27 June 1724, when she played Abigail in *The Drummer* at Richmond. At the same theatre she was seen as Lady Bountiful in *The Stratagem* on 29 June, Isabinda in *The Busy Body* on 11 July, and the Queen in *The Spanish Fryar* on 18 July. After that she dropped from sight.

Gull, Mr ₁*fl. 1789–1792₁*, *actor.*

Mr Gull played at Richmond on 13 July 1789 when *The Beggar's Opera* and *The Author* were performed. On 7 March 1791 he acted Whisper in *The Busy Body* at the Haymarket Theatre in London; then, in July of that year he performed at the Duke Street Theatre in Brighton. He returned to the Haymarket on 20 February 1792 to appear as Launcelot in *The Merchant of Venice* and Sir Francis Gripe in *The Busy Body*.

"Gulliver, Captain" ₁*fl. 1737₁*, *manager?*

At the Lincoln's Inn Fields Theatre on 7 May 1737 "Capt. Gulliver's Company of Lilliputians" performed *The Honest Yorkshireman*. The pseudonym may have been used by the master of the children's troupe, or the title may have been pure publicity.

Gum. *See* **Gom.**

Gunn, John *c. 1765–c. 1824, violoncellist, flutist, music essayist.*

John Gunn, born about 1765 at Edin-

burgh, taught cello at Cambridge until he moved to London in 1790. There he taught cello and flute and published in 1793 *Forty Scotch Airs arranged as trios for flute, violin, and violoncello* and *The Theory and Practice of Fingering for the Violoncello.*

In 1794, Gunn was listed in Doane's *Musical Directory* as living in Rathbone Place and participating in Salomon's concerts and the Handelian performances at Westminster Abbey. In 1795, Gunn returned to Edinburgh to write and teach. He died there about 1824.

Gunn's writings include an *Essay Theoretical and Practical, on the Application of Harmony, Thorough-bass, and Modulation to the Violoncello* (1801) and *An Historical Inquiry respecting the Performance on the Harp in the Highlands of Scotland from the earliest Times until it was discontinued about the Year 1734* (1807).

His wife Anne (née Young) was, according to Grove, "an eminent pianist," and the author of *An Introduction to Music . . . illustrated by Musical Games and Apparatus and fully and familiarly explained* (Edinburgh, c. 1803). John Gunn perhaps was related to Barnabas Gunn (c. 1680–1753), the composer and organist successively at St Philip's Church, Birmingham, and Gloucester Cathedral, who is noticed in Grove.

Gunning, Mrs J. *See* **Campbell, Miss** ₁*fl. 1799–1806?₁*.

Gunthony. *See* **Ganthony.**

Gurion. *See* **Gauron.**

Gurnie, Mlle ₁*fl. 1787₁*, *dancer.*

At the beginning of the Royal Circus season in April 1787 a bill announced that Mademoiselle Gurnie would be one of the principal dancers, but no specific assignments are known for her.

Gurrelli. *See* **Garrelli.**

Gurrini. *See also* **Guerini.**

Gurrini, Mauro *[fl. 1763–1764]*, singer, manager.

As Sybil Rosenfeld related in her *Foreign Theatrical Companies in Great Britain*, Edinburgh was visited in the summer of 1763 by an Italian burletta troupe managed by a Signor Mauro Gurrini (or Guirini). The company opened on 21 June with *La serva padrona,* in which Mauro and Signora Rose Gurrini sang principal parts. The *Evening Courant* the following day reported that

The action of Signor Gurrini, who play'd the part of the old man, was particularly excellent; and Signora Gurrini, who played the part of his maidservant, sung several songs with uncommon approbation; the duets in particular were remarkably fine; and the last, where humour and harmony were so happily blended, was encored and repeated to the general applause of every person.

During their stay in Edinburgh the Gurrinis also appeared in *Il giocatore* on 27 June and *L'ucellatrice, or the Female Bird-catcher* on 20 July. Gurrini had a benefit on 30 July, the final night of the season. The troupe then performed in Newcastle, where the players were advertised as passing through "on their way to London." After spending early September in Newcastle, they moved on to Durham, then performed in York during most of October. By 6 December they were expected in Manchester, where they were to perform "in the same manner as at the Theatre in the Haymarket, London." Presumably they acted in London some time between 25 October and 6 December, though *The London Stage* lists no performances by the troupe at any London theatre at any time. We should suppose that their London playbills have not survived.

Dublin saw the Gurrini company in 1764 at the Crow Street Theatre. *La serva padrona* was still in the repertory, along with *Gli amanti gelosi.*

Gurrini, Signora Mauro, Rose *[fl. 1763–1764]*, singer. See GURRINI, MAURO.

Guy, Mr *[fl. 1793]*, tailor.

The Drury Lane accounts contain an entry dated 4 July 1793: Mr Guy, a tailor, was paid £1 16s. for working one week after the close of the season.

Gwatkin, Abraham *[fl. 1785–1805]*, instrumentalist.

On 3 July 1785 Abraham "Gwathin," son of the trumpeter Thomas, petitioned the Royal Society of Musicians for an allowance to cover his father's burial expenses. He also informed the Society that his mother had died on 16 June. A grant of £5 was approved. Doane's *Musical Directory* of 1794 listed Abraham Gwatkin, of No 2, Bartlet Buildings, Holborn, as a trumpeter, violinist, and horn player who participated in concerts presented by the New Musical Fund. He was still a subscriber to that society in 1805.

Gwatkin, Thomas *d. 1785, trumpeter.*

Thomas Gwatkin, a bachelor, married Ann Powles, a spinster, at St Marylebone on 3 December 1759. Gwatkin was certainly the trumpeter of that name who was active in the 1770s. In 1776 Joseph Probart, the royal sergeant trumpeter, gave Gwatkin power of attorney to collect sums due Probart from the crown. Probart described Gwatkin as a "Household trumpeter" then living in Little Castle Street in the parish of St Marylebone. On 4 May 1777 Gwatkin was admitted to the Royal Society of Musicians. He stated that at that time he was married and had three children, two of them over 15 years of age. He said he had practised music for a livelihood for over seven years. The St Marylebone registers show that Ann Gwatkin, a spinster and certainly the daughter of Thomas and Ann Gwatkin, married James William Miller, a bachelor, on 18 October

1784. The registers contain no information about the rest of the Gwatkin family.

In 1785 Thomas Gwatkin died: on 3 July of that year the Society granted £5 to his son Abraham (also a musician) for funeral expenses. Thomas Gwatkin's wife had died on 16 June 1785.

Gwatkins, William ₍fl. 1706₎, *singer.*

"Wm Gwatkins, late Child of Chapel Royal," was given a clothing allowance on 14 May 1706, according to a warrant among the Lord Chamberlain's papers in the Public Record Office.

Gwillim, John ₍fl. c. 1752–1777₎, *musician.*

John Gwillim, a musician, lived in Ratcliff Cross in 1777, but nothing is known to us of his career. His two sons, John Gwillim (b. c. 1752) and Thomas Gwillim (b. c. 1763), also musicians, are noticed separately on these pages.

Gwillim, John *b. c. 1752, violinist.*

The violinist John Gwillim was admitted as Freeman to the Worshipfull Company of Musicians on 9 December 1773, presumably after completing an apprenticeship of seven years. Since apprenticeships usually began at the age of 14, John's year of birth can be put at about 1752. At the time of his admission to the Company, Gwillim was living at No 3, Green Dragon Court, Snow Hill. He was no doubt the son of a musician of the same name who lived in Ratcliff Cross in 1777. Burney listed the younger John as one of the first violins for the Handel Memorial Concerts at Westminster Abbey and the Pantheon in May and June of 1784. Gwillim was a regular player at the Covent Garden spring oratorios between 1792 and 1800.

By 1789 Gwillim was a member of the Royal Society of Musicians, for in May of that year he played at the Society's annual concert at St Paul's; he had similar assignments in 1790, 1792, 1793, 1802, and 1803. In 1806 and 1807 he served as a Governor of the Society. Gwillim was listed in 1794 in Doane's *Musical Directory*; in addition to the associations already given, Doane described him as a violinist at Sadler's Wells Theatre, with an address at Cross Street, Hatton Garden.

John Gwillim was married at least twice. By his first wife Sarah he had at least one child, John Gwillim, born in 1776, who became a musician and is entered here separately. John's first wife seems to have died by 1784, for on 7 December of that year he married Ann Halliday at St Marylebone. No issue from his second marriage is known. John's brother Thomas Gwillim (b. c. 1763) was bound his apprentice on 10 February 1777.

On 6 March 1825, the Royal Society of Musicians granted £5 5s. to John Gwillim "for relief." Presumably the violinist was unable to work. He received a "full allowance" of £4 4s. from the Society on 6 January 1828. He was still alive on 4 February 1838, on which date he sent his thanks to the Society for its Christmas donation.

Gwillim, John *1776–1808, instrumentalist.*

John Gwillim, the son of the violinist of the same name (b. c. 1752) and his first wife Sarah, was born on 9 November 1776 and was baptized at St Sepulchre, London, on 6 December, following. He was bound an apprentice to his father on 26 November 1790, at which time they were living at Cross Street, Hatton Garden. The Gwillims were still at that address in 1794 when young John was listed in Doane's *Musical Directory* as a violinist and a participant in the Handelian Memorial Concerts at Westminster Abbey.

On 17 February 1798 Gwillim was made a Freeman of the Worshipfull Company of Musicians. Several weeks earlier, on 4 February, he had been recommended by his father for admission to the Royal Society of Musicians, at which time it was declared that the son played the piano, violin, viola, and clarinet, and was a single man with "a good deal of Business." John was unanimously elected on 6 May 1798 and within a few days played the violin at the Society's annual concert at St Paul's. He played at similar concerts in 1799, 1800, 1804, and 1805.

Gwillim died in the latter months of 1808, and on 1 January 1809 his widow, Susanna Gwillim (whom he had married between 1798 and 1800) petitioned the Society for assistance. She was granted the usual allowance of £12 12s. 6d. per month, plus £1 1s. per month for each of her two children: John, born on 10 March 1801, and Susanna, born on 12 December 1802. The son John was bound apprentice to William Jones, a goldsmith of Dean Street, on 3 September 1815, and the daughter Susanna was placed with Mr Graham, a dressmaker, on 5 January 1817. On 5 July 1835, John Gwillim's widow Susanna was granted £5 "medical aid" by the Royal Society of Musicians. She was still alive on 4 February 1838, on which date she sent thanks to the Society for its Christmas donation.

Gwillim, Thomas *b. c. 1763, musician.*

On 10 February 1777, Thomas Gwillim, the son of John Gwillim of Ratcliff Cross, was bound apprentice to his brother John Gwillim (b. c. 1752), a musician at Snow Hill. Since apprenticeships usually commenced at the age of 14, Thomas's year of birth can be put at about 1763. On 18 February 1784, described as a musician of No 12, Turnagain Lane, having finished his apprenticeship, he was made free of the Worshipfull Company of Musicians.

Gwinn. *See also* GWYN, GWYNN.

Gwinn, Mr *[fl. 1716], house servant? See* GWINN, WILLIAM.

Gwinn, Mr *[fl. 1724–1748], pit doorkeeper.*

Mr Gwinn the pit doorkeeper at the Lincoln's Inn Fields playhouse and later at Covent Garden was surely the son of William Gwinn, who also served those theatres. The Lincoln's Inn Fields accounts refer on 25 September 1724 to "Gwin, Jr" as a member of the company earning 5s. daily. Similar citations on 16 September 1726 and 9 June 1727 show him to have been given a raise to 7s. 6d. The theatre's free list in 1726–27, 1727–28, and 1728–29 occasionally mentions "Y. Gwin" (Young Gwinn?), "Mrs Gwin Junr.," and "Young M^rs. Gwin." The younger Gwinn's wife seems not to have worked at the theatre, however. On 21 May 1730 Gwinn shared a benefit with two other members of the troupe.

The accounts do not mention Gwinn again until 1735–36, when he was paid an unspecified sum for working 179 days at Covent Garden; he was again identified as Gwinn, Junior. We have no way of knowing whether or not Gwinn was steadily employed at the theatre between 1730 and 1735, but he probably was, and it is also likely that he continued working there in the late 1730s even though the accounts do not cite him again until 21 May 1740. On that date he shared a benefit at Covent Garden with two boxkeepers. He was described as a pit doorkeeper. He was not called Junior, for the elder Gwinn, William, had died about 1738 and a distinction was now unnecessary. The younger Gwinn continuing serving as pit doorkeeper at least through 1747–48, sharing annual benefits.

Gwinn, William *d. c. 1738, boxkeeper, pit doorkeeper.*

It is probable that the "Young Gwinn" who shared a benefit with two others at Lincoln's Inn Fields on 18 July 1716 was William, who was a boxkeeper and pit doorkeeper at that playhouse and at Covent

Garden. The designation "Young" suggests that another Gwinn, doubtless William's father also served at the theatre. Gwinn, no longer called "Young," shared a benefit on 13 May 1719, as he did every spring through 12 May 1737. We would guess that between the summer of 1716 and May 1719 William's father had died. In the benefit bills William Gwinn was referred to as a pit doorkeeper in 1725, as a boxkeeper from 1735 on, but again, after his death, as a pit doorkeeper.

His shared benefits were usually well attended, as was often the case with employees who worked in the house and were in constant contact with theatregoers. On 10 May 1721, for instance, he and the prompter Stede shared £121 5s. 6d.; in 1726 he and three others shared £197 19s. 6d.; and in 1736 with two others he shared £146 4s. 6d.

The free list for 1726–27 through 1728–29 at Lincoln's Inn Fields, preserved at Harvard, mentions Mrs Gwinn, Gwinn's daughter (not named), and Gwinn's maid. The free list also supplies us with Gwinn's Christian name. William's wife, Lucy, was also employed at the theatre. William Gwinn died between his last benefit on 12 May 1737 and a benefit given his widow on 15 May 1738.

Gwinn, Mrs William, Lucy [fl. 1727–1763], _wardrobe keeper._

Lucy Gwinn, the wife of the pit doorkeeper and boxkeeper William Gwinn, was cited in the free list at Lincoln's Inn Fields in May and December 1727; in both instances her Christian name was given, and, on 30 May 1727, she was called "M^{rs}. Lucy Gwin – The Engenier." The meaning of that is not clear, but since Lucy was in later years cited as a silk dyer, perhaps in 1727 she was doing some work for the theatre that qualified her as an inventor or designer.

Lucy was not mentioned again in surviving documents until 15 May 1738, when she shared a benefit with the boxkeeper

Vaughan at Covent Garden and was identified as "Gwinn's widow, the late Pit Doorkeeper." When Lalauze had a benefit on 9 April 1739 he made his tickets available from Widow Gwinn the silk dyer in Drury Lane; later that season, on 23 May, Widow Gwinn shared a benefit at Covent Garden with Mrs Atkins. It would appear that Lucy Gwinn was earning a living dying silk, selling benefit tickets, and running a boarding house where Lalauze, among others, lived. On 1 March 1742 Lalauze gave his lodging as Mrs Gwinn's house in Drury Lane near the Castle Tavern, as he did again in 1744 and 1745.

The evidence thus far would not indicate that Mrs Gwinn worked at the theatre, though as a silk dyer she may have done work for the players. However, on 4 May 1754 and again in 1756, 1757, 1758, 1760, 1761, 1762, and 1763 Mrs Gwinn's benefit tickets were taken at Covent Garden; she was serving at the theatre those years (if not earlier) as an assistant wardrobe keeper at 1s. 6d. daily. The accounts show that on 8 December 1759 she was paid 17s. for cleaning silks, so in addition to her chores at the playhouse she may have kept up her silk-dying business. The last mention of Lucy Gwinn in the benefit bills was on 14 May 1763.

Gwyn, Eleanor _1642?–1687, actress, dancer._

"The Manager's Note-Book" claimed that Nell Gwyn was born in 1642, and it will be seen that that date fits best with other information we have about her life. But according to her horoscope at the Bodleian Library, Nell was born at six in the morning on 2 February 1650. Elias Ashmole cast her horoscope, and his information on the time and date of her birth he presumably got from Nell herself; oddly, though she was remarkably exact about when she was born, she was apparently blank about where. The two most likely places are Coal Yard Alley, east of Drury

National Portrait Gallery

ELEANOR GWYN

studio of Lely, c. 1675

Lane in London, or Pipewell Lane in Hereford. Perhaps she was born in Hereford and moved to London at an early age. Oxford has also been put forward as her birthplace, but the evidence is too flimsy to have convinced many of Nell's biographers.

Nell's father may have been, as Frederick Van Bossen wrote in 1688, "Thomas Gwine, a captaine of ane antient family in Wales." Her mother Ellen or Eleanor (Nell, too, was called both) may have been born Smith. Nell had a sister Rose, who became Mrs John Cassells and later Mrs Guy Forster. Doran in his *Annals* suggested that Nell's real name was Margaret Simcott or Symcott, but there seems to be no evidence to support that, and Doran did not say where he found the name. In her later years Nell was of the parish of St Martin-in-the-Fields in London; a search of the registers there reveals a number of Gwyns, Guins, Guyns, and Gwins, especially in the 1670s when Nell was at her most notorious. The recurrence of the name Eleanor is especially interesting: Ann Gwin the daughter of William and Eleonara was christened on 12 April 1640; Francis Guin the son of Richard and Eleanor was born on 15 April 1671 and christened five days later; Edward Guyn the son of Richard and Eleanor was born on 22 June 1672 and christened on the twenty-sixth; Elianora Gwyn ("Mulier") was buried on 20 January 1673; Elianora Gwyn ("Puella") was buried on 20 December 1674; and Elinor Gwin (our Nell) was buried on 17 November 1687. There is no way to tell whether or not those several Eleanors were related to Nell, but some may have been.

Many satirical poems of the late seventeenth century allude to Nell, her parents, and her early years, and in some of the scribbling there were probably a few grains of truth. But winnowing them out is about as difficult as identifying the authors of some of the poems. "A Panegyric" (1681) in *Poems on Affairs of State* was attributed to Rochester but was probably not by him:

> From Oxford prisons many did she free,
> There di'd her father, and there glori'd she,
> In giving others life and liberty.

About 1686 or slightly later was written "The Lady of Pleasure or the Life of Nelly Truly Shown from Hopgard'n, to the Throne, Till the grave she tumbled down." It is among the Harleian manuscripts at the British Museum, and it was published in Buckingham's *Works* in 1715, attributed to Etherege:

> The Pious Mother of that flaming Whore,
> Maid, Punk, and Bawd full Sixty Years & more,
> Dy'd Drunk with Brandy in a common-shore—
> No matter that, nor what we were must shame us,
> 'Tis what we last arrive to, that must fame us,
> Fam'd be the Cellar then, wherein the Babe
> Was first brought forth to be a Monarch's Drab.

Biographers have sifted such poems for clues to Nell's background; they note, for example, that Hereford is "Hopgard'n" country and argue for her birth there. Easier to corroborate is the reference to Nell's mother dying drunk, as we shall see.

A "Satire" (1677) in *Poems on Affairs of State* was printed in editions of Rochester's works but was probably not by him. It tells of the early life of Nell, but how much of it is based on fact?

> Whose first employment was, with open throat
> To cry fresh herrings e'en at ten a groat,
> Then was by Madam Ross [the procuress] expos'd to town,
> (I mean to those who will give half a crown),
> Next in the playhouse she took her degree,

As men commence in th'university:
No doctors, till they've masters been
*   before,*
Nor any player but she's first a whore.

Nell may well have hawked herring in the streets, for as legend has it, her father vended fruit. Pepys said that Nell "was brought up in a bawdy house to fill strong waters to the guests"—and Nell admitted to that.

Our heroine's next (after which of the above?) employment, according to "A Panegyric," was as an orange girl at the theatre: "This first step rais'd, to th'wond'-ring Pit she sold/ The lovely fruit, smiling with streaks of gold." Indeed, Nell worked under Mary Meggs—"Orange Moll"—at the Bridges Street Theatre, which would have given a gregarious girl ample opportunity to become acquainted with the players on the one hand and the nobility and gentry in the audience on the other. She began working at the playhouse not long after it opened in May 1663; she would have been only 13 if we accept 1650 as her birth year, but 21 if we accept 1642. In any case, within a year and a half or so Nell moved from orange girl to actress.

"The Lady of Pleasure," attributed (erroneously?) to Etherege in Buckingham's *Works* in 1715, said:

Then Entred Nelly on the publick Stage
Harlot of Harlots, Lais of the Age;
But there what Lacy's fumbling Age
*   abus'd,*
Harts sprightly Vigor more robustly us'd.

Who helped Nell to a stage career? *The History of the English Stage* (1741) contains an account by Oldys which says a merchant named Robert Duncan (or Dungan, Dongan) helped Nell; "Madam Nelley's Complaint" (in Buckingham's *Works*, 1715) also alludes to Duncan and names Mary Knight as having had a hand in Nell's introduction to the stage. Colley Cib-

ber, on the other hand, writing in 1740, remembered Nell's patron as the leading actor in the King's Company, Charles Hart (to whom that last poem alluded). It is not unlikely that several people aided Nell, but Hart, who became her lover and her leading man and who was in a position to hire her, seems the likeliest candidate. He was probably her tutor in acting, just as John Lacy (also alluded to in the poem above) became her dancing teacher. Cibber suggested Lacy as Nell's first paramour and Hart her second—within the playhouse, that is. Duncan may have enjoyed her first, just as through her later influence she helped him enjoy a commission in the guards.

Since a bit player is not often mentioned in cast lists or playgoers' diaries, we cannot be certain when Nell made her first stage appearance. Possibly it was during the 1664–65 season. The Bodleian manuscript of *The Siege of Urbin*, which was probably performed at Bridges Street that season, has "Mrs. Nell" down for Pedro (Melina—a maid servant in breeches). "Mrs. Nell" could refer to some other woman in the troupe, of course, but it is what Nell Gwyn was sometimes called later. And "Nelle" was intended by the company proprietor Thomas Killigrew to play the small role of the courtesan Paulina in his *Thomaso* in November 1664. Once again, a birth-date of 1650 seems less likely than 1642; the use of "Mrs." would be more appropriate (it merely meant over 21 then, not necessarily married) and the roles would be more suitable.

The prompter Downes of the rival Duke's Company wrote in 1708 that Nell acted Panthea in *A King and No King* and Cydaria in *The Indian Emperor* when she first came on the stage, but it is not likely that she acted those important roles until later in the 1660s. John Harold Wilson in *All the King's Ladies* sensibly guesses that Nell may have played no important parts before the plague closed the theatres in May 1665. But Nell was around and about. Pepys went to see *Mustapha* at the rival Lincoln's Inn Fields playhouse on 3 April 1665, and in the audience was "pretty witty Nell" of the King's Company, with Rebecca Marshall, another actress. They "sat next to us; which pleased me mightily." That Pepys identified Nell as a member of the King's troupe assures us that, even if her roles were not large in 1664–65, she had made herself noticed.

After the plague and fire Nell's stage career is easier to trace, though the information is woefully incomplete. Pepys tells us that Nell was Lady Wealthy in *The English Monsieur* on 8 December 1666 at the Bridges Street playhouse. The diarist said "the women do very well; but above all, little Nelly. . . ." Flecknoe intended her as Lysette in *Damoiselles à la Mode*, which may have been performed in 1666–67 and was certainly given on 14 September 1668. Another role Nell attempted was Caelia in *The Humorous Lieutenant* on 23 January 1667. Pepys was there, and his actress friend Mrs Knepp took his party backstage "and brought to us Nelly, a most pretty woman, who acted the great part of Coelia to-day very fine, and did it pretty well: I kissed her, and so did my wife; and a mighty pretty soul she is." That Pepys called Nell a "woman" and not a girl is perhaps another argument for a birth date in 1642.

On 14 February 1667 the King's troupe acted either *Flora's Vagaries* or *Rule a Wife and Have a Wife* at court; we know that Nell played Flora a few months later, but we do not know whether or not she had a part in *Rule a Wife*. Wilson suggests that Nell may have acted the Second Constantia in *The Chances* in February 1667, and she certainly played the breeches part of Florimel in *Secret Love* when it opened in late February (the first certain performance on record was 2 March). In *Secret Love* Dryden had Celadon describe Florimel, and since the playwright may well have had

Nell in mind when he created the part, perhaps the following is descriptive of her:

A turn'd up nose, that gives an air to your face: Oh, I find I am more and more in love with you! a full neather-lip, an out-mouth [pout?], that makes mine water at it: the bottom of your cheeks, a little blub, and two dimples when you smile: for your stature 'tis well; and for your wit, 'twas given you by one that knew it had been thrown away upon an ill face: Come, you are handsome, there's no denying it.

Florimel describes herself obliquely as "five and twenty"—which Nell would have been when the play opened if she had been born in 1642.

Pepys saw *Secret Love* on 2 March and was all agog:

[T]here is a comical part done by Nell, which is Florimell, that I never can hope ever to see the like done again, by man or woman. . . . But so great performance of a comical part was never, I believe, in the world before as Nell do this, both as a mad girle, then most and best of all when she comes in like a young gallant; and hath the motions and carriage of a spark the most that ever I saw any man have. It makes me, I confess, admire her.

But Nell was not perfect. Pepys saw her dancing, probably in *Secret Love*, and then on 7 March 1667 he went to the Duke's theatre and saw Moll Davis: "the truth is, there is no comparison between Nell's dancing the other day at the King's house in boy's clothes and this, this being infinitely beyond the other."

Nell spoke the prologue to *The Knight of the Burning Pestle*, probably about March 1667, Wilson thinks. It is likely that she acted Samira in *The Surprisal* on 8 April, and Wilson guesses that about May she played Mirida in *All Mistaken*. On 1 May Pepys "saw pretty Nelly standing at her lodgings' door in Drury Lane in her smock sleeves and bodice, looking upon one: she seemed a mighty pretty creature."

Her lodgings, according to her earliest serious biographer, Cunningham, were at the Cock and Pie on the west side of Drury Lane, opposite Wych Street.

It was probably inevitable that some nobleman should lure Nell from the stage. Charles Sackville, Lord Buckhurst, later the sixth Earl of Dorset, was the first to do so. He apparently was struck by her charms when he saw her with John Lacy rolling about the stage floor in *All Mistaken*. "The Lady of Pleasure" described the occasion:

> *Yet* Hart *more manners had than not to tender,*
> *When noble* B[uckhurst] *begg's him to Surrender:*
> *He saw her roll the Stage from side to side,—*
> *And thro' her Draw'rs the powerful Charm Decry'd,*
> Take her my Lord, *quoth* Hart since you're so mean,
> To take a Player's leavings for your Q[ueen].

Poor Pepys was crushed to hear from his friend Mr Pierce on 13 July 1667 that Nell had been, as Downes would have said, "by force of love erept the stage." He confided to his diary: "what troubles me, that my Lord Buckhurst hath got Nell away from the King's house, lies with her, and gives her £100 a year, so as she hath sent her parts to the [play]house, and will act no more." One wonders, incidentally, how Nell managed her roles in the first place: she was illiterate, or nearly so, as her own comments prove. She may have had someone read her her lines; if she did, she must have had a remarkable ear and memory.

It should not come as a surprise to learn that the day after Pepys heard of Nell's taking up with Buckhurst, the curious diarist contrived to be at the King's Head in Epsom: "Here we called for drink, and bespoke dinner; and hear that my Lord Buckhurst and Nelly are lodged at the next house, and Sir Charles Sidly with them:

and keep a merry house. Poor girl! I pity her; but more the loss of her at the King's [play]house."

Pepys had no need to fear. On 22 August 1667 Nell was back at the Bridges Street playhouse, acting Cydaria in *The Indian Emperor*: "I find Nell come again, which I am glad of; but was most infinitely displeased with her being put to act the Emperour's daughter, which is a great and serious part, which she do most basely." His judgment seems to have been valid; Nell Gwyn was not cut out for serious roles. On 26 August Pepys reported that his friend Orange Moll at the King's playhouse assured him "that Nell is already left by my Lord Buckhurst, and that he makes sport of her, and swears she hath all she could get of him; and Hart, her great admirer, now hates her; and that she is very poor, and hath lost my Lady Castlemayne, who was her great friend also: but she is come to the [play]House, but is neglected by them all." Her chastisement seems not to have lasted long.

On 20 September 1667 she acted Mirida in *All Mistaken*. She took the title part in *Flora's Vagaries* on 5 October, and after that performance Pepys was taken my Mrs Knepp "up into the tiring-rooms: and to the women's shift, where Nell was dressing herself, and was all unready, and is very pretty, prettier than I thought. . . . But Lord! to see how they were both painted would make a man mad, and did make me loathe them; and what base company of men comes among them, and how lewdly they talk!" But he thought it "was pretty" to "see how Nell cursed, for having so few people in the pit." On 19 October Nell may have been Alizia in *The Black Prince*; then, on 16 November she played Bellario in *Philaster* (she may well have acted it earlier), a breeches part, opposite Charles Hart. Years later, in 1695, Settle wrote a prologue to his revision of the play, remembering the 1667 revival of the original:

Philaster and Belario, let me tell ye,
For these Bold Parts we have no Hart,
*   no Nelly;*
Those Darlings of the Stage, that charm'd
*   you there.*

On 11 November 1667 Pepys tried *The Indian Emperor* again but was still disenchanted: "above all things Nell's ill speaking of a great part made me mad." Again on 26 December at *The Surprisal* he was unhappy, "especially Nell's acting of a serious part [Samira], which she spoils." Two days later at *All Mistaken,* "Nell's and Hart's mad parts are most excellently done, but especially her's: which makes it a miracle to me to think how ill she do any serious part, as the other day, just like a fool or changeling; and in a mad part, do beyond all imitation almost."

On 20 February 1668 Pepys saw *The Duke of Lerma (The Great Favourite)* and enjoyed Mrs Knepp and Nell in the prologue; Nell spoke the epilogue as well. On 27 February Nell acted Angelo, the good angel, in *The Virgin Martyr;* she was Cydaria in *The Indian Emperor* again on 28 March; and on 17 April, probably, she repeated her role of Samira in *The Surprisal.* When Pepys saw *The Virgin Martyr* on 7 May he met Rebecca Marshall and Nell after the play; he found Nell "in her boy's clothes, mighty pretty. But, Lord! their confidence! and how many men do hover about them as soon as they come off the stage, and how confident they are in their talk!" Early in May 1668, according to Nell's recent biographer, Bevan, she played Lucilla in *The Man's the Master,* but that seems very unlikely, for the work belonged to the rival Duke's Company. Wilson suggests that Nell may have acted Olivia in *The Mulberry Garden* in May (18 May?). She certainly played Donna Jacintha in *An Evening's Love* on 12 June.

When *Damoiselles à la Mode* was acted in September 1668 Nell played the waiting woman, Lysette; on 18 December "Mrs Nell" spoke the prologue and epilogue to

Catiline; on 7 January 1669 she was seen by Pepys "in an upper box" watching *The Island Princess.* Pepys and his party were in the next box, and "the jade Nell," "a bold merry slut," "lay laughing there upon people" with one of her friends from the Duke's troupe. At performances of *Horace* beginning on 16 January, Nell and John Lacy offered a farce and dances of Lacy's composition between the acts; on 6 May, according to a manuscript cast in a Harvard copy of *A King and No King,* Nell played Penthea; and on 24 June she acted Valeria and spoke the epilogue to *Tyrannick Love.* That epilogue by Dryden had Nell left as dead at the end of the play and about to be carried off when:

Hold, are you mad? you damn'd con-
*   founded dog!*
I am to rise and speak the epilogue.
. . . .
Here Nelly lies, who, though she liv'd a
*   Slater'n,*
Yet dy'd a Princess acting in S. Cathar'n.

After her appearance in *Tyrannick Love* Nell was again erept the stage. "A Panegyric" said, "There's Hart's and Rowley's [King Charles's] soul she did ensnare,/ And made a King the rival to a play'r." It is not certain just when Nell became one of the mistresses of Charles II, but she certainly was one by the summer of 1669. She remained a member of the acting troupe, however; a warrant in the Lord Chamberlain's accounts dated 2 October 1669 confirms that she was granted livery for 1668–70. But she was heavy with child and gave birth to a son, Charles, later Duke of St Albans, on 8 May 1670—or so said Malone. Anthony à Wood wrote that "About 14 or 15 [June 1670], Elianor Quin, one that belongs to the King's play hous, was brought to bed of a boy in her house in Lyncoln's Inns feilds, next to Whetstones Park—the King's bastard."

Nell returned to the stage in December 1670 to speak the prologue to Dryden's

The Conquest of Granada "in a broad-brim'd hat, and Wastbelt" to ridicule Nokes of the Duke's Company, who had worn oversized accoutrements when acting in *Sir Salomon* at Dover. Nell also acted Alma-hide in both parts of Dryden's work, which ran on alternate days into February 1671. After that she left the stage for good (the roles erroneously assigned to her in later years belonged to Ann Marshall Quinn).

Nell Gwyn caused a remarkable stir after she became the King's mistress. On 20 June 1670, for example, the actress Peg Hughes's brother, who was a servant to Prince Rupert, was killed in a dispute over whether Nell or Peg was the hand-somer, and in 1671 the satirical scribblers turned out a plethora of poems alluding to Nell. Many of them were published in *Poems on Affairs of State*. One, a clever piece attributed to Marvell but probably not by him, was "A Ballad called the Hay-market Hectors" (1671) which reads in part:

> Our good King Charles the Second,
> Too flippant of treasure and moisture,
>   Stoop'd from the Queen infecund
> To wench of orange and oyster.
> Consulting his cazzo, he found it ex-
>   pedient
> To engender Don Johns on Nell the co-
>   median.

The final stanza of the ballad refers to Nell's sister:

> If the sister of Rose
> Be a whore so anointed
>   That the Parliament's nose
> Must for her be disjointed,
> Should you but name the prerogative
>   whore,
> How the bullets would whistle, the can-
>   non would roar!

(The prerogative whore was the Duchess of Cleveland.)

Another satirical poem of 1671, "On the Prorogation," suggested that Parliament should meet to vote Nell's new baby a clout (diaper):

> Nell's in again, we hear, though we are
>   out.
> Methinks we might have met to give a
>   clout
> And then prorogue again: our wont hath
>   been
> Never to miss a session 'gainst lying in.

The poem went on to castigate Charles for spending money on his "dunghill wench" instead of preparing for war against the Dutch.

As a "sleeping partner in the ship of State," as Nell called herself, she was con-tent to live in the house on Pall Mall (No 79) that the King provided for her, buy pretty things, be entertaining at court, please the King on demand, and stay out of politics. A satire of 1669 titled simply "Nell Gwynne" reported that

> Hard by Pall Mall lives a wench call'd
>   Nell.
>   King Charles the Second he kept her.
> She hath got a trick to handle his p——,
>   But never lays hands on his sceptre.
> All matters of state from her soul she
>   does hate,
>   And leave[s] to the politic bitches.
> The whore's in the right, for 'tis her de-
>   light
>   To be scratching just where it itches.

But sometimes Nell could not keep her-self aloof from political matters. Bevan quotes a contemporary account of Nell and the Duke of Monmouth:

Nelly dus the Duck of Monmouth all the kindness shee can, but her interest is nothing. Nell Gwinn begg'd hard of his Maj^tie to see him, telling him he was grown pale, wan, lean and long-visag'd merely because he was in disfavour; but the King bid her be quiet for he w^d not see him.

On 1 March 1671 John Evelyn recorded in his diary that he was walking through

St James's Park to the Garden with King Charles and heard "a very familar discourse betweene — — & Mrs. Nellie as they cal'd an impudent Comedian, she looking out of her Garden on a Terrace at the top of the Wall, & — — standing on the greene Walke under it: I was heartily sorry at this scene." Bishop Gilbert Burnet found Nell "the indiscreetest and wildest creature that ever was in Court."

In his *History of My Own Time* Burnet claimed that at first Nell asked only £500 a year, though the King ultimately gave her over £60,000. She was a spendthrift, but she seems not to have been avaricious; much of the money she gained by her mistresshood she squandered or gave away. She aided the poor, helped to free prisoners, gambled wildly (she is said by Lucas in his *Authentic Memoirs* to have lost 1400 guineas to the Duchess of Mazarin in one night, playing basset), bought luxuries (she paid Peg Hughes £4250 for a pearl necklace Prince Rupert had given her), and enjoyed passing her afternoons at the theatre (we know of at least 55 visits over a two-year period). But though the King paid her bills, he "never treated her with the decencies of a mistress," Burnet wrote, "but rather with the lewdness of a prostitute, as she had been indeed to a great many; and therefore she called the King her Charles the Third, since she has been formerly kept by two of that name" — Hart and Sackville.

Nell's second son by the King, James, Lord Beauclerk, was born on 25 December 1671. He died in Paris in September 1680. Nell's first son, Charles, was created Baron Headington and Earl of Burford (both in Oxfordshire, which encouraged some biographers to support the theory that Nell had been born there). Charles became Duke of St Albans in 1684; he died at Bath in 1726.

At court Nell had to contend with three strong rivals for the King's favor: Barbara Palmer (Lady Castlemaine, then Duchess of Cleveland), Louise de Kéroualle (Baroness of Petersfield, Countess of Farnham, and Duchess of Portsmouth), and Hortense Mancini (Duchess Mazarin). For a while there were just Nell and Louise; on 11 September 1675 the Marchioness de Sévigné wrote to her daughter:

[Louise] did not forsee that she should find a young actress in her way, whom the King doats on; and she had it not in her power to withdraw from her. He divides his care, his time, and his health between these two. The actress is as haughty as Mademoiselle; she insults her, she makes grimaces at her, she attacks her, she frequently steals the King from her, and boasts whenever he gives her the preference. She is young, indiscreet, confident, wild, and of an agreeable humour; she sings, she dances, she acts her part with a good grace. She has a son by the King, and hopes to have him acknowledged.

Earlier, on 14 July 1673, Henry Ball had written to Sir Joseph Williamson of the competition at court:

A pleasant rediculous story in this weeke blazed about, that the King had given Nell Gwinn 20,000 *l.*, which angrying much my Lady Cleaveland and Mademoiselle Carwell [as the English often spelled Kéroualle], they made a supper at Berkshire House, wither shee being invited was, as they were drinking, suddainly almost choaked with a napkin, of which shee was since dead; and this idle thing runs so hott that Mr. Philips askt me the truth of it, believing it, but I assured him I saw her yester night in the Parke.

On 25 August 1673 Ball wrote Williamson:

The people say, Madam Guinn complains she has no house yett [i.e., no title], and they will needs have it she is promised to be Countess of Plymouth as soon as they can see how the people will relish itt; so accordingly it's reported shee is so made, but how farr this motion is gone I cannot learne.

It did not go anywhere, nor did the proposal that Nell should be made Countess

By permission of the Board of the British Library

Ballad concerning ELEANOR GWYN and the Duchess of Portland

of Greenwich. She was, as of 1675, one of the ladies of the Queen's Privy Chamber, but that may have been as much of a title as Nell ever achieved.

Property she gained, however. At first she was not granted her Pall Mall house, but in 1676 that freehold was given to William Chiffinch, the King's page of the backstairs, and to Martin Folkes; they, as trustees of the estate of the Earl of St Albans, in turn granted the freehold to Nell's trustees in 1677. The property was settled on Nell for life, then upon her younger son, James. In addition to her house in Pall Mall, Nell is said to have had some disputed lands in Ireland, of which Rochester was her trustee; Sandford House in Chelsea; a house in Leyton, Essex; a house in Princes Street, Leicester Square; a summer residence in Bagnigge Wells; and Burford House in Windsor. A house at Mill Hill,

near Hendon, sometimes said to have been hers, she seems not to have owned.

At which one of those lodgings might the following have taken place? Colley Cibber remembered a story about Nell, told him by the actor-singer John Boman. The incident probably occurred, if at all, in the 1670s:

Boman, then a Youth, and fam'd for his Voice, was appointed to sing some part of a Concert of Musick at the private Lodgings of Mrs *Gwin*; at which were only present the King, the Duke of *York*, and one or two more who were usually admitted upon those detach'd Parties of Pleasure. When the Performance was ended, the King express'd himself highly pleased, and gave it extraordinary Commendations: Then, Sir, said the Lady, to shew you don't speak like a Courtier, I hope you will make the Performers a handsome Present: The King said he had no Money about him, and ask'd the Duke if he had any? To which the Duke reply'd, I believe, Sir, not above a Guinea or two. Upon which the laughing Lady, turning to the People about her, and making bold with the King's common Expression, cry'd, *Od's Fish! what Company am I got into!*

In addition to the King and his immediate circle, Nell was on friendly terms with many notables of her day: Henry Killigrew, Henry Savile, Laurence Hyde, and a group Andrew Marvell dubbed "The Merry Gang": the second Duke of Buckingham, the Earl of Mulgrave, Lord Buckhurst, Sir George Etherege, the Earl of Rochester, and others. Through a secretary (who seems to have been only a little more literate than Nell herself) Nell wrote a chatty letter to one of those friends, Laurence Hyde, son of the Earl of Clarendon and one of the King's advisors, in June 1678:

pray Dear Mr Hide forgive me for not writeing to you before now for the reasone is I have been sick thre months & sinse I recoverd I have had nothing to intertaine you withall nor have nothing now worth writing but that I can holde no longer to let you know I never have ben in any companie wethout drinking your health for I love you with all my soule the pel mel is now for me a dismale plase sinse I have uterly lost Sr Car Scrope never to be recovrd agane for he tould me he could not live allways at this rate & so begune to be a littel uncivil which I could not suffer from an uglye baux garscon Mrs Knights Lady mothers dead & she has put up a scutchin no beiger then my Lady grins scunchis My lord Rochester is gon in the cuntrie Mr Savil has got a misfortune but is upon recovery & is to mary an aires who I thinke wont wont [sic] have an ill time ont if he holds up his thumb My lord of Dorscit apiers wonse in thre munths for he drinkes aile with Shadwell [the playwright] & Mr Haris [the actor] at the Dukes [play?]house all day long my lord Burford [Nell's son Charles] remimbers his sarvis to you my Lord Bauclaire [her son James] is

is [sic] goeing into France we are a goeing to supe with the king at whithale & my Lady Harvie The king remembers his sarvis to you now lets talk of state affairs for we never caried things so cunningly as now for we dont know whether we shall have peece or war but I am for war for no other reason but that you may come home [from the Hague] I have a thousand merry conseets but I cant make her [the secretary] write um & therfore you must take the will for the deed god bye your most loveing obedient faithful & humbel

sarvant

E G

Nell proudly signed her initials herself. She was not completely illiterate, it seems; in November 1679 Sir Robert Howard, another one of her friends, wrote to the Duke of Ormonde to say that Nell "presents you with her real acknowledgments for all your favours, and protests she would write in her own hand but her wild characters she says would distract you."

An exchange of letters between Henry Savile and the Earl of Rochester in June 1678 indicates how concerned about Nell her aristocratic friends sometimes became. Savile, in disgrace at the time, wrote to Rochester on 4 June that

one who is allways your friend [Nell] and sometimes (Espeacially now) mine, has a part in [an intrigue] that makes her now laughed att and may one day turne to her infinite disadvantage. The case stands thus if I am rightly informed: — My Lady Hervey who allwayes loves one civill plott more, is working body and soule to bring Mrs. Jenny Middleton into play [with the King]. How dangerous a new one is to all old ones I need not tell you, but her Ladyship, having little opportunity of seeing Charlemayne upon her owne account, wheadles poor Mrs. Nelly into supping twice or thrice a week at W. C[hiffinch']s and carryeing her with her; soe that in good earnest this poor creature is betrayed by her Ladyship to pimp against herselfe, for there her Ladyship whispers and contrives all matters to her owne ends, as the other might easily percieve if she were not too giddy to mistrust a false friend.

To which Rochester responded:

my Advice to the Lady you wot of [Nell], has ever been this, Take your measures just contrary to your Rivals, live in Peace with all the World, and easily with the King: Never be so Ill-natur'd to stir up his Anger against others, but let him forget the use of a Passion, which is never to do you good: Cherish his Love where-ever it inclines, and be assur'd you can't commit greater Folly than pretending to be jealous; but, on the contrary, with Hand, Body, Head, Heart and all the Faculties you have, contribute to his Pleasure all you can, and comply with his Desires throughout: And, for new Intrigues, so you be at one end 'tis no matter which: Make Sport when you can, at other times help it.

Nell seems to have gotten on remarkably well with everyone, perhaps because she followed Rochester's sensible advice.

On 16 October 1678 she was entertained at Cambridge "by certaine scholars," wrote Anthony à Wood, and "had verses presented to her." She visited Oxford frequently, though there is no record of the scholars there honoring her. But in Oxford in March 1681 her carriage was mistaken for that of the papist Duchess of Portsmouth; when the mob began to attack, her defense was, "Pray, good people, be civil —I am the *Protestant* whore." Indeed, Nell was a staunch support of Protestantism. She was friendly with the Duke of Monmouth, whom she dubbed prophetically "Prince Perkin" (Warbeck). John Evelyn, when he saw Nell and John Dryden attending mass (in January 1686), convinced himself that they were proselytes and "no great loss to the Church," but Nell remained a Protestant to her death.

In 1679 Aphra Behn dedicated *The Feign'd Curtizans* to Nell. The Epistle Dedicatory was typically flowery in its praises, but there was doubtless truth in Mrs Behn's description of Nell as "infinitely fair, witty, and deserving." You "never appear," said she, "but you glad the hearts of all that have the happy fortune to see you, as if you were made on purpose to put the whole world into good Humour."

Nell's mother "Helena" died, according to Musgrave, on 20 July 1679 at the age of 56. Wood reported that "Elen Gwynne commonly called Old Madam Gwynne, being drunk with brandy, fell in a ditch neare the neat houses London and was stifled." Though that sounds very like fiction, it may have been close to the truth. Certainly the satirists thought it true enough: in "The Lady of Pleasure" Mrs Gwyn "Dy'd drunk with Brandy in a Common-shore" and "A Panegyric" called her "the martyr of the ditch." In 1679 was published *A True Account Of the late most doleful, and lamentable Tragedy of Old Maddam Gwinn, Mother To Maddam Elenor Gwinn; Who Was unfortunately drowned, in a Fish-Pond, at her own Mansion-House, Near The Neat-Houses*. That work made great sport of her death, saying that Nell's mother injected brandy into some bread and made pellets of the loaf, which she then cast into her pond to catch some fish; in a drunken haze, thinking the pond was brandy, she "floundered in" and, since the fish were also drunk and couldn't aid her, she drowned. However she may have died, her daughter gave her a burial with much pomp at St Martin-in-the-Fields on 30 July 1679. Said "A Panegyric,"

> Nor was her mother's funeral less her care,
> No cost, no velvet did the daughter spare.
> Fine gilded scutcheons did the hearse enrich
> To celebrate this martyr of the ditch.

Thomas Otway became the tutor of Nell's son Charles when the boy was about ten. On 1 June 1680 Otway witnessed a

D. E. Bower Collection, Chiddingstone Castle, Kent

ELEANOR GWYN

by Lely

power of attorney which allowed Nell to receive her pension, and he may have rendered her other services. "An Essay of Scandal" is a poem among the Harleian manuscripts that touches upon Otway's work for Nell:

> *Then for that cub, her son and heir,*
> *Let him remain in Otway's care,*
> *To make him (if that's possible to be)*
> *A viler Poet, and more dull than he.*

By the 1680s, though Nell would have been in the prime of her life whichever birthdate one accepts, her heyday was close to an end. The satirists spoke less and less about her, though they did not neglect her. *A Dialogue Between The Duchess of Portsmouth, and Madam Gwin, at parting* was published in 1682. It is as scurrilous as most such poems, but it has a past-tense flavor:

> Gw.
> *You never suffered Nell to come in Play*
> *Whilst you had left but one Meridian-*
> *Ray,*
> *And yet by Turns I did my self that*
> *Right,*
> *If you enjoy'd the Day, I rul'd the Night.*
> . . . .
> Port.
> *What, tho I was his only Miss before*

*I was your Kings, you had a thousand
    more.
Who Fame Reports did Squeeze you o're
    and o're
Before you came to be a Royal-Whore.*

. . . .

                    Gw.
*My Name thou Jezebel of Pride and
    Malice,
Whose Father had a Hog-stey for his
    Pallace,
In my clear Veins best Brittish Bloud
    does flow
Whilst thou like a French Tode-stool
    first did grow,
And from a Birth as poor as thy Delight
Sprung up a Mushroom-Dutchess in a
    Night,
Nor did I ever with the Brats I bore,
The Royal Standard Stein in Monstrous
    gore,
Which makes thee fly to France, where
    thou must rot,
Or cure the Ulcers which the Bath cou'd
    not.*

Nell's finances, as will be seen, were unstable, as was her health. On 14 April
1684, when she was at Burford House in
Windsor, she sent a letter to a Madame
Jennings, very likely the mother of Frances
and Sarah Jennings (Sarah became the
Duchess of Marlborough). Nell complained of her poor financial state at that
time and also of her health: "I have continued extreme ill ever since you left me,
and I am so still. I have sent to London for
a Doctor. I believe I shall die. My service
to the Duchess of Norfolk, and tell her, I
am as sick as her grace, but do not know
what I ail, although she does, which I am
overjoyed that she does with her great
belly."

Charles II died on 6 February 1685.
John Evelyn, two days before, wrote in his
diary that the King "spake to the Duke to
be kind to the Duchess of Cleveland, and
especially Portsmouth, . and that Nelly
might not starve." Bishop Burnet's version
was only slightly different: Charles recom-

mended to the Duke of York's care "over
and over again, Lady Portsmouth and her
son, the Duke of Richmond, and desiring
him to be kind to his other children, and
not let poor Nelly starve; but he said not
one word of his Queen. . . ." What we
know of Nell's income would suggest that
she was not in financial difficulty or in any
danger of starving after Charles died.
Among the treasury papers preserved at
Harvard is an order signed by Sir Robert
Howard for a payment of £1250 to Nell
in June 1683; the payment was her quarterly annuity, the annual stipend being
£5000 (granted by the King on 11 July
1679). But Nell was such a spendthrift
that she apparently went through her stipend with ease, and she was too giddy to
manage her finances sensibly. King James
gave Nell a bounty of £1000 on 26 December 1685, and though he continued her
annual pension, it dropped, according to
Akerman, to £1500.

About April or May 1685 Nell sent
King James a letter in which she discussed
King Charles:

had hee lived hee tould me before hee dyed
that the world shuld see by what hee did for
me that hee had both love and value for me
and that hee did not doe for me, as my mad
lady woster, hee was my frind and alowed me
to tell him all my grifes and did like a frind
advise me and tould me who was my frind
and who was not

Nell went on to thank James for a recent
present which helped to "releeve me out
of the last extremety."

That Charles died of a venereal disease
seems now fairly certain, and we may guess
that Nell's illness which she mentioned to
Laurence Hyde in 1678 may have been
the beginning of her own bout with what
they called the pox. During 1687 Nell was
very ill. In March part of her body was
completely paralyzed, and in the John Ellis
correspondence is a letter saying, "Mrs
Nelly is dying of an apoplexy." On 9 July

1687 she made her will, adding codicils the following 18 October. The bulk of her estate she left to her son, the Duke of St Albans—or in trust for him with her executors, Laurence Hyde (the Earl of Rochester), Thomas Earl of Pembroke, Sir Robert Sawyer the Attorney General, and Henry Sidney. To each of her executors she bequeathed £100.

The first codicil was described as a "last request of Mrs. Ellenr. Gwynn to his Grace the Duke of St. Albans. . . ." She requested burial at St Martin-in-the-Fields and a funeral sermon by Dr Tenison (who obliged her at some risk to his reputation; the sermon has not survived). Nell also asked that a pulpit cloth and cushion be given to the church and that £100 be distributed to the poor of that parish and the parish of St James, Westminster. Dr Tenison was asked to use some of the money to take poor debtors of his parish out of prison and clothe them. Nell wished £50 to be given to any two Catholics in the parish of St James, to show "my charity to those who differ from me in religion." She left £200 to her sister Rose, then Mrs Guy Forster. To "Jo." her porter she left £10. She remembered with bequests her nurses, servants, Lady Fairborne, her chaplain John Warner, Lady Hollyman, and her kinsman Mr Cholmley (probably William Cholmondeley). Nell asked that another £50 be used to release debtors from prison every Christmas.

The second codicil added another £200 for Rose Forster and £40 for Rose's husband. Nell made bequests to her doctors (Christian Harrell and "le Febure" [Lefevre]), to Dr Harrell's nephew Dr Derrick, to Mrs Edling, and to Nell's servant Bridget Long. The legend that Nell asked for the ringing of church bells every Monday has no substantiation in her will.

Henry Muddiman's newsletter, dated 15 November, stated that "On the 14th, about ten of the clock, Madam Ellen Gwyn, after a long and wasting sicknesse died at her house in Pall Mall, whither her son the Duke of St. Albans is now removing from his lodgings in Whitehall." Narcissus Luttrell jotted down the information that "Mrs. Ellen Gwyn was buried the 17th November at St. Martins; she hath left a considerable estate to her son, the Duke of St. Albans." At St Martin's the clerk recorded the burial of "Elinor Gwin, W." Wigmore wrote to Etherege the following day (he called her "Mad. Ellen Gwyn") saying,

She has made a very formal will, and died richer than she seemed to be whilst she lived. She is said to have died piously and penitently; and as she dispensed several charities in her lifetime, so she left several legacies at her death; but what is much admired is she died worth and left the D. of St. Albans vivis et modis, about 1,000,000 *l.* stirling, a great many say more, few less.

Nell's will was proved on 7 December 1687. Her balance at Child's Bank was reported to be well over four figures, and she possessed almost 15,000 ounces of plate. Perhaps most of her wealth was in trust or not in liquid assets; that might explain why the rich girl was so poor.

Shortly after Nell's death a broadside elegy appeared entitled *Madam Ellenor Gwinn, Who Departed this Life on the 14th of November, Anno. Dom. 1687.* It spoke of Nell as one who had been "Curteous even to the Poor," a "Glorious Beauty," and "Witty and gay." She "did much Abound / In Charity" and "refus'd and hated Flattery."

Nell Gwyn has probably received more attention from biographers than any other performer in history (Garrick excepted), and some of her admirers have not helped matters by mixing fact and legend. She received brief notices within such larger works as Tom Brown's *Amusements Serious and Comical* (1700) and *Letters from the Dead to the Living* (1703), Buckingham's *Works* (1715), *The History of the English Stage* (1741, probably by Curll), and then full treatment in an anonymous *Memoirs of the Life of Eleanor Gwinn* (1752), Cunningham's *The Story of Nell Gwyn* (1852), Cecil Chesterton's *Nell Gwyn* (1912), Noel Williams's *Rival Sultanas* (1915), Melville's *Nell Gwyn* (1923), Dasent's *Nell Gwynne* (1924), Bax's *Pretty Witty Nell* (1932), John Harold Wilson's *Nell Gwyn* (1952), and Bryan Bevan's *Nell Gwyn* (1969). "The Story of Nell Gwynne," a four volume collection begun in 1884 and finished in 1891 by Zaehnsdorf is at the Army and Navy Club, where many of Nell's household bills have been preserved. Nell also inspired such fictional works as Edward Jerningham's comedy *The Peckham Frolic, Or Nell Gwyn* (1799; never acted), Thomas Horton's historical play *Nell Gwynne*, and Kathleen Winsor's *Forever Amber*. It surely would have pleased Nell, who came from common stock, to know that common folk today who might look blank at the names of Burbage, Betterton, Garrick, Kemble, or Siddons might well recognize the name of Nell Gwyn—and recognize her not just as a famous whore, but a famous actress.

The task of separating the authentic portraits of Nell from those that picture someone else seems to be impossible. Piper's catalogue of seventeenth-century paintings at the National Portrait Gallery notes that the portrait of Nell with a lamb, and variants of it, and the Lely portrait of Nell nude with her son Charles (as Venus and Cupid) are the only ones with much authority, though that claim is made by others who have portraits said to be of Nell. The list below, then, which undoubtedly includes some duplications, should be treated with caution. Attributions to Lely should be understood as not necessarily by Sir Peter himself but by his studio.

1. By Mary Beale. In the collection of the Earl of Bradford.

2. Miniature by S. Cooper, dated about 1670, now lost. Engraved by F. W. Pail-thorpe, G. Valck, R. Earlom, and several anonymous engravers.

3. By Henri Gascar, showing Nell with her two sons, pictured as cupids supporting draperies, and Charles II in the background. Engraved by Masson, Annan and Swan, E. Stodart, and an anonymous engraver.

4. Pencil drawing by S. Harding. At the Huntington Library.

5. By Lely. At Hatfield House.

6. A copy, probably of the above Lely. At Hatfield House.

7. By Lely, showing Nell three-quarter length, seated; dated about 1675. At the National Portrait Gallery.

8. By Lely, showing Nell nude, as Venus, with her son Charles as Cupid; dated about 1671. In the collection of Denys E. Bower. In 1721 George Vertue gave an account of the Lely portrait:

Nell Guin naked leaning on a bed. with her child. by Sr Peter Lilly. this picture was painted at the express command of King Charles 2^d. Nay he came to Sr Peter Lillys house to see it painted. when she was naked on purpose. Afterwards this picture was at Court. Where the Duke of Buckingham took it from, (when K. James went away,) as many others did the like.

This portrait, or a variant of it, was probably the work written about in *Notes and Queries* in 1858. In February Edward Rimbault wrote of a letter by William Huddesford which referred to a portrait of Nell at the lodgings of Dr Leyborn; "probably now it is at Westwell, near Burford, in the possession of Mr. Taylor, his nephew. It was, I am told, drawn by a famous flower-painter (my intelligencer forgot the name) [query: Lely? a pun?], whom King Charles *forced* to draw it. It had a most amazing softness." In March another correspondent suggested that the portrait in question may have been the one in the gallery at Littlecot, near Hungerford.

9. Variant of the above Lely, probably by one of his assistants. Once in the collec-

tion of James II, now at the Army and Navy Club. The variant had a sliding piece covering it, on which was a copy by Danckers of Van Dyke's portrait of the Countess of Dorset—though another history has it that the Danckers cover may have been of the Duchess of Cleveland.

10. By Lely or from his studio, showing Nell with a lamb. At the National Portrait Gallery. Engraved by G. Valck, J. Ogborne, T. Wright, Green, J. McArdell, and an anonymous engraver.

11. Variant of the above Lely, probably from the studio of Lely. In the de Saumarez collection at Shrublands; dated about 1675. Probably once in the collection of Baptist May. Engraved by G. Valck and by Ogborne.

12. From the Lely school, showing Nell half-length in a blue and red dress. In the collection of Richard Cavendish.

13. Attributed to Lely, showing Nell dressed in white with a blue overdress and blue scarf, seated in a rocky niche; pearls in her hair and a large pearl earring. Listed in the Augustin Daly sale catalogue and used as a frontispiece to it. This and the Verelst portrait may be identical.

14. (By Lely?), showing Nell with left hand to shoulder, curls over right shoulder. In the collection of Charles Richard Cammell. Engraved by A. DeBlois?

15. By Lely, showing Nell waist length, seated, legs crossed and hand in lap. Engraved by P. Van Bleeck and by H. R. Cook.

16. By Lely, showing Nell seated, with her two sons standing beside her, one holding a dove. Engraved by R. Thompson and, reversed, by C. Allard. This is much like the Gascar engraving.

17. By Lely, showing Nell seated, the upper part of her body nude. Engraved by V. Green.

18. By Lely, showing Nell full face, holding a drapery to her breast with her left hand; wearing a pearl necklace and an earring on her right ear. Engraved by

Scheneker, J. Thomson, and F. W. Fairholt.

19. By Lely, showing Nell standing, holding a drapery with her right hand, with her left arm at her side; hair in curls over her ears. Engraved by E. Scriven.

20. Portrait by Lely, three-quarter length, showing Nell standing, with her hands on a table at left, with flowers. In the collection of the Marquis of Hastings. Engraved anonymously.

Portraits of Nell by Lely or from the Lely studio are at the Metropolitan Museum of Art, Abercairny House, Easton Neston, Mentmore, in the Spencer collection at Althorp, in the Mansell collection, at the Garrick Club, and in the Lely room at Hampton Court. A portrait by Lely long thought to show Nell has now been tentatively identified as a portrait of Katherine Sedley, Countess of Dorchester; it is at the National Portrait Gallery. A painting at Knole by Lely, showing Charles II, the Duchess of Cleveland, and Nell (supposedly), as Cymon, Iphigenia, and her attendant, seems not to be a likeness of Nell, and Ronald Beckett in his *Lely* (1951) does not cite it as showing her.

21. By Tempest. Engraved by R. B. Parkes.

22. By Simon Verelst; dated about 1670. In the collection of Arnold Wiggins.

23. Called Nell Gwyn, by Verelst, showing a woman looking at the spectator, with pearls in her hair and a pearl necklace, wearing a frilled, white, low-cut gown; dated about 1690. On loan to H. M. Ministry of Works from the National Portrait Gallery. The identification has been seriously questioned, and the picture may be identical with No 13 by Lely, above.

24. By Verelst, called Nell Gwyn, showing a woman head and shoulders, her head to the left, with dark brown hair, a maroon dress and low chemise. At the Garrick Club. This may be a variant of the above.

25. Perhaps by Verelst, bust, face to right. Engraved anonymously.

26. Portrait from the Dutch school,

showing Nell three-quarter length behind a table, a black servant behind her. In the collection of Richard Cavendish.

27. Small portrait by an unknown artist. Originally in the Mathews Collection and listed in the Garrick Club Catalogue. Present location unknown.

28. By an unknown artist, supposedly of Nell. Once in the collection of the Duke of Portland at Welbeck Abbey. Destroyed by the fifth Duke's direction as one of 82 "much decayed canvases."

29. Miniature on copper by an unknown artist, called Nell Gwyn. In a case with 30 cover dresses in talc showing Nell in different characters. Advertised for sale in the 23 March 1901 issue of *The Lady's Pictorial*. Summers in his edition of Otway's *Works* said the picture was not of Nell.

30. Bust by an unknown artist. In the collection of Sir Charles Dick.

31. As Sir Patient Fancy, delivering an epilogue, hat in hand. By D. Dodd; engraved by T. Cook and an anonymous engraver. Reproduced in Woodcock's *Incomparable Aphra* and in Summers's *The Playhouse of Pepys*.

32. As Cupid. Drawing by P. Cross. Published by R. Thompson.

33. Engraving by P. Tempest.

34. Engraving by B. Spenser.

35. Satirical print dated 16 October 1756: "Nell Gw(eye)nn 2 the Hungary (Hare)lot 1756." At the British Museum. Portrait supposed to show Nell; an engraved letter below the picture.

The Dictionary of National Biography reported portraits of Nell by different hands at Goodwood, Elvaston, Welbeck, Sudbury, "&c."

Gwynn. *See also* **GWINN.**

Gwynn, Mr ₁*fl. 1751–1753*₁, *harper, singer.*

The blind Welsh harper Parry shared a benefit with his fellow Welsh harper Gwynn at the Haymarket Theatre on 14 March 1751, an event not listed in *The London Stage* but preserved among Latreille's transcriptions of bills. The following 4 May at Drury Lane "Gwinn" performed, and he is surely the singer Gwinn listed by *The London Stage* as in the Drury Lane company in 1750–51. Gwynn sang and played his harp at Covent Garden in 1752–53, though the first mention of him in the bills there was late in the season, on 28 April 1753.

Gyles, Mr ₁*fl. 1769*₁, *singer.*

In September 1769 the singer Gyles performed in *The Harlot's Progress* at Sadler's Wells. During that summer season Gyles, without the concurrence of the proprietors, printed bills and tickets for his benefit, and the management of the Wells announced that his tickets would not be accepted that season.

Gyngell, ₁**Daniel?**₁ ₁*fl. 1794–1821*₁, *conjuror, singer, performer on musical glasses, manager.*

Gyngell the showman seems to have been one of those entertainers of the populace whose perambulations and personalities were well known to all in their day but who operated so much on the fringes of the larger theatrical enterprise that most of their activities went unrecorded.

He was first noticed at Bartholomew Fair in 1794, "at Flockton's original Theatre up the Greyhound Yard, Smithfield," in partnership with Mrs Sarah Flint, long-time assistant of the recently deceased John Flockton, who had inherited Flockton's fantoccini and other theatrical properties. Gyngell and Mrs Flint performed jointly at fair time (August and September) for several years. In other seasons they operated in taverns and inns, one known occasion and place being 21 July 1800 at the George Inn, Chiswick. There in the Great Room they gave their varied entertainments under the heading "Machinic Theatre." Their bill presented Gyngell's playing on the musical

The Widow FLINT & GYNGELL Beg leave to return their Sincere thanks to the Ladies and Gentlemen of Chiswick and its Vicinity for the many liberal favors they Experienced Laſt Seaſon and hope by unſeaſed Exertion to merit a Continuance of their favors which will be ever thought the higheſt honour to deſerve

By Deſire of Several Ladies and Gentlemen of CHISWICK,

MACHINIC THEATRE,
GREAT ROOM.

At the GEORGE INN, CHISWICK;

This preſent Evening, MONDAY, JULY the 21st. 1800,

The Widow Flint and Gyngell,

Will EXHIBIT their much Admired

ENTERTAINMENTS,

Which have been Honored with the Preſence of the Royal Family and moſt of the Nobility of this Kingdom.

Firſt Mr. GYNGELL,

Will Display his Astonishing Performances,

He will Exhibit with

Japan'd Caſkets	Watches	Swords	Letters
Rings	Pocket Pieces	Numbers	Silver Cups
Ear-Rings	Thandis	Medals	&c. &c.

Alſo, a Variety of uncommon Experiments with CARDS, never Exhibited by any one but Himſelf.

SINGING by Mrs. GYNGELL.

A Loyal Piece, called

BIRTH DAY; or, the BRITISH VOLUNTEERS,

REPRESENTING Hyde Park as it appeared on the Fourth of June laſt, in which is Repreſented the general Aſſemblage of the different Corps formed in Battallion, with the King and his Attendants, Complimenting each Battallion as they paſs.

☞ This Piece is Performed with near ONE THOUSAND FIGURES.

FANTOCCINI, from Sadler's Wells;

Consisting of Tumbling and Stage Dancing, Military Exercise, Comic Performances, &c.

By Deſire of a Gentleman, Mr GINGELL will ſing the Comit Song of ABRAHAM NEWLAND.

The Whole to Conclude with

A New and Grand NAVAL Spectacle, repreſenting the Action between the ENGLISH and FRENCH FLEETS, at the

BATTLE OF THE NILE.

The Scenery, Machinery and Decorations Entirely New; and Good MUSIC to accompany the Performance.

PIT 1s. GALLERY 6d. The Doors to be Opened at SEVEN and Begin at Half-paſt SEVEN.

Meſſrs. FLINT & GYNGELL take the old Engliſh maxim of depending on their Sea & Land Forces for Protection and Support, as from the vaſt Quantity of Recruits they have had this Seaſon they are ſtronger in Finance than ever; and, tho' ſurrounded by Enemies of ſuperior Number, like Little England, they bid Defiance to all.

⁎ Muſical Inſtruments Bought, Sold and Repaired. Harpſichords and Piano Fortes Tuned on the ſhorteſt Notice.

HAMMOND, PRINTER, No. 12, ST. MARTIN's LANE, LONDON.

Harvard Theatre Collection

Playbill: Entertainments at George Inn, Chiswick, 21 July 1800, by WIDOW FLINT and MR GYNGELL

glasses, singing, and sleight-of-hand, Mrs Gyngell's singing, and Mrs Flint's fantoccini. Later bills also included Flockton's Grand Musical Clock, which motivated "upwards of Nine Hundred Figures, at Work in their respective Trades and Callings." Perhaps that was what was meant by "Machinic."

In 1810, according to the Lord Chamberlain's records, one Daniel Gyngell, presum-

Harvard Theatre Collection

MR GYNGELL, at Bartholomew Fair

artist unknown

ably the subject of this entry, was granted a license for music and dancing at the rooms at No 5, Princess Street, Leicester Fields, during the period 2 March to 31 May.

In a review in the *Examiner* for 6 August 1815 William Hazlitt spoke of "our old friend Mr. Gyngell, the celebrated itinerant manager, and the only showman in England, who, after the festivity of the week, makes a point of staying the Sunday over, and goes with all his family to church." Hazlitt had lately (according to a playbill of 16 February 1815) had an opportunity of viewing the family Gyngell at the little theatre in Catherine Street, the Strand, where they returned on 10 March 1816.

A newspaper notice of the New Jubilee Pavillion, dated 1 September 1816, in the Harvard Theatre Collection is given in full to show what Gyngell's typical offerings were like in his later years:

Mr. GYNGELL, sen, having returned from a Country tour through the principal Cities and Towns in England, where his MECHANICAL and SCIENTIFIC Entertainments so peculiar to himself were received with unbounded applause, intends introducing them at BARTHOLOMEW FAIR, West Smithfield, on TUESDAY Next, and three following Days, consisting of his inimitable Card and other Deceptions, astonishing pieces of Mechanism, wonderful live Birds, Harmonized Musical Glasses; also the matchless feats of YOUNG GYNGELL on the Swinging Wire, Balancing, &c. To conclude with the Original FANTOCCINI, or Automaton performers, whose feats resemble life itself—Adjoining to the Jubilee Pavillion will be exhibited Mr. PAAP, the celebrated Dutch Dwarf—the Smallest Man in the World, who has received the unqualified approbation of all the Sovereigns in Europe.

When he toured through Canterbury, Ramsgate, Margate, and the Isle of Thanet in December 1821 Gyngell declared in his bills that it had been four years since he had exhibited "in this County." That is the latest date we find him performing. Another clipping at Harvard identifies his family (none of whom, presumably, performed in London during the eighteenth century) as Joseph, a juggler and equilibrist, Horatio, a dancer and painter, George, a pyrotechnist, and Louisa, a beautiful tightrope dancer. That source also names Nelson Lee, a juggler, as a nineteenth-century member of the Gyngell company.

Gyngell was pictured in an anonymous engraving which showed him performing at Bartholomew Fair in 1815. His Bartholomew Fair booth was shown in an engraving by J. Nixon, after Rowlandson.

Gyngell, Mrs ₁Daniel?₁ ₁*fl. 1794–1821?*₁, *singer. See* **GYNGELL, ₁DANIEL?₁.**

Illustrations

PLAYBILLS, TICKETS, ACCOUNTS, AND CASTS

Theatre checks and tickets, 1671–1817
from Wilkinson's *Londina Illustrata*, 1819–25

Ticket for Handel's *Samson* at Covent Garden Theatre,
11 March 1752
probably designed by John Devoto

AT the *Queens-Arms-*Tavern, in *Southwark*, during a Fortnight, (the usual time of the Fair) will be presented an excellent Droll, call'd,

The Exile of the Earl of Huntington,

Commonly known by the Name of

ROBIN HOOD.

With the Merry Conceits of Little *John*,

And the Humours of the Jolly PINDAR of WAKEFIELD.

With Variety of Singing and Dancing, New Scenes and Machine, he like was never seen in the Fair before.

VIVANT REX & REGINA.

✿✿✿✿✿✿✿✿✿✿✿✿✿✿✿✿✿✿✿✿✿✿✿✿✿✿✿✿✿

Never Acted but once.

AT the THEATRE ROYALL, in *Drury-Lane*, this prefent *Wenfday* being the Nineth day of *November*, will be prefented,

A New Play called,

HENRY the Second King of England.

No money to be return'd after the curtain is drawn.

By their Majefties Servants. *Vivant Rex & Regina.*

Courtesy of Sir Ralph Verney
Drury Lane Theatre playbill, 9 November 1692
from the Verney manuscripts

Folger Shakespeare Library
Lincoln's Inn Fields Theatre playbill, 28 October 1697

Never Acted but twice.

AT the THEATRE ROYAL in *Drury-Lane*, this present *Tuesday* being the 13th day of *April*, will be presented,

A New Comedy call'd,

The Fair Example, Or, The Modish Citizens.

To begin exactly at half an hour after Five.
No Money to be Return'd after the Curtain is drawn up.
By Her Majesty's Servants.   *Vivat Regina.*

Folger Shakespeare Library
Drury Lane Theatre playbill, 13 April 1703

At the *Theatre* in *Lincolns-Inn-Fields*.
TUESDAY, *June* the Fifth, 1716.
A COMEDY call'd,
Old Batchelor.
For the Benefit of LOVELACE and WHITE, Box-Keepers.

BOX.

Harvard Theatre Collection
Lincoln's Inn Fields Theatre ticket, 5 June 1716

By *Subscription.*

AT THE

QUEEN's THEATRE

In the *Hay-Market* :
On *Wenſday* next, being the
Second Day of *March*, will be
preſented,

A New OPERA, call'd,

CLOTILDA.

The Boxes to be open'd to the Pit. And no Perſon to
be Admitted, but by the Subſcribers Tickets ; which
will be delivered on Tueſday and Wenſday Morning
next, at Mr. *Whites's Chocolate-Houſe* in St. *James's-ſtreet.*

Boxes upon the Stage 15 s. Firſt Gallery 5 s. Upper
Gallery 2 s.

To begin exactly at Six a Clock.

And by Command. No Perſon to ſtand upon the Stage,

Vivat Regina.

Theatre Collection, The New York Public Library at Lincoln Center
Queen's Theatre playbill, 2 March 1709

(1725)

For the Benefit of Mrs SAUNDERS.

By His Majesty's Company of Comedians. *1725.*

AT THE

THEATRE ROYAL

In *Drury-Lane* :

On MONDAY the 14th Day of *April*,
will be presented, *(In the Time of Mills; and his outfield)*

A COMEDY call'd,

Rule a Wife, *and Have a* Wife.

With Entertainments of Singing and Dancing,
as will be Express'd in the Great Bill.

To begin exactly at Six a Clock.

~~~ties Command, No Persons are to be admitted behind the~~~
~~~~~~~y to be Return'd afte~~~

Enthoven Collection, Theatre Museum
Drury Lane Theatre playbill, 14 April 1718

BY PARTICULAR DESIRE.

For the Benefit of Mr. LALAUZE,

AT THE

THEATRE ROYAL in *Covent-Garden*,

On WEDNESDAY next, the 1st of *MAY*, 1745

Will be presented a TRAGEDY, call'd

THE ORPHAN.

The Part of *CASTALIO* to be perform'd

By Mr. BARRY,

Acasto by Mr. SPARKS,

Polydore by Mr. SMITH,

Chamont by Mr. DYER,

And the Part of *MONIMIA* to be perform'd

By Miſs BELLAMY.

To which will be added a *Grotesque* PANTOMIME (*Not perform'd there*
theſe Six Years) call'd

COLOMBINE COURTEZAN:

Or, *HARLEQUIN* RESTOR'D.

Magician by Mr. HOWARD,

Harlequin by Mr. PHILLIPS,

Spaniard by Mr. BENCRAFT,   *Colombine* by Mrs. BAKER,

The Character of PIERROT by Mr. LALAUZE,

And the Other PARTS to the Beſt Advantage.

With ſeveral Entertainments of DANCING

Particularly, *By Deſire*, A BALL MINUET

By Mr. LALAUZE and a SCHOLAR of His,

of Nine Years of Age, who never appear'd before.

Boxes 5 *s.*   Pit 3 *s.*   Firſt Gallery 2 *s.*   Upper Gallery 1 *s.*

TICKETS *to be had of Mr.* LALAUZE, *at his Houſe in Great* Suffolk-Street, *near the Hay-*
Market; *and of Mr.* CRUDGE, *at the Stage-Door, where* PLACES *may be taken.*

Folger Shakespeare Library
Covent Garden Theatre playbill, 1 May 1745

For the Benefit of Mr. BRANSON, Mrs. LAMPE,
Mrs. JONES, and Miſs BESFORD.

At the Theatre-Royal Covent-Garden,
This preſent WEDNESDAY, MAY 19, 1773,

H A M L E T.

Hamlet by Mr. S M I T H,
King by Mr. G A R D N E R,
Ghoſt by Mr. B E N S L E Y,
Horatio by Mr. H U L L,
Oſtrick by Mr. D Y E R,
Laertes by Mr. D A V I S,
Polonius by Mr. S H U T E R,
G R A V E D I G G E R S,
MrDUNSTALL, M. STOPPELAER,
Ophelia by Mrs. M A T T O C K S.
Queen by Miſs M I L L E R.

of Aɕt End I. a new Dance, by Maſt. LANGRISH, and Miſs BESFORD.
End of Aɕt III. the Highland Reel, Mr. ALDRIDGE, Sig. MANESIERE and Miſs BESFORD.
To which will be added an Entertainment (not aɕted theſe Five Years) called

POLLY HONEYCOMBE.

Scribble by Mr. L E W E S,
Being his FIRST APPEARANCE in that Charaɕter.
Mr. Honeycombe by Mr. Q U I C K,
Ledger by Mr. D U N S T A L L,
Mrs. Honeycombe, Mrs. PITT, Nurſe, Mrs. COPIN,
P O L L Y H O N E Y C O M B E (with the Original Eqilogue)
By Miſs B E S F O R D,
Being her FIRST APPEARANCE as an ACTRESS.
Tickets delivered by Mr. ROFFE will be taken.

To-morrow, KING RICHARD the THIRD, With the CITIZEN.
For the Benefit of Mr. WIGNELL, and Mr. DAVIS.

Folger Shakespeare Library
Covent Garden Theatre playbill, 19 May 1773

NEVER PERFORM'D.

At the Theatre-Royal, Covent-Garden

This prefent TUESDAY, JANUARY 17, 1775,
Will be prefented a NEW COMEDY, call'd

The RIVALS

The CHARACTERS, by

Mr. WOODWARD,

Mr. SHUTER,

Mr. LEE,

Mr. LEWIS,

Mr. QUICK,

Mr. LEE LEWES,

Mr. DUNSTALL,

Mr. FEARON,

Mrs. GREEN,

Mifs BARSANTI,

Mrs. LESSINGHAM,

And Mrs. BULKLEY.

With a PROLOGUE and EPILOGUE.
And NEW SCENES and DRESSES.
To which will be added the MUSICAL ENTERTAINMENT of

The CHAPLET.

Damon by Mr. MATTOCKS,

Palemon by Mr. DU-BELLAMY,

Paftora by Mrs. BAKER,

Laura by Mrs. MATTOCKS.

Ladies and Gentlemen are defired to fend their Servants by Four
o'Clock, to the Stage-Door, to keep Places.

Huntington Library
Covent Garden Theatre playbill, 17 January 1775

At the Theatre-Royal, Covent-Garden,

This prefent FRIDAY, FEBRUARY 24, 1775,
Will be prefented a COMIC OPERA, call'd

LOVE in a VILLAGE.

Juftice Woodcock by Mr. SHUTER,
Hawthorn by Mr. REINHOLD,
Young Meadows, Mr. MATTOCKS,
Sir W. Meadows, Mr. THOMPSON,
Euftace by Mr. YOUNG,
Hodge by Mr. DUNSTALL,
Deborah by Mrs. PITT,
Margery by Mrs. BAKER,
Lucinda by Mrs. MATTOCKS,
Rofetta by Mifs CATLEY.

To which will be added (the FORTY SIXTH TIME)

The DRUIDS.

With the ALTERATIONS, the LAST NEW SCENE, and
ADDITIONAL PERFORMANCES,
By Signor ROSSIGNOL,
The CHARACTERS of the
PANTOMIME and DANCES as USUAL.
With NEW MUSIC, SCENES, MACHINES, HABITS and DECORATIONS.
The MUSIC compofed by Mr. FISHER.
The Scenes painted by Meffrs. DALL, RICHARDS, and CARVER.
NOTHING under FULL PRICE will be taken.
NEW BOOKS of the Songs, Choruffes, &c. will be fold in the THEATRE.
The Doors to be opened at FIVE o'Clock.
To begin exactly at SIX   Vivant Rex & Regina.

To-morrow, SHE STOOPS to CONQUER,
With the Mafque of COMUS.

Folger Shakespeare Library
Covent Garden Theatre playbill, 24 February 1775

By His MAJESTY's COMPANY,
At the Theatre Royal in Drury-Lane,
This present MONDAY, May 27, 1776,
Will be presented a TRAGEDY, call'd
KING RICHARD the THIRD.
King Richard by Mr. GARRICK,
(Being his First Appearance in that Character these 4 Years)
Richmond by Mr. PALMER,
Buckingham by Mr. JEFFERSON,
Tressel. by Mr. DAVIES,
Lord Stanley by Mr. BRANSBY,
Norfolk by Mr. HURST,
Catesby by Mr. PACKER,
Prince Edward by Miss P. HOPKINS,
Duke of York Master PULLEY, Lord Mayor Mr GRIFFITHS,
Ratcliffe by Mr. WRIGHT, Lieutenant by Mr. FAWCETT,
King Henry by Mr. REDDISH,
Lady Anne (First Time) Mrs. SIDDONS,
Dutchess of York by Mrs. JOHNSTON,
Queen by Mrs. HOPKINS.
To which will be added
The DEVIL to PAY.
By Charles Coffey
Sir John Loverule by Mr. VERNON,
Jobson by Mr. MOODY,
Lady Loverule by Mrs. JOHNSTON,
Nell by Mrs. WRIGHTEN.
Ladies are desired to send their Servants a little after 5 to keep Places, to prevent Confusion.
The Doors will be opened at Half after FIVE o'Clock.
To begin exactly at Half after SIX o'Clock.   Vivant Rex & Regina.
To-morrow, (by particular Desire) BRAGANZA, with Bon Ton, or High Life above Stair.
(Being the last Time of performing them this Season.)
And Dancing by Mr. SLINGSBY and Signora PACINI,

Theatre Collection, The New York Public Library at Lincoln Center
Drury Lane Theatre playbill, 27 May 1776

Dramatis Personæ.

Mr. *Dorimant*,		m*r* *Betterton*
Mr. *Medley*,		m*r* *Hodgson*
Old *Bellair*,	Gentlemen.	m*r* *Ant*: *Leigh*
Young *Bellair*,		m*r* *Mich*: *Lee*
Sir *Fopling Flutter*,		m*r* *Bowman*
Lady *Townley*,		m*rs*
Emilia,		m*rs* *Lassells*
Mrs. *Loveit*,		m*rs* *Barry*
Bellinda,	Gentlewomen.	m*rs* *Butler*
Lady *Woodvil*, and		m*rs* *Lee*
Harriet her Daugh-		m*rs* *Mountfort*
ter,		
Pert,		m*rs* *Richardson*
and	Waiting Women.	m*rs* *Perring*
Busy,		
A *Shoomaker*.		m*r* *Bowson*
An *Orange-woman*.		m*r* *Bright*

Three *Slovenly Bullies*.
Two *Chair-men*.
Mr. *Smirk*, a *Parson*. ——— m*r* *Powell*
Handy, a *Valet de Chambre*.
Pages, Footmen, &c.

THE

Harvard Theatre Collection
Manuscript cast for Etherege's *The Man of Mode*, 1684

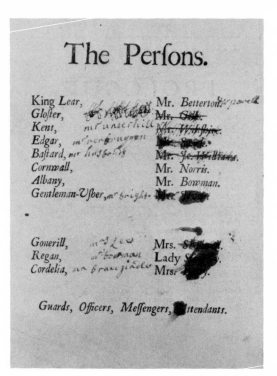

The Perfons.

King Lear,	Mr. Betterton.
Glofter,	Mr. Gill.
Kent,	Mr. Wilfhire.
Edgar,	
Baftard,	Mr. Jo. Williams.
Cornwall,	Mr. Norris.
Albany,	Mr. Bowman.
Gentleman-Ufher,	

Gonerill,	Mrs. S.
Regan,	Lady S.
Cordelia,	Mrs.

Guards, Officers, Meffengers, Attendants.

[7]

The PERSONS.

Myrtillo,	Mrs. *Marg. de L'Epine*
Laura,	Mrs. *Barbier.*
Lycon,	Mr. *Burkhead.*
Mopfa,	Mrs. *Willis.*

CHORUS of Shepherds.

MYRTILLO.

LAURA *alone.*

LAURA.

LOVE! with what fantaftick Sway
Thou mak'ft poor Mortal Hearts Obey !
I Love, and am Belov'd again,
Yet treat my Lover with Difdain.
Whene'er he's nigh me,
I undoe him ;
Yet, fhou'd he flie me,

An Accompt of moneys paid to Mr Thomas Betterton &
Mr Wm Smith for manageme[nt] of the Affaires of ye
Theater over & besides wt was pd to them & comprehended
in the day Bookes of Accompt of the Theatres And also an
Accompt of ye moneys since they left the s[ai]d Manageme[nt]
hath bin pd to Mr Thomas Davenant for ye same
over & besides wt was pd to him & comprehended in
the day Bookes of the said Theater &c 4th of
Augt 1692

1682:		£	s	d
May 13	paid to Mr E. Betterton & Mr Smith towards the said manageme[nt] for 6: dayes	1:	0:	0
20	paid more for 6: dayes	1:	0:	0
27	paid more	1:	0:	0
June 3	paid more	1:	0:	0
10	paid more	1:	0:	0
17	paid more	1:	0:	0
24	paid more	1:	0:	0
July 1	paid more	1:	0:	0
8	paid more	1:	0:	0
Augt 7	paid more for 4: weekes & 1: day	4:	3:	4
Oct 7	paid more for 11: dayes	1:	16:	0
14	paid more for 6: dayes	1:	0:	0
21	paid more	1:	0:	0
28	paid more	1:	0:	0
Novr 4	paid more	1:	0:	0
11	paid more	1:	0:	0
18	paid more	1:	0:	0
25	paid more	1:	0:	0
Der 2	paid more	1:	0:	0
9	paid more	1:	0:	0
16	paid more	1:	0:	0
23	paid more	1:	0:	0
30	paid more for 5: dayes	0:	16:	8

Courtesy of the Public Record Office
United Company accounts, 1682

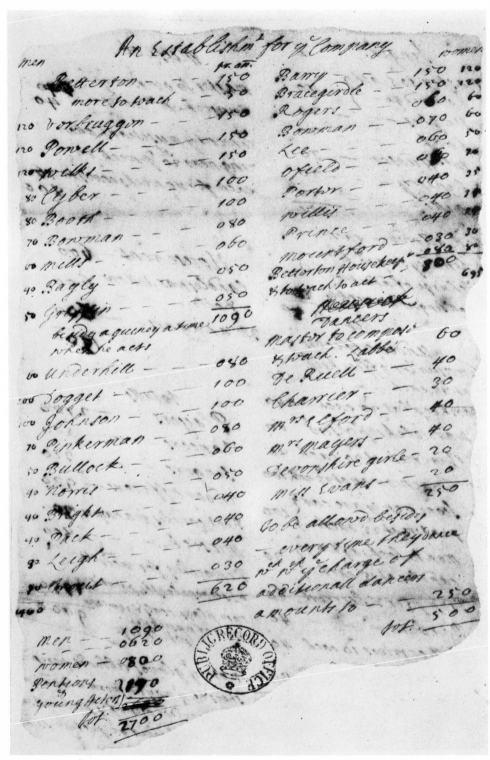

Courtesy of the Public Record Office
Proposed salary schedule for a new acting company, c. 1703

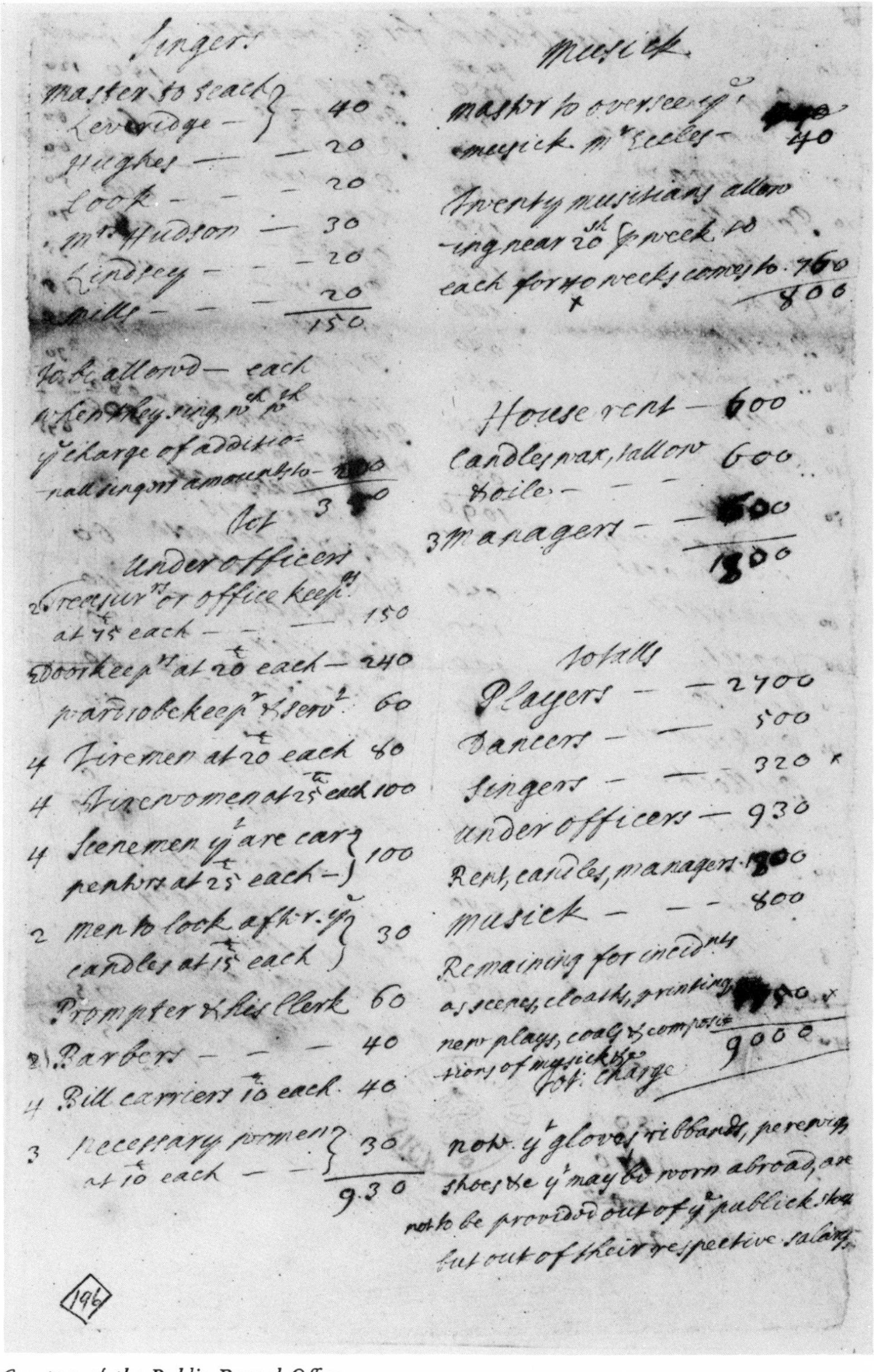

Singers

master to teach
Leveridge — 40
Hughes — 20
Cook — 20
mr Hudson — 30
Lindsey — 20
Mills — 20
150

To be allowed — each
when they sing wth ye
ye charge of additio-
nall singers amounts to —
lot 3

Under officers
2 Treasurer or office keep'rs
at 75 each — 150
Doorkeep'rs at 20 each — 240
p'r wardrobekeep'r & serv't 60
4 Firemen at 20 each 80
4 firewomen at 25 each 100
4 Scenemen yt are carr
penters at 25 each 100
2 men to look after ye
candles at 15 each 30
Prompter & his Clerk 60
2 Barbers — 40
4 Bill carriers 10 each 40
3 necessary women
at 10 each — 30
930

Musick

master to oversee ye
musick mr Eccles — 40

Twenty musicians allow-
ing near 20sh p'r week to
each for 40 weeks comes to 760
800

House rent — 600
Candles, wax, tallow 600
& oile — 600
3 managers — 600
1800

Totalls
Players — 2700
Dancers — 500
Singers — 320
under officers — 930
Rent, candles, managers 1800
musick — 800
Remaining for incidents
as scenes, cloaths, printing
new plays, coals & compositions of musick &c 9000
tot. charge 9000

note yt gloves, ribbands, perewigs
shoes &c yt may be worn abroad, are
not to be provided out of ye publick sto.
but out of their respective salary

Courtesy of the Public Record Office
Proposed personnel for a new acting company, c. 1703

The House Taylor his Bill
February ye 6 = 171¾

omitted 2 Shillings given to
The Taylors by Mr Wilks order } 0 : 2 : 0

ffor 8 mene Monday, and
Monday Night and Teuesday } :02 : 00 : 00
3 dayes Each

ffor 2 men 3 Dayes Each
to Loyne Mr Booth Coat and } 00 : 10 : 00
Mr Rayes Waskutt and other woark

ffor 2 Dayes for my Selfe — 00 : 05 : 00

ffor 4 Eles of Canvis for
Mr Bowmans waskutt and Breches } 00 : 04 : 00

ffor 3 yds of Buckeram — 00 : 03 : 00

ffor 5 yds and e'halfe of Dimety
to Loyne Mr Bowmans waskutt } 00 : 05 : 00
and Breches

ffor Thread and Silke — 00 : 04 : 00

given to the men to Drink the
Night thay felt up by Mr Wilks order } 00 : 02 : 06

For Breakfast for Taylors — 00 : 05 : 04

Tho Lewis
04 = 00 = 10

four pound
act Wilks Rbooth Cibber

Folger Shakespeare Library
Drury Lane Theatre accounts, 1714

Nov. 1714:

The Launderis her Bill :

Friday y 19 } 11 opeacis : A Shurt and wascult : 0 : 1 : 7

Saterday y 20 } 3 Double Ruffer ———— 0 : 1 : 6
A pr Silk Stokens and a Shurt : 0 : 0 : 6
20 peacis ———— 0 : 1 : 8

Monday y 22 } 4 Surplis and a Shurt — 0 : 2 : 3
2 pare of Silk Stokens — 0 : 0 : 6
21 peacis ———— 0 : 1 : 9

Tuesday y 23 } 14 opeacis and a pr of yarn Stok. — 0 : 1 : 4
A pare of Silk Stokens — 0 : 0 : 3

Wednesday y 24 } 8 peacis ———— 0 : 0 : 8

Thursday y 25 } 2 pare of Silk Stokens — 0 : 0 : 6
6 peacis ———— 0 : 0 : 6

Tho Goble

00 = 13 : 00

The womens Bill

Friday — A Shurt and 6 Towells : 0 : 0 : 6

Saterday — 4 Towells and a Dressingay : 0 : 0 : 3

Monday — 2 Surplis 2 Bands ——— } 0 : 1 : 3
A pare of Threed minting }
6 Towells ———— 0 : 0 : 3

Tuesday : A Night Raile and 4 Towell : 0 : 0 : 4

Wednesday : 4 Towell ———— 0 : 0 : 2

Thursday : 4 Towelles A Shurt and apr : 0 : 0 : 8

00 : 03 : 05

Y.d 4...

(17)

m

It is agreed that Mrs Booth
be allow'd fifty pounds per annum
in consideration of her providing
Cloaths for her self in all Parts
of Tragedy Comedy, ~~and Dancing~~
~~and~~ Boys Cloaths witness our hand
this present 22 of Sepr 1722

Clibber.

Mr Castelman   Rob: Wilks

RBooth

Add Twenty Shillings to mr
Shaw's Salary from this day.

Sep: 22. 1722

RBooth

Rob: Wilks

Clibber.

Folger Shakespeare Library
Drury Lane Theatre accounts, 1722

Mr Casselman

Tri: 9.th Sep.r (24) 1726

Strike out the Name of Mr Ray, of Mr Roberts, Mr Savage, Mr Roberts, from the Constant Charge, and reduce the Sallary of Mr Dupar to 2.s 6.d per diem of the two willis's to 5.s per diem of the Constable to two Shill: &c

Cibber.
B Booth
Rob Wilks   Sep.r 9.th 1726.

Mr Casselman
Put down the Name of Mr Clark at 13.s — 4.d per diem in the Constant Charge

Cibber.
B Booth
Rob Wilks

Folger Shakespeare Library
Drury Lane Theatre accounts, 1726

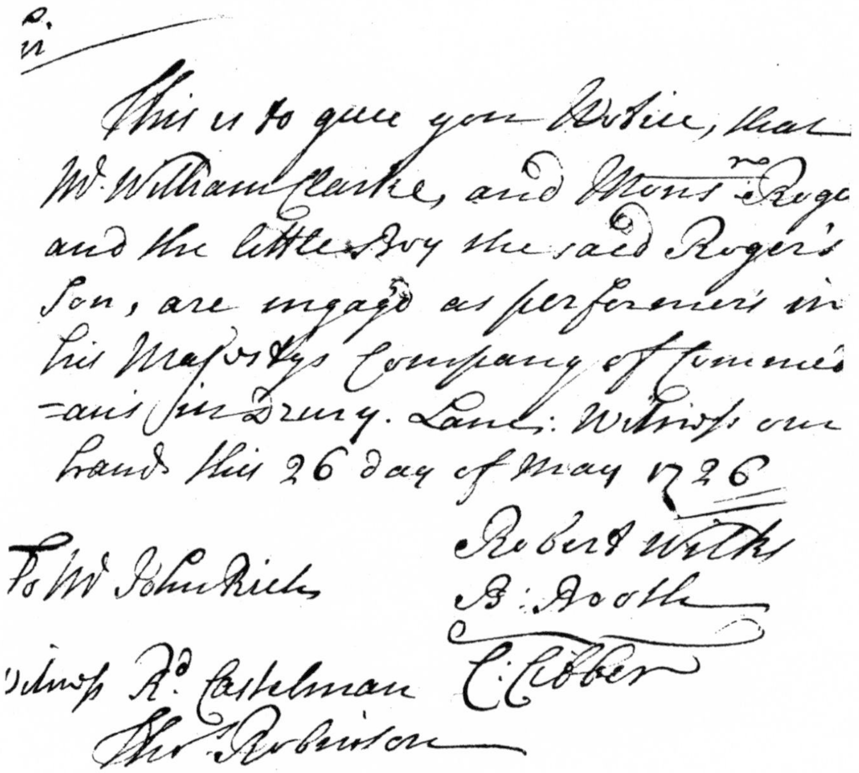

P.
ii

This is to give you Notice, that
M*r* William Clarke, and Mons*r* Roger
and the little Boy the said Roger's
Son, are engag'd as performers in
his Majestys Company of Comedi's
=ans for Drury. Lane: Witness our
hand this 26 day of May 1726

Robert Wilks
B: Booth
C. Cibber

To M*r* John Rich

witness R*d* Castelman
Tho*s* Robinson

Folger Shakespeare Library
Letter from the managers Cibber, Wilks and Booth of Drury
Lane Theatre to their rival John Rich, 1726

499

1727. Monday April 10ᵗʰ Woman's a Riddle for Mr. Bullock

Wilmot — 6 — 10 — 0
Redfern 3 — 15 — 0
Lawrence 1 — 15 — 0
Taylor 0 — 0 — 0
Atkins — 2 — 0 — 0

14 — 0 — 0

Stage — 1 — 5 — 0

Gwin 26
Gallant 25 } 7 — 13 — 0
Pitt 51

Boxes { Shafto 2 } 0 — 4 — 0
      { Tubman } 0 — 0 — 0

Fr. Gall. 41. Maine 4 — 2 — 0

Uppʳ G. 59 Aylet 2 — 19 — 0

First acct. — 30 — 3 — 0
Seals — 2 — 2 — 0
After Money 1 — 3 — 0

Total 33 — 8 — 0

After Money

Gwin — 0 — 4 — 0
Gallant 0 — 1 — 0
Maine — 0 — 8 — 0
Verhuyck 0 — 5 — 0
Redfern 0 — 5 — 0

1 — 3 — 0

Money 33 — 8 — 0
Tickets 71 — 18 — 0

105 — 6 — 0

Seal Tickets	Box	Pitt	Gall.	
Wilmot	24	4	—	0 — 3 — 0
Redfern	14			
Lawrence	18			
Taylor	16			
Atkins	2			
Stage	11	8		0 — 6 — 0
Gwin	13	70	9	0 — 17 — 0
Gallant	8	72	15	0 — 3 — 0
Shafto		2	3	
Tubman			2	
Maine	13	30	102	0 — 13 — 0
Aylet	2	4	8	
	121	185	139	2 — 2 — 0

Harvard Theatre Collection
Lincoln's Inn Fields Theatre accounts, 1727

500

1727 Tuesday April 11th Merry Wives & Proserpine

114. Clarkson	28 – 10 – 0		83 Vaughan	20 – 15 – 0
43 Verhuyck	10 – 15 – 0		43 Webb	10 – 15 – 0
42 Wood	10 – 10 – 0		60 Gwin	15 – 0 – 0
36. Harrison	9 – 0 – 0		49 Gallant	12 – 5 – 0
	58 – 15 – 0			58 – 15 – 0

In the pitt and Box.s
Mr Colebrane. Mr Middlemore. Mr J. Rich's Note 2
Office 1. Mr Scott. Mr Chambers Mr J. Rich. Coll:
Hubert Mr Ravenall. Mr Hippesley Mr S. Clark.
Mr R. Clark Mr Salle in the Entertainment
Mr Ch. Rich by Mr Hitchcock 2. Mr J. Riche
Note 2. Mrs Younger 2. Mrs Chambers 1. Mr
Walker 1.

Slips 22 { Shaftoe 9 } 1 – 2 – 6 Mr Ch. Rich by Mr Hays 2. Office by Mr Giles 1. Mr
{ } Tasboroughs 2 Servants.
{ Tilman 13 } 1 – 12 – 6 Office 1. Mr J. Rich by Redfern 1

1st G. 223. Main 27 – 17 – 6 Notes Mr J. Rich. 2. Mr Wood 3. Mr Laundy 1.
Ord.n Mr Gwins Notes and 1. by Leonard
Mr Norris by Mr Giles.

Upp. G. 135. Aft 10 – 2 – 6

99 – 10 – 0

Orders
22 Boxes – 5 – 10 – 0
7 Slips – 0 – 17 – 6
9 1st Gall. 1 – 2 – 6
Upp. G – 0 – 0 – 0
7 – 10 – 0

R.

Per Contra _____ C^r

1759		Bro forw^d - - - - - -		632 15. 3
October 11	By Band of Musick - - - -	4. 9. 2	66	
	By Wardrobe bill - - - -	-. 16. 6	70	
	By Properties - - - -	-. 12. 6	72	
	By Mr Sarjant ½ in Salary to Michs	10. -. -	50	15 10 2
12	By Band of Musick - - - -	4. 9. 2	66	
	By Wardrobe bill - - - -	-. 16. 6	70	
	By Properties - - - -	-. 7. 6	72	5 13 2
13	By Guards 5 Nights - - - -	3. 10. —	65	
	By Barber 5 Nights - - -	1. 6. 0	65	
	By Band of Musick - - -	4. 9. 2	66	
	By Bill Setters p bill - -	3. 15. 6	70	
	By Wardrobe bill - - - -	-. 16. 6	70	
	By Properties - - - -	-. 13. —	72	
	By Mr Rich 5 Nights - - -	26. 5. —	74	
	By Mr C. Rich 5 Nights - -	5. -. —	74	
	By Miss Brent Entr^d the 9th inst. inclusive, 4 Nights at 13.4 p N^t —	2. 13. 4	11	
	By M^r & Mrs Tariot Entred D^o. 4 Nights at 5^s each p N^t - -	2. -. —	20	
	By Mr Stephens advanc'd to 5 p N^t from D^o. - 5 N^{ts} Salary -	1. 5. —	33	
	By Mr Dall on Acc^o of salary -	1. 10. —	47	
	By Mr Austin 6 Days - - -	-. 12. —	40	
	By D^o - - p bill - -	-. 7. 6	40	
	By Mr Dyer for 1st weeks acting -	7. —. —	5	
	By Mrs Abegg omitted in List - 10 Nights —	2. 10. —	29	
	By Mr Means p bill - -	1. 9. -	76	
	By Mr Gum for Scene Mrⁿ p bill - -	6. 19. 0	66	
	By Performers 5 Nights - - -	10 10. 10		
	By Servants - 5 Nights - - -	19 16. 2		276 9. 4
	Carried forward - - - -		£	930 15. 11

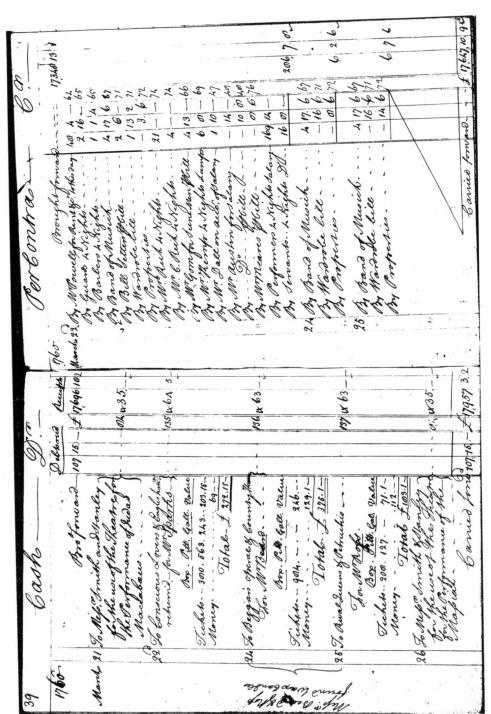

Folger Shakespeare Library
Covent Garden Theatre accounts, 1760

Mr. Garrick first play'd Affron } very fine — G: applause }

108	Mon 8:	Venice preserv'd & L. Valet	195
109	Tue 9	Kind Imposter & Miss in her teens	150
110	Wed 10	Othello & Damon	140
111	Th 11	Provok'd Wife & Flora	130
112	Fry 12	Love for Love & Dragon	080
113	Sat 13	The Foundling	200
114	Mon 15	Do	170
115	Tue 16	Do (Fast day)	160
116	Th 16	Do	170
117	Fry 19	Do	150
118	Sat 20	Do	170
119	Mon 22	Do	170

This comedy was wrote by Mr. Moor, & except ye part of Fiddle met with universal applause [ye Authors first play]

(great SHOW) for ye Author

for ye Author

There was a report that my Lord Hubbard had made a party this night to hiss the Foundling off the Stage, that ye Reason was it ran too long, or they wanted variety of Shakespeare — Mr Garrick was sent for, he met em, & so far prevail'd that they promis'd peace till after ye 9th night. however there was an attempt made by one catcall, & an apple thrown at Macklin & some other other efforts made by a few but without effect—greatly hiss'd us given out

Folger Shakespeare Library
Pages from the "Prompter's Diary" of Richard Cross,
Drury Lane Theatre, February 1748

	100	Fry 18	Ditto & Ditto —————— 180
	101	Sat: 19	Rule a Wife & High Life —— 190
	102	Mon 21	Alchymist & Harl: Invasion — 160
	103	Tues 22	Rule a Wife & Do ———— 160
3 off.e Young Princefes / There — not sufi.t Bills	104	Wed 23.	Douglas & Love ala Mode —
	105.	Thus 24	Desert Island & Way to keep him
		Frid 25	Do ... Do
		Sat 26	Ditto ... Do
Two Entertainments by Mr Murphy / of 3 Acts each		Mond 28	Ditto ... Do
		Tues 29	Ditto ... Do
		Wed 30	Ditto ... Do
		Thurs 31	Ditto ... Do
			February
		Frid 1	Desert Island & Way to keep him
	106.	Sat 2	Ditto ... Do
	107	Mon 4	Ditto ... Do
	108	Tues: 5	Ditto ... Do
		Wed 6	Comedy & No Love, A la Mode.
		Sun 7	James & Ditto ...
	109	Friday 8	Funeral & Ditto ...
	110	Saturday 9	Desert Island & Way to keep him.

Folger Shakespeare Library

Pages from the Cross-Hopkins "Prompter's Diary,"
showing Cross's last entry on 23 January 1760